Occult Imperium

OXFORD STUDIES IN WESTERN ESOTERICISM

Series Editor
Henrik Bogdan, University of Gothenburg

Editorial Board
Jean-Pierre Brach, École Pratique des Hautes Études
Carole Cusack, University of Sydney
Christine Ferguson, University of Stirling
Olav Hammer, University of Southern Denmark
Wouter Hanegraaff, University of Amsterdam
Ronald Hutton, University of Bristol
Jeffrey Kripal, Rice University
James R. Lewis, University of Tromsø
Michael Stausberg, University of Bergen
Egil Asprem, University of Stockholm
Dylan Burns, Freie Universität Berlin
Gordan Djurdjevic, Siimon Fraser University
Peter Forshaw, University of Amsterdam
Jesper Aa. Petersen, Norwegian University of Science and Technology

CHILDREN OF LUCIFER
The Origins of Modern Religious Satanism
Ruben van Luijk

SATANIC FEMINISM
Lucifer as the Liberator of Woman in Nineteenth-Century Culture
Per Faxneld

THE SIBLYS OF LONDON
A Family on the Esoteric Fringes of Georgian England
Susan Sommers

WHAT IS IT LIKE TO BE DEAD?
Near-Death Experiences, Christianity, and the Occult
Jens Schlieter

AMONG THE SCIENTOLOGISTS
History, Theology, and Praxis
Donald A. Westbrook

RECYCLED LIVES
A History of Reincarnation in Blavatsky's Theosophy
Julie Chajes

THE ELOQUENT BLOOD
The Goddess Babalon and the Construction of Femininities in Western Esotericism
Manon Hedenborg White

GURDJIEFF
Mysticism, Contemplation, and Exercises
Joseph Azize

INITIATING THE MILLENNIUM
The Avignon Society and Illuminism in Europe
Robert Collis and Natalie Bayer

IMAGINING THE EAST
The Early Philosophical Society
Tim Rudbog and Erik Sand

SPIRITUAL ALCHEMY
From the Age of Jacob Boehme to Mary Anne Atwood, 1600–1910
Mike A. Zuber

MYSTIFYING KABBALAH
Academic Scholarship, National Theology, and New Age Spirituality
Boaz Huss

OCCULT IMPERIUM
Arturo Reghini, Roman Traditionalism, and the Anti-Modern Reaction in Fascist Italy
Christian Giudice

Occult Imperium

Arturo Reghini, Roman Traditionalism, and the Anti-Modern Reaction in Fascist Italy

CHRISTIAN GIUDICE

OXFORD
UNIVERSITY PRESS

Oxford University Press is a department of the University of Oxford. It furthers
the University's objective of excellence in research, scholarship, and education
by publishing worldwide. Oxford is a registered trade mark of Oxford University
Press in the UK and certain other countries.

Published in the United States of America by Oxford University Press
198 Madison Avenue, New York, NY 10016, United States of America.

© Oxford University Press 2022

All rights reserved. No part of this publication may be reproduced, stored in
a retrieval system, or transmitted, in any form or by any means, without the
prior permission in writing of Oxford University Press, or as expressly permitted
by law, by license, or under terms agreed with the appropriate reproduction
rights organization. Inquiries concerning reproduction outside the scope of the
above should be sent to the Rights Department, Oxford University Press, at the
address above.

You must not circulate this work in any other form
and you must impose this same condition on any acquirer.

CIP data is on file at the Library of Congress
ISBN 978-0-19-761024-4

DOI: 10.1093/oso/9780197610244.001.0001

1 3 5 7 9 8 6 4 2

Printed by Integrated Books International, United States of America

All that is gold does not glitter, not all those who wander are lost;
the old that is strong does not wither, deep roots are not reached by
the frost.

—J. R. R. Tolkien, *The Fellowship of the Ring*

Contents

Acknowledgments ... xi

1. The Anti-Modern Side of Modernity ... 1
    1.1. Anti-Modern Sentiments in Modern Italy ... 1
    1.2. The Metaphysics of Dunces? ... 6
        1.2.1. Occultism and Modernity: Strange Bedfellows? ... 6
        1.2.2. From Yates to Eternity ... 11
        1.2.3. Enter Tradition and Traditionalism ... 13
        1.2.4. Paganism versus Christianity in Traditionalism ... 16
    1.3. Reghini through the Modern Looking Glass ... 18
        1.3.1. Multiple Modernities and Occultism ... 18
        1.3.2. The Invention of Sacred Traditions and the Occult ... 20
    1.4. Overview of the Book's Chapters ... 21
        1.4.1. The Italian Occult Milieu at the Turn of the Century ... 21
        1.4.2. The Early Years (1898–1910): Avant-Garde, Theosophy, and Modernity ... 21
        1.4.3. *Schola Italica* and the *Rito Filosofico Italiano* (1910–1915) ... 22
        1.4.4. The Great War and *Imperialismo Pagano*: A Clash between the Modern and the Traditional (1915–1920) ... 23
        1.4.5. Fascism and Traditionalism (1920–1925) ... 24
        1.4.6. The *Ur* Group and the End of a Dream (1925–1929) ... 24
        1.4.7. *Silentium post Clamores*: The Final Years (1930–1946) ... 25
    1.5. Conclusion ... 26
    Appendix: *Imperialismo Pagano* ... 26

2. *Risorgimento* Italy: Occultism, Politics, the Rise of the Nation State, and Roman Traditionalism ... 27
    2.1. A Historical Overview of the *Risorgimento* ... 27
        2.1.1. A Brief Outline ... 27
        2.1.2. *Risorgimento* as Roman Tradition and the Role of Freemasonry in the Unification Process ... 32
        2.1.3. Freemasonry in Italy in the Second Half of the Nineteenth Century ... 33
    2.2. Pope Pius IX and the Roman Question ... 35
    2.3. Italy and Nineteenth-Century Occultism ... 36
        2.3.1. The Origins and Spread of Spiritualism ... 37
        2.3.2. Spiritualism and Spiritism among the *Risorgimento* Elite ... 40

	2.4.	The Naples School and the Occult Italo/Roman Primacy	42
		2.4.1. The Metanarrative of Primacy: Mazzoldi and Mengozzi	42
		2.4.2. Occultism in Nineteenth-Century Naples	44
3.	The Early Years (1902–1910): Avant-Garde, Theosophy, and Anti-Modernism		49
	3.1.	Reghini's Early Life and the Reghini Di Pontremoli Family	50
	3.2.	The Crisis of Positivism and the Rise of Neo-Idealism	51
		3.2.1. Italian Philosophy in the Late Nineteenth Century	51
		3.2.2. Benedetto Croce and Idealism as Counterpositivism	53
	3.3.	The Florentine Avant-Garde: The Case of *Leonardo*	56
		3.3.1. Birth and Characteristics of the Florentine Avant-Garde	56
		3.3.2. The Three Lives of *Leonardo* and Its Occultist Phase	57
		3.3.3. Rehnini and *Leonardo*	60
	3.4.	Reghini between Avant-Garde and the Theosophical Society	60
		3.4.1. The Theosophical Society in Italy	61
		3.4.2. The Theosophical Library	62
		3.4.3. The Roots of Roman Traditionalism in Theosophy	64
		3.4.4. Reghini's Theosophical Writings	66
4.	The *Schola Italica* and the *Rito Filosofico Italiano* (1910–1914): Initiation and Invention of Tradition in Modern Italy		70
	4.1.	The Role of Freemasonry in Modern Italy	71
		4.1.1. A Brief History of Italian Freemasonry (1861–1914)	71
		4.1.2. Anti-Clericalism within Italian Freemasonry	73
		4.1.3. Nationalism and Irredentism within Freemasonry	75
		4.1.4. Fringe Masonry in Italy	77
	4.2.	Meeting Ara and Reghini's Masonic Past	78
		4.2.1. Enter Freemasonry: From *Rigeneratori* to *Lucifero*	78
		4.2.2. A Mysterious Gentleman: Amedeo Rocco Armentano	80
		4.2.3. Reghini's Initiation into the *Schola Italica*	82
		4.2.4. Invented Traditions as an Epistemological Strategy	84
	4.3.	Enter Frosini: A Singular Ally	86
		4.3.1. The *Rito Filosofico Italiano*	86
		4.3.2. Changes within the *Rito Filosofico* and the Its Short Life	88
5.	The Great War and "Pagan Imperialism" (1914–1920): A Clash between the Modern and the Traditional		91
	5.1.	Interventionism and Nationalism in Italy (1910–1914)	91
		5.1.1. The Larger Picture: Italy and Nationalism	91
		5.1.2. Reghini and Roman Traditionalist Volunteers	93
	5.2.	1914: Pagan Imperialism: A Textual Analysis	96
		5.2.1. The Context of "Imperialismo Pagano"	96
		5.2.2. "Introduction"	99
		5.2.3. "Impero e Cristianesimo" ("Empire and Christendom")	101

  5.2.4. "La Tradizione Imperiale Romana" ("The Roman Imperial
    Tradition")   104
  5.2.5. "L'Idea Imperiale Dopo Dante"
    ("The Imperial Idea after Dante")   107

6. Fascism and Traditionalism: Modernity and Anti-Modernity
 (1920–1925)   111
 6.1. The Larger Picture: A Historical Overview   111
  6.1.1. Benito Mussolini and the March on Rome   111
  6.1.2. Fascism and Roman Traditionalism: Anti-Modern or Modern?   114
  6.1.3. Social Occult Modernism   118
 6.2. Occultism and Fascism: A Real Partnership?   120
  6.2.1. The Fascist Link with Occultism: The 1920s   122
 6.3. Guénonian Traditionalism   125
  6.3.1. Guénon and the Birth of Traditionalism   125
  6.3.2. Guénon and Traditionalism in 1920s Italy   130
  6.3.3. The Reghini-Guénon Correspondence (1923–1926)   133
 6.4. Roman Traditionalism from 1920 to 1925   138
  6.4.1. The End of the Beginning   138
  6.4.2. The Beginning of the End   141

7. The *Ur* Group and the End of a Dream (1923–1929)   142
 7.1. *Le Parole Sacre Di Passo* Published by *Atanòr* (1922)   142
  7.1.1. Meeting Ciro Alvi and the *Atanòr* Publishing House   142
  7.1.2. *Le Parole*: Reghini's First Monograph (1922)   144
 7.2. The Journals *Atanòr* (1924) and *Ignis* (1925)   150
  7.2.1. Reghini's First Journal: *Atanòr*   150
  7.2.2. *Ignis*   155
 7.3. *Ur* and the *Ur* Group: Practical Occultism   158
  7.3.1. The *Ur* Journal (1927–1928)   158
  7.3.2. The *Ur* Group and the Break with Evola   160

8. Silentium Post Clamores (1930–1946)   163
 8.1. Troubles in the Capital: 1929–1938   163
 8.2. Reghini's Works in the 1930s and 1940s   166
  8.2.1. "Il Fascio Littorio" (1934)   166
  8.2.2. *Per La Restituzione Della Geometria Pitagorica* (1935)   170
  8.2.3. *Dei Numrti Pitagorici* (1936–1944)   172
 8.3. The Final Years (1939–1946)   179

9. Concluding Remarks   183

Appendix: English Translation of Imperialismo Pagano   193
Notes   203
Bibliography   285
Index   317

Acknowledgments

First of all, my foremost thanks go to two scholars, without whom this book would not be in your hands right now: the late professor Nicholas Goodrick-Clarke, who encouraged me to take my first uncertain steps in the world of academia, after having marked my master's thesis on post-Crowleyan magic and having suggested I didn't waste my "academic potential on petty chaos magic." To him I owe more than I was ever able to tell him. Great thanks go to my supervisor Professor Henrik Bogdan (University of Gothenburg), who, first welcomed me to Göteborg and made me feel at home in my new working environment, and then consistently supported my efforts throughout these four years, with his knowledge of Western esotericism and his helpful comments on my book.

I also would like to acknowledge Professor Marco Pasi (UvA), for his invaluable help throughout the writing of the book, which would become this book, and Professor Mark Sedgwick (Aarhus University) for reading the draft version of my book and giving me his feedback and welcome comments on the subject of Traditionalism and Western esotericism in general.

Spending four years at the Department of Literature, History of Ideas and Religion means that feedback, suggestions, and constructive criticism came to me from scholars in the most disparate fields. I therefore want to thank my colleagues for their generous input of ideas: Professor Göran Larsson; PhD candidates Giulia Giubergia, Jonatan Bäckelie, and Per Ahlström; Lisa Schmidt, PhD; Wilhelm Kardemark; and Jessica Moberg. Special thanks go to Department Head Cecilia Rosengren for her continued support and Department Secretary Pernilla Josefson for her assistance.

Many thanks are due to those interested in Italian occultism who have helped me with their suggestions and criticism, sometimes unearthing literary material I had lost all hope of finding: independent scholar H. T. Hakl, Sandro Consolato, Dr. Michele Olzi, Dr. Francesco Baroni, and Luca Valentini. Friend and expert on Roman Traditionalism Francesco Naio, especially, has been a veritable goldmine of suggestions and information.

Heartfelt thanks also go to Antonio Girardi of the Italian section of the Theosophical Society, for providing me with some of Reghini's early articles on Theosophical matters; Professor Lidia Reghini di Pontremoli, for sharing some family memories of her great-uncle Arturo; the heirs to the Guénon Estate for providing me with unpublished correspondence between Guénon and Reghini;

xii ACKNOWLEDGMENTS

Dr. Letizia Lanzetta at the *Instituto Nazionale di Studi Romani*; and the staff at the *Archivio di Stato* in Rome for their invaluable help.

To Maria Liberg, Peter Olsson, and Daniel Abrahamsson, fellow students of Western esotericism at the University of Gothenburg, who welcomed me since my first day in Sweden and helped me through the toughest periods, my sincere thanks.

Last, but certainly not least, to Margaret Jessop, the only Mahātmā I have ever encountered, and Vincenzo Giudice, who transmitted his love for twentieth-century Italian history to me. This book is dedicated to them.

1
The Anti-Modern Side of Modernity

> Progress is equivalent to non-being.[1]
> —Amedeo Rocco Armentano

1.1. Anti-Modern Sentiments in Modern Italy

In 1914, one year before Italy's involvement in the Great War, an article appeared in *Salamandra* (*Salamander*, est. 1914), a cultural publication with a small following of enthusiasts, signed by a then relatively obscure occultist, mathematician, essayist, and self-avowed neo-Pythagorean: Arturo Reghini (1878–1946). The author's contribution to the literary periodical was entitled "Imperialismo Pagano" ("Pagan Imperialism"), and it vividly contrasted the positivist, progressive worldview, which permeated a vast section of the Italian modern culture of the day.[2] The article denounced some of the very staples of what sociologists, from Max Weber to Anthony Giddens, have, through the decades, judged to be intrinsic to modern culture: mass democracy, secularization, the detraditionalization of society, and the idea of a "disenchanted West," to name but a few.[3] Modern society as "a progressive force promising to liberate humankind from ignorance and irrationality" was by no means the *weltanshaaung* advocated by the article.[4] In it Reghini vehemently attacked the Vatican and the Catholic nationalists, guilty of wielding too much political power, and deplored the "universal suffrage," which had "granted access to active politics to almost all of the illiterate and malleable mass of the nation."[5] More importantly, and relevant for the purposes of my book, Reghini wrote about the existence of an uninterrupted chain of initiates, from King Numa Pompilius (753–673 BCE) to Vergil (50–19 BCE), from Dante Alighieri (1265–1321) to Giuseppe Mazzini (1805–1872), who had been the custodians of a Pagan Roman Tradition, from the foundation of the Eternal City right up to the early twentieth century.[6] This Tradition, secretly handed down through the generations, would prove essential to the twentieth-century alleged manifestation of the institution that has been called by its advocates the *Schola Italica* (*Italic School*), an anti-modern, neo-Pythagorean, initiatory order, which sought to restore order to what was perceived as a modern chaotic Italian society, through a return to the traditional ideals of Ancient Rome to be applied in the early twentieth century.[7]

Occult Imperium. Christian Giudice, Oxford University Press. © Oxford University Press 2022.
DOI: 10.1093/oso/9780197610244.003.0001

But who was Arturo Reghini, a self-proclaimed anti-modern intellectual? What were his links to the Traditionalist movement called *Schola Italica*, which he wrote about in many articles and publications? Was he a lone Don Quixote in his fight against the windmills of modernity, and was he alone, in days when most sought occult wisdom in foreign authors and Eastern texts, to crave for a return to a pristine autochthone tradition in order to escape from Weber's infamous *stahlhartes Gehäuse*?[8] Contemporary studies on the interaction between modernity and occultism have proven beyond a shadow of doubt that, indeed, occultism cannot be simply seen only as a reaction by alienated individuals who resented objective reality and "try to elicit meaning from it by saying abracadabra,"[9] thus culminating in James Webb's definition of occultism as a "flight from reason."[10] Yet, however well the theories may fit one author's agenda, such claims are not universal and must not lead to a pernicious tendency to overgeneralize, since the impact of modernity on occultism, as will be seen, varied sensibly from country to country, from one occult milieu to another. To quote sociologist Jeffrey Herf, "[t]here is no such thing as modernity in general. There are only national societies, each of which becomes modern in its own fashion."[11] Therefore, it will be up to this volume to demonstrate that some aspects seen to be thoroughly compatible with modernity in an occult order in Great Britain, the Hermetic Order of the Golden Dawn (est. 1888), for example, do not apply to a country like Italy and an esoteric Tradition like the one represented by Reghini's writings.[12]

Contemporary scholars, such as Alex Owen, Marco Pasi, Corinna Treitel, and David Harvey, to cite the most prominent who have analyzed the complex relationship between the surge of interest in occultism and the allegedly positivist, secularist, Enlightenment-inspired qualities of modernity, *pace* Theodor Adorno and Max Horkheimer, have almost unanimously viewed occultism as a progressive, integral aspect of the modern world, and indeed as a forum in which new social conquests (emancipation of woman and democratization of access to knowledge, to name but two key factors) would make their first appearance, before slowly trickling down to mass society:[13] the reason for this trend is relatively straightforward, if one only considers the extremely multifaceted nature of the terms used and the malleability of these concepts (in contrast to Zygmunt Bauman's idea of a rigidly characterized *heavy* modernity opposed to a postmodern, fragmented, and *liquid* one) have allowed authors to describe modernity as everything and its opposite.[14]

Sociologist Marshall Berman, acutely aware of this conundrum, has attempted a description of the slippery, almost intangible qualities of modern life, which may aid the reader not only in his comprehension of modernity's qualities per se but also in acknowledging the existence of individuals and groups of people strongly opposed to the effects of modernity: Berman describes the "maelstrom of modern" life as being characterized by scientific discoveries; a massive increase of industrialization; the creation of new human environments which end up phagocytizing old ones; demographic upheavals (which, as I have written earlier, were a strong concern for Reghini); and the rise of national states and of a capitalist world market, for example.[15] Berman's depiction of twentieth-century modernity as a world in which "everything is pregnant with its contrary" will be crucial in trying to understand certain underlying tensions, between the progressive and the reactionary, in Reghini's writings:[16] if all contains a germ of its opposite, it is also quite true that early twentieth-century modernity, in Berman's view, is either accepted wholly with enthusiasm or else is "condemned with a neo-Olympian remoteness and contempt."[17] Although this may seem an extreme position to hold, it does help bolster a critical assumption in this book: my hypothesis is that elitist, anti-modern, Traditionalist milieus, sometimes even prone to totalitarian political ideas, obviously *did* actually exist in modern times and that a balance must be struck between the older theoretical constructs which bound occultism to a one-way journey to irrational and totalitarian ideas a priori, and the newer, more nuanced, scholarship which views occultism as an integral part of modernity, but seems to ignore some facets of modern expression, since even anti-modernism, in this case, must be seen as a modern phenomenon, albeit less congenial to its theses. Another useful distinction is given by Roger Griffin, in his division between epiphanic and progressive modernism: the first is seen as a revolt against modernity merely confined to "aesthetic, religious and spiritual quests, articulated in both literature and painting, for ephemeral experiences."[18] Griffin's description of programmatic modernism resembles the spirit found in Reghini's writings in a much more potent way:

> A quite different face of modernism manifests itself when the creative *élan* towards a higher *subjectively* perceived plane of existence becomes sufficiently intense to break free from the modern "slough of despond" altogether, and mutates into the sustained aspiration to create a new *objective*, external world, a new future premised on the radical rejection of and opposition to prevailing reality.

Est modus in rebus, quoth Horace (65–8 BCE) in his *Satires* (35 BCE), and it is my firm conviction that the study of anti-modern writings like Reghini's will help paint a clearer picture of this intricate relationship than has been presented to date.[19] In attempting to provide a definition of reactionary modernism in Weimar Germany, Herf writes of "nationalists who turned the romantic capitalism of the German Right away from backward-looking pastoralism, pointing instead to the outline of a beautiful new order replacing the formless chaos due to capitalism in a united [. . .] nation."[20] Reghini was acutely aware of the modern world he lived in and, through his writings, conveyed a sense of modernity itself providing the opportunity of a new beginning, which had been building up since the final years of the *Risorgimento*, an historical phase in Italian history culminating in the unification of the peninsula, and which would manifest itself, on the political plane, with the rise of the Fascist regime.[21] What marked the difference between his Traditionalist brand of occultism and other occultist movements was not a mere, irrational rejection of modernity tout court, but the deep-felt need to employ traditional tools for the spiritual reconstruction of modern Italy. Hence, the core question of my work can be thus formulated: *How and why did Arturo Reghini and his circles of friends react so vehemntly against the Modern, and what can the analysis of his life and writings offer to the ongoing debate regarding the intricate relationship between occultism and modernity?*[22] It is my hypothesis that Reghini's writings are not only a way to penetrate the oft-neglected anti-modern occultist Italian milieu specifically, but will prove to be of great relevance in the wider study of that section of population, which indeed opposed notions of progress and modernization, and acutely felt the seemingly nefarious effects to be found in what scholar Jeffrey C. Alexander has defined "the dark side of modernity."[23]

As discussed, my work will focus on Italian occultism, specifically on Arturo Reghini and, to a lesser degree, on his mentor Amedeo Rocco Armentano (1886–1966). The chapters of the dissertation will have a triple function: first, the study of Reghini's writings will help flesh out a solid biographical account, whose main purpose will be that of providing a *fil rouge* for the reader to follow; second, in each chapter I will endeavor to intertwine Reghini's life with some of modernity's major elements, opening up to the wider field of sociology of religions, and therefore focusing on the "dark-side" elements of modern, or anti-modern, life of the early twentieth century: the reaction to positivism, the rise of avant-gardes, the relationship between occult orders and the Vatican, and the Fascist regime's repression of occultism. In this way I will paint a wider picture of the many nuances in which Italy differed from other European countries when analyzing how anti-modernists may have experienced what philosopher Charles Taylor defined as the "malaise of modernity."[24] Through Reghini's biography and writings, I will thus aim to typify the discomfort caused by modernity, suffered not only by the Florentine thinker himself, but by some of his close associates belonging to nonoccult wider intellectual circles, whether members of the countercultural Florentine *Scapigliatura* such as journalists and writers Giovanni Papini (1881–1856) and Giuseppe Prezzolini (1882–1982) or Freemasons battling against Fascist censorship. Third, it is my belief that such an approach to Reghini's writings will help me better shed light on a segment of occultism which has yet to receive due attention in the smaller field of Western esotericism: that of Traditionalism, in general, and Roman Traditionalism in particular. In the study of Italian esotericism, the last century witnesses a depressing dearth of scholarship in the English language.[25] Whether the reason might be found in the vitality and progressive nature of other contemporary occult expressions abroad, or to some links to Fascism, which still looms over Italian history as a menacing taboo, I am nevertheless convinced that an etic approach to the subject material will be found to be vital for a better understanding of the idea of anti-modernity in Reghini's private dimension, in the more contained domain of Western esotericism, and in the wider field of religious studies.

Aside from the wide-ranging approaches that my work will employ, it is my intention to focus on the relevance of the writings of Arturo Reghini to the English-speaking world, since only a handful of articles, which are completely devoted to him, to date, have been published in foreign academic journals.[26] Both academic and nonscholarly studies of Reghini's writings have been severely lacking in Italy, too. While the right-wing culture, which in the postwar period hailed Julius Evola (1898–1974) as its main philosophical referent, rejected Reghini because of his Masonic ties, Freemasonry dismissed his work because of his neo-Pagan and anti-clerical stance. An anti-Christian approach, writes historian of Freemasonry Natale Mario Di Luca, "inevitably brought him to an ideological anti-Semitism," since Reghini had given Christianity the definition of "semitic disease."[27] This caused Reghini to be completely forgotten until the turn of the century, when his works started to enjoy increasing success and two biographies have been devoted to him. But while Di Luca takes a reductionist stance when judging Reghini's occult writings, lamenting "a marvelous manifestation of collective narcissistic pathology [. . .] on the verge of delusions of grandeur,"[28] Roberto Sestito, a neo-Pythagorean follower of Reghini's Roman Traditionalism, employs an overtly religionist stance that mars an otherwise well-researched work.

As independent scholar Dana Lloyd Thomas argues, Reghini "was a key figure in 20th century Italian esotericism."[29] His first-hand experience in the establishment of one of the first groups of the Theosophical Society in Italy, his role in attempting to restore the spiritual traditions of Freemasonry, his revival of neo-Pythagorean philosophy, and his deep interest in occult matters definitely make Reghini a key figure, with ties to almost every aspect of the Italian esoteric environment of his time. By studying Reghini's life and writings, we also study the developments of the esoteric discourse in Italy at the beginning of the twentieth century. Through his journals, "a landmark in Italian esoteric literature,"[30] Reghini drew together the most varied fringes of occultist expression, from the therapeutic masonic circle gathered around Giuliano Kremmerz (1861–1930) to Italian exponents of anthroposophy such as Giovanni Antonio Colonna di Cesarò (1878–1940) and Giovanni Colazza (1877–1953); from the

Traditionalists Julius Evola and Guido de Giorgio (1890-1957) to neo-Pagans and neo-Pythagoreans Amedeo Armentano and Giulio Parise (1902-1970).[31]

Before moving on to an analysis of the previous research available to me, I would briefly like to list the different elements that form the *Corpus Reghinianum*. The first part of his career is focused mainly on articles written on journals, the Florentine *La Voce* (1906) and *Leonardo* (1906-1907), the Futurist *Lacerba* (1913-1915), the more politically oriented *Salamandra* (1914) and *Patria* (1914), the theosophical journal *Ultra* (1914), the masonic *Rassegna Massonica* (1923-1924), and his 1907 and 1908 lectures at the *Biblioteca Filosofica* in Florence; his substantial introduction to Cornelius Agrippa's *De Occulta Philosophia* (1927) will no doubt offer a new insight to the interrelationship between science, religion, and magic in modern-day Italy, as will his works on occult journals edited by him such as *Atanòr* (1924), *Ignis* (1925), and *Ur* (1927-1928). His book *Le parole sacre di passo dei primi tre gradi ed il massimo mistero massonico* (*The Sacred Passwords of the First Three Grades and the Greatest Masonic Mystery*, 1922), will provide a less thorough approach to political and social issues but will prove to be a veritable gold mine when analyzing the author's Traditionalist views. Private correspondence between Reghini and some of his colleagues will be priceless when trying to come to terms with Reghini as an anti-modern thinker living in a modern world. Such correspondence includes hitherto unpublished letters sent to the putative father of the Traditionalist School: René Guénon (1886-1951).

1.2. The Metaphysics of Dunces?

1.2.1. Occultism and Modernity: Strange Bedfellows?

Right up to the mid-1980s, occultism in the light of modernity had been perceived as a nuisance, which bothered most sociologists and historians of religions: described as an irrational yearning caused by the rational and progressive nature of modernity itself, occultism was perceived to be an unsound element, worthy of being readily tossed in the "conceptual waste-basket of rejected knowledge."[32] In three sentences, in his *Theses*, Theodor Adorno had summed up his ideas on the irrationality within the discourse between occultism and modernity:

> Occultism is the metaphysic of dunces. The mediocrity of the mediums is no more accidental than the apocryphal triviality of the revelations. Since the early days of spiritualism the Beyond has communicated nothing more significant than the dead grandmother's greetings and the prophecy of an imminent journey.[33]

It must be stressed that Adorno's, or Marcello Truzzi's, knowledge of occultism was almost nonexistent. Adorno's approach to the subject matter was never that of a rigorous scholar, but that of a theorist who needed an element of ridicule in order to prove his theories, and found it in the horoscopes of mainstream newspapers, or, in Truzzi's case, in the 1960s boom of sales of Ouija boards, which, according to him, for a period of time, outsold the board game *Monopoly*.[34] This trend witnessed a change in the seriousness of the approach to it when the independent scholar James Webb's published his *Flight from Reason*. Despite being a well-researched and scholarly work, from the first sentence of the first chapter, the author elucidated his beliefs on occultism with a statement that almost reads as an epitaph: "[a]fter the Age of Reason, came the Age of the Irrational."[35] But in the eyes of cultural critics, Italy's Fascist regime did not possess the same connection to occultism that Nazi Germany provided, and the anti-esoteric rhetoric in Italy was sensibly less present in the postwar period.[36] Thus postwar Italy, while witnessing an obvious backlash against all things that remotely drew the mind to the Fascist period, definitely lacked the brand of sensationalist authors such as Louis Pauwels, Jacques Bergier, or Trevor Ravenscroft, an ominous presence with their writings on the Third Reich, willing to perpetuate the idea of occult ties between occultists and politics:[37] to quote author Gianfranco de Turris, "we cannot speak—no matter what some people may think—of a 'fascist esotericism,' that is to say, neither an official or off-the-record esoteric dimension of fascism."[38]

In recent scholarship, occultism has been defined with a wide array of definitions, although I will be using Wouter J. Hanegraaff's definition of occultism, seen as comprising

> all attempts by esotericists to come to terms with a disenchanted world, or, alternatively, by people in general to make sense of esotericism from the perspective of a disenchanted world.[39]

Marco Pasi characterizes occultism by some distinguishing traits that may be found in Reghini's theories, such as the overcoming of the conflict between science and religion, an anti-Christian stance that led occultists to fulfill their spiritual needs in pagan traditions, and the great relevance played by the "spiritual realization of the individual."[40]

Since the beginning of the new millennium, studies have mostly provided a more sympathetic approach to the subject matter: academics have striven to swing the pendulum between the rational and the irrational as far away from Adorno and other postwar theorists as possible, creating, in my opinion, an even greater imbalance of judgment when dealing with the occultism-modernity connection. In scholar Alison Butler's words, "most of the recent scholarship on nineteenth-century occultism in Britain, France and Germany contribute to a current challenge to debunk the long-standing equation of modernity with disenchantment."[41] In their eagerness to validate occultism as a respectable field of enquiry, they have followed Hanegraaff's theory, according to which magic survived the disenchantment of the world by adapting to the new mechanics and worldviews of modernity,[42] but oversimplifying the globalizing elements of occultism, thus almost treating occultism like any other bourgeois commodity of the period.[43] An example is Marco Pasi, who in his article "The Modernity of Occultism," first states the intention to draw conclusions "about the way the ways which esotericism has interacted with modern Western society and culture,"[44] only to the restrict his scope to the well-known Theosophical Society (est. 1875) and Hermetic Order of the Golden Dawn: admittedly they were two among the most innovative occult establishments of their day, but hardly representative of "modern Western society and culture" as a whole.[45] It must be said, in fairness, that Treitel, Harvey, and Owen, for example, have been more careful in delimiting their field of research to particular countries and occult orders. While other authors have tried to provide a more balanced approach, albeit only through review articles, it is my intention to seek to strike a middle ground between the occultist seen as the epitome of irrationalism and that of the occultist depicted as the cutting-edge progressive modern individual, by employing Reghini in the Italian milieu as a counterexample that may allow us to appreciate both sides of the coin, when researching occultism's flourishing in modern times.[46] If it is understandable to see why, among the debris left behind after the fall of the National-Socialist regime, theorists of the Frankfurt School saw that the enemy of rationality had to be found in occultism, in order to justify the theorem according to which all that stands against rationality must be irrational, and that all that is irrational must be condemned,[47] I find it harder to understand the opposite tendency to focus on the positivist and scientist traits as the only aspects of the occult in line with modernity's qualities, in contemporary scholarship. Of course, the Hermetic Order of the Golden Dawn is, without doubt, one of the most utilized structures employed to convince the reader of the compatibility of modernity with occultism, among fin-de-siècle practitioners. For example, Pasi writes about the "exceptional status that women enjoyed in these occultist organizations,"[48] and Owen too describes the freedom enjoyed by female initiates within the English order.[49] Undoubtably, women in this specific order and in this specific country did enjoy a modicum of freedom and equal rights. Yet William Wynn Westcott (1948–1925), cofounder of the Order, and among the first to recognize the need to admit women in the higher echelons of the organization, still complained about women not cleaning the rooms of the Second Order quarters well enough, and Golden Dawn initiate Frederick Leigh Gardner (1857–1930) was reassured by the head of the Bradford lodge, that "no petticoat-government will do for us in any way."[50]

In the very first pages of his work on neo-Martinist movements in modern France, *Beyond Enlightenment: Occultism and Politics in Modern France* (2005), David Allan Harvey makes a statement, which I find to be very convincing:

> While [Helena Petrovna] Blavatsky's Theosophical Society was the dominant influence over the occult subcultures that emerged in the United States, Britain, and Germany, neo-Martinism developed as a reaction to English speaking Theosophy, one that rejected many of the latter's tenets in the name of doctrines and traditions native to France.[51]

Although Harvey never actually does compare the occultist circles in France to those abroad, his point is clear: what may be hailed as a social conquest of occultism in one country, or even of a single occultist order within a country, cannot be held to be true in another European nation. Just to use an example, what would the progressive female magicians of the Golden Dawn have thought of Julius Evola's article "Woman as a Thing"?[52] Or of his statement according to which "The absolute woman not only does not possess that 'I,' but would not know what to do with it, she cannot even conceive it and its presence would act in an extremely disturbing matter when concerning every genuine manifestation of her deepest nature?"[53] What would they have made of his physical abuse toward Italy's most prominent feminist activist Sibilla Aleramo (1876–1970), with whom he had had a brief love affair?[54] These are but few examples within the restricted domain of the relationship between women's emancipation and occultism, but really do apply to other aspects of society at large, when confronting two enormously different countries such as the United Kingdom and Italy.

It is definitely not my intention to belittle the work of any of the contemporary authors who have previously tackled the interrelation between occultism and modernity. Alex Owen's theory of "seeking the infinite in a newly psychologized but potentially divine self"[55] and Treitel's ideas on the diffusion of occultism within German society are fundamental landmarks in the field. Some occultist circles in the early twentieth century indeed possessed many characteristics that define their notion of modernity, but there was a whole range of occultists, lodges, and orders, in Italy, Germany, and France, for example, which do not fit into this dominating framework. To quote Laqueur in describing the Western occultist milieus:

> But there is also something not modern in the whole story [. . .]. Certain early twentieth-century figures understood this explicitly. The self-proclaimed "traditionalism" of René Guénon, for example, exploited sources of precisely the same sort and grew from the same roots as the supposedly modernist movements of Owen and Treitel. It had its origins in nineteenth-century occult,

was fuelled by Masonic Lodges, [. . .] and thought to save the West from its impoverished materialism.[56]

Maybe the use of the term *non-modern* by Laqueur is not entirely accurate, since, as I have argued before, even anti-modernists were a clear product of modernity, but, ill choice of the term aside, his point is nonetheless valid. In his groundbreaking work on race and anthroposophy in Nazi Germany and Fascist Italy, Peter Staudenmaier acknowledges the fact that both perspectives on occultism, the postwar cry for its irrationalism and its recent rehabilitating efforts by contemporary scholars, "reveal significant facets of the modern occult revival, and the contrasts between them indicate the historical work that still needs to be done towards a more comprehensive understanding of the phenomenon."[57] It is exactly my aim to further the studies within this field, by examining a reactionary modern occultist movement. Therefore, I will not be arguing for a new occult dimension in contrast with those previously analyzed by other scholars, but will merely endeavor to contribute fruitfully to the discourse by covering its most neglected facet.

Anti-modernity, compared to its positivist counterpart, has been a neglected field of study in social sciences: still, in order to delineate ideas and values ascribed to Reghini and his coterie, a theoretical framework is necessary. Scholar Peter King provides just such a framework in his *The Antimodern Condition: An Argument against Progess* (2014).[58] In this work, King describes four key elements to anti-modernism, which, as we will see, seem to apply perfectly to Reghini, Armentano, and the other members of the *Schola Italica*: first, we find the urge to focus on "accepted and habitual ways of acting and doing": this factor is coupled with an interest to maintain such an outlook while at the same time embracing newer trends and vogues, in Reghini's case. But it is nevertheless true that a rhythm of life, which rejected the frenzied mechanization and fast-paced life championed by the Futurists, for example, may definitely be found within Reghini. Second, the need for a common culture "which pre-dates us and will reach beyond us," giving life within such culture a "significance that transcends our everyday concerns"; the third element, according to King's fourfold division, is the stress on the idea of transmission: the key concepts of such culture are to be passed from generation to generation in order to remain valid and resistant to change. A strong parallel may be made with the claims of the Italic Tradition allegedly being handed down throughout the millennia, in an unbroken chain from Pythagoras to Reghini; finally, and this factor touches upon Reghini's political involvement, King argues for a government whose main aim is that of preserving "institutions, traditions and practices that allow the common culture to thrive."[59] Reghini's plan for an intellectual elite to initiate the masses into age-old traditions through the help of a Pagan state overseeing its cultural development is a fundamental thesis backed by the Florentine thinker, and it will constitute the fulcrum of his "mission."

1.2.2. From Yates to Eternity

A rigorous study of Western esotericism can be said to begin in the 1930s, in Italy, with the studies of Paul Oskar Kristeller on Marsilio Ficino and Lodovico Lazzarelli (1447–1500),[60] and with a different, more religionist approach in Ascona, Switzerland, thanks to meetings among scholars in what, from 1933, became known as the *Eranos* meetings.[61] The organization of these meetings derived by "a willingness to take *myth and symbolism* seriously, and explore their relevance to history and modern culture."[62] Among the most distinguished names of the participants of the *Eranos* meetings throughout the years, we find Jewish Kabbalah scholar Gershom Sholem, Islamicist and theorist of the *mundus imaginalis* Henri Corbin, future representative of the so-called Chicago School Mircea Eliade, and future scholar of Western esotericism Antoine Faivre. What characterized the subject matter of the papers presented during these meetings was a marked inclination toward occult traditions, which tended to be religionist in their approach. Many times the scholars did not distance themselves from the subject of their writings, resulting, at times, in open polemics against the dangers of historical reductionism.

The real breakthrough in the academic study of hermetic and esoteric currents was to be achieved in 1964, the year of publication of Dame Frances Yates's (1899–1981) *Giordano Bruno and the Hermetic Tradition*;[63] in this book, which captured the imagination of many readers among the countercultural movements of the 1960s, Yates proposed her theory that the Florentine Renaissance had been made possible mainly because of the employment of magic and because of the revival of hermeticism, due to the translation of the *Corpus Hermeticum* (trans. 1471) made by Ficino at the court of the Medici family. The hermetic tradition of the Renaissance, promoted by Yates, was characterized as

> a tradition dominated by magic, personal religious experience, and the powers of imagination; [. . .] it reflected a confident, optimistic, forward-looking perspective that emphasized humanities' potential to operate on the world and create a better, more harmonious, more beautiful society.[64]

Yates's works, though appealing to the general public, presented two main problems: first, Dame Yates's concept of Hermetic Tradition was depicted as an almost autonomous undercurrent, in a constant struggle against both Christianity and the scientific worldview, simplifying complex interrelations in a manner that was deemed unacceptable by her contemporary colleagues;[65] second, her writing betrayed an idea of magic as a static, scientifically antiquated realm, which nevertheless provided the sixteenth and seventeenth centuries with the necessary tools for a scientific revolution and a modern idea of progress. Luckily, as Hanegraaff pointed out, we are no longer dependent on legitimizing the study of Western esotericism by characterizing it as progressive; therefore, even currents, such as the one analyzed in this book, "deserve serious attention whether they happen to be progressive or not."[66]

In a recent review article on the introductory texts to Western esotericism available in 2013, Hanegraaff, making an analogy to the updating of computer software, referred to this initial part of the history of the study of such currents as "Western esotericism 1.0."[67] The update, so to speak, to "Western esotericism 2.0" was marked by two distinct events which are still very relevant to contemporary scholars of Western esotericism: they are Antoine Faivre's publication of his seminal study *L'Ésotérisme* in 1992, and a consequent shift toward an empirical approach to the subject matter, away from the religionist approach of the *Eranos* meetings and the Chicago School, and from Yates's oversimplifying theories.[68] For the first time in the history of the academic field of Western esotericism, Faivre attempted to define esotericism as a domain of academic research: what he offered to the reader in *l'Ésotérisme* was the now popular definition of esotericism as a form of thought, characterized by the presence of four intrinsic qualities (correspondences; living nature; imagination; transmutation) and the possible presence of two nonintrinsic ones (practice of concordance; transmission).[69] Furthermore, the increasing preponderance posited on empiricism and critical historiography made it possible for "Western esotericism 2.0" to begin to be accepted as a legitimate field of enquiry within academia, fueling ever-increasing discussions on methodological and theoretical debates among the pioneering scholars of the field.[70]

The greater acceptance of Western esotericism as a valid subject of enquiry has brought some scholars in the field to scrutinize Western esotericism through theories and methods successful in the field of religious studies in general. The most significant example was the relatively recent use of discourse analysis within the field of Western esotericism: Olav Hammer, in his *Claiming Knowledge: Strategies of Epistemology from Theosophy to the New Age* (2001), applied a scrupulous analysis to three different strategies of epistemology within movements such as Theosophy and the New Age: namely the appeal to tradition, to science, and to experience. Another strong advocate of this approach to the field was Kocku von Stuckrad, whose most recent application of discourse analysis may be found in his *Locations of Knowledge in Medieval and Early Modern Europe* (2010): in it, the break from Faivre's definition of Western esotericism as a form of thought is definitive, and the author argued against the idea of "Western esotericism [being] an objectively identifiable 'tradition' or 'coherent' system of thought and doctrine," that constituted an academic field per se.[71] By steering away from the idea of a Christian-centric view of Europe, advocating for an integration of Islamic and Jewish narrative, von Stuckrad focused on "esoteric discourses" that ended up blurring or transcending altogether the margins between the three religions of the book, thus, in my opinion, transforming his subject of enquiry from esotericism to a European history of religion, which includes many more topics than Western esotericism alone. This being the case, as Hanegraaff argues, all is reduced to "an exclusivist and reductionist subtext that automatically devalues 'contents and ideas' in favor of 'structures,' makes history subservient to theory, and ends up promoting discursive approaches as the *only* valid methodology in the study of religion, esoteric or otherwise," implicitly forcing the historian of Western esotericism into a seemingly inescapable cul de sac.[72] Other, more recent publications have followed a similar postmodern approach to Western esotericism, with some scholars proposing to drop the "Western" in Western esotericism completely:[73] these often self-referential and vacuous theories and methodologies proposed in what has been defined the 3.0 postmodern mutation of (Western) esotericic studies are not picked up in this work and are only cited for the sake of completion.

At the beginning of this new phase in the study of Western esotericism, having overcome overt religionist agendas, as in the Eranos meetings and Chicago School, and being aware of the ever-evolving approaches to Western esotericism, including reductionist methodologies, it is my opinion that contemporary scholarship should maintain an empirical approach. However, at the same time it should widen the scope of enquiry and embrace a multidisciplinary approach, which may increase the relevance of the field with respect to more established disciplines and avoid the possibility of the field itself remaining a niche area of study for few devoted enthusiasts.

1.2.3. Enter Tradition and Traditionalism

Since the Renaissance, the transmission of ancient traditions and their reception have been among the foremost problems tackled by magicians and mystics.[74] Prominent thinkers, such as Florentine theologian Marsilio Ficino (1433–1499) and *enfant prodige* philosopher Pico della Mirandola (1463–1494) both "tried to harmonise different ancient traditions."[75] Fictional and historical figures of antiquity, such as Zoroaster, Hermes Trismegistus, Orpheus, Aglaophemus, Moses, Pythagoras, and Plato, were envisaged as being part of a chain of initiates, which had propagated a *prisca philosophia* (ancient, or primordial philosophy) deriving from a single *fons perennis* (eternal spring, or source).[76] To the existing source material at their disposal, Ficino argued for an addition of a *philosophia occulta* (occult philosophy) or *magia*, which strongly resounded with Trismegistus's *Corpus Hermeticum* (II–III c. AD), while Pico tried to highlight the concordances of ancient philosophy with the Jewish kabbalah.[77] It was the Vatican librarian Agostino Steuco (1497–1548), in his *De Perenni Philosophia* (1540), who first introduced the notion of a progressive degradation of the human spirit: the *prisca philosophia*, handed down by God himself, which had become more and more diluted and impure with each passage of transmission. This concept would be further expounded on by twentieth-century Traditionalist thinkers.[78] Far from being an interest limited to the early modern period, a search for a continuous and perennial source of wisdom was undertaken by intellectuals even after the Enlightenment; thus, terms such as "the primitive Tradition" appeared in Louis-Claude de Saint-Martin's writings (1743–1803), both in his *Des Erreurs et de la Vérité ou les Hommes Rappeliés au Principe Universel de la Science* (*Of Errors and Truths, or Men Related to the Universal Principal of Science*) of 1775 and *Tableau Naturel des Rapports qui Unissent Dieu, l'Homme et l'Universe* (*A Natural Table of the Relationships which unite God, Man and the Universe*), published in 1781;[79] Johann Friedrich Kleuker (1749–1827) published an exegesis of Saint-Martin's work entitled *Magikon* (1784), in which Plato's ideas and biblical narratives could be found in Kleuker's addition to the list of Kabbalists and Christian theosophists, which represented his major contribution to the Traditionalist discourse.[80] During the French occult revival of the nineteenth century, a prominent occultist such as Eliphas Lévi (1810–1875), in his seminal *Dogme et Rituel de Haute Magie* (*Trancendental Magic, Its Doctrine and Ritual*, 1854–1856) states as his major intention for the book, that of discovering "the great secrets of religion and of the primitive knowledge of the magicians and the unity of universal dogma."[81] Faivre justifies this attempt to seek transcendental secrets of religion and magic "in order to discover elements of legitimization for their [the occultists of the nineteenth century] crusade versus rising materialism, elements against which the teachings of the Churches, they deemed, argued insufficiently."[82]

At the dawn of the twentieth century, with the ever-increasing quickening of the rise of the traits of modernity, a perennialist current, placing Traditionalist beliefs at its core, was born. Scholars within the field of Western esotericism have debated whether or not to include this school of thought within the folds of their area of enquiry and while, as an academic concept, perennialism, or Traditionalism, has been deemed unfit because of its emic connotations,[83] nevertheless I tend to agree with Faivre, when he insists on *pérennialisme* as being part of the modern Western esoteric milieu, since Traditionalism and occultist currents are in many ways intertwined.[84] In modern times, the terms "Perennialism" and "Traditionalism" refer mainly to the thought current initiated by Réné Guénon, and the two terms have been used interchangeably by scholars.[85] I shall be using the term "capitalized" when refering to a specific tradition, be that Reghini's Roman-Pagan one or Guénon's Sufi-Islamic blend. When referring to traditions in general, the term will not be capitalized. Guénon's ideas on Traditionalism have been ingeniously summarized by Mark Sedgwick in three distinct categories: first, there is a belief in a *philosophia perennis*, which, according to Guénon, and following Steuco's idea, had degenerated and become almost inaccessible in the West. The first point brings us directly to the second, and most important from an occultist perspective: the idea of counterinitiation. Guénon, as Reghini in Italy, had been involved in several occult orders in his youth, in an attempt to rediscover the lost perennial philosophy. His two books *Le Théosophisme: Histoire d'une pseudo-religion* (*Theosophism: History of a Pseudo-religion*, 1921) and *L'Erreur Spirite* (*The Spiritist Fallacy*, 1923) denounced the degenerate nature of the teachings of the Theosophical Society and of the spiritualist movement, judging them as counterinitiatory, that is, guiding the initiate in a 180-degree turn away from the goal of knowledge of an authentic, ancient tradition.[86] These two volumes are the fruits of Guénon's frequentation of the Parisian occultist milieu between 1906 and 1912, a period that almost coincided with Reghini's involvement in the Italian occultist scene (1898–1929). Extant correspondence between the two Traditionalist thinkers shows that both were aware of what they perceived to be their follies of youth, and, as I will demonstrate in the following chapters, Guénon was just as instrumental in inspiring Reghini with Traditionalist ideas as Reghini and his mentor Armentano were to Guénon.[87] The third point, the most important aspect of Traditionalism relating to the overall subject of this book, is that of inversion. Inversion is "seen as an all-pervasive characteristic of modernity. While all that really matters is in fact in decline, people foolishly suppose they see progress."[88] By 1924, with the publication of *Orient et Occident* (*East and West*), Guénon seemed to have lost all hope in finding a true initiatory access to the ancient wisdom in the West and advocated for an embracing of Oriental traditions. The West was not depicted as inherently lost; rather, it was equated with modernity, while the East was identified with a land in which tradition was still available to the seeker.

But what were Traditional beliefs in the early twentieth century and what did Traditionalist thinkers such as Guénon and Reghini seek from a return to tradition?

Sociologist Edward Shils gives a definition that I am inclined to agree with:

> Traditional beliefs are deferential. They express an attitude of piety not only towards earthly authorities, towards the elders and ancestors but also to the invisible forces which control earthly life. Holy men and priests are prized by traditional attitudes as is the learning of sacred texts.[89]

Both Guénon and Reghini sought a higher metaphysical principle that would guide them through the dangers of modernity; both actually sought to create an intellectual élite, which would function as the medium between the transcendent and the common people. But while Guénon looked East, finally converting to Islam and moving to Cairo, Reghini was unshakable in his belief in the superiority of his autochthone traditions. He perceived Tradition to be intrinsically particularistic, paying constant allegiance to the ideas of lineage, ethnicity, "and the cultural sublimations of primordial ties in linguistic communities and national societies."[90] His idea of the need for an order as a metaphysical realm of existence, no doubt influenced by his Pythagorean studies, is summarized eloquently in some of Armentano's anti-modern aphorisms, such as "where there is order, there can't be progress," or "in human matters, order is almost always threatened by disorder," or finally "social disorder is a consequence of believing in progress and of the desire to become other than what we are."[91] It is my hope, with these examples, to have made clear that Traditionalists saw in the idea of progress, scientific and social, the main enemy that had been brought by the advent of modernity, and that the tool to overcome the perceived disorder was Tradition itself, a return to the past in order to create an ordinate future.

1.2.4. Paganism versus Christianity in Traditionalism

Studies on the phenomenon of Roman Traditionalism have only recently begun to flourish, and this dissertation will be the first exhaustive depiction of its characters and traits in the English language.[92]

In his break with Guénon, Reghini continued promoting his ideals for the resurgence of Roman Traditionalism, a national brand of ancient wisdom, which would reintegrate a state of order, in what he considered a country ravaged by modernity and spiritually ruled by Christianity, a religion he considered as a foreign anomaly in the Roman-Italian history. Author Piero di Vona has provided a definition of Roman Traditionalism, which I agree with wholeheartedly:

> We will call this brand of traditionalism Roman, firstly because it depended on people, who wrote on journals that were published and circulated in Rome, and belonged to the cultural milieu of the capital, secondly because it was inspired by the pagan and Roman tradition, or at least it assumed that the idea of Rome was still alive and still had a function in our [the twentieth] century.[93]

Reghini saw in the reformation of Freemasonry, via traditional values, to its alleged pristine state before being co-opted by foreign countries, as the only way in which Italy could be saved from its decaying status. To do so, he recognized his role as the human agent, but was convinced of being backed by the primordial powers of the Roman Tradition: "above men and initiates stand the great fates which tower over the Gods themselves; and initiates can only aspire to recognise them and consciously and intelligently collaborate for their manifestation in the world of mortals."[94] His mission, in his eyes, was backed by the forces which had made Rome great, and if he were to succeed, would make the city great again in the future, concurrently with the first stirrings of the Fascist movement, which would aspire to create a new Roman Empire, and could be seen looming on the horizon in the late 1910s. Already in 1906, his relationship with dogmatic faith and scientific epistemology were very clearly expressed in one of his lectures at Florence's *Biblioteca Filosofica*: "Dogmatic religion opposes this [Traditional] view in name of a higher revelation; and science too, so-called positive, takes a hostile view, demanding absolute monopoly of scientific enquiry, declaring as anti-scientific all researches which are not conducted with the means and criteria fashionable today."[95] Much more will be written about Reghini's approach to metaphysical questions throughout the work, and for the purpose of this introduction, this last quotation about the magical essence of Rome and its soil itself, which clearly implies ethnonationalist sentiments, may suffice:

> Language and race are not the causes of this metaphysical superiority, it appears to be linked to the nature of the place, to the soil, to the very air. Rome, Rome *caput mundi, the eternal city, historically manifests itself as one of these magnetic regions of our earth* [italics mine].[96]

In the journal *Ur*, which Reghini coedited with Julius Evola and his disciple Giulio Parise, the ties between this group of occultists and an allegedly ancient form of Roman Tradition were made, if possible, even more clear: this Roman *traditio*, in a way similar to Jewish Kabbalah, was said to have been handed down through the centuries from master to student, in order to keep alive a pagan initiatic center that would remain powerful and alive through two millennia of Christianity. In the Reghini-Guénon correspondence, although skeptical toward the idea of pursuing a Western form of tradition, Guénon agreed with Reghini of the "possible persistence of a Western tradition."[97] As shall be seen in Chapter 2 in greater detail, the fascination with the glory of ancient Rome had captured poets, painters, nationalists, politicians, and occultists: the ground was certainly fertile for such ideas to be cultivated, and, within a closed circle, developed according to anti-modern, elitist standards.[98]

1.3. Reghini through the Modern Looking Glass

1.3.1. Multiple Modernities and Occultism

As I have hinted at repeatedly in the first two subchapters of this introduction, it is my opinion that the conditions for the development of occult milieus in different European countries were greatly varied, and inasmuch as no specific occult group in the south of Europe could bear similarities with the British occult scene, for example, it is my intention to embrace, on a wider level, S. N. Eisenstadt's theories on multiple modernities: according to Eisenstadt, and, as we shall see, to a number of other scholars, "the notion of 'multiple modernities' denotes a certain view of the contemporary world—indeed, of the history and characteristics of the modern era—that goes against the views long present in scholarly and general discourse."[99] The idea is that, while a very general pattern of modernity obviously did affect Europe between the nineteenth and twentieth centuries, in the social fabric of family life, the work environment, and so on, the very ways through which modernity itself bubbled to the surface varied vastly, from the timing in which certain aspects would rise, right up to the ideologies which would support or adverse these innovations. As Eisenstadt aptly noticed, "many of the movements that developed [. . .] articulated anti-Western or even anti-modern themes, yet all were distinctively modern. This was true [. . .] of the various nationalist or traditionalist movements that emerged in these societies from the middle of the nineteenth century until after World War II."[100] Eisenstadt's theories, and those of his colleagues, mostly touch upon contemporary frictions between a generalized idea of Western modern traits being at odds with non-European cultures, escalating to Samuel P. Huntington's famous concept of "clash of civilizations."[101] It is quite simple to imagine, though, that as the author himself puts it, "there was an inherent tension between the culture of modernity, the modern 'rational' model of the Enlightenment that emerged as hegemonic in certain periods and places and others construed as reflecting the more 'authentic' cultural traditions of specific societies."[102] The adaptation of the idea of multiple modernities to the more circumscribed and specific field of different occult milieus is quite simple: while some countries, such as Great Britain, Germany, or the Scandinavian nations, in general, can be considered as harboring more progressive and modern occult communities, countries like Italy, Greece, or Spain, for multiple reasons, were not as advanced in many fields as their Nordic counterparts, and thus at times symbolized those cultures reflecting "the more 'authentic' cultural traditions" of their land.[103] At the turn of the century, a comparison between a Central or North European country with Italy would have brought out all the differences between the modern countries and the more traditional ones: in 1921, industrialization was still in its infancy in Italy, and only one person out of one thousand owned a car; life expectancy had slowly crept from 35 in 1881 to 50 in 1921; 69 people out of 100 were illiterate in 1871, when Italy was reunited, while the ratio had gone down to 48.5 at the turn of the century; when Mussolini took power in 1922, 52 percent of workers were employed in the agricultural sector, which for long after remained Italy's main source of revenue; only 5 percent of women possessed a degree in 1900, and the right to vote was extended to them only in 1945.[104] It is therefore plausible to accept the theories of Eisenstadt or those of sociologist Volker H. Schmidt, when the latter wrote that

> Not only are there [. . .] several paths to modernity, but different historical trajectories and sociocultural backgrounds also give rise to highly distinct forms of modernity in different parts of the world. *In fact, even Europe, where it all began, exhibits a great deal of cultural and institutional diversity.* [italics mine][105]

Volker goes on to explain that, as there are different accounts of modernities outside the Western Hemisphere, there exist multiple modernities within the Western Hemisphere itself: "Thus, French modernity differs from German modernity differs from Scandinavian modernity differs from English modernity differs from American modernity and so on."[106] Sociologist Björn Wittrock suggested that the fact that Greece, Portugal, and Spain only comparatively recently adopted a democratic political system sets their expressions of modernity light years away from those of the countries in Central and Northern Europe.[107]

Although I will not be continuously comparing the Italian esoteric milieu with that of other countries dealt with in previous research, I will use the theoretical framework provided by the "multiple modernities" thesis in order to consider the flourishing of an anti-modern expression of occultism in Italy at the turn of the century and well into the 1930s. This development, if we are to accept the theories posited by S. N. Eisenstadt and others should not come as a surprise, and it should enable my research to balance out the view of European occultism being inherently progressive and, as it were, coincident to an idea of a homogenous modernity affecting the whole of Europe in the same way. Sociologist Ibrahim Kaya has suggested that "[t]otalising theories of modernity stem from the belief that modernity is driven by unilinear progress, absolute truths, the rational planning of ideal social orders and the standardization of knowledge and production."[108] The necessity to take a step back and reassess the multiplicity of modernities is paramount, and this concept also applies to parts of modernity, such as anti-modern sentiments, which are obviously a product of their time and thus thoroughly modern. Therefore, by using this theoretical framework, I will argue that Reghini's Traditionalist circle fits perfectly in such an analysis of modernity, and his focus on ancient Roman customs as the sole instruments with which to remodel the modern world, were at once modern, but unlike anything produced by Britain, Germany, or the Nordic countries. The anti-modern, I will prove, is but the flip side of the modern, even in the smaller field of Western esotericism, and it is my intention to use this framework in order to assess the exaggerated idea of occultism as an exclusively progressive force within modernity. As Raymond R. M. Lee has suggested:

> Each identity involved in this struggle is free to invoke traditions as essential to the reworking of modernity. The role of traditions in organising identity suggests that multiple modernities can be perceived as specific expressions of culture. It implies that the conditions under which modernity is reorganised and represented have symbolic value insofar as they come to encompass cultural meanings vital to identity needs.[109]

1.3.2. The Invention of Sacred Traditions and the Occult

Eric Hobsbawm and Terence Ranger's theory on the invention of traditions, of the creation of ad hoc myths tied to historical events in order to bolster the credibility of certain movements, is almost a corollary to the notions on the transmission of traditions, which I wish to employ in my exposition.[110] James R. Lewis argued that, in a religious setting, traditions are invented and obtain legitimacy through the recreation of an ideal past, when Weberian charismatic leaders were still alive.[111] In Reghini's case this past was to be found during the lives of Pythagoras and of the first kings of Rome, and such magico-religious Tradition, according to the representatives of the *Schola Italica*, had been handed down from generation to generation of secret initiates. Olav Hammer also argues that an emic historiography is often created in order to make the traditions more authentic and believable; thus, according to Hammer "different movements vary in their wish or ability to counter the claims of historical-critical research. [...] The Esoteric Tradition is no exception."[112] It may suffice, in this introductory chapter, to remember Reghini's presumed uninterrupted line of initiates, including Pythagoras (570 BCE–495 BCE), King Numa, Dante Alighieri, Pomponius Leto (1428–1498), Giordano Bruno (1548–1600), Tommaso Campanella (1568–1639), Giuseppe Mazzini, and Amedeo Armentano.

It is through these two theoretical frameworks that I will shed more light on modernity and occultism, in general, and on Reghini's writings on Tradition and modernity, specifically.

1.4. Overview of the Book's Chapters

1.4.1. The Italian Occult Milieu at the Turn of the Century

In order to fully appreciate the changes brought forth by the re-elaboration of positivist epistemology and the influence on the Italian occultist milieu that irrationalist currents exerted, an introductory panorama of occultist manifestations at the end of the nineteenth century is fundamental. Many of the most important political figures who were involved in the unification of Italy were partial to occult practices: Freemasonry, in particular, appealed to Giuseppe Garibaldi, at one stage Grand Master of the Grand Orient of Italy; Camillo Benso, Count of Cavour (1810–1861), was an enthusiastic spiritualist, as was the prominent scientist Cesare Lombroso (1835–1909), founder of the Italian School of Positivist Criminology and, later in his life, a staunch supporter of Eusapia Palladino (1854–1918), without doubt the most famous medium in Italy. In the world of arts, Giosué Carducci (1835–1907) was a long-standing Freemason, and so was Carlo Collodi (1826–1890), author of what is considered to be one of Italy's finest initiatory novels: *Pinocchio*.[113] When the crisis of modernity reached Italy, occultism, as previously discussed, provided one way out of the Weberian cage of disenchantment, and it was in this climate that the young Reghini grew up. Therefore, after a brief outline of the *Risorgimento* phenomenon, which brought Italy's unification, I will analyze traits of nineteenth-century culture, which obviously inspired Reghini, seeping into the following century. Such traits may be found in the great influence that Spiritualism had among the *Risorgimento* élite. The chapter will be closed with an analysis of the nebulous occult milieu called by scholars "the Neapolitan School," which allegedly represented the fin de siècle torchbearers of a perennial Roman Tradition and had as its major exponents Domenico Bocchini (1775–1840), Giustiniano Lebano (1832–1910), and, obviously, Giuliano Kremmerz (1861–1930). Although sources on the Neapolitan schools are scant, it will be necessary to roughly sketch its history because of the great influence it would have on the neo-Pythagoreans and their idea of a *Schola Italica*

1.4.2. The Early Years (1898–1910): Avant-Garde, Theosophy, and Modernity

After a brief foray into the Reghini family history and the Florentine's thinker's early life, this chapter will charter Reghini's first experiences in the world of occultism, with his active role in the founding one of the first Italian Theosophical centers with Isabel Cooper-Oakley (1853/1854–1914), his subsequent delusion with this foreign brand of occultism, and his first studies on the subject of Roman Tradition. The analysis of the broader Theosophical movement in Italy, in clear contrast with Amedeo Armentano's school of thought, will prompt a wider discussion on Reghini's seemingly contradictory involvement with the artistic and cultural avant-gardes and his yearning for an older, pristine tradition. While being a prominent figure at the *Biblioteca Teosofica* in Florence and at the cultural *Caffé Giubbe Rosse*,[114] writing for Giovanni Papini's *Leonardo* and the futurist journal *Lacerba*, Reghini was nevertheless anchored to the idea of a tradition, and yet yearning for a new form of spirituality. By treating the Florentine thinker's writings as studies on the interaction between tradition and avant-garde, I will be able to scrutinize that shift of consciousness Alex Owen refers to, when writing: "committed to a rationalised understanding of the irrational, involved with the elaboration of a worldview that claimed allegiance to much older religious and magical traditions, and caught up in some of the most avant-garde preoccupations of the day, *fin de siècle* occultism exemplified the spiritualized investments of modern disenchanted subjectivity."[115]

1.4.3. *Schola Italica* and the *Rito Filosofico Italiano* (1910–1915)

Reghini's involvement with Freemasonry was constant between 1902 and 1925, the year in which masonic organizations were banned by the Fascist regime. It was within fringe Freemasonry that Reghini found fertile ground for his ideas concerning a reform of modern Freemasonry which invoked a return to origins, and which the Florentine occultist considered to be Italian. Reghini's involvement with Eduardo Frosini (1879–?) will be documented, and the brief history of the *Rito Filosofico Italiano* (*Italian Philosophical Rite*),[116] created to convey the ideals of Roman Traditionalism, will be discussed in detail. Reghini's attempt to bring autochthone ideas and rites into fringe masonry will provide an effective means to widen the scope of the discourse of a Western Tradition opposed to the oriental vogue of the early 1900s.[117] Italy, as was the case of other European countries, witnessed an increased fascination with Oriental philosophies and cultures. Among the most influential scholars who devoted their energies to the study of Eastern cultures, many were also drawn to occultism: Leone Caetani (1869–1935), author of *Annali dell'Islam* (*Annals of Islam*, 1905–1926), was very close to the Roman pagan movements in Rome; Giuseppe Tucci (1894–1984), who began focusing on Eastern cultures by contributing to a Theosophical organization run by Decio Calvari; Julius Evola, who, as Thomas Hakl has rightly emphasized, was in contact with Sir John Woodroffe (1865–1936) and published the first Italian text on Tantra: *L'Uomo come Potenza* (*Man as Power*, 1925). A resurgence of interest in the traditions of Ancient Rome was not limited to

Reghini's circle, though, as can be testified by Roggero Musmeci Ferrari Bravo (1866–1937) and his play *Rumon* (1929), and the diffusion of plays and novels dedicated to Roman themes (viz. Ciro Alvi's *Incendio di Roma*). In this chapter I will also scrutinize Reghini's meeting with his master Armentano, the nature of his initiation, and their common forays in the world of Freemasonry. Space will be devoted to the concept of invented traditions, in this case the *Schola*, as a strategy of epistemology. The brief history of the *Philosophical Rite* will be discussed as the closest Reghini ever got to creating a Roman Traditionalist masonic order.

1.4.4. The Great War and *Imperialismo Pagano*: A Clash between the Modern and the Traditional (1915–1920)

Reghini's most popular article, "Imperialismo Pagano," published in 1914 for the *rivista La Salamandra* and republished in 1924 in *Atanòr*, shall be scrutinized as the most effective and inspiring of Reghini's writings concerning Roman Traditionalism.

Prior to World War I, nationalist sentiments, derived largely from ideals of the *Risorgimento*, had been conveyed into the formation of the *Associazione Nazionalisti Italiani* (*Italian Nationalist Association*) in 1910. Through the writings of Enrico Corradini (1865–1931) and Luigi Federzoni (1878–1967), nationalism acquired a vast number of followers among the bourgeois, with its strong anti-socialist, anti-democratic, and anti-parliamentary sentiments. The main aim of the nationalists was the creation of a monarchy that would enact an imperialist policy. But nationalist ideals also had space in the agenda of occult groups: Arturo Reghini and his closest followers, most of them greatly involved in avant-garde movements, were staunch supporters of Italian nationalism. The main reason for supporting a nationalist agenda went beyond political sympathies, though: Reghini believed that only through the conquest of lands, which had been originally part of the Italian peninsula during the Roman Empire, the energies which had made Rome great in the past would be summoned again. Reghini, Armentano, Papini, and Giulio Parise all enlisted as volunteers for the purpose of being able to harness the occult powers of a reunified Italy.

A large part of the chapter will be a textual analysis of Reghini's most influential article, "Imperialismo Pagano": the subjects of discussion will be manifold: who the readers of the article were, the theories espoused therein, the idea of a *prisca sapientia Romana*, which could still bring Italy its past glory back. The bearers and transmitters of such knowledge will be described, and the metahistory created by Reghini in the article will be contextualized in its time and place of publication.

1.4.5. Fascism and Traditionalism (1920–1925)

With the rise of Fascist power in the 1920s, the State's attitude toward masonic or other secret societies exacerbated and in a memorable speech on the June 21, 1921, Benito Mussolini (1883–1945) declared that Fascism did not share Freemasonry's ideals, claiming that Freemasonry was a "big windbreak behind which hide little men."[118] In 1923, he declared that belonging to a lodge or occult order prevented a person from being a member of the Fascist party, while in 1925, with the Bodrero bill, Freemasonry was banned, and many lodges were ransacked and destroyed by Mussolini's squads. After a historical introduction, in which I will describe Mussolini's rise to power and his march on Rome, I will use Roger Griffin's and Frank Kermode's theories in order to highlight the two sides of Fascism: the ultra-modern one and the traditionalist aspect. The concept of "social occult modernism," created by Griffin, will be expounded on and its functionality to my ideas of an anti-modern approach to occultism in modern times will be assessed. Next, the idea of an Occult Fascism will be compared to that of Nazi Occultism, and I will discuss the pros and cons of holding the idea of the existence of an occult aspect to Fascism or not.

I will then argue how, throughout the 1910s, René Guénon's theories for the rise of an *élite intellectuelle* were taken into consideration by Reghini, Amedeo Armentano, and the circle of associates close to them. Such an elite was to provide the esoteric and spiritual foundation on which to rebuild Western civilization. While the relationship between elitism and occultism is much looser in other countries, an analysis of Reghini's writings and those of the *Gruppo di Ur* (*Ur Group*) will be pivotal in showing how a culture soon to be permeated by the concept of elitism, such as the Italian one in the 1920s and 1930s, would co-opt the very concept of elite in its esoteric expressions, too. A thorough analysis of hitherto unpublished correspondence between Guénon and Reghini will close the chapter, and a mutual influence between the two Traditionalist thinkers will be highlighted: as will be seen, Reghini, in the 1920s, seems to have influenced Guénon's ideas on Traditionalism in the West, as can be gleaned from the Frenchman's writings on the journals edited by the Italian occultist in the following chapter.

1.4.6. The *Ur* Group and the End of a Dream (1925–1929)

Occultism has often been related to the concept of elitism. Both Adorno and Webb refer to a restricted number of individuals who embraced occult ideas in open defiance of Enlightenment ideals. While scholars such as Joscelyn Godwin, Corinna Treitel, and Marco Pasi have done much to promote the idea of a democratization of occultism in the modern world, it is important to notice how, alongside more easily accessible societies such as the Theosophical and the Anthroposophical societies, elitist occult movements existed in early twentieth-century Italy. Indeed, the concept of élite itself was the subject of many debates among Italian occultists. These diatribes were often hosted on occult reviews, on which Reghini was one of the most active agitators. In 1924, Reghini founded his first *rivista* (journal, *Atanòr*), and would later involve the *haut monde* of occultism in his subsequent endeavors, *Ignis* and *Ur*. Out of the long list of contributors to these journals, one may cite René Guénon, Julius Evola, Giuliano Kremmerz, Aniceto Del Massa (1898–1975), Leone Caetani, and Giovanni Antonio Colonna di Cesarò. The *Gruppo di Ur*[119] was the most significant coterie combining an elitist aristocratism and occultism in 1920s Italy.

The ultimate blow to shatter Reghini's dream of Pagan Imperialism under the guide of Mussolini took place in 1929, when, with the Concordat, the Vatican State reacquired temporal power and was declared the official religion of the budding Fascist empire. The rift between Roman Traditionalists and the Catholic Church had been evident from the early years of the twentieth century. As Alex Owen has noticed in her study on modern British occultism, in the modern age "many of the most spiritually inclined no longer identified in any way with formal Christian observance, [and] turned instead to the heterodox spirituality of Occultism."[120] If this was the case for Britain, studying the reaction to orthodox Christianity in Italy is even more revealing: Reghini's attempt at a restoration of Roman pagan ideals is a striking example of how anti-Christian and anti-clerical feelings permeated sections of the Italian occult milieu of the day. A return to the Roman Way to the gods could therefore be seen as an individual and subjective choice before the advancing crisis of religious institution, which still regarded itself as an omnipresent, exclusive way of access to the divine.

1.4.7. *Silentium post Clamores*: The Final Years (1930–1946)

In 1929, Reghini abandoned Rome for what I argue are three important reasons: first, the end of his hopes for a pagan Renaissance had created great discomfort, and the idea of continuing operating in Rome was, in the light of socio-political developments, impractical; second, his mentor Armentano had long left Italy for Sao Paulo, Brazil, for reasons both political and economic, and many of Reghini's remaining relationships had soured (most importantly, his collaboration and friendship with Evola had ended abruptly); third, Reghini was subject to the constant attention of the Fascist secret police OVRA. His ill-standing with the regime meant that his only hope of gaining an income was to teach in a private school, and this he did in Budrio, near Bologna, at the Quirico Filopanti private institute, from 1937 to 1946, the year of his death. In his final years, great attention was paid by the occultist to Pythagorean mathematics. His interest in mathematics had been a constant throughout his life, and he was often to be found alone, with an abacus, pen, and paper, for, as Roberto Sestito notes in his biography, "it was through the science of numbers that he grasped some of those never-disclosed secrets of the ancient *Schola Italica*."[121]

1.5. Conclusion

A final section in which I will draw my conclusions will close the work: in it I will pick up all the strands developed in the separate chapters and weave them into a coherent structure, attempting, in the first place, to describe a novel interaction between occultism and modernity in an Italian context, following the theory of multiple modernities, and in the second, to prove Reghini's pivotal role in the history of Italian occultism, showing him to be a fundamental figure in the development of Traditionalist thought, Italian Freemasonry, occult reviews, the neo-Pagan tenets of the *Schola Italica*, and mathematics.

Appendix: *Imperialismo Pagano*

A translation of Reghini's seminal article into the English language will be presented as an appendix, in order to provide the reader with the complete text, thus aiding his understanding of the main tenets of the *Schola Italica*.

2
Risorgimento Italy

Occultism, Politics, the Rise of the Nation State, and Roman Traditionalism

> The Fatherland is the sign of the mission that God
> gave to you to realise among Humanity.[1]
> —Giuseppe Mazzini

Before dealing with Reghini and his life and works, an introductory chapter on the Italian *Risorgimento*, in all its multifaceted expressions, is necessary: not only will it help shed light on the historical processes which shaped Reghini's youth and political beliefs, but a more focused analysis on the Roman question and the proliferation of occult milieus within the Italian peninsula will also help explain Reghini's lifelong anti-clerical and pro-Masonic leanings. It is fundamental to notice that most of Reghini's ideas were not born in a vacuum, and that the nineteenth-century occult and literary milieus had already formulated some of the key themes, which would later blossom in the Roman Traditionalist current.

2.1. A Historical Overview of the *Risorgimento*

2.1.1. A Brief Outline

When writing about the Italian *Risorgimento* (literally translated as Resurgence or Resurrection), the two main questions that need to be answered in order to aid readers less familiar with Italian history are as follows: (1) what is the timeframe in which the *Risorgimento* occurred? and (2) what do historians mean by this term? The first question has been debated by many scholars, and the general consensus is to fix the date for the beginning of the *Risorgimento* as the immediate aftermath of the Congress of Vienna held in Schoenbrunn Castle from November 1814 to June 1815, after the fall of Napoleon Bonaparte (1769–1821). During the Congress, it was decided that post-Napoleonic Italy would remain very much as it had been "since the sixteenth century, a plaything of the European Powers."[2] What is now Italy was then divided into five large states: Piedmont,

Lombardy-Venetia, the Grand Duchy of Tuscany, The Papal States, and the Kingdom of the Two Sicilies with Naples as the capital. The year of the end of the *Risorgimento* process has been debated more often. While it has been commonplace to choose 1861 as a key date, there are numerous others considered to mark the end: following Giuseppe Garibaldi's conquest of the Two Sicilies; the annexations of Tuscany, Emilia, Marches, and Umbria by Piedmont; the plebiscites' vote of 1860-1861; or the election of the first Italian Parliament in January of that year. Other scholars have shifted the date to 1871 after Rome had been conquered by the army led by General Luigi Cadorna (1850-1928) and the "eternal city" had been proclaimed the capital of the country.[3] A third date, less popular, but, as we shall see, fundamental to Reghini and his associates, was 1918, the end of World War I, when the Italians had annexed the cities of Trento and Trieste, thus effectively concluding the process of complete unification of the peninsula.[4]

As to the what the *Risorgimento* actually represented, modern scholarship tends to reject the common idea, mostly still taught in Italian schools today and fundamental to Reghini's early twentieth-century understanding of history, that the *Risorgimento* was a movement that concerned small and circumscribed elites, leading the people to independence by the determination of the four great personalities of the time: Camillo Benso Count of Cavour (1810-1861), King Vittorio Emanuele II (1820-1878), Giuseppe Garibaldi (1835-1871), and Giuseppe Mazzini (1807-1872). The revisionism on this stock description of the *Risorgimento* is too vast a subject to discuss in this chapter, and it includes new interpretations of economic, political, geographical, and, most of all, social factors. What is important to stress, though, is that contemporary scholars, such as Alberto Mario Banti, Paul Ginsborg, Derek Beals, and Gigi di Fiore, to mention a few, have convincingly argued that the idea of Italy was not, as famously described by Austrian diplomat Klement von Metternich (1773-1859), "a mere geographical expression."[5] Rather than being a political and economic process supported by very few individuals, the *Risorgimento* has been more recently described as a larger movement than previously argued. It is true that Italy's inhabitants in the nineteenth century were mostly illiterate, with literacy rates barely reaching 2.5 percent and the number of local dialects being the main form of expression, but it is also equally true that

> [i]n the context of a largely illiterate society [. . .] the number of people affiliated to sects [i.e. secret societies], of the rebels of '20-21, the members of the *Giovane Italia* [Young Italy, Mazzini's secret society in favour of Italy's unification], of those who take to the piazzas or voluntarily go to war or fight with the regular army of the Kingdom of Sardinia or set-up hospitals or communication lines in 1848-9, who plot schemes of insurrection in the early fifties, who fight

as volunteers in 1859, 1860 and 1866, who go and vote during the plebiscites, who participate en masse to the funerals of Mazzini, of Vittorio Emanuele, of Garibaldi and others, is *absolutely impressive* [italics added].[6]

In his numerous studies on the phenomenon of the *Risorgimento*, Banti treated this popular movement in the light of George Mosse's study of German patriotic nationalism.[7] Banti described *Risorgimento* agitations as a manifestation of new politics, born from the French Revolution, which "conceptually, even before than factually, posits at the centre of the public arena the *people/nation*, as principal depository of sovereignty."[8] As such, he formulated three main ideas, which, to German nationalism scholars, will appear familiar, as characteristics of the *Risorgimento* rhetoric that would spur the masses into action: the love for the Fatherland, the sacralization of heroes, and the concept of blood and soil, all popularized by German romantics and nationalists as the *blut und boden* ideology.[9] With other wording, Banti proposed this tripartite romantic ideal in other works. In *Per una Nuova Storia del Risorgimento* (*For a New History of the Risorgimento*, 2007), for example, he formulated the idea of profound figures, *figure profonde*, which he defined as "allegoric systems, narrative constellations, which incorporate a specific chart of values, offered as the fundamental one that gives meaning to the proposed conceptual system," meaning in this case, that the ideas behind the *Risorgimento* were backed by a vast movement.[10] These three ideas were love/honor/virtue (*amore/onore/virtù*), sacrifice (*sacrificio*), and kinship (*parentela*). Of course, in most cases, the three ideas are intricately intertwined, and it is not easy to find a speech, poem, melodrama, or newspaper article that does not mix all three. It will, therefore, be more useful to find examples that range from the political arena of rhetoric, to poetry, to narrative in popular books in which the reader can find aspects of these profound archetypes.

On March 25, 1861, just months prior to his death, Cavour delivered one of his most famous speeches to the newly formed Parliament in Turin. Replete with nationalistic rhetoric, Cavour's address touched upon the very themes, which had characterized the entire period of the *Risorgimento*: the love for the united Fatherland and the need to conquer Rome and make it Italy's capital once again. From the minutes of the Parliamentary session, it is easy to see that the speech was a triumph, uniting both Left and Right in its propositions: parenthesized comments from the audience can be found throughout the written copy of the speech, such as "(On the left: Good!), (Approval), (Applause) or (Laughter and signs of approval)."[11] But, as one of Cavour's most celebrated interventions in the newly created Parliament, what was the content of the talk? The rhetoric of the greatness of ancient Rome, which Reghini and Armentano would make great use of in the twentieth century, can already be found in 1861:

[A]ll the historical, intellectual, moral circumstances that must determine the conditions of the capital of a great country all converge in Rome. Rome is the only city, which does not only have memories of being a municipality; all of Rome's history, from the days of the Caesars to this very day, is the history of a city whose importance extends infinitely beyond its territory, of a city, I mean, destined to be the capital of a great State.[12]

Later on, a more sociopolitical bent was given to the speech when Cavour asserted that Rome must be annexed with two conditions: (1) an alliance must be forged with the French against the Austrians and (2) the numerous Catholics in the country must be reassured that a move of the capital to Rome would in no case represent an act of servitude toward the Vatican.[13] The rest of Cavour's talk dealt with the Roman question, and how, as Italians, the population should be free to practice the Christian religion even though the Kingdom of Italy was not ready to grant temporal power to Pius IX (1792-1878).

Such sentiments, the love for the Fatherland and for the ideals of the *Risorgimento*, were not confined to the Parliamentary halls of Turin. They also seemed to pervade popular literature even long after the annexation of Rome and the reunification of Italy. Possibly the most noticeable example, which impressed *Risorgimento* values upon the mind of many young readers, was Edmondo de Amicis's (1846-1908) "*Cuore*" (*Heart*, 1886), a book aimed at young children, replete with *Risorgimento* values and their celebration thereof.[14] The success of the book was so astounding that three years after its first publication, the publishers, the Treves brothers, had put out the 100th reprint. The text followed the life of an elementary school class in Turin throughout the 1881-1882 school year and confronted themes, such as the condition of southern Italians who had emigrated North in search of work and the teaching of civic virtues in the newly formed Kingdom, including the love for the Fatherland, heroism, charity, and a stoic endurance of adversities. Interspersed between the diary entries of the protagonist, Enrico Bottini, we find *Risorgimento* stories regarding young children and their contribution to the Italian cause. These characters, who excelled in virtue and heroic valor, such as *il piccolo scrivano fiorentino* (the little Florentine writer), *la piccola vedetta lombarda* (the little Lombard lookout), or *il piccolo tamburino sardo* (the little Sardinian tamborine), all represented examples of extreme bravery, endurance during wartime, and an example to follow for the young Bottini and his classmates.[15] The most striking example of a strict adherence to the value of the *Risorgimento*, though, can be found in Bottini's father's letter to his son, verging on the subject of the love of the Fatherland. In it, the reader may find a sum of what it meant for adherents to the *Risorgimento* to be Italian:

I love Italy because my mother is Italian; because the blood that flows in my veins is Italian; because the soil in which our dead are buried whom my mother mourns and whom my father venerates is Italian; because the town in which I was born, the language that I speak, the books that educate me, because my brother, my sister, my comrades, the great people among whom I live, and the beautiful nature which surrounds me, and all that I see, that I love, that I study, that I admire, is Italian.[16]

Bottini's father ends his letter admonishing his son never to neglect his duty toward the Fatherland: "May I one day see you return to safety from a battle fought for her [Italy, . . .] but if I should learn that you have preserved your life because you were concealed from death [. . .] I shall never be able to love you again, and I shall die with that dagger in my heart."[17]

Similar sentiments are also felt in loftier literary expressions, such as poetry, and more modest entertainment, such as popular songs. Alessandro Manzoni (1875–1873), author of the novel *I Promessi Sposi* (*The Betrothed*, 1827), was among the first to pen an ode spurring Piedimontese and Lombard forces to unite against the common enemy.[18] In his *1821*, published only in 1848, Manzoni wrote, "They swore: May it be that this wave never / again may flow amongst two foreign banks: / May there be no place where barriers will rise / Between Italy and Italy, never!"[19] Giovanni Berchet (1783–1851) was another poet who embraced the patriotism of the *Risorgimento* wholeheartedly.[20] His *All'Armi! All'Armi* (*To Arms! to Arms*, 1830) later became the hymn of Mazzini's *Giovane Italia* and represented one of the most rousing examples of *Risorgimento* poetry: the first verses sing:

> Come on. Sons of Italy! Come on, at arms! [Be] brave!
> The soil here is ours: of our heritage
> The terrible barter of kings ends.
> A people divided in seven destinies,
> Broken in seven by seven borders,
> Melts into one, a serf no more.[21]

Teobaldo Ciconi (1824–1863), patriot, author, journalist, and poet, penned some of the *Risorgimento*'s most recognisable lyrics, and in a very short time, they were adapted to music and achieved fame as popular songs.[22] His *Passa la Ronda* (*The Patrol Comes Around*, 1848) quickly became soldiers' favorite, with its easy to memorise lyrics:

> Hush, silence! Who's there?
> The patrol comes around. Hail the patrol:

> Long live Italy, freedom!
> We are the guards of the three colours,
> Green, the hope of our hearts,
> White, the faith we keep amongst us,
> Red, the wounds of our heroes![23]

2.1.2. *Risorgimento* as Roman Tradition and the Role of Freemasonry in the Unification Process

In his work on Roman Traditionalist strands in the *Risorgimento*, *Dell'Elmo di Scipio: Risorgimento, Storia d'Italia e Memoria di Roma* (*By Scipio's Helm: Risorgimento, Italian History and the Remembrance of Rome*, 2012), author and Roman Traditionalist Sandro Consolato, following the footsteps of the ideas of the members of Reghini's *Schola Italica*, sought to demonstrate that "the Italian *Risorgimento* was a spiritual and political event, *indigenous* in its deep essence, and, *as such*, readable within the categories of the 'World of Tradition' [...] and, in particular, of the Roman-Italic tradition."[24] Even though it lays beyond the strict boundaries of an etic approach to the subject matter, Consolato's work is key to familiarize oneself with ideas that successfully circulated in Reghini's group—ideas that would drastically shape the Florentine occultist's life pursuit. Moreover, the choice of using an emic source as the subject of discussion is only dictated by the fact that by reading Consolato, the reader may more easily understand Reghini's patriotism and nationalism.[25] With this interpretative key, the nineteenth-century movement can be seen as a product of the modern age (with the rise of the nation states; the emancipation of a bourgeois class; the rampant secularisation of religion; and the seemingly unstoppable upsurge of Positivist thought), but it is an "aspirazione antica," an ancient vocation, which just happened to take place in the modern era.[26] Consolato then proceeds chronologically to map the great figures of Italian thought who, throughout the centuries, allegedly wished for an Italian unification. Again, the characters enunciated are the same that present themselves in Reghini's "Imperialismo Pagano." Dante Alighieri (1285–1321), the so-called father of the Italian language, is of course among the very first to be considered with his contemporary Francesco Petrarca (1304–1374), being praised even more for abandoning the idea of the link of Italian independence with that of the Catholic Holy Roman Empire.[27] In his poem *Italia mia, perché 'l parlar sia indarno* (*Oh my Italy, Though Speaking [of unity] is Fruitless*, 1344–1345), Petrarca dreams of a united Italy from the Alps to Sicily but realizes the impossibility of the task at hand in his day.[28] The following two characters linked to a unified nation and an Italian renaissance are old acquaintances of scholars of Western esotericism—the Calabrian theologian

Tommaso Campanella (1568–1639) and the Dominican mystic Giordano Bruno (1548–1600).[29] During the *Risorgimento* proper, one of the greatest advocates for a united Italy with Rome as its capital was Mazzini:

> There aren't five Italies, four Italies, three Italies. There is but one Italy. God, who in creating her smiled upon her, gave her as boundaries the two most sublime barriers he ever set in Europe, symbols of eternal Strength and eternal Motion, the Alps and the Sea. Thrice accursed, by you and those who come after you, he who would assume to give her other boundaries.[30]

Mazzini's influence on Reghini can never be overstated. As is seen in his magnum opus "Imperialismo Pagano," some of Mazzini's writings seemed to be almost memorized by Reghini, who would then reinterpret them according to his Traditionalist ideas: "Many cities perished on earth and all may in their turn perish, but Rome, by design of Providence, and realized by its people, is the Eternal City, like that to which the mission to divulge to the world the word of Unity was given," wrote the leader of the *Giovane Italia*.[31]

Giuseppe Garibaldi was the second fundamental figure in the reunification of Italy, noted for his role as a liberator of South American countries, which had made him a world-recognized hero. As Alessandro Colonna Walewski has proclaimed, "Garibaldi is a man capable triumphing in any feat."[32] Upon Garibaldi's return to Italy, he, along with Mazzini, was one of the major figures of the *Risorgimento*. Garibaldi's motto of "O Roma, o Morte!" ("Rome, or Death!") symbolizes the importance given by the leader of the redshirts to the conquest of the capital. Ippolito Nievo (1831–1861), author and one of Garibaldi's most staunch supporters, wrote in his *Le Confessioni di un Italiano* (*The Confessions of an Italian*, 1867): "Rome is the Gordian Knot of our destinies, Rome is the grandiose and many-shaped symbol of our race, Rome is our ark of salvation, which with its light dissipates the fog of all the crooked and confused thoughts of the Italians."[33] As formidable a leader as Garibaldi was, it is in the light of his strong links with Freemasonry that his influence must be scrutinized.

2.1.3. Freemasonry in Italy in the Second Half of the Nineteenth Century

The institutional history of Italian Freemasonry has a fixed date of birth against which no scholar has argued, December 20, 1859.[34] In Turin, on the second floor of the building in *Via Stampatori* 18, seven masons met and decided to create "an Italian Grand Orient under the name of Great Orient of *Ausonia*."[35] After Napoleon's (1769–1821) debacle, and the successive return to smaller duchies and kingdoms in 1816, Freemasonry had been banned for its subversive potential by the rulers of the various states. This does not mean that other secret societies did not thrive or have weight in the political events of the first half of the nineteenth century. On the contrary, the *Carbonari* (Charcoal Burners) had been fundamental in some of the early uprisings of 1821 and 1831 in the Kingdom of Naples and the Papal States. *Carboneria* was a loosely organized group of secret societies with a vague resemblance to Freemasonry, and most of the important figures of the *Risorgimento* have been positively linked to this movement.[36] Mazzini was a member as far back as 1827 when he was only twenty-two, and Garibaldi was associated with what we can consider the first active element of a revolt in the history of the *Risorgimento*.[37] As Sandro Consolato noted, patriot Santorre di Santa Rosa (1783–1825) was probably the first to write about the key role played by the *Carbonari* in the insurrections that took place in Piedmont, Veneto, Lombardy, the Papal States, and the Kingdom of Naples: "This revolution is the first attempted in Italy in many centuries without the aid and the intervention of foreigners; it's the first to have shown two Italian peoples that replied to one another from the two extremities of the peninsula."[38] Despite their attempts to revolt, the *Carbonari* were too far removed from the average population, who, more often than not, did not join in the revolutionary actions, which were swiftly culled with much bloodshed.[39]

Some of the founding members of the newly formed *Ausonia* Lodge had had experiences with the *Carboneria* and other secret societies of a similar kind. Sisto Anfossi (n.d.), doctor and revolutionary fighter, had been a member of the *Franchi Muratori* (Free Masons, est. 1825) and successively of *I Cavalieri della Libertà* (The Knights of Liberty, est. 1830–1831), two societies with much in common with the *Carboneria*.[40] After the creation of the Italian state in 1861, the founders of the Italian Grand Orient (henceforth GOI) preferred to assume a moderate position in the political arena of the day, succeeding in deterring the more democratic members from electing Garibaldi as Grand Master. The Cavourian Filippo Cordova (1811–1868), ex-Minister of Agriculture and among the most conservative of the moderate wing of GOI, was elected instead.[41] In 1864, Garibaldi was assigned an Honorary Grand Master title, and the next head of GOI was the left-wing Member of Parliament Francesco de Luca (1811–1875). As noted by historian of Freemasonry Augusto Comba, "with 1865 and the movement of the capital to Florence, a 30-year period begins during which there will be a strong identification between that political sector (the left wing) and the leadership of Italian Freemasonry."[42] Within this timeframe, the number of lodges throughout Italy increased exponentially. In 1860, a new Supreme Council of GOI was founded in Palermo with the creation of the lodge *I Rigeneratori* (The Regenerators), a lodge in which, incidentally, Reghini would be initiated in 1902. The reasons behind this sudden popularity of Freemasonry are obviously to be found in the newly formed state in which freedom of expression was more openly tolerated, but it is my opinion that it was the link with politics that proved to be Freemasonry's fortune. Many key ideas that were upheld within cultural and political circles of the 1850s and 1860s were identical to those that could be found in a lodge: political ideologies, sacralization of politics and of the nation-state, and the edification of a new country as one people, for example.[43]

A *vexata quaestio*, which always seems to crop up when Freemasonry is analyzed in relation to the *Risorgimento*, is the apparent major role that Freemasonry played in the unification of the country. Following Consolato's idea, which goes as far as calling it a "plot theory," I postulate that we must focus on the historical data we possess to be able to draw a sound conclusion. If there were only eight people in 1859 who wanted to start GOI, and a negligible number of "irregular" Masonic lodges scattered throughout Italy, and Freemasonry had been banned in all of the peninsula after the Congress of Vienna, we are left with the smaller secret societies and offshoots of the *Carboneria*, which had to operate under the constant threat of being disbanded and its members incarcerated or killed.[44] The identity between the new bourgeois class and members of Freemasonry had undermined the nation states restored after Vienna, but after the failure of the revolts in 1820–1821 and 1830–1831, the new political climate excluded Freemasonry from any public activity. Freemasonry only seemed to pick up in the 1860s, when most of Italy was unified and the only state resisting annexation was the Vatican. But before then, there are simply no documents to support a thesis of a huge Masonic entity pulling the strings and deciding the fate of Italy. Ernesto Nathan (1848–1921), Grand Master of GOI at the turn of the century, had himself admitted that "with the fall of the Napoleonic dominion, the age of maximum splendour for Freemasonry ended and, in part, as a consequence of the rise of the *Carbonari*, who were falsely equated with Freemasons, severe prohibitions were applied [. . .] Freemasonry did not rise again until the middle of the nineteenth century," as will be further discussed in Chapter 4.[45]

2.2. Pope Pius IX and the Roman Question

Before his death in 1861, Cavour had made the importance of the conquest of Rome and its annexation to the Kingdom of Italy clear, especially during the time of the newly formed government in March 1861, where he claimed that Rome "is the necessary capital of Italy, since without Rome being united to Italy as its capital, Italy could never hold a stable position."[46] In these decades, Italy witnessed the rise of a group that has been defined as Neo-Guelph. According to historian Luigi Bulfiretti, "the Neo-Guelphs are those who consider, as a basic element of the national-political resurgence, the Pope, who should head an Italian confederation of princes [. . .] for the fight against the Turks or the foreigner hostile to the Church."[47] The Neo-Guelphs, who had rallied around Vincenzo Gioberti (1801–1852) and the tenets of his *Del Primato Morale e Civile degli Italiani* (*Of the Moral and Civil Primacy of the Italians*, 1845),[48] were more and more cornered by the other nationalist movements. This ever-growing consensus, through the propaganda of left-wing papers in Piedmont, especially, rallied for the abolition of clerical orders, the abolition of the first article of the Albertine statute, which declared Catholicism as the "State-Religion" and the introduction of civil marriage into the constitution.[49] However, what was it of Pope Pius IX that so angered the citizens of the newly founded reign of Italy? In 1868, two years before being held captive on Vatican soil, the Pope had issued the bill, *Non Expedit*, which forbade all Catholics from voting in elections or taking an active political role in the Kingdom of Italy.[50] The government also proceeded to emanate laws that were grouped under the heading of *Liquidazione dell'Asse Ecclesiastico*, or *Liquidation of the Ecclesiastic Fund*, which, according to decree 3036 of July 7, 1866 and law 3848 of the following year, enforced the coerced closure of religious corporations and the sale of the goods acquired thereby.[51] During the inauguration of the new quarters of the very first Masonic lodge in Italy, Turin's *Loggia Ausonia*, on January 1, 1860, Lodge Master Filippo Delpino (1779–1860) had said: "Rome, once ruler of the world, then left for centuries tainted by many crimes at the hands of the nefarious activities of its rulers [i.e., the Papacy], pastors in savage wolves' clothing, stretches its supplicant hands toward this blessed corner of Italy where, adored by his subjects, Vittorio Emanuele II reigns."[52] The importance of the annexation of Rome to the Kingdom cannot be stressed enough: in Reghini's day, first, because, as we shall see, only a unified Italy, in the eyes of Roman Traditionalists, could let loose the latent occult powers of the land, which would bring Italy to rule the world once more; second, in the years succeeding 1861, too, nationalistic fervor and rampant anticlericalism made the conquest of Rome a priority. Rome, as we have seen in previous paragraphs, was a symbol, a rallying point around which many politicians and military leaders had constructed their fortunes. Both the general public and the more educated elites saw papacy as the final barrier between what was perceived as centuries of temporal despotism and a future of glory for the newly unified country. This topic will be dealt with more thoroughly in the second half of Chapter 7.

2.3. Italy and Nineteenth-Century Occultism

In order to fully appreciate the importance of occultism in Italian society during the historical period analyzed in this chapter, a cursory research into foreign forms of occult manifestation must be accounted for and described. The three most important strands of occult influence, which touched Italian society in all of its strata, were, as we have already seen, Freemasonry, Spiritualism, and Theosophy. Seeing that the Theosophical Society (est. 1875), which was to have a massive influence on the young Reghini, who played a pivotal role in its expansion on Italian soil, was only founded close to the end of the nineteenth century, I shall be discussing this phenomenon more thoroughly in the following chapter. Since Freemasonry, and all of its ties with the political turmoil of nineteenth-century Italy, has already been discussed to some degree and will be more thoroughly examined in Chapter 4, most of this subchapter will primarily focus on Spiritualism, its history outside of Italy, its spread on Italian soil, and the great interest it garnered among the higher social, as well as the lowest, classes. As shall be seen, most of those whom we consider to be the primary actors in *Risorgimento*'s history shared a deep interest in the practices dictated by Spiritualist beliefs.

Before delving into the history of this phenomenon, it is important to provide a working definition of Spiritualism, not to mention its differences with Spiritism. While Spiritualism refers to the movement that gained momentum in the United States at around the middle of the nineteenth century before spreading to England and other European countries, Spiritism is represented by a corpus of doctrinal teachings defined by its founding figure, pedagog and author Hippolyte Léon Denizard Rivail, better known by his "channelled" druidic name Allan Kardec (1804–1869). He described Spiritism as "science that deals with the nature, origin, and destiny of spirits, and their relation with the corporeal world."[53] But in order to make chronological sense in the *mare magnum* of spirits, séances, and dancing tables, we must start our narration from a small town in upstate New York in 1848.

2.3.1. The Origins and Spread of Spiritualism

As historian of occultism James Webb wrote at the very beginning of his first chapter of *The Flight from Reason: The Age of the Irrational*: "[t]he gods came down to earth again on 31 March 1848 [. . .] It was a small wooden cottage at Hydesville, Arcadia, near New York."[54] Here the sisters Leah (1814–1890), Margaret, (1833–1893), and Kate (1837–1892) Fox claimed to have found a way to communicate with a spirit who made his presence known through "rappings" or "raps" on the walls and the ceiling.[55] Before two years had passed, the Fox sisters were performing in New York City, where they gave three séances in three days for one and a half dollars per ticket.[56] Spiritualism became a sensation, and the Fox sisters, once the phenomenon had spread nationwide, were largely forgotten until 1888 when a journalist offered Margaret the sum of $1500 in order for her to expose her séances as a fraud. In front of a packed New York Academy, Margaret proceeded to uncover one of the biggest hoaxes of modern history. According to Amy Lehman, "in 1888, the sisters confessed that they had faked the ghostly rapping, which precipitated the age of spirit contact. They claimed to have produced knocking sounds by manipulating and cracking the joints in their feet and knees. For a while, they made money giving lectures about this 'deathblow' to Spiritualism."[57] But it was a story that believers were not interested in. While the fame of the sisters had waned considerably, Spiritualism had spread across the United States, and the raps were alternated by feats of automatic writing, states of trance in which the medium was overtaken by a spirit who spoke through the human vessel it occupied. Musical mediums could make instruments float in mid-air and play tunes, while others manifested ectoplasm, the residue substance left behind by manifesting spirits.[58] It was a matter of time before the Spiritualist craze would touch European shores, as the continental countries had been long since fascinated by the magnetic experiments led by the likes of Franz Anton Mesmer (1734–1815) and his disciple Armand Chastenet (1751–1825). With all their talk of latent powers and faculties lying within a hypnotized person, Spiritualism certainly had the way paved by such pre-existent phenomena.[59] To understand the magnitude of the omnipresence of Spiritualism, one must concur with Simona Cigliana, when she stated:

> It is very difficult, nowadays, to realise with full comprehension the intensity and the extension of the debate, which took place in the XIX century, especially in the Positivistic era when a thirst for all things marvellous seemed to almost universally spread into all social strata, of the passion with which Positivist science devoted itself to somnambulist women and turning tables, manifestations out of thin air and ectoplasms, alternating episodes of *pochade* with spectacular conversions, riding the wave of the so-called Hydesville phenomena.[60]

In 1852, the first American medium to set foot on European soil was Maria B. Hayden (1826–1883), who had discovered her mediumistic powers the year before during a séance held by her husband.[61] The medium, who had been invited to take part in the séance at the Hayden's residence, was none other than an eighteen-year-old Daniel Dunglas Home (1833–1886), who would proceed to become one of the most controversial and popular mediums of his time. While Hayden's stay in England proved to be unsuccessful, her sojourn lasting but a year, Home's fortunes were to prove more enduring.[62] Suffering from ill health, in his memoir *Incidents in my Life* (1874), Home confessed that he did not expect to survive more than a month after his move to London. Against all odds, he was welcomed by a fervent Spiritualist named William Cox (n.d.), who took the man into his care and gave him free lodging in his large hotel on 53-55 Jermyn

Street.[63] Immediately, and within less than a month, Home had more clients attending his séances than he could have ever thought of and was earning incredible amounts of money: "my time was fully occupied, notwithstanding my delicate health, in giving séances to anxious enquirers of all ranks and classes, from the peer to the artisan, including men of all the professions high in art, science and literature."[64] Soon, Home was sought after in other countries, and his voyages took him to France, Russia, and Italy, where he contributed greatly to the flaring up of the Spiritualist mania.

In Italy, the Spiritualist vogue bloomed slightly later, but from 1864 the *Annali di Spiritismo in Italia* (*Annals of Spiritualism in Italy*, 1864–1898), edited by Professor Vincenzo Scarpa (1835–1912) under the pseudonym of Niceforo Filalete, one-time secretary of the Count of Cavour, provided the ever-increasing readership with "many mediumistic 'communications,' and brief excerpts of dialogues with the 'deceased.'"[65] Scarpa's efforts were not limited to the publication of the *Annali*. In 1863, he published a translation of Allan Kardec's classic *Le Spiritisme à sa plus Simple Expression* (*Spiritism at Its Most Simple Expression*, 1963), where *Filalete*, in the preface, informed the reader: "both in Paris and Lyon, the two biggest cities in France, it has been noticed that all workers, strong-hands and day labourers who consecrated themselves to Spiritism soon abandoned their old guilty habits of carelessness and squandering, have become laborious and frugal, and live honourably trusting in God and in the certainty of a better life."[66] Scarpa's work was not merely limited to the occult: as Cigliana noted,

> The "Annals of Spiritism" were [...] the periodical of the heroic years of spiritism in Italy. [... S]piritism covered an important role, along with Freemasonry, in upholding the spiritual needs of the progressive party, anti-clerical and lay, favouring, also, as a consequence of the Holy See's uncompromising attitude on the subject of temporal power, the heading of religious aspirations towards a transcendent horizon not bound to the Church.[67]

Since the late 1850s, Italy witnessed a marked increase in the number of societies and clubs constituted around mediums. Turin was probably still the most exciting city in terms of variety in which Spiritualists and Spiritists manifested their beliefs. In 1856, the Vice-President of the House of Parliament, Gaetano de Marchi (1792–1868), along with a number of experts and rich landowners, founded one of the very first of such societies on Italian soil. Once this group was dissolved, the *Società Torinese di Studi Spiritici* (*Turin Society for Spiritists Studies*) was founded in 1863 with Scarpa as a member and Enrico Dalmazzo (n.d.) as an allegedly talented medium and future editor of *Annali*.[68] Soon, the Turin society was joined by the *Società Spirituale* (*Spiritual Society*) in Naples, the *Società Spiritica* (*Spiritic Society*) in Palermo, the *Società di Scordia* (*Society* of *Scordia*) based in the Sicilian town by the same name, and the famous *Società Spiritica*, in Florence, run by patriot and author Felice Scifoni (1802–1883).[69]

2.3.2. Spiritualism and Spiritism among the *Risorgimento* Elite

As can be seen by Scarpa's comment on the working class, the lower strata of society were intrigued by séances and spirit manifestations, but it would be a mistake to limit the area of influence to the working class alone. Working class aside, well-read bourgeois representatives, such as scientists, professors, artists, and the higher echelons of Italian society, were also swept away by the Spiritualist craze. Judging by the reigning house of Savoy in Piedmont, the list of high-tier active participants in séances is surprising: King Umberto I (1844–1900) and his wife Margherita of Savoy (1851–1926) had their first experience with a rapping table as guests in Naples;[70] Umberto's father, Vittorio Emanuele II, was considered to be a "convinced Spiritualist."[71] It is among the intellectual elite, though, that the mediumistic vogue involved its most influential adepts: Massimo d'Azeglio (1798–1866), author and Prime Minister of the Kingdom of Sardinia before Cavour, was very touched by the alleged revelation of spirits. After a brief, but influential foray into the world of politics, d'Azeglio chose to retire and spend his days in isolation in Cannero, a small town by Lake Maggiore, from the summer of 1864 until his death. Biographers Giorgio Martellini and Maria Teresa Pichetto described his new life in Cannero:

> By a chance initiation from a non-descript "Signor Romano," d'Azeglio becomes close, in the nocturnal silence of his small villa overlooking the Verbano [a local name for Lake Maggiore], to the practices of Spiritism. With the mysterious guest, with the painter Gaetano Ferri, who lives nearby, and an anonymous damsel with great abilities with the piano, not to mention a medium of rare sensibility, he spends entire evenings sat at the three-legged table, evoking otherworldly presences.[72]

D'Azeglio was not the only intellectual enthralled by such practices. Other major figures of the cultural milieu of the time include author Luigi Capuana (1839–1915), author of books such as *Spiritismo?* (*Spiritism?*, 1884) and *Mondo Occulto* (*Occult World*, 1896);[73] Antonio Fogazzaro (1842–1911), whose novel *Malombra* (1881) is centered on a woman convinced of being a reincarnated spirit; and members of the Milan literary movement the *Scapigliatura*, an 1870s literary circle, were all extremely enamored with occult themes.[74]

What really stands out, though, in the age of Positivism and empirical data as the ultimate proof for experiments dealing with séances, was the conversion of some of the leading scientists of the day to the Spiritualist cause: as many other trends, Positivism had reached Italy later than Northern European countries, and its tenets only peaked in Italian universities in the 1880s and 1890s.[75] For the sake of brevity, I will only be dealing with the most famous case, which, I am sure, will aid in comprehending the extraordinary influence Spiritualism exercised in nineteenth-century Italy's scientific milieu. If one man were to be named, among those who most tried to adapt the Positivist method, it certainly would be Cesare Lombroso (1835–1909).[76] Doctor, anthropologist, criminologist, and full professor in legal medicine at Turin University, Lombroso was a pioneer in the studies of phrenology, physiognomics, and social Darwinism.[77] His academic interest in mediumistic phenomena was dictated by his research in the field of hypnosis as a cure for hysteria. Yet, at this stage of his career, he denied any truth in theories of spirit interventions during séances or hysteria, which he disparagingly called "the spirits of mirrors and armchairs," and he was extremely preoccupied by what he considered to be a regression from the findings of science: "remember that by this way we go back to the Totem, to the Fetish."[78] In the 1890s, though, a semi-illiterate woman from Naples, Eusapia Palladino (1854–1918), was causing a *furore* with her séances, which baffled even the most sceptical of attendees.[79] After having been invited by Palladino's *impresario* to one of the lady's séances, Lombroso's whole view on Positivism and spirit life was shattered. Lombroso, the Positivist university professor, declared himself "ashamed and sorry to have fought with such tenacity the possibility of so-called spiritual facts [...] I say facts because I am still opposed to the theory. But facts exist, and I take pride in being a slave to facts."[80] How much Lombroso's opinion counted in making men of science decide between Palladino's status as a fraud or a genuine medium and maybe even how much the crisis of positive science was beginning to surface in Italy, was highlighted by this event, which Massimo Biondi summarized eloquently:

> Within few years, among those interested in her [Eusapia Palladino], we'd encounter Charles Richet, the Parisian physiologist, who was ALREADY interested in spiritual "facts" and would go on to earn a Nobel prize in 1913 for his studies on immunology; Myers, Sidgwick, Barrett, meaning the group belonging to the English *Society for Psychic Research*; Wagner, professor of zoology in [St.] Petersburg [...] Ochorowicz, professor of psychology and philosophy in Warsaw; the Curies and Flammarion [...] A semi-illiterate made the best names of European science and culture spin around her.[81]

2.4. The Naples School and the Occult Italo/Roman Primacy

The vast reservoir of myths and legends concerning the transmission of a *prisca sapientia italica* (ancient Italic wisdom) from the days predating the ancient Roman monarchy became a subject of great interest in the nineteenth century, and it was represented in a literary strand that would influence the *Risorgimento* culture greatly. The first author to put forth such a theory can be traced as early as the fifteenth century, as the brilliant research of Fabrizio Giorgio has evidenced in his two-volume history on Roman Traditionalism, *Roma Renovata Resurgat*.[82] The Dominican monk, Annio da Viterbo (1437–1502), had written extensively on the pre-eminence of the Etruscan people, whose leader, Noah-Janus-Vertumnus, had led his people to a life of humility and fraternity: "*Ergo Ianus docuit humiles urbes et coetus et communionem politicam, non ad pompam et dominationis libidinem.*"[83] Other authors, through the centuries had picked up the thread left by Annius, and in 1710, Neapolitan philosopher Gianbattista Vico (1668–1744) had written his *De Antiquissima Italorum Sapientia ex Linguae Latinae Originibus Eruenda* (*On the Most Ancient Wisdom of the Italians: Unearthed from the Origins of the Latin Language*).[84] In it, he defended the antiquity of the Etruscan people's sacred knowledge, which he dated as antecedent to that of the Greeks or Egyptians, and he mentioned the hero of these narratives in a direct fashion: "I strongly insist on saying that Pythagoras did not bring his doctrine from Ionia to Italy."[85] Such an interest in the Etruscan primacy in the Italian peninsula was rekindled in the nineteenth century when a group of authors whom scholar Paolo Galiano calls "Tyrreno-Pelasgian" picked up strands of the myth and posited the Pelasgian people as the forebears of the Etruscans, while giving the narrative a nationalist twist, a detail vastly appreciated during the *Risorgimento*.[86]

2.4.1. The Metanarrative of Primacy: Mazzoldi and Mengozzi

Among the *Risorgimento* retelling of the myths ascribing an ancient wisdom to Italian soil, there are chiefly four concordant elements that I have found. These ideas would fuel Reghini's notions of an Italic superiority. First, in primordial times, people inhabiting the Italian peninsula were imbued with some degree of divine wisdom, giving them a sense of pre-eminence over neighboring people; therefore, Italian primacy was, authors believed, founded on sacred knowledge. Second, this blessed race of human beings had witnessed what authors soon agreed to call *Cataclisma Italico*, a cataclysm of seismic nature, which changed the face of the Italian landscape with large masses of land being sunk by floods and others rising from the sea as a result of earthquakes. Third, these people, whom many nineteenth-century authors identified as the Pelasgians, were forced to emigrate to Egypt and Greece, bringing with them only fragments of the ancient sacred lore, only to come back to the peninsula centuries later and settle in the center of Italy, as the people we identify as Etruscans today. Finally, the uniting figure of all these myths was Pythagoras, depicted as an Italian who had restored the sacred mores after the cataclysm.

The first, and probably, most famous of the Tyrreno-Pelasgian authors is Angelo Mazzoldi (1802–1864).[87] In his *Delle Origini Italiche* (*On Italic Origins*) of 1840, Mazzoldi put forth the theory that the first inhabitants of the Italian peninsula practiced monotheism and adored "a single divinity, an arcane cause of the universe."[88] Furthermore, he identified the civilization of ancient Italy with the Atlantean one that Plato (428 BCE–348 BCE) had described in his *Timaeus* (ca. 360 BCE).[89] It is necessary to remember that, while the *Risorgimento* was mainly a sociopolitical phenomenon, aspects of the sphere of the sacred were equally important to a smaller cultural elite. As Renato Del Ponte, one of the foremost representatives of modern-day Roman Traditionalism and one-time disciple of Julius Evola (1898–1974), pointed out, the renewed value given to ancient sacred wisdom: "it was and remains an *indispensable* and *necessary* condition in order to go back to a geopolitical reality of Augustus's (or Dante's) Italy; hence, for a new manifestation in the *Saturnia tellus* of those divine powers which *ab origine* are tied to that geographic reality—consecrated from the will of the primordial Roman gods."[90] As we have already seen, the *Risorgimento* wars had already been given this sacral characteristic. It would seem that Mazzoldi's writings then provided a theoretical backdrop, which would justify such enthusiasm and be used as a basis for the elaboration of further theories.[91] Benedetto Croce (1866–1952), arguably the greatest Italian philosopher of the first half of the twentieth century and Nobel Prize candidate, remembered Mazzoldi's publication as being largely praised: "Mazzoldi's book was generally greeted with respect and studied with seriousness."[92]

The second author whose works I will briefly analyze before moving onto the occult manifestations in Naples, and who claimed to work with these ancient energies, was Giovanni Ettore Mengozzi (1811–1882). Mengozzi, in 1860, soon after the Bourbons were expelled from Naples, founded an association, which he named *Accademia Nazionale, la Scuola Italica* (*National Academy, Italic School*), for the study of medicine, philosophy, and literature.[93] The aim of the society was to rid Italian culture from what was perceived as noxious foreign elements to create a new national philosophy based on what both Mazzoldi and Mengozzi considered the loftiest of Italic philosophers: Pythagoras.[94] As the editing board of the journal *Roma Etrusca* wrote in their launch issue:

The Tyrrenian Pythagoras, back from the Orient, initiated in those arcane doctrines, and having grasped the ancient knowledge of Etruscan Rome (promoted and nobly represented by Numa), decided to rekindle the Italian glory in philosophy, going to Kroton, where he knew a philosophical school existed, uncorrupted in the days that the Italian culture was fought and corrupted in Greek Elea, and thus, for our Pythagoras, the best arena for his glory [was to be found] in Italy rather than elsewhere.[95]

The association experienced a resounding success, and many popular figures of the *Risorgimento* period were involved: King Vittorio Emanuele II granted the association the title of *Accademia Reale*, or Royal Academy; journalist and linguist Nicolò Tommaseo (1802–1874) and statesman Count Terenzio Mamiani della Rovere (1799–1885) were at one point respectively chairs of the philosophical and literary section of the Academy. Among the honorary members of the *Anziani Pitagorici*, the *Pythagorean Elders*, figured naturalist and geologist Charles Darwin (1802–1874).[96] Mengozzi also drew in politicians and generals who had made the history of the *Risorgimento* when he sponsored the creation of an *Alleanza Monoteistica*, or *Monotheistic Alliance*, in 1870. The aim was to limit Papal power with a religious reform that could bring the Italians closer to the Etruscan sacred roots they had neglected for centuries.[97] Garibaldi himself, enthused by the idea of an anti-Papal movement, wrote to Mengozzi: "I completely adhere to monotheism, whose aim is the cult of truth, the brotherhood of nations and the destruction in Italy, and around the world, of Papacy, representative of ignorance and slavery."[98] Other than Garibaldi, Mengozzi was also in touch with the Masonic milieu of Naples, being a high-degree Mason himself and holding an affiliation with the *Loggia Sebezia*, which, as we shall see, played a pivotal role in the development of an occult discourse related to the antiquity and primacy of the Italic people.[99]

2.4.2. Occultism in Nineteenth-Century Naples

As has been hinted at, the origins of a distinctive Egyptian hermetic tradition in Italy had its roots in the Neapolitan Masonic tradition,[100] of which the most prominent examples can be noted in the Egyptian Traditional Rite founded by Raimondo di Sangro (1710–1771), the seventh Prince of San Severo, in the mid-seventeenth century.[101] In the words of author Federico d'Andrea:

> Accurate researches, undertaken in selected archives, attest to the foundation of an *Antiquus Ordo Egypti* by Raimondo di Sangro, an order in which a *Rite of Misraim seu Aegypti* operated on 10 December 1747. Research, conducted

by various scholars following successful findings, has demonstrated the creation by Prince di Sangro of a secret lodge with clear hermetic and Rosicrucian leanings, named *Rosa d'Ordine Magno* [Rose of the Great Order].[102]

Unfortunately, such claims are rarely backed by documentary evidence, so this particular facet of Italian occultism seems destined to remain outside the domain of serious etic research. Nevertheless, it is important to state that such stirrings were present in Naples and that they almost certainly had an influence on Armentano's and Reghini's future Roman Traditionalist outlook.

Such a link to Egypt and initiatory knowledge, though, is much older, as can be attested by the statue representing an anthropomorphic rendition of the river Nile, commissioned by Egyptian Alexandrine immigrants in the second or third century CE. To this date, it can be seen in Naples located almost adjacent to a small square named *Piazzetta Nilo*, or *Nile Square*, in the proximity of which we can find a building, in whose subterranean chambers the remains of the ancient temple of Isis in Naples are allegedly to be found, that had belonged to Di Sangro.[103] It may be pure chance but not for the seventeenth- and nineteenth-century occultists who believed in inherent hermetic powers, that two of the most remarkable early modern Italian thinkers, namely Giordano Bruno and Tommaso Campanella, had both studied at the Convent of *San Domenico*, a stone's throw from *Piazzetta Nilo*. It was in a building overlooking the very same square that one of the most famous occultists of the turn of the century, Ciro Formisano (1861–1930),[104] better known by his hyeronym Giuliano Kremmerz, was allegedly initiated into the Egyptian Great Orient in the presence of one of the great figures of nineteenth-century Italian occultism, Giustiniano Lebano (1832–1910). The *Ordine Egizio* (Egyptian Order) had seemingly been a Masonic structure, which oversaw the cultural input in the various Egyptian lodges in Naples, although, again, the lack of conclusive evidence prevents the serious scholar from agreeing wholeheartedly with the conducted research.[105] Fabrizio Giorgio has written on the topic that "the contribution that such milieus gave to the Unitarian movement wasn't, in any case, just of a cultural nature, since all those who are described as the major exponents of the Egyptian Order of the time participated, 'with true Roman spirit,' to the insurrections of the *Risorgimento*."[106] Foremost among the members of the *Ordine Egizio*, and one of the most mysterious occultists of the Naples milieu, was Domenico Bocchini (1775–1840), who allegedly led the order until the day of his death. He published a short-lived journal, *Il Geronta Sebezio* (*The Wise Man of the Sebetus*, est. 1835), which specialized in the arcane origins of the Pelasgians and their link to ancient Rome.[107] Bocchini's teachings were rarely straightforward, and what still remains of his writings shows an erudite partial to the primordial Italic Tradition:

The Roman Labyrinth of which the classics speak of was the [secret] sovereign Palladium of Rome of which Eusebius spoke to the plebs [. . .] And Pliny says, that for having just spoken about it, Valerius Soranus had lost his head [. . .] We think that for Italian Labyrinth we must understand all the Orphic elements in the whole of Italy.[108]

And on Pythagoras, too, Bocchini seemed to have great intuitions: "[s]o it seems that the name Pythagoras was like that of Zoroaster, of Aliced, of Jupiter, of Mercury Trismegistus and other primeval *hyerophants* for whom the name was [constituted by] their Ministry and not [by] the person. And with this idea, we reconcile an infinite quantity of anachronisms that we find in Greek and Latin poets."[109] Upon Bocchini's death, after a brief *interregnum* during which a mysterious character only known by the name of Mamo-Rosar-Amru took a position of leadership, and after the death of Mamo-Rosar-Amru's successor Pasquale de Servis (1818–1893), Giustiniano Lebano, who had married Bocchini's niece, allegedly became his successor as leader of the *Ordine Egizio*.[110]

Lebano, according to Mengozzi, had been a very high-ranking member of the *Sebezia* Lodge, where the author had gained the highest degree achievable. He was a key figure of the Neapolitan occult milieu, acting as a *trait d'union* between the various Egyptian orders, such as the Egyptian Great Orient and the mysterious *Ordine Egizio Osirideo* (*Osirian Egyptian Order*), and its more Italic-Traditionalist approach, which later found a receptive center in Rome under the aegis of neo-Pagan occultists Armentano and Reghini.[111] In the second part of the nineteenth century, Naples was a renowned center for the European occult intelligentsia, and many figures connected to the occult world paid Lebano a visit, according to the theories of Kremmerzian scholars, from Dr Franz Hartmann (1838–1912), to Sir Bulwer-Lytton (1803–1873), in need of inspiration for his *The Last Days of Pompeii* (1834), to the young Giuliano Kremmerz himself.[112] Lebano may have been an inspiration to Kremmerz in the field of therapeutic magic, too. Having lost all of his male sons to epidemics of cholera between 1867 and 1884, he had developed theories on the origins of the disease, which, according to him, came from "areas of Tartarus, created by magical arts of foreign priests."[113] Lebano's wife took her life by setting herself and her husband's extensive occult collection on fire, making the extent of Lebano's influence on his followers difficult to ascertain. In any case, it is fair to say that interest in medicine and the treatment of diseases was a particular aspect common to Neapolitan occultists. Lebano's subdivision of healers into two categories: the *Ippocrati* (*Hippocrates*), divinely inspired healers, and the *Ipocrati* (*Hipocrates*), medics with a university degree, certainly seems to point toward the belief in the superiority of a hermetic therapeutic treatment over the scientific one.[114] Lebano's alleged contacts with Bulwer-Lytton, the

French occultist Eliphas Levi (1810–1875), and author Freemason, and supporter of the Garibaldine cause Alexandre Dumas (1802–1870) seemed to have transformed Naples into one of the occult centers of Europe for a short period of time.[115]

Lebano's teachings, consultable in manuscript form only until very recently, can give us an idea as to the quality and quantity of theories tied to the *prisca sapientia* that the order passed down to the more receptive Masonic organisations in Naples. "We know where precious metals are," wrote Lebano, "the Sacred Signs and Sacred Objects of the Fathers of Rome. In due time, we will reveal where they are; for now the times are not ripe."[116] Lebano was instrumental in suffusing the Egyptian Masonic scene in Naples with the tenets of the ancient Italic wisdom, which he saw as corrupt and sorely lacking a rigorous practical application. It was through him, chiefly, that Mazzoldi's and Mengozzi's theories were able to mix with the alleged Egyptian Freemasonry of Raimondo di Sangro, and subsequently influence Arturo Reghini, his Master Armentano, and the Roman Traditionalist milieu. A short mention must be made in this chapter of Giuliano Kremmerz, or Kremm-Erz, as the last great representative of the Neapolitan school, and because of the great influence his work had on twentieth-century occultists. If Lebano made the Italic traditions re-emerge in the Neapolitan occult circles, Kremmerz was the person who divulged the information in highly successful, but short-lived journals. In *Commentarium* (1910–1911), a journal Kremmerz edited, his ideas on the grandiosity of Rome were evident, and Kremmerz seemed to have learned the esoteric teachings of his Masters: "Of the prophecies on Rome I know many, [I] have known them for a long time [. . .] There is one, for example, that foretells nothing less than an Imperial Rome and the resurrection of the Latin Glory and of the mission of justice of the great civilisation of the third lay Rome."[117] This was written only twelve years before Mussolini's rise to power. In another of his works, Kremmerz adopted even more nationalistic tones when it came to defending the occult primacy of his country, an aspect that would definitely not have been lost on Reghini, Armentano, Parise, and the other members of the their group:

> If the occult Urbs knew the secrets of the science of the human psyche as an Etruscan and Graeco-Egyptian inheritance, can't the poetic mythology of our ancestors have hidden the truth of a concrete science of the spirit of man? Why is it preferable to play at being an Indian with symbols of Budda [sic], of Brama, of the Parsi, when Jupiter and the major deities of the Latin Olympus can honourably hold their ground?[118]

***

Now that we have introduced the reader to the nineteenth-century political and occult vogues which were to influence Reghini's life, his early years and first writings may be discussed, analyzed, and interpreted with greater ease. Once the dual aim of this chapter has been met, that of giving an informative outline of the last thirty years of nineteenth-century Italian history and that of providing a clear introduction to the basics of Roman Traditionalist ideas, we may now tackle the eventful years of Reghini's Theosophical period, where Tradition and avant-garde seemed to coexist in a highly dynamic intellectual environment.

3
The Early Years (1902–1910)
Avant-Garde, Theosophy, and Anti-Modernism

> New religion is in line with modernity:
> it has no apostles, but journals,
> no martyrs, but victims who end up
> filling psychiatric hospitals with their
> brains shocked by nervous exaltations.
>
> —Luigi Capuana[1]

In order to provide the reader with the tools necessary to appreciate the elitist, anti-modern, and anti-Positivist character of the milieu in which the young Reghini lived, this chapter will approach three distinct topics: first, I will strive to provide the reader with a comprehensive introduction to the Italian philosophical milieus of the beginning of the twentieth century: a special focus will be given to Benedetto Croce (1866–1952), the Neapolitan Idealist who, more than anybody, shaped the philosophical discourse of the day, and to the phenomenon called *Florentine Scapigliatura*,[2] of which Giovanni Papini (1881–1956) and Giuseppe Prezzolini (1882–1982) were the main movers, with their literary/philosophical journals.[3] With regard to the first two decades of the century, Florence, the city in which Reghini grew and developed long-lasting friendships, was one of Italy's cultural capitals, and many of the avant-garde movements that successively developed in other regions owe much to the exciting and vibrant atmosphere of the Tuscan city. The second and most important section of this chapter will highlight the anti-modern, aristocratic, and Traditionalist traits present within Florence's learned society, which, in my opinion, shaped the views of the young Reghini and that Reghini himself manifested quite clearly in his first writings.[4] Reghini, along with Papini, Prezzolini, and many others, seemed to straddle the seemingly far-fetched concepts of avant-garde and Tradition, and, through an analysis of his contributions to journals of the time, correspondence, and presentations delivered at the *Biblioteca Teosofica*, I will show how early nineteenth-century occultism, in its Italian Theosophical and Traditionalist variant, definitely did not verge "towards the progressive, liberal pole of the cultural and political spectrum" as its British counterpart probably did.[5] The germs of what Guénon would later refer to as the missing, yet fundamental existence of an *élite intellectuelle*, granted access to occult knowledge in virtue of a superior intellectual capacity and destined to form the minds of the masses, was somewhat bubbling to the surface in 1900s Florence.[6] Finally, I will focus on Reghini and his membership within the Theosophical Society:[7] previous research had claimed this period to be just a trivial, inconsequential one for the formation of young Reghini.[8] I stand against this simplistic interpretation of Reghini's Theosophical years and firmly place his adherence to the Theosophical Society in the vaster framework of his Traditionalist views. Reghini, as documentation with very high-ranking members of the Society and his pivotal role as curator of the *Biblioteca Teosofica* show, played a key role in the cultural, intellectual, and occult coteries of the time.

3.1. Reghini's Early Life and the Reghini Di Pontremoli Family

A brief analysis of Reghini's early life, or what can be surmised from the scant evidence, should be attempted at this point in order to better position the figure of the Florentine thinker at the turn of the century. Before a new interest in the Florentine mathematician captivated the curiosity of Italian researchers and scholars, Reghini's life, as his works, had mainly remained shrouded in mystery.[9] Most of the biographical anecdotes were slight variations of Giulio Parise's *Nota sulla Vita e l'Attività Massonica dell'Autore* (*Note on the Life and Masonic Activity of the Author*), which was published in a scarce posthumous edition of Reghini's *Considerations*.[10] Even this brief introduction is replete with details and dates, which, upon closer scrutiny, do not seem to match. Some examples had the wrong given date for his involvement in the Theosophical Society, and his role within the Society itself, whose first group Parise told us the Florentine philosopher helped found in 1898. Archival research on his family background and illustrious history may give glimpses of Reghini's upbringing and allow us to speculate, where we have no available documentation whatsoever, about his status, the quality of his upbringing and the prestige of his family.[11] Biographer Mario Natale de Luca tells us very little about Reghini's origins; he is only able to ascertain that the Reghini di Pontremoli, Arturo's town of provenance, were a noble family with a long history.[12] Roberto Sestito, in his biography, begins analyzing Reghini's life from 1906.[13] The Reghini family and its influence in the area around the town of Pontremoli may be traced without interruption back to the thirteenth century.[14] The first historical figure we can be absolutely certain of is Petricciolo Reghini (n.d.), Deputy to the Bishop of Luni, who was cited in a document dated 1317.[15] Petricciolo would be the first of a very long list of Reghini's descendants linked to the clergy or more directly to the Vatican. One of these descendants was Cesare Reghini (1580–1658), who was made Bishop of the town of Sarsina by Pope Innocent X (1574–1665); author Emanuele Gerini wrote that, three years after his death, when the holy man's body was exhumed, it had defied the process of decomposition and was as pristine as on the day it had been buried.[16] On April 14, 1778, the city of Pontremoli had been decreed to be a "Noble City" by the Grand Duke of Tuscany, and the Reghini family had become part of the local aristocracy by decree on November 27, 1782.[17] The constant characteristics of the Reghini family, across the centuries, were its status, its wealth, and its close ties to the Catholic Church. Although not all Reghinis were as saintly as Cesare had been, as in the case of Teodoro Reghini (n.d.), who "escaped to Genoa, climbing down a window of the seminar" in order to reach Garibaldi and his red shirts.[18] Because of the close ties between the Reghini family and the Vatican, Marcello Reghini (b. 1920), Arturo's nephew, taking into account his strong anti-clerical views, confessed to Roman Traditionalist Renato del Ponte that Arturo had always been considered the black sheep of the family.[19]

Summing up these lamentably few notions gleaned from his genealogy and from the social standing of the family, we can venture to hypothesize that Reghini grew up in a noble, privileged environment, where he had the time and possibility to learn five languages and enroll at the University of Pisa, where he obtained a degree in Mathematics. It is probably worth highlighting the fact that in 1900, 79 percent of Italians could not read or write, with illiteracy peaks of 90 percent in the south of the country.[20] The amount of detail and the erudition showed even in his very first writings; as we shall see, all point to Reghini belonging to the privileged few families in early twentieth-century Florence. The great number of foreign visitors to Florence that Reghini was in contact with, mostly because of their links to the Theosophical Society, is another piece of evidence to his privileged status of a noble man and belonging to Florence's aristocracy. It is understandable, then, that with such an upbringing, Reghini's anti-democratic, anti-modern, and elitist ideas might have developed from a very early age and might have represented a heritage derived from his own family.

3.2. The Crisis of Positivism and the Rise of Neo-Idealism

3.2.1. Italian Philosophy in the Late Nineteenth Century

As will be seen later in this chapter, Reghini was very much influenced by the philosophical debate that blossomed during the early years of the twentieth century. In order to understand his stance better, and that of his companions, a brief analysis of the philosophical trends in nineteenth- and early twentieth-century Italy is necessary.

The philosophical systems that had enjoyed the greatest favor in Italy during the first half of the nineteenth century had all possessed a religious underpinning and had provided the ideological fodder to the so-called Catholic-liberal movement. Its main proponents were without a doubt Antonio Rosmini-Serbati (1797–1855) and, to a lesser extent, Vincenzo Gioberti (1801–1852).[21] The main strands of Rosmini's philosophy strove to unite a Platonic-Augustinian view of the world with the more recent theories of Emmanuel Kant (1724–1804).[22] Rosmini's two main contributions to the philosophical debate of his time were essentially the concept that true dialectic had to be based on the idea of creation and of a primal cause, and that such dialectic would provide a *coniunctio oppositorum*, which would harmonize the opposites that had resulted from creation itself. Rosmini's theories fell out of favor in the 1830s when philosophical speculations began to be formulated hand in hand with ideas of national liberation. This period represented the first apparition of Positivist thought on Italian soil, its main theoreticians being Carlo Cattaneo (1801–1869) and Giuseppe Ferrari (1811–1876).[23] Supporting the democratic and republican instances that were being elaborated in those years, Cattaneo and Ferrari elaborated theories on social revolution, on the connection between the material essence of civilization and progress, and, not least, on the link between production and class interaction.[24] A further characteristic of this republican wing of Positivist thought was, of course, a complete rejection of Rosmini's theories and an anti-clericalism very typical of the historical period in question.[25]

After the unification of Italy between 1861 and 1870, Italian Positivism began to be challenged by what, at least in the peninsula, represented a brand new school of thought: the Neapolitan Hegelian School.[26] Blossoming during the 1840s, when, for example, Georg Hegel's (1770–1831) theories in Germany had been already supplanted by the then cutting-edge theories of Karl Marx (1818–1883), this Hegelian School was soon split into two seemingly antithetical positions: a more leftist one, represented by brothers Bertrando (1817–1883) and Silvio (1822–1893) Spaventa and Francesco de Sanctis (1817–1883), and a more Idealist wing, more conservative in nature, which would give life to neo-Hegelian Idealism.[27] While this conservative neo-Hegelian Idealism will be dealt with in detail in the following paragraph, it will suffice to say that the long-term aims of the Spaventa brothers and their fellow thinkers were that of a final embrace of Hegelian ideas only if intertwined with materialist propositions. It is fair to say, though, that the dominating philosophical current to impose itself upon the Italian culture and bourgeoisie, at the end of the nineteenth century, was without a doubt Positivism. This new brand of Positivism was vastly different from Cattaneo's and Ferraris's, though, since the well-known cult of science had begun to mingle with Phenomenalism and a less philosophically rigorous approach.[28] Its major proponent, both praised and criticized at the same time, was Roberto Ardigò (1828–1920), who appeared to want to unite a subjectivist view of the world as psychophysical reality with an extreme mechanistic view of nature as the creator of itself.[29]

For a brief while, at the end of the nineteenth century, as scholar Eugenio Garin so clearly put it, there was a genuine belief that "truly Italy had witnessed the birth of the philosopher of the new age, the theoretician of the lay State, and it would be even better to say, with a fortunate expression, the theologian of the new democratic and anti-clerical Italy."[30] With the turn of the century though, the Positivist model would enter a crisis from which it would never recover. As scholar Antonio Banfi wrote, more and more members belonging to the higher strata of society began seeing through the cracks of Positivism, thus paving the way for the imminent anti-Positivist intellectual barrage of the first decade of the century: "the heirs of Positivism were contrite [philosophers] in search for absolution, aiming at diluting bourgeois progressivism and social-democracy with a humanitarianism [typical of] an amateur rally."[31] The crisis of Positivism of the 1890s and 1900s has been analyzed by intellectual historians and philosophers alike. It is not the scope of this chapter to analyze the reasons for the anti-Positivist backlash. However, as far as the Italian situation is concerned, Eugenio Garin synthesizes the historical moment very succinctly and precisely when noting that the main cause of the fall of Positivism in the peninsula was a sharp break between science and philosophy, where the philosophers were at most amateur scientists, and the scientists were completely devoid of any philosophical baggage whatsoever.

> [T]he [. . .] real people responsible were, not the Idealists, like some obtuse divulgers like to say, but those hapless Positivists, who, with their generic insinuations, caused the lack of trust in the real scientists and the critique of the most alert philosophers, who would then sweep away, not science—as some believed—but the simple metaphysics that was being smuggled behind a scientific dressing.[32]

It was up to Idealism, in all its forms of expressions, to pick up the clunky mantle dropped by the automatons of progress.

3.2.2. Benedetto Croce and Idealism as Counterpositivism

The beginning of the twentieth century marked a sensible shift in the cultural and philosophical outlook of Italian thinkers and in the way they expressed their condition within modern society. The year 1903 may be pinpointed as a pivotal year, as this year saw the launch of three journals, different, yet linked in many ways. The first was *Leonardo* (1903–1907) founded by Giovanni Papini (1881–1956) and Giuseppe Prezzolini (1882–1982) in Florence; the second one was *Il Regno* (*The Kingdom*, 1903–1906) founded by nationalist Enrico Corradini (1865–1931);[33] and the third was *La Critica* (*The Critique*, 1903–1944) founded by Benedetto Croce in Naples, which became the vehicle of the Hegelian neo-Idealism, and would soon become the main opponent of the stagnant Positivist theories. This section will focus on the figure of Benedetto Croce (1866–1952), arguably the most prominent Italian philosopher of the first half of the twentieth century and by far the most respected exponent of the Neapolitan Hegelian School. The exclusion from this analysis of the other giant of Italian Idealism, Giovanni Gentile (1875–1944), is dictated not by his lesser relevance within the philosophical milieu of the time, but because Croce dealt more closely with the Florentine *Scapigliati* with whom Reghini began his career as an author.[34]

Croce's philosophy, after a brief flirtation with Marxist ideas at the end of the nineteenth century, no doubt influenced by his teacher Antonio Labriola (1943–1904), was a complete reinterpretation of Hegelian principles in order to create a reactionary philosophy, which could keep both Socialism and Positivism at bay.[35] His critique of science was emblematic. For Croce, as is the case of Gentile, Hegel should have negated all value to natural science and mathematics, which were seen to possess only practical and utilitarian value. Only Idealism could represent a real, trustworthy science.[36] As a direct consequence, Croce denounced Hegel's triad of Idea, Nature, and Spirit, granting a higher status to Spirit only. This reform of Hegelian philosophy would marginalize Positivists at least until the end of World War II. It is important to note, though, that, while Benedetto Croce rapidly became a giant within Italian culture, his ideas were acceptable only within Italian confines since Italy was, at the turn of the century, decades behind other Western European countries and the United States. What Positivism represented in these other states, the ideology of industrialization and imperialism born in the mid-1800s, could not be transferred to Italy, an industrially underdeveloped landscape with a very weak colonial power.[37] Croce's attack on Marxist philosophy, beginning as early as his 1900 *Materialismo Storico ed Economia Marxistica* (*Historical Materialism and Marxist Economy*), was equally met with little opposition. Labriola, the only Italian Marxist thinker of that time, simply did not have a sufficient theoretical backing. Croce's ideas on Marxism, chiefly its role as a pseudoscience in the realm of economy, a utopia in the field of politics, and its definition as nonphilosophy, went largely uncontested. The first decade of the twentieth century saw Croce returning to his critique of Marxism and Socialism so many times that a pattern may be found in the object of his critique. First, he simply negated the validity of surplus capital gain; second, he argued against the dependency of the cultural and ideal plane of history to the practical one; and third, historical materialism was only seen as useful when considering economic factors.[38] Finally, when discussing Hegelian philosophy, Croce's main achievements were those of elevating the role of history, literature, and aesthetics, having judged Hegel's approach too abstract and metaphysical.

In a nutshell, Croce's neo-Idealism was a philosophical system that can be summed up, in my opinion, in four major points: (1) the fight against Marxism and Positivism; (2) the backing of the sociopolitical status quo, which had taken shape after the unification of Italy; (3) the defence of different strands of conservative ideologies; and (4) the championing of a lay, bourgeois society, protected from the influence of religion.[39] Hegelian neo-Idealism had been conceived in England during the previous century, but only as one of many philosophical approaches to the modern world. Italy was, in this case, a unique example in which this precise array of philosophical ideas influenced academics, schoolteachers, and the entire scholastic system, and most of all the young and upcoming generation of thinkers of which Reghini, Papini, Prezzolini, and Corradini were all part.[40]

In his journal *La Critica*, published between 1903 and 1944, Croce would discuss all the aforementioned topics, along with others he is possibly more famous for: historiography, literary criticism, and aesthetics. Within his journal, though, his philosophical ideas were made very clear. In the introduction to the first issue of *La Critica*, Croce wrote:

> And, since philosophy may not be anything but Idealism, he [Croce] is a follower of *Idealism*: ready to recognise that new Idealism since it moves more cautiously than before and likes to account for every step it takes, can be easily defined as critical Idealism, or as realistic Idealism, and even (where with the term metaphysics, we refer to arbitrary forms of thought) as anti-metaphysical Idealism.[41]

What was the core idea, which in the beginning brought Croce to be almost idolized by Papini and his circle? If I were to choose one concept, it would be the freedom and autonomy of culture, as a manifestation of man in history devoid of all that is not directly related to the subject.[42] He even enthusiastically mentioned the editors of *Leonardo* in his own journal:

> The authors of *Leonardo* are bound to each other by a philosophical conception, which is Idealism, taken in in the form that one of the most delicate French contemporary thinkers gave it, Bergson, as a philosophy of contingency, of freedom, of action. And they are joyous and determined authors, souls that are shaken and inebriated by the virtue of ideas; not lowly copiers of other people's

articles and sentences to which they add their own frigid comments for a scholastic and professional purpose, such as usually fill up philosophical journals. This may only aid in strongly attracting our sympathy.[43]

Reghini, who, as we shall see, was closely linked to the group of thinkers writing for the journal *Leonardo*, would be clearly influenced by the emerging Idealist trends. Just like Papini and Prezzolini, Reghini's contributions to *Leonardo* were deeply imbued with the anti-Positivist and Idealist attitude that Croce helped spread in Italy.

3.3. The Florentine Avant-Garde: The Case of *Leonardo*

3.3.1. Birth and Characteristics of the Florentine Avant-Garde

In his *Lo Spaccio dei Maghi* (*The Dispatch of the Magicians*, 1929), author Mario Manlio Rossi vividly described the milieu of Florentine avant-gardists, enflamed by touches of mysticism, neo-Romanticism, and Spiritualism:

> In the commotion, once in a while some dark illumination. Now, the voluminous whiteness of Besant's hair at the *Giubbe Rosse*. Now the scientific astrology of an anglo-American named Dodsworth [...]. Over everything, the remarkable height, the Buddhist monk-like face, the lordly and childish kindness of the wizard Reghini, who was probably my best friend.[44]

Rossi's book represents an author's memoir of a particular phase of Florentine history, where new poetics, Wagner and Nietzsche, Pragmatism and Croce's neo-Idealism, Oriental religions, and occultism did, for a short number of years, seem to be able to all go hand in hand. A generation of young self-taught intellectuals was on the rise, and the manifestation of their protean ideas was to be found in literary and political journals. We have seen how 1903 saw the birth of Croce's *La Critica* and Enrico Corradini's political-nationalist publication *Il Regno*. The collaboration between editors and authors of these various journals would last for the whole decade, as "between '*Hermes*', '*Leonardo*' and '*Il Regno*' there would be a mutual collaboration. '*Leonardo*' in a more philosophical environment, '*Il Regno*' in a strictly more political capacity, forwarding instances not too far and different from the ones in '*Hermes*'. The three brothers will each tend to their own fields, like good neighbours do."[45] In a letter to Prezzolini, cofounder Giuseppe Papini, echoing the sentiments that were rife in Florentine cultural circles, wrote on November 17, 1902: "My dearest friend, I am creating a scientific function: I institute an experience. I'm not talking about residues with barbarous names or harmless rabbits, but of men and supermen. I'm talking, as you understand, of 'Leonardo.'"[46] The stance that Papini and Prezzolini, under the pseudonyms of *Gianfalco* and *Giuliano il Sofista*, took, was uncompromising from the beginning, creating an "us versus them," "present versus past"-like climate. While the two were more than happy to host guest authors they endorsed, which, through the years varied from poet and military leader Gabriele d'Annunzio (1863–1938)[47] to philosopher William James (1842–1910),[48] from authors Miguel de Unamuno (1864–1936)[49] to Benedetto Croce,[50] the editors of *Leonardo* were all too eager to express their discontent with what went against their new idea of the world. Through their anonymous column "*Schermaglie*" ("*Skirmishes*"), Papini and Prezzolini would belittle established authors, such as Giosué Carducci[51] and Giovanni Pascoli, considered to be too old to be appreciated by the younger generation, or launched attacks against Catholicism, Positivism, the bourgeoisie, and the modern world.[52] Having established what *Leonardo* was against, it is imperative to clearly state, in the words of the authors, what they thought of themselves and which instances they were in favor of. In his opening words in the first issue of the journal, Papini clearly explained who this "group of youths" was:[53]

> In Life, they are pagan and individualists—lovers of intelligence and beauty [...]. In Thought, they are personalists and Idealists, so as to mean superior to every system and every limit, convinced that every philosophy is nothing but a personal lifestyle—deniers of any other existence outside thought. In Art, they love the ideal transfiguration of life and fight against its lower forms.[54]

Prezzolini's article "L'Ideale Imperialista" ("The Imperial Ideal"), immediately following Papini's introduction, would have certainly enthused a young Reghini, who in the future would make great use of the concepts of intellectual elite, Paganism, imperialism, and other terms dear to the *Leonardians*, within his own *weltanshauung*. Reghini's collaboration with Papini and Prezzolini was limited to five articles and two reviews, and they would only manifest in the last year of the journal's publication when its articles began to touch upon occultist and Orientalist themes.[55] A short history of the evolution of the journal is now necessary if we are to appreciate the speed with which the Florentine avant-garde accepted new ideas before tossing them away and arriving at their final mystic-occultist phase.

3.3.2. The Three Lives of *Leonardo* and Its Occultist Phase

Leonardo was published every fortnight, starting from January 4, 1903, when it made its debut in selected Florentine bookshops. The first noticeable detail in the very first phase of the journal's life was an almost complete absence of political articles. The few that were present were nationalistic in essence and very hostile toward the budding Socialist Italian milieu. The reason behind this attitude was explained clearly by sociologist Paolo Casini: "the answer is to be sought in the myths of Positivism which entered after the crisis of *post-Risorgimento* forms of thought: the spread of social-Darwinist theories, the exaltation of the superman, the rise of a more aggressive feeling towards the Fatherland and one's social class."[56] The innate cultural elitism was evident in Prezzolini's "Imperialismo Intellettuale" ("Intellectual Imperialism"), where he scolded the editors of other philosophical journals reminding them that "you assert that you are enemies of democracy, bourgeoisie, bourgeois and democratic civilisation and progress. Now we are rabid enemies of such things, but we are not nor will we be with you [. . .]. We aim for a bigger and more dignified prey: for the intellectual imperialism of all the essences of the universe."[57] This period, coupled with Papini's statement that nothing existed outside the mind, created a fracture between the small group at the *Leonardo* and the few avant-gardists who had come before them. Such attitude, although limited to a magazine, which, at its peak, printed six hundred copies, caught the attention of the main philosophers on both sides of the Alps, including French philosopher Henri Bergson (1859–1941), whose theories on intuition and vitalism had influenced both Papini and Prezzolini, therefore, fitting perfectly in *Leonardo*. Papini and Bergson actually shared a short, but amicable correspondence, relating to the articles on Bergson's philosophy appearing in the *Leonardo*.[58]

The second phase of the journal's life coincided with its second series and what Borgese described as a depuration from "all the dross that weighed it down in the first issues."[59] The "dross" implied referred to the group of aesthetes who had joined *Leonardo* only to jump ship after a short time in search of the next big thing in Florentine publishing. Prezzolini, from issue 10 to 14, published in 1904, was free to pursue his new passion, Pragmatism, which he shared with his friend and correspondent F. C. S. Schiller (1864–1937). In his three articles all dated 1904, "La Filosofia che Muore" ("The Dying Philosophy"), "Morte e Resurrezione della Filosofia" ("Death and Resurrection of Philosophy"), and "Marta e Maria (dalla Contemplazione all'Azione)" ("Martha and Mary [from Contemplation to Action]"), Prezzolini made it clear that *Leonardo* had acquired a new direction and a new father figure, who was no longer Croce, but William James (1842–1910).[60] Pragmatism and Bergsonism conveyed the new idea that action was required in order to experience the world, but that it was still an action supported by intellect/intuition over rational theories. In other words, for the *Leonardians*, there was no epistemological difference between what is and what should be. James briefly took Papini and Prezzolini under his wing and published articles about the two thinkers and their journal.[61] After

1904, along with their anti-Positivist battle, the "Florentine Band of Leonardists," as James had called them, operated on a new front against Croce's speculative neo-Idealism. "Hegelian" had suddenly become a bad word in the Florentine Pragmatist milieu. James's psychology had won Papini's and Prezzolini's hearts, the former, after a Pragmatist conference held in Rome, writing enthusiastically in issue 17 of *Leonardo*:

> Today, the issue is not whether to choose one name or another, it concerns the augmentation of our power of action [...]. The winner of this Congress, therefore, should have been Pragmatism, which, really, has triumphed in Rome in the person of one of its greatest exponents, William James.[62]

James's theory of a stream of consciousness and his 1902 classic *The Varieties of Religious Experience: A Study in Human Nature* brought the *Leonardians* closer and closer to an apology of religion, "understood as a social and psychological phenomenon, which is autonomous from the supposed hegemony of the neo-Idealists, but also as a personal vocation."[63] During this third and last phase of *Leonardo*'s brief existence, as Paolo Casini rightly observed, "it is not easy to distinguish between "scientific" intent of that research and its lapses or theosophical, initiatic, esoteric adherence, which were omnipresent in the early XX century."[64] The attraction that the occult exercised on the two authors was great by this time. As Papini himself would later write: "the famous Pragmatism didn't really matter to me [...] I looked beyond. A thaumaturgic dream arose in me. The need, the will to purify and strengthen the spirit in order to enable it to act upon things [...] and to thus reach the miracle, omnipotence."[65] Reghini, introduced to Papini by future author and politician Giorgio Amendola (1907–1980), immediately felt at home in the new dimension acquired by *Leonardo*. The relationship between Reghini and Papini would last long after the experience of the journal. Papini would write in his diaries that Reghini had asked him, more than once in the 1910s, to be initiated into his neo-Pythagorean group,[66] and Papini himself had referred to Reghini as not being "one of the usual *dilettante* charlatans of magical science, but he was an acute spirit, enriched by a great erudition, sharpened by the exercise of mathematical analysis."[67] During the last year of the *Leonardo* experience, articles and reviews on occult themes and publications abounded, and Papini publicized Reghini's *Biblioteca*, of which I will write about shortly, in each and every issue of the last series of *Leonardo*. Issue 24 was entirely dedicated to occultism and New Thought with articles by Papini, Reghini, and anthroposophist Roberto Assagioli (1888–1974). The subject of the articles varied greatly from Arianism to the *Upanishads*, and from Blavatsky to nineteenth-century occultist Eliphas Levi (1810–1875). The twenty-fifth and final issue of *Leonardo* marked the end of Papini's and Prezzolini's brief flirtation with occultism, too. Within the short space of four years, the two avant-gardists had moved from a neo-Idealist stance to James's Pragmatism, ending up among occultists "from whom we have definitely distanced ourselves," as Papini wrote to Prezzolini in 1907.[68]

3.3.3. Rehnini and *Leonardo*

Having established the fact that Papini and Prezzolini did not cherish any enduring experience after their flirtation with occultist circles, we have to consider what Reghini might have gained by frequenting the Florentine avant-gardist milieu. What is clear is that Reghini, Papini, and Prezzolini used the same language, the same key words and ideas to captivate their audience. Most of these ideas on individualism, elitism, imperialism, mysticism, occultism, anti-democratic and reactionary impulses, formed the basic core around which all three thinkers built their philosophical edifices. Reghini would have definitely appreciated Prezzolini's passage in his "Alle Sorgenti dello Spirito" ("At the Sources of Spirit," 1903):

> All this stink of phenic acid, of fat and smoke, of common people's sweat, this clanging of machines, this commercial busybodying, this loudness of adverts, are things that are not only tied together rationally but also are holding each other's hands, close by virtue of a sentimental tie, which would make us disdain them if they were far away but makes us hate them because they are near to us.[69]

3.4. Reghini between Avant-Garde and the Theosophical Society

Such was the brief, but intense history of the journal *Leonardo*, the literary and philosophical review where Arturo Reghini debuted as an author. Before analyzing Reghini's writings of this period, in order to extrapolate his ideas and proclivities at this early stage in his life, it is necessary to cover a fundamental aspect of the Florentine thinker's spiritual path in the first decade of the twentieth century: his ties to the Theosophical Society.

Official evidence of Arturo Reghini's membership within the Society in the early years of the twentieth century is overwhelming.[70] Both biographers of the Florentine thinker, Roberto Sestito and Natale Mario Di Luca, devoted entire chapters to this short but rich period in his life, although usually practicing a *caesura* between the youthful period and the subsequent Traditionalist direction Reghini took. Gennaro d'Uva, arguably the most engaging of Reghini experts, wryly referred to Arturo's early years as those of adherence "to the universalist theoretical premises of theosophism," with the embrace of its major tenets: "the 'universal', a naïve and vulgar theory of reincarnation; the tendency to valorise and master Oriental philosophies; the youthful indulgence towards practical-sentimental postulates [...] of Christian ethics."[71]

What are we to make of Reghini's period within the folds of the Theosophical Society? While, as we have seen, Gennaro d'Uva saw the embrace of the main tenets of Blavatsky's occult system as a youthful error, biographer Roberto Sestito viewed the Theosophical years, a period in which Reghini was already very aware of Theosophy's ideas and infatuation with the Orient, as a meaningless stepping stone toward more serious Traditional pursuits.[72] What I propose in this section is to strike a middle ground between these two theories, and I argue that, while d'Uva's approach was correct to some extent, the use of material not employed by Sestito, Di Luca, or d'Uva will allow us to picture young Reghini already researching autochthone forms of occult and religious expression with the blessings of the higher echelons of the Society. This portrays a brief, but necessary, period of absorption of both Western and Eastern occult influences before Reghini smoothly moved onto his more focused formulation of his brand of Traditionalism.

3.4.1. The Theosophical Society in Italy

As in most European countries, the Theosophical Society was quickly established in Italy's major cities mostly through the coordinating efforts of distinguished foreign members. The reasons for such a resounding success on Italian soil are to be found in the novel character of Helena Blavatsky's (1831–1891) theories, which allegedly based themselves on a renovation of values that blended ancient lore and modern science, effectively providing an alternative to the stifling Positivistic outlook that the avant-garde in Florence was against.[73] As Marco Pasi has written: "One of the fixed points in this longed-for renovation was the critique of the prevailing materialism, countered by the rediscovery of the spiritual values of a primordial and perennial tradition. Such values were also seen in contrast to the dogmatism and sclerotisation of the dominant religious faiths."[74] Not only did the Theosophical Society provide a way out from the Positivist-Marxist conundrum, but it also provided enquirers with an alternative to Catholicism and other mainstream Christian denominations, which lay in a "longstanding crisis."[75] Reghini's virulent anti-Christian stance would have been accepted by many, in a Society founded by a woman, Blavatsky, who had devoted her life to unmasking the wrongdoings of Christianity.[76] The first certain trace of the Theosophical Society in Italy can be found in Rome when in 1894,

Countess Ulla Wachtmeister (1838–1910) made a donation in order to open a Theosophical library in the capital.[77] Four years later, in 1898, although not a founding member of the first Italian section, Reghini would figure among the first adherents to the Roman nucleus of the Society. While 1898 was the date provided by Reghini biographer Di Luca, both Pasi and author Paola Giovetti postponed the date of the creation of an official Italian section to 1902.[78] According to Giulio Parise, a disciple of Reghini and author of the first biographical note on his Master, the Florentine thinker himself was among the founding members, although his name does not appear in the rosters of the Theosophical Society.[79] Parise also mentions Reghini founding the publishing house *Ars Regia* with fellow Theosophist Giuseppe Sulli-Rao (1869–1935). *Ars Regia*, whose headquarters Parise located in Turin instead of Milan, would be of pivotal importance in translating foreign Theosophical texts and newer Italian contributions.[80]

The key figure for the establishment of the Theosophical Society in Rome, first, and the rest of Italy later, was undoubtedly Isabel Cooper-Oakley (1853/1854–1914), one of Blavatsky's first disciples in Europe. Beginning in 1897, Cooper-Oakley had been present in the Italian Theosophical milieu, helping different cities network more effectively and representing a strong *fulcrum*, albeit sometimes lacking the social niceties usually attributed to the English upper-class, around which early enthusiasts rallied.[81] Thanks to her, the most prestigious international members of the Society lectured widely in Italy, including figures, such as Henry Steel Olcott (1832–1907), Curupullumage Jinarajadasa (1875–1953), Annie Besant (1947–1933), and Charles Leadbeater (1854–1934). Notwithstanding Cooper-Oakley's uncompromising demeanor and resolute character, many documents attest to the benevolence of the Italian Theosophists in her regards.[82] A special friendship with Cooper-Oakley seems to have been entertained by a relative of Arturo Reghini's, Ida Carlotta (n.d.). It was Ida Carlotta Reghini, who took it upon herself to write the obituary on the national Theosophical bulletin when Cooper-Oakley died in Hungary in 1914. The enthusiasm and love for her transpires at every line penned: "she was among those who with their magic wand let water flow from the rocks, and this magic wand was her will, her unbound devotion to the cause of the Theosophical Society, to her Master." Moreover, "in her you could feel the reflection of those heroic times, which demanded an absolute and complete dedication of one's being. We owe it to these great workers if today we may lean on and take respite upon the great truths of Theosophy."[83]

3.4.2. The Theosophical Library

Rome and Milan certainly witnessed Reghini's involvement with the dissemination of Theosophical ideas; however, it was in his native Florence that he

THE EARLY YEARS (1902-1910)   63

really became a major asset to the Society. In 1903, thanks to the financial aid of Theosophist Giulia H. Scott (n.d.), Reghini was able to open and manage his own Theosophical library, amassing a great number of volumes on alchemy, Freemasonry, and Theosophy in a very short time. By 1906, the library offered two thousand volumes, and by 1908, the number of available books had risen to five thousand.[84] The time at which Reghini started his activity as a conference organizer at the *Biblioteca Teosofica* coincided with great social and cultural turmoil. As Guido Ferrando (1883-1969) had written in the journal *La Voce* (*The Voice*, est. 1908): "the Theosophical Society arose when materialism in both philosophy and science had reached its higher status and when already one could witness the first and isolated protests against the extremely novel doctrine that reduced all life to a mechanism and negated any free activity to the spirit."[85] Ferrando's thoughts inexorably posited that the Florentine avant-garde ideas were close to the Theosophical Society, and Reghini was one of the focal contact points between the two. Reghini was not alone in his desire to reaffirm the fundamental role of the spirit; his influence on the younger generation of intellectuals who met at the *Giubbe Rosse* café was fundamental: along with the already mentioned Papini and Prezzolini, Reghini also rubbed shoulders with other frequenters of this particular café: Giovanni Amendola (1882-1926), journalist and member of the Theosophical Society, and Ardengo Soffici (1879-1964), painter and future Minister during Mussolini's first government among them. It was at the *Giubbe Rosse* that a violent fistfight erupted in 1913 between members of the Florentine literary avant-garde and Filippo Tommaso Marinetti (1876-1944) and his following of Futurist artists.[86] This intellectual milieu was the ideal surrounding for Reghini, the *Giubbe Rosse* café being described by a scholar as "a place where mysteries were at hand" at which one could see "the closed spaces of magical Idealism, Evolian initiatic movements, in which one would talk of Pagan imperialism, of superior races destined to dominion and all the Nietzschean manias of traditional esotericism vibrated."[87] The periods just quoted, penned by avant-garde journals expert Marino Biondi, really exemplify the close tie between far-reaching avant-gardist ideas and esoteric traditions deeply rooted in the past, which was a common trait among the young *élite intellectuele* of the day. In writing about this historical period, and Reghini's library in particular, Simona Cigliana wrote:

> [O]ne ends up asking oneself what part and how big of a role did Arturo Reghini's [. . .] [l]ibrary play on the circulation of some ideas which then seemed to radicate themselves into Italian culture, in the shape of key words or ideas, the same that went on to enrich the substratum of much "irrationalism" and "idealistic" confusion until they constituted, on the one hand, some of the

ideological directives for the involution of Italian politics, on the other, some of the leitmotivs of the literary-avant-gardist elaboration of Futurism.[88]

Due to disagreements with Cooper-Oakley and the then leader of the Society Annie Besant, the name of the library was changed to *Biblioteca Filosofica* in 1905, and Amendola became the new chief librarian and conference organizer.[89] This allowed Reghini more time to write and present his own papers, such as *Il Dominio dell'Anima* (*The Dominion of the Soul*) in 1907, *La Vita dello Spirito* (*The Way of the Spirit*) of the same year, and *Per una Concezione Spirituale della Vita* (*For a Spiritual Understanding of Life*) in 1908. Within the confines of the Florentine avant-garde stirrings, including Papini's and Prezzolini's *Scapigliatura* and the Futurist artistic and literary movements, Reghini was a central figure that many intellectuals turned to for an opinion or an endorsement.[90] Never again, in my opinion, would his influence on mainstream culture be so incisive. It is significant that it was during his brief Theosophical period that we have the most references to Reghini in other authors' works, thus giving us a fleshed-out and more human depiction of the Florentine Theosophist. According to Augusto Hermet, "Reghini belonged to the kind of aristocrat of great culture, an ideal image for young people wishing to elevate themselves above the masses [...] who made a programmatic point of their intellectual journey out of aristocracy."[91] Nicola Lisi gives us a major insight into the man's metaphysical interests: "Reghini, and by now most of us know it, was a philosopher/mathematician following the example of the ancients. A Pythagorean, as he liked to define himself."[92] Coveted by the day's cultural intelligentsia, Reghini exerted a great influence on the young generation of anti-Positivist thinkers, who were all too ready to assimilate the "aristocratic and anti-democratic elements" in Reghini's occult views.[93] It seems that an early strain of anti-democratic feeling and a belief in the superiority of an elitist form of occultism was already present in Reghini during his days as a member of the Theosophical Society.

3.4.3. The Roots of Roman Traditionalism in Theosophy

To the scholar of fin de siècle occultism, it comes as no surprise that Theosophy postulated the existence of a perennial philosophy, which, harkening back through the ages, could provide the Theosophist with a pristine understanding of an immutable sacred wisdom. In Theosophical circles, the idea of a *philosophia perennis* acquired the names of Ancient Wisdom or Wisdom-Religion.[94] The efforts of the Theosophical Society in bridging the gap between Western and Eastern ideas of knowledge effectively made Eastern theories known in the West, A. P. Sinnett's (1840–1921) *Esoteric Buddhism* (1883) being an early example of this trend.[95] Early in the Society's history, the original interest had been in hermetic philosophy and Western occult lore, and Hindu and Buddhist doctrines encountered in the East were seen as "belonging to the same corpus of writings that included the *Corpus Hermeticum*, or Giordano Bruno's writings."[96] The mention of Bruno is of vital importance here. Reghini's first-ever article in *Leonardo*, "Giordano Bruno smentisce Rastignac" ("Giordano Bruno Refutes Rastignac, 1906), is a paean to the esoteric and mystical aspects of the Nolan philosopher, who had until then been hailed as a champion of 'free thought and modern science."[97]

Reghini's brief involvement with Theosophy has been readily dismissed by biographers and scholars alike as a "necessary mistake," given the occultist's youth and Theosophy being at the time the most approachable access to the world of occultism, Idealism, and spiritual transformations. Traditionalist circles did not value Theosophy greatly, and in René Guenon's (1886-1951) and Reghini's correspondence, there is no evidence to show that the Italian disagreed with the French thinker's vitriolic remarks on Blavatsky's movement. Even Julius Evola (1898-1974) would only have words of praise for Reghini for having advised him against joining the Society.[98] Every residue of Reghini's past connection with Cooper-Oakley and her circle seems to be swept away by his initiation into the folds of the purportedly ancient *Schola Italica* in 1910 by Amedeo Rocco Armentano.[99] In successive years, mentions of the Theosophical Society are scarce to say the least. But all is not what it seems.

In the light of newly found material, it is my intention to discuss the extent to which Reghini's Theosophical past influenced his future thoughts and actions. I certainly believe that even though Reghini did not disdain to take the occasional jab at the Society as an institution, he nevertheless started his journey toward the ancient tenets of Roman traditions as a member of the Theosophical Society before his meeting with Armentano. During the first years of the Theosophical presence in Rome, and this fundamental aspect has to date been highlighted only by Marco Pasi, members of the Society embarked on the search for local roots of esoteric knowledge that could be researced alongside the Eastern approaches more typical of the Society. Such endeavors were seen as "connected to the concept of a hermetic-Italic school that took shape during these years in Giuliano Kremmerz's circle and likened to that of a Pythagorean-Italic tradition that was later expanded on by Reghini and his associates."[100] Although I do not agree completely with Pasi about the actual extent of the Theosophical influence on Giuliano Kremmerz, I do think that such an important statement cannot be underestimated. During the First Annual Congress of the Federation of the European Sections of the Theosophical Society held in 1904, where Reghini presented the paper *Il Meccanismo della Visione e la Quarta Dimensione* (*The Mechanism of Vision and the Fourth Dimension*), Decio Calvari (1863-1937),

Theosophist and future Secretary General of the Italian Parliament, made the public aware of an important initiative to take place in Italy in the near future:

> Another kind of work has begun, which will be further developed in the next autumn. It consists of the study of our [that is, Italian] mystical tradition, which offers such a great number of points in common with our [that is, of the Theosophical Society] teaching, as the research on the great authors and thinkers of the Renaissance demonstrates. Through the creation of a philosophical-religious library and a Society for the creation of Public Conferences, we will try to bring back to life, in Florence, the great neo-Platonic idea that in the fifteenth century boasted representatives, such as Marsilio Ficino and Leonardo da Vinci.[101]

I realize that Marsilio Ficino (1433–1499) and Leonardo da Vinci (1452–1519) were hardly the precursors of a Pythagorean school of thought, which Reghini later claimed to represent, but, after all, Reghini himself wrote that "the philosophy of the *Schola Italica* left its indelible and strong mark in all of the subsequent Platonic and neo-Platonic philosophy, and, therefore, on all classical thought."[102] Nevertheless a new and more nuanced understanding of Reghini's years is necessary, and the years leading up to his initiation into the Pythagorean *Schola* in 1910 represent, in my eyes, a progression toward what would become known as Roman Traditionalism, which had already started in the Theosophical Society. I will now analyze Reghini's writings from the period covered in this chapter and try to highlight the genuine avant-gardist and equally fervid Theosophical enthusiasm, which characterized this period of his life.

3.4.4. Reghini's Theosophical Writings

A brief analysis of the pseudonyms Reghini chose while writing articles during his *Leonardian*/Theosophical period would probably suffice to show Reghini's genuine interest in Theosophical lore. In "Mors Osculi" ("Death by a Kiss," 1906), he signs his contribution as *Alaya*, and in "Istituzioni di Scienza Occulta" ("Institutions of Occult Sciences," 1906), Reghini chose the name *Svasamdevana*.[103] The word *Alaya* is a term that appears recurrently in Blavatsky's *The Secret Doctrine* (1888) and *The Voice of the Silence* (1889).[104] The first mention of *Alaya* in the *Stanzas of Dzyan* signifies unbound consciousness,[105] and in Blavatsky's *The Voice of the Silence* (1889), we read: "behold how like the moon, reflected in the tranquil waves, Alaya is reflected by the small and by the great, is mirrored in the tiniest atoms, yet fails to reach the heart of all."[106] Reghini's *"Mors Osculi"* is the depiction of the journey of the soul after its fall. After encountering the elements, the sun, the moon, a panpipe playing a mystical tune, Soul is finally at rest and may sleep for seven eternities. In the article, Reghini mentions the heroic frenzies (*eroici furori*) of *Anima*, the Soul, and this has brought some authors to attach great importance to Giordano Bruno's (1548–1600) philosophy[107] and the role it would play in Reghini's future development of an idea of unbroken initiates propagating the Roman *prisca sapientia* in the company of "Virgil, Dante, Campanella, Mazzini."[108] In my opinion, the reference to Bruno in this passage owes more to Reghini's early view of Bruno as an occultist, as opposed to the then common view of the Nolan philosopher as a martyr for a modern view of the world. Another reason for Bruno's inclusion in the article is that Annie Besant, leader of the Society after the death of Blavatsky and with whom Reghini corresponded, was firm in her belief of being the reincarnation of Giordano Bruno.[109] What "Mors Osculi" more closely reminds the reader of is the classics of Romantic *Naturphilosophie* and the Vitalist approach of German *Lebensphilosophie*. This would find a welcome space in the last series of *Leonardo*: Reghini's *Anima* is closely reminiscent of Ludwig Klages's (1872–1956) *Seele*'s struggle to find its place in a modern logocentric world.[110] Furthermore, the personification of the soul within the narrative brings to mind the epic poems of another member of the Munich Cosmic circle, Albert Mombert (1872–1942). Reghini's *Anima*, its trials and tribulations, can be seen to parallel closely Mombert's *Aeon: Dramatische Trilogie* (1907–1911) with the music being played by a panpipe and the "seven eternities of slumber" echoing closely the post-Nietzschean sensibility of the Munich circle.[111]

In the second article I will briefly analyze, "Istituzioni di Scienza Occulta" ("Institutions of Occult Science," 1906), Reghini uses the pseudonym *Svasamvedana*, a Sanskrit term that is usually utilized to express self-awareness or the reflexive nature of awareness. Of course, Blavatsky, and other Theosophists after her, had explained the term in their works, and Reghini probably borrowed this nom de plume from English Theosophical writings. A passage where the term is used may be found in Blavatsky's *Fall of Ideas*, where she compares the teachings of the Gnostics to those of the Buddha: "the solution of the two systems was identical in that they traced the Cause of Sorrow to Ignorance, and to remove this, pointed out the Path to Self-knowledge. *The Mind was to instruct the Mind: 'self-analysing reflection' was to be the Way*. The Material Mind (Kāma-Manas) was to be purified and so become one with the Spiritual Mind (Buddhi-Manas)."[112] This self-awareness, according to Reghini, was to be achieved by yogic practices and meditation. We know Reghini actually practiced these techniques taught by the Theosophical Society from a letter Annie Besant had sent to the Florentine occultist from her lodgings in Benares. The letter is dated April 24, 1903, and it is a response to Reghini's complaints of physical pain while performing his practices. Besant's advice is not too clear to the noninitiated, but the two could have been discussing astral travel: "the pain you are feeling demonstrates that you are not ready to free the energies concentrated to arrive to the higher plexus [. . .]. You should go back to simple meditation, continuing to train the mind, the body. After this, time will come when you will be able to exit the body at no risk."[113] Not only does this letter prove Reghini's attempts at following the series of exercises prescribed by Theosophical theories, but it also indicates that, in knowing and corresponding directly with Annie Besant, he must have been a most influential and well-known member of the Italian Theosophical community and possibly a member of the Esoteric School section of the Society, whose membership is still a secret today. His efforts to make occult teachings available to a wider public were easily discernible in his writings on this period: "[We must] draw a bridge above the abyss that separates modern thought from its scientific-Positivist prejudices from the old and yet always new esoteric thought; tear away the reader from a wrong and ordinary idea of life and initiate him into the spirit of occultism."[114]

In the three lectures Reghini gave at the *Biblioteca Teosofica/Filosofica*, namely *La Vita dello Spirito* (*The Life of the Spirit*, 1907), *Il Dominio dell'Anima* (*Control of the Soul*, 1907), and *Per una Concezione Spirituale della Vita* (*For a Spiritual Understanding of Life*, 1908), the influence of Theosophical teachings was also omnipresent.[115] In *Dominio*, after having defined the essential questions of the talk as concerning "the problem of death, of nature and of the survival of the soul,"[116] Reghini went on to describe the inadequacy of both science and religion with the core problems of humankind, highlighting possible methods reminiscent of the first Theosophers' writings:[117]

> But there is still another category of souls, whose thirst for knowledge is not satisfied by either springs [i.e. Science or Religion]. These souls, and they are more numerous than you think, do not deem it necessary to choose between science and religion; they do not judge either indispensable but think of them as inadequate, either separate or united, to extinguish the divine thirst for knowing completely.[118]

He then continued, quoting *The Light on the Path*, and praises the virtues of yogic practice in order to still the mind and enhance the soul's capacities. Post-Theosophical Reghini would no doubt use another terminology altogether, trying to fit the introspective aspects of yoga within a Pythagorean and Western frame, but in 1907, he exhorted his audience to "concentrate our [energies] on the evolution of our conscience, both following with will, faith and heroic frenzy the natural impulse and the various techniques of evolution and of yoga."[119] The conclusion of *Il Dominio* is a masterpiece in Theosophical rhetoric, leaping beyond the present limits of human consciousness one partakes in, and of universal consciousness, of the whole, the one, mighty Brahman, of whom "only silence expresses the ineffable name."[120] In *La Vita dello Spirito*, the arguments are similar, and yoga and meditative techniques are advised so that "each one of us may try and reach the vast Ocean of Consciousness and feel its immense immanence."[121] Reghini's knowledge of Theosophy and Eastern doctrines is palpable when he mentions the poet and philosopher Sadhak Ramprasad Sen (c. 1723–c. 1775), a shakta poet who "made the banks of the Ganges resound a century ago with the sound of his *vina*."[122] In describing the goddess Kali and the god Shiva, the latter's use of his third eye and the former's role as destructor of nature, Reghini showed he possessed more than just rudiments of Oriental lore. *Per una Concezione Spirituale della Vita* proceeds on the same trajectory as his previous talks: yogic practice, reincarnation, Oriental influences, all woven together in a Theosophical tapestry, which previous studies of Reghini have vastly underestimated.

***

Now that Reghini's Theosophical period has been re-evaluated as a necessary stepping stone toward his Traditionalist phase, we may move on and cover the Florentine thinker's involvement with Freemasonry, and his fateful meeting with his Master, Amedeo Armentano. As will be seen, the Masonic milieu of the late 1900s was vibrant and multifaceted, and within it, Reghini and Armentano saw the possibility to organize the teachings of the *Schola Italica* in a more structured manner, accessible to the Italian intellectual elite of the day.

4
The *Schola Italica* and the *Rito Filosofico Italiano* (1910–1914)

Initiation and Invention of Tradition in Modern Italy

> Oh, great spirit of Pythagoras [. . .]
> forgive the poor profane who defile
> initiation, turning it into empty
> choreography, forgive them!
>
> —Eduardo Frosini[1]

The years leading up to the Great War were fundamental to Reghini's development as a Roman Traditionalist for three distinct reasons: first, the meeting with Armentano really helped Reghini rise from a period of apathy and uncertainty he had experienced after leaving the Theosophical Society and move his occult efforts in a new and exciting direction; second, the initiation into the *Schola Italica* dated December 21,1910, changed Reghini's life forever and provided him with a mission he would pursue for the rest of his days: namely, the propagation of the teachings of the *Schola* via the channels of Freemasonry; third, this period witnesses Reghini's and Armentano's most concrete attempt at practically creating an elitist, anti-modern, anti-Positivist, and anti-Catholic Masonic body within the folds of the *Rito Filosofico Italiano*,[2] a true Italian autochthone Rite,[3] and with the help of the enigmatic figure of Eduardo Frosini.

It is my opinion that, within the more peripheral Rites, often cataloged under the term of "fringe Masonry" such as the *Rito Filosofico*, initiates who sought a more elitist path that would go beyond the Enlightenment ideals of *liberté*, *egalité*, and *fraternité* could further their agendas in a secret society, abandon the secularized and disenchanted approach to Freemasonry, and remain virtually unnoticed by other brothers and the world at large,[4] although it must be noted that within and outside of Italy, even more established Rites, with a large following did possess occult overtones.[5]

4.1. The Role of Freemasonry in Modern Italy

4.1.1. A Brief History of Italian Freemasonry (1861–1914)

After the foundation of the *Loggia Ausonia* in Turin in 1859, which I referred to in the second chapter, Freemasonry seemed to blossom in Italy.[6] Founded two years later and promoted by most of the creators of the *Ausonia* Lodge, the Italian Grand Orient (GOI) enabled lodges, which were to rise across the peninsula, to share a common observance in accordance with international Masonic laws.[7] As explained in Chapter 2, though, the GOI was born in tumultuous times in Italian history: the Reign of Italy had just been proclaimed, Garibaldi had yet to confront the Kingdom of the Two Sicilies, and General Cadorna would not conquer Rome for another eleven years. Therefore, James Anderson's (1680–1739) *Constitutions* (1723), which were considered the blueprint for all international Masonic bodies, forbidding lodge members from engaging in political affairs, were largely dismissed by Italian brothers.[8] Politicians with visible public profiles, thus, were inclined to mix their political activism with their Masonic militancy. Notable examples of this included *Risorgimento* hero Giuseppe la Farina (1815–1853), President of the Italian Chamber of Deputies Michele Coppino (1922–1901), university professor and politician Pier Carlo Boggio (1827–1866), and Foreign Minister Costantino Nigra (1828–1907).[9] When the first twenty-three lodges met in Turin in December 1862, three main aims for the Italian Freemasonry were ratified: "a) Independence and unity of individual nations, and fraternity among the same—nationality being sacred; b) Tolerance of every religion, and equality among beliefs; [...] and c) Moral and material progress of all social classes."[10] It is clear right from the beginning that Reghini would not have appreciated the "fraternity," the "tolerance," and the "material progress" of the masses, and thus, it is not surprising that he would always take alternative approaches when it came to affiliations to Masonic bodies.

After having traced the basic direction in which to steer GOI, the major representatives of the *Grand Orient* wrote a statute, which was not particularly strict where membership requirements were concerned, as it aimed at gaining the largest number of members in the shortest time possible.[11] Soon, GOI was characterized by Italian traits that were not present in foreign Grand Lodges. The Deist Great Architect of the Universe and its religious tolerance were soon substituted by a well-documented presence of lay sentiments, bordering on the anti-clerical, a clear legacy of the earlier years of the *Risorgimento*. As scholar Fulvio Conti wrote,

> Consequently, the cosmopolitan universalism, which had been paraded in the constitutions, slowly gave way to a [form of] patriotism, which, at least at the head of the obedience, never knew decline or second thoughts.[12]

In a speech held in Reggio Calabria in 1885, the Grand Master of GOI Adriano Lemmi (1822–1906) made a clear distinction between internal affairs and nationalism, which had by now come to occupy a prominent place in the minds of Italian Freemasons. The international solidarity program was first proposed in 1861, and it expected Masonic bodies to help foreign lodges in times of need:

> First of all, we have to provide for ourselves, then to outside needs. Other peoples do not think nor act differently. Would we be more Italian than humanitarian this way? I believe not [. . .]. Regardless, I know that the love for family is the first source of love of the Fatherland: given this, could he who did not love his own Fatherland love humanity?[13]

The differences between the Masonic movements of the seventeenth and eighteenth century and fin de siècle Italian Freemasonry were noticeable: the weight had shifted to a definite national-political standpoint, the esoteric and initiatic dimensions cast aside, and many members would also attend public events in Masonic regalia, diminishing the divide between bourgeois would-be affiliates and the higher strata of the Masonic milieu.[14]

A complete unity of all Masonic lodges in Italy seemed to be impossible, though, since, in the southern regions of the country, other institutions, which would not bow down to the Turin GOI, had already been founded. The most important of these was the *Supremo Consiglio Grande Oriente d'Italia dell' Antico e Accettato Rito Scozzese* (*Supreme Council Grand Orient of Italy of the Antient and Accepted Scottish Rite*) based in Palermo, which had been founded in 1860 by a group of Sicilian democrats, who had among its supporters future Prime Minister Francesco Crispi (1818–1901) and the greatest of *Risorgimento* heroes Giuseppe Garibaldi (1807–1882).[15] There were two essential reasons of contrast between the two factions. While the Turin group was by all means pro-government and had adopted only the first three degrees of Freemasonry (that of "Entered Apprentice," "Fellowcraft," and "Master Mason"), the Palermo Freemasons were democratic, still followed Mazzini's and Garibaldi's *Risorgimento* ideals, and had thirty-three working degrees in their system. In 1864, though, during a plenary of all Northern GOI lodges in Florence, the democratic wing gained most of the positions of power, and they were, thus, able to create a dialogue with Palermo. The catalyst for the two competing bodies coming together was the election of Francesco de Luca (1811–1875), a southern democratic Mason, as Grand Master. It was only in April 1872 that the process of unification of all Italian lodges became a reality during the plenary session at the *Argentina* theater in Rome. Giuseppe Mazzoni (1808–1880), member of the left wing in the Kingdom of Italy's Parliament, was elected Grand Master, and sixteen out of twenty-one members of GOI's council were Freemasons and representatives of Parliament.[16] The democratization of Freemasonry was proceeding at considerable speed. Conti shows us that from documents dating back to 1874, that almost one-third of the Italian Masons by then belonged to the middle class, "the larger nucleus (23%) was represented by clerks, teachers and pensioners, followed by traders, shopkeepers and merchants, which constituted 17.5% of the sum."[17] Membership to the official, recognized Freemasonry, therefore, possessed qualities that could appeal to a large number of the Italian bourgeoisie. Despite its shared consensus among most classes of Italian society, it nevertheless maintained its own identity in two major qualities: its strong anti-clerical stance and its irredentist and nationalist thrust, setting it apart from foreign Masonic manifestations.[18] Both these factors, present in the wider political spectrum too, were, as we shall see, to influence Reghini in his sociopolitical and occultist development.

4.1.2. Anti-Clericalism within Italian Freemasonry

Many researchers, including scholar of Freemasonry Aldo Mola and author Beatrice Bisogni, have brought attention to the phenomenon of widespread anti-clericalism within the GOI.[19] According to Conti,

> One of the binding elements of Masonic activism in the second half of the nineteenth century was without doubt anti-clericalism. The aversion towards the Catholic Church and the role it covered in social and political life—a feeling moreover corresponded by analogous sentiments on the ecclesiastical front—manifested in particularly bitter tones [...].[20]

Among the social battles inspired by Freemasonry were the strenuous defense of laity within education, the political struggle to keep religious formation outside of public schools, and the extension of compulsory education to a higher age, in order to defeat the pressing issue of illiteracy.[21] Clerical reaction was always vehement, the most evident manifestation of it being registered in 1896 when the Vatican organized what it had defined as "the last crusade,"[22] the *Primo Congresso Internazionale Antimassonico di Trento* (*First International Anti-Masonic Congress of Trento*), spanning a full five days from September 26 to 30.[23] The aim of the congress was to "strengthen the lay Catholic organisations since only with a united force [...] could the now well-known enemy have been fought."[24] Trento was a great choice on behalf of the Papacy: an Italian city on Austrian soil, where

Freemasonry had been banned, and the Habsburg rulers had been more than happy to host the event, thus enflaming the hearts of Freemasonry, which was being challenged both in their enlightenment-derived beliefs and in their irredentist yearnings. The major Papal press organ, the *Osservatore Romano* (*Roman Observer*, est. 1861), mocked the Masons from its safe geographic position:

> Oh, welcome be the Anti-Masonic Congress, and the new Crusade it undertakes against the guilty sect, may this be the new dawn of that lucky day in which, once the enemies of our holy religion have been dispersed from the face of the earth, the sweet reign of Jesus Christ may return upon all men.[25]

During the five days of the Congress, attacks against the illuministic principles professed by Freemasons, which were obviously the early object of scrutiny, moved to an "incredible battle against the worshippers of Lucifer, against the bloodthirsty ones who did not disdain to plot against legitimate power in the dungeons, in which the most unworthy and shameful things for a human being were being devised."[26] As Aldo Mola wrote, while commenting upon the saturation of the social climate by the superstition and fantasies of the Church:

> Not much more troublesome were the recurring "revelations" of ecclesiastic representatives who, once every so often, "discovered" the true plot and occult pacts devised in view of the imminent universal revolution, destined to swipe away every order, institution, moral foundation. Beyond the esoteric preoccupations of the *fin de siècle*, discussed with anguish between a sensual hysteria, mystical excitations, stimuli that would exude a makeshift naturalism and religious morbidity (refer to the classic *Là-Bas* by Joril-Karl Huysmans), tasting the exaggerated delight of heresy slithering among Catholics, 'tempted' like never before by the allure of the "Adversary."[27]

This was but a culmination of a clash that had known other momentous instances in the past. Pope Leo XII's (1810–1903) bull *Humanum Genus* (1884) had defined Freemasonry as "Satan's synagogue" and ex-Mason merry pranksters and Catholic extremists, such as Leo Taxil (1854–1907) and Domenico Margiotta (1858–?), did nothing to ameliorate the lot of Freemasons.[28] In 1904 when Ettore Ferrari (1845–1929), a Rome-based sculptor and deputy of the Italian Parliament, was elected Grand Master, his new cabinet was even more interested in intertwining politics and Freemasonry, and this approach only accentuated the anti-clerical stance.[29] This left-leaning stance, though, created fractures within the GOI, as many Freemasons were of a more moderate leaning and more interested in following the English model, which preached a detachment from politics and religion. The schism took place in 1908, and two years later, a new obedience, named *Gran Loggia d'Italia* (*Grand Lodge of Italy*) or *Piazza del Gesù*, from the name of the Piazza where the headquarters were located in Rome, was created. Head of the schismatic faction was a Protestant Pastor named Saverio Fera (1850-1915).[30]

4.1.3. Nationalism and Irredentism within Freemasonry

While the concept of Italian nationalism must by now be very clear to the reader, the concept of irredentism might be a new one. By irredentism, I will refer to the nationalistic kind of political and cultural orientation, aiming to annex to the Fatherland territories that were linked to it because of culture, customs, and language, but that politically belonged to another country. With regard to Italy, I refer to the northeastern regions of Trentino, Friuli, Istria, and Dalmatia.

Reghini, Armentano, and the other members of the *Schola Italica* were both nationalists and irredentists, thus justifying a section to analyze the interaction between Freemasonry and semi-clandestine irredentist circles.[31] As far as nationalism is concerned, it is true that in the twentieth century a sincere hatred for Masonry was rife among the cultural-political circles, which were gearing up toward an armed intervention in World War I. Freemasonry incarnated all that nationalists saw as wrong within the sociopolitical milieu of the day, as it was "[b]ourgeois reformism, a visceral, lay, humanitarian, internationalist approach, which seemed to stifle any expansionistic aim for the country. A tendency to compromise, which [. . .] was bringing Italy towards a moral and spiritual degeneration."[32] As I have written, though, Italian Freemasonry was much more involved in politics than its European counterparts, and as the war neared, it was clear that a sense of patriotism remained very strong among politicians involved with Freemasonry, and, when having to decide in favor of the imperialistic expansion in Tripolitania in 1911 or for an intervention in World War I in 1915, the nationalist ideal always prevailed upon ideas of European internationalist compromise.[33] Nationalism had been one of the rising forces within the Italian intellectual and cultural milieus with intellectuals, such as poets Giosué Carduccci (1835-1907) and Gabriele d'Annunzio (1863-1938), adhering to its cause. Nationalist sentiment had become a force to be reckoned with from 1910 when Enrico Corradini and Luigi Federzoni (1878-1967) founded the *Associazione Nazionalista Italiana* (*Italian Nationalist Association*). As we have seen in the previous chapter, Corradini, with Papini and others, had founded the nationalist journal *Il Regno*, which was followed by *L'Idea Nazionale* (*The National Idea*) in 1911. It has already been argued that Reghini and Armentano knew and approved of Corradini's ideas. However, they differed when it came to the thorny issue of religion: while Corradini despised Christianity for its Semitic connotations, just like the Roman Traditionalists, he nevertheless upheld the principles of Catholicism, which he viewed as Romanised, and thus, in his opinion, a sanitized, version of Christianity.[34]

Freemasonry's ties regarding irredentism are much more complicated to synthesize, but they may be divided into two main groups for the sake of clarity. On the one hand, there were legally created associations, such as *Lega Nazionale* (*National League*), *Pro Patria* (*For the Fatherland*), and the *Circolo Dante Alighieri* (*Dante Alighieri Circle*), which based their activities on a series of cultural events that would promote the cause of reannexation of the lost lands through non-violent means and intellectual debates.[35] The GOI, particularly its most moderate wing, was very close to these associations, and for the *Dante Alighieri* in particular, we have many examples of interaction between the two entities. On the other hand, there were secret societies, mostly composed of young people with more Republican and revolutionary political views in nature: GOI did not officially approve of these formations, although it followed their development closely, and some individual Republican Masons may have lent their support on an individual basis. The Mazzinian and Garibaldian inspiration of these groups often brought them to put real demonstrative actions, which would often end in violence, into practice with:

> the detonation of explosives and make-shift bombs in front of edifices representing the Austrian State; the distribution of flyers and pamphlets exalting Italy during theatrical representations or visits of official representatives of the Austrian government.[36]

Such demonstrative actions are beautifully represented during the opening scenes of Luchino Visconti's (1906–1966) film *Senso* (1954), where a myriad of glimmering green, white, and red leaflets were thrown from the balconies of a theater to the dismay of the Austrian soldiers sitting below.[37]

No matter how strong the ties between GOI and the irredentist circles were, be they moderate or more active, GOI's role was essentially that of mollifying the most turbulent groups through the intercession of the more moderate circles, such as the *Dante Alighieri*.[38] Such a stance, as may be imaginable, was not entertained by the Roman Traditionalists, who would resort to fringe Masonic obediences to pursue their goals thanks to a less visible profile and a greater liberty within said obediences. Reghini especially, as I will document in this chapter and in Chapter 6, would resort to fringe Masonry because of the less intrusive presence of universalist ideas, outspoken proselytism among the bourgeoisie, and left-leaning political sympathies.

4.1.4. Fringe Masonry in Italy

Fringe obediences in Italy would appear to be, to the scholar of Western esotericism, of much greater interest, being more imbued with occult lore and elaborate rituals. Not only was the esoteric and initiatic aspect not ignored, like in GOI, but in many cases it constituted the fundamental aspect that provided spiritual nourishment to those, such as Reghini, who had by the early 1900s come to see mainstream Masonry as completely devoid of any spiritual or intellectual aspect whatsoever. His idea of regular Freemasons was clear in 1906, on the pages of *Leonardo* he had written:

> A new coat of green paint is not enough to transform into free-thinkers some marionettes who have always thought with someone else's brain, and to tilt their head left and right is not more intelligent than making it oscillate from top to bottom.[39]

And from the conclusion of the same article:

> The Masons of our time prefer to remain rough stone rather than becoming polished stone; and if Plato were alive, he would refuse once again to teach to these unworthy initiates the secret of the cubic stone. By explaining it, he would expose the hermetic cross, and Freemasons would mistake it with the Catholic Church's cross.[40]

Reghini's frustration is palpable in these passages. The fact that even members of Masonic orders did not show an interest in the occult traditions he was pursuing must have outraged him, just as much as the opening of Freemasonry toward a wider, and, thus, less elitist, membership. The left-wing tendencies of mainstream Freemasonry left him and his companions very little to work with, hence, the decision to resort to the smaller rites of fringe Masonry. What then could fringe Masonry provide Reghini with that regular obediences could not? Beatrice Bisogni, an Italian Masonic researcher, describes the rise of "irregular" Masonic groups that were more interested in spirituality than politics, as a moment of global crisis, which, according to her, kick-started individual spiritual impasses. When man finds it too difficult to find adequate answers in the preexisting systems, be they political, philosophical, or religious: "[a]s always," she writes, "it happens that some energies may agitate themselves in a convulsive and confused manner, and yet in their apparent and too often accepted irrationality, testify to a rebellious behaviour and a gnoseological will."[41] Despite the extremely emic approach of the quote, it is my opinion that if Bisogni were right, such an aspiration to a gnoseological dimension must have transcended the often mundane practices of the official rites, and this, I posit, could be the reason why Armentano and Reghini sought their approach to Freemasonry through the fringes. Bisogni focuses on five distinct rites, which, being beyond the scope of the book, I will only list, without delving into their history: the *Antico e Primitivo Rito Orientale di Memphis-Mizraim* (Antient and Primitive Oriental Rite of Memphis-Misraim); the *Antico e Primitivo Rito Orientale Di Memphis* (Antient and Primitive Oriental Rite of Memphis); the *Rito Egiziano Riformato* (Reformed Egyptian Rite); the *Rito di Memphis Riformato* (Reformed Memphis Rite); and the *Rito Filosofico Italiano* (Italian Philosophical Rite).[42] As we shall see, it will be the last Rite that Armentano and Reghini chose to infuse with their Roman Traditionalist theories.[43]

4.2. Meeting Ara and Reghini's Masonic Past

4.2.1. Enter Freemasonry: From *Rigeneratori* to *Lucifero*

Arturo Reghini showed a strong interest toward Freemasonry from a very young age. In 1902, in the same year he joined the Theosophical Society through his friend Giuseppe Sulli-Rao, whom I have mentioned in the previous chapter, Reghini was admitted to the *I Rigeneratori* (The Restorers) lodge of Palermo. The lodge belonged to the Oriental Rite of Memphis, a Rite that Napoleon Bonaparte (1769–1821) had allegedly been the first European to be initiated in at the feet of the Great Pyramid in 1798. The first documented lodge of this Rite in Europe had been established by Napoleonic officers who had come back to France from Egypt. On April 30, 1815, Samuel Honis (n.d.), Gabriel Mathieu Marconis de Négre (1795–1868) and Thomas-Alexander Dumas (1762–1806) founded the mother lodge *Les Disciples de Memphis* (The Disciples of Memphis).[44] The *I Rigeneratori* lodge was subsequently founded in Palermo by Baron Nicola Giuseppe Spedalieri (1812–1898) in 1876. The regeneration, which was implied by the name of the lodge, referred to the revolt of January 12, 1848, when political activists Rosolino Pilo (1820–1860), Francesco Crispi, and Salvatore Spinuzza (1829–1857) had organized the uprisings in Sicily, which had hastened Garibaldi's expedition. Clearly an irregular Rite, it accepted both men and women and added further grades to the usual three, which contained the more esoteric teachings. *I Rigeneratori* was highly valued as an initiatic center. Among its most notable members, through its fin de siècle activities, we find Abbot Domenico Angherà (1803–1873), founder of the *Sebezia* lodge in Naples; Giuseppe Garibaldi and his second in command, Nino Bixio (1821–1873); John Yarker (1833–1913), who covered the position of Great Hierophant and International Head of the Order from November 1902; his successor, from 1913, was Gérard Encausse, better known by his hieronym Papus. Whether Reghini ever actually travelled to Palermo is still not clear, as his disciple and first biographer Giulio Parise (1902–1969) and Eduardo Frosini (1879–?), imply he did, while the *Encyclopédie de la Franc-Maçonnerie* clearly states that Reghini was initiated by Sulli-Rao "on the sword," or by proxy.[45]

The great distance between Florence and Palermo forced Reghini to find another Masonic entity that could satisfy his needs for occult studies. In 1903, he joined the *Michele di Lando* lodge in Florence, and in 1904, he was one of the main reorganizers of the lodge along with Eduardo Frosini and the brothers Pietro (n.d.) and Giovanni Mori (n.d.): the lodge was rebaptized *Lucifero* (*Lucifer*). The lodge, following the *Rito Simbolico Italiano* (*Italian Symbolic Rite*), owed its obedience to GOI and when Ettore Ferrari was elected Grand Master on February 15, 1904, a new statute was issued, which would once again thwart Reghini's plans for a more spiritual and elitist manifestation of Freemasonry. According to the statute, the aims of GOI were to be found in a

> Democratisation of Masonry, through the cutting of fees, so that intellectuals without means may be enabled to join; the reformation of the symbol: To the Glory of the Great Architect of the Universe; a reduction of the formalities [i.e., rituals] of the Rite; a greater development of Masonry's presence in public life, while keeping its character intact [. . .].[46]

The modernist wing of GOI, much to Reghini's chagrin, had gained the majority, and after his re-election on February 26, 1906, Ferrari had added a sentence to the first article of the GOI's constitution: "The Italian Community, closely adhering to the principles and goals that the World Order professes and fights for the democratic principle in the social and political order."[47] Reghini's reactions were crystalized in the following statement:

> Having the Monists, the Positivists, the Socialists taken over the Cabalists and the mystics, the clear waters of esotericism have been roiled, and it is difficult to recognise the origin of that mud-puddle that is today's Freemasonry.[48]

Deeply disillusioned by what could be gained by early twentieth-century Freemasonry, again, Reghini had to look elsewhere. In 1907, a musician from Calabria was initiated into the *Lucifero* lodge. This mysterious composer from southern Italy was about to change the Florentine thinker's life forever: his name was Amedeo Rocco Armentano (1886–1966).

4.2.2. A Mysterious Gentleman: Amedeo Rocco Armentano

Not much is known about Amedeo Armentano. Born in Scalea, near Cosenza, on February 6, 1886, he was raised by his father Giuseppe Armentano, a wealthy landowner, and his mother Maria Alario.[49] In 1905, at the age of nineteen, he moved to Florence to study the violin at the prestigious *Regio Istituto Musicale* (*Royal Musical Institute*, est. 1860), and, as noted earlier, was initiated into Freemasonry in 1907.[50] Just like Reghini, who quickly fell under the spell of the man eight years his junior, he frequented the literary cafés *Giubbe Rosse* and *Paskowski* and has been remembered by the many literary figures who met him. Author Nicola Lisi, when writing about Reghini and his authority among the frequenters of the literary cafés in Florence, noted: "Only once did Reghini renounce with simplicity in his conviction to his investiture as magus, which, by the way, was congenial to him. It happened every time that a strong and singular character whose name was Armentano came to the café. His early life was ignored by all, by Reghini, too, I think. What was known [. . .] was that he lived in a castle on a hill off the coast of Calabria."[51] Augusto Hermet (1889–1954), in his memoirs relating to the first decade of the twentieth century, wrote about Reghini and Armentano with his usual wit:

> Reghini then, according to his metaphysical principal derived from the Hermetic-Pythagorean-Orphic-Eleusinian-Daoist-Zoharian tradition, said: "*Non cogito, ergo sum.*" And the brotherly hierophant, sturdy, with a red leonine head and athletic jaw, the man with the mace with the huge ivory knob, negligent musician and devourer of hams, applauded him saying: "*Nihil nihil.*" In the grottos below his castle on the sea of Calabria, the surviving sirens sung.[52]

The castle in question is without a doubt the *Torre Talao* (*Talao Tower*) in Scalea near Cosenza, a sixteenth-century coastal fortification that the Spanish had built during their reign over the region of Calabria. Armentano had bought it and transformed it into his living quarters, and he hosted many of his Pythagorean disciples during the summer months, and with all members of the *Schola* he would also practice mysterious rituals and meditations.[53]

It is clear that Armentano had shaken Reghini out of his disappointing early forays into occultism. In a letter written to an anonymous *sorella* (sister, no doubt a high-ranking female member of the *Schola*), presumably in 1907, Reghini wrote that "Amedeo has simply brought me back to life. When Amedeo came to see me, I had already resigned myself to a life without aim, without a goal, without hope."[54] In the same letter, Reghini insisted that "even in my first dreams of occultism when the only things I desired were a contact with the Brotherhood, I would have never thought to have the daily happiness of an ever-increasing communion with my friend, brother and Master."[55] What do we know about the relationship between the two with regards to occultism? What can be said of the period between 1907, when the two first met, and 1910, the year in which Reghini was initiated into the *Schola Italica* where Armentano appeared to be the visible head?

Di Luca, a Reghini biographer, synthesizes the many changes in Reghini's outlook on life, politics, and occult matters in two broad categories, which I agree with on a general basis. First, from the very beginning of the friendship between master and pupil, Reghini became convinced, and remained so until his death, about an uninterrupted Pythagorean Tradition that was allegedly passed down through the ages from master to disciple since the days in which Pythagoras taught his followers in Kroton. Second, the strong conviction that such a Tradition was intimately bound to a form of Freemasonry that predated the Enlightenment and, therefore, could be brought back to its pristine state by eliminating all the profane and misinformed changes that had been made since the advent of modern times.[56] Such ideas were also entertained by other thinkers, the most important of whom was the founding figure of Traditionalism, René Guénon (1886–1951). According to Guénon, whom Armentano knew intimately and corresponded with frequently, Dante had been profoundly influenced by Pythagoras in the use of numbers in his works and in his *Ésotérisme de Dante* (*Dante's Esotericism*, 1925) claimed that "from Pythagoras to Virgil, from Virgil to Dante, the 'chain of tradition' had not been broken on Italian soil."[57] Armentano's introduction of Guénon to Reghini helped the Florentine mathematician solve many theoretical problems, which plagued his occult *weltanschaaung* and, in my opinion, paved the way for a modern reformulation or reinvention of an autochthone Italian/Roman Tradition. In a 1914 article titled "Del Simbolismo e della Filologia in Rapporto alla Scienza Metafisica" ("On Symbolism and Philology in Relation to Metaphysic Science"), Reghini gave his readers the first clues about the *Schola Italica*:

> The Italic School never had myths; its symbolism was as pure and abstract as possible, numeric symbolism. Within it very few ceremonies, despite the Italic origin of this word; a hard spiritual training ground; a mysticism of the senses, integral, empirical and transcendent, a metaphysical and yet social view, and the light serenity of the pure sky of Calabria.[58]

In his introduction to his translation of Heinrich Cornelius Agrippa's (1486–1535) *De Occulta Philosophia Libri Tres* (*Three Books on The Occult Philosophy*, 1531–1533), Reghini noted that "there exists an oral tradition of hidden knowledge, which may not be transmitted through words (perceived and understood in a profane way). There is still a serious tradition in the West, which has nothing to do with the circus noise, the parody and the imitation of the so-called occultism of today."[59] A pseudonymous author, writing under the pen-name *Rumon*, in commenting on Armentano's *Schola Italica* has pointed out the fact that it aimed to teach an integral idea of man, which belonged to the classical world and which the Renaissance admirably made its own:

> The Roman man, like the Pythagorean, cannot fathom a disconnection between the various dimensions in which the human personality manifests itself, from esotericism to politics, the political being, according to some, the last degree of expertise in the Pythagorean school [...]. It would not be improper to claim that the aim of the Pythagorean school was to constitute an élite founded within the Sacred, that is rooted in the direct knowledge of the Sacred.[60]

With a continuous, slow, and laborious work of purification of oneself, the group, which gathered around Armentano, sought to emulate and become the Pythagorean and Roman man in order to bring esoteric and political glory and excellence back to Italy in general, and Rome, in particular. Because, as Reghini wrote in *Del Simbolismo e Filologia* (*On Symbolism and Philology*), "[l]anguage and race are not the causes of this metaphysical superiority, this appears to belong to the place, to the land, to the air itself. Rome, Rome *caput mundi*, the eternal city, manifests itself, even historically, as one of these magnetic regions of the earth."[61]

In sum, the *Schola* aimed to create an élite of metaphysically and politically superior men, who could manipulate, through magical practice and political intervention, the fate of Italy to bring the country back to its former glory. While Armentano had been the person who claimed to have aligned himself to this Tradition, it was up to Reghini to formulate the practicalities of this Traditionalist revolution.

4.2.3. Reghini's Initiation into the *Schola Italica*

Before moving onto the brief experience of the *Rito Filosofico Italiano* (*Italian Philosophical Rite*), a brief discussion on Reghini's initiation into the *Schola Italica* is necessary. Three years after meeting at the *Lucifero* lodge, Armentano finally decided to initiate Reghini into his Tradition. The date was set on the winter solstice of 1910; the chosen place was the *Passo del Vestito*, or *Vestito Pass*, a small, rickety path that connected the Western side of the Apuan Alps to their Eastern slopes.[62] Author and local mountaineer Disioniso D. Bertolorenzi has written about the difficulty of reaching such a pass, and if one thinks that the two Pythagoreans set out toward the location during a winter night, through thickets, icy slopes, and a vast quantity of snow, the trek to the spot must have been in itself an ordeal.[63] In the same article, Bertolorenzi pointed to a more spiritual dimension behind the choice of the pass itself:

> The Apuan [Alps] are to be found in the exact spot where the Italian Peninsula detaches itself from the continent. A place of change, a threshold and a meeting point for very diverse environmental conditions. This peculiarity turned these mounts into a "bridge" and passage area for many different cultures and peoples.[64]

During a very emic *excursus*, Bertilorenzi, native of the zone, wrote that "the pass, a small grove in a wood, is right on the limit of an abyss," whereby abyss we are meant to think of a deep chasm or ravine.[65] Sestito described this chasm as "a frightening gorge, an abyss, a leap of hundreds of meters."[66] What exactly happened on that night is not entirely clear and probably never will be. According to Sestito, Reghini was dropped into the abyss, in "the obscure chasm of the flabbergasted and lost consciousness."[67] The idea that Reghini must have been lowered down into the "abyss" by the use of a rope tied to his body, and left at the mercy of the elements, is the most probable, but is not mentioned in detail by any of the main sources, Parise, Sestito, or De Luca.[68] Author Piero Fenili, in comparing the figure of Giustiniano Lebano and Amedeo Armentano, has written that "to the interior abyss [. . .] of the initiate, there can be a correspondent external one, as a *theatrum dramatis*, either a deep subterranean cavity, or an Alpine ravine, if we agree that such physical external environments have only the aim to stimulate an experience that consumes itself uniquely *sub specie interioritatis.*"[69]

Despite not knowing what exactly happened on the night of the winter solstice, it is clear that the initiation into the *Schola Italica* marked a fundamental change in Reghini's outlook on his own spiritual progress and on life in general. In Henrik Bogdan's, *From Darkness to Light* (2003), he describes the idea of initiation in great detail. In the second chapter, he quotes scholar of religions Mircea Eliade (1907–1986) at length, especially when dealing with different kinds of initiatory processes.[70] In it Bogdan summarizes Eliade's threefold division of initiatory experiences: (1) the *rites de passage*, which are usually tied to the maturing and ageing of an initiate; (2) the initiation within a secret society; and (3) the heroic and shamanic initiations, where an ecstatic state is reached by the initiate.[71] It is my hypothesis that Reghini experienced the second and third types of initiation listed by Eliade. He was at once ushered into the *Schola Italica* as a full and supposedly high-ranking member, and he seemed to have experienced some kind of revelatory or ecstatic experience, which changed his outlook on many different aspects of life. The first case is easy to explain. Reghini was ushered into a new life within a secret society, which had as its main goals "the reconciliation of Freemasonry with its initiatic function, pruning away its polluting elements in order to steer society towards an order based on spiritual values."[72] The second kind of initiation is harder to demonstrate, and in order to describe the change that took place within Reghini, a closer investigation of his correspondence is necessary. In a letter dated 1911 and quoted in Sestito's biography, Reghini wrote to his Master:

> I feel that I could maybe take interest and sink into one of my old stupid small passions again, but I also feel that no matter how much I sank I could never drown the perception that is budding in me of a new life, serene and lacking the base pleasures and pains of that ego that is refusing to give up.[73]

And again, referring also to the first kind of initiation granted to him: "I need occultism like a plant needs water [...]. What would I do with my life if I did not have before me the sublime task that you have shown me, that you have comforted me again to see and admire with wonder?"[74]

Reghini's introduction into the mysterious *Schola Italica* represented a culmination of his search for an autochthone form of wisdom, which he could learn and transmit, and this seemed to go hand in hand with his elitist view of society, his accentuated nationalism and the need to reform Italian society by harnessing an ancient Italic Tradition.

4.2.4. Invented Traditions as an Epistemological Strategy

In the remarkable work by religious scholar Olav Hammer, *Claiming Knowledge: Strategies of Epistemology from Theosophy to the New Age* (2004), the fourth chapter is devoted entirely to the "Appeal to Tradition."[75] In it, starting from Eric Hobsbawm's theories of the creation of Traditions, Hammer delves deeply into his theory, while simultaneously offering the reader some practical examples that may make his theories clearer. It is my opinion that the *Schola Italica* could be subjected to the same analysis as the one employed by Hammer with Theosophy and other movements. In order for the esoteric school of the *Schola Italica* to be successful, Armentano, even before Reghini's enrolment would have had to create an ever-continuing unbroken chain of occult transmission, which would in turn give birth to a solid emic history that could bolster his claims. As Hammer writes, "For spokespersons [in this case Armentano and then later Reghini] [...] in a modern, post-Enlightenment context, critical and well-documented historical accounts will be readily available. Different movements vary in their wish or ability to counter the claims of historical critical research."[76] Both Armentano and Reghini went to great lengths not to counter, but to offer, a novel interpretation of historical events, which, seen through the lenses of Roman Traditionalism, would show patterns that would validate their claims: some examples can be readily found in Reghini's works. In his first extant article, "Giordano Bruno Smentisce Rastignac" ("Giordano Bruno Refutes Rastignac"), for example, Reghini wrote in order to refute Rastignac's (pseudonym of Vincenzo Morello, 1860–1933) ideas that he had enunciated during a conference on the figure of Giordano Bruno. There, Morello had presented Bruno as a precursor of the Positivist thought and determinism.[77] Reghini wrote,

> He wasn't a precursor of determinism but a mystic and an occultist. Some of the essentially mystical works are the *Eroici Furori*, the *Sigillus Sigillorum*, and the book of *Thirty Sigils*, not to mention others. He also believed that "the reign of God is within us and that divinity dwells in us because of a reformed intellect and will" [...]. The *De Monade* and *Cabala* were nothing but tractates on cabalistic and Pythagorean philosophy; and he consecrated to magic three whole works and many excerpts of other works.[78]

In articles regarding Freemasonry, Reghini insisted on this institution deriving from the ancient Roman builders and claims that "it is an undeniable fact that the Rosicrucian rituals redacted by Elias Ashmole [...] are based on the Egyptian mysteries, such as Iamblichus handed them down to us."[79] Every aspect of occultism, and especially Freemasonry, was drawn together to create a "new" tradition that harkened back more than two thousand years. In quoting Richard Hofstader, Hammer evidences this point in the clearest of manners, writing that "in an effort to bolster a pre-existing frame of understanding with a historical background, isolated and almost unrelated events and elements are juxtaposed and combined into a new edifice."[80] Even Pythagoras, the founder of the so-called Roman Tradition, was made "more Romanized" than he actually had been. Pythagoras, according to Armentano's 129th Maxim, published in his *Massime di Scienza Iniziatica* (*Maxims of Initiatic Science*, 1992), was "Tuscan [i.e. Etruscan] and not from Samos, a disciple of Numa and not vice versa,"[81] with Reghini echoing these sentiments in an article printed in *Atanòr*.[82]

Hobsbawm, in his introduction to *The Invention of Tradition*, explained his idea of invented traditions, writing that "[i]nvented tradition is taken to mean a set of practices [...] which seek to inculcate certain values and norms of behaviour, which automatically imply continuity with the past."[83] Such a definition fits well with Armentano and Reghini, who never seem to use malice in the construction of their Tradition but genuinely "attempt to establish continuity with a suitable historic path."[84] The elitist approach of the *Schola* is also covered by

Hobsbawm and echoes of his statement may be found in Armentano's *Massime* and Reghini's "Imperialismo Pagano" ("Pagan Imperialism"):

> More commonly they [i.e., invented traditions] may foster the corporate sense of superiority of elites—particularly when these had been recruited from those who did not already possess it by birth or ascription—rather than by inculcating a sense of obedience in inferiors. This might be done by assimilating elites to pre-bourgeois ruling groups or authorities, whether in the militaristic/bureaucratic form [... or the non-militarised] "moralised gentry."[85]

Armentano peppered his *Massime* with cold, crystal-clear sentences, which left no room for imagination as to his political views: "58—Men are equal before God and aren't among themselves. 170—Democracy is a word without real meaning; it's an ironic idea of government. 171—People and Government are two antithetical terms. 221—In order for them to be true, things needn't be known by commoners."[86] In more elaborate and ornate sentences, Reghini often makes sure that his elitist message comes out clearly. A prime example of this is his "Imperialismo Pagano," which will be analyzed in depth in the next chapter.

4.3. Enter Frosini: A Singular Ally

4.3.1. The *Rito Filosofico Italiano*

Throughout the mid-1900s and the 1910s, a singular character acquired prominence in the Italian Masonic milieu, Eduardo Frosini. He was also known by his nom de plume *Dr. Hermes*, a travelling salesman, whose business card instead introduced him as Dott. Eduardo Frosini, *Professore di Scienze Sociali ed Antropologiche (Professor of Social and Anthropologic Sciences)*.[87] His passion, within the world of Freemasonry, had been the most occult-leaning Rites, which would include the teachings of the great French occultists, such as Eliphas Lévi (1810–1875), Josephin Péladan (1859–1918), Stanislas the Guaïta (1861–1897), and, of course, the seemingly omnipresent Papus.[88] Usually pitted against the Eastern lore promoted by the Theosophical Society, such Rites were in favor of a restoration of a supposed lost Western Tradition. Di Luca, Reghini biographer and expert in Italian Freemasonry, lists some of them:

> The *Societas Rosacruciana in Anglia*, the Order of the Golden Dawn in Outer [sic.], the Rite of Memphis and Mizraim, the National Iberian Rite, the Swedenborgian Rite, the *Ordo Templi Orientis*, etc. Usually there were only a handful of followers of these monikers, amongst whom "grades,"

grand-sounding titles and similar dignities were shared, handed out with the same ease to *ad honorem* members and foreign representatives.[89]

In January 1908, Frosini, who had been all but disenchanted by the Italian GOI, was nominated *Gran Rappresentante* (*Grand Representative*) of the *Grande Loggia Simbolica di Spagna* (*Grand Symbolic Lodge of Spain*) in Italy. He had been granted the authority to create his own lodge by the head of the Grand Symbolic Lodge of Spain, Villarino del Villar (n.d.).[90] His other charters included that of the Antient and Primitive Order of Memphis Misraim by decree of John Yarker, the post as Secretary of the newly created *Federazione Massonica Universale* (*Universal Masonic Federation*), and, during the second part of the year, he founded his own lodge of the Rite of Memphis and Misraim with autonomous day-to-day running:

> So robustly bolstered by "patents," even if they came from "irregular" expressions of Freemasonry, in March 1909 in Florence, he proceeded to found with some followers a *loggia centrale Ausonia* (central Ausonia lodge) and a *Supremo Gran Consiglio Generale dell'Ordine Antico e Primitivo di Memphis e Mizraim* (Supreme Grand Council General of the Antient and Primitive Rite of Memphis and Mizraim) under the denomination of *Rito Filosofico Italiano*.[91]

To better promote his newly founded body, Frosini published a voluminous book entitled *Massoneria Italiana e Tradizione Iniziatica* (*Italian Freemasonry and Initiatic Tradition*, 1911).[92] In it, Frosini's theories seemed to have caught the attention of Reghini and Armentano, who had met Frosini back in the days of the *Michele di Lando* lodge.[93] Frosini's theories, in a style that is scarcely enjoyable and seems not to have undergone any major editing,[94] are, in my opinion, to be summed up in these major points. First, the idea that Mazzini's philosophical and religious theories had great points in common with "the esoteric theories handed down to us by ancient initiatory orders [. . .]. The integration of the Italian School with the Symbolic tradition would have happened already if the philosophical background had been there."[95] Second, the primacy of Italy, which according to Mazzini, "has within the school of Giordano Bruno, Telesio, Campanella, the *seeds* of a brotherhood between Philosophy and Religion, from which the institutions that can make our fatherland great again will descend."[96] Third, the Roman character of Freemasonry, clear heritage of the *Risorgimento*: "Papus is a mystical-esoteric Christian and supports synarchy. We, of the *Italian School*, Pythagorean and followers of Mazzini, are cosmic-humanist Theosophers, and we oppose isocracy to synarchy."[97] Such statements clearly caught the attention of Reghini and Armentano, who had wanted to propagate their theories to a small number of initiates. The Roman character of the *Rito Filosofico Italiano* made it the best option for the two Roman Traditionalists, who had become disillusioned with the workings at the *loggia Lucifero* and wanted to start working towards the awakening of the masses on behalf of an elite with matters concerning Roman Tradition, both in its theoretical and practical-operative aspects.

4.3.2. Changes within the *Rito Filosofico* and the Its Short Life

The contacts regarding a possible entrance of Reghini and Armentano into the *Rito Filosofico Italiano* (RFI) began in early 1912.[98] With all his patents and high titles, Frosini still thought that he needed something, or someone, more in order to be taken seriously in the Masonic world. Hence, in the spring of 1912, Frosini and his treasurer Guido Bolaffi (n.d.) tried to recruit Reghini, and through him, Armentano.[99] In a letter dated May 1, 1912, Reghini informed his Master: "Frosini is offering me a place in the Supreme Council of the Philosophical Rite with full autonomy in the work," and, in another letter dated May 4, Reghini expressed optimism at what could be done by the Roman Traditionalists in the *Rito Filosofico*: "in any case, the Philosophical Rite, and all things related to it, is in our hands since Bolaffi is responsible, and he is ours [sympathizer or member of the *Schola*] already."[100] The two Traditionalists decided to enter, Armentano under the pseudonym *Ermete Cosentino* (*Hermes of Cosenza*), and by the summer of the same year, the two had opened the *Quirico Filopanti* lodge in Bologna, which, "alongside the "Hermes" [lodge] in Florence, the "*I Pitagorici*" ["The Pythagoreans"] in Milan and the Sebezia of Naples, [were] among the most dynamic and attended [lodges]."[101] On April 21, 1913, to celebrate the anniversary of the foundation of Rome, the Hermes lodge was "consecrated," and *Ermete Cosentino* delivered a speech, which clearly defined the programmatic ideas of the *Rito Filosofico*: "Rome has always risen like the *Phoenix* and [. . .] Italy has always woken up, fought in Masonic manner and won through the Gribaldine saga and the apostolate of Mazzini."[102] In a crescendo of Roman exaltation, Armentano continued:

> And it is for this living and immanent tradition if Italy, guided by the principles, which we, of the Italian Philosophic Rite support and defend, will rise to that greatness and that moral domination of the world that Eternal Rome and all of the glorious Italic thought point to, aspire to, desire and will have![103]

The expansion of the *Rito* was noticeable, and after John Yarker's death in 1913, lodges as distant as New York, Chicago, and Alexandria, Egypt, asked Frosini to be able to stand under the tutelage of the *Rito Filosofico*. With the new year, Frosini left his job in order to concentrate his efforts fully toward his Masonic endeavors.[104] His first major aim was to publish a journal, which was going to be named *Pitagora* (*Pythagoras*), but the chronic lack of funds made it so the journal never saw the light of the day. By the end of the year, two incidents forced Reghini and Armentano to leave the *Rito* hastily and distance themselves from Frosini and Bolaffi. On the one hand, Frosini, in an article on a literary journal, falsely declared he had been initiated into the *Schola Italica* and could speak on its behalf;[105] while on the other hand, the Treasurer, Bolaffi, was found guilty of embezzlement—a strong blow against the credibility of the whole *Rito*.[106] While Bolaffi's expulsion from the *Rito* was swift, Reghini could not leave Frosini's claims unchecked, and in an issue of the Theosophical journal *Ultra* (est. 1906), Reghini was allowed to retort, claiming that "our work, purely metaphysical and thus naturally esoteric, has always been voluntarily secret. We did not need to make the existence of this School public, and if Frosini, hadn't by chance, made a step that could cause equivocations, we would have stayed in our shadows."[107] Reghini resigned from the *Rito* at the end of 1913, and a Masonic decree barred him and Bolaffi from ever communicating to their ex-brothers again: "The civil death (Masonic burning) has been inflicted upon the lawyer Guido Bolaffi and Dr. Arturo Reghini for HIGH TREASON. From the 14 January 1914, these two gentlemen HAVE NOTHING TO DO WITH OUR FAMILY."[108]

Reghini's expulsion did not seem to affect the Florentine Traditionalist, as already in January 1914, he had set out to work and write a series of important articles to be published in the short-lived journal *Salamandra*. It is in my opinion, though, that beyond the surface, a great chance to propagate the tenets of Roman Traditionalism through the vehicle of Freemasonry had been a great chance for the *Schola* to hand pick its choice adherents carefully. While Reghini, in a letter dated November 24, 1913, described Frosini as having "neither esoteric nor exoteric value" and lacking any knowledge in science, philosophy, or classical culture, Armentano was more reluctant to leave the Rite he had been put in charge of, and, at the end of his lifetime, in an interview in Brazil, conducted by Nino Daniele, had admitted:

> Yes, that was our trumpet call—by that I mean that the Italian Philosophical Rite (which, more than a Rite, was a real school, Masonic, but up to a certain measure)—for a serious Pagan imperialism.[109]

***

The year 1914 witnessed an event, which would momentarily put a halt to all of the *Schola Italica* members' attempts at infiltrating Masonic bodies in order to promote their tenets, and it would soon scatter the tight-knit group of occultists all over the Italian border. July 28, 1914, saw the beginning of World War I, and, while Italy would not participate in the conflict until a year later, most members of the Schola were only waiting for the moment when they could volunteer in an effort to help the Italian forces defend their borders and annex the northwestern irredentist lands.

5
The Great War and "Pagan Imperialism" (1914–1920)

A Clash between the Modern and the Traditional

> Rightly did Dante say that [...] the world
> was destroyed by Constantine
>
> —Julius Evola[1]

5.1. Interventionism and Nationalism in Italy (1910–1914)

5.1.1. The Larger Picture: Italy and Nationalism

During the celebrations in Florence on the night of December 31, 1913, a group of young revelers, no doubt after an evening of merriment at one of the literary cafés in the city center, marched through the streets chanting: "Long live imperialism!"[2] Among the boisterous youths were *Lacerba* collaborator Italo Tavolato (1889–1963),[3] future essayist and novelist Aldo Palazzeschi (1885–1974),[4] Teodor Daubler (1876–1934), and, leading the group, Arturo Reghini. This scene perfectly captures the feelings and hopes of many young intellectuals who had constantly grown in number from the beginning of the century and had now become, on an intellectual level if not on a political one, a force to be reckoned with. What had essentially changed, in the ten years leading up to 1914, were the perspectives and aims of the Italian Nationalists. Under the governments led by Francesco Crispi (1818–1901) and Giovanni Giolitti (1842–1928), expansionism had created more problems than it had solved, and the gains had been negligible. An attempt to conquest Ethiopia on March 1, 1896, was met with a crushing defeat for the Italian forces led by Oreste Baratieri (1841–1901) near the city of Adua.[5] On May 2, 1889, with the Treaty of Uccialli, Ethiopia and Italy agreed on Eritrea becoming an Italian protectorate.[6] In the war against the Turks between the years 1911 and 1912, Italy managed to annex Libya and the Dodecanese Islands, an archipelago between Greece and Turkey. A pyrrhic victory if ever there was one, the sun seemed to set very quickly over the Italian "empire."

The attention of the Nationalists thus moved toward the irredentist cause, dealt with in the previous chapter, brought on by an exasperation of the political climate, which had the effect of overshadowing any other political problem Italy may have had. To exemplify the multifaceted positions that were taken by some of the most prominent figures, a quote by future Fascist Minister of Justice, Alfredo Rocco (1875–1935), extrapolated from his pamphlet *Che cos'è il Nazionalismo e Cosa Vogliono i Nazionalisti* (*What Nationalism Is and What Nationalists Want*, 1914), will hopefully be explicative:

> Nationalists, therefore, aren't liberal moderates, or better they are not essentially liberal moderates, aren't conservatives, aren't clerical, aren't democratic, neither radical nor republicans; they are not, finally, Socialists; while not dismissing the value of the problems that some of these parties put forth (which explains how with some of these, sometimes, they may agree) they remain, characteristically nationalist since they only give absolute value to the national problem and consider all others as subordinate to it.[7]

Following the evolution of nationalist thought embodied by thinkers, such as Corradini and Federzoni, the nationalist idea seems to have gone through two distinct phases. The first one was propagated by journals, such as *Il Regno* and *La Voce* in the early years of the twentieth century, when avant-garde and nationalist sentiments began mixing and complementing each other. The second one was where Corradini's Association of Italian Nationalists joined the political fray in the early 1910s. During the first part, Corradini and others were more interested in critiquing Positivism, materialism, "contemporary cowardice," and "ignoble socialism," proposing nationalism as an intellectual crusade against "moral decay."[8] The second phase was marked by a more realistic approach to the problems Italy was facing: a poor economic situation, a disastrous imperialist campaign, a shaky political environment (Nationalists under the Giolitti government used to refer to Italy as *Italietta*, "poor little Italy"), and a rise in unrest among the workers' syndicates.[9] The process of coagulating a stream of irrationalist ideas and creating a movement that could stand up to the parties in the government was reached by pure force and iconoclasm. The Nationalist movement's greatest successes were reached through a strong opposition to contemporary politics rather than for the cohesion of its ideas. Therefore, after having gained their first seats during the 1913 elections, Corradini and his followers synthesized their program in the reannexation of the Italian-speaking regions, which were still under foreign rule:

> Italy knows that within the borders, *immutably prescribed by its history and by its glory*, there is a population of heroes who for the defence of the hearth

and of blood desperately fight the fiercest war ever fought, alone and beautiful. Italy knows that from Trieste to Pola, from Capo d'Istria to Trento, from Split to Fiume, one is the language, one the soul, one the hope that urges the help of all Italians to our last defence.[10]

Now that the stance of the Italian Nationalist Association has been roughly sketched, it may be natural to ask oneself: what was the relationship between members of the *Schola Italica* and Corradini's coterie? As I will write in my analysis of Reghini's "Imperialismo Pagano," the one main difference was the link to the Catholic Church. In 1912, universal suffrage had widened the bracket of voters to more than 8.5 million men, and the new voters, mostly members of the working class, against whom Reghini railed in his articles, were likely to vote for the *Partito Socialista Italiano* (*Italian Socialist Party*).[11] To avoid a surge in power of the Socialists, Giolitti had conferred with an aristocrat and representative of the Italian Catholic Electoral Union, Vincenzo Ottorino Gentiloni (1865–1916). The aim was to create a joint front between Catholics and Liberals against the rising Socialist force and, while Giolitti promised to include Catholics of the Electoral Union in his future government, Gentiloni, after whom this agreement took its name, would scrutinize Giolitti's candidates and choose the ones who adhered most to Catholic ideals. The result was a landslide victory for Giolitti, which left democratic Catholics, such as don Luigi Sturzo (1871–1959) and don Romolo Mutti (1870–1944), outside of the coalition and without allies.[12] While the Catholics in Parliament were in favor of an intervention alongside the Austro-Hungarian Empire and Germany, both the Nationalists and Democratic Catholics vied for an alliance with England and France.

5.1.2. Reghini and Roman Traditionalist Volunteers

In this key period of Italian history, Reghini was busy writing new articles for *Salamandra*, which had been much in demand after the publication of "Imperialismo Pagano" in the first issue. His frequentation of the cafés in Piazza dell'Unità, the *Giubbe Rosse* and *Pazkowsky*, were the only moments during which the Florentine thinker connected with the outside world to discuss current affairs with his friends. In a letter to Armentano, dated May 27, 1914, he had written:

> The political situation is again serious. We will end up going to war with Austria; it seems like Austria wants it immediately because we have not recovered from Libya yet, and Russia is not ready [. . .]. One thing is for sure: no ten days pass without some new problem rising.[13]

In another document, his anti-clerical sentiments are excited once more. Again, in corresponding with Armentano, he wrote that

> You will have probably seen that the Nationalist Congress in Milan has accentuated the clerical aspect of this party; a new daily nationalist newspaper will see the light of day under the auspices of the Bank of Rome.[14]

The letter ends with an enigmatic sentence by Reghini: "The time might have come to act in the imperial sense."[15] What exactly was meant by this is left to speculation, and it is unclear whether Reghini is speaking about occult magical operations or about something more mundane. What is true, as I will discuss, is that Reghini credited Armentano and his magic for some of the success Italy had during the Great War, so the idea of a use of magical powers in order to allegedly bolster the imperial idea is not so far-fetched.

Reghini, with his Master, spent the summer in Scalea practicing magic and discussing politics, esotericism, and Freemasonry. There they were joined by many guests, most of whom were interested in Armentano's and Reghini's Pagan-imperialist ideas; Augusto Hermet (1889–1956), Giorgio Amendola (1907–1980), and Enrico Salvi (n.d.) were only a few of the people who went to the *Schola*'s headquarters in Calabria. It seems safe to say that these prewar years represented the height of Armentano's and the School's prestige. As Roberto Sestito aptly summarizes,

> [I]t was a summer full of meetings and reunions, during which discussions on politics intertwined with historical and philosophical debates on the spiritual union of the Italians, while the European war knocked heavily on the irredentist borders of the Motherland.[16]

By the beginning of 1915, Reghini, writing to Armentano, confided that all his friends had received a warning to be prepared to leave at very short notice to join the war effort. Reghini's brother was ready to go, too, and all members of the *Schola Italica* had volunteered to be among the first to go to the front line. Reghini was shocked when, during the military medical examination, he was rejected and deemed unfit to participate in the conflict.[17] Armentano, Giulio Guerrieri (1885–1963), and futurist author Ottone Rosai (1895–1958) were the first among Reghini's friends to leave, abandoning their companion in Florence; Reghini would then decide to spend his time focusing on methods of clairvoyance to use once at the front.[18] By using a secret substance, called *ortica mistica* (*mystic nettle*), possibly containing hashish and other mind-altering substances, which had been used with Armentano in Scalea, Reghini was sure that he had achieved a proficient level:

You realise it can work against Jesuits and Austrians. I would put myself at the service of General Cadorna after having proven its validity to him. Do not think that I am exaggerating or that I have lost my mind. I just wanted to try; the thing worked. At least there is a direct transmission of thought, which is something.[19]

When the last of his friends had left and joined the military, Reghini was in a state of constant isolation. It was a chance for him to observe how the tenets expressed in his "Imperialismo Pagano" fared from the outside when confronted with the harsh reality of war. In a letter to Armentano, dated July 11, 1915, he wrote, "If there weren't the possibility to forget everything within my philological research, I'd be going through bad times [. . .] but I have faith in all that prodigious transcendence with which we've had contact many times!"[20]

Reghini carried on with his occult experiments, and, in July, wrote to Armentano, who was stationed on the Austrian front, detailing his experiments with the few friends had still not been conscripted: "suffice to say that at my first *fiat lux* [i.e., let there be light] an electric lamp which was three meters away from us switched itself on; and later at another *fiat lux*, it switched on and off along with all the lighting in the street."[21] During another summer evening, Reghini had tried to visualise Armentano through the following experiment:

> Yesterday I hypnotised Vitali. Without telling him a single word, with the simple contact of your letter on his forehead, he managed to see you. The vision was so clear, that at one point I had to wake him up. He saw you laughing in the trenches with a man with a short black beard, whom he later recognised as Rossaro. He saw you in battle: the Austrians were close to the small church, behind a graveyard (?!) [. . .]. What is true about this? Rest assured that I didn't speak a word to him, and that it all happened in a few minutes. Did anything similar happen on 13 July?[22]

Reghini spent the rest of the summer in Armetano's *Torre Talao*, writing articles on metaphysics, practicing the rites of the *Schola*, his only company being an Englishwoman by the name of Myriam Southgate (n.d.), whom Armentano had hired as a nanny to look after his young son Lorenzo.

Toward the end of 1916, Reghini had applied for a position of official in the Italian Army, but had been denied, since he had only worked very sporadically as a substitute teacher, and not a full-time one. His time had come to go and fight for his country, but as a common infantryman. His disgust is very clear in this letter to Armentano dated November 28, 1916:

> So I am condemned to be a private soldier. Two dimes a day and the prolonged promiscuity with my peers! Think about what it would be for me to live

in continued promiscuity with a mass of brutes, and, without fault, without reason, being the brunt of their jokes, and what jokes, without being able to flee, or rebel![23]

Reghini asked his friend Amendola, who had by then moved to Rome and become the head of the Roman office of the national paper *Corriere della Sera* (Evening Courier, est. 1876). On November 1, 1917 he enrolled in the Military Academy of Turin to undertake a course, which would make him noncommissioned officer of the Engineering Corps.[24] Even when close to the enemy lines, he devoted all his spare time to his culture, and taught himself German by reading *Thus Spake Zarathustra* (1885), an ancient Egyptian grammar, and the Greek classics.[25] His old friend from the Giubbe Rosse period, Nicola Lisi, remembers meeting him in the fog of war, where Lisi had been bed-ridden due to a sprained ankle:

> I was thus alone, lying down while complaining, when I saw, descending from above and coming toward me, someone who, it appeared to me, looked more like a magician than an official. All of a sudden I recognised him as Reghini. I sprung up, having forgotten even of the effects of my sprain. Certain I would make him happy, I told him that while he walked toward me he had appeared to me like Cagliostro reincarnated [. . .]. Before leaving each other [. . .] I set up a meeting with Reghini for the following Thursday night, to read, or re-read in his case, Plato.[26]

One of Reghini's last letters from the front, dated October 1918, ended with a prophetic and enigmatic message to Armentano: "DUE TO OUR WORK, AUSTRIA DIES."[27] After the end of the Great War, Reghini was transferred from Florence to Rome, and soon after resumed life in the capital on permanent leave.

5.2. 1914: Pagan Imperialism: A Textual Analysis

5.2.1. The Context of "Imperialismo Pagano"

Before delving into the analysis of "Pagan Imperialism," I would like to present the work in its context, answering a series of questions, which were formulated by communication theorist Harold Lasswell in 1948. According to Lasswell, "a convenient way to describe an act of communication is to answer the following questions: 'Who / Says What / In Which Channel / To Whom / With What Effect.'"[28] This method may be dated, and it will not be used as a methodology to examine the text in question, but I believe that answering these questions will embed my textual analysis into a clearer context, making it easier to follow the interpretation of the writing at hand.[29]

By 1914, Reghini had reached a unique position in the cultural milieu of his native Florence and of certain Roman circles: he was hailed as one of the greatest thinkers of his time by the Futurists, who wrote for the journal *Lacerba*. About Reghini's position, Sestito has written: "In Florence, rumour had it that he was the true leader of the Futurists and that Futurism wasn't just a movement animated by artistic and literary motivations, but that within it hid a philosophical and Pagan soul."[30] Moreover, he was widely revered by the small group of fellow Pythagoreans of the *Schola*, who had accepted Armentano's decision to make Reghini the official spokesman for his coterie of occultists, a position, which Reghini had accepted gladly.[31] Most of the people he frequented at literary cafés and journals' editorial offices, from Papini to Däubler,[32] from *Schola* member Giulio Guerrieri to friend, Theosophist, and irredentist Augusto Agabiti (1879–1918),[33] all shared a Pagan, elitist, and imperialist political outlook. As none of these had the right qualities to jot down these political ideas in a succinct and coherent manifesto, this task was left to Reghini, who, in a letter dated September 12, 1913, had written to Armentano that he would be dedicating himself to a *serio lavoro*, a serious task, in the last months of the year.[34] In this letter, Reghini expressed the urgency of writing something with impact that could create a future political base to build upon, and seeing that "Imperialismo Pagano" was published in January 1914, it is natural to think that the topic of conversation was most probably the article itself. Reghini had spent his summer at the *Schola*'s headquarters in Scalea, and the main topic of debate had been, as we can glean from the correspondence dating from September to December 1913, the constitution of a political movement founded upon the Italic Tradition.[35] The article itself was divided into four distinct sections: a brief introduction, where Reghini grounded his theoretical framework in the historical period of the day; "Empire and Christendom," where he discussed the fall of the Roman Empire and the alleged major role played by the rise of Christianity; a third part called "The Imperial Tradition," where Reghini went at lengths to provide his reader with the idea of an unbroken chain of imperialists, including Vergil, Dante, and Petrarch; a final fourth one, in which Reghini continued with his list of imperialist thinkers throughout the centuries, citing Machiavelli, Bruno, Campanella, and, of course, Garibaldi and Mazzini. A short, half-page epilogue wrapped up the article, with Reghini's considerations on the present day, his critique of Italian nationalism, and his usual dose of anti-clericalism.

The Roman journal *Salamandra*, described as "amorphous" by Augusto Hermet, was edited by Giovanni Mori, who had been, as we have seen in previous chapters, a Masonic brother and good friend of Reghini.[36] The adjective amorphous was probably used by Hermet because, before the journal's ideology and direction could take shape, Mori had abandoned the project after only three issues.[37] Its short life span, though, was characterized by a moderately wide readership and a lively reader-editor letter exchange. Reghini would pen "La Tragedia del Tempio" ("The Tragedy of the Temple"), an article on the Knights Templar, for the second issue, and a critique of Theosophy, which anticipated Guénon's *Le Théosophisme* by seven years, had been in the works for the third.[38] Its title was supposed to have been "I Santi Padri della Teosofia: Besant, Leadbeater, Steiner" ("The Holy Fathers of Theosophy: Besant, Leadbeater, Steiner"), but the interruption of *Salamandra*'s publication forced Reghini, who felt he could not publish it elsewhere, to abandon this project at a very early draft.[39]

The reaction to the publication of "Imperialismo Pagano" was noticeable in Roman and Florentine circles but also abroad. As Sestito writes, "[The publication] brought upon him, as was expected, the critiques of the vast majority of readers, who did not possess a background in classical and Pagan culture."[40] The strong anti-Christian character of the article was denounced by most of the critics, especially from his old Theosophical friends, who were always precariously balancing the ideas of Christianity and Eastern traditions.[41] Reghini's response to his critics was harsh and brief. With the author's typically dry wit on February 4, 1914, he had written to Armentano: "[I despise] this universal tomfoolery. The will to make things take their course will prevail against everyone and everything; by that, I mean imposing oneself by means of culture, art and fist-fights."[42] The Italian Italian Grand Orient (GOI) pressured Mori to include a leaflet that stated clearly that GOI distanced itself from the imperialist ideas of the author.[43] Even Papini, one of Reghini's oldest friends, criticized the archaizing structure of the ideas contained in "Imperialismo Pagano," but "many youths who frequented the literary cafés of Florence were fascinated by his patriotism, and we will witness Däubler, a refined lyric poet overwhelmed by a new imperialist mysticism, compose his exuberantly beautiful *Inni all'Italia* [sic] (Hymns to Italy, 1916)."[44] According to Sestito, and I concur with his conclusion:

> *Pagan Imperialism* was the article that was destined to signal a change in the Italian esoteric world because it broke with a habit of fear and a submission of Italian pride and dignity towards political and religious powers, mostly foreign or of foreign origin, a rupture modelled on the thought of the great national seers.[45]

Who these so-called seers were for Reghini and his friends will be clearer in the next paragraphs. Now that I have briefly tackled the "Who / said what / in which channel / to whom / with what effect" in a very cursory, but I hope satisfactory, manner, an analysis of the text itself is necessary.

5.2.2. "Introduction"

The article begins with an epigraph from Dante Alighieri's (1265–1321) *Monarchia* (*Monarchy*, 1308–1312/1313); the epigraph, taken from the second book of Dante's work, reads, "The Roman people were appointed to rule by nature." Since the beginning, by the use of this sentence, Reghini put no doubt in the Roman character of his endeavor. Not only did his idea of imperialism have to be Pagan in nature, but it also had to stem from a tradition of which Dante was one of the greatest representatives, and much will be written about him in the next paragraph.[46]

The introduction offers a panoramic view of the Italian political milieu, paving the way for an analysis of a new form of Imperialism to be postulated by Reghini. This section focuses on two main issues: the critique of democracy and the Catholic Church, and his opening comment on democracy needs to be quoted in full:

> In the recent political elections, universal suffrage, extreme corollary of democratic postulates, has brought us to the triumph of oversimplification. The two parties, thus, who have seen their votes rise the most, are without doubt the clerical and the Socialist. Evident sign that the arguments and the promises utilised were by nature more accessible and welcomed by the vast, illiterate majority of voters, much more than the ideas of other parties could be.[47]

Several considerations may be made about this opening statement. First, from a strictly political point of view, it seems clear that, without the support of said masses, any party would have struggled to emerge, and if indeed Reghini would have presented a new, elitist, anti-democratic and anti-Socialist party in a country that would have remained a democracy until 1923, the chances of a political victory would have been drastically low. From a sociological point of view, the fracture between the maybe three hundred people to whom this article was directed paled when compared to the democratic electorate, which Reghini treated as mere statistical numbers. The gap between these two groups was profound in terms of culture, competence, desires, and expectations.[48] Lumping all of his most disliked political traits into one sentence, Reghini lamented that "illiteracy, oversimplification and internationalisation, bound together, have therefore won the greater glory of the Parliamentary regime."[49] Reghini then continued to criticize the first of his two targets: the variety of Nationalist groups, which gravitated toward Corradini's Italian Nationalist Association. While never mentioning the name of the association or of its President, Reghini was adamant in stating that there was "no party to this date in Italy with which the national conscience can identify itself trustingly."[50] Reghini, possibly moulding reality to suit his needs, attributed a clerical element to Corradini's Nationalists. As we have seen, the movement had started following a strict, *Risorgimento* way of conjugating the politics of their time with a very lay approach, but it had ultimately abandoned those positions in lieu of less extreme manifestations of political expression. In the years between 1908 and 1910, Corradini had preached in favor of a "Nazione Proletaria" ("Proletarian Nation"); however, just before the elections of 1913, his nationalist movement had co-opted industrialist magnates and members of the bourgeoisie, and a movement more moderate, clerical, and anti-Socialist in nature was born, the *Conservatori Nazionali* (*National Conservatives*).[51] Their aspirations can be summed up in this quote by their leader, Ezio Maria Grey (1885–1969), from a 1914 newspaper article: "We affirm the necessity of an association, which may take to the defence of the grand national institute threatened by Socialism. All class interests will be judged, not by way of their separation, but in their union coordinated with the national interest."[52] Gray would later become an important figure in the budding Fascist regime, and he participated in the March on Rome that ultimately brought Fascism to power.[53] In sum, if the *Associazione Nazionalisti Italiani* had any reason to be considered on the same side as Pope Pius X (1835–1914), it is because both shared an utter distaste for the direction, which lay society, on the one hand, and clerical modernism, on the other, were heading. Pius X was by all means an upholder of traditional Christianity with his aim being to bring back the Church from what he considered to be the greatest danger of all for the Vatican: Theological Modernism.[54] While talking of modernist priests, the Pope's ideas were very clear, and his resolve was unwavering: "they [the Vatican clergy] want them to be treated with oil, soap and caresses. But they should be beaten with fists. In a duel, you don't count or measure the blows, you strike as you can."[55] Catholicism, as I shall also point out in the next two chapters, was an obsession for Reghini and an evil that had to be extirpated before the possibility of a pagan imperialist movement could even be born. Catholicism's presence was everywhere, according to the Florentine philosopher, and it seemed that little could be done to stop its expansion in temporal power:

> Bad times are upon us! And the progress of Catholicism in Protestant countries is a meagre consolation for so many ailments: in Germany where the Emperor needs the votes of the Catholic centre; in England and the United States where the Catholic cult, more *picturesque* than the various Protestant cults, is continuously gaining ground.[56]

Reghini then summed up his introduction with the individuation of two changes in Italian society, which made the Church look like the biggest enemy for pagan imperialism: (1) war, which had awoken nationalistic sentiments, and

(2) universal suffrage, which had made the voting masses easily manipulated by the *longa manus* of the clerical activists engaged in politics. By not asking for an official return of temporal power to the Vatican, Reghini saw the Church's involvement in politics as a shrewd, cunning move. Talking as a hypothetical member of the clergy, Reghini concluded his introduction writing: "[I]n this way, even the worst among troubles that has befallen the Church of Rome, the formation of Italy as a united and independent country, will end up benefiting us [the Church of Rome]."[57]

5.2.3. "Impero e Cristianesimo" ("Empire and Christendom")

The first section of "Pagan Imperialism" opened with a full-frontal attack against the Church of Rome and the malleable masses, which the Church so easily, according to the author, managed to entice and bring to submission.[58] In order to be a true nationalist, the good of the State and the good of the Church must never cross paths. Here lied Reghini's first crucial point of "Pagan Imperialism," one that he would reiterate for the rest of his career as an author and public speaker:

> Now in our case, there is a natural, fatal, deep, irreconcilable contrast. In the long succession of the centuries, from the foundation of the Church of Rome onwards, Papacy has always been the natural enemy of Rome and Italy. Latin civilisation, eclectic, serene, open, in a word *gentile*, and the Roman empire with it, was suffocated by the exotic, intolerant, fanatic, dogmatic mentality of Christianity. And this is a crime that still awaits its expiation.[59]

The alleged negative influence of the Church of Rome was called to account for the failure of the imperial idea, which, according to Reghini, was a well-oiled machine of tolerance and acceptance before one god upon many was chosen to be favored.[60]

Reghini then introduced, the second of the greatest predecessors in the exaltation of Roman imperial ideas, second only to Dante: Publius Virgilius Maro (70 BCE–19 BCE), more commonly known as Vergil: Rome's own epic poet. It is curious that the first work to be cited in "Imperialismo" is not the epic classic *Aeneid* (29 BCE–19 BCE), considered by most Roman Traditionalists as the bible of Roman Imperialism, but a verse from the fourth of his *Eclogues*. This is a verse that has intrigued and fascinated a great number of thinkers throughout the centuries. Verse IV:6 is quoted in full by Reghini: "*Jam redit et Virgo, redeunt Saturnia regna.*"[61] From the years following the composition of the fourth *Eclogue*, many scholars have wondered about what the *Saturnia regna* referred to, and the later mention of a *puer*—a child who would bring back a Golden Age—sparked the curiosity of many a reader.[62] The nature of the Golden Age in this passage has been analyzed by many classical scholars, *in primis* Kenneth Reckford, who linked Vergil's verses to the Hesiodic narration of an Age in which men lived with gods and did not have to toil in order to earn a living until a progressive degeneration of man, at some point, forced the gods to withdraw, leaving man to fend for himself. Such an anti-evolutionist approach to history would have no doubt tantalized Reghini, as a close comparison between Hesiod's myth and the doctrine of the Hindu *yugas* will prove. The idea of a spiraling condition of man was later adopted by Stoic philosophers, who believed in a cataclysmic "destruction of the world by fire (*ekpyrosis*) [that] facilitated the acceptance of a cyclical view."[63] Vergil's IV *Eclogue* is not the only place where the reign of Augustus is seen as ushering a new Golden Age: *Aeneid* 1. 291–296 and 6. 791–794 are just as potent and convincing that the poet was simply doing his job as a political propagandist at the court of the Emperor.[64] Who then was the child who would usher in this age? For some scholars, it was Asinius Gallus (d. 33 CE), son of Asinius Pollio (d. 4 CE) and one of Vergil's patrons; while for others it was the future child of Augustus himself and his wife Scribonia (68–16 BCE). Nevertheless, no matter how plausible these theories may be, from the time of Constantine,

> [T]here has long been a persistent belief that the child was Christ, and that Vergil in this little poem was prophesying something greater than the birth of a son to his friend Pollio or to the imperial house of Rome.[65]

The interpretation of most Latin scholars considered the "Virgin" to represent "Justice," bringing a King, representing the beginning of imperial power in the figure of a child. Constantine begged to differ: as Bourne writes, "the *virgo* is, of course, the Virgin Mary; she brings the king, who is Christ."[66] After Constantine, many notable Church historians agreed with this thesis, including Lactantius (240–320), Augustine of Hippo (354–430), Abelard (1079–1142), and, of course, Dante, in his XX *Canto* of Purgatory.[67]

Reghini introduced this verse from Vergil because his main aim, in this article, was to establish a chain of Roman imperialist thinkers who would buttress his ideas, and losing Vergil and Dante in one fell swoop would have meant an instant defeat of his argument. He, thus, proceeded to ridicule the Christian interpretation of Vergil's verses in the IV *Eclogue*. The passage deserves to be quoted in full to appreciate the virulence of Reghini's rhetoric:

> Vergil, the great poet, had just sung the return of the golden age
>
> *Jam redit et Virgo, redeunt Saturnia Regna,*

and prophesised the coming of a *veltro* [a greyhound] which the destroyers of the Vergilian ideal had the impudence of identifying with Jesus. Here we have a megalomaniac, hypochondriac and sentimental, whose vision of the world created by his God moved to compassion and tears, thought himself the one and only wise man to live in this vale of tears, and made the brand new discovery that in order to fix humanity's affairs, all one needed was to make men better.[68]

While accompanying Dante through hell in the *Divina Commedia*, Vergil talked about the greyhound in Dante's *Inferno*, telling his newly found disciple that "he shall not feed on either land or wealth, but wisdom, love and power shall be his food."[69] The identity of the greyhound has been debated for centuries, but for many interpreters, the allusion referred to an emperor who in the future would save Italy from the greedy hands of the she-wolf with which Dante associated the Papal States.[70] Thus, with one powerful paragraph, Reghini began to delineate the lineage of his Roman imperial thought. By linking two great Masters of Roman and Italian culture under the imperialist flag, Reghini was ready to move on to fiercer criticism toward the Church upholstered by the figures of Vergil and Dante. In the following passages, Reghini endeavored to explain the reason why the alien religion of Christianity took hold in the empire, and, according to him, began to corrode it from the inside. The Roman Empire, wrote Reghini, was founded on common law, untouched by matters of religion, and founded its power and existence upon the knowledge of the empirical problems of life with no theological speculation or abstraction.[71] Christianity seems to have sneaked up from Judaea all the way to the heart of the empire; according to Reghini: "when the emperors became aware of the new trend, it was too late. The infection had spread rapidly across the Empire, had reached the Urbs [Rome], and even if the violence [literally iron and fire] had been used even more generously than unfortunately it had been, it could not have saved the West."[72] To Reghini, this is the crux behind the decline of the West: Christianity, always alluded to by the Florentine author as a disease, a malaise, an exotic syndrome, which had managed to find its way through the Roman Empire's chinks of armor and had rotted the giant's corpse from the inside. "A sentimental morbid mysticism drowned the healthy and serene Italian practicality, the Italian *prudentia* [Latin for foresight], and the Roman eagle, accustomed to long flights, smeared its talons in the sticky sweetness of universal love."[73] The paragraph ends with Reghini pointing to the Church's appropriation of certain magical symbols, allowing Rome to prosper for centuries, and with a short list of events perpetrated by the Church, which helped facilitate the destruction of the Roman Empire. In the first instance, Reghini prominently refers to the magical force that I have referred to throughout this book, which he thought permeated the soil and air of the city of Rome itself, before alluding to the keys of Janus. The keys of Janus had become the keys of

Peter, and the Roman institution of the *pontifex maximus*—the highest post in Republican Rome—was taken by the Church and used to this day to refer to the Pope.[74] The second grievance Reghini expressed regarded the first actions of the Church. Once in a position of influence, which derived from the creation of the Oriental Roman or Byzantine Empire, the Church, according to Reghini, brought a quick collapse of the Western empire: "political unity and the loss of the conscience of an Italian national unity for centuries upon end, the destruction of culture, thought, letters, arts [...]."[75]

5.2.4. "La Tradizione Imperiale Romana" ("The Roman Imperial Tradition")

The second main section of "Imperialismo" began on a very somber note: Christianity had spread across the whole of Europe, and any trace of a Pagan community seemed to have disappeared. Any attempt by the barbarian kings to re-establish a temporal realm in Rome had, in one way or another, failed. The Italian imperial authority seemed to have disappeared forever. "Nevertheless," Reghini wrote, "even facts themselves took it onto themselves to show its necessity [i.e., of imperialism]."[76]

> Another religion, being born from Judaism and Christianity, threatened from Asia. Muslim fanaticism did not pale in comparison to the Christian one; from the remotest Arabia, the Asian hordes made their way north towards Europe, and, along the road, they converted and overran people with the persuasion of their scimitar.[77]

It is the Muslim migration westward, which, according to Reghini, rekindled a sense of necessity of an empire in the West that could put a stop to the seemingly invincible Islamic threat. Charlemagne (742–814) represented a pivotal figure in Reghini's narration on the development of the imperial idea in Europe.[78] Reghini, thus, saw the advent of the Holy Roman Empire as a necessity felt by those who did not feel at ease with the domination of the Catholic Church: "the idea of a Roman empire, put in effect by Charlemagne, remained present in the conscience of peoples and little by little became the secret hope of all the heretics, the ultimate goal of all secret societies that flourished in all of Europe from the 1000 to 1400."[79] The modern scholar of Western esotericism may be surprised to read about a surge in the number of secret societies in these years, but in the following paragraph, Reghini provided a clear idea of what he meant in his text:

It is not possible to penetrate within the true spirit of those changes without knowledge of Gnosticism, of Manicheism, of the Paganism of most of the heresies of the day, without having divined the mystical and political secret of chivalry, without having understood the gay science of the troubadours, and the jargon of the secret societies, and without having discovered the affinities and occult ties that bound together heretics and Ghibellines, inhabitants of Lombardy and Toulouse, wandering priests, troubadours and the Knights Templar.[80]

The usually bleakly characterized epoch of the Dark Ages was here enchanted by Reghini, who, against the unconditional rule of the Church, saw many varied expressions of people oriented toward imperial temporal power. It was of no concern as to whether the Cathars, the Knights Templar, and the Manicheans actually did share a belief in the importance of the presence a strong temporal power in Europe. From an anti-clerical perspective, there was no doubt that this would have helped such persecuted groups. What mattered most to the author of "Imperialismo" was the creation of a strong imperialist and anti-clerical narrative, which would bolster Reghini's conclusion, making it appear as if the idea of a lay or Pagan imperialism had always been present throughout European history.

After Charlemagne, Reghini turned once again to Dante—the Florentine poet of the *Divine Comedy*. According to Reghini, it was with Dante that an idea of a Pythagorean-Roman monarchy, which would become the Italian imperialist tradition, first became conscious of the importance of its existence. Dante was, thus, inserted within the tradition of the great imperialists of the past, which had inspired Reghini and his group of friends: namely, King Numa, Pythagoras, Julius Caesar, Vergil, Augustus, "and the other great Italians who came later on."[81] The creation of a clear and plausible string of wise Pagan imperialists began to take shape at the very center of "Imperialismo." Reghini's Traditionalism needs both a *prisca sapientia*, but most importantly a respectable list of *prisci sapientes*, who could justify the Roman Traditionalists' return to the ways of old. The rest of the second chapter of "Imperialismo" focuses on two legitimization strategies related to Dante and his work.

First, Reghini refuted the idea of a Christian Dante, explaining that he was forced to pose as a Christian in thirteenth-century Florence in order to compose his works in relative tranquillity. The fact that his *Monarchia* had been successively banned by the Church and his frequent words of devotion to Vergil were proof to Reghini of the Pagan nature of Dante's message: "[b]ecause Dante, by great Jove and the good Apollo that he used to invoke, was not a Catholic and his imperialism was Pagan and Roman!"[82] Reghini continuously reminded his reader of the link between Vergil and Dante, especially by drawing parallels between the prophetic *Aeneid VI* and the *Comedy* itself: "[t]he isagoge is the same in both, it is the allegorical and sometimes categorical exposition of the metamorphosis of man in God; politically, furthermore, Vergil and Dante don't do anything apart from exalting the Roman Empire."[83] The VI book of Vergil's magnum opus talks about Aeneas's descent into the underworld in order to see his father Anchises and experience visions, which fit well with the imperial propaganda that Vergil had peppered his poem with: to the startled Aeneas, Anchises shows the glorious future of Rome:

> Turn your two eyes
> This way and see this people, your own Romans.
> Here is Caesar, and all the line of Iulus,
> All who shall one day pass under the dome
> Of the great sky: this is the man, this one,
> Of whom so often you have heard the promise,
> Caesar Augustus, son of the deified,
> Who shall bring once again an Age of Gold
> To Latium, to the land where Saturn reigned
> In early times.[84]

Secondly, Reghini insisted on the present symbolism in the *Divina Commedia* as being imperial in essence. He described the two most important symbols of Dante's *Paradiso* as the eagle "the sacred bird that made the Romans revered in the world" and the rosy-cross, "which is not the mystic rose but the sectarian rose of the *Roman de la Rose*."[85] The eagle, carried atop every military standard within the Roman army, was, thus, seen as the very symbol of imperialism, which united Reghini's present to the glorious past he was trying to evoke. The rosy-cross, which Reghini later linked to the *Fraternity of the Rose-Croix* and to the eighteenth Masonic degree in the Antient and Accepted Scottish Rite, that of the *Sovereign Prince Rose Croix*, most probably alluded to the troubadors, and the alleged heretic imperialists in the south of France. The *Roman de la Rose* (ca. 1230) was a manual on courtly love written in France in medieval times, which probably enticed Reghini for the same thematic connection with the Italian *Fedeli d'Amore (The Pledged to Love)*.[86] Without going into too much detail, the *Fedeli d'Amore* was a supposed closed group of artists whose work revolved around the allegory of love as a way to the divine, active in Italy during the end of the thirteenth century. Such an approach to poetry would definitely have been influenced by the French troubadors just mentioned, and the French heresy of the Cathars, the so-called Church of Love, wiped out by the Catholic Church during the Albigensian Crusade of 1209–1229.[87] Scholar William Anderson describes the *Fedeli* as

> Rare spirits who were struggling to devise a code of life that retained from chivalry the idea of nobility, while making it depend on personal virtue instead of inherited wealth and breeding, and that preserved spiritual aspirations not unlike those of some mendicants without demanding a life of withdrawal or celibacy [... and forming] a closed brotherhood devoted to achieving a harmony between the sexual and emotional sides of their natures and their intellectual and mystical aspirations.[88]

According to Dante scholar Luigi Valli (1878–1931) and the Traditionalist thinker René Guénon, Dante had gotten in touch with this group and had incorporated their ideas into his poetry. This obviously gave rise to a completely new school of interpretation of Dante whereby the Florentine poet's works appear to have an esoteric core, which would elude the common interpreter of Dante's verses, as can be seen in books by Valli, Guénon, and Reghini (in "Imperialismo"). If these authors were then to be believed, the *Commedia* would be a universal story of man's struggle to achieve a close proximity to God through love, with an imperialist twist thrown in for just measure, in Reghini's case.[89] As if realizing the fact that he had probably thrown in too many obscure references in an attempt to make clear what was supposed to be a short and to the point article, Reghini ends the second section of his "Imperialismo" by writing: "but we will more diffusely deal with Paganism and the imperialism of Dante some other time."[90]

5.2.5. "L'Idea Imperiale Dopo Dante" ("The Imperial Idea after Dante")

The third section of "Imperialismo" aimed to bring his reader up to date with regard to the imperial idea from Dante to Reghini's day. Reghini started by painting a dire picture of the political situation in Italy, alluding to a triumphant Church and the rise of the *comuni* and of the republics of Venice and Florence as too fragmented to really foster an imperialist idea.[91] There were individuals, though, who carried on the imperial ideal, overtly or secretly embedding it in their writings, and such a list of characters formed the main part of the third section of "Imperialismo." The first to be applauded by Reghini is Francesco Petrarca (1304–1374), who was a very close friend of Cola de Rienzi, otherwise known as Cola di Rienzo (1313–1354), a fourteenth-century politician of great prestige, who had advocated for the abolition of Papal temporal power and had sought to bring back Rome to its former imperial splendour.[92] That Petrarca had shared similar ideas is a fact highlighted in the studies devoted to his figure.[93] Perhaps not surprisingly, the next figure to be exalted as the forbearer of imperialist theories was the famous author and political thinker Niccolo' Machiavelli (1469–1527). Rather than a mere return to a pristine form of greatness, Machiavelli could see the fragility of an Italian peninsula divided into many small city-states and advocated for the advent of an illuminated prince, who would take it upon himself to reunite the warring cities in Italy.[94] But, Reghini wrote, "as Dante had never seen the pregnant Vatican she-wolf, Machiavelli too died without any prince heeding his call, and Machiavellian politics were taken and applied by the Company of Jesus to the detriment, and not to the betterment, of Italy and of the imperialist idea."[95]

Reghini then turned to his Renaissance heroes, whom he credited with the survival of the imperial idea in the southern part of Italy, namely Campania. It was the "Southern neo-Pythagoreans":[96] Giordano Bruno,[97] Bernardino Telesio,[98] and Tommaso Campanella,[99] who, by revolting against Aristotelianism, then the most common approach to scholastic interpretation of Church ideas and dogmas, gave birth to a western lay culture, which, Reghini added,

> is slowly disinfecting European mentality from Christianity. These mystics of the senses, these precursors and initiators of European philosophy, were not part of those lazy saints who retired to a Thebaide or a hermitage; they were fierce and brave men of action.[100]

After the brief reference to these three ecclesiastical figures, it was the turn of one of the embodiments of imperialism in the eighteenth- and nineteenth-century politics: Napoleon Bonaparte (1769–1821). Reghini considered Napoleon as "another Italian" since his birthplace, Ajaccio, Corsica, in ancient times had been part of the Italian province of the Roman Empire.[101] In the brief number of lines devoted to Napoleon, the reader could glean the great respect, almost a veneration, that the Florentine author had for the Corsican leader:

> The Roman eagle flew high once again with the Napoleonic legions, and Italy found freedom again even in provinces that today are oppressed, the Latin spirit triumphed and Rome had a King once more. And it was the imperial idea, Roman, Pagan notwithstanding the Concordat [with the Vatican], which between the fires of revolution reconstituted after many centuries, Italy's unity.[102]

To the modern reader, the use of Napoleon as a figure that could be venerated by Roman Traditionalists may seem strange, given Napoleon's nationality, his nationalistic aims of expansion, and his alliance with the Holy See. Nevertheless, the fact that an Emperor had finally reunited the peninsula under one rule was a fact so exceptional that Reghini and his friends, and other politicians responsible for the independence and final unity of Italy during the *Risorgimento*, were more than happy not to throw the baby out with the bath water and to hold onto both vigorously.

Giuseppe Mazzini and Giuseppe Garibaldi were, finally, mentioned as the incarnation of imperialist ideas in Italy. Reghini really wanted to ensure that his writing would celebrate these two figures as Pagan, or at least lay, imperialists.[103] About Mazzini, whom Reghini does not hesitate to call a "seer," Reghini wrote, "He too, like Virgil and Dante, who loved, studied and understood more than many illustrious professors, said that Italy was destined by God to dominate over the populations, to give to the world, from Rome, the light of a third civilisation."[104] The end of the third section brought the reader to the twentieth century, where Reghini stated that "[M]asonic democracy today dreams of a confederate republic of Latin countries headed, it is obvious, by France, with the fated city of Bern as a capital, just to make the internationalist yokels happy."[105]

In the brief, half-page afterword, Reghini summed up the major points of his writing in order for them to stick in the mind of his reader. First, choosing Catholic Nationalism was equal to distancing oneself from a three-thousand-year-old tradition of Pagan imperialism, preferring an exotic creed like Christianity to the autochthone Italian Tradition. Second, none of the parties who vied for attention and votes before World War I possessed the Pagan character sought by Reghini: "[b]ut the attempt is wrong because the momentary conditions of the parties are unimportant in front of the age-old and fatal revolutions of the spirits."[106] The afterword ended with a final admonition to the Catholic Nationalists:

[T]he others may do what they want. We know they cannot win. What reassures us is our faith in the destiny of the Eternal City, and we remind, and will continue to remind, to the overt and hidden enemies of pagan imperialism the Latin maxim: Destiny leads on those who are willing to follow and drags along those who aren't.[107]

The importance of "Imperialismo Pagano" to the political aims of the *Schola* has been sorely neglected, and this is the first thorough analysis of the text. Its importance to members of the *Schola* itself is undeniable, as it was the only article that Reghini deemed worthy of republishing in his own journal *Atanòr* (1924). What permeates "Imperialismo" is no clear-cut political strategy. It is not a manifesto for the creation of a party. I see it more as an attempt to take stock of the situation within the Roman Traditional milieu, written the year before the Great War. With

World War I in mind, it was a rallying point before the years 1915–1918 for the *elite intellectuelle* which Armentano and Reghini firmly believed they represented. The great representatives of the past were celebrated one by one, almost creating a pantheon from which to take inspiration. An odd pantheon at that; one where Giuseppe Mazzini, Giordano Bruno, and Napoleon were made to belong to the same tradition of Pagan imperialists, who had, in one way or another, held the greatness of Italy in great esteem and loathed the backward thinking of the Church and its temporal power. The reprint of the article in 1924, as we shall see in the next chapter, is also significant. Mussolini had taken power and installed himself as the Dux, the leader of the Italian people, and, thanks to Fascism, talks about the birth of a Third Rome, which had long circulated in the small Roman Traditionalist milieu, now hit the headlines of most newspapers and were the subject of discussion among the most celebrated Italian intellectuals. "Imperialismo Pagano," in 1924, more than in 1914, would represent a great tool for Reghini and others to become acquainted with Mussolini and, in the following years, practice magic with the aim of helping him succeed in his expansionistic endeavors.

"Imperialismo Pagano," on a smaller scale, also helped pinpoint the *Schola Italica* in the Italian occult milieu. In the comparatively small environment, occultists would oftentimes be members of various orders at the same time: Reghini himself had, in the past, been a member of the Theosophical Society and Freemasonry. The *Schola* brought in an element of elitism that had previously been unheard of: it could be joined by invitation only, and it distanced itself from all other occult manifestations, claiming to be the only Italic valid way to reach certain goals. Some of its members were all too happy to disregard Theosophists, Anthroposophists, Freemasons, and other occultists, labeling them as charlatans. "Imperialismo," more than any of Reghini's writings, showcased the existence of a small, but vocal, elitist, right-wing, Traditionalist occult presence in Italy. In a subculture where Christianity still represented the superstructure against which occult theories were formulated, "Imperialismo" shocked and was condemned by bourgeois occultists, who, at least in Italy, always tried to amalgamate religion and occultism. It represented a novel way of interaction between politics, occult activism, and cultural Traditionalism, making Reghini and his small coterie of friends stand out from the more mainstream expressions of the occult even to this date.

6
Fascism and Traditionalism
Modernity and Anti-Modernity (1920–1925)

> After the Rome of the Caesars, that of the Popes,
> there exists today a Rome, the Fascist one, which,
> with the concurrency of the ancient and the modern
> imposes itself to the admiration of the world.
> —Benito Mussolini[1]

6.1. The Larger Picture: A Historical Overview

6.1.1. Benito Mussolini and the March on Rome

On October 28, 1922, tens of thousands of Fascist militants belonging to the *Partito Nazionale Fascista* (*National Fascist Party*) converged upon Rome in order to force the then King Victor Emmanuel III (1869–1947) to dissolve Parliament and grant their leader Benito Mussolini a chance to create a new government.[2] The events that took place between October 27 and October 30, 1922, would, in the future, be considered as the prologue to the Fascist revolution, and October 28 would, under the Fascist regime, mark the beginning of the Fascist year. A brief excursus on the figure of Benito Mussolini is now necessary in order to understand better the historical events that were to shape Italy in the 1920s and the fascination on behalf of intellectuals, such as Reghini, Giovanni Amendola, and Giuseppe Prezzolini, who all, at some stage, believed in the possibility of a new beginning for Italy under Mussolini's new leadership.[3]

Benito Amilcare Andrea Mussolini was born in 1883 in Dovia di Predappio, son of a Socialist blacksmith and a Catholic elementary school teacher. Mussolini shared his father's passion for politics, and in 1900, he officially registered with the *Partito Socialista Italiano* (*Italian Socialist Party*), which, as we have seen in the previous chapter, would play a vital role in the first twenty years of Italian politics.[4] Due to the inability to find a full-time job as a schoolteacher, and to avoid conscription into the Italian military service, Mussolini decided to relocate to Lausanne, Switzerland, on July 9, 1902, where he soon became head of the local Worker's Union as well as penning his first articles for local newspapers. While in Lausanne, Mussolini was able to attend the university lectures of one Vilfredo Pareto (1848–1923), professor in economics and political sciences. The two soon bonded and Mussolini adopted Pareto's theories on elites and on wealth redistribution.[5] Back in Italy after the moratorium on his crime, Mussolini, in 1910, became Secretary of the *Federazione Socialista Forlivese* (*Forlì' Socialist Federation*) and became editor of his first weekly paper: *L'Idea Socialista* (*The Socialist Idea*).[6] In 1912, he became editor of the main Socialist papers of the time, the *Avanti!* (*Forward!*), and in 1913, he ran for the elections discussed in the previous chapter but was defeated by his Republican opponent Giuseppe Gaudenzi (1872–1936).[7] With the beginning of World War I, Mussolini changed his Socialist views on neutrality in the conflict, and on October 18, he published a three-page article entitled "Dalla Neutralità Assoluta alla Neutralità Attiva e Operante" ("From Absolute Neutrality to Active and Operating Neutrality").[8] The article argued for voting in favor of a war among nations, which would have armed the Italian people and successively transformed the arming of the people for war purposes to an armed revolution against the eternal enemy, the bourgeoisie:

> That democracy would, therefore, have the faculty to declare war, clearly ignoring the will of the people (and in case of resistance, may they violently attack the people). The will of the people, if consulted, would very rarely coincide with that of kings, but [the idea] that Socialists accept the system of bourgeois governments is absurd. That's why the masses needed to be consulted, not least so that the Government could have a clear indication of the feelings of a great part of public opinion.[9]

The article had devastating effects on Mussolini's Socialist career. On November 29 of the same year, he was expelled from the Socialist Party, but he had managed, through the financing of important industrial sectors, to found his own paper, *Il Popolo d'Italia* (*The Italian People*) from which he harshly criticised his ex-colleagues. In 1915, he was present at the foundation of the extra-parliamentary political group *Fasci di Azione Rivoluzionaria* (*Fasces of Revolutionary Action*), led by unionist Filippo Corridoni (1887–1915), with whom Mussolini shared the hatred of the Parliament and bourgeois State institutions.[10] In a speech dated May 15, 1915, Mussolini's authoritarian drift was already becoming apparent:

> As for myself, I am always more firmly convinced that for the safety of Italy, a few dozen members of Parliament should be shot, and I do mean shot, in the back, and some ex-Ministers, at least, should be sent into exile. Not only this, but I believe with ever increasing faith that the Parliament in Italy is a contagious wart. It needs to be extirpated.[11]

Back in Milan after the war, where he had distinguished himself for acts of valor,[12] Mussolini was ready to create the Italian answer to the German *Freikorps*. In *Piazza San Sepolcro* (*Holy Sepulchre Piazza*) in Milan, on March 23, 1919, Mussolini gave a speech before the first fifty adherents to the *Fasci Italiani di Combattimento* (*Italian Fighting Fasces*).[13] After another speech held on the April 15, a mob of *Fasci* assaulted the headquarters of the Socialist *Avanti!*, while Mussolini stocked the newsroom of his *Popolo d'Italia* with weapons, fearing retaliation from comprehensibly disgruntled Socialists.[14]

On November 16 of the same year, the *Fasci di Combattimento* chose to run on their own in the elections, with some of the biggest names on the Italian political scene, such as Mussolini and Marinetti, focusing on gaining votes in Milan. The result was a fiasco, and no seat in Parliament was won, the party gaining a measly 4,675 votes in the Milan constituency.[15] Realizing their failure to make an impression on the left-wing electorate, Mussolini subsequently sought alliances with more conservative powers. In the following elections of 1921, he struck an alliance with the anti-Socialist giant in Italian politics, the liberal Giovanni Giolitti (1942-1927), who had served as Prime Minister of Italy five times between 1892 and 1921.[16] Giolitti had convinced Mussolini to join the *Blocchi Nazionali* (*National Blocks*), a political group formed by the Liberals, Nationalists, and some minor parties.[17] The result was a triumph for the Fascists if compared to the disastrous campaign conducted just two years previously: the Blocks obtained 105 seats in Parliament with Mussolini's party gaining 35 of those.[18] The elections were undertaken in a violent climate, and many times, possibly with the connivance of the police, Mussolini's *squadristi* (*squads*) were able to interrupt political rallies of opposing parties with the use of violence.[19] At the end of 1919, Mussolini transformed his *Fasci di Combattimento* into a more democratic sounding *Partito Nazionale Fascista* (*Fascist National Party*), and on New Year's Day of 1922, he founded the party's official newspaper, *Gerarchia* (*Hierarchy*). In February, Luigi Facta (1861-1930), a modest representative of Giolitti's political ideals, was elected Prime Minister. All the while, in August, the Socialists and Communists organized a strike against the increasing violence against rival political factions by Mussolini's *squadristi*.[20] It is my opinion that this was the exact moment that the political climate in Italy degenerated since Mussolini was probably only waiting for such disorders to happen in order to exercise a firmer grip on domestic policy.[21] At the beginning of September the *squadristi* illegally and violently occupied the town halls of several cities, including Milan, Genoa, Leghorn, and Trento. This was the beginning of what would subsequently be called *La Rivoluzione Fascista* (*The Fascist Revolution*). The last step before an affirmative action against the democratic institutions of the State was a sizeable rally held in Naples on October 24, 1922, just four days prior to the most important date in Fascist history. There, Mussolini urged his supporters to march toward Rome and to seize the power that, in his words, was rightfully theirs.[22]

In a secret meeting with Giolitti on October 23 in Turin's *Hotel Bologne*, the Popular Party representative Giovanni Battista Bertone (1874–1967) had tried to convince the ex-Prime Minister to take his post once more in the wake of Facta's objective inability to contain the Fascist revolution. During the Naples rally, Mussolini is alleged to have said to his mass of followers that "either they will give us the government, or we will take it marching on Rome."[23] Thus, on the night between October 27 and 28, almost 25,000 men headed toward Rome from many different locations, confiscating and appropriating themselves of trains and of the railway lines. On the morning of October 28, Mussolini got in touch with Antonio Salandra (1853–1931), right-wing politician and, later, a distinguished member of the Fascist intelligentsia and professor at the University of Rome.[24] While Salandra had urged veteran politician Vittorio Emanuele Orlando (1860–1952), Prime Minister between 1916 and 1919, to form a new government, King Vittorio Emanuele III (1869–1947) suggested that Mussolini create a new group of ministers under the supervision of Salandra himself, whom he knew Mussolini admired.[25] Mussolini refused the idea of a joint rule and urged the king to send him a telegram, in which he would be granted the possibility to govern on his own. Mussolini only met Vittorio Emanuele III on November 4, as Mussolini's trip from Milan to Rome was delayed at almost every station by sympathizers and militants belonging to his *squadre*. Once in Rome, a total of 70,000 men marched in front of Mussolini and Vittorio Emanuele III, activist numbers having doubled in merely a week.[26] Later that day, Mussolini promised he would create a government composed of Fascist and non-Fascist elements, although his antipathy for the Socialist and the newly created Communist Party would remain evident for all to see. Thus, with political intrigue, intimidation, and violence, Mussolini had become the Prime Minister of Italy.

6.1.2. Fascism and Roman Traditionalism: Anti-Modern or Modern?

In his ground-breaking work, *Modernism and Fascism: A Sense of a New Beginning under Mussolini and Hitler* (2006), Professor Roger Griffin declared the very concepts of Modernism and Fascism to be "antithetical and oxymoronic" when dealt with in the two major incarnations of Fascist theories of the first part of the twentieth century: Fascism and Nazism.[27] His work, which I will refer to frequently in this subsection, posited great emphasis on "modernist Fascism" and the sense of a new beginning that the Fascist regimes of Italy and Germany provided to their populace. The work is a counterargument of sorts to the theories presented in Professor Frank Kermode's *The Sense of an Ending: Studies in the Theories of Fiction* (1966). In this collection of essays, literary critic Kermode focused more on the idea of crisis and on the concept of apocalyptic times as a central theme to modernist literature, ascribing any foray of modernist poets into the realm of politics as a dangerous fall into the noxious world of the irrational. No doubt perturbed and influenced by the writings of members of the Frankfurt School, Kermode wrote, when tackling the issue of the poetical treatment of concepts of crisis and transition at the turn of the twentieth century: "Its ideological expression is Fascism; its practical consequence the Final Solution."[28] While oftentimes Kermode's conclusions seem to be solely influenced by texts, such as *The Authoritarian Personality* (1950), which is famous for its inclusion of an F-Scale (Fascist Scale) to measure a person's inclination toward irrational and Fascist ideas, I still think his work is of paramount importance, especially when paired with Griffin's, if we want to analyze the Fascist phenomenon, and, on a smaller scale, Roman Traditionalism and both their links to modernity and anti-modernity.[29] In his lecture "Apocalyptic Modernity," Kermode tackled the subject of modernist poets coming to grips with aspects of contemporary reality.[30] To do so, he employed the oft-quoted poem *Second Coming* (1919) by poet William Butler Yeats (1865–1939),[31] where the composition is usually used to signify the disaggregation of values and certainties that the modern world forces upon man, and I think the first stanza is worth quoting in this context.

> Turning and turning in the widening gyre
> The falcon cannot hear the falconer;
> Things fall apart; the centre cannot hold;
> Mere anarchy is loosed upon the world,
> The blood-dimmed tide is loosed, and everywhere
> The ceremony of innocence is drowned.[32]

For Kermode, there are two ways of articulating one's feelings toward the crisis. The noxious one, according to Kermode, is represented by living through "the difference between poetic *fictions* used by the artists to illuminate or articulate elusive aspects of contemporary reality, and politicised *myths*, which become incorporated into the ideological rationale for attempts to engineer radical transformations of that reality."[33] Yeats's enthusiasm for Italian Fascism, and the Irish variant of the Blue Shirts, is a testament to his passage to his ideological and political dimension, which Kermode dismisses as a slipping over into "the invisible border into the realm of the political."[34] Griffin argues that Fascism cannot be understood without taking into account the crisis of Positivism, secularization, and all the aspects that we have grown accustomed to associating with early twentieth-century Western culture.[35] At the same time, though, he denies the hegemonic feeling of crisis or despair put forth by Kermode, and postulates that

> In the immediate aftermath of the First World War not just the avant-garde, but millions of "ordinary people" felt they were witnessing the birth pangs of a new world under an ideological and political regime whose nature was yet to be decided.[36]

Griffin's definition of modernism, which, as we shall note, can be seen to include even seemingly anti-modern movements, such as Fascism and Roman Traditionalism, appears to be threefold. First, it needs a view of the process of modernization as one that is constantly eroding "a stable sense of 'tradition' and promotes the rise of 'reflexivity.'"[37] Second, it identifies modernity with a shift in the conception of time, which becomes itself more reflexive and open to the possibility of a new and better future. Third, it characterizes modernity of the mid- to late nineteenth century as a period of a loss of interest in the trope of progress, favoring that of decadence, to which Yeats's *Second Coming* tellingly alludes.[38] Griffin, on the backdrop of his analysis of Fascism, also gave a definition of the concept of tradition, which serves the reader to understand Roman Traditionalism in modern times: "[t]radition [. . .] is to be considered not as a static, timeless entity but as a dynamically evolving, in some cases historically recent, set of beliefs and practices."[39] Such a myth was constructed precisely by people, such as Reghini and Armentano, who "feel thrown into an age of chaos of decline" where the perceived view of stability and security appeared to be threatened by the tropes of modernity to which we have grown accustomed: the rise of rationalism, secularization, liberalism, capitalism, the idea of progress, and so on.[40]

The idea of anti-modern movements existing in modern times and even being a direct product of modernity is, therefore, not an outrageous or illegitimate idea to entertain. It is my idea that both the agents of Roman Traditionalism and the early Fascist regime shared the ambivalent quality of thrusting themselves against the classical facets of modernity, viewing them as decaying and useless for their idea of the traditional man, hence, the appeal to tradition, the longing for a mythical past, and the creation of a somewhat mythical present, which are connected by great historical narratives in order to be validated. As Malcolm Bradbury and James McFarlane have written:

> Modernism was in most countries [, and certainly in Italy,] an extraordinary compound of the futuristic and the nihilistic, the revolutionary and the conservative, the naturalistic and the symbolistic, the romantic and the classical. It was a celebration of a technological age and condemnation of it; an excited

acceptance of the belief that old regimes of culture were over, and a deep despair in the face of that fear.[41]

What Fascism and Roman Traditionalism did not incarnate, in my opinion, was the regression of reason and a death-wish plunge into the realms of the irrational, which Theodor Adorno and Max Horkheimer bemoan in their *Dialektik der Aufklärung* (*Dialectic of Enlightenment*, 1947). Both Fascism and Roman Traditionalism looked to the future with optimism; the modern present had to be transcended in order to provide a new, more stable, future to the Italian population. Mussolini pointed to this very important aspect in many of his speeches and writings. In front of the apocalyptic present, as described by Kermode, Mussolini would wish: "Make it so that the glories of the past may be surpassed by the glories of the coming age."[42] During a speech delivered soon after the March on Rome, Mussolini argued about Fascism being a revitalizing element in the life of modern Italians:

> Democracy has taken away "style" to the life of the people. Fascism brings back "style" into the lives of the people: [I mean] a line of conduct; colour, strength, the picturesque; the unexpected; the mystical; to sum up, all that matters in the hearts of the multitudes.[43]

In order to regain this style, this Nietzschean leap against the *taedium vivere*, this Bergsonian *élan vital*, everything had to be tried in order to subdue the contrary tide of modernity. War and violence, if necessary, tended to be seen as acceptable from artists and politicians alike. The Futurist Filippo Tommaso Marinetti, in the *Manifesto of the Futurist Movement* published on *Le Figaro* (1909),[44] auspicated the arrival of a war as the "only hygiene of the world"; Reghini advocated the use of force in his anti-democratic and anti-clerical "Imperialismo Pagano" (1914); Gabriele d'Annunzio (1863–1938) led three thousand men to the conquest of the irredentist city of Fiume in 1919;[45] and to Frank Kermode's great distress, English-writing modernist poets seemed to embrace Fascist ideologies. Two great examples are the mentioned Yeats, and the American Ezra Pound (1885–1972), who would go on to work for Mussolini and radiobroadcast tirades against Italian Jews and their supposed involvement with usury and President Roosevelt (1882–1945).[46]

Finally, another scholar whose work fits neatly with my idea of Roman Traditionalism and Fascism as anti-modern expressions of modernism is Walter Adamson: he seems to endorse Griffin's theories on the subject, by characterizing the anti-democratic aspects of modernism as "adversary culture or other modernity that challenged the 'modernising forces' of science, commerce and industry, usually in the name of some more 'spiritual' alternative."[47] This in turn brought some thinkers of the modern period to adhere wholeheartedly to the recreation of the primordial, of the mythical, of the traditional in what Adamson has defined as "a messianic mood of frenzy, despair and apocalyptic hope."[48] The hope for Reghini and the Roman Traditionalists, but also for Mussolini and his Fascist revolution, was that their actions and ideas would play a "central role [...] in the creation and organisation of a regenerated culture."[49]

Both early Fascism and Roman Traditionalism employed similar tropes in order to further their agenda, and it is clear how, with the grand narrative of the creation of the Third Rome, Reghini and Armentano would have been fascinated by this movement with which they shared many influences, supporters, and ideologues. Both, as I have shown, are effective anti-modern manifestations of what Adamson defines as "other" modernity when compared to the definition of modernity to which we are accustomed. Neither, though, followed Adorno's and Horkheimer's theories of a regression of reason into the realms of the nihilistic and irrational. Both movements, albeit with different aims, sought a new beginning to alleviate the perceived noxious elements of modernity and connect man to his natural space and time on earth, subduing, once and for all, the sense of alienation described and suffered by many. While much has been written about the interaction between the modern and totalitarian regimes, especially in the years immediately following World War II, I think that it would benefit the reader to indulge more on the concept of social occult modernism developed by Griffin in order to validate my original claim that Traditionalism, as understood by Reghini, Armentano, and Evola, was one facet of the modern world, which, although anti-modern or reactionary in nature, was nevertheless a product of its time.

6.1.3. Social Occult Modernism

In his chapter "A Primordialist Definition of Modernity," Griffin tackled the issue of what he defined as "the Myth of Transition on Modernity."[50] Taking cue from Kermode's literary criticism of modernist literature, Griffin singled out two key elements in what Kermode had defined as the "apocalyptic paradigm": "a deep conviction in decadence and a prophetic confidence of renovation."[51] Griffin then further singled out a particular mode of transition in modern times: the Rite of Passage.[52] The outcome of the rite of passage, according to anthropologist Maurice Bloch, is never "seen as a return to the condition left behind in the first stage, but as an aggressive consumption of a vitality that is *different* in origin from that which had originally been lost."[53] Anthropologist pioneer Arnold van Gennep had divided the process culminating to the rite of passage in three distinct stages, and these distinctions are going to make it easier for me to apply this framework to Fascism and Traditionalism. First, there is a stage of separation in which a group, or a single person, detaches from the prevailing social conditions. The elitist, secretive, and anti-democratic nature of the *Schola Italica* makes this concept absolutely clear when it comes to Reghini and Armentano. It can also be seen with Mussolini leaving the Socialist Party in 1914 and founding his own paper and political movement, successively. Second, van Gennep theorises the idea of the margin, or the liminal, when the old position has been abandoned, but the new one has not yet been reached.[54] Chronologically, in the *Schola*'s case, the margin goes from the months succeeding the meeting between Armentano and Reghini at the *Lucifero* lodge in Florence in the last years of the 1910s and the first publication of "*Imperialismo Pagano*" in 1914; while Mussolini's liminal stage may run from the creation of the *Fasci di Azione Rivoluzionaria* with Corridoni in 1915 until his rise to power in 1922. Finally, the third stage is defined as aggregation or postliminal, when the participants to the rite of passage acquire and work according to their renewed vision of the world.[55] This period, for the *Schola* stretches from 1914 to 1929, the year of the Lateran Accords between Fascism and the Vatican, while Mussolini's postliminal stage could be stretched from 1922 to 1945, the year of his death and of the end of World War II.

Anglo-American anthropologist Victor Turner has described this process in a very succinct but precise way:

> People who are similar in one characteristic [. . .] withdraw symbolically, even actually, from the total system, from which they may in various degrees feel themselves "alienated" to seek the glow of a *communitas*. Through the route of "social category," they escape the alienating structure of a "social system" into "*communitas*" or social anti-structure.[56]

Having introduced the concept of a rite of passage as a form of revitalization, Griffin briefly, but significantly, touches upon the occult with his theory of occultist social modernism, a category that this book will benefit from greatly.[57] In selecting Theosophy as the sample occult movement of choice, Griffin argues that what Theosophy provided to the Western man was "a horizon once more framed by myth."[58] There was, in other words, a sense of transcendence and order, which sought to bring about a revitalized humanity away from the ills of modernity.[59] A facet that Griffin explores very thoroughly is that of a necessity to go back to the primordial sources in order to recreate a future, "to go 'back to the future'" in a process that Conservative Revolutionary Arthur Möller van den Bruck (1876–1925) was to call "a reconnection *forwards*."[60] To the reader, it will be clear that Roman Traditionalism, as represented by the *Schola Italica*, sought to do just that, seeking for the Perennial Pythagorean Tradition, which would illumine the path to a more ordered future. Mussolini's extensive references to the myth of the third Rome and the iconography used by his party and regime also seem to point in the same direction.[61] Griffin, therefore, concluded, having provided us with a new tool with which to read modernism: "it is when occultism serves as the principal vehicle for a regenerating civilisation allegedly dying from the poison fruits of progress, that it can be seen as a form of social modernism in its own right."[62]

Griffin also briefly touches upon the idea of a rightist social modernism. In describing the other side of the coin of modernity, which Jeffrey Alexander has aptly described as "the dark side of modernity," Griffin very briefly mentions Traditionalism and its being based on the idea of a *philosophia perennis* (perennial philosophy), starting with Guénon, and picked up by Aldous Huxley (1894–1963) in the interwar period and by Ananda Coomaraswamy (1877–1947) and Fritjof Schuon (1907–1977) later on.[63] It is a short section in which Griffin does little more than name-drop before introducing the figure of Julius Evola, as we have seen in previous chapters, arguably the most controversial of Traditionalists. Guénon and Evola are evoked as being representatives of that very dark side of modernity, which counters Coomaraswamy's leftist approach to the subject. While Guénon's work *La Crise du Monde Moderne* (*The Crisis of the Modern World*, 1927) is described as condemning materialism and containing "a conspicuous component of elitism, anti-liberalism, anti-communism and anti-democracy,"[64] Evola is depicted as allying himself overtly to totalitarianism, misogyny, anti-Semitism, racism, imperialism, and biopolitics, hence becoming an accomplice to the most elitist, uncompromizing, and terroristic forms of Fascism and Nazism.[65]

To conclude, for Griffin, and myself, too, it appeared absolutely natural that some forms of occult expressions could be progressive and fit in with standardized ideas of modernity (and in this, I refer once more to Marco Pasi's "The Modernity of Occultism"), but in certain scenarios, an occult, anti-modern, and rightist way of envisioning the world could blossom and win over adherents. Certainly, the *Schola Italica*, growing during the interwar milieu that led to Fascism, is a clear example of such a movement.

6.2. Occultism and Fascism: A Real Partnership?

Before moving onto an analysis of the relationship between occult movements and the Fascist regime, it will be helpful to provide a general introduction to the academic study of another totalitarian regime's ties with occultism, namely the National Socialist movement in Germany. From the 1960s to this day, it has been a widespread notion, outside of academic circles, that "the Nazis were principally inspired and directed by occult agencies from 1920 to 1945."[66] The cause of this widespread belief, no doubt, blossomed in the year 1960 with the publication of Louis Pauwels's and Jacques Bergier's *Le Matin Des Magiciens* (*The Morning of the Magicians*, 1960), an allegedly nonfiction exposé of occult influences on historical events, conspiracy theories, and what may be defined as proto-ancient astronaut theories, all wrapped into a retelling of a secret history of the world where facts and fiction were crudely blended to create an overarching narrative, which helped kick-start the budding New Age movement.[67] The entire second section of the book was dedicated to the Third Reich, "under the suggestive title, 'A Few Years in the Absolute Elsewhere.'"[68] In it, small secret societies of little effective influence, such as the *Thule Gesellschaft* (*Thule Society*, est. 1918), were granted paramount importance in the development of Nazi theories and politics. Other secret coteries, such as the *Vril Gesellschaft* (*Vril Society*), were inspired from fiction and have never existed, but in *Le Matin*, they seemed to cover a pivotal role in the years in which the Reich was in power. People who had played a marginal role in Hitler's life were given almost supernatural status. Two glaring examples of this were Dietrich Eckart (1868–1923) and Professor Karl Haushofer (1869–1946): Eckart's role, according to the authors, was that of mediating the contacts between Hitler and higher, invisible chiefs who were eager to provide the Führer with unlimited powers.[69] The second, who had served as an attaché in Japan and had devoted his studies to Oriental cultures, supposedly had urged Hitler to focus on the conquest of the East, rekindling the myth, propagated by many occult authors, such as Joseph Saint-Yves d'Alveydre (1842–1909) and Ferdynand Ossendowski (1876–1945), that somewhere in the Gobi Desert or the Tibetan Himalayas lay the entrance to an underground world inhabited by creatures vastly superior to man in intellect and power.[70] Building upon this hodgepodge of tall stories and fanciful elaborations of the truth, other authors had followed the footsteps of Pauwels and Bergier: Dietrich Bronder, in 1964, published his *Bevor Hitler Kam* (*Before Hitler Came*) in which he picked the topic of the *Thule Gesellschaft* and developed it to unprecedented levels of spuriousness.[71] The membership roster of this tiny Bavarian group, which had been born under the name of *Studiengruppe für Germanisches Altertum* (*Study Group for Germanic Antiquity*) under Bronder's penmanship, had been inflated to include almost everyone who would play a role in the future Third Reich. According to Bronder, Ariosophists Guido von List (1848–1919) and Lanz von Liebenfels (1874–1954) rubbed shoulders with Benito Mussolini and Adolf Hitler (1889–1945), Heinrich Himmler (1900–1945), and Rudolf Hess (1894–1987). Academic studies, such as Goodricke-Clarke's, have since then proven that Hitler, although living in Munich at the time, never participated in any of the Thule meetings, that Mussolini throughout the 1910s never visited Bavaria, and that the presence of other future members of the Reich was doubtful to say the least.[72]

Other authors followed this extremely lucrative niche market, the most notable being Trevor Ravenscroft with his *The Spear of Destiny* (1972), no doubt the biggest inspiration for the Indiana Jones franchise,[73] Michael-Jean Angbert's *Les Mystiques du Soleil* (*The Mystics of the Sun*, 1971),[74] and Alan Baker's under-researched *Invisible Eagle—The History of Nazi Occultism* (2000).[75]

In 1985, Professor Nicholas Goodrick-Clarke published his magnum opus, *The Occult Roots of Nazism*. This ground-breaking work endeavored to wipe away all of the fallacies that had accumulated on the topic in the previous twenty-five years, using only archival sources and keeping speculation to an absolute minimum. The result is a work that has stood the test of time, and it is still today considered as one of the most important works on the topic.[76] Goodrick-Clarke ascribed the success of his book from the realization that Nazism had been a political religion, and that "its eschatological vision of genocide, clearly demonstrated the irrelevance of a Marxist analysis based on a critique of capitalism, economic factors, and class interest."[77] The occult influence, where present, was not downplayed, but assigned its natural role with no extra emphasis or added sensationalist claims. It being a political religion, in Goodrick-Clarke's mind, he decided to analyze the antecedents of the Third Reich, which could have provided it with a doctrinal basis, and he found what he was looking for in the Ariosophist circle. This coterie had developed in Austria between the 1890s and the 1930s around the mentioned figures of Guido von List and Lanz von Liebenfels. In this movement, an interest in runes and sacred symbols, including the Swastika, was joined with a Theosophical approach to the doctrine of the Aryan man, and further mixing with strong anti-Semitic sentiments.[78] Goodrick-Clarke's book concludes by admitting that, so far as Ariosophy is concerned, some members of the Third Reich were indeed influenced by reading the garbled writings of List and Liebenfels, but that was where the line must be drawn.

Having analyzed, albeit very briefly, the relationship between occultism and the Third Reich, it is natural to ask the question: Did Italian Fascism grow with certain ideas born from occultist milieus? The answer is far easier to reply to than that of the German case.

6.2.1. The Fascist Link with Occultism: The 1920s

If Adolf Hitler, even if only to a certain degree, was influenced by the Ariosophists in matters of race, the use of symbols, and other minor aspects, Mussolini was most certainly not. Mussolini is reported to have said of his major ally in the war: "Hitler possesses a heart of steel [. . .] of indomitable steel. His brain, however, is confused. He has something of the wizard and of the market-hall philosopher. He has created, for his own aims, a history, a politic, a geography of the world, and he only drinks from that well."[79] In the preface to the first collection of articles to study the connection between esotericism and Fascism, Gianfranco de Turris asked the question of whether it is possible to talk about an esoteric Fascism. His answer to the question is worth quoting in full because it provides a definitive, and, in my opinion, correct answer from which the scholar may begin any further enquiries into the subject.

> If we can talk, without erring too much, about a "Nazi esotericism," given that many documents surfaced after the incredible but generic statements of *The Morning of the Magicians* by Louis Pauwels and Jacques Bergier, the same may not be said—no matter what some may think—of a "Fascist esotericism," that is to say of an esoteric dimension, which is neither officially or unofficially, fascist: the personalities who led the movement, their culture and their spiritual predisposition (despite the many ties to Freemasonry) weren't able to give life to an "esoteric," "occult" and by no means a "traditional" dimension of Fascism.[80]

Having stated this, de Turris is quick to say that there were, within the Fascist regime, personalities highly invested in the occult, which failed to influence, or to steer, Mussolini's movement into an occult direction. Nevertheless, the consolidation of Mussolini's power was also in part due to the elimination of any group or association, which could, behind closed doors, be working to undermine the new regime; therefore, the 1920s witnessed a harsh lockdown on all Masonic bodies, the prime targets for Mussolini, who despised the secretive nature of Freemasonry.

On November 9, 1925, Emilio Bodrero, Minister of Education, penned an introduction to a collection of surveys that had been conducted in the years 1912–1913 by the nationalist paper *Idea Nazionale*. The paper had interviewed high-ranking members of the academic, military, and political milieus, asking three short questions: (1) whether a secret society such as Freemasonry still possessed a raison d'être compatible with modern public life; (2) whether materialistic rationalism and an internationalist ideology, typical of Freemasonry, corresponded to the ideals of contemporary society; and finally, (3) whether the secret influence of Freemasonry in the educational system, the military, and in the legal system may have been a benefit or cause of damage to Italy.[81] The replies to the questionnaire vary from the very lengthy to the very succinct. Orientalist and University Professor Francesco Beguinot (1879–1953) stated laconically that "to the three questions I answer with three no's."[82] Others, like Reghini's friend Giovanni Amendola, were more articulate and wrote of the "futility of secrets in modern political life" and that "the ideology of today's democratic parties contrast greatly with the needs and goals of Italian society."[83] Archaeologist Giacomo Boni (1859–1925) went back to ancient Roman customs, writing that "like ancient Rome—in 186 BCE—with the *Senatus Consultum de Bacchanalibus* [Deliberation of the Senate regarding Bacchanalia], so our Rome should thrust upwards towards the sunshine any remains of a clandestine society: *the sun kills those invisible*."[84] Finally, even popular author Giovanni Verga (1840–1922) declared his opposition of the existence of Freemasonry in modern Italy, answering no to all three questions.[85]

The interviews were over a decade old, but Bodrero's new introduction made them appear relevant to the very year the book was published. This, of course, brought a tightening grip on secret societies and, to part of the readership, the content of the book seemed to justify the use of drastic measures. Interviewed by German-American war journalist Karl Henry von Wiegand (1874–1961), Mussolini had spoken against Italian Freemasonry in no uncertain terms:

> In Germany, in England, in America, the Masons are a charitable and philanthropic confraternity. In Italy, instead, Masons constitute a secret police. Even more and worse, they depend completely on the Grand Orient of Paris. I hope the Italian Masons may become what the English and Americans are: a brotherly apolitical benefit [to] society.[86]

The Nationalist movement had been the first to manifest serious animosity toward Freemasonry, and it had made its ideas clear through the publishing of the questionnaire, which would constitute *Inchiesta sulla Massoneria* (*Enquiry into Freemasonry*, 1925), to which Bodrero had added his introduction.[87] Once the Fascist regime had gained power, it had been quick to declare the incompatibility between Fascism and Freemasonry. A law passed in February 1923 invited:

> All Fascists who are also Freemasons to choose whether to belong to the Fascist National Party or to Freemasonry since for a Fascist there is but one discipline, the discipline of Fascism; but one hierarchy, the hierarchy of Fascism; but one, absolute, devoted and daily obedience to the Head and heads of Fascism.[88]

Already in 1923, the newspaper *Cremona Nuova* allowed the State to gain access to the names of local Freemasons in order "to shoot them en masse as traitors of the fatherland."[89] Soon the masonic temples in Turin, Pistoia, Lucca, Leghorn, Siena, Florence, Bari, and Ancona were destroyed completely and set on fire by Fascist *squadristi*. The Grand Lodge in Piazza del Gesù in Rome was destroyed on October 11, 1925, and in this tense political climate, the law to ban Freemasonry was passed with 239 votes in favor and only 4 against. The law was then ratified by the Senate on November 20 of the same year. Although the name of the law, never explicitly mentioned Freemasonry, it was certainly its main aim and caused many Freemasons to seek refuge abroad.[90] For instance, on November 22, the Grand Master of GOI, Domizio Torrigiani (1876–1932), dissolved all of the lodges under his authority and quit the publication of the prestigious Masonic journal *Rassegna Massonica* before being forced into exile by the regime.[91]

6.3. Guénonian Traditionalism

Before moving onto a specific analysis of how the laws against secret societies impacted the work of Reghini and Armentano, a section must be devoted to the philosopher who is considered to be the founding figure of Traditionalism by most scholars in the field: René Guénon (1886–1951).[92] The importance of Guénon needs to be made clear, especially when we know of his friendship and correspondence with both Armentano and Guerrieri, who both visited the French thinker in his Paris abode before World War I,[93] even before the formulation of his first Traditional theories, some of which would end up influencing the *Schola Italica*, too. Thus, a short biography will precede his main theories, followed by a brief analysis of his publications up to 1925. The final part of this section will be devoted exclusively to the analysis of the correspondence between Guénon and Reghini, which started in January 1923 and continued at least until 1935. In it, one will appreciate the cross-pollination of ideas between Guénon, who had already devoted himself to Eastern forms of spirituality to propagate his theories, and Arturo Reghini, who, while admiring the scope of Guénon's knowledge, preferred a more restricted and autochthone idea of Tradition. While the difference between the two thinkers is obvious when tackling subjects such as Guénon's choice of the East as the sole remaining repository for unaltered initiatic knowledge, one will be surprised at the commonalities between the two thinkers. The correspondence shows Reghini as a sincere student of Eastern lore but strong enough in his convictions to stand up to Guénon when writing about the alleged decline of Western initiation systems. I suggest that, in the light of this hitherto unpublished correspondence, there has indeed been a process of exchange of ideas, which influenced both Guénonian Traditionalism and Roman Traditionalism.

6.3.1. Guénon and the Birth of Traditionalism

René Guénon was born in the town of Blois, France, on November 15, 1886, to architect Jean-Baptiste Guénon and Anna-Léontine Jolly and raised in a very strict Roman Catholic household.[94] Guénon scholar David Bisson has conveniently classified the French philosopher's life into three distinct periods.[95] Although there are many overlaps and some problems with dating the end or the beginning of said periods, the divisions are very functional for the short biographical introduction I intend to provide. The first phase of Guénon's life is, therefore, referred to as *l'Intuition Gnostique* (the Gnostic Intuition) and spanned from 1906 to the beginning of the Great War in 1914; the second phase, referred to as *l'Exposé Orientale* (The Exposition to the Orient), lasted from 1914 to his one-way trip to Egypt in 1930; finally, the last part of his life was classified under the heading *La Synthese Traditionelle* (The Traditional Synthesis), spanning the years 1930–1951.

Early education was left to his aunt Mme. Duru (n.d.), who would homeschool young René throughout elementary school, because of his fragile health. Throughout his boyhood, Guénon then frequented Jesuit-owned institutes, where he was noticed for his shy, yet proud, demeanor and where he seemed to excel in mathematics and philosophy.[96] In 1904, he moved to Paris in order to join the prestigious *École Polytechnique* (Polytechnic Institute, est. 1794). Having received his degree in mathematics, possibly seduced by the variety of options offered by Paris during the *Belle Époque*, Guénon decided against pursuing his academic career further and moved into a small flat at 51 rue Saint-Louis-en-l'Île, where he would entertain the friends he had made at the *École*.[97] As Bisson correctly states, "two major currents crossed the intellectual field from side to side: socialism as a way of political realisation and occultism as a way of individual salvation."[98] For Guénon, who had always been interested in the ultimate causes of human existence and the seemingly infinite capabilities of the human intellect, the choice of occultism was an obvious one. There seem to be many commonalities in the early career of Guénon and Reghini, and this might help to explain why their long-distance friendship was never troubled by arguments or major disagreements. Both held degrees in mathematics and yet were deeply spiritual beings in their early approach to occult lore; both were to go through membership of many occult orders before setting themselves free from milieus that they would virulently attack in their later years, distancing themselves from the mistakes made in their youth. Frequenting occult circles in Paris at the beginning of the twentieth century meant rubbing elbows with one of the greatest figures of French, and may I venture to say European, occultism, Gérard Encausse, better known by his magical name, Papus.[99] Papus can well be seen in this context as the "catalyser of culture in full swing."[100] Under Papus's tutelage, Guénon joined the *Ordre Martiniste* (Martinist Order, est. 1884)[101] and Isis, a lodge that derived directly from the Theosophical Society.[102] Both of these societies, as Mark Sedgwick has argued, were important sources for Guénon's theories on Vedanta and Perennialism, and they must have influenced Guénon's future formulation of Traditionalism.[103] In 1908, Guénon abandoned both orders run by Papus and strove to achieve what he considered the most important tasks for an occult initiate in the West: "to restore the Western tradition and turn occultism into a science that could be compared to the ones normally studied at university."[104] In order to do so, he joined another occult order, the *Église Gnostique de France* (The French Gnostic Church)—a Christian body which had been founded in 1890 and had been revived in 1906 as a cultural association—this one not run by Papus or his associates, as they had become increasingly targeted by the anti-Masonic press.[105] Through his membership in this Church, Guénon made three fundamental connections that were to influence the rest of his life vastly. First, in 1908, he met Albert de Pouvourville (1861–1939), an adventurer best known by the name Matgioi, who had travelled through China extensively and had elucidated on Daoist doctrines in his twin volumes *La Voie Métaphysique* (*The Metaphysical Path*, 1905) and *La Voie Rationelle* (*The Rational Path*, 1907). The books, a curious interpretation of Lao Tsu's (b. ca. 590 BCE) theories, posited the existence of a primordial and untainted tradition in the East. Second, Guénon met Léon Champrenaud (1870–1925), best known by his Arab name Abdul-Haqq, who shared his knowledge of Sufism with Guénon, and was considered instrumental in Guénon's future conversion to Islam. Third, and most importantly, Guénon, in those years met Swedish painter and Sufi Ivan Aguéli (1869–1917), one of the first Westerners to approach the more mystical side of Islam.[106] It was through Aguéli, known also as Abdul Hâdi, with whom Guénon became great friends, that he was finally initiated to Sufism under the name Abd-el Wâhed Yahia in 1911.[107] The effect produced by these encounters in a Gnostic occult framework would start Guénon on his search for a pristine Tradition he could employ to arrive at the very source of the divine, and they would provide him with three main theories that were to accompany him for the rest of his life: "the divine and immemorial origin of a tradition, a world [the Western one] governed by evil, and the necessity of an initiatic conversion."[108]

Having been dismissed by the military for his poor health, Guénon was able to find a job as a teacher in Sétif, Algeria, where he was nominated Professor of Philosophy at the *College de Saint-Germain* on September 20, 1917. According to both Bisson and Jean-Pierre Laurant, during the period spent in Algeria, Guénon was able to meditate on two very important factors that would strongly influence his future writings. The first one was his critique of the dominant Comtean Positivistic outlook on life; the second was the substitution of the term *gnose* (gnosis) for *métaphysique* (metaphysics) in his writings. While the first point is intuitive, the second probably needs some explanation when it comes to the use of the word *métaphysique*. To Guénon, metaphysics was not simply a branch of philosophy studying the fundamental idea of being, as the term was utilized by Aristotle (384–322 BCE).[109] To Guénon, metaphysics is the knowledge of the Perennial Truth, which lies behind exoteric forms of religion. In essence, though changing the nomenclature, Guénon still retained a Gnostic element to his approach to the word *métaphysique*, implying at all times a direct connection to a source of primordial knowledge, which has remained uncorrupted throughout the ages.[110] In 1921, Guénon published his first book, *Introduction Générale à l'Étude des Doctrines Hindoues* (*A General Introduction to the Study of Hindu Doctrines*).[111] The work is unconventional in that it does not rely as heavily as other contemporary works on the subject on footnotes and quotations of Hindu texts. In the work, Guénon criticized the "vogue of texts, of sources, of a bibliography" and approaches the subject matter in his own style.[112] Faithful to the title of the work, Guénon gave his own definitions of the most important concepts connected to Hinduism: Vedanta and its nondualist (*Advaita*) expression were constantly lauded, and his conclusion was that *atman* (the Self) is the only reality on which the philosopher has to operate in the hope of achieving *moksa*, an ascetic deliverance from the material world.[113] Moreover, it is in *Introduction* that we first read of another Guénonian leitmotif, the praise of the Brahminic caste, which should be entrusted the mission of maintaining pristine religious doctrine against the various attacks from the modern world.[114] As Bisson notes, Guénon inaugurates an original reading of the East, which does not found itself on a [Edward Said's] "system of ideological fiction" but rather on an idealized traditional model. The historical, geographic, and religious complexity of India is reduced to an organic and spiritual unity.[115]

In the early 1920s, René Guénon celebrated his complete detachment from the Parisian occult milieu with the publication of two texts: *Le Théosophisme, Histoire d'une Pseudo-Religion* (*Theosophism: History of a Pseudo-Religion*, 1921), and *L'Erreur Spirite* (*The Spiritist Error*, 1923).[116] The texts are an extraordinary tour-de-force aimed at dismantling the theories propagated by the Theosophical Society, on one hand, and the Spiritualist movement, on the other. The main object of Guénon's ironic lambasting is without doubt Helena Petrovna Blavatsky, but other figures like Allen Kardec (1804–1869) with regard to Spiritism also get their fair share. Such a crude distancing from the milieu that had introduced him to the valuable ideas, which he subsequently would elaborate on and reformulate, may seem quite excessive. To Guénon, the history of these two movements was a clear example of mental deviation brought on by the agencies of the modern world.[117] In 1924, having cleared the way from his past allegiances and influences, Guénon published what is considered to be his first works of substance: *Orient et Occident* (*East and West*, 1924) and *La Crise du Monde Moderne* (*The Crisis of the Modern World*, 1925). The French thinker developed his theories about a terminally ill West and a salvific East toward which modern man must turn.[118] Influenced no doubt by the success of Oswald Spengler's (1880–1935) *Der Untergang des Abendlandes* (*The Decline of the West, 1918–1922*), Guénon explored various avenues when thinking about how to save the West; the idea of an intellectual elite, which Reghini had also written about in the 1910s, was brought forth by the French author. According to Guénon, a small number of people should achieve a connection with the source of the Primordial Tradition in the East and try and revive any moribund tradition that was still alive in the West.[119] In *Orient et Occident*, writing about this supposed elite, Guénon noted:

> We have already alluded to the role that an intellectual elite may play, if it will be able to create itself in the Western world, or if it will function as a "ferment" to prepare and lead in the most favourable sense a mental transformation, which will become necessary one day or another, whether we like it or not.[120]

1925 also marked the peak of Guénon's fame, as he was invited by the Sorbonne to deliver a lecture on Oriental metaphysics in which, once again, Guénon opposed the idea of a materialist West to the notion of a spiritual East.[121] As we shall see later on in this chapter, Guénon's exchange of ideas with Reghini would culminate with the French author's collaboration on Reghini's journals. One of such collaborations, *l'Ésotérisme de Dante* (*Dante's Esotericism*, 1925), seemed to follow theories that Reghini had already developed in "Imperialismo Pagano" and other writings prior to 1925. Guénon agreed with the representatives of the *Schola Italica* that the *Divina Commedia*, along with the *Aeneid* and other classics, represented a "metaphysical-esoteric allegory, which veils and unveils at the same time the various phases through which the conscience of the initiate must pass in order to achieve immortality."[122]

In 1930, Guénon travelled to Egypt for what should have only been a trip to collect Sufi texts, but, through a series of unpredictable events, he remained in Cairo for the rest of his life, never to return to his homeland. In the first three years of residency in Cairo, Guénon published two works, *Symbolisme de la Croix* (*Symbolism of the Cross*, 1931), an expansion on a series of articles published years before on the journal *Gnose*, and *États Multiples de l'Être* (*Multiple States of Being*, 1932), a study on the necessity of a "metaphysical *Infinity*" and its relationship with "universal Possibility."[123] In the early 1930s, Guénon met Sheikh Salama Hassan ar-Radi (n.d.), founder of the Hamidiya Shadiliya Sufi order, which he joined, and soon after another Sufi, Sheikh Mohammad Ibrahim, whose daughter Guénon married in 1934. Guénon died in 1951, survived by his wife and four children.[124]

Guénon's work, especially his contributions during the 1920s, has been considerable when taking into account the development of Traditionalist theories. Of course, the idea of a *philosophia perennis* handed down through the ages has been discussed in the introduction and other chapters of this book, and we are by now familiar with this theory. It was Guénon's fascination with Eastern doctrines that made him a giant of twentieth-century Traditionalist thought. His focus on *Advaita-Vedanta* and nondualistic thought; his rejection of a Western form of spirituality in favor of Islam and Sufism; the creation of the idea of an *elite intellectuelle*; the supratemporal, metaphysical conception of Tradition; the concept of cyclical time and the correspondence of Modernity with the lowest of the Hindu time cycles—the Kali Yuga; and the idea of counterinitiation: all composed the varied tapestry of Guénon's writings and, it is most likely, as we shall see later, that Reghini was influenced by some of these ideas.

6.3.2. Guénon and Traditionalism in 1920s Italy

Guénon was very active in his contacts and collaboration with different exponents of the Roman Traditionalist milieu. The very first acquaintances go back to the early 1910s when Armentano and Guerrieri had personally met the French thinker in his apartment in Paris. Guénon's ties with Guerrieri became even closer, as the member of the *Schola Italica* was wont to spend extended periods of time in the French capital, most of the time as an honored guest in the Guénon household. Roberto Sestito mentioned letters that attest to the great esteem Armentano was held in by the French thinker, but, unfortunately, he failed to reveal the exact sources. Guénon and Reghini had definitely known about each other before beginning their correspondence, and despite the common taste for mathematics, calculus, and literature, Reghini, until 1922, kept an ambivalent stance toward the French philosopher: an interesting case in point can be found in the criticism brought forth by the Florentine thinker toward Guénon's exclusion of the *Schola Italica* among the few Western traditions worthy of saving. In his *Le Parole Sacre e di Passo dei Primi Tre Gradi ed il Massimo Mistero Massonico—Studio Critico e Iniziatico* (*The Sacred Words and Pass-Words of the First Three Degrees and the Greatest Masonic Mystery: Critical and Initiatic Study*, 1922), Reghini was quite critical of Guénon, when he wrote:

> The reader, with the right intentions, may thus choose. All Traditions are at his disposal; the Indian, the Chinese, the Jewish, the Rosicrucian, the druidic, the Arab, since all people have been masters of civilisation and have produced masters and initiates, except of course Italy![125]

In a note on the same page, Reghini targeted Guénon personally: "[w]ith some astonishment, we realise that even GUENON shares this appreciation. And yet he recognises that a movement that will bring the West and the East closer again, with regards to the metaphysic tradition, cannot start but from Latin countries [...]. Excluding Italy, the mission is evidently in France's hands. *Cicero pro domo sua?*"[126] In the eleventh issue of the journal *Atanòr* (1925), Reghini reviewed Guénon's *Orient et Occident*, and there are very few doctrinal divergences in what otherwise is a highly positive survey of the Frenchman's work.[127] First,

Reghini criticizes Guénon for denying a Traditional continuity in the West going up to their days. Reghini, of course, felt strongly about the validity of his lineage of initiation and could not let this detail slip; second, Guénon talks about Scholasticism in Medieval times as the last manifestation of a genuine Tradition in the West. Guénon, between the years 1925 and 1927, collaborated with a journal titled *Regnabit: Revue Universelle du Sacré-Coeur* (*Regnabit: Universal Journal of the Sacred Heart*, 1921–1929), and he was very interested, for a period of time, in finding a Christian Tradition that could help resurrect the West from its alleged terminal state. Reghini, of course, defended his idea of a Roman-Pythagorean unbroken chain, which was more than ready to awaken Westerners from their slumber. Third, quoting Guénon, he wrote: "he unfortunately thinks that it is extremely improbable that individualities, even isolated, may exist in the West,"[128] and finally, Reghini criticized Guénon because of his statement about the West not having representatives of the symbolic "centre of the world."[129]

My opinion is that Guénon was very aware of the gray areas on which Reghini had commented and had been voluntarily vague and pessimistic in his judgment of the West because he wanted those "isolated individualities" to manifest. Guénon had thrown down the gauntlet and was waiting to see if anyone would stand up to refute his views on the West expressed in *Orient et Occident*; specifically, it was the subject of the creation of an intellectual elite in the West, which could stir the European continent out of the morass of modernity. But what exactly was this "*elite intellectuelle*," which Guénon wrote about throughout his early works and in *Orient et Occident* specifically? Guénon himself was very vague about the concept even though he did give multiple definitions of what characterized the intellectual elite, he envisaged: "The aptitudes we have in mind when we talk about an elite, are in the domain of pure intellect, cannot be determined [. . .] by any exterior *criterium*, and they are things which do not appear in 'profane' instruction [. . .]"[130] It seems that Guénon was referring to the ability to possess some transcendental knowledge, which could bring the members of the elite closer to the core of Tradition, although, in the West, Guénon considered such elite to be "non-existent" and the exceptions to the case being "too few and too isolated" from each other.[131] What is clear to Guénon is that the intellectual elite will never take the form of "a society with statutes, rules, reunions, and all the other exterior manifestations that this word entails."[132] Nevertheless, the position Guénon took in his text was that of extreme pessimism:

> It is only in the East that one can actually find examples to aspire to; we have reason to believe that in the Middle Ages, the West also had organisations of the same type, but it is quite doubtful that sufficient traces survived for one to be able to begin to have a clear idea other than by analogy with those that exist in

the East, an analogy based in any case, not on wanton suppositions, but on signs that do not deceive when one already knows certain things.[133]

On September 1, 1924, Reghini had been intrigued by a revival of the Western Tradition according to the *Schola*'s line even if influenced by Eastern Traditionalism. He had written to Armentano asking him if he had read Guénon's book and if he had received Guenon's letter: "What measures do I have to take in regard to his [Guénon's] manifest proposal to include us into an intellectual elite in order for the West to receive the Oriental Tradition?"[134] So, after all, Guénon had individuated some thinkers in the West that he thought would be well enough prepared to be part of his elite. In a letter dated December 12, 1924, Reghini told Armentano of Guénon's willingness to "organise something together," given his great appreciation of the *Schola*'s work.[135] Armentano had advised caution to Reghini, as he had preferred to wait to see how things would unfold without committing the *Schola* to any rash decision. Reghini, over the years, had become more and more confused with Guénon's apparent flirtation with the Christian church. After he had translated *Le Roi du Monde* (*The King of the World*, 1927), an alarmed Reghini had again written to Armentano: "You must have seen in 'The King of the World' with what indulgence and good disposition he treats Christianity, and maybe I wouldn't have proposed to translate his work if I could have predicted he would have gone so far down this line."[136] The idea of an intellectual elite gradually slipped from both Guénon's and Reghini's minds until Reghini heard through mutual friends about the difficulties that Guénon was going through, which characterized Guénon's life at the end of the 1920s. These difficulties can be summed up as health and financial issues: the death of his first wife and a supposed boycott the Catholic Church had forced on his works after the publication of *La Crise du Monde Moderne*. "I have heard from others," wrote Reghini to Armentano:

> Of his difficult situation in Paris; he has been heard pronouncing my name often, as a sort of invocation, and I think that showing him true and intelligent sympathy other than being the right thing to do may also be a good way to make him realise that his attempt was illusory, and that it is not with priests that he can create an elite that he yearns for and neither obtain a *reddressement* of the West.[137]

As many scholars interested in Guénon's work have noted, Guénon had in fact located possible members of an intellectual elite in the Catholic Church. He was also working on a theory of a Western elite although this no longer concerned him personally. As early as 1910, Guénon had converted to Islam and later joined a Sufi order. Soon after his problematic period in France, which Reghini described to Armentano in the previously quoted letter, the French philosopher would move to Cairo, never to return to his native land. It was, therefore, a problem worth writing about but one that did not affect Guénon himself. However, Reghini lived in a country in which, as we have seen in the previous chapter, everything seemed to point to a renaissance of ancient Roman aesthetics, architecture, vogue, and values. The sudden appearance on the scene of the Fascist regime, with its knowing nod to the greatness of Ancient Rome, seemed to happen at a perfect time. To Reghini, it was necessary to create an intellectual elite that could provide the new state with a renewed spiritual foundation in order to make Italy great again. As Sestito wrote, "while Guénon, and other esotericists like him, theorised on the *western tradition* sitting idly while waiting for the coming of miraculous 'avatars,' Reghini in Rome entered the arena with the overt aim to coagulate the pure forces of culture and of Western intellectuality in his journals."[138] The differences between the more contemplative Guénon and the more militant Reghini were many, as were their interpretations of concepts, such as the crisis of the West and of the intellectual elite. While Guénon had located the last period of adherence to Tradition with the scholastic Middle Ages, Reghini had seen, in the Renaissance and in the following centuries, a gradual but constant flowering of Pagan values and ideas, which seemed to have come to possible fruition with the rise of the new regime in mid-1920s Italy.[139] Far from escaping eastward, Reghini had intuited that the time had come for a positive reactivation of the ancient Roman mores in order to provide the new Fascist state with a solid, Pagan and Pythagorean base on which to build a new empire.

The following subsection, which will close this part of the chapter, is an analysis of hitherto unpublished missives sent by Reghini to Guénon and vice versa. An analysis of such correspondence will be useful in order to show how Guénon was probably more influenced by theories circulating among members of the *Schola* than the Italian Traditionalists were inspired by the better known Guénon. In these missives, one can almost notice a sort of veneration toward Guerrieri and Armentano on Guénon's behalf and a very respectful tone toward Reghini, who, by the mid-1920s, had published only articles and one single monograph compared to the plethora of writings already published by Guénon.

6.3.3. The Reghini-Guénon Correspondence (1923–1926)

The correspondence exchanged between Arturo Reghini and René Guénon sheds lights on many factors concerning the relationship between these two thinkers, who, pitted against financial difficulties, never had the chance to meet each other in person. Guénon's letters had been previously published by scholar Gastone Ventura as an appendix to the reprint of the *Atanòr* journal and by

Mariano Bizzarri in his collection of Guenonian essays entitled *Il Risveglio della Tradizione Occidentale* (*The Awakening of the Western Tradition*, 2003).[140] Most of Reghini's responses to these letters have hitherto been unpublished but provide a clearer insight to Guénon's missives, filling in the gaps of the narrative, as it were.[141] The subjects dealt with in this ten-year correspondence are obviously many, ranging from the discussion on symbolism to the decline of the West, an analysis of Christianity as a possible vehicle for the restoration of the West, to more mundane matters. One could even venture to call them plain gossiping around the subject of the active occult circles at the time. For the sake of convenience, I have selected three nodal points in their correspondence that I think will successfully summarize the voluminous corpus of exchanged letters. First, the great respect each man had for the other's work is the paramount subject I shall be highlighting; second, I will specifically target Guénon's *Le Roi du Monde*, its impact on Reghini, and the exchange they had around this fascinating work; finally, a focus on the figure of Julius Evola will exemplify the gossip-like aspect of part of the missives, which seem to anticipate the sharp break between the Florentine philosopher and the Roman Baron in the years to come.

Since Reghini's first letter sent on December 17, 1923, the figures of Armentano and Guerrieri seemed to provide the *trait d'union* between the two thinkers. Correspondence dating back to 1910 between Guénon and the other two members of the *Schola* is still extant, and Guénon appears to hold both in the highest esteem. It is entirely possible that Reghini's connection with Armentano and Guerrieri facilitated the beginning of this long epistolary friendship.[142] Reghini's appreciation of Guénon's work seems mostly to cover the entire spectrum of Guénon's literary interest. On January 8, 1924, Reghini wrote to send his appreciation of Guénon's work on *Vedanta*. Having read the first instalments of the work on the revue *La Gnose*, Reghini declared himself to be "*enchanté*" regarding the possibility of a monograph devoted to the subject.[143] On March 16 of the same year, while translating Guénon's articles into Italian in order to publish them in the journal *Atanòr*, Reghini wrote that he had "already read and translated his article with a true pleasure of the spirit." "Your writings," continued Reghini, "are by now so familiar to me that I can appreciate even the nuances, and I enjoy your discrete irony."[144] Guénon, on his side, was just as lavish with compliments as his Italian correspondent. The most important endorsement, which has impressive repercussions if analyzed correctly, is to be found in a missive dated June 19, 1924. Here Guénon was discussing the corrections Reghini made about the article that would then form the basis for the work *L'Éstoterisme du Dante*. The French author seemed to treat Reghini as an equal when it came to the discussion of Traditional thought and, more than that, seemed to relinquish any will or possibility of knowing more than Reghini in the domain of Western Traditions and the possibilities to revive them:

Thank you for what you say about my study; I notice that we always agree on the essential. On the subject that you submit to me about the existence of a Western tradition, this is very correct and corresponds to an issue that worries me just as it worries you; if, today, authentic representatives of this tradition exist, how is it possible to gain contact with them? *Here is a difficulty that you are in a much better place to overcome since, under the intellectual point of view, I am much closer to the Orient than I am to the Occident. Would you be so kind as to tell me your thoughts on this subject* [italics added for emphasis]?[145]

The importance of this quote cannot be underestimated: the main representative of twentieth-century Traditionalism seemed to be treating Arturo Reghini as an equal in one of the thorniest subjects at hand. Not only did he profess his disadvantage because of his intellectual framework, but Guénon also seemed to see in Reghini somebody who could possibly illumine his theories with fresh input from the Roman Traditionalist perspective.

While Guénon's work on the idea of esotericism within Dante's work was received favorably by Reghini, it is Guénon's *Le Roi du Monde* that seems to have resonated more strongly with the Florentine author. The day after finishing the translation of the complete work, September 14, 1926, Reghini wrote intense words of praise for the booklet, describing it as "a small volume with a great importance."[146] Reghini had been greatly stimulated by the idea of the "existence, nowadays [. . .] of a supreme spiritual centre" and by "the many arguments used to bolster your [Guénon's] 'revelation.' "[147] Such an idea probably opened Reghini to the concept of a universal Tradition, which the Roman one was but a single facet of, bringing him, as we shall see in the following quote, almost full circle with his Theosophical period. The existence of such a center, Agartha, had been postulated previously by Alexandre Saint-Yves d-Alveydre, French occultist, and Ferdynand Ossendowski, and Reghini mentioned this to Guénon in a missive dated November 5, 1924.[148] In the same letter, Reghini discussed the possibility of Helena Petrovna Blavatsky (1831–1891) having written about the same subject in her *The Secret Doctrine* (1888), thus showing good familiarity with the subject at hand.

The majority of the corpus of letters deals with Reghini's corrections to the translations of Guénon's works, the exchange of French and Italian journals that could be of interest to either author, and, in a smaller part, more serious takes on the issues of occultism or Traditionalism. It is amusing to find, peppered here and there in the letters, allusion to contemporary events within the Italian and French occult milieus, and the witty and eager way with which both authors seem to have tackled these subjects provides them with a more human side hitherto left unscrutinized. Among the many figures which fell under the sharp pens of Reghini and Guénon were Martinists, such as Giulio Sacchi, French

Anthroposophists, and Benito Mussolini himself. As we shall see in more detail in the following chapter, Mussolini, under the pseudonym *Fermi*, had written an article on the paper *Gerarchia* (*Hierarchy*, est. 1922), a publication that Mussolini himself had founded.[149] In it, he took a strong defence of Catholic ideas, perhaps writing on subjects he was not too familiar with. The article was a response to a previous piece written by Reghini titled "Campidoglio e Golgota" ("Capitol Hill and Golgotha," 1924).[150] Neither Reghini nor Guénon seemed to be aware of who was actually writing behind the pseudonym *Fermi*, but Guénon's comment on the article was nevertheless scathing:

> Whoever the author of the article may be, he clearly shows towards the end that he has not understood the essential distinctions between metaphysical and initiatic knowledge and profane knowledge (when he talks about the "*Nuova Accademia*" etc.) and similarly, that he knows nothing of Oriental doctrines: his classification of "mystical" works and "moral" works is quite funny![151]

Not even Mussolini was spared from Guénon's humor. But the target of most of the two authors' jibes was without a doubt the young and upcoming Traditionalist and colleague, Julius Evola. As we shall see in the next chapter, Evola's break with Reghini was an important event in the lives of both Italian thinkers, and it can possibly be the proof of all the allegations Reghini and Guénon made in the previous year: that Evola's fame may have overshadowed his dastardly behavior. The first letter to contain a remark on Evola is dated June 19, 1924, and it contains a critique of Evola's excessive attachment to the theories of German philosophers:

> The sixth issue of *Atanòr* arrived the day after you wrote. As you had predicted, I only have some reserves on Evola's article even though you presented it in the best of ways. What need is there to complicate things with all those considerations copied from German philosophy?[152]

Soon in the correspondence, the attacks on Evola become increasingly hostile, and, in Reghini's letter to Guénon dated December 13, 1924, he wrote:

> Regarding Evola, who is very young and much persuaded of being something special, I'll tell you that before reading *Orient et Occident*, he criticised you claiming that you are a rationalist. According to him, one must bring oneself to such a point that the will becomes absolutely powerful.[153]

In a later letter, Reghini, while informing Guénon of Evola's intention of writing a book on Tantra, *L'Uomo e la Potenza* (*Man and Power*, 1926), cannot resist a dig toward the younger philosopher: "Do you know Evola is preparing a work on Tantra and he doesn't know Sanskrit? He must know Greek and Latin very badly since he never pursued classical studies, and so what a [poor] display of Greek!"[154] Guénon would take up this very subject in his letter dated April 21, 1925, where he asks Reghini about news on Evola's tantric work and an evaluation of Evola's translation of the *Tao Te Ching* (1923):

> Mister [Guido] De Giorgio asks me what value Evola's translation of the *Tao Te Ching* might have; I have not read it, I don't trust him since the author does not know the language. Regarding Evola, how is his work on Tantra going? It will without a doubt be a reproduction of the works of Sir John Woodroffe; unfortunately, even he knows very little Sanskrit and what is even more peculiar is that he makes incredible blunders even when writing in English, which, if I am not mistaken, is his mother-tongue.[155]

What can we infer from the correspondence between these two fundamental figures in the history of Traditionalism? Certainly, both treated each other as equals and were equally interested in the other's opinion on a vast array of matters. Sestito has written: "An influence, even indirect, of Guénon on Reghini must be excluded," keeping the exchange of information of two colleagues out of the equation. My opinion is more nuanced than Sestito's. Guénon definitely influenced Reghini on two main factors: first with theories concerning the intellectual elite, which Reghini had hinted at but had never set into a coherent theoretical framework like Guénon had in *Orient et Occident*; second, the publication of *Le Roi du Monde* seemed to change some of Reghini's perspectives. The correspondence, in the earlier quoted passages, seems to confirm this change from the belief of a particular Tradition, higher and nobler than the others, namely the Roman Tradition, to a more Universalist approach to the validity of other, Eastern traditions. This is a subject, which would deserve a study of its own, but it is clear from the correspondence that Reghini had matured enough to recognize the validity of other religious Traditions with regard to initiation and to the reversal of the tide of modernity. Guénon, however, had already devoted his life to Islamic mysticism years before his first contact with Reghini. The question of the West seemed to interest him greatly, but it does not appear to constitute a problem that threatened him personally. In the correspondence, he was more than happy to consider Reghini the expert when dealing with Western traditions, and he clearly seemed to be content with his choice of preferring Mecca over Rome. Nevertheless, Reghini's erudition on Western religious traditions and his expertise on the esoteric Dante influenced his future writings and Guénon, in my opinion, came away just as enriched as Reghini had, with what concerns their respective intellectual pursuits. What appears from the letters is a friendship, which could have produced much more interesting developments if the two had ever had the chance to meet in person, but for this and other reasons, remained until 1935, the year of the last letters between the two, a mere epistolary relationship.

6.4. Roman Traditionalism from 1920 to 1925

6.4.1. The End of the Beginning

Once the war was over, Reghini began what is considered to be the most prolific decade of his life in terms of writing and publishing: the 1920s. Between the end of 1919 and the beginning of 1920, the philosopher travelled to Armentano's tower in Scalea in order to discuss future possibilities for the *Schola*'s manifestation in the public and political sphere. Once back in Rome in the spring of 1920, Reghini obtained the permanent position of professor at the *Scuola Tecnica di Portoferraio* (*Portoferraio Technical School*) on the Isle of Elba in Tuscany.[156] In the period starting from February and going on to September, when his teaching position started, he moved to Rome and obtained a contract for the translation of Robert Louis Stevenson's (1850–1894) masterpiece *The Strange Case of Dr. Jekyll and Mr. Hyde* (1886). In addition to his work as a translator, Reghini also found time to pen his first book, *Le Parole Sacre e di Passo*. As Sestito rightly noted in his biography, Reghini's book is a classic among twentieth-century Masonic literature, and it is probably the main reason Reghini is remembered by a wider Masonic audience nowadays. In it, Reghini urges for a *restitutio ad pristinum*, a return to the origins, as it were, of Freemasonry, and in his incipit, he quotes Niccolò Machiavelli, the famous Renaissance humanist and political theorist: "If we want a sect or a republic to live long, it is necessary to pull it back towards its beginning" and "these alterations are to the benefit of those who reduce them to their own principles."[157] In his book, Reghini criticizes the degeneration of Freemasonry in the previous two centuries and advocates for a return to the origins according to the ideals propounded by the *Schola Italica*. The idea of bringing Freemasonry back to its origins did not represent a mere nostalgic need by Reghini. Throughout the text, he seems to be clear that real knowledge is definitely not hidden in texts, scrolls, or books. In Reghini's mind though, in a very Pythagorean fashion, "it is supremely important to give back to the words, to the ceremonies, their real traditional value, so that, through their help, the intellect may learn self-discipline and how to penetrate their hidden value."[158] One of the most fascinating theories Reghini put forth was that of a distinction between a "critical" and an "initiatic study" of the *Passwords* (*Parole di Passo*), considering the initiatic study of them the only tool that could bring the realization that "the central idea is, therefore, the ancient Mediterranean idea of privileged survival, of resurrection to the immortality from death, of palingenesis attained through the mystic death."[159] The discourse of privileged initiation is omnipresent, and Reghini also gives us a definition of initiation, which, as Sestito remarks, must include four factors: "knowledge; immortality; beatitude and perfection."[160] Reghini had discovered and copied Tommaso Campanella's *La Prattica dell'Estasi Filosofica* (*The Practise of Philosophical Extasy*, n.d.) from a manuscript that had been found in the early 1910s at the Magliabecchiana library in Florence.[161] Reghini recognized in Campanella a member of the unbroken chain of representatives of the *Schola Italica* and had practiced the exercises prescribed in *La Prattica* for at least ten years before writing the book. In *Le Parole Sacre*, Reghini described the technique used to help gain higher knowledge or philosophical ecstasy:

> It is an unsurpassed page of the technical initiatic literature, and the Western esoteric tradition casts glimmers of light thanks to this neo-Pyhagorean from Southern Italy, heroically fighting Christian ferocity and ignorance. We don't think that among the French [lit. Transalpini] there are many that may hope to compete in the realms of metaphysical knowledge with this heir and exponent of the Schola Italica.[162]

Reghini's attempt to link the origins of Masonic words to the Eleusinian mysteries and other Mediterranean traditions may appear naïve to those who have studied the Judeo-Christian provenance of most Masonic passwords, but the chance to sponsor his own heritage and to downplay Christianity and Judaism at the same time, in my opinion, was regarded as too good to turn down.

Reghini's position regarding which Masonic body to join, among the two main obediences, was settled in Scalea. After a long deliberation with his Master, Armentano, and on September 20, 1921, Reghini joined the Scottish Rite, which at the time was led by Raul Palermi (1864–1948). His induction was followed by a speech of the newly initiated Reghini, who, according to Sestito, went back to the figure of Dante and left no doubts on his political inclination toward his heathen brand of imperialism. His old enemy Frosini had tried to create obstacles and thwart Reghini's initiation into the Scottish Rite, but Frosini was expelled more or less at the same time as the Florentine philosopher was initiated. Biographer di Luca suspects a *longa manu* intervention on behalf of Armentano from his quarters in Scalea, in aspects concerning Reghini's successful initiation.[163] Reghini, always one who would have the last word, had written an article titled "Due Parole al Dott. Frosini" ("A Few Words to Dr. Frosini," 1921) in the pages of the *Rassegna Massonica*, which he had just been nominated editor of:

> I own a small booklet in which [. . .] I write down all the doodling and the idiotic statements printed by various Masonic authors. At the head of the list is Br.

Ulisse Bacci, but Frosini does not lag that far away, and since he is still young and his intelligence is developing floridly, I believe that even in this he will end up being ahead of everyone. It is only a matter of time [. . .].[164]

When the law of February 14, 1923—effectively outlawing Freemasonry—came out, while Raul Palermi faltered, a splinter group that would oppose the Fascist regime's decision was created, and that group itself launched its own journal, *Fenice* (*Phoenix*, est. 1923). Although Reghini was tempted to join the secessionist group, which he had hoped to influence with his political and esoteric ideas, Armentano had called him to remain faithful to the oaths made at the time of his initiation. Reghini ended up staying in the Scottish Rite, abandoned by some of his closest friends, such as Moretto Mori, and trying to coexist with Raul Palermi, who had by then lost control of his lodges. Reghini tried to keep Palermi away from the pressures of the clerical-Fascist power and closer to his Roman imperialist ideas, but Palermi still believed in his chances of striking a deal with the regime.[165] Reghini's vicinity to Palermi made him a prime target for the newly born *Fenice*, which, in an article, had branded Reghini, out of all the Freemasons, as filo-Jesuit.[166] The other main reason behind these accusations, beyond Regini's close proximity to the Head of the Scottish Rite, Raul Palermi, are to be found in the Masonic political stances taken by the Grand Master of GOI, Domizio Torrigiani: while Torregiani had immediately suggested that all Fascists leave the Grand Orient, Palermi had published an official announcement on February 15, stating that his Masons

> Devotedly obey the Fascist hierarchy, superior to all contingencies, and, thus, may continue to serve the fatherland and the Fascist organisation, loyal and disciplined towards the supreme leader, Benito Mussolini.[167]

Still, Reghini seemed to maintain faith in Mussolini's anti-Catholic stance, and in his article "L'Intolleranza Cattolica e lo Stato" ("Catholic Intolerance and the State," 1923), had written that even though "Catholics, nationalists, Jesuits, and all the sons of priests" tried to impose themselves on the new government and take advantage of Freemasonry's crisis, he continued saying, "the idea that a devotion of Italian politics towards the clerical demands may be in the intentions of Mussolini does not appear to us an idea that may be entertained honestly."[168] In between the accusations of being a friend of the Jesuits and causing the fall of all Masonic bodies, Reghini decided to leave Rome for the more relaxed environment of Scalea to spend the summer months with his Master Armentano. There, new ideas were concocted to manifest the *Schola Italica* in the public world. Marco Rossi, in his analysis of these incredibly complicated years, has written:

Reghini finds himself far away from the lodge of Palazzo Giustiniani because of his Fascist sympathies and his anti-democratic convictions, which explains his activities in the supreme Scottish counsel of Piazza del Gesù; but, at the same time, he does not follow the line of Mussolini devoted to finding an agreement with the Catholic Church, a line [...] that his superior Palermi approved of unconditionally.[169]

6.4.2. The Beginning of the End

Back from Scalea, it was decided that Reghini and the other representatives of the *Schola Italica* would create a Pythagorean association in Rome. In October 1923, Reghini informed Armentano of the situation at hand. The owner of the hotel *Des Étrangers* in Rome, Gino Gori (1876–1952), who offered a place for the group to meet in his hotel, had also offered the monthly sum of 200 lire to finance an independent journal that would cover themes dear to the *Schola*. In his letter, Reghini wrote: "I think the moment has come in which we have a small base and the times are ripening for the institution of a movement, of a Journal of an Order of ours."[170] As Sestito noted, Reghini was convinced that by granting the new Order an imperialist and thoroughly Italic connotation, he could bypass Mussolini's ban on Masonic bodies. A delegation of representatives from the Scottish Rite met Mussolini on November 9, 1923. Again, Armentano was informed by letter that "Mussolini showed much cordiality, and there was an important exchange of ideas and projects."[171] On December 18, 1923, the *Associazione Pitagorica* (*Pythagorean Association*) was created with Reghini at its head, and the decision to publish a journal was voted for—the journal would be called *Atanòr, Rivista di Studi Iniziatici* (*Atanòr, Journal of Initiatic Studies*, 1924). Other participants included old members of the *Rito Filosofico* and the *Schola Italica*, such as Mori, Guerrieri, Salvi, and Procacci. The culminating period called by author Augusto Hermet *La Ventura delle Riviste* (*The Destiny of Journals*, 1941) was about to start, and in five fiery years, Reghini would have directed three journals dealing with Pythagoreanism, imperialism, Paganism, and occultism. The contrasts between editors like Reghini and the regime, though, were about to hit the most critical point.

7
The *Ur* Group and the End of a Dream (1923–1929)

> For the man of Tradition,
> looking towards the past
> and not Skyward would mean
> preferring to drink from the pond,
> rather than from the spring.
>
> —Gruppo dei Dioscuri[1]

7.1. *Le Parole Sacre Di Passo* Published by *Atanòr* (1922)

7.1.1. Meeting Ciro Alvi and the *Atanòr* Publishing House

In a letter to his mentor Amedeo Armentano dated June 25, 1914, after a meeting with Ciro Alvi (1872–1944), Reghini wrote:

> Alvi is a good author and has been one of our fighters for idealism during these past 15 years. We agreed upon everything. He, too, wants the Empire and the primacy of the Italians [...] In short he appeared to me as the person naturally closer to us than all the ones we met so far. I invited him, too, to come and visit us in Scalea.[2]

Biographical data on Alvi are very scarce.[3] He was born in the Umbrian town of Todi in 1872, and his family belonged to the local aristocracy. Although obtaining a degree in Law, his passions were the Latin and Greek classics, which would shape his view of the world drastically. He was a member of the the Italian Grand Orient (GOI) from a very young age, although his name does not figure in its roll call, and his highest degree achieved is to this day unknown.[4] With anti-clerical and strong Socialist leanings, Alvi was forced into exile in Switzerland during 1898–1899 after the Socialist uprisings had been repressed. This seems to be a fundamental moment in Alvi's life, as he abandoned his political activism and focused on his career as an author of novels and on his spiritual development. His first two books, *Verso la Purificazione* (*Towards Purification*, 1899) and *La*

Via Nuova (*The New Way*, 1901), suggest, even by their titles, a spiritual yearning in the author's writings.[5] His following novel, *S. Francesco d'Assisi* (*St. Francis of Assisi*, 1903), possibly his most well-known work, was considered heretical for its strong anti-Christian sentiments, and it was banned by the Catholic Church:[6] "much discussed by critics, it was published in more than one edition. It was banned."[7] In 1911 along with his cousins Armando and Giorgio Comez (nd.), Alvi founded *Atanòr*, the publishing house that more than any other in Italy would strive to put out texts dealing with occultism, Freemasonry, Hermeticism, and similar topics.[8] The publishing house was initially very successful, and according to Mariano Bianca:

> Its founding, which represented the satisfaction of a need of the day's Italian culture, set itself within a wide cultural movement, promoted also by the strengthening and European consolidation of Freemasonry, of its institution and its thought, which also put great relevance on the esoteric and spiritual dimension that seemed to lose itself within the diffusion of science and Positivist thought or even more in the various religious doctrines and practices.[9]

Alvi, behind the wider scope of the diffusion of a vast array of esoteric subjects, was primarily focused on texts that would promote a Roman imperialist view of the world years before his first meeting with Reghini in 1912.[10] Reghini himself, in 1913, had established contact with Alvi and had intended to go to Todi, where he had recognized similar intents and ideas in Alvi's circle, before he himself had joined Armentano in Scalea.[11] The trip never manifested, but it is clear that the small Todi Roman Traditionalist milieu, which gravitated around Alvi, the Comez brothers and their publishing house, was on very similar political and spiritual positions as Armentano and his *Schola*, so a meeting between the two groups seemed inevitable. Alvi's career as a novelist also seemed to take a Roman Traditionalist bend, especially in his *Per lo Spirito la Carne Esaltare* (*To Exalt the Flesh for the Spirit*, 1923), which I will deal with more thoroughly in the section devoted to the journal *Atanòr*.[12] The novel is a utopia, where the main characters, returning from a long voyage abroad that had put them face to face with the most extreme consequences of modernity, come back to a new imperialist Italy they barely recognized. The novel is filled with patriotic rhetoric and a feeling that the restoration of the old aristocratic mores and Roman traditions was the best thing for Italy in its current state: "The first citizens took care of public welfare, those favoured by the Gods, and only they were allowed to work for the material wealth of the modest."[13] However, Alvi also seemed to share Reghini's repulsion toward Christianity, as can be clearly gleaned from reading his 1928 novel *L'Incendio di Roma* (*The Fire of Rome*). The story is based on the popular, now outdated theory, that it was the Christians who started the fire, which ravaged Rome on July 18 and 19, 64 CE.[14] An example, short and to the point, can be seen on page 29 of the work when the Christian Apollonio tells his friend Fabio Gemino: "Listen Fabio Gemino. Ponder this. For us christians [sic.], Rome is the enemy, the abomination, it is the reign of Satan."[15]

When Alvi agreed to publish a monograph by Reghini's, Alvi was writing Roman Traditionalism-inspired novels and *Atanòr*, as a publishing house, was in full swing publishing texts like ex-member of the *Rito Filosofico* Vittore Marchi's (1892–1981) *La Missione di Roma nel Mondo* (*Rome's Mission in the World*, 1915) and Enrico Caporali's (1838–1918) *La Sapienza Italica* (*The Italic Wisdom*, 1914–1916).[16] *Le Parole Sacre e di Passo* seemed to fit perfectly in this publication schedule, in order for *Atanòr* to promote Roman Traditionalism in all of its aspects. Finally, it seemed that the members of the *Schola*, and Reghini in particular, appeared to have found a strong and far-reaching outlet for their imperialist ideas.

7.1.2. *Le Parole*: Reghini's First Monograph (1922)

In 1920, Alvi relocated his publishing house to Rome, the epicenter of the cultural and political ferment in the country. His most important publication within the subject of Freemasonry manifested in 1922 when, nine years after their first meeting, Alvi decided to publish Reghini's *Le Parole Sacre e di Passo*. As Fabrizio Giorgio has pointed out, "it was certainly the shared faith in the Pagan-imperialist ideals that drove Alvi to commit, in such a delicate political moment, to an editorial venture so risky that it exposed both him and his publishing house."[17] Perhaps, just like Armentano and Reghini, Alvi had realized that such a period of unrest was the best time to push the imperialist agenda forward, and the march on Rome later that year, with its authoritarian bend, probably convinced him further that he was indeed right. Reghini had begun writing his work during the summer stay at Scalea in 1919, and it was in 1921 that he met the man who was destined to become his prized disciple and early biographer: Giulio Parise (1902–1969).[18] Upon meeting Reghini at the young age of nineteen, the young student Parise fondly remembers Reghini and his Spartan flat in Rome: "I met A.R. when he was preparing his volume on 'The Sacred Words and Pass-Words and the Greatest Masonic Mystery,' published in 1922. Back then, he lived in a modest room, where the most interesting thing apart from him was a small shelf containing his books."[19] His first copy of the book was obviously inscribed to his friend and Master Armentano, bearing the dedication: "Dear Master, this book is the fruit of our combined work. I hope I will not have to do without your future guidance to complete another work even more worthy of you. Arturo Reghini."[20] The reason behind my quoting other members of the *Schola Italica* is to underline the fact that although Arturo Reghini was the sole author of the book, it was only through a joint effort between master, disciple, and publisher that the work came to have the importance it serves even nowadays among Italian Masons. The 1920s, in my opinion, were seen as the last possible attempt for the *Schola* to influence the cultural and political milieu of the capital to adopt a Pagan imperialist stance, and throughout the correspondences between Reghini and Alvi or Reghini and Armentano, the consistent idea that the times were ripe for a final "now or never" push of their ideas was an omnipresent feeling of urgency that permeated every communication. One example might be a letter the Pagan imperialist Mario Gallinaro (n.d.) wrote to Armentano expressing all of his excitement for Reghini's work while at the same time harboring some doubts on the excess of the Florentine's author proverbial caustic wit:

> I very much enjoyed reading the book by our Arturo. There are pages of real, ingenious depth; as a whole, I consider it politically unmanageable since it would hurt many sensibilities, nay, all of them. Maybe it would have been better to smooth out some polemical asperities in the first edition and save them for a second volume when the really superior authority of the author in the field of initiatic esotericism would not have become undoubted and un-doubtable.[21]

What then is the content of Reghini's book? It appears to me that within the author's plan, the text is a continuous invitation to bring back Freemasonry to its primordial initiatic splendor. The *restitutio ad pristinum*, a restoration according to the mores of the ancient Roman world, had been a *fil rouge*, which has traversed every chapter of this current book. Now Reghini made a case for Freemasonry, which, since the *Rito Filosofico Italiano* (RFI), he had viewed as the best vehicle for the esoteric teachings of the *Schola Italica*. If the RFI had been a failure, mostly because of loose cannon Eduardo Frosini, *Le Parole* approached Freemasonry from a more general point of view.[22] The preface to the work opens with a programmatic quote from Niccolò Machiavelli's (1469–1527) *Discorsi sulla Prima Deca di Tito Livio* (*Discourses on the First Deca of Titus Livius*, 1531), where Machiavelli argues that in order for a sect or a republic to live long, it will often need to be brought back to its early state.[23] As we have seen, Machiavelli, along with Vergil, Dante, and Mazzini, had been one of the champions of "Pagan Imperialism," Reghini's most successful writing so far. The return to basics, in this case, was argued in favor of Freemasonry, which Reghini saw as corrupt, devoid of any initiatory qualities and too modern to do any candidate any good. In his preface, Reghini argued that

> The analysis of the ceremonies and the ritual legends of the various degrees evidently shows the inspiration from the Pagan Mysteries, the Eleusynian and

Isiaic ones especially, and Anderson's constitutions faithfully maintain the healthy rationalist spirit that infused the Order with life at its very beginnings (1717).[24]

The book was divided into five chapters: the first one dealing with a philological analysis of the Masonic passwords; the second with the sacred words of the first and second degree; the third with the sacred word of the third degree; the fourth with the passwords; the fifth with the concept of initiatic resurrection as the foundation of true Freemasonry; the appendix, much to the benefit of this chapter, dealt with the then thorny issue of Freemasonry and Christianity.

From the outset of the first chapter, two things were apparent to the reader. Reghini's vast erudition on the topic of Freemasonry and his desire, from the first page, to illustrate how Freemasonry, allegedly, was inextricably linked to the Pagan mysteries to which he desperately wanted to bring Masonic lore back. Reghini, though using outdated sources for his research, still provided the reader with an array of scholarly theories that surpassed, in finesse and philological clarity, those of any other Italian Freemasons of his day: from Jean-Marie Ragon (1781–1862) to Gottfried Findel (1828–1905), from Eliphas Lévi (1810–1875) to the Baron of Tschoudy (1727–1769), from Richard Hely-Hutchinson (1756–1825) to Samuel Pritchard (n.d.): Reghini showed an outstanding grasp of the subject, chiding one author's gullibility one moment and praising the philological work of another a couple of lines further down.[25] The second factor apparent is Reghini's motives for writing the book. Immediately, at the inception of the first chapter, he claimed that along the words derived from an architectonic background that are expected to be found in Freemasonry, "it is easy to see within the Masonic lingo a number of words and sentences, whose symbolism retain a philosophical character that is deeper and more determined."[26] His allusion is to the three passwords, which he believes are not Jewish in origin. However, he does not contest the "Jewishness" of the sacred words Boaz, Jachin, and Mac-benah, which are strictly correlated to the history of the biblical building of the Temple of Solomon and closely linked with the legend of Hiram Abif—the mythical architect entrusted with the construction of the temple—who is slain by some of his disciples, as the third degree ritual of any Masonic obedience recounts. It is the very slaying and resurrection of Hiram, which, according to Reghini, confirms the Pagan origin of Freemasonry:

> Hiram dies and is reborn and in such a way he becomes a Master. Similarly, Osiris, Dionysus, Jesus were slain, proceeded down to hell, resurrected and became immortal.

Having attributed this kind of function to Hiram shows the evident intention to reconnect the Masonic initiation to the classical ones, especially the Isiac and Eleusynian.[27]

To elucidate his point even further, Reghini reverted to examples in classical mythology, which may link to Hiram's story: the first mythological case tackled by the author was the legend of Aeneas's descent into the realm of the dead. Reghini likened the Trojan prince's necessity to procure a Golden Bough in order to be able to pass by the guardians of the netherworld to the sprig of acacia wood that was placed on Hiram's burial site.[28] The importance of the *Aeneid* as a sacred text of Roman Traditionalist lore and customs has been discussed before in this book, as has the importance of Vergil as Dante's psychopomp.[29] Another myth, also found in Vergil, was that of the young Polidorus killed by King Polymestor because of the youth's wealth and buried under a bush by a hillside: according to Vergil, Aeneas, while visiting Polymestor, had accidentally snapped a branch from the bush, and the gruesome discovery of the body had ensued.[30] Reghini, thus, concluded his second chapter by stating that the Masonic mysteries have one central concept, which harkens back to the Mediterranean idea of the survival of the soul after death acquired through a mystical death: "it is the Egyptian, Orphic, Pythagorean, Hermetic idea; it is the main reason behind the mysteries of Eleusis, of Ceres, of Mithras."[31]

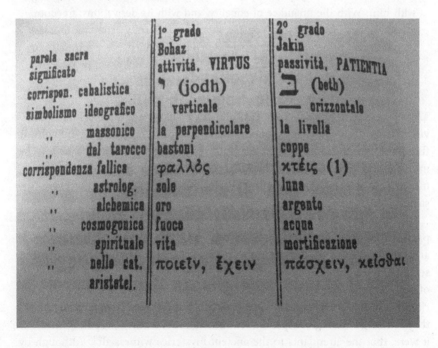

The third and fourth chapters of *La Parole* will only be reviewed briefly because a philological analysis of Hebrew words is outside of the scope of this work. Reghini's competence in dealing with ancient languages, though, must be highlighted. Whether discussing the ancient Hebrew suffixes of the words *Boaz* or *Jakin* or trying to find Greek alternatives behind the sacred word *Tubalcain*, the author seemed at ease with Egyptian, Hebrew, Greek, and Latin, and he used his knowledge to prove his main hypothesis. In sections of the text, his use of comparative tables and correspondences could remind his reader of Eliphas Lévi or Aleister Crowley (1875–1947) and their attempts at synthesizing occult lore. The graph shown here, for example, is highly reminiscent of some tables charted by Crowley in his Kabbalistic work *777*.[32] The central focus, the central drive of the book remained the same: to reconnect modern Freemasonry to the ancient Mediterranean mysteries. To do that, Reghini used his wide knowledge of classical sources to point to similarities between the two, from Pherecides of Syros (ca. 580 BCE–ca. 520 BCE) to Plutarch (46–127 CE) and from Pliny (29–79 CE) to Catullus (84 BCE–54 BCE).[33] Of course, within his treatment of the subject of Freemasonry, Reghini manifested his usual dissatisfaction with the way occult secrets were approached, as was made abundantly clear from the following quote:

> Nowadays, it is thought that truth may be gained through discussion, and it seems natural that the pupil may put himself on a level with his Master, arguing with him. With the prejudice of equality, and with its derivations: freedom, human rights, sovereignty of people, compulsory fraternity, economic utopias, etc. etc., every principle of authority has been undermined, every spiritual and intellectual superiority has been trivialised, hierarchy unknown or reversed, and deference and reverence to a master have vanished.[34]

The concepts of hierarchy, secrecy, elitism, a distancing of the higher individual from the plebeian mass of uninitiated people were a constant in Reghini's thoughts, and in *Le Parole*, his attempt to resacralize Freemasonry needs to be understood from the point of view of a man trying to involve a detached, antimodern readership, who had allegedly lost all contact with, or interest in, the sacred.

The fifth and closing chapter of *Le Parole* summed up the theoretical apparatus that in the previous four sections had been mingled with philological analysis. It was a departure from the exquisitely rational study of the first four sections, toward a more mystical and spiritual exegesis of the central messages of Freemasonry. The chapter posed one fundamental question: Were Masonic rituals just innocuous ceremonial reenactments with no spiritual value, or did the initiate go through a spiritual transformation, a mystical palingenesis, as it were, that the attendants to the ancient mysteries witnessed?[35] Although by the fifth chapter this appeared to be a rhetorical question, Reghini went to great lengths to convince his reader of the strength of his arguments. Initially, the author went through examples of physical cases of apparent death and subsequent "return" to life as a metaphor for death being just another state of being after life, "as night follows day, sleep is followed by awakening, winter by spring."[36] He then went back to the ancient mysteries and states that even then great ritual ceremonies were performed, but Reghini argued that these must have been "the only ones, which the great masses attended to," and that the bigger ceremonies did not confer "those interior effects, of which Apuleius and Plutarch talk about."[37] The chapter then went onto undermining the authority of other occultist groups' claims to possess the keys to access the sacred and that of scientists, who belittle the benefits of "real" initiation. In the first instance, Reghini complained that occultists had cropped up like proverbial weeds in early twentieth-century Italy. He lists "freemasons, rosicrucians, templars, gnostics, hermetists, kabbalists, astrologers, alchemists, theosophists, anthroposophists," concluding that with such an abundance of true wise men "within a couple of decades, they will all be initiates!"[38] Reghini, here, was clearly staking his ground, and that of the Schola's, as the only true repository of initiatic knowledge, which could be traced back to antiquity. The validation by antiquity with which he invested his reformed version of Freemasonry was clearly different from all other Masonic obediences, since Freemasons were the first in the above quoted list that the author lampooned. Modern Freemasons were no more than members of an exclusive club in the eyes of Reghini, and the democratization of occultism was to blame for the situation at hand. The chapter, and the book, closed with a warning to the second group of people Reghini wished to attack, those who preferred to explain every phenomenon through science, the rationalists, the believers in progress:

> We could allow you to experience, if you ever wished so, one of the feelings spoken about by Apuleius and Plutarch; we'll content ourselves with laughing at you when at the first tottering of *your* psyche, you will give manifest signs of having understood that the open waters of the seafarers are no route for small boats.[39]

The appendix entitled "Freemasonry and Christianity" ("Massoneria e Cristianesimo") did not share the same dialectic vigor of the rest of the work, although it did fit in with the increasing anti-clerical stance taken by Reghini in the 1920s. Very briefly, it represented a call to arms for Freemasons all around Italy to unite against the increasing power of the clergy. After accusing British Freemasonry of being completely corrupted by Christianity "insofar that it takes the form of one of the many Protestant sects that took hold there," Reghini urged Italian Freemasons to unite against the greater evil "if we do not want to leave the Order and the country at the mercy of [sic] christianity."[40] The appendix, in essence, ideally represents the thread that runs through this entire chapter. Horrified by the idea of Christianity gaining more and more influence since its loss of temporal power in 1870, Reghini urged Freemasons, whom he still saw as the group least corrupted by religion and the malaise of modernity, to join him in a return to the sources of initiation, the Pagan mysteries, and thereby bringing Italy back to a position of preeminence in both spiritual and political domains. After having accused the Young Men's Christian Assocation and Salvation Army of tainting men through their institutions, Reghini then pointed his finger toward Christian Science, New Thought, and his repudiated alma mater, the Theosophical Society.[41] All these institutions had worsened the spiritual condition of English occultists and freethinkers because of their "anglo-saxon super-Idealism."[42] Reghini hoped that Christianity, which had made its way into the British occult milieus, would not do the same thing in Italy:

> But we are Pagan; [a]nd we remind the Italian Freemasons once again that Masonic science has nothing to do with the religion of Jesus, or any other; it is instead the same wisdom that classical civilisation cherished and transmitted through its sacred mysteries.[43]

As to Reghini's first monograph, the work can be said to have been written in a clear and concise matter: to the reader of previous material written by the author, the themes were definitely not new, and the same motifs were repeated again throughout the work: the value of Freemasonry as a vehicle of Traditional transmission; the origins of Freemasonry to be found in the ancient mystery cults; the aim of all esoteric endeavors within Freemasonry, namely palingenesis and self-deification. These three points, along with a superb philological analysis made by the author on the passwords themselves, have prompted Reghini biographer and Masonic researcher di Luca to state that "Reghini has been the first author in Italy to discuss, with knowledge of his sources, of this subject and of authors like Hutchinson, Hawkins, Mackey, Findel, Preston, Tschoudy, Thory, de Bonville, Oliver, Pike."[44]

7.2. The Journals *Atanòr* (1924) and *Ignis* (1925)

7.2.1. Reghini's First Journal: *Atanòr*

By 1924, the *Atanòr* publishing house had established itself as the major distributor of books related to Freemasonry and occultism. In a review of Reghini's *Le Parole Sacre*, an anonymous journalist had playfully written, joking on the large occult movement in tiny Umbria: "This work of our terrible friends Arturo Reghini, author, and Ciro Alvi, publisher, scares us like the many others published by the wizard of Umbria [Alvi]. Which was a verdant [land], but with so many fumigations must have, by now, have become smoky-black."[45] It did not take much on Reghini's behalf to convince Alvi to publish a monthly magazine dedicated to the esoteric with a particular focus on the Italic, tradition, which both Reghini and Alvi felt the need to promote the most. As mentioned in the previous chapter, Reghini had already written to his teacher Armentano about the necessity of propagating their ideas through a journal, but by 1924, the magus of Scalea seemed to have more pressing concerns at hand. The scandal created by his marriage to his extremely young niece Giselda Perrone (nd.) during one of his trips to Brazil in 1921 and the crash of his revenue from the land he owned, due to the postwar economic crisis, forced Armentano to seek refuge in Brazil, where rich relatives were ready to take care of the Italian side of the family.[46] On May 3, 1924, Amedeo and Giselda Armentano left Italy for what should have been a relatively short stay in South America but ended up being a one-way voyage. Armentano, for one reason or another, would never set foot in Italy again. Reghini took it upon himself, therefore, to carry on with the divulgation of the *Schola*'s idea, and a journal seemed like the perfect medium to address the various issues most pressing to the Roman Traditionalists. After all, Marco Rossi, an expert on Italian journals of the time, has written, "there existed an ambiguous and yet organic link between the spiritual and cultural research of the artistic avant-gardes, the milieu of esoteric Freemasonry and the origins of the fascist movement."[47] Thus, through Alvi's publishing house, 1924 saw the publication of nine issues (including three double issues) of *Atanòr: Rivista di Studi Iniziatici* (*Atanòr: Journal of Initiatic Studies*). The editorial board was composed of a veritable who's who in the esoteric Italian milieu of the day: in addition to Ciro Alvi, Arturo Reghini, and his recently recruited disciple Giulio Parise, the roster included the names of René Guénon, Giuliano Kremmerz, Julius Evola, anthroposophist Aniceto del Massa, Armando Comes, Amedeo Armentano, and Alberto Russo Frattasi—all of whom have been mentioned before within this book. The presence of Kremmerz and Frattasi on the editorial board is purely nominal, as they did not seem to have been involved in any of the nine published issues. It is my idea that Reghini simply wanted to gather all established esoteric thinkers who were in line with his Italic theories of magical primacy, in order to be able to focus better on the inevitable attacks of other occultist groups, the Theosophical Society or the Martinist Order *in primis*. Generally speaking, the articles and columns in *Atanòr* may be divided into three categories, through my own subdivision, in order to elucidate better the issues tackled by the various authors, something that is not necessarily readily apparent to the casual reader of the journal. The first group of writings concerned themselves with the promulgation of the Pythagorean and Italic ideals of the *Schola Italica*, and the authors clearly made use of the journal as a vehicle for esoteric knowledge toward people who already had a vague idea of occultist and Traditionalist themes. Second, we have the articles, which most times seem to be talking about esoteric themes, but they are truly reflections and comments on the political situation of the day. Such articles were mostly penned by Reghini and were directed toward either the Christian Church or Benito Mussolini and his regime. Third, *Atanòr* also contained many personal attacks to the exponents of other occult movements, chiefly the Theosophical and Martinist ones. Although Reghini's pen was definitely mightier than the sword, and although it may seem that he was writing such articles for the amusement of the authors and his readers, it will become readily apparent that the main focus of his writing was represented by his tactic of using ridicule aimed at establishing his neo-Pythagorean ideas as the only ones valid, and discrediting those of the other movements, which were in those days fashionable.

The most important group of articles, from the scholar of Roman Traditionalism's point of view, is without doubt the first. Right from the first editorial of the first issue, "Ai Lettori" ("To the Readers"), Reghini was direct, and clearly stated the intents of the newly founded journal.[48] The theme covering the majority of the articles dealt with "the Italian tradition, from Pythagoras to our days" and its core goal was to provide the diffusion of such ideas without preference to a particular religion or occult system: "[t]o the frantic hunger for new trends, the original the wonderful, [this journal] will prefer the examination of facts and the ascertainment of truth, old or new."[49] The double "warfront" against science and religion was postulated at the end of Reghini's first article when he clearly stated that he was arguing both against science and religion:

> We cannot accept the claim of those religions or beliefs that think they can evade science and claim the dominion of spiritual enquiry from faith. Neither can we agree with the abdications of a science that wants to arbitrarily exclude from the field of scientific experience the spiritual experiences, neither the unreasonable obstinacy in wanting necessarily to impose in this field criteria and methods that are not functional, subordinating the subject in need of study to a system of enquiry and vice-versa.[50]

This method of approach to spiritual knowledge is reflected nowadays in the theory of diversification of religion, science, and gnosis (spiritual first-hand knowledge) brought forward by many scholars in the field of Western esotericism. To cite but one, Wouter J. Hanegraaff, in his *Western Esotericism: A Guide for the Perplexed* (2013), devotes a chapter to the concept of knowledge, which he divides into products of reason, faith, and gnosis.[51] He then proceeds to illustrate two characteristics that pertain to all three groups of knowledge that are considered: communicability and testability of the gained knowledge. While scientific knowledge, therefore, is both communicable and testable, and religion is definitely communicable but inevitably not testable, gnosis, or direct access to a higher state of knowledge, is neither transmittable nor testable.[52] The themes of the journal *Atanòr*, then, were those systems, which provided the individual with a personal, unmediated access to "divine" knowledge. The journal did not aim at explaining states of gnosis because it is impossible to do so, yet Reghini, as Hanegraff, one hundred years later, thought of the distinction between science, faith, and Italic Pythagorean gnosis, as a paramount division to present the readers with right from the outset.

Other major articles, which, in my opinion, belonged to this category, were René Guénon's: some of his works, thanks to Reghini's diligent translations, would be printed in Italy even before their publication in France, and such articles constituted the core writings of every issue of *Atanòr*. Besides, having Guénon on board provided the journal with a more universalistic approach to the subject matter, in my opinion, making the journal as a whole more interesting for a wider audience. The first attempts at this can be seen already in the first issue in his "L'Insegnamento Iniziatico" ("Initiatic Teaching," 1924), where Guénon argued that there could be no two identical initiations and no two identical initiates.[53] In his eyes, "the unity and immutability of the principle do not require unity and immutability, which would be impossible to realise, of the exterior forms."[54] In other words, Guénon opened to a plurality of approaches to the sacred, not limited, as in Reghini's case, to the Italic mysteric way. In this way, Guénon was paving the way for a generation of Traditionalists after him, such as Frithjof Schuon (1907–1997), for example, whose first work would be programmatically titled *The Transcendent Unity of Religions* (1952).[55] The other articles by Guénon, already discussed in detail in the previous chapter, are "L'Esoterismo di Dante" ("Dante's Esotericism, 1924") and "Il Re del Mondo" ("The King of the World," 1924).[56] Reghini's contribution was predictably much more specific in its subject matter. His first writing on esoteric subjects was entitled "L'Impronta Pitagorica nella Massoneria" ("Pythagorean Imprint in Freemasonry," 1924).[57] Here Reghini made use of his mastery of both mathematics and Pythagorean philosophy, showing links between states of being, numbers, musical notes, and stages of Masonic initiation. The reading is not of the easiest, but if the editors of the journal wanted to keep the standards of the articles high, then Reghini's first contribution could be considered as a convoluted, but ingenious, introduction to modern neo-Pythagorean theories and their links to the degrees of Freemasonry. Of course, there were more easily approachable writings, such as Aniceto del Massa's "Palingenesi e Reincarnazione" ("Palingenesis and Reincarnation," 1924), in which the contributor went through all the theories of reincarnation in the pre-Socratic West and East, focusing then on Pythagoras's idea on the topic, quoting Aristoxenus (c. 375 BCE–335 fl. BCE):

> For the Pythagoreans, the aim of man is to become similar to God. The key to the Pythagorean system is to follow God [...] The authority of Aristotle allows us to say that Pythagoreans divided rational living things into Gods, men and those similar to Pythagoras.[58]

The article, of course, then quoted the final couplet in Pythagoras's *Golden Verses*, where man is promised immortality: "And when, after having deprived yourself of your mortal body, you arrived at the purest Aither, you shall be a God, immortal, incorruptible, and Death shall have no more dominion over you."[59]

The second section, as explained earlier, dealt with Reghini's turbulent relationship with the Catholic Church and Mussolini's regime. The articles are, most of the time, thinly disguised as esoteric in nature, but more often than not Reghini's lack of subtlety in his invectives gave the game away from the onset. In the third issue of the journal, after pressures by colleagues in the *Schola Italica*, Reghini decided to republish his most famous article, "Imperialismo Pagano" ("Pagan Imperialism," 1924), which was deemed to be very revealing for the current times, even ten years after its first publication.[60] Reghini, nevertheless, did not think a mere republication of the article would be enough and, thus, penned an introduction to the article to make it even more in line with current events. In it, he spared no blows toward the Church: writing about a change of attitude toward modern contraptions in politics and religion, which would favor a spiritual approach, Reghini wrote:

> Neither is such a question without importance even from a political point of view, especially when one talks or thinks about imperial politics, and one may wish to set the country in motion towards a spiritual revolution and not only a mercantile one. And one would be wise to think about this, especially when the official religion, lacking or forgetful of initiatic wisdom, usurps on earth "my empty space" [quotation marks added], as Dante used to say talking about Papacy, leaving Italy and the West, at least as far as appearances go, in a position of spiritual inferiority.[61]

An example of a more direct attack on the Italian Head of State was Reghini's one-page article, "Campidoglio e Golgota" ("Capitol Hill and Golgotha," 1924), in which Mussolini appeared to be dangerously close, in Reghini's eyes, to the ideals of the Catholic Church.[62] While exalting the qualities of ancient Rome and the return of Fascism to such a golden age for Italy, Mussolini pronounced the sentence that incensed Reghini: "*The Capitol Hill,*" he said, "after the Golgotha, *is certainly from centuries back the most sacred [hill] for civilised people.*"[63] Outraged, Reghini had written in response that "we refuse to subordinate the sacred mound of the Capitol Hill to an Asian hillock," remembering how his concept of empire harmonized with names, by now familiar: Vergil, Dante, Frederick II, and Nicholas of Cusa.[64] In "Morale e Peccato" ("Morals and Sin," 1924), the opening article to the sixth issue of *Atanòr*, Reghini launched a full frontal attack against the Church.[65] The crux of the problem, according to Reghini, was that, while under the Pagan creed, many different religions managed to coexist peacefully, Christianity and Judaism were nefarious for a peaceful coexistence between different people:

> The Christian religion, which derives from the Jewish, essentially a *political* one, by changing territory has made itself *apolitical* or *non-political*. While [back] in Rome, the attack on religion meant an attack on the State, in Christian countries, one thinks that the Church may be separate from the State, and this highlights a jealous theory of supremacy over the State.[66]

7.2.2. Ignis

The economic problems plaguing Ciro Alvi and his publishing house put a halt to the publication of *Atanòr*, which, thus, had a lifespan of exactly one year from January to December 1924.[67] Undeterred, Reghini launched another journal in 1925, *Ignis* (Latin for *Fire*), which bore very few differences to *Atanòr*. *Ignis* had fewer collaborators, but this granted Reghini the ability to write the majority of the articles, therefore, proposing a more homogeneous set of writings and sparing him financial expenses that he probably could not afford. In his opening article "Ai Lettori" ("To the Readers," 1925), Reghini explained that only "the title and the postal address" had changed compared to his previous revue, and the new journal was to deal solely with initiatic studies, abandoning the previous focus on politics and religion.[68] If he did keep his word on the first point, the precipitous events in 1925 Italy made sure Reghini would also deal with the two subjects he had declared taboo. Reghini's writings appeared in *Ignis* under his real name and under the pseudonyms *Maximus* and *Il Vicario di Satana* (*Satan's Vicar*), while the few who collaborated included his disciple Giulio Parise, Aniceto del Massa, Julius Evola and, to a lesser degree, René Guénon. Thus, while Reghini did not inquire the link between Pythagoreanism and Freemasonry into any further, he certainly devoted himself to the study and rediscovery of some lesser known alchemists, Masons, and occultists. His studies on Cagliostro or Oswald Crollius (1563–1603), for example, were the first to tackle these figures seriously, in a professional and scholarly way, and these articles, appearing in the early issues, were followed by thorough research on Alexander Seton (1555–1622) and his alleged disciple Michael Sendivogius (1566–1636).[69] Reghini's studies on such figures, just like his detailed research on the works of Agrippa, Bruno, and Campanella, put him in a position that predated scholars like Eugenio Garin and Paul Kristeller, who would only seriously tackle the subject of esotericism nearly two decades later. It is true that Reghini sometimes was prone to emic blunders, which occurred when he tried to link his school to such authors, but overall the rigorousness of Reghini's research in his writings was, at the time, something new, captivating, and appreciated by members of the occult community.[70] Julius Evola, then aged twenty-seven, began to make his mark on the journals of the day, as he contributed to *Ignis* with articles containing his typical dry wit, his remoteness and disdain for what he considered to be lower forms of initiates: the two articles that best represent this phase of Evola's life are the infamous "La Donna come Cosa" ("Woman as a Thing," 1925) and "Che Cosa Vuole l'Antroposofia di Steiner" ("What Steiner's Anthroposophy Wants," 1925).[71] In his first article, his demolition of womanhood is jarring. In the introduction, he states that "her substance is purely negative—not living for herself [. . .], but for the death of perfect life—for the decomposition and impurity—she is contingent to herself."[72] Later, casting aside all philosophical jargon, Evola makes his misogyny clear to all readers:

> Experience shows that only passion has made possible whatever woman employed to elevate herself from an amorphous and obtuse life. The same female mysticism is mostly justifiable with a deviated or repelled sensuality, which explains the fact—noticed by many authors—of the absolute mediocrity (not to say inexistence) of feminine works in domains, such as science, philosophy, the creation of religions etc. etc., which imply a principle of mediation and positive initiative.[73]

In his article on Rudolf Steiner (1861–1925), in the year of the German founder of Anthroposophy's death, Evola is, as usual, scathing: "it is a distortion and flawed understanding of eastern wisdom, made worse, comparing it to theosophy proper [Blavatsky's Theosophy is intended here], on the one hand from Christian prejudice, on the other from what worse there is in the West, that is to say a Positivist-empirical and progressive-humanitarian mentality."[74] For these articles to be published in *Ignis*, they must have certainly have been read by the editor prior to printing. Although it must be said that Reghini himself had specified within his preface to "Ai Lettori," in the first issue, that the editor was only responsible for the general direction the journal would take and not of the content of the contributors' articles.

Halfway through 1925, though, Reghini had to forego his promise not to write about religion or politics. The events, sometimes violent, leading to the Bodrero bill necessitated Reghini's attention. In the June/July double issue, within the rubric *Associazioni Vecchie e Nuove* (*Associations Old and New*), Reghini railed against Mussolini's law of May 16, 1925, against secret societies.[75] Reghini's article was entirely aimed against the Italian Head of State and Bodrero's superficial definition of "Masonic institutions" accused of promoting "a doctrine inspired by a kind of mystic rationalism, which, in itself absurd, is most antithetical one can imagine to the fundamental character of the Italian sentiment and thought."[76] Reghini clarified his position and that of his companions in a long passage worth quoting in full:

> We, imperialists since 1910 (when a lot of people whose name is superfluous to state followed foreign and internationalist ideologies and laughed at the very name imperialism); we who first in Italy in 1912 celebrated the birth of Rome (when many famous hypernationalists of today didn't even know what it meant), we, the very first interventionists, we who went to the front voluntarily, we aristocrats who do not accept the concept of nation for the very reason [of being] imperialists, we always thought that no declaration could absolve those who renounced Italian lands in the name of democracy, in the same way that we cannot applaud so-called nationalists for handing over Italy to the priests.[77]

The target of the article was clearly Mussolini, who had, as we shall see in the section dedicated to Lateran accords, already interacted with Reghini via journalistic diatribes and certainly knew who he was and what he stood for. Mussolini's Socialist past was brought up as a ghost to haunt the Head of State, and the Catholic nationalists like Corradini were not spared vitriolic words. The article, connecting to a previous, already analyzed, publication that appeared in *Atanòr*, was concluded once again with what had become one of Reghini's greatest bones of contention with Mussolini: "And we do not consider the Capitol Hill less glorious than the Golgotha. On the contrary!"[78] Although proceeding with the publication of many articles on esoteric subjects, the final numbers of the journal, from October to December 1925, were more concerned with Italian politics and religion than Reghini had promised when launching the premiere issue. In his article "Eccessi di Parte Guelfa" ("Excesses on Guelfs' Behalf," 1925), Reghini lamented the damage caused to the Masonic temples by anti-Masonic and Fascist sympathizers in the cities of Florence, Rome, and Leghorn.[79] Truly alarmed by the violence, which Reghini was convinced was encouraged by Jesuits and other members of the clergy, he wrote:

The Government, which alarms itself in an exaggerated and unjustified way for the possible interventions of the Masonic hierarchy against that [hierarchy] of the State and a fascist one (which are not and should not be the same thing), could do with looking a bit closer to the consequences to which it is exposed, (and with it the country) by the inference of another hierarchy, more subtle and close, which prefers its confessional interests to the Italian interests since the true leaders are foreign, and the true instigator [the Pope] has an international and markedly anti-Italian character.[80]

The political climate at the end of 1925 had escalated. Tito Zanaboni (1883–1960), a Socialist activist, attempted to assassinate Mussolini with a precision rifle from a hotel overlooking *Palazzo Chigi*, the building where the Fascist government had taken office.[81] The violent actions of the Fascist police escalated, and Reghini soon realized that the December issue of *Ignis* was going to be the last he would edit, for fear of retaliation from the authorities.

7.3. *Ur* and the *Ur* Group: Practical Occultism

7.3.1. The *Ur* Journal (1927–1928)

The year 1926 began with a collaboration among Reghini, his disciple Giulio Parise, and Julius Evola. The anti-Masonic propaganda, and the consequent violence and destruction aimed at the Masonic temples and affiliates, forced Reghini to share his responsibilities as an editor. In a very short time span, *Atanòr* and *Ignis* had been shut down, Freemasonry had been banned, and Reghini's idea of *Imperium* did not attract many sympathies outside of the *Schola*; all the while, Mussolini's regime and the Vatican were slowly, but progressively, getting closer to an agreement that would give back temporal power to the Pope and help Mussolini morally reunite the whole of Italy under the Catholic faith. After long deliberations, the three decided to start a new journal and name it *Ur*, where Arturo Reghini would be the secret gray eminence, Evola would take care of the political and administrative side of things, and Parise, the wealthiest of the three, would be Secretary and Treasurer.[82] The first issue of *Ur: Rivista di Indirizzi di una Scienza per l'Io* (*Ur: Journal of Orientations Towards a Science for the I*) was published in January 1927. The contributors to the journal came from the most disparate esoteric backgrounds, and, for the sake of convenience, they have been categorized into three main groups by researcher Renato del Ponte: first, even at an editorial level, the Pythagoreans Reghini and Parise, joined by Aniceto del Massa, represented a strong presence within the multifaceted currents of the contributors. The idea of writing under pseudonyms in order for the texts not to be judged by readers' personal biases toward individual authors followed a strictly Pythagorean tradition, and all seemed to accept the idea happily. Thus, Reghini wrote as Pietro Negri or Henìocos Àristos, Parise as Luce, and del Massa as Sagittario. Evola appeared under many different guises, Agarda, Arvo, Ea, and Iagla, and even other anonymous articles that have been accredited to him by del Ponte, Gianfranco de Turris, and Hans Thomas Hakl.[83] The second group, quite surprisingly, given Evola's opinion on Steiner, were the Antroposophists: Giovanni Colazza as Leo, poet Arturo Onofri (1885-1928) as Oso, and Corrado Reginelli (1905-?) as Taurulus. The third biggest influence came from the Kremmerzian milieu, especially through the contributions of Ercole Quadrelli (n.d.). However, it is important to note that, as for *Atanòr* and *Ignis*, a contribution could be submitted by men only. As Hakl explains, "[t]he reasoning behind this was very simple: esoterically [according to the editorial board], only men are bound with the 'sky' and, thus, with transcendence; whereas women are bound to the earth. Just as a man is responsible for spiritual 'fertility,' a woman is responsible for earthly fertility."[84]

In its first editorial, the character of *Ur* is clearly stated as: "initiatic, hierarchical, traditional, Western, and elitist."[85] Del Ponte conveniently divides the subject matter of the articles into four major groups. First, there were those referring to "esoteric doctrine and culture," which delved into practical methods and symbology of esoteric practice; second, there were articles devoted to "practice" and to the narration of personal experiences in practicing magic; third, we can circumscribe a group of articles dealing with the "editing or translation of classic or rare esoteric texts"; and fourth, there were articles devoted to "doctrinal synthetic overviews" of various esoteric traditions.[86] The Pythagoreans, headed by Reghini, contributed to all of the aforementioned sections, and some of Reghini's articles are worthy of being analyzed more scrupulously. In his "Della Tradizione Occidentale" ("On the Western Tradition," 1928), Reghini synthesized the main arguments that constituted his main theories regarding the existence of a Tradition in the West. According to him, Paganism had been devalued because of the increasing, and finally totalising, influence of the Church on European history through the centuries.[87] In his writings, Reghini opposed "1) the Western character of Christianity; 2) the Christian character of the Western initiatic tradition."[88] Reghini's erudition on a cultural level has been attested to throughout this book, and not much more needs to be said about it or about his ideas on matters of religion and politics. Reghini's *Ur* contributions shone when they provided the reader with hands-on instructions for the practice of magic and personal experiences while practicing it. Here, we can glean more about the nature of the rituals employed by Reghini, as in the short article "Avventure e Disavventure in Magia" ("Adventures and Misadventures in Magic," 1927). In this article, Reghini describes all the practicalities of actually performing a ritual: having narrated his trip to a subterranean vault at three in the morning, Reghini describes the rest of his evening, the matches dampened by humidity, his having to kneel and crawl in order to get to the ritual vault:

> I grab the sword according to the ritual, wear my glasses, use my left [hand] to hold a roll of paper prepared for the occasion in order to unravel it with one hand and read the long invocation written on it, I turn eastwards, poise the sword in the direction of the sign of the operation and well aware of what I am doing, I begin to say slowly and loudly: "Greatest power of every power" [. . .] I gladly notice that the lamplight allows me to read the words of the invocation and that everything is proceeding. But what now? What is this wind? Why does it pick up now to sway the flames and disturb my reading!? And what now? I can't see anymore! For all the Gods of Olympus, my glasses clouded over![89]

This article, in some parts amusing, was actually an important presence in the journal for it attested to practical workings and made clear that the purpose of *Ur* was not that of satisfying armchair magicians, but that it wanted to inspire the few people it could captivate to practice magic and work toward transcendence. This raises the questions: given the nature of this, and other important articles in the two years of publication of the journal, did its contributors practice magic together? And if so, of what nature?

7.3.2. The *Ur* Group and the Break with Evola

Despite the multitude of articles being dismissed as a "hodgepodge collection," members of what was called the *Ur* Group definitely practiced the magic they wrote about.[90] The ultimate goal was "the realisation of oneself, and, in itself, of Existence. This, or nothing."[91] This was the reason the contributors to the journal scoured every text on traditional knowledge they could find: "ancient theurgical texts as well as hermetical and alchemical works of the Middle Ages and the early modern era. The teachings of yoga, tantra, Taoism and Buddhism were likewise studied."[92] Both Hakl and del Ponte agree in stating that the magic that was practiced by the members of the *Ur* Group was not of a ceremonial type, or certainly not only of a ceremonial nature: "Ur strove to 'High Magic,' which can be described as 'practical metaphysics' with the goal of self-deification."[93] We are thus very far from the aims of the Masonic and occult orders of the day, and it was the Group's end game, along with its peculiar brand of "practical metaphysics," which makes this coterie stand out even to this day.

Beyond the experiences of the larger group of collaborators to the *Ur* Group, there was also an inner circle of those who wanted to achieve bigger goals. The members of this inner group were very few, consisting, in Rome, of Evola, Reghini, Parise, Quadrelli, and Colazza.[94] The aim for this Group's magic rituals was that of creating an *egregore*, a collective mass of psychic force, which could attract other higher energies to it. In more simple words, the group rituals were enacted in order to raise an energy powerful enough to influence not only the individual's development, but that of the world at large, and, in particular, of the political situation of the day, which saw Mussolini steadily drifting away from Roman imperialist ideas, drawing closer and closer to a pact with the Vatican.[95] As Evola writes in his memoires:

> There was a more ambitious objective that an influence from above, through evocation, could be formed over the kind of psychic body that we wanted to create. In such a case, we wouldn't have excluded the possibility to exert, behind the scenes, an action even on the predominant forces in the general world of the day. As to the direction of such action, the main points of reference would have been more or less those of "Imperialismo Pagano" and of the "Roman" ideals of Arturo Reghini.[96]

The Imperialismo Pagano (Pagan Imperialism, 1928) mentioned by Evola was not the oft-quoted article by Reghini, published in 1914 and republished in 1924, but a new book written by Evola and published in 1928.[97] The publication of this work was the beginning of the rift that was going to separate the Pythagoreans and Evola forever. Other accidents had marred the relationship between the two members of the *Schola* and Evola, such as the Masonic connection of Parise and Reghini, which Evola had always criticized as only being a bourgeois pursuit; Parise's affair with Sibilla Aleramo and the publication of her *Amo dunque Sono* had only exacerbated Evola's problematic relationship with Parise. For a while, Evola produced articles on various journals slandering both Aleramo and Parise until Parise decided to settle scores via a fist fight, in which Evola allegedly ended up bruised and battered.[98] However, the tipping point was the publication of Evola's new book, which plagiarized not only the title of Reghini's article but also, according to the Florentine occultist, the contents and ideas contained therein.[99] The three editors ended the *Ur* experience with the 1928 December issue. In 1929, Reghini and Parise launched a new version of *Ignis*, but due to financial problems, the new journal never went past the first issue. A lawsuit followed, and the attention gained by Reghini made it so that his name was put on the list the secret police were to gather information on and to follow. The numerous articles by Evola, denouncing Reghini as a Freemason, also made Reghini *persona non grata* to the government. In the end, Reghini won the lawsuit, and Evola had to publish a letter of apology in the *Roma Fascista* (*Fascist Rome*, est. 1924) paper, but the damage to his reputation had been made.[100] Bigger problems seemed to loom over the Pagan imperialists' heads, though, as Mussolini and the Vatican were always closer to a collaboration, which would represent the end of Reghini's Pagan dream.

8
Silentium Post Clamores (1930–1946)

Therefore, I believe in the one that contains all,
motion, strength, intelligence, good, love and death.
I believe in the ascension of man to the infinite one,
in the universal law of all that was, is and eternally will be.

—Giuliano Kremmerz[1]

8.1. Troubles in the Capital: 1929–1938

Even though Reghini had won the legal battle against Julius Evola, who had been forced to write a formal apology on a national paper, his employment opportunities had suffered a serious blow:[2] after all, the idea of employing an ex Freemason and Pagan imperialist would have been a daunting one for any high school headmaster looking for a simple mathematics teacher.

In November 1926, he had obtained a temporary job as a substitute at the "Leonardo da Vinci" Technical Institute, but his job was pending on Reghini's promise that he would not engage in any activity that could upset the political status quo of the day.[3] For the meagre sum of 475 lire a month, Reghini reluctantly agreed, and on a surface level, complied to the restrictions imposed upon him, as we can surmise from a letter to Armentano dating November 2, 1926: "to avoid any possible trouble I also had to stop any form of activity in other fields."[4] The year 1927, therefore, was dedicated to something that Reghini had always put on the backburner for his entire life: his professional career and his financial wellbeing. With his master on the other side of the ocean, and his other close friends keeping a low profile for the same reasons as his, Reghini would not have had any chance of receiving financial help, had he lost this job, too. In a very brief period of time, Reghini had established himself as a successful and charismatic teacher, both among his pupils and his colleagues. In his biographical "Nota," Parise had vouched for Reghini's success, writing that "his high value, the knowledge of the subject and [his] didactic method had made him rank amongst the very first, when it came to the esteem of his pupils, of his peers, of scientists."[5] Toward the end of the year Reghini moved to a bigger flat the very central Via del Teatro Valle 71, and when printing his new letter headed paper he had added a new title next to his name: "doctor in mathematics."[6]

Occult Imperium. Christian Giudice, Oxford University Press. © Oxford University Press 2022.
DOI: 10.1093/oso/9780197610244.003.0008

Even though he wrote all of his articles for *Ur* under the pseudonym of Pietro Negri, the agents in OVRA, (Organizzazione per la Vigilanza e la Repressione dell'Antifascismo, Organization for Vigilance and Repression of Anti-Fascism, est. 1927), whose job it was to keep a keen eye on publications of dubious affiliation to Mussolini's movement, had identified Reghini's caustic style and dry wit. Father Pietro Tacchi Venturi (1861–1956), a Jesuit priest of high influence who was very close to Mussolini, had included Reghini as the first name on a long list of dissidents he wanted Mussolini to banish from Italian soil.[7] Mussolini's response will not come as a shock to the reader, after we have disentangled ten years of fiery, but honest relationship between the Duce and Reghini, as the latter wrote to Armentano in late 1927:

> From what I was told, Mussolini is said to have shouted: No, I know this imperialist. [...] As you can see, we can't say that the pioneers of imperialism have not collected the fruits [of their labor]. You will say that they're small things, and I'll reply that I am happy enough.[8]

Such an endorsement from Mussolini allowed Reghini to live in relative tranquility for the beginning of 1928, and his major plans in the first half of the year had been to organize his annual retreat to the Torre Talao in Scalea, in order to write the final section of his article series on the Western Tradition published in *Ur*, for which, Sestito, warns us, "simple erudition alone was not sufficient."[9] After the *debacle* of his collaboration with Evola and the court case that dragged on until 1929, Armentano explicitly invited Reghini to move to Sao Paulo and live with him and his family. In December 1929 the Concordat had been signed, Reghini's professional career did not seem to thrive as he had hoped, and there was very little time left for him to devote to his esoteric endeavors. In order to fully appreciate the reasons behind Reghini's refusal to leave Italy, Reghini's last letter to Armentano written from Rome must be quoted extensively:

> As to my trip to Brazil I am convinced that I would benefit from it completely since here one breaks his back to earn the strict necessary. But there are two reasons that will probably keep me here; one is my mother to whom I would give a disappointment that she could definitely not be able to bare and in no way would I want the blame to have killed her; and the other is that in spite of all the wars and hardships and in spite of the incredible triumphs of the enemies of romanity, I hope and think that there is still some work to do; and since up to now I haven't switched allegiance nor have I abandoned the camp, I wish to proceed in the same manner until it will be impossible for me to live in Rome.[10]

In the beginning of 1930, we find Reghini deciding to definitely cut any ties with his Masonic past and downsizing his circle of friends considerably. His communications with Armentano, now permanently living in Sao Paulo, Brazil, became more and more difficult since the Fascist secret police had opened a permanent file on him and monitored his movements and correspondence constantly.[11] The few letters that he did send to Armentano would be redirected to the exiled master from Bianchini and Mori, who had been less involved in Masonic endeavors in the 1910s and 1920s, and thus benefited from more relaxed supervision by the secret police. Reghini's adherence to Fascism never seemed in doubt, although his ideas were considered by informants and agents to be problematic, and his morality, and that of Armentano, was often questioned: "the Head of Government may absolutely believe to use these people for immediate gains, but it is not a useless endeavour to tell you that we are talking about men without scruples who parade their disgust for moral laws, who obey secular sectarian [i.e., Masonic] goals [. . .]."[12] Reghini's ideas, in the end, were considered impractical and slightly eccentric, the same informant concluding with a critique of "unattainable things in this historical period (for example the evaluation of Pagan myths as facts)."[13] It is, therefore, certain that Mussolini and the secret police knew, albeit in a confused manner, of the aims of the *Schola Italica* and the first quote showed that the possibility of using the neo-Ghibelline contingent was real, had the Vatican exaggerated on their post-Concordat demands.

The relationship between the Vatican and Fascism was even more consolidated in the 1930s, making the members of the *Schola Italica*, who had until then entertained a modicum of freedom, expendable. It has recently been discovered that Vittorio Falorsi (n.d.) and Amerigo Bianchini (n.d.), two of Reghini's few remaining friends, were informants to Mussolini's secret police: Reghini had briefly shared a flat in Rome with Bianchini.[14] Despite such changes in the political scene, Reghini still believed in the possibility of a Traditionalist alliance with the regime, and in 1933, for the first time, he became a card-carrying member of the *Partito Nazionale Fascista*.[15] Even though we are, therefore, certain of Reghini's seemingly privileged status under the regime, most of the time spent in Rome during the 1930s saw the Florentine thinker moving from school to school, teaching algebra and trying to make ends meet.[16] The break with Evola had had repercussions on his career as a teacher, and Reghini found it increasingly difficult to find a position as a teacher in Roman state schools. In Parise's famous biographical note, we find a slice of life of what the Pythagoreans remaining in Rome did to pass the time:

> We played chess, we reasoned on the political ills of the day, but mostly we talked about what was closest to our hearts: of the possibility, still very far away, but certain, of better future forms of civic life, of a return of Freemasonry.[17]

Like di Luca, I am inclined to think that, even though working in total secrecy, Reghini still had a Pythagorean nucleus gravitating around him, a group of people who still met and practiced the *Schola*'s rituals.[18] In Aniceto del Massa's *Pagine Esoteriche*, a diary of the Anthroposophist's interactions with the occult, we find a very telling passage that corroborates this hypothesis:

> This evening [July 25, 1933] Reghini was here, in my studio [. . .] When I go to Rome, I hope to be admitted to the experiences that take place in a circle headed by him and about which he briefly spoke to me.[19]

During the 1930s, although Reghini's life appeared to be more simple and uneventful, ill health plagued him throughout the decade: he suffered from two severe pneumonias, which kept him bedridden for months, and toward the end of the 1930s, while on a trip to Florence, he fell and broke his arm, and, due to a prolonged convalescence, he lost the job at the lyceum where he was teaching.[20] One aspect of his life that really benefited from his relative lack of interest in politics and Freemasonry was his literary output. The first work that Reghini managed to publish in a relatively obscure journal was a small article titled "Il Fascio Littorio" (The *Lictoriae* Fasces, 1934).[21] This brief article was soon followed by a more lengthy study on Geometry and Pythagoreanism by the title of *Per la Restituzione della Geometria Pitagorica* (*For the Restitution of Pythagorean Geometry*, 1935).[22] The final work, definitely his magnum opus in the realm of mathematics, was *Dei Numeri Pitagorici: Libri Sette* (*On Pythagorean Numbers: Seven Volumes*, 1936–1944) and took Reghini eight years to complete and was never published in his lifetime.[23] It was bequeathed to his friend Moretto Mori, who in turned left it to his sons. Since 1991, through a joint effort by publishing houses *Ignis* and *Arché*, the work has been slowly published. The mathematical volumes, while solving arithmetical conundrums, which had remained irresolvable for centuries, are beyond the scope of this volume, but the prologue, which Reghini uses to embed his whole work into a philosophical and occult substratum, will be scrutinized in the next subchapter.

8.2. Reghini's Works in the 1930s and 1940s

8.2.1. "Il Fascio Littorio" (1934)

Reghini's first published article in the 1930s was titled "Il Fascio Littorio" and represented a very detailed analysis on the occult qualities of the fasces employed as a symbol of the Fascist Regime.[24] The chosen subject was in line with his renewed interest in Fascism and his request to join the party in 1933. In the study of the fasces, it is Reghini's intent to underline "the traditional and occult value of the glorious lictoriae fasces."[25] The twelve rods that compose the bundle of reeds from which the fasces are made, along with the twelve carriers of the fasces in ancient Rome,[26] suggested, to Reghini, a connection with the magic and religion of ancient people, and, therefore, the presence of a symbol handed down from antiquity, representing a link between ancient Rome and the Fascist regime.[27] The whole article is devoted to two subjects: the mathematical link of the fasces to Roman and Etruscan tradition to the number twelve and the consequent imperial and universal value of said fasces, which did not pair as well with the Vatican as it did with the autochthone Roman Tradition:

> [I am] very happy to see the lictoriae fasces being honoured again, which we venerate deeply, with Pagan spirit, immune from exotic infections, we hope their fate will be favourable; we hope for an ever more conscious and deep return to romanity, in all respects, without submitting the fasces to adverse or different influences.[28]

The article, at a first glance, seems to be simply an archeological and philological reconstruction of an ancient tool, which had been used since the Etruscans had reigned in central Italy, but by now the reader will easily be able to spot certain subtexts, which point subtly to the Italic Tradition and to Reghini's and Armentano's *Schola*.

As we have seen in previous chapters, Reghini and other authors had pushed for an Etruscan origin for Pythagoras, who had then imparted his knowledge on King Numa, thus creating the first link in the chain perpetuated through the ages by the *Schola Italica*.[29] Historian and author Massimiliano Vittori shed more details on what the fasces actually looked like:

> The fascis was composed by 12 reeds of elm or birch, 150 cm long, held together by red leather strips (symbol of courage and love), on top of which an ax head was inserted, on its side or on top of it. It was carried on the left shoulder by the lictors (lat. *lictor*, maybe from *licére*, "to sue"), who were subordinate officials at the service of Roman magistrates or some priests.[30]

Vittori also added another consideration, which no doubt Reghini was aware of, as we shall see: he extended the use of the fasces to other "similar peoples and civilizations, marked by the same symbols and cults. It is the case of the Cretan-Micenean or Pre-Hellenic civilization, which had Crete as its center before the year 1000 BC."[31] Reghini himself mentioned this tie with other ancient civilizations and a common use of the fasces, agreeing with ancient Latin author Silius Italicus (25–101) and writing that "Vetulonia [an ancient Etruscan city] was at one point home to the Meonian people (that is, from Lidia): it was the first city to let the 12 fasces march forth and to attach to them, with silent terror, the same number of axe heads."[32] Later on in this article, Reghini claimed that the number twelve appeared so many times in Roman and Etruscan culture, including in sacred or traditional aspects, that "it is necessary to find a determination of a deeper reason and of a less contingent nature even when explaining its presence in the lictoriae fasces."[33] In his attempt to tie the political significance to the spiritual, and even magical dimension, Reghini went back to the sources he was most familiar with: the supposed links in the chain of the *Schola Italica*'s tradition. In order to justify his subsequent statement, he quoted Giambattista Vico and his *Principi di Scienza Nuova* (*Principles of New Sience*, 1725), when he wrote that the fathers of the Etruscan people "with such staffs, having received the omens, that they may command them, inflicted punishments to their sons."[34] Reghini saw in this statement the threefold nature of the augural Estruscan staff: the symbol of the commander, the symbol of lawmaker, and the symbol of the augur, or magician. In summing up the fasces' power, Reghini added that "it is not strange that the king's staff was at the same time the royal sceptre, the cane of justice, and the magical lituus or wand."[35]

The author then analyzed the more spiritual essence of the number twelve, and it is in this section that Reghini's vast knowledge of the traditions and religious customs of many civilizations really shines: by choosing the Etruscan people as a point of departure, he claimed that the symbol of the Etruscan people was the Dodekapolis, or confederation of twelve cities, which had existed since the beginning of Etruscan civilization: he then quotes Livy (59 BCE–17 CE) writing that "Etruria is a religious nation par excellence" and links the twelve cities of the Etruscan confederation to the main pantheon of Etruscan gods, made of twelve deities.[36] The Roman gods had very similar characteristics to the Etruscan gods, and the main group of deities consisted of twelve individuals, as did the gods of Ancient Greece, which, according to Herodotus, had been influenced by the twelve main divinities of Egypt.[37] He then followed Diodorus Siculus (91 BCE–30 ca. BCE) in linking the Chaldean-Babylonian pantheon, constituted by twelve major deities, with the twelve signs of the zodiac and the twelve months of the year.[38] As if trying to find a universal trait in the tradition of the religious use of the number twelve, Reghini also noted that there were several different Eastern countries, which had adopted twelve months for their calendar:

> China, Japan, Siam use a lunar calendar of twelve months and a lunar-solar calendar with a thirteenth lunation. A savage East-African tribe, the *kikuyos*, divide the year in twelve parts too. In India, finally, we find the twelve *adityas*, forms and emblems of the sun for every month of the year, that Hindu mythology reports as generated by Aditi and Casyapa [. . .]. The correspondence

between the 12 Hindu *adityas* and the 12 main gods of the Roman-Greek-Etruscan pantheon is evident.[39]

This is Reghini at his best: combining his great knowledge of the Italic classics and his expertise in Eastern religions and traditions acquired during his activity within the Theosophical Society, the author managed to weave a tapestry that, as René Guénon and other Traditionalists after him were wont to do, tied together disparate notions and wove them in a coherent whole.

The last couple of pages of "Il Fascio" tried to drive the point through even more intensely: moving back to ancient Rome, Reghini listed other sacred institutions tied to the number twelve: the Arval Brethren, a body of priests who offered annual sacrifices to the gods in exchange for bountiful harvests were twelve in number, as were the Salii, or "leaping priests," who were always constituted by twelve patrician youths, once a year would walk around the perimeter of Rome singing the archaic *Carmen Saliare* (eighth century BCE), which was already considered outdated by Ovid.[40] In the ancient myth, Romulus had seen twelve vultures fly above him during the foundation of Rome, and twelve was the number of the *duodecim tabulae*, or twelve Tables that formed the core of Roman law. All these aspects, wrote Reghini, "are facts and elements of the greatest importance, and the fact that twelve was the number of the *lictorii* that preceded kings and consuls cannot be considered in isolation, but must be evidently framed within this consideration and veneration for the number twelve that may be found in the very origin of foundation of Rome."[41] Reghini concluded the article with a very brief foray into hermeticism, claiming that the number twelve could be found in the *12 Gates* (1471) by George Ripley (d. 1490), the *12 Keys* (1599) of Basil Valentine (1394–1450), and the twelve tracts of the *De Lapide Philosophorum* (1604) attributed to Andreas Libavius (1555–1616) or Michael Sendovigius (1566–1636).[42] "Il Fascio" was published in one of the innumerable journals of the day, and we cannot expect it to have created the stir that "Imperialismo Pagano" had caused in 1913 and 1924, both because of the subject matter and because of the time in which it was published. Neglected by many critics, I find it to be a fundamental writing in the corpus of Reghini's writings, since it shows without a doubt that the Florentine thinker, while not being involved in any official occult group activity, still held the same ideas of an Italic Tradition, symbolized, in this article, by the emblem of the Fascist regime. The fasces had also been employed during the *Risorgimento* as a symbol of national unity by Mazzini and other patriots, whom Reghini, as we know, considered to be the torchbearers of the Italic Tradition in the nineteenth century.[43] One of the few people who lauded Reghini for this brief article was his long-time friend René Guénon, who had most certainly received it by Reghini himself: in the May 1935 issue of the French journal *Le Voile d'Isis*, Guénon reviewed it favorably, focusing on the idea of the connection between the twelve deities and the signs of the zodiac.[44]

8.2.2. *Per La Restituzione Della Geometria Pitagorica* (1935)

As we have already seen, from 1930 onward Reghini lived in Rome and worked as a mathematics teacher, dedicating most of his time to activities related to his job and trying to elude the attentions of the Fascist secret police, who still observed his every action.[45] As noted earlier, Bianchini and Falorsi collaborated with the Fascist police and promised to keep an eye on Reghini's activity, but the fact that they helped him send his letters to Armentano undetected, more than once, attests to the fact that his two friends protected the math teacher from OVRA rather than posing a real threat.[46] In 1935, Reghini finished writing his first mathematical tract, to which he gave the title of *Per la Restituzione della Geometria Pitagorica*: lacking the funds to publish it himself, Reghini sought Parise's help, who created the Casa Editrice IGNIS (Ignis Publishing House, est. 1935) for the sole publication of the volume.[47] The publication, though distributed in a very limited edition, garnered the praise of the academic milieu of the day, and the *Reale Accademia d'Italia* (*Royal Italian Academy*, est. 1929) paid homage to the author by awarding him a prestigious literary prize.[48] Members of the *Accademia* included literary giants of the day, such as Luigi Pirandello (1867–1936) and Gabriele d'Annunzio, as well as world-renowned scientists such as Enrico Fermi (1901–1954) and Guglielmo Marconi (1874–1937), both Nobel Prize winners for the contribution in the field in applied physics. His old friends from the Florentine *scapigliatura* Giovanni Papini and Ardengo Soffici were members of the committee, too.[49]

Per la Restituzione is not an easy read: one should really be an expert in mathematics, philosophy, Euclidean geometry, and ancient history, in order to appreciate Reghini's genius in full. It is, for all purposes, a reappraisal of Pythagorean mathematics applied to Euclidean geometry, and it is easy for the neophyte to lose himself in the plethora of complex formulas and the overabundance of triangles, squares, and other geometric shapes. In order to elucidate the point further, one only needs to look at the chapter titles: "Il Teorema di Pitagora" ("Pythagoras's Theorem"), "I Poliedri Regolari" ("Regular Polyhedrons"), or "Dimostrazione del Postulato di Euclide" ("Demonstration of Euclid's Postulate").[50] A quote will suffice to prove the impenetrable nature of the work:

> Let AH be the height of an ABC right triangle, and let m, n be the projections CH and HB of the two legs. By indicating for mere convenience, rectangles

and squares with modern notations (but without introducing with them the concepts of proportion and measures), from our ABC triangle we have:

$$m^2 + h^2 = b^2$$

And thus:
$$m^2 + h^2 + c^2 = b^2 + c^2$$

On the other hand:
$$a = m + n$$

So that:
$$m^2 + n^2 + 2mn = a^2$$

But
$$b^2 + c^2 = a^2$$

So also:
$$m^2 + h^2 + c^2 = m^2 + n^2 + 2mn$$

Luckily, not all of the book is as hard to follow as most parts are, and Reghini's passion for the philosophical and hermetic aspects of Pythagoreanism shines through in some sections. In the chapter dedicated to the Pythagorean symbol par excellence, the pentalpha, or five-pointed star, Reghini wrote that "not all the reasons for which the pentalpha was chosen as a symbol of our School are geometrical in nature," and he goes on to add that the reason must have been much deeper, "given the connection between geometry, the other sciences and Pythagorean cosmology."[51] Toward the end of the same chapter, Reghini connected the pentalpha as a symbol of salvation and immortality, "that salvation and privileged survival pointed at in the last of the 'Golden Verses' [of Pythagoras]."[52] Here the author is basically trying to provide a mathematical foundation to the doctrine of immortality, or pure life after death. Not a small feat for a mathematical treaty! Reghini continued:

> This ancient Pythagorean symbol crops up here and there in the Western esoteric tradition, often designated as "Pythagoras's shape." Sometimes in its centre we find the letter G inscribed, the initial for Geometry, for example in the flaming Star of a well-known Western Order [i.e., Freemasonry] that has as its aim the perfection of man, that is literally, the *teleté* of the mysteries.[53]

The chapter ends with Reghini summing up the core teaching of his 1930s writings: "we'll only say [. . .] that the pentalpha and the *lictoriae* fasces (between which there are more than a few ties) are the only important truly spiritual Western symbols. The rest, for good or bad, comes from the East."[54] These comments, well-hidden between pages and pages of calculus, show that, to

Reghini, the Italic Tradition and its survival still mattered, and if we are to believe Aniceto del Massa in his *Pagine Esoteriche* (*Esoteric Pages*, 2001), there were still some activities of the *Schola*.

Writing something as complex as *Per la Restituzione* was not just a scientific endeavor that kept Reghini occupied during his spare time during his teaching years in Rome: it was a true attempt at a "restitution" of the Pythagorean tradition to a place of prominence and of dignity within the cultural milieu of the day. Writing about the *lictoriae* fasces and the pentalpha did not only involve Reghini's mathematical genius or his encyclopedic occult knowledge: it was a way to reify and ground his esoteric theories on the power of certain primordial symbols and ideas of which he was one of the last repositories. Writing about the pentalpha and the fasces was a way of showing Guénon and all of his followers that an autochtone esoteric Tradition had resisted in the West, and it had nothing to do with Eastern influences. It had been there since time immemorial, at least from the time in which Pythagoras had allegedly taught King Numa Pompilius, and manifested itself through rituals, which Reghini and his friends performed at the Torre Talao, first, and in Rome, at a later date, and through doctrinal teachings that Reghini made available through writings such as "Imperialismo Pagano," "La Tradizione Occidentale," "Il Fascio Littorio," and *Per la Restituzione della Geometria Pitagorica*.

8.2.3. *Dei Numrti Pitagorici* (1936–1944)

In 1936, in a state of prolonged hardship imposed by his chronic lack of money and ill health, Reghini began writing what is today considered his magnum opus, if only for the sheer scope of the work, which spanned the length of seven volumes. His *Dei Numeri Pitagorici* is a work of pure mathematics, introduced by a lengthy prologue, in which the author tried to connect the abstract nature of his oeuvre with the subjects of philosophy, occultism, and Italic Tradition. But it would be a mistake to consider *Dei Numeri Pitagorici* anything other than a mathematical treaty of incredible breadth and scope. Roberto Sestito writes:

> The Reghini *doctor mathematicus*[55] that we want to remember is obviously the author of "Dei Numeri Pitagorici" and not the indefatigable professor who earned his living with difficulty teaching algebra and equations in the schools of Rome. It is that mysterious Archimedes who perplexed his friends who had convened with him for the spiritual retreats at the Torre Talao when they saw him alone, with an abacus in his hand, sitting on the shores of the Tyrrenian Sea immersed in calculations and in geometrical patterns.

SILENTIUM POST CLAMORES (1930–1946)   173

This passage is quite revealing, in that it hints at the fact that some of the ideas taught to him by Armentano could only be grasped through the aid of a more rational, mathematical mind. We are reminded of Parise, who, in his "Ricordo di Arturo Reghini" had noted how "the last fifteen years were devoted to a prevalently scientific activity, which tried to restore the values and research methods of the Scuola Italica."[56] We know a lot about the values of the *Schola*, and have written about them throughout this book, but, what the research methods so closely linked to mathematics could be can only be speculated upon: about this topic, Sestito writes:

> We must believe, according to what his friends wrote about him, that he devoted himself to the "research of numbers" avoiding the interference of unrelated people; it would be easy to attribute the observance to such jealous discretion to his "esoteric" personality or his natural coyness, but it was through the science of numbers that he grasped some of those never-revealed secrets of the ancient Scuola Italica and that because of their ineffable quality remained buried deep within his soul.[57]

Dei Numeri Pitagorici was a mathematical treatise just like *Per La Restituzione* was: in it Reghini proved to have found a simple method to solve every indeterminate second-degree standard equation with two-integer variables, a problem that had stumped previous mathematicians such as Joseph-Louis Lagrange (1736–1813), the founder of the calculus of variations, who had found a method of maximizing and minimizing functionals in a way similar to finding extrema of functions in the field of mathematics and number theory.[58] Given the remoteness of the subject matter from the text at hand, I will only be analyzing the *Prologo* (*Prologue*, 1936–1944), the 120-page-long first volume of his work, which Reghini had written to introduce the lay reader to the insidiously abstract topic of the rest of the book. About the *Prologo*, Reghini had written to his friend Moretto Mori, in 1942:

> [It is] a prologue of a philosophical and cultural character where the subject of Pythagorean arithmetic is embedded into Pythagoreanism in general [...]. It cost me two years of work, and I don't really care about others' judgement on the matter since I know nobody who can give one considering all the aspects does not exist apart from, maybe, Guénon.[59]

Reghini was obviously conscious of the impenetrable nature of the text that had taken him eight years to write, and the necessity of an introduction that would in some way help *Dei Numeri* sit coherently with the rest of his writings was most certainly just as evident. The lengthy prologue covered a startling array of subjects, from the concept of Pythagorean triad in the spoken language to a theoretical approach to the generation of numbers; from the alphabetical system of written numeration to the Pythagorean idea of the perfection of the number three. For convenience, I have decided to focus on three main topics, which the author wove throughout the introduction as a way to familiarize the reader with the complex topic ahead: first, I will be analyzing Reghini's idea of the Pythagorean triad; second, the presence of Pythagorean numbers in the sciences and the arts; finally, I will be tackling the topic of the Pythagorean technique of anamnesis, which, in my opinion, was central to the teachings of the *Schola Italica*. These three subjects are not chosen arbitrarily, but because they are the ones that have most connections to the neo-Pythagorean knowledge shared by members of the *Schola*, and because, in a way, by writing about these specific topics, Reghini comes full circle in his exposition of the ancient Roman Tradition of which he was one of the last representatives.

When tackling the issue of the Pythagorean triad, Reghini provided the reader with the theory of the inhabitants of Kroton descending from the Dorians, who were described by Homer as τριχάϊκες, divided into three, and were actually separated into three distinct tribes.[60] When looking for the special place held by the number three in Pythagorean doctrines, Reghini pointed to a more metaphysical answer, though:

> The intervention of another more important influence, proper to the genius of the school, that is the immediate, spiritual recognition of the great universal law of the ternary, of which the reflection and the manifestation in language and in magic, seems to us a plausible and natural [explanation].[61]

Reghini continued writing his metaphysical argumentations, implying that "the existence of a Pythagorean esotericism" should not be discounted and how they were the first among men to be called philosophers, or lovers of knowledge.[62] When describing the initiators of the Italic Tradition that he felt he represented, he went to great lengths to convince the reader that the first Pythagoreans had used every method possible to attain a specific kind of knowledge "which modern science ignores or abhors."[63] This idea, that of a knowledge higher than that of science or religion, is a concept that Reghini had held dear since his first meetings with Armentano and is still expressed with passion, thirty-five years later: this is the very idea that had caused him to grow disillusioned with Theosophy and other occult movements of the day. The Theosophical pursuit to unite science and religion under one banner appeared ludicrous, once Reghini had realized that the ultimate Truths were above both. And in this invective against modern science, he is quick to indicate these ways to knowledge that science spurns: "intuition, aesthetic sense, anamnesis, inner experience and the practices of the mysteries."[64] In the same chapter, he criticizes ancient Greek scholars and historians such as Paul Antoine Meillet (1866–1936) and Abel Rey (1873–1940), who accused Pythagoras's imposition of strict rules in his circles to be the same sort of moralism which the philosopher supposedly manifested.[65] To this Reghini argued that this supposed moralism of the Pythagoreans was not a hodgepodge of "sentimental residues, of hardened beliefs and sexual taboos."[66] "The moralism of the Pythagoreans," Reghini admonished, "is nothing else than an esoteric spiritual technique":[67] their self-imposed dietary restrictions and their bizarre customs, of which that of abstaining from fava beans being the most infamous, are not a form of religiosity, but the path toward the attainment of immortality, which, as we have seen earlier, the *Golden Verses* point to in their final lines. Reghini quoted the neo-Platonic philosophers Iamblichus (245–325) and Prophyry (233–305), who considered the ultimate goal of man that of reaching the gods.[68] Reghini also made clear that Greek religion per se did not concern itself with any eschatological preoccupation, but that such a grave matter was left to the Orphic, Pythagorean, and Eleusinian mysteries: "Orphism made [the mysteries] the object of religious practices, and provided its dead with a 'viaticum,' Pythagoreanism used them as objects of experience and spiritual exercise to lead their living to palingenesis."[69] At the end of this train of thought, Reghini concluded with what I believe to be the most clear exposition of what the goals of the *Schola Italica* were, put in plain language for all to read:

> Reacting against all that is vaguely redolent of initiatic or esoteric and confining itself in the position one entrenches and defends oneself, [that is,] Western modern thought, one necessarily dooms himself to an incomprehension of other mentalities and in particular of the Pythagorean spirit. By adopting the same behaviour and practicing the same rites, it must, or should at least, evidently, be at least possible to reach identical or similar results and to correspondent conclusions.[70]

Reghini then went on writing about the allegedly bizarre habits of Pythagoras's followers and mentioned the Pythagorean practice of silence: this, he likened to Eastern forms of meditation, concluding that "even for us Westerners, by seriously practicing, on a daily basis, certain rites and spiritual exercises [. . .], it is possible, after months, years or decades, to reach the perception of inner silence."[71] Such a state of inner silence, according to Reghini, was the prerequisite for leaving one's body behind and, just like in the last two *Golden Verses*, become immortal, similar to god. Reghini called this process *indiamento*, which could be translated as progressively becoming godlike, and cites famous followers of Pythagoras, who had allegedly reached this stage during their lifetime: Hermotimus of Clazomenae (ca. sixth century BCE), Epimenides of Cnossos (ca. seventh–sixth century BCE), and the pre-Socratic philosopher Empedocles (ca. 494–434). Throughout the process, the duality between the body and the soul is transcended, reintegrating itself in the Pythagorean monad, the perfection of the perfected one. After this process, Reghini wrote, "there is nothing else. Summing up, the experience of ascending brings to a progressive recognizing of the monad, of the dyad and the triad."[72] Such was the Pythagorean, and neo-Pythagorean, path to immortality.

The second part of the *Prologo* that I would briefly like to analyze is Reghini's association between the harmony of Pythagorean geometry and numbers with the arts and sciences. By heavily leaning on the lessons imparted by Romanian Prince Matila G. Ghyka (1881–1965) in his *Esthétique des Proportions dans la Nature et dans les Arts* (*Aesthetics of Proportions in Nature and Art*, 1927), Reghini was enamored with the concept that the natural world possessed geometric qualities that were subconsciously reproduced by artists, in an attempt to capture the perfection of creation.[73] Reghini even went so far as praising a passage from the Bible, in order to better express what he meant: "The Pythagorean idea [of harmony] is close to the Bible's when it claims that God made all things by number, weight and measure; and it is also expressed by Plato according to whom God geometrises always (always and not only back in the day)."[74] It is easy to see how neo-Pythagoreans like Armentano or Reghini would be unable to tolerate the apparent lack of harmony created by progress, mechanization, 1920s and 1930s architectural aesthetics, in one concept, by the modern world. The chapter in *Prologo*, which had started with an exaltation of the harmonious nature of Pythagorean thought, quickly moved to the relations between man and man, and the ideal form of government. Reghini broached the subject thus:

> Pythagoreanism also aimed among other things to harmonise individuals among themselves, to harmonise society and to attune the single individual with the whole, without sacrificing moreover the individual to the mass [. . .]. Harmony and number are the foundations of Pythagoreanism.[75]

As we have seen throughout this book, Reghini's hatred for the masses stemmed from the suppression of the individual: the hordes of illiterates, which, according to Reghini, had symbolized the democratic nature of Western countries, were to blame because they were not harmonized with the world, and primarily because they stifled the expression of the superior individual. Reghini dedicated pages of his *Prologue*, noticing how, before him, Ghyka had described the original Pythagorean Institute as "Esoteric Fascism," while economist and sociologist Salvatore Cognetti de Martiis (1844–1901) had described it as "Communism," likening it to the proto-Christian societies, which shared all possessions.[76] Reghini argues against both theories, claiming that it was a hierarchical regime: "Founded and directed by Pythagoras, an extremely spiritually elevated man, modelled according to nature and the example of the celestial brotherhoods, ordered and lead according to the sacred order and cemented by spiritual similarities, it seems to belong to legend rather than history."[77] It is quite fitting for the neo-Pythagorean narrative that such a quasi-mythical "hierarchical regime," according to Reghini's reconstruction, was destroyed by a democratic uprising. Buried in one of the notes of the chapter, we find one of Reghini's strongest digs against the Christian concept of equality:

> According to many modern endorsers of equality, all men are equal because they are sons of the same Father; but even if this sentence, typically Anglo-Saxon and Christian, had an intelligible and real meaning, this still would not be a good reason for in a family not even twins are equal [...]. Jesus, like almost every Jew, considered the Jews as the chosen people; and called the sons of Jews "children" and called the sons of non-Jews "sons of dogs."[78]

In a very important passage, which I think sheds light on the aims and activities of Armentano's and Reghini's *Schola*, the author wrote about spiritual health being the most pressing preoccupation among the first Pythagoreans. According to Reghini, spiritual health was reached through "palingenesis, or rebirth, or new birth or birth to the new life."[79] Such a rebirth should not be confused with "metempsychosis or metemsomatosis, nor with migration [. . .]."[80] More importantly, according to Reghini, it was not a state that could be achieved in passive contemplation or by the grace of some god. He considers it to be "a work," rather the "great work," enacted deliberately and technically according to a proper rite or τέχνη [craft] that Plato and Maximus of Tyre call "the royal art."[81] Reghini then reviewed the various metaphors used throughout the centuries to refer to this exact process of perfection in rebirth, citing the transmutation of base metal into gold of alchemical lore, and the working of the rough stone into a polished one of Masonic tradition. The clues that Reghini left in the *Prologue* create an intriguing set of questions that we unfortunately will never know the answer to: what, among these techniques, or τέχνη, were Armentano and his associates practicing in the Torre Talao in the summer months when the *Schola* congregated there? Were specific rites prescribed to members of the *Schola* to help them achieve the return to the monad, the palingenesis of which Reghini wrote? If so, what was the provenance of these rites, and who were Armentano's teachers? From what we know about Reghini's initiation into the *Schola* in 1910, the rituals employed by Armentano and his followers were very peculiar and did not share any similarity with any known Masonic initiation rituals that were conducted in Italy in that historical period. Were these rituals part of the "creation of a tradition" that Hobsbawm writes about, or was there a legitimate corpus of rites and rituals passed down to Armentano by unknown superiors, which were later passed on to Reghini? What we do know is that the *Prologo* is the closest we get to deciphering what Reghini had only written about in a cryptic way in previous articles, and that the original Pythagorean Institute seems to share many similarities with the intellectual elite that Armentano and Reghini wanted to create in Italy.

The third and final part of the *Prologo* that I briefly want to analyze is that dedicated to the subject of Pythagorean anamnesis: this section is a paean to the virtues of the irrational and of intuition, even in the rigid and logical fields of mathematics and geometry. In it, Reghini professed to being unable to side with those who insist that one could reach mathematical truths only by logical speculation, and not through direct contemplation. As an example, Reghini quoted those prodigies who were able to solve mathematical calculations in the matter of seconds "in a very mysterious and in some cases obviously irrational manner."[82] Taking inspiration from L. E. Dickson's *The History of the Theory of Numbers* (1919–1923), Reghini lauded the few who possessed the ability to access mathematical truths by "irrational" means, and he quotes the American author at length:

> The conventional stories which take for granted that every fact has been discovered through a natural series of deductions from previous elements and devote considerable space to try and reconstruct such a concatenation. But the experts in research know that the germs of many important results at least were discovered through a sudden and mysterious intuition, maybe a result of a subconscious mental feat, even if such intuitions must be later put to the test of critical faculties.[83]

The use of this passage was not employed by the author to justify a more lax use of mere fantasies within the scientific method, but to prove that, sometimes, the human mind is able to raise itself to the level of divine science and consciousness and to reach scientific conclusions via nonscientific methods. Later, in the same chapter, Reghini makes his argument even more clear, when he argues against the possibility of reducing divine knowledge to any human philosophical path:

> Therefore, divine knowledge cannot be reduced to a philosophical system; it is so to speak necessarily "uncertain," and cannot be humanely *comprehended*. Understanding this is a great step already because one must know his limits in order to transcend them. The divine knowledge or "wisdom" which the Pythagoreans professed themselves friends of is then only reachable by surpassing the physical state, surpassing that must be made not *through words* but essentially through palingenesis that from the human worm forms the angelic butterfly which flies toward justice with no barriers.[84]

Reghini then quoted extensively from Plato's dialogues and proved that the journey toward knowledge was not conducted through reasoning but through the process of remembering, or anamnesis. Learning was therefore associated the function of memory, which is the reason, according to the author, for those instant flashes of genius or idea association which bring great scientific results but are not themselves scientific in nature. Was there a way to infuse this knowledge into the minds of neo-Pythagoreans, who wanted to have experiences similar to those of their forebears? Reghini's answer was that it could indeed be possible following the instructions of a short manuscript, which the *Schola* had recovered, titled *Prattica dell'Estasi Filosofica*, which in Reghini's days was attributed to philosopher Tommaso Campanella.[85] The text explained a meditation technique that allows one to look directly at the facet of divine knowledge that one wants to understand better, and "when the soul finds itself purified, put this [thought] ahead of oneself, and then he will think to have a crystal clear and shining lamp, through which no truth will be hidden from him."[86] In order to explain the complex process to the reader in a clearer fashion, Reghini summed the whole process up in three distinct stages: first, the intellectual contemplation of the world of ideas, which the author considered a perception, or experience, of the mind; second, the transmission of this vision, knowledge, or idea, to the mind, so that the meditation and its results may be easily related from the intellect to the physical brain; finally, the fixation of this infused knowledge in the physical realm by writing down immediately what has been obtained from the world of ideas. Reghini explained that such retrievals were like dreams, and they tended to fade rapidly if not committed to paper immediately.[87]

The *Prologo* is one of Reghini's most surprising works: what, in the other six volumes, is a dry treatise on advanced mathematics, is introduced by one of the most revealing pieces of writing by the Florentine thinker: there is more in the *Prologo* about the practical rituals and customs of the *Schola Italica* than in any other writing by Reghini. It is possible that the knowledge of the fact that the book would not be published during his lifetime had caused him to be less cautious and cryptic, when writing about the activities of the *Schola*, or that his final years spent in solitude (vide infra) allowed him to write more freely on the subject. Whatever the case may be, the *Prologo* contains some hidden gems that shed more light on the *Schola*'s heydays and make it easier for the scholar of Western esotericism to put at least more of the pieces together.

8.3. The Final Years (1939–1946)

"I saw Arturo a couple of evenings ago, and he regretfully told me that in a matter of days he will be moving to Bologna to teach at the Scuola Italica which is still active and is kept running by miss Partengo, who has remained devoted to Salvi."[88] In this letter dated October 12, 1939, Bianchini updated Armentano on Reghini's life and working arrangements. Enrico Salvi (d. 1937), a close friend of the members of the *Schola*, had founded a private school in Bologna, but, after having died of a heart attack in 1937, the school had been supervised by Camilla Partengo (1887–1970), a close friend of Salvi.[89] Bianchini also wrote to Armentano that Partengo knew most of the members of the *Schola*, and shared their ideals, and had been particularly close to Guerrieri, who had lost his wife about the time when Salvi had passed. Once Bianchini died in 1945, it would be Moretto Mori who would keep an eye on Reghini and communicate with Armentano. In a letter dated November 3, 1945, Mori told Armentano that Reghini was in Budrio, teaching in Partengo's institute and living with her in Villa Giacomelli, and that he had finished writing a work on Pythagorean mathematics, which

> Will allow to practice a form of Geometry based on Pythagoras's Theorem and that will once again reaffirm the Italian primacy in the scale of values, when the current rampant atomistic craze, in which technical progress and the perfection toward which humanity yearns are synonymous with massacre, will have left its place to a predominant spiritual order.[90]

It is fascinating to notice how, at the end of World War II, the ideals of members of the *Schola Italica* are still the same as they were in 1910, when Reghini had been initiated by Armentano: in this passage we find an opposition to progress, culminated in the invention of nuclear devices; a disdain toward the masses, who are always yearning for a skewed idea of perfection; the idea of the modern world and its technologization as fundamentally evil; and finally the idea that one single book or an elite of initiates may usher in a new order, which will be spiritual in nature. Because of the secret police following Reghini's moves and intercepting a large part of his correspondence, we don't have many letters between him and Armentano: one, though, remains, and was sent by Reghini on April 21 1946, the anniversary of the foundation of Rome. The letter was sent only two weeks before Reghini's death and covers a large span of time, where the Reghini wrote about his occult visions, his more mundane job, and many other subjects. His hardships in Budrio make up a substantial section of the letter and tell of difficult times for him and Camilla Partengo:

> During the first years things went well, also thanks to the help of the City Council. Then the Secretary of the Republican Fasces kicked us out in the street by force; and that's when hardships and hostility of every kind began: the Fascists, those who had been evacuated, the Germans who made camp in our

house for ten months and forced us to shut the school (I earned 80 liras in a year!) then the air raids during the day and during the nights and in the end the German and English artillery bombing for four days and four nights without a break.[91]

The closing of the letter expresses all of the sadness of a man left to his own devices in a provincial town in postwar Italy: "Of all the friends who were supposed to give me a hand, nobody managed; Cavalli committed suicide, Moretto went bankrupt, you are where you are, others have abandoned me."[92] The rest of the letter is replete with sincere thanks toward Armentano and a foreboding feeling of his impending death, which Reghini himself judged almost as a blessing, since in this difficult position, he did not feel that he could contribute in any useful way to the *Schola*'s cause.[93] His health, too, had rapidly declined. In the span of very few years, he had broken both of his arms and had an tumor on his left cheek, which at the time of writing the letter, he was treating with radiation therapy in a hospital in Bologna; of course, he made sure his mentor knew that "intelligence, memory and resistance to work [are] the same as before."[94]

Arturo Reghini died on July 1, 1946 in his home in Budrio. The first-hand account we have of his death is Parise's *Nota*, where one may find what seem to be the final sentences of a hagiography. The many employed stylistic artifices to detail the deaths of Mazzini or Garibaldi, for example, are abundantly used, and the impression that Parise wanted to leave to his reader was definitely not that of the death of a common man, but the death of a man who had gone through his palingenesis and could serenely look forward to the next stage of his life. Camilla Partengo, too, in describing Reghini's last days, wrote: "He was an example of that spiritual calm typical of one who lives in a superior world and doesn't fear anything."[95] Roberto Sestito himself, biographer and follower of Reghini, writes at the end of his biography that Reghini can best be described as a hero: "Hero, in the language of classical tradition, was not only the tutelary deity of cities or families but also the Master of Magic who had attained immortality in life and post-mortem."[96] Going back to Parise's account, the tone is not much different:

> The first day of July of 1946, the spirit of Arturo Reghini released its corporeal bonds and passed into the Eternal Light. It was the fifth hour of the afternoon. The sign had appeared. Arturo Reghini turned towards the dying sun for the final salute, for the final rite; then he leant on the shelf with his right hand, bent his gigantic stature towards the Great Mother, his back straight; and he was free.[97]

Curiously, the epic tone of this story reminded me of the death of one of Reghini's bitter enemies: Julius Evola. Stories regarding Evola's death are very similar, and a comparison of how both Traditionalists spent the last moments of their life is intriguing. In 1974, in his house in Corso Vittorio Emanuele 197 in Rome, Evola died while assisted by some of his closest friends and disciples. He had demanded to "be brought 'standing' [Evola had been confined to a wheelchair since being hit by shrapnel during bombings in Vienna in 1945] in front of the window facing the Gianicolo hill, and there his strong fibre had surrendered."[98] Mario Coen Belifanti (b. 1925), who had visited Evola just two days prior to his death, writes that the modality of his death was not a coincidence, but Evola wanted to salute the sun one last time before his death.[99] Arturo Reghini is buried in the Budrio cemetery, his memorial plaque celebrating his ties to his two great loves: Pythagoreanism and Freemasonry.

9
Concluding Remarks

In Chapter 1, the core questions of my book were enunciated and, for convenience, will be posed once more here: *How and why did Arturo Reghini react so vehemently to the modern, and what can the analysis of his writings offer to the ongoing debate regarding the intricate relationship between occultism and modernity?*

Like many Italian occultists of his age, Reghini had an upper-class background and naturally saw himself as a step (or two) above the teeming and malleable masses. Having grown up with the ideals of the *Risorgimento*, Reghini saw a world where heroes, above-average human beings, had succeeded in accomplishing what was for many decades thought to be impossible: the reunification of all Italian territories under one rule. Thus, characters such as Garibaldi and Mazzini must have influenced young Reghini's mind significantly, so much so that, in "Imperialismo Pagano," he included them in the list of greats who had helped keep the Italic-Pythagorean Tradition alive through uncertain times. This elitist attitude of separating the collective from the individual was probably the first of Reghini's displays of reaction against what he perceived as the pernicious tendencies of the modern. Since many pages have passed from when I first asked the core questions that I have endeavored to answer in this work, I think it will be useful for the reader to recall Reghini's, and the *Schola*'s in general, reaction toward the seemingly unstoppable malaise of modernity.

The first aspects, which would have definitely influenced both Armentano and Reghini in their longing for the past glories of ancient Rome and the toutcourt rejection of the customs and cultural manifestations of the day, can already be found, as written earlier, in the *Risorgimento* period. The exaltation of Rome could be witnessed not only in the discourses of the great politicians of the day, such as Cavour or King Vittorio Emanuele, but also in the arts and literature of the day: in Chapter 2, I gave De Amicis's *Cuore* and Manzoni's *Promessi Sposi* as examples of best-selling novels peppered with *Risorgimento* ideals such as the love for one's country and the rise of the three core values of the day, admirably summarized by Alberto Mario Banti in the combination of love/honor/virtue (*amore/onore/virtù*), sacrifice (*sacrificio*), and kinship (*parentela*). A list of war heroes was provided to the youth like Reghini, growing up in post-*Risorgimento* Italy: Garibaldi, the man capable of triumphing in any feat; Mazzini, who baptized Rome as the imperishable eternal city; and other minor figures such as Ippolito Nievo, who had called Rome the Gordian knot of the Italians' destinies.

Another idea that was readily available for young people of Reghini's generation was the role played by Freemasonry: many readers of Reghini, including biographer Natale di Luca, have asked themselves why Reghini and the *Schola* wished to transmit the teaching of a supposedly age-old tradition through often short-lived and chaotic Masonic manifestations, such as the *Rito Filosofico Italiano*. The answer, in my opinion, lies in the exaggerated role that Freemasonry attributed to itself in the unification of Italy, which has by now been discredited by scholars of Italian history and Freemasonry alike. In Reghini's days, and in the postunification years, though, the allure of Italian Freemasonry was still very much alive, and that is why we see Reghini joining the *I Rigeneratori* lodge of Palermo as early as 1902. As we have seen, Garibaldi had been assigned an Honorary Grand Master title by the Italian Grand Orient (GOI), and many politicians, who were active in the years leading up to and after the reunification of Italy, were members of a Masonic lodge. To Reghini, belonging to a secret society meant being able to discuss everyday issues with his peers, while learning esoteric secrets that could help him advance spiritually: this is why he was so shocked and appalled by GOI's decision to open its ranks to the bourgeoisie. Masonic orders were supposed to be the training ground of the elite, in Reghini's possibly outdated view, not a place to meet up and exchange calling cards with members of lower classes. Another aspect of *Risorgimento* Freemasonry, which no doubt Reghini approved of, was its strong anti-clerical stance against the temporal power of the Papacy in Rome. As we have seen, this would be a nonnegotiable aspect of Reghini's personality, which he no doubt picked up from the post-*Risorgimento* cultural heritage.

Another inclination that Reghini, maybe subconsciously, adopted from post-*Risorgimento* culture was his fascination with the occult. If we are to believe Parise, who first published Reghini's biographical sketch, Reghini had helped found the first Theosophical Lodge in 1897, which would have made him nineteen at the time, and travelling from Florence to Rome for that purpose. Such an early predisposition toward the occult sciences was shared by many others that he would start frequenting in the cultural cafes of Florence at the turn of the century, and it appears that, back at the beginning of the twentieth century, occultism was possibly more widespread and less problematic than it is today. Many of Reghini's friends were, to varying degrees, interested in the occult: from Theosophists Giovanni Amendola and Augusto Agabiti, to foreign residents in Florence such as Alexey Dodsworth, Theodor Daubler, and Annie Besant, to the Masonic contingent composed, among others, by Moretto Mori and Amerigo Bianchini. The diversity of the youngsters belonging to the blossoming avant-garde movements meant that Reghini was also active in other circles and rubbed shoulders both with the Idealists of the *Leonardo*, Giuseppe Papini and Giuseppe Prezzolini, and with Filippo Tommaso Marinetti and the members of the Futurist movement. Reghini also contributed to *Leonardo* in its brief occult, post-Nietzschean period, in which Papini seemed willing to try any avenue possible in order to elevate his everyday being to a higher status (perhaps influenced by the theory of the Übermensch). Reghini was a central figure within the Florentine Theosophical movement, when he worked as the director of the Theosophical library, and through his short stay within the Society, he managed to develop an interest for Eastern traditions, which the other members of the *Schola* never did. This is possibly the reason why, in later years, he would get on so well with René Guénon, who, as we have seen, had abandoned all hope for a spiritual revival of the West. Ideas predominant within the Theosophical milieu would end up intriguing Reghini for the rest of his life, even after he had severed all ties and gone on to study under Armentano's tutelage: to name but two, Reghini would always be interested in the concept of the Hindu cycles of time, the Yugas, and the mythical subterranean city of Agarthi, hidden beneath the mountains of Tibet, and ruled by the mysterious King of the World. Another aspect of Theosophical activity in Italy, though, would be of paramount importance to Reghini's development: Decio Calvari's decision to focus on more autochthone manifestations of the secret wisdom, which immediately excited Reghini because of the possibility of linking his love for ancient Italy and his passion for occultism. This Theosophical beginning of Reghini's pursuit for a Roman Tradition has been overlooked by all previous scholars and must not be underestimated.

In Chapter 4 we have another series of clues that point toward Reghini's rejection of modernity, that are to be found especially within his Masonic misadventures. Reghini had joined the *Michele di Lando* (later rebaptized *Lucifero*) lodge in 1904, but he had been outraged by the new direction all lodges under GOI were moving toward: the democratization of Freemasonry, though the lowering of the fees had been the first episode to cause annoyance within Reghini's circle of friends. This had rapidly been followed by a reduction in the ritualistic aspect of GOI, which was primarily the reason Reghini had joined Freemasonry in the first place. When the head of GOI, Ettore Ferrari, had argued in favor of a greater involvement of Freemasons in Italy's public life, Reghini developed a lifelong disgust for GOI and its progressive initiatives. When, in 1906, Ferrari had added a commitment toward the world order and a willingness to fight for the democratic principle in the social and political sphere, Reghini abandoned the lodge. Luckily for him, just before leaving the *Lucifero* lodge, he had met Armentano and had immediately begun to study under his tutorage. If we were to summarize Armentano's teachings to Reghini, we could condense them in two key points: first, that a Pythagorean Tradition was passed down through the ages from master to disciple since the days in which Pythagoras taught his followers in ancient Kroton. Second, that such a Tradition was intimately bound to a form of Freemasonry that predated the Enlightenment and, therefore, could be brought back to its pristine state by eliminating all the profane and misinformed changes that had been made since the advent of modern times. In Armentano, Reghini had found a great ally in his war against the modern world: one of his most popular maxims had been that progress was equivalent to nonbeing, and that where order was, progress could not be. Hailing from an aristocratic Italian family, which had made its fortunes in Brazil, Reghini found in Armentano a mentor, a friend, and a fellow anti-modernist. As the Pythagoreans before him, Armentano taught that it was impossible to disconnect the various planes of a man's existence. According to him, the magical could not be disjoined from the political, the intellectual from the practical. It is clear, then, that Armentano and Reghini were in diametrical opposition against the process of progress and democratization that the modern world was beginning to manifest in 1910s Italy. The two were in favor of the eternal, the fixed, the orderly, while the modern world offered a maelstrom of protean changes in social, economic, and spiritual issues. The pair's attempt at taking over the *Rito Filosofico Italiano* failed quickly: according to Reghini, it was due to the incompetence of the third head of the lodge, Eduardo Frosini. It might just be that to manifest what the *Schola* taught in a mundane environment such as a Masonic order in 1910s Italy was an endeavor doomed to failure.

The fifth chapter is possibly the most significant, when it comes to finding examples of Reghini's many reactions against the modern world, and also the most rewarding when looking for the reasons for such vitriolic retorts. The analysis of "Imperialismo Pagano" brings all of Reghini's grievances to surface, and none of his enemies are spared. To him, the nationalists were too imbued with Catholic propaganda, and the masses had no appeal. At the same time, a small group of intellectuals possessed a patriotic, pagan, elitist, and anti-clerical sentiment, and this minute coterie rallied around Reghini and Armentano: Reghini was rumored to be the invisible head of the Florentine Futurists, the other members of the *Schola Italica* had happily accepted Reghini's role as their official spokesperson, and a good part of the Florentine cultural milieu shared Reghini's pagan, elitist, and imperialist political outlook. While small in number, the people for whom Reghini wrote "Imperialismo" were a vocal and influential aspect of the Italian prewar cultural scene. Reghini's publication was critiqued by the many who did not share his vast culture and knowledge of ancient Greek and Roman literature and customs. And the anti-Christian character of the article was denounced by members of GOI and his ex-Theosophist friends. The arguments contained in "Imperialismo" can be grouped in three distinct sections, for convenience: the first includes the overarching narrative, which includes Vergil, Dante, Bruno, Campanella, Garibaldi, and Mazzini as its main actors, of the transmission of an Italic-Pythagorean, imperial, pagan, anti-democratic, and anti-modern Tradition, which Reghini represented and that

CONCLUDING REMARKS 187

"Imperialismo Pagano" sought to present to the public on the eve of the Great War; the second cluster of arguments relates to the anti-clerical aspect of the *Schola*'s teachings: not only did Reghini blame Christianity for the fall of the Roman Empire, but he also found that, behind any historical crisis of Italian imperial power, the culprit was the Catholic Church, which Reghini famously described as a "Semitic cult"; the third, more hidden cluster of ideas, is the rallying call for the creation of an intellectual elite that could divert the disastrous direction Italy was going in, by influencing the political climate of the day, through both political *and* magical means. The performance of rites to influence the events in Italian politics was something that Reghini continued to implement right until his break with Evola in 1929, and much of the practical work of the *Ur* Group was dedicated to this effort. "Imperialismo Pagano" could then be seen as a call to action, in order for Armentano and Reghini to see who was really ready to usher in a new age for Italy by any means possible, and it is reflected in the war correspondence between the two, ending with Reghini's statement that because of their work Austria had perished.

The themes of Chapter 6 and 7 may be considered together, as both sections deal with the more practical manifestations of Roman Traditionalist ideas. The three main events to influence the movement in the 1920s were without a doubt (1) Mussolini's rise to power, which so enflamed the hearts of the Roman Traditionalist milieu, with its imperial trappings and reference to ancient Rome and its grandeur; (2) a first, brusque awakening in 1925 with the regime's approval of the Bodrero bill, which effectively outlawed secret societies and dealt a huge blow to the dream of recreating a Masonic vehicle for Roman Traditionalist ideas, and which contributed to the voluntary exile of many of the core members of the *Schola*, including Armentano; and finally, (3) the tangible experience of occult practices of the *Ur* Group, in which groups or chains of initiates worked secretly to steer Mussolini's ideas toward the neo-Pagan stance shared by the members of this secret coterie. The concept of social occult modernism coined by Roger Griffin was used to express two key elements that preoccupied both the members of the *Schola* and the newly installed Fascist regime: the conviction of the decadence of the days they were living in, on the one hand, and a prophetic confidence in a renewal of ancient customs, which would benefit Italy as a whole, on the other. Victor Turner's idea of the individual abandoning society to form a smaller *communitas* was also explored in correspondence of the *Schola* and of the first group of Fascists: both were deeply disillusioned by what they saw as a decadent age of ever-increasing mechanization, alienation of the individual, and erosion of social values. Both the *Schola* and the early Fascist regime argued for the creation of a new man, who would incarnate ancient ideals and who could bring forth a new, brighter future, or what Conservative Revolutionary Arthur Möller van den Bruck would call a reconnection *forward*. Although the thrill of having found in Mussolini a kindred spirit who *had* to share their same views on the Italic Tradition only lasted for approximately four or five years, the *Schola's* enthusiasm and Reghini's literary output both witnessed a significant boost. With the ban on Masonic organizations, Reghini realized that the ally they had sought in Mussolini had turned his back on them, and his Concordat with the Vatican, which granted the Pope temporal power again, after an absence from the political scene which lasted sixty years, smashed any dream of a new pagan Rome that was left. We are reminded once again of de Turris's conclusions that, if the National-Socialist regime did have occult roots, to be found in the volk-isch and Ariosophist movements, the Fascist government never allowed occult expressions to thrive, from Mussolini's rise to power in 1923, until his downfall in 1945. The fact that some occultists attempted to favor his political endeavors through the use of magical rites can be seen as one minor expression of adherence to Mussolini's ideals of the foundation of the Third Rome, but the Duce himself did certainly not imagine his Rome to be influenced by Reghini's intellectual elite: he already had his Fascist elite, which ruled the country with an iron fist.

The previous chapter, covering the years spanning from 1930 to Reghini's death in 1946, shows two major themes running parallel: the first one is Reghini's idea that something could still be gained from Mussolini's regime, and that the declaration of the Catholic creed as the official religion of the country did not seem to bother him too much. In 1933 he became a card-carrying member of the *Partito* and he wrote on the virtues and symbolism of Fascism's main symbol, the *lictores fasces*. Such enthusiasm, though, would steadily wane throughout the 1930s, and by the start of the war, Reghini's preoccupations became more practical in nature. With little or no money, abandoned by his closest friends, who possibly lived under circumstances as bad as his, Reghini spent the last years of his life far away from his beloved Rome. The second major theme, which he developed especially in his *Dei Numeri Pitagorici*, was an even more intricate exploration of the Pythagorean Tradition that Armentano had initiated him to: right up to two years prior to his death, Reghini worked on his magnum opus and continued to practice the Pythagorean techniques, which would eventually allow him to experience palingenesis. Even in the most desperate of times, Reghini never lost the enthusiasm for the Italic-Pythagoean Tradition, which he did not see as remote and static, but as the only lens to see the world through: throughout the bombings, the Nazi raids of his house, poverty, and illness, Reghini saw the world as a perfect reflection of the Pythagorean monad, inspiring Camilla Partengo to write to Armentano, once Reghini had passed, about how "he was the example of that spiritual calm that belongs to he who lives in a higher plane and does not fear anything."[1]

Throughout this book, I have provided a unique and novel approach that has demonstrated the existence of a manifestation of the occult, which defies both extreme characterizations as described earlier and creates a significantly important bridge. As to the ideas of the first group of social scientists, the anti-modern stance adopted by Reghini and the Roman Traditionalists is clearly anti-Positivist, against any idea of linear progress and to a certain extent irrational in that they do not seek to link science and spirituality in a novel, *modern* fashion. Nevertheless, entertaining the idea that anti-modern occult circles paved the way for the rise of Fascism is ludicrous. The Fascist entourage never viewed occult circles with favor, and the ban on secret societies in 1925 and the Concordat with the Vatican in 1929 went against all Reghini represented. His correspondences with René Guénon, Amedeo Armentano, and other Traditionalists and his published books and articles have provided innumerable examples of Reghini's anti-modern, pro-Masonic, and anti-Christian dispositions. If one of the two parties had ever been eager to jump on one's bandwagon, it was the Roman Traditionalists, and certainly not Mussolini, whose affection toward the idea of imperial Rome was of a propagandistic nature, not a spiritual one. The differences with the conclusions reached by authors to cite only the most prominent scholars, like Alex Owen, Corinna Treitel, and Marco Pasi, who are involved in the contemporary debate on the intersection between occultism and modernity, could not be more evident, as we will see in the following paragraph. The aforementioned authors have all dealt with Mitteleuropean and Northern European countries, and it is my opinion that because they have dealt with a different kind of modernity, to put it with Eisenstadt, than the one that manifested in southern European countries, the results are necessarily very different.

In this book I have argued that, far from what can be surmised from the most recent scholarship in the field, the interaction between occultism and modernity was hardly always a progressive, Positivist hub in which occult circles stood at the forefront of social emancipation. Indeed, my main argument has been that there were, and still are, occult milieus that were reactionary, nonprogressive, anti-Positivist, anti-democratic: in a word, anti-modern. By using Eisenstadt's theory of multiple modernities, I have argued that if a rose-tinted version of progressive occultism was a reality in more northern European countries, where the process of modernization had started sooner and had produced more encouraging results, the same could not be said about countries in southern Europe, and especially Italy, which at the turn of the century was lagging behind most other European countries in both scientific fields and the humanities. However, it is clear by now that occultism does not equate to irrationality, as the Frankfurt School, but even more recent and better-informed scholars such as James Webb, have posited. While the idea of progressive occultism has been researched and argued with success by scholars such as Treitel and Owen, it is my opinion that the simplistic approach to the field of occultism seen as the embodiment of the irrational may be finally discarded and its idea considered passé and absolutely inaccurate.

By using Reghini's writings and those of other Traditionalists of the early part of the twentieth century as empirical material, I have defended the idea of the existence of a different expression of occultism, which I have termed anti-modern occultism, and given multiple examples in order to bolster my main theoretical framework. The most significant result of my research is that of having pinpointed a more obscure, oft-neglected facet of occultism in modern society, which almost forms the point of a triangle, it being equidistant from Adorno's theory of occult irrationality and that of modern scholars' progressive occultism. Indeed, this neglected facet has yet to be researched in depth, and it does not limit itself to the *Schola Italica* or Italy.

The Different Approaches to Occultism
Anti-modern Occultism

Occultism as   *Progressive*
Irrationality   *Occultism*

If we were to do away with the idea of occultism as irrationality altogether, as I suggest, a line would be formed, with manifestations such as Reghini's *Schola Italica*, on the one hand, and more progressive examples of occult manifestations such as the Theosophical Society, on the other. This dark side of occultism at the turn of the century had been previously ignored, and the many publications on fin de siècle occultism had all endeavored to show how in line with the major tropes of modernity the Occult Revival actually was. This had created a disproportionate imbalance, which I can only believe was pursued in order to create a sanitized version of the occult, which would make it acceptable for academic interdisciplinary studies in the future: by doing so, though, the academics who have highlighted the positive (or Positivist?) aspects of the occult, while sweeping what didn't fit with their theories under the proverbial rug, ended up providing a disservice to anyone interested in the whole story. As I mentioned many times in the course of this book, anti-modern occultism was not only represented by Reghini's *Schola Italica*. We find examples of it everywhere in Europe: in France, with Alexandre Saint-Yves d'Alveydre and his idea of an occult synarchy as the perfect form of government; in Austria, with Guido von List and Lanz von Liebenfels, and the tenets of Ariosophy; in Switzerland, France, England, and Italy, with the Traditonalist School shaped by René Guénon and developed in different directions by Julius Evola, Frithjof Schuon, Martin Lings, and others, with their fierce critique of modernity, materialism, progressivism, psychologism, scientism, empiricism, agnosticism, and atheism.

Progressive Occultism — *Anti-Modern Occultism*

Anti-modern occultism is certainly a challenging topic, and its relationship with modernity raises many issues, some of which I have tackled in this work: research on this facet on occultism, when compared to the more "socially acceptable" esoteric manifestations covered by previous scholars, who have investigated the intersection between the occult and the modern, has been sorely lacking. It is my hope that this work, and the handful of others dedicated to anti-modern occultism, will inspire other scholars to readdress the balance.

Appendix: English Translation of *Imperialismo Pagano*

Pagan Imperialism[1]
By Arturo Reghini
Atanór 1, no. 3, pp. 69–85

Introduction

> Populus Romanus natura ordinatus
> Fuit ad imperandum.[2]
> —Dante Alighieri, *De Mon.*

In the recent political elections, universal suffrage, extreme corollary of democratic postulates, has brought us to the triumph of oversimplification. The two parties, thus, who have seen their votes rise the most are without doubt the clerical and the socialist. An evident sign that the arguments and the promises they utilised were by their own nature more accessible and welcomed by the vast, illiterate majority of voters, much more than the ideas of other parties could. The farmers of [71] Veneto and Brianza, whose primitive soul is governed by the priest who uses and abuses their strong christian faith and helps himself with the less spiritual topic of the catholic banks, if in need; the farmers of Emilia and Romagna and the workers of the great cities, having drunk at the inexhaustible spring of clichés and by now polluted by democratic eloquence, reducing everything to their narrow class selfishness in order to win an immediate miserable gain, proud of feeling evolved, convinced they represent Progress, the new fantastic God. Both banking on the strength of sheep-like discipline and the strength of numerous leagues, they have used their sovereign right voting for the two great internationalist parties.

Illiteracy, oversimplification and internationalism, bound together, have therefore won to the greater glory of the parliamentary regime.

On the other hand the nationalist party, though, emerging victorious from some of the battles; was not able to obtain a success proportional to the strength which the Italian national consciousness has awakened equipped with. What then happened to that overwhelming nationalist tide that wanted the (italian-turkish) war and that elevated Italy from the degrading and humiliating condition of Cinderella among nations? If we do not want to believe that all this energy has simply vanished into thin air, we must admit that it was not able to express itself because of the conditions of the parties in Italy, being there no party to this date in Italy with which the national conscience can identify itself trustingly. And truthfully that party that defines itself nationalist does not give the italian soul any assurance on its absolutely italian character; the deep intuition of race isn't persuaded, and it hesitates and refuses to call itself nationalist if nationalist must mean clerical.

Instinctively, we do not trust nationalism nor clericalism.

The change has been too fast, too smooth not to stink like a machination at a first sniff. We do not want to bore the reader by repeating extremely well-known facts; still we cannot abstain from bringing up the aversion of our own and foreign clericals towards our country; in Belgium, Austria, Spain, Germany, in their congresses the eternal italian question was debated; only yesterday the [72] Secretary of State was protesting against he who detains, and the tears of the faithful for the imprisonment haven't even dried dried yet, the Pope. And now, all of a sudden, changes ahoy; to the faithful in St. Peter's square who shout long live the Pope-king, Pius X himself gestures for them to be silent, an archbishop in a clearly official speech, which cannot diminish in worth because of recent repentance, declares that the time of temporal vindications is past, the clericals monopolise nationalism; everywhere at the hands of clericals new journals are born, weeklies, daily papers with a nationalist flag. Has the monk become the devil? Already another time we witnessed a Pope asking God to bless Italy, and he was probably sincere. But it was a short agreement with no consequences. The Papacy is an essentially international institution, openly catholic, clericals in the everyday political life of all peoples represent the army of this institution; to become nationalists is for them to lose their own nature. Therefore, we do not believe in the sincerity of this sudden change from which very evidently a jesuit plot transpires; and in any case because of a natural fatality of things, we don't think it will last long; and lastly, sincere or not, we see in it a damage and a danger for the future of Italy.

It is not hard, after all, to guess which considerations must have brought the company of Jesus to this apparent change of politics regarding Italy.

The international and national conditions made this move appropriate and almost necessary.

France, precious ally against Italy in the days of Leo XIII, once the nationalist clerical military attempt had failed because of the unlucky Dreyfus affair, is today in the hands of Freemasonry; and, if it takes action against Italy, it does it through Palazzo Giustiniani and democracy, and not through the Vatican anymore. Austria certainly doesn't procure us of these problems; the clerical party here is very strong at court, in the army, in bureaucracy: the hereditary archduke and the not so princely consort are in great relationships with the Company, Austria after all is always old Austria; but it has too many internal issues and too many threats along the borders to be able to afford a policy that goes against Italy. In Spain, it is necessary that willingly or unwillingly, Alphonse XIII shows himself [73] as a liberal if he doesn't want to end up like his colleague in Lisbon; and the formation of a Poland [that may be] independent, catholic and with a king possibly hailing from the Habsburg house doesn't seem too close. On the other hand, atheism, materialism, socialism are spreading through the working masses and even among the farmers of Europe more and more.

Bad times are upon us! And the progress of Catholicism in protestant countries is a meagre consolation for so many ailments; in Germany where the Emperor needs the votes of the catholic centre; in England and the United States where the catholic cult, more *picturesque* than the various protestant cults, is continuously gaining ground.

On the other hand, Italy has witnessed two important unexpected changes. War with its associated diplomatic competitions, which has awakened the nationalist feeling of the country; and universal suffrage, which has brought most of the uneducated and malleable masses of the country to participate in political activities. Wouldn't it be a masterstroke, must have said the old foxes of the papal *Curia*, if, instead of continuing to ask from an ever-increasingly strong Italy an always less-probable restitution (!), we tried to direct the unexpected events in our favour and little by little we took over not only Rome but the whole of Italy? We have a clergy, young and combative, who isn't allowed to be overpowered by the fireworks of socialist orators; it will be able to recruit columns and columns of farmers; we will exploit the great renaissance of nationalism taking advantage of the universal economic infatuation of all democratic parties, which in order to shout out their sacrosanct principles of '89 are so blind as to go against the contingencies of reality, and so kind as to leave us the monopoly over this great current; count Gentiloni will take it upon himself to import into Italy the secret-pact system that worked so well for us in the United States; and the ship of St. Peter will be able to sail even with a stormy sea and an obstinately unfavourable wind. In this way even the biggest trouble to have ever hit the Church of Rome, the formation of Italy as a united and independent nation, will end up benefiting us.

The Church is not wrong, therefore, if it deems exploiting nationalism convenient. What needs to be seen is if and how much this selfless help may aid the non-clerical nationalists.

[74] Empire and Christendom

We have already said that we do not believe in the sincerity of clerical nationalism. We do not believe in it because we know about the wily schemes of our enemies all too well, and because it is all too evident that for personal interest and necessity they have been forced into this masquerade. May nobody come and speak to us about catholics that are not clerical. The mentality, the sentimentalism, the faith of a catholic are grounds too fertile for the intensive cultivation of clericalism for it to be slept upon; priests exert such an ascendant upon the believers" character that as and when necessary they will always be able to do whatever they want with the uncivilised and faithful masses, and it would be then but a mere consolation to realise that the distinction between catholic and clerical would have allowed some semi-independent figure to act of his own accord.

A nationalist must desire the good of the nation above all other things. Adding or *implying* the adjective catholic shows the existence of a mental restriction, shows that it desires the good of the nation if and because it works in favour of a certain particular belief. Therefore one may be a sincere nationalist only if the two purposes are never at odds with each other.

Now in our case there is a natural, fatal, deep, irreconcilable contrast. In the long course of the centuries, from the foundation of the Church of Rome onwards, Papacy, forever and ever, has been the natural enemy of Rome and Italy.

Latin civilisation, eclectic, serene, open, in a word *gentile*, and together with it, the roman empire were smothered by the exotic, intolerant, fanatical, dogmatic mentality of christendom.

And this is a crime that still awaits its expiation.

Vergil, the great imperial poet, had but just sung about the return to the golden age,

Jam redit et Virgo, redeunt Saturnia regna[3]

and prophesised, the arrival of a *hound*, which the destroyers of the Vergilian idea have had the impudence to associate with Jesus: so [75] here we have a hypochondriac and sentimental megalomaniac, whose vision of the world created by his God, moved to compassion and tears, who thought himself the first and only sage who appeared in this valley of tears, and made the farfetched discovery that to accommodate the lot of mankind, it was only necessary to make men better. Having found this out, all that was left was to persuade them to love one another.

Less wise than Faust, he tricked himself into believing that he knew what was necessary to teach.

Die Menschen zu bessern und zu bekehren[4]

and so began that nefarious predication of love for one's neighbour and of christian charity, honey- and liqueur-based universal cure-all, true manna for all the sentimental languors of humanity. This preaching should have enjoyed inevitable success; as a matter of fact, the paradise promised to the faithful, a blessed future life in which the wrongs of this life would be made right and the evils compensated assured by the preachings of a meek Jesus the consensus of those who felt the mental need to validate the regularity of a divine justice made in the image and likeness of their miserable human criterion.

There will be occasion to examine the splendours of christian charity and the merits of love towards one's neighbour. The theological hatred, the blind fanaticism, the persecutions, the excommunications, the religious wars unknown to pagan humanity, were the natural consequences of this mad propaganda. The fault of men our Christian readers will possibly claim; Jesus's fault we say, for if he had really been wise he should have predicted that human beings would never be able to practice his superhuman maxims. To do so, they should have stopped being men, and it is impossible to change what is by persuading it not to be.

But let us go back to our main argument and see how and why the first Roman emperors failed to defend the empire from christian peril.

The first emperors maybe never understood the particular nature of this danger. Used to the most serene tolerance of all cults and sects, which coexisted and [76] peacefully prospered side by side without proselytism and claims of monopoly, they never thought that in some crazy mind the absurd idea could form that truth could be attained and happiness conquered by just following a religion. No pagan cult had ever laid such claims; and in all antiquity in Rome and in other places wisdom was not obtained through belief and cults, but participating in the Mysteries.

Moreover the state, essentially lay, used to estrange itself from the various cults and founded its administrative wisdom upon social necessities and pure law.

A law, free from any kind of religious character, did not rely on any theoretical morals from theories, postulates and prejudices; but it was based upon a healthy empirical knowledge of the practical necessities of life. *"Neminem laedere, unicuique suum tribuere, honeste vivere"*;[5] without the scaffolding of religious or philosophical morals, without classifications of good and evil.

The state in this way stood above all cults, and its authority had no limits. Even that small, greedy and riotous people, who did not believe it impossible that the Lord God had for them a special predilection, closed itself in its haughty conviction and did not feel the itch of the propaganda. How could one imagine that a man, exciting the sentimental hysteria, dulling the intelligence, promising the earth, sea and sky and even heaven to those who would follow him blindly, could create the missionary mania, that is the holy zeal of the spirit of proselytism?

When the emperors became aware of this new reality it was too late. The infection had rapidly spread throughout the Empire, it had reached Rome; and fire and brimstone used even more generously than was the norm could not have saved the West. Thus, while the *pax romana* assured a great part of humanity a condition of wealth and happiness which, according to Gibbon, was never reached again, throughout the empire the inundation of milk and honey spread.

A sentimental morbid mysticism drowned the healthy and serene Italian practicality, the italic *prudentia*;[6] and the roman eagle, used to [77] long flights, got its claws sticky in the syrupy sweetness of universal love. The greatest part of the strength of Rome was to be found in its proud, realistic, hard and austere character of the roman citizen; and the tender and innocent bleat of the christian lamb was not what was needed to keep the barbarians who were pushing at the borders at bay.

It is not enough either. Establishing itself solidly in Rome, the new religion snatches, turning it to its benefit, the strength itself and the ascendant inherent to the land, the air, the sacred name of Rome. It stole from the ancient and indigent cult of Janus, the keys and out of it made the shuttle of St. Peter; it stole from archaic Masonic symbolism the very name of the high priest himself, usurping the name and the functions of the *pontifex maximus*; and almost as if to hide its insane original exoticism it proclaimed itself roman.

The first effect of the Christian predominance and of the servitude of the imperial authority to the new authority was the abandonment of the unitarian pythagorean idea of the roman state through the creation of the Eastern Empire. And, soon after, a great number of misfortunes: the fall of the Western Empire, the political unity and the sense of Italian national unity lost for centuries to come, the shipwreck of culture, of thought, of literature, of arts; christian barbarism in sum substituted by pagan civilisation. Rightly so did Dante (Par. XX) say that the world was in such a way destroyed by Constantine.

And let us not cast upon the barbarians the responsibility of such ruin; for during the first centuries of the *vulgar* era, Alexandria was the centre of graeco-roman culture; and it wasn't the Vandals or the Visigoths who destroyed the Library and the Museum and persecuted and killed the neoplatonists and the gnostics, the mathematicians and the hermetists.

The Roman Imperial Tradition

Once established in Rome with its dual spiritual and temporal authority, the Catholic Church had to inevitably oppose with all its strength the rise of any political authority in Rome independent from it.

But it looked like the church could exist uncontested. [78] Christianity had spread through the great part of Europe, and every remain of a pagan community had disappeared; the barbarian kings' efforts to reconstitute a united Italy had failed, as had the efforts of the byzantine kings to re-instate imperial authority in Italy; the sects and the heresies weren't born yet or prosperous enough, and the idea of the empire was but a memory. Even so historical events forced the imperial idea to make its necessity felt.

Another religion, stemming from judaism and christianity, threatened Asia. Muslim fanaticism did not pale in comparison to its christian counterpart; from the remotest Araby the Asian hordes made their way up towards Europe, and as they marched along, they converted and conquered people with the persuasion of the scimitar.

In the East the Empire held its stance and resisted against the islamic fury for centuries; in the West, once Africa had been conquered, the arabs threatened the islands and all the coasts of the peninsula, broke through into Spain and crossed the Pyrenees. The perception of danger made a political unity feel necessary even for the West; and thus the Empire sprung back to life. The capital though was not in Rome, and the authority of the Papacy wasn't threatened; on the other hand the Empire could not avoid basing its tenets on the catholic faith, which was then universally accepted in Italy, in France and in the greater part of Germany. But the marriage between the Catholic church and Roman Empire was essentially against nature and would repeat itself sincerely only once more, with Carl V, and last for a very short time. Meanwhile, the idea of the roman empire, put into practice by Charlemagne, was by now ingrained in the minds of the people and little by little became the last hope of all heretics, the final aim of all the secret societies that from the year one thousand to the four hundreds took hold in all of Europe. The history of this great period is not entirely unwritten, but certainly misunderstood. It is impossible to penetrate within the true spirit of the revolutions of that time without knowledge of gnosticism, manicheanism, of the paganism of almost all of the heresies of the day, without having divined the mystical and political secret of knighthood, without having understood the gay science of love of the troubadours, and the language and symbolism of the secret societies, and without having found the affinity and the occult links that intertwined together the heretics and the ghibellines, the lombards and the natives of Toulouse, monks, troubadours and knights of the Temple.

[79] The church, painted as the apocalyptic beast of babylonian abomination by troubadours and love poets (including Dante), felt greatly threatened and defended itself by every mean. The first apostles

dell'Evangelio féron scudi e lance[7]

but the bloody hands of St. Dominic and his peers used real swords to propagate the christian faith and charity. The fire and iron had overcome the heresy from Toulouse; fraud and torture and the inquisition toppled the vastly powerful Order of the Temple, which threatened to overturn from its foundation the temporal and spiritual authority of the Church of Rome all at once.

The onslaught had been terrible, the defence ruthless. The greatest among Italians [Dante] was scared of and suffered for this, and he invoked the help of the Emperor and the vengeance of God.

With Dante, the monarchic roman-pythagorean ideal, which had become the italic imperialist tradition, became visibly aware of itself. This great idea ties Numa, Pythagoras, Caesar, Vergil, Augustus, Dante and the other great italians who came at a later date.

And those catholic nationalists who want to put Dante across as a christian as if he almost had never been persecuted and prosecuted as a heretic, and who pride themselves in not doubting the orthodoxy of Dante's imperialism, as if the *De Monarchia* itself hadn't been indexed, may they look for another Christopher Columbus to parade as a catholic glory to humankind! Because Dante, by the great Jove and the good Apollo whom he invoked, was not a catholic and his imperialism was pagan and roman!

As he himself writes, his only Master is Vergil, but he himself had

umani corpi già veduti accesi[8]

living torches for the greater glory of the meek and forgiving Lord, he knew his value and did not certainly want vainly to surrender his great work in sacrifice; necessity forced him to become christian, but it wasn't but a great Comedy. He is pagan and never misses a chance to make us [80] catch glimpses of it; right from the first canto of the sacred poem Dante invokes the Sun, divine Apollo, initiator of Hercules and Aeneas; and it is well known how the Divine Comedy relies on the sixth book of the Aeneid.

In both we see the same isagoge, it is the allegorical and sometimes categorical exposition of the metamorphosis of man in God; politically, after all, Vergil and Dante do nothing more than exalt the Roman Empire.

The ever-present enemy, perennial object of Dante's formidable invective is the Church, symbolised by the wolf in the inferno, by the apocalyptic beast in purgatory; while he finds the way to cast down to hell even the two popes still-living during his mystical voyage, he uses the words heretic and catholic only once in the whole poem, almost trying to dodge the accusation of having avoided them on purpose, as one avoids those who are plagued by sickness.

All the defeats and the imperialist and ghibelline misfortunes cause him to suffer. One has the feeling that he curses the ill-fated and mysterious tragedy that took from Frederick his ministry; Manfredi and Conradin have all his sympathy. And for the killing of Conradin and the treason against the templars, as soon as he can he hurls abuse at France, the Capetian dynasty, the house of Angiò and especially at Philip the Fair.

Naturally Dante could in no way drag Vergil with him in Heaven. His guides, as is well known, follow one another in this order: Vergil, pythagorean and imperialist; Statius, whom he named Toulousan *motu proprio*, a simple hypostasis of Vergil; Beatrice, symbol of philosophy; and finally St. Bernard.

St. Bernard, so orthodox at a first glance, deserves such honours for having founded the rule of the Templars. Dante, who does not forget to define him *contemplator*, dresses him with the *white vestments*, the garb of the knights templar; the very same item of clothing worn by the blessed who constitute the rose of Heaven around the big templar cross, and seeing this immense cross, he speaks these meaningful words:

> qual è colui che tace e dicer vuole/
> mi trasse Beatrice, e disse: mira
> quanto è il convento delle bianche stole[9]

where the word *convento* is the technical traditional term for the great meetings of secret societies, and its just right to [81] use it when talking of white stoles and the whole vision brings Valentinus's gnostic prayer to mind.

Adeste visiones stolis albis candidae[10]

The two great symbols of Heaven are the eagle, the sacred bird which made the Romans revered by the world, and the rosy-cross, which is not the mystical rose but the sectarian rose of the "*Roman del la rose*", where the art of love is all hidden, and the fundamental symbol of the mysterious fraternity of the rosy-cross, and of the 18th degree of the scottish rite.

The emperor earned his title by divine right, and since Dante made the legitimacy of the germanic emperor derive from that of divine Augustus, who had certainly not received it from the Pope, it follows that *even spiritually imperial authority was independent from that of the Pope*. One should only read the *De Monarchia* and compare it with Cicero's *De Republica* (Book I-XXXVII and Book II-XXIII) to realise that both support the thesis of the excellency of monarchic (universal) rule over any other basing their assumptions on the great unitarian pythagorean principle; like Cicero and Vergil, Dante was faithful to the great immortal tradition of the Scuola Italica, chronologically and essentially anti-christian.

But we will focus in more detail on Dante's Paganism and imperialism some other time.

The Imperial Debate after Dante

The great Florentine died in exile never seeing his hopes and prayers fulfilled by Henry of Luxembourg. The Church triumphed, the guelphs took an uncontested lead in Italy, and the blossoming of the italian communes, of the republics of Venice and Florence especially made it impossible to accomplish the imperial ideal and political unity of Italy.

The idea did not disappear. The great spirits kept their faith. Petrarch, the chronichler of Cola di Rienzi, carried on the tradition. We'll make a passing mention, and we direct the reader towards a wider treatment of the roman imperialism of Petrarch by Bartoli (Storia della Letter. Italiana 1884 – Vol. VII, pag. 135–146).

[82] Machiavelli, who saw the perils of a political divide in Italy, while other peoples created political unity, asked for a prince who would know how and would want to complete the unification. He too took inspiration from the idea of roman imperialism, as has been noted by Villari (N. Machiavelli – Vol III, page 370–82, 1877 Edition).

But just like Dante had not seen the Vatican wolf die while giving birth, Machiavelli too died without a prince who would listen to him; and the Machiavellian politics were later taken up and applied by the Company of Jesus to the harm and not to the benefit of Italy and of the imperialist idea.

In the meantime neo-platonic humanism and the later rise of experimental sciences, and the revolt against aristotelianism, especially by the hands of the southern neo-pythagoreans Bruno, Telesio Campanella gave way to the western lay culture, which is slowly disinfecting Christianity from the European mentality. These mystics of the senses, these precursors and inventors of European philosophy, were not some lazy saints who would take refuge in a Thebaides or a hermitage; they were fiery and brave men of action. Campanella, alone, misunderstood, at a time in which the sun never set on the domains of the most christian Spain, first dared to put into practice his ideal of Monarchy, not christian of course, as written in his *Città del Sole*, seeking help even amongst the Turks. Betrayed, tried, tortured by the same Reverend Jesuit Fathers who took care of Giordano Bruno with great zeal, he never betrayed himself or changed his mind, and, buried for 27 years in a rotting cell, he carried on hoping and prophesising the accomplishment of his great ideal.

Campanella died in Paris and as if to give a tangible manifestation of the occult tie that binds men and things across the ages, from the house in which he died came the first voice of the french revolution. The revolution that was the result, it is known, of the practical intervention of secret societies, freemasonry and the illuminati more than others, all animated by a very profound anti-christian sentiment. But what is unknown is in what part the work of another great italian, which the Jesuit cunning and calumny made to pass as a charlatan. We are talking about Giuseppe Balsamo, better known as the Count of Cagliostro, the wonderful representative [83] of italian esotericism. To be convinced of this one need only remember his absolutely unassailable prophecy of the conquest and destruction of the Bastille which had been made in London by Cagliostro himself, and one need only think of the touching concern of the french masonic officials, when, in 1797, they passed by San Leo, and above all [one need only remember] the fierce fury of catholic authors even to this day who are against him. The authors of the *Rivista Massonica* of the Grand Orient of Italy who aren't ashamed to print the disgusting lies against Cagliostro circulated by the Jesuits around the time of his trial in Rome, should rather study the magnificent and well-documented recent work by Dr Marc Haven before reviling the memory of one of their great brothers! They would then begin to see why those contemporaries who knew him called him the divine Cagliostro.

Another Italian piloted and dominated the french revolution and, from the immense energy that he unleashed became an instrument to create the empire. Indeed, one must observe, as Carducci writes, "that what Dante only thought to do, another Italian, Napoleon I tried in his own way to put into effect". And if Carducci had realised how right Foscolo's claim had been, that Dante wanted to establish a new religious school in Europe, he probably wouldn't have hated, pagan as he was, Dante's holy empire.

Yet again the Roman eagle flew high with the Napoleonic legions; even in provinces that are captive today, Italy was freed again latinity triumphed and Rome had a King once more. This was the Roman imperial ideal; pagan despite the mistake of the Concordat, which after many centuries amidst the fire of the revolution built a united Italy.

Once the empire fell, catholic, lutheran and orthodox christianity came back with the Holy Alliance to weigh upon the whole of Europe. But it was only a short break. Napoleon was not dead yet, and already two generous youths entertained the ancient immortal ideal in their minds. What profound roots the faith in the imperial idea had in the soul of Giuseppe Mazzini, anyone with some familiarity with the Genoan seer's writings will know well. He too, like Vergil and Dante, who loved, studied and understood more than many illustrious professors, said that Italy had been destined by God to rule over peoples, to give from Rome to the world the light of [84] a third civilisation; he proclaimed the name and the soil of Rome as sacred, and in 1849 was eager to defend it together with Garibaldi from the french and the austrians united to uphold Catholicism.

Giuseppe Garibaldi always held Rome highly in his thoughts; he thought about Rome while fighting at Volturno, about Rome in '62 and '67; and disbanding his legion in San Marino, he said "in Rome, we will see each other again in Rome". His motto "Rome or death" shows how clear the transcendental importance of Rome was for the destiny of Italy for him.

Oh! Were it that the example of these two great figures, not suspected of christianity, was followed by those republicans, who have abandoned mazzinian spiritualism for the materialist theories imported from Germany, and who throw away the great idealistic force of the italic tradition in order to mimic the socialists, who care only about secondary and transitory economic issues!

Oh! Were it that the word of Mazzini, who admonished the Italians not to trust France: "dangerous for the sympathy it inspires among us", was heard by those democrats who on the altar of the God-given principles of 89, and in the name of a latin fraternity always in France's favour, try to hinder, every time that Italy is forced to defend its rights and its destiny from the arrogance which comes from the other side of the Alps!

But today, democratic freemasonry dreams of a confederation of latin republics led, obviously, by France, with the fateful city of Berne as a capital, just in order to make the internationalist idiots happy; and Mazzini may be read by Indian and Polish revolutionaries since they seem to care!

***

In this short overview, we have often been compelled to use simple sentences or incomplete examples; but what we really cared about was to show the immutable paganism of italian imperialism in a synthetic vision.

From what we have seen, it is clear that enacting a catholic nationalism is equal to tearing onself away from a 3000-year-old tradition, purely italic, just to cater to the interests of an exotic religion, deeply repugnant to all sense of romanity, and which has always been the bane of Italy over the past 2000 years.

[85] *But the attempt is politically wrong; because the fleeting conditions of today's parties do not matter in the face of secular and fated revolutions of the spirits*; and a sharp and artificial deviation cannot change the direction of the great courses of history.

Nationalism and Catholicism are antithetical terms even on an etymological basis! Historically and intrinsically a catholic nationalism is an absurdity! We invite those sincere Italians not to give credence to the Roman Church's tricks; and to constitute a lay, pagan, ghibelline imperialist party that takes inspiration from the italic tradition of Vergil, Dante, Campanella, Mazzini.

The rest may do what they like. We know they cannot win; our faith in the destiny of the Eternal City makes us certain of this, and to the known and the hidden enemies of pagan imperialism, we remind them and will carry on reminding them of the latin sentence:

Ducunt volentem fata, nolentem trahunt.[11]

Notes

Chapter 1

1. Amedeo Rocco Armentano, "Progredire è lo stesso che non essere," *Massime di Scienze Iniziatica* (Ancona: Ignis, 1992), p. 146.
2. Arturo Reghini, "Imperialismo Pagano," in *Salamandra* 1:1 (1914), republished in *Atanòr* 1, no. 3 (1924), pp. 69-85. I will be referring to the *Atanòr* version throughout the dissertation, an edition expanded and revised by the author himself. For other writings of Reghini, which challenged the modern status quo in the early part of his career, see "La Tradizione Italica," *Ultra* 7, no. 2 (1914), pp. 68-70; "Trascendenza di Spazio e di Tempo," *Mondo Occulto* 6, no. 6 (1926), pp. 69-107; "Istituzioni di Scienze Occulte," *Leonardo* 4, no. 2 (1906), pp. 155-160; "La Massoneria come Fattore Individuale," *Leonardo* 4, no. 4 (1906), pp. 297-310; "Il Punto di Vista dell'Occultismo," *Leonardo* 5, no. 2 (1907), pp. 144-156. It is fundamental to notice that occultists were by no means the only authors to rebel against the tenets of the modern world with a staunch antipositivist attitude: as we shall see, Benedetto Croce (1866-1952) and his idealist philosophy permeated much of the antipositivist discourse of the time. See Chapter 3 for an exhaustive coverage of Croce's influence on Italian culture in general, and Reghini and his fellow intellectuals, in particular.
3. Max Weber, *The Sociology of Religion* (Boston: Beacon Press, 1964 [1922]), pp. 270-272, and Anthony Giddens, *Modernity and Self-Identity: Self and Society in the Late Modern Age* (Cambridge: Polity Press, 1991), pp. 10-34. See also James Beckford, "The Disenchantment of Postmodernity," *New Blackfriars* 73, no. 913 (2007), pp. 121-128; Ralph Schroeder, "Disenchantment and its Discontents," *Sociological Review* 43, no. 2 (1995), pp. 227-250; Gilbert G. Germain, *A Discourse on Disenchantment: Reflections on Politics and Technology* (Albany: SUNY Press, 1993); Wouter J. Hanegraaff, "How Magic Survived the Disenchantment of the World," *Religion* 33 (2003), pp. 357-380; Kristina Karin Shull, "Has the Magic Gone? Weber's Disenchantment of the World and Its Implications for Art in Today's World," *Anamesa: An Interdisciplinary Journal* 3, no. 2 (2005), pp. 61-73; Egil Asprem, *The Problem of Disenchantment: Scientific Naturalism and Esoteric Discourse, 1900-1939* (Leiden: Brill, 2015); Shull, "The Disenchantment of Problems: Musings on a Cognitive Turn in Intellectual History," *Journal of Religion in Europe* 8 (2015), pp. 304-319; see also the recent Jason Storm, *The Myth of Disenchantment: Magic, Modernity and the Birth of the Human Sciences* (Chicago: University of Chicago Press, 2017).
4. Pauline Marie Rosenau, *Post-Modernism and the Social Sciences: Insights. Inroads, Intrusions* (Princeton, NJ: Princeton University Press, 1992), p. 5.

5. "il suffragio universale che ha condotto a partecipare all'attività politica quasi tutta la massa incolta e malleabile della nazione," in Reghini, "Imperialismo," p. 71.
6. The strategy of using an unbroken chain of transmission as a means of legitimization of Reghini's discourse, an Italic autochthone one, will be fully analyzed later in the volume.
7. The survival of Pythagorean thought in Italy throughout the centuries does not apply to the twentieth century and Reghini's coterie only: it is a wide and extensive phenomenon, which appears to have ancient roots: Pythagoras's birthplace, usually attributed to the Greek island of Samos, has been questioned by many Italian authors, through the centuries: Pythagoras is considered Italian tout court by works such as Vincenzo Capparelli, *Il Messaggio di Pitagora: Il Pitagorismo nel Tempo* (Rome: Edizioni Mediterranee, [1944] 2003), where Tommaso Campanella, Giordano Bruno, and Bernardino Telesio are all said to have been inspired by the pre-Socratic philosopher: "Have Bruno, Campanella and Telesio thought to reconnect themselves, as their precursors, to Saint Thomas, Saint Augustine, to Plotinus, or rather to the Pythagoreans and Eleatics?" (p. 192); other works in a similar vein include both scholarly literature and works with a more emic approach:, among the first, see Dominic J. O'Meara, *Pythagoras Revived* (Oxford: Oxford University Press, 1989); Christoph Riedweg, *Pythagoras: His Life, Teaching and Influence* (Ithaca, NY: Cornell University Press, 2005); Christiane L. Joost-Gaugier, *Measuring Heaven, Pythagoras and His Influence on Thought and Art in Antiquity and the Middle Ages* (Ithaca, NY: Cornell University Press, 2006); Kitty Ferguson, *Pythagoras, His Life and the Legacy of a Rational Universe* (London: Walker, 2008); for a more "insider" approach, see Paolo Galliano, *Roma prima di Roma: Metastoria della Tradizione Italica* (Rome: Simmetria Edizioni, 2011); Giuseppe Lo Monaco, *L'Ordine Osirideo Egizio e la Trasmissione Pitagorica* (Bassano del Grappa: np, 1999); Paolo Casini, *L'Antica Sapienza Italica* (Bologna: Il Mulino, 1998).
8. Three biographies have been published in Italian on Reghini: the first, by his disciple Giulio Parise, may be found in Arturo Reghini, *Considerazioni sul Rituale dell'Apprendista Muratore, con una nota sulla vita e sull'Attività' Massonica dell'Autore* (Naples: Edizioni di Studi Iniziatici, 1946), pp. v–xv. For decades these scant pages have been the only biographical material at the disposal of the general reader, until the following biographies were published in the new millennium: Roberto Sestito, *Il Figlio del Sole: Vita e Opere di Arturo Reghini Filosofo e Matematico* (Ancona: Associazione Culturale Ignis, 2006) and Natale Mario di Luca, *Arturo Reghini: Un Intellettuale Neo-Pitagorico tra Massoneria e Fascismo* (Rome: Atanor, 2003).
9. Theodor Adorno, "Theses Against Occultism," in *The Stars Down to Earth and Other Essays on the Irrational in Culture*, ed. and intro. by Stephen Crook (London: Routledge, [1974] 1994), p. 174.
10. James Webb, *Flight From Reason* (London: MacDonald & Co., 1971).
11. Jeffrey Herf, *Reactionary Modernism: Technology, Culture and Politics in Weimar and the Third Reich* (Cambridge: Cambridge University Press, [1984] 1998), p. 1.
12. See the theoretical framework of my dissertation on multiple modernities, which I will discuss later in the chapter.

13. For more on the individual scholars and their theses on occultism and modernism, see section 1.2 of this chapter.
14. One example, out of many, is Leszek Kolakowski, "Modernity on Endless Trial," *Encounter* 66 (1986), pp. 8–12, where the author expressedly admits (p. 9) that "we have no idea what Modernity is." Bruno Latour, *Nous n'Avons Jamais Été Modernes: Essai d'Anthropologie Symétrique* (Cambridge, MA: Harvard University Press, [1991] 1993), p. 10, states that "modernity comes in as many versions as there are thinkers or journalists."
15. Marshall Berman, *All That Is Solid Melts into Air: The Experience of Modernity* (London: Verso, [1982] 2010), p. 16.
16. Ibid., p. 24.
17. Ibid., p. 24.
18. Roger Griffin, "Modernity, Modernism, and Fascism: A Mazeway Resynthesis," *Modernism/Modernity* 15, no. 1 (2008), pp. 9–24 (p. 11).
19. "There is a measure in things," Quintus Horatius Flaccus, *Satyrarum Libri*, book I, v. 106.
20. Herf, *Reactionary Modernism*, p. 2.
21. See Roger Griffin's seminal *Modernism and Fascism: The Sense of a New Beginning under Hitler and Mussolini* (Basingstoke, UK: Palgrave Macmillan, 2007); Walter Adamson, "Modernism and Fascism: The Politics of Culture in Italy, 1903–1922," *The American Historical Review* 95, no. 2 (1990), pp. 359–390; David Crowley, "Nationalist Modernisms," in *Modernism 1914–1939: Designing a New World*, ed. Christopher Wilk (London: V&A Publications, 2006), pp. 371–373; Emilio Gentile, "The Myth of National Regeneration in Italy. From Modernist Avant-garde to Fascism," in *Fascist Visions*, ed. Matthew Affron and Mark Antliff (Princeton, NJ: Princeton University Press, 1997), pp. 25–45.
22. A section dedicated to Traditionalism and Roman Traditionalism, in particular, will follow shortly.
23. Jeffrey C. Alexander, *The Dark Side of Modernity* (Malden, MA: Polity, 2013).
24. Charles Taylor, *The Malaise of Modernity* (Toronto: Anansi Press, 1991). A precise division of chapters and outline of the thesis will be provided in section 1.4, at the end of the present chapter.
25. Notable exceptions to the rule are Marco Pasi, "Theosophy and Anthroposophy in Italy during the First Half of the Twentieth Century," *Theosophical History, a Quarterly Journal of Research* 16, no. 2 (2012), pp. 81–119; Hans Thomas Hakl, "The Theory and Practice of Sexual Magic, Exemplified by Four Magical Groups in the Early Twentieth Century," in *Hidden Intercourse: Eros and Sexuality in the History of Western Esotericism*, ed. Wouter J. Hanegraaff and Jeffrey J. Kripal (Leiden: Brill 2008), pp. 445–478; Hakl, "Julius Evola and the UR Group," *Aries* 12, no. 1 (Leiden: Brill 2012), pp. 53–90; Hakl, "Nazionalsocialismo ed Occultismo," *Arthos* 1, no. 1 (1997), pp. 16–27 and 1, no. 2 (1997), pp. 57–75; Peter Staudenmaier, *Between Occultism and Fascism: Anthroposophy and the Politics of Race in the Fascist Era* (Brill: Leiden, 2014); Mark Sedgwick, *Against the Modern World: Traditionalism and the Secret Intellectual History of the Twentieth Century* (New York: Oxford University Press, 2004);

Sedgwick, "How Traditional Are the Traditionalists? The Case of the Guenonian Sufis," *Aries* 22 (1999), pp. 3–24; Roberto Bacci, *La Trasmutazione della Coscienza nell'Esoterismo Italiano del Periodo Fascista: Spaccio dei Maghi (1929) Di Mario Manlio Rossi e Maschera e Volto dello Spiritualismo Contemporaneo (1932) Di Julius Evola*, unpublished PhD dissertation.

26. Dana Lloyd Thomas, "Arturo Reghini: A Modern Pythagorean," *Gnosis* 44 (1997), pp. 52–59; Thomas, "Arturo Reghini," in *Dictionary of Gnosis and Western Esotericism*, ed. Wouter J. Hanegraaff, Antoine Faivre, Roelof van den Broek, and Jean-Pierre Brach (Brill: Leiden, 2006), pp. 979–980; Lazlo Toth, "Arturo Reghini," *Politica Hermetica*, 1 (1987), pp. 143–155.

27. Di Luca, *Reghini*, p. 158: "Lo portò inevitabilmente ad un antisemitismo ideologico."

28. Ibid., p. 105. "un impressionante manifestazione d'invasamento narcisistico [. . .], ai limiti del delirio di onnipotenza."

29. Thomas, "Arturo Reghini," p. 789.

30. Ibid., p. 780.

31. See Michele Beraldo, "Le Riviste Spiritualistiche, Occultiste ed Esoteriche durante il Regime," in *Esoterismo e Fascismo*, ed. Gianfranco de Turris (Rome: Mediterranee, 2006), pp. 383–387; Marco Rossi, "L'Interventismo Politico-Culturale delle Riviste Tradizionaliste negli Anni Venti," *Storia Contemporanea* 18, no. 3 (1987), pp. 457–504; Francesco Saverio Festa, "Teosofia ed Esoterismo nelle Riviste Italiane della Prima Metà del 900," in *Pioniere, Poeten, Professoren: Eranos und der Monte Verità in der Zivilisationgeschichte des 20 Jahrhunderts,* ed. Elisabetta Barone, Matthias Riedl, and Alexandra Tischel (Wurzburg: Konigshausen & Neumann, 2004), pp. 143–154.

32. Wouter J. Hanegraaff, *Esotericism and the Academy: Rejected Knowledge in Western Culture* (Cambridge: Cambridge University Press, 2012), p. 221.

33. Adorno, *Theses*, p. 241: "Okkultismus ist die Metaphysik der dummen Kerle. Die Subalternität der Medien ist so wenig zufällig wie das Apokryphe, Läppische des Geoffenbarten. Seit den frühen Tagen des Spiritismus hat das Jenseits nichts Erheblicheres kundgetan als Grüße der verstorbenen Großmutter nebst der Prophezeiung, eine Reise stünde bevor." Adorno was obviously not the only critic of occultism as an irrational anomaly within the larger framwork of modernity; see also Marcello Truzzi, "The Occult Revival as Popular Culture: Some Random Observations on the Old and Nouveau Witch," *The Sociological Quarterly* 13 (1972), pp. 16–36; Andrew M. Greeley, "Implications for the Sociology of Reason of Occult Behaviour in the Youth Culture," in *On the Margin of the Visible: Sociology, the Esoteric and the Occult*, ed. Edward A. Tiryakian (New York: Wiley, 1974), pp. 295–302; John Straude, "Alienated Youth and the Cult of the Occult," in *Sociology for the Seventies*, ed. Morris Medley and James E. Conyers (New York, Wiley, 1970).

34. Truzzi, "Occult Revival," p. 20.

35. Webb, *Flight*, p. 1. See also Hugh Trevor-Ropers's theories in *The Last Days of Hitler* (London: Macmillan, 1974) or *Consciousness and Society: The Reorientation of European Social Thought, 1890–1930* (London: Transaction, 2002): "How can the reaction against positivism avoid the very irrationalism that positivism had not been

able to avert once it fell prey to social Darwinism, 'heredity' and 'environment' [...]?," p. xiii.
36. Perhaps the most vehement attack against occultism in Italian language may be found in the works of Benedetto Croce, who, after a brief support for the regime, ended up considering Fascism to be a "moral disease": see Francesco Baroni, *Benedetto Croce e l'Esoterismo* (Bologna: Il Mulino, 2011): "The radical refusal on Croce's behalf [...], of the esoteric manifestations of *fin-de-siécle* esotericism, derives from seeing in them a degenerative form of 'irrationalism,'" p. 12; Benedetto Croce, *Storia d'Italia. Dal 1871 al 1915*, ed. Giuseppe Galasso (Milan: Adelphi, 1991 [1928]); see also Cecilia Gatto Trocchi, the works most interesting for my research being *Storia Esoterica d'Italia* (Milano: Piemme, 2001); *Il Risorgimento Esoterico, Storia Esoterica d'Italia da Mazzini ai Giorni Nostri* (Milano: Mondadori, 1996); *Viaggio nella Magia: La Cultura Esoterica nell'Italia di Oggi* (Rome: Laterza, 1996); a more intriguing theory on "Ur-Fascism" or "Eternal Fascism" is provided by Umberto Eco in his *Cinque Scritti Morali* (Milan: Bompiani, 1997) and *Il Fascismo Eterno* (Milan: Bompiani, 1997) and Furio Jesi, *Cultura di destra. Con tre inediti e un'intervista*, ed. Andrea Cavalletti (Rome: Nottetempo, [1993] 2011), in which the irrational attraction to totalitarianism is tackled by these two thinkers.
37. See the Nazi occultism theories in Louis Pauwels and Jacques Bergier, *Le Matin des Magiciens* (Paris: Gallimard, 1960); Trevor Ravenscroft, *The Spear of Destiny* (New York: Bantam, 1974); these are but two examples of literature aiming to connect Nazi ideology and occultism: for a thorough treatment of the phenomenon, see Nicholas Goodrick-Clarke, "The Modern Mythology of Nazi Occultism," in Goodrick-Clarke, *The Occult Roots of Nazism: Aryan Cults and their Influence on Nazi Ideology* (Albany: SUNY Press, 2004), pp. 217–226.
38. *Esoterismo e Fascismo*, p. 10. "non si può invece parlare—checché ne possa pensare qualcuno—di un 'esoterismo fascista,' vale a dire di una dimensione esoterica né ufficiale né ufficiosa del fascismo."
39. Wouter J. Hanegraaff, *New Age Religion and Western Culture: Esotericism in the Mirror of Secular Thought* (Albany: SUNY Press, 1998), p. 422.
40. Marco Pasi, "Occultism," in *The Brill Dictionary of Religion*, ed. Kocku Von Stuckrad, trans. Robert R. Barr, Vol. III (Leiden: Brill, 2006), p. 1366. For earlier definitions of the term, see Antoine Faivre, *Access to Western Esotericism* (Albany: SUNY Press, 1994); Antoine Faivre, "Questions of Terminology Proper to Study of Esoteric Currents in Modern and Contemporary Europe," in *Western Esotericism and the Science of Religion*, ed. Antoine Faivre and Wouter J. Hanegraaff (Louvain: Peeters, 1998), pp. 1–10; Robert Galbreath, "Explaining Modern Occultism," in *The Occult in America: New Historical Perspectives*, ed. Howard Kerr and Charles L. Crow (Chicago: University of Illinois Press, 1983), pp. 11–37; Edward A. Tiryakian, "Toward the Sociology of Esoteric Culture," in *On the Margin of the Visible: Sociology, the Esoteric, and the Occult*, ed. Edward A. Tiryakian (New York: Wiley, 1974).
41. Alison Butler, *Victorian Occultism and the Making of Modern Magic: Invoking Tradition* (New York: Palgrave Macmillan, 2011), p. x.
42. See Hanegraaff, "How Magic."

43. See Butler, *Victorian Occultism*; Alison Butler, "Making Magic Modern: Nineteenth-Century Adaptations," *The Pomegranate* 6, no. 2 (2004), pp. 212-230; *The Occult in America*; Alex Owen, *The Disenchantment of the West: British Occultism and the Culture of the Modern* (Chicago: University Press of Chicago, 2004); Marco Pasi, "The Modernity of Occultism: Reflections on Some Crucial Aspects," in *Hermes in the Academy: Ten Years' Study of Western Esotericism at the University of Amsterdam*, ed. Wouter J. Hanegraaff and Joyce Pijnenburg (Leiden: Brill, 1999), pp. 59-74; *The Occult in Russian and Soviet Culture*, ed. Bernice Rosenthal (Ithaca, NY: Cornell University Press, 2005); Randall Styers, *Making Magic: Religion, Magic and Science in the Modern World* (Oxford: Oxford University Press, 2004); Corinna Treitel, *A Science for the Soul: Occultism and the Genesis of the German Modern* (Baltimore: John Hopkins University); Bradford Verter, *Dark Star Rising: The Emergence of Modern Occultism*, unpublished PhD dissertation.
44. Pasi, "Modernity," p. 59.
45. Ibid., p. 63.
46. The two articles which most influenced my reasoning on the topic of occultism and modernity are the review articles: Thomas Laqueur, "Why Margins Matter: Occultism and the Making of Modernity," *Modern Intellectual History* 3, no. 1 (2006), pp. 111-135; and John Wayne Monroe, "The Way We Believe Now: Modernity and the Occult," *Magic, Ritual and Witchcraft* 2, no. 1 (2007), pp. 68-78.
47. See Arthur Versluis, "The New Inquisitions: Heretic Hunting and the Intellectual Origins of Modern Totalitarianism," in *Theodor Adorno and the 'Occult'* (Oxford: Oxford University Press, 2011), pp. 1-14.
48. Pasi, "Modernity," p. 64.
49. Owen, *Place*, p. 90. "As Dorothea Hunter, 'Deo Date' of the Golden Dawn, later remarked, 'the Order was my University.'"
50. Ibid., p. 72 and p. 91.
51. David Allen Harvey, *Beyond Enlightenment: Occultism and Politics in Modern France* (DeKalb: Northern Illinois University Press, 2005), p. 6.
    Helena P. Blavatsky (1831-1891) was the one of the founding members of the Theosophical Society and among the most influential occultist of her generation.
52. Julius Evola, "La Donna Come Cosa," *Ignis* 1, no. 1-2 (1925), pp. 13-14.
53. "La donna assoluta non solo non possiede quell'Io, ma non saprebbe nemmeno che farsene, essa non sa nemmeno concepirlo e la sua presenza agirebbe in modo estremamente disturbatore presso a ogni genuina estrinsecazione della di lei più profonda natura," Julius Evola, *La Metafisica del Sesso* (Rome: Mediterranee [1958] 1996), p. 196.
54. It is Evola who lies behind the fictional character of the shady Bruno Tellegra in Sibilla Aleramo's biographical novel, *Amo Dunque Sono* (Milano: Mondadori, 1927), p. 145 ff. "Exiting the villa he asked me if we could walk some more along the deserted road that runs close to the gates. The year before I had begged him for the same thing and he had declined. 'Let's walk,' I replied. All of a sudden, in a patch of darkness, he grabbed me by the arm, and buried his fingers in my velvet hair. My hair, which I had cut short because he didn't like it long. I moved away. But he grabbed my wrists, throwing his

body onto mine, trying to kiss me. Silent struggle against the dark trunk of a tree, and high up there, among the foliage, some star was dreaming. I bit his hands, I felt I had turned into a panther, with no hate, happy, I manage to free myself, triumphant. 'You are strong. I did not believe you to be this strong,' he muttered. He escorted me back to the hotel entrance. He will send me a copy of Der Golem, which you told me of. He will call me to know if I will stay or leave. The night swallowed him up again [. . .]." Never become like him! May you be safe from the curse within him! May you repeat to me that "in my goodness is my strength, in my capacity to love, my glory." See also Simone Caltabellotta, *Un'Amore degli Anni Venti: Storia Erotica e Magica di Sibilla Aleramo e Giulio Parise* (Milan: Adriano Salani, 2015).
55. Owen, *Place*, p. 249.
56. Laqueur, "Margins," p. 127.
57. Staudenmaier, *Occultism*, p. 10.
58. Peter King, *The Antimodern Condition: An Argument against Progess* (London: Ashgate, 2014); other works useful for this stance against modernity are David Harvey, *The Condition of Postmodernity* (Oxford: Blackwell, 1989); Arthur Versluis, "Antimodernism," *Telos* 132 (2006), pp. 96–130.
59. Ibid., pp. 18–19.
60. Paul Oskar Kristeller, *Supplementum Ficinianum: Marsilii Ficini Florentini Philosophi Platonici Opuscula Inedita et Dispersa Primum Collegit et ex Fontibus Plerumque Manuscriptis Edidit*, 2 vols. (Florence: Olschki, 1937); Paul Oskar Kristeller, "Marsilio Ficino e Lodovico Lazzarelli: Contributo alla Diffusione delle Idee Ermetiche nel Rinascimento," *Annali della R. Scuola Normale Superiore di Pas, Lettere, Storia e Filosofia* 2 (1938), pp. 237–262; see also Christopher S. Celenza, "Paul Oskar Kristeller and the Hermetic Tradition," in *Kristeller Reconsidered: Essays on his Life and Scholarship*, ed. John Monfasani (New York: Italica Press, 2006), pp. 71–80.
61. For a comprehensive study on the Eranos meetings, see Hans Thomas Hakl, *Eranos, an Alternative Intellectual History of the Twentieth Century* (Durham, NC: Acumen Press, 2013).
62. Hanegraaff, *Esotericism and the Academy*, p. 278.
63. Frances A. Yates, *Giordano Bruno and the Hermetic Tradition* (Chicago: University of Chicago Press, 1964); see also her following books: *The Art of Memory* (Chicago: University of Chicago Press, 1966); *The Rosicrucian Enlightenment* (London: Routledge & Kegan Paul, 1972); *The Occult Philosophy in the Elizabethan Age* (London: Routledge & Kegan Paul, 1979).
64. Hanegraaff, *Esotericism and the Academy*, p. 327.
65. Eugenio Garin, "Divagazioni Ermetiche," *Rivista Critica di Storia della Filosofia* 31 (1979), pp. 462–466.
66. Wouter J. Hanegraaff, "Beyond the Yates Paradigm: the Study of Western Esotericism between Counterculture and new Complexity," *Aries* 1, no. 1 (2001), pp. 5–37 [17].
67. Wouter J. Hanegraaff, "Textbooks and Introductions to Western Esotericism," *Religion* (2012), pp. 1–23 [2].
68. Antoine Faivre, *L'Ésotérisme* (Paris: Presses Universitaires de France, 1992).
69. Ibid., p. 4.

70. See, among the many papers devoted to theory and method, Wouter J. Hanegraaff, "On the Construction of Esoteric Traditions," in *Western Esotericism and the Science of Religion*, ed. Wouter J. Hanegraaff and Antoine Faivre (Leuven: Peeters, 1998); Hanegraaff, "Beyond the Yates Paradigm: the Study of Western Esotericism between Counterculture and New Complexity," *Aries* 1, no. 1 (2001), pp. 5–37; Arthur Versluis, "What Is Esoteric," *Esoterica* 4 (2002), pp. 1–15; Kocku von Stuckrad, *Western Esotericism: A Brief History of Secret Knowledge*, trans. Nicholas Goodrick-Clarke (London: Equinox, [2005] 2009), pp. 1–12; Marco Pasi, "Il Problema della Definizione dell'Esoterismo: Analisi Critica e Proposte per la Ricerca Futura," in *Forme e Correnti dell'Esoterismo Occidentale*, ed. Alessandro Grossato (Milan: Medusa, 2008), pp. 205–228; Michael Bergunder, "What Is Esotericism? Cultural Studies, Approaches and the Problem of Definition in Religious Studies," *Method & Theory in the Study of Religion* 22 (2010), pp. 9–36.

71. Kocku von Stuckrad, *Locations of Knowledge in Medieval and Early Modern Europe* (Leiden: Brill, 2010), pp. x–xi. Also see von Stuckrad, "Discursive Study of Religion: From States of the Mind to Communication and Action," *Method & Theory in the Study of Religion* 15 (2003), pp. 255–271; von Stuckrad, "Reflections on the Limits of Reflection: An Invitation to the Discursive Study of Religion," *Method & Theory in the Study of Religion* 22 (2010), pp.156–169.

72. Hanegraaff, *Esotericism and the Academy*, p. 365.

73. See, for example, *New Approaches to the Study of Western Esotericism*, ed. Egil Asprem and Julian Strube (Leiden: Brill, 2021).

74. The clearest and most persuasive work, in my opinion, on the concept of tradition and its central role in Western esotericism, from the Renaissance to modern times, is Antoine Faivre, "Histoire de la Notion Moderne de Tradition dans ses rapports avec les courants ésotériques (XVe–XXe siècles)," *Filiation et Emprunts, Aries Special Issue* (Milan: Archè/La Table d'Émeraude, 1999), pp. 4–47. Also see Faivre, *Theosophy, Imagination, Tradition* (Albany: State University of New York Press, 2000), pp. 171–248, and *Esoterismo e Tradizione* (Torino: Elledici, 1999).

75. Antoine Faivre, "tentent de metre en consonance diverses traditions anciennes," "Histoire de la Notion Moderne," p. 9.

76. "hunc [. . .] perennem fontem," quoted in Charles Schmitt's article "Perennial Philosophy: Steuco to Leibniz," *Journal of the History of Ideas* 27 (1966), pp. 505–532.

77. For a comprehensive commentary on the *Corpus Hermeticum*, see Brian P. Copenhaver, *Hermetica: The Greek Corpus Hermeticum and the Latin Asclepius in a New English Translation, with Notes and Introduction* (Cambridge: Cambridge University Press, 1995); Joscelyn Godwin, *The Golden Thread: The Ageless Wisdom of the Western Mystery Traditions* (Wheaton, IL: Quest Books, 2007); Yates, *Giordano Bruno*. For Pico's Theses, see *Syncretism in the West: Pico's 900 Theses (1486): The Evolution of Traditional Religious and Philosophical Systems*, ed. and trans. S. A. Farmer (Tempe, AZ: Medieval and Renaissance Texts and Studies, 1998).

78. Agostino Steuco, *De Perenni Philosophia* (New York: Johnson Reprint Corp., 1972); also see Ronald K. Delph, "Renovatio, Reformatio, and Humanist Ambition in Rome," in *Heresy, Culture and Religion in Early Modern Religion*, ed. Ronald K.

Delph, Michelle M. Fontaine, and John Jeffries Martin (Kirksville, MO: Truman State University Press, 2006), pp. 73–92.
79. Louis-Claude de Saint-Martin, *Des Erreurs et de la Vérité ou les Hommes Rappeliés au Principe Universel de la Science* (Edinburgh: np, 1775); *Tableau Naturel des Rapports qui Unissent Dieu, l'Homme et l'Universe* (Edinburgh: np, 1782).
80. Johann Friedrich Kleuker, *Magikon oder das Geheime System einer Gesellschaft Unbekannter Philosophen* (Hannover: np, 1784).
81. "La decouvérte des grand secrets de la religion et de la science primitive des mages et l'unité du dogme universel," Eliphas Levi, *Dogme et Rituel de Haute Magie* (Paris: Librairie Medical de Germer Ballière, 1856), p. xi.
82. "c'est afin d'y trouver des éléments de légitimation de leur croisade contre le matérialisme montant, éléments que les enseignements des Églises leur paraissant insuffisants à fournir," Antoine Faivre, "Histoire de la Notion Moderne," p. 25.
83. Hanegraaff, "On the Construction of Esoteric Traditions," pp. 26–27.
84. Faivre, "Histoire de Notion Moderne," p. 31.
85. Among Guénon's classic texts that form the basis for his Traditionalist ideas, see René Guénon, *Orient et Occident* (Paris: Payot, 1924); Guénon, *La Crise du Monde Moderne* (Paris: Bossard, 1927); Guénon, *Le Règne de la Quantité et les Signes des Temps* (Paris: Gallimard, 1945); Guénon, *Aperçus sur l'Initiation* (Paris: Éditions Traditionelles, 1946); two essential works on Guénon and the Traditionalist movement are Sedgwick, *Modern World* and the recent David Bisson, *René Guénon: Une Politique de l'Esprit* (Paris: Pierre-Guillaume de Roux, 2013). Where Sedgwick's text succeeds in delineating a complete picture of Traditionalism in the last century, with the only downside of a very scarse use of primary sources, Bisson's work focuses on Guénon alone, with a plethora of primary material being used, from published works to articles and corresponence. On Traditionalism, see William W. Quinn, *The Only Tradition* (Albany: State University of New York Press, 1997); Kenneth Oldmeadow, *Traditionalism: Religion in the Light of Perennial Philosophy*, 2nd ed. (San Rafael, CA: Sophia Perennis, [2000] 2011; Aldous Huxley, *The Perennial Philosophy* (New York: Harper & Brothers, 1945); VVAA, *Politica Hermetica: Doctrine de la Race et Tradition* 2 (1988); Jean Borella, *Esotérisme Guénonien et Mystère Chrétien* (Lausanne: L'Age d'Homme, 1997); Marco Pallis, *A Treasury of Traditional Wisdom: An Encyclopedia of Humankind's Spiritual Truth* (Louisville, KY: Fons Vitae, 2000); Huston Smith, *The World's Religions: Our Great Wisdom* Traditions (New York: Harper & Brothers, 1958); Jean-Pierre Laurant, *Guénon* (Paris: Éditions de l'Herne, 1985); Laurant, *René Guénon, Les Enjeux d'une Lecture* (Paris: Dervy, 2006); Antoine Compagnon, *Les Antimodernes. De Joseph de Maistre à Roland Barthes* (Paris: Gallimard, 2005), pp. 7–14.
86. René Guénon, *Le Théosophisme, Histoire d'une pseudo-Religion* (Paris: Editiones Traditionelles, 1921); Guénon, *L'Erreur Spirite* (Paris: Editiones Traditionelles, 1923)
87. For published correspondence between Guénon and Reghini, see René Guénon, "La Corrispondenza di Réné Guénon con Arturo Reghini," in *Il Risveglio della Tradizione Occidentale*, ed. Mariano Bizzarri (Rome: Atanòr, 2003), pp. 105–143.
88. Sedgwick, *Modern World*, pp. 24–25.

89. Edward Shils, "Tradition," *Comparative Studies in Society and History: Special Issue on Tradition and Modernity* 13, no. 2 (1971), pp. 122–159 [137].
90. Sedgwick, *Against the Modern World*, p. 137.
91. "La' dove vi é ordine non vi puo' essere progresso"; "Nelle cose umane l'ordine é quasi sempre insidiato dal disordine," "Il disordine sociale é una conseguenza della credenza nel progresso e del desiderio di voler divenire diversi da cio' che siamo," Amedeo Armentano, *Massime*, pp. 146–147.
92. For sources in Italian, see Giorgio, *Roma* and Renato del Ponte, *Il Movimento Tradizionalista Romano nel 900* (Scandiano: SeaR, 1987).
93. "Questo tradizionalismo lo diremo Romano, sia perché fece capo a persone, che scrivevano su riviste che si pubblicavano e circolavano a Roma, ed appartenevano all'ambiente culturale della capitale, sia perché fu ispirato alla tradizione romana, o almeno partì dal presupposto che l'idea di Roma fosse ancora viva, e avesse ancora una funzione nel nostro secolo," Piero di Vona, *Evola, Guénon, De Giorgio* (Borzano: SeaR, 1993), p. 219.
94. "al disopra degli uomini e degli iniziati stanno i grandi fati che sovrastano anche gli Dei; e gli iniziati possono solo ambire a riconoscerli ed a collaborare consciamente e intelligentemente alla loro manifestazione nel mondo dei mortali," in Arturo Reghini, "Libertà e Gerarchia," quoted in Di Luca, *Reghini*, p. 77.
95. "La religione dommatica si oppone a questa ricerca in nome di una rivelazione superiore; ed anche la scienza, così detta positiva, vi si dimostra ostile, pretendendo al monopolio fdell'indagine scientifica, e dichiarando anti-scientifiche tutte le indagini che non siano condotte conquei mezzi e criteri presentemente in auge," Arturo Reghini, "Il Dominio dell'Anima," in *Paganesimo, Pitagorismo e Massoneria*, ed. Gennaro d'Uva (Furnari: Societa' Editrice Mantinea, 1988), p. 3.
96. "Il linguaggio e la razza non sono le cause di questa superiorità metafisica, essa appare connaturata al luogo, al suolo, all'aria stessa. Roma, Roma caput mundi, la città eterna, si manifesta storicamente come una di queste regioni magnetiche della terra" in Arturo Reghini, "Del Simbolismo e della Filologia in Rapporto alla Sapienza Metafisica," *Ultra* August (1914), p. 13.
97. Letter from Guénon to Reghini, July 13, 1924, Guénon collection.
98. For an idea of the general climate concerning the idea of imperial Rome, see Giorgio, *Roma*, pp. 228–312; Christian Giudice, "Rome Was Rebuilt in a Play: Roggero Musmeci Ferrari Bravo and the Representation of *Rumon*," *Pomegranate: Journal for Pagan Studies* 14, no. 2 (2012), pp. 212–232.
99. S. N. Eisenstadt, "Multiple Modernities," *Daedalus* 129, no. 1 (2000), pp. 1–29; see also *The Origins and Diversity of the Axial-Age Civilizations*, ed. S. N. Eisenstadt (Albany: State University of New York, 1986); Alex Inkeles and David H. Smith, *Becoming Modern: Individual Change in Six Developing Countries* (Cambridge, MA: Harvard University Press, 1974); Johann P. Arnason, "The Theory of Modernity and the Problematic of Democracy," *Thesis Eleven* 26 (1990), pp. 20–46; *Education and Fascism: Political Identity and Social Education in Nazi Germany*, ed. Heinz Sunker and Hans-Uwe Otto (London: Falmer Press, 1997).
100. Eisenstadt, "Multiple Modernities," p. 2.

101. Samuel P. Huntington, *The Clash of Civilization and the Remaking of World Order* (New York: Simon and Schuster, 1996).
102. Eisenstadt, "Multiple Modernities," p. 12.
103. Ibid., p. 10.
104. ISTAT, "Italia in Cifre," last accessed October 5, 2020. This survey, by Italy's major center for statistics, was made public for the 150th anniversary of the Unification of Italy in 1861.
105. Volker H. Schmidt, "Multiple Modernities or Varieties of Modernity?," *Current Sociology* 54, no. 1 (2006), pp. 77–97. Italics mine.
106. Ibid., p. 80.
107. Björn Wittrock, "Modernity: One, None, or Many? European Origins and Modernity as Global Condition," *Daedalus* 129, no. 1 (2000), pp. 31–60.
108. Ibrahim Kaya, "Modernity, Openness, Interpretation: A Perspective of Multiple Modernities," *Social Science Information* 43, no. 1 (2004), pp. 35–57.
109. Raymond L.M. Lee, "Reinventing Modernity: Reflexive Modernity vs Liquid Modernity vs Multiple Modernities," *European Journal of Social Theory* 9, no. 3 (2006), pp. 355–368 [364].
110. *The Invention of Tradition*, ed. Eric Hobsbawm and Terence Ranger (Cambridge: Cambridge University Press, 1992), pp. 1–14
111. *The Invention of Sacred Tradition*, ed. James R. Lewis and Olav Hammer (Cambridge: Cambridge University Press, 2007), pp. 10–12.
112. Olav Hammer, *Claiming Knowledge: Strategies of Epistemology from Theosophy to the New Age* (Leiden: Brill, 2001), p. 69.
113. Élemire Zolla, in his *Uscite dal Mondo* (Milano: Adelphi, 1992), wrote of *Pinocchio* as "a literary miracle of an almost intolerable esoteric profundity."
114. *Ritorno alle Giubbe Rosse*, ed. Roberto Sestito (Ancona: Associazione Culturale Ignis, 2006).
115. Alex Owen, *The Place of Enchantment*, p. 257.
116. See Eduardo Frosini, *Massoneria Italiana e Tradizione Iniziatica* (Ancona: np, 1911); Roberto Sestito, *Storia del Rito Filosofico Italiano e dell'Ordine Orientale Antico e Primitivo* (Firenze: Libreria Chiari, 2003).
117. Arturo Reghini, "Campidoglio e Golgota," *Atanor* 1, no. 5 (1924), p. 14.
118. Quoted in Renzo de Felice, *Benito Mussolini: Il Fascista: la Conquista del Potere (1921-1925)* (Turin: Einaudi, 1966), p. 145: "Un grande paravento dietro cui si nascondono piccoli uomini."
119. See Renato del Ponte, *Evola e il magico Gruppo di Ur. Studi e documenti per servire alla storia di Ur-Krur* (Borzano: SeaR, 1994) and Hans Thomas Hakl, "Julius Evola and the UR Group."
120. Owen, *Place*, p. 266.
121. Roberto Sestito, *Il Figlio del Sole*, p. 242.

Chapter 2

1. Giuseppe Mazzini, *Dei Doveri dell'Uomo* (Milan: RCS Libri, [1860] 2010), p. 72: "La Patria è il segno della missione che Dio v'ha dato da compiere nell'Umanità."
2. Martin Clark, *The Italian Risorgimento*, 2nd ed. (New York: Routledge, 2013), p. 19.
3. See Edgar Holt, *The Making of Italy 1815–1870* (New York: Atheneum, 1971) and Lucy Riall, *Il Risorgimento: Storia e Interpretazioni* (Roma: Donzelli, 1997) for the alternative years suggested.
4. From the website of the Ministry of Defence: "L'Unità d'Italia (1861–1918)," difesa.it, http://www.difesa.it/Content/150anniversario/Pagine/Unit%C3%A0dItalia.aspx: "the process of unification continued with the third independence war (1866), the second of Garibaldi's expeditions to Rome (1867) and the annexion of Rome (1870). With the first world war (1915–1918) the process of reunification which brought to contemporary Italy was concluded."
5. Klement von Metternich, quoted in Clark, *Italian Risorgimento*, p. 4.
6. Alberto Mario Banti and Paul Ginsborg, "Per una Nuova Storia del Risorgimento," in *Storia d'Italia Gli Annali 22, Il Risorgimento*, ed. Alberto Mario Banti and Paul Ginsborg (Turin: Giulio Einaudi Editore, 2007), pp. xxiii–xxiv: "Nel contesto di una società largamente analfabeta [. . .] il numero di affiliati alle sette, dei rivoltosi del '20–'21, degli iscritti alla Giovane Italia, di coloro che scendono in piazza o partono volontari o guerreggiano nell'esercito regolare del Regno di Sardegna o organizzano ospedali o servizi di collegamento nel 1848–49, che tessono trame insurrezionali nei primi anni cinquanta, che si arruolano volontari nel 1859, nel 1860 e nel 1866, che vanno a votare ai plebisciti, che si affollano ai funerali di Mazzini, di Vittorio Emanuele, di Garibaldi e di altri ancora, è assolutamente imponente."
7. Alberto Mario Banti, *Nel nome dell'Italia. Il Risorgimento nelle Testimonianze, nei Documenti e nelle Immagini* (Bari: Laterza, 2010); Banti, *Immagini della Nazione nell'Italia del Risorgimento*, ed. Roberto Bizzocchi (Roma: Carocci, 2002); Banti, *La Nazione del Risorgimento. Parentela, Santità ed Onore alle Origini dell'Italia Unita* (Turin: Einaudi, 2000); Banti, *Il Risorgimento Italiano* (Bari: Laterza, 2004).
8. Banti. *Questioni*, p. xxiv: "concettualmente, ancor prima che fattualmente, pone al centro dell'arena pubblica il popolo/nazione, depositario principale della sovranità."
9. Alberto Mario Banti, *Sublime Patria Nostra: la Nazione Italiana dal Risorgimento al Fascismo* (Bari: Giuseppe Laterza e Figli, 2011), chapters 2, 3, and 4.
10. Alberto Mario Banti and Paul Ginsborg, "Per una Nuova Storia del Risorgimento," p. xxviii. "delle immagini, dei sistemi allegorici, delle costellazioni narrative, che incorporano una tavola valoriale specifica, offerta come fondamentale che da senso al sistema concettuale proposto."
11. Conte Camillo di Cavour, *Discorsi Parlamentari Del Conte Camillo di Cavour Raccolti e Pubblicati per Ordine della Camera dei Deputati* (Rome: Eredi Botta, 1872), pp. 314-334: "(Alla sinistra: Bene!), (Approvazione), (Applausi), (Si ride e segni di Approvazione)."
12. Ibid., p. 318: "in Roma concorrono tutte le circostanze storiche, intellettuali, morali che devono determinare le condizioni di una capitale di un grande Stato . Rome è la

sola città d'Italia che non abbia memorie esclusivamente municipali; tutta la storia di Roma dal tempo dei Cesari al giorno d'oggi è la storia di una città la cui importanza si estende aldilà del suo territorio, di una città, cioè, destinata ad essere la capitale di un grande Stato."

13. Ibid., p. 319.

14. Edmondo de Amicis, *Cuore* (Milano: Fratelli Treves, 1886). For more on the author, see Luigi Cepparrone, "Patria e questione sociale nel primo De Amicis," in *Aspettando il Risorgimento. Atti del convegno*, ed. S. Teucci (Florence: Cesati, 2010) pp. 109–132; Antonio Carrannante, "De Amicis nella storia della scuola italiana," *Rivista di Studi Italiani* (2007), pp. 49–68.

15. These sections of *Cuore* captured the hearts and the imagination of early cinema directors, and in the early twentieth century, when Reghini was in his twenties, early motion pictures such as *Il Piccolo Garibaldino* (*The Little Garibaldi Soldier*, 1909), directed by future Fascist Filoteo Alberini (1867–1937), also director of *La Presa di Roma* (*The Conquest of Rome*, 1909), helped keep the *Risorgimento* ideas alive in the new century. See Giovanna Lombardi: *Filoteo Alberini, L'Inventore del Cinema* (Rome: Arduino Sacco, 2008) and Sergio Toffetti e Mario Musumeci, *Da La presa di Roma a Il Piccolo Garibaldino* (Rome: Gangemi Editore, 2007).

16. de Amicis, *Cuore*, p. 104: "Io amo l'Italia perché mia madre è italiana, perché il sangue che mi scorre nelle vene è italiano perché è italiana la terra dove son sepolti i morti che mia madre piange e che mio padre venera, perché la città dove son nato, la lingua che parlo, i libri che m'educano, perché mio fratello, mia sorella, i miei compagni, e il grande popolo in mezzo a cui vivo, e la bella natura che mi circonda, e tutto ciò che vedo, che amo, che studio, che ammiro, è italiano."

17. Ibid., p. 105: "se un giorno io vedessi te tornar salvo da una battaglia combattuta per essa, [...] e sapessi che hai conservato la vita perché ti sei nascosto alla morte, io [...] non potrei amarti mai più, e morirei con quel pugnale nel cuore."

18. The poems of the three authors that follow have been placed in the volume Associazione Amici Accademia dei Lincei, *Canti e Poesie per un Italia Unita–1821–1861*, ed. Pierluigi Ridolfi, pref. Carlo Azeglio Ciampi (Rome: Accademia dei Lincei, 2011), and as such, the pages referring to the poems and songs chosen will refer to this booklet. For more on the figure of Manzoni, see Giorgio Bonfiglioli, *Manzoni, la Vita e le Opere* (Milan: Genio, 1949); Alberto Giordano, *Manzoni. La Vita il Pensiero i Testi Esemplari* (Milan: Accademia, 1973); Giuseppe Langella, *Manzoni e Altra Letteratura del Risorgimento* (Novara: Interlinea, 2005); Silvia M. Tatti, *Il Risorgimento dei Letterati* (Rome: Storia e Letteratura, 2011).

19. Alessandro Manzoni, "1821," *in* Associazione, *Canti e Poesie*, pp. 13–17, vv. 5–8: "Han giurato: Non fia che quest'onda / Scorra più tra due rive straniere: / Non fia loco ove sorgan barriere / Tra l'Italia e l'Italia, mai più!"

20. For more on Giovanni Berchet, see Italo Bertelli, *L'itinerario umano e poetico di Giovanni Berchet* (Ghezzano: Giardini, 2005) and Alberto Cadioli, *Introduzione a Berchet* (Bari: Laterza, 1991).

21. Giovanni Berchet, "All'Armi! All'Armi," in *Canti e Poesie*, pp. 25–6, vv. 1–6: "Su. Figli d'Italia! Su, in armi! Coraggio! / Il suolo qui è nostro: del nostro retaggio / Il turpe

mercato finisce pei re. Un popol diviso per sette destini, / In sette spezzato da sette confini, Si fonde in un solo, piu' servo non è."
22. For songs and hymns of the *Risorgimento*, see Giangiacomo Palermo, *Inni e canti del Risorgimento* (Milan: Mondadori, 2012); Tersilla Gatto Chanu, *Canti Popolar del Vecchio Piemonte* (Rome: Newton Compton, 2007); Oreste Marcoaldi, *Canti Popolari Inediti Umbri, Liguri, Piceni, Piemontesi, Latini* (Genoa: Forni, [1855] 1997).
23. "Zitti, silenzio! Chi passa là? / Passa la ronda. Viva la ronda: / Viva l'Italia, la libertà! / Siamo le guardie dai tre colori, / Verde la speme dei nostri cori, / Bianco, la fede stretta fra noi, / Rosso, le piaghe dei nostri eroi."
24. Sandro Consolato, *Dell'Elmo di Scipio: Risorgemento, Storia d'Italia e Memoria di Roma*, e-book (Rome: flower-ed, 2012), Chapter 1, Section 1, Paragraph 2: "il Risorgimento italiano fu un fatto spirituale e politico *indigeno* nella sua essenza profonda, e, *come tale*, leggibile all'interno dellle Categorie del 'Mondo della Tradizione," [...] e, in particolare, della tradizione romano-italica."
25. For works from academics belonging to the Traditionalist school, see, for example, Sayed Nasr Hossein, *The Need for a Sacred Science* (Albany: SUNY Press, 1993) and William W. Quinn Jr., *The Sacred Tradition* (Albany: SUNY Press, 1997).
26. Sandro Consolato, *Dell'Elmo di Scipio*, Chapter 1, Section 1, Paragraph 3.
27. Among the scholarly secondary sources, see Gian Mario Cazzaniga, "Dante Profeta dell Unità d'Italia," in *Storia d'Italia Annali 25 L'Esoterismo* (Turin: Einaudi, 2010), pp. 455–476; Stefano Salzani, *Luigi Valli e l'Esoterismo di Dante* (Verona: Il Cerchio, 2014); see especially Maria Pia Pozzato, "Due casi di interpretazione aberrante di Dante. Luigi Valli e i 'Fedeli d'amore,'" in *L'Ansia dell'Interpretazione* (Modena: Mucchi, 1989), pp. 181–203; Pia Pozzato, *L'idea Deforme. Interpretazioni Esoteriche di Dante* (Milan: Bompiani, 1989). For primary sources on the treatment of Dante and the idea of him as an esoteric author, see René Guénon, *L'Ésotérisme de Dante* (Paris: Ch. Bosse Libraire, 1925); Luigi Valli, *Il Linguggio Segreto di Dante e i Fedeli d'Amore* (Milan: Luni, 1994); Luigi Valli, *L'Allegoria di Dante Secondo Pascoli* (Bologna: Zanichelli, 1922); and Luigi Valli, *La Chiave della Divina Commedia* (Bologna: Zanichelli, 1929).
28. Francesco Petrarca, "Italia Mia Perché 'l Parlar sia Indarno," in *Sonetti, Canzoni e Trionfi* (Firenze: Giovanniantonio de Nicolini da Sabio, 1541), p. 89.
29. For the standard work on the subject, see Yates, *Giordano Bruno*.
30. Quoted in Sandro Consolato, *Dell'Elmo di Scipio*, n.602. "Non vi sono cinque Italie, quattro Italie, tre Italie. Non vi è che un'Italia. Dio che, creandola, sorrise sovr'essa, le assegnò per confine le due più sublimi cose che ponesse in Europa, simboli dell'eterna Forza ed dell'eterno moto, l'Alpi e il Mare. Sia tre volte maledetto da voi e da quanti verranno dopo di voi qualunque presumesse di segnarle confini diversi."
31. Quoted in Gaetano Salvemini, *La politica estera dell'Italia (1871–1914)* (Turin: Barbera Editore, 1944), p. 214: "molte città perirono sulla terra e tutte possono alla lor volta perire; Roma, per disegno di Provvidenza indovinato dai popoli, è città eterna, come quella alla quale fu affidata la missione di diffondere al mondo la parola d'Unità."
32. "Garibaldi è un uomo capace di trionfare in qualsiasi impresa," in Jacques Duprey, *Un fils de Napoleón dans les pays de la Plata au temps de Rosas* (Paris-Montevideo: Casa Barrero y Ramos, 1937), p. 164

33. Ippolito Nievo, *Le Confessioni di un Italiano* (Turin: Einaudi, [1867] 1964), p. 708, "Roma è il nodo gordiano dei nostri destini, Roma è il simbolo grandioso e multiforme della nostra schiatta, Roma è la nostra arca di salvazione, che colla sua luce snebbia d'improvviso tutte le storte e confuse immaginazioni italiane."

34. It must be said that masonic bodies existed in Italy before this date: the affiliation to foreign obediences and the development of the Masonic bodies as we know them today, though, can be said to begin on the date provided. See especially Carlo Francovich, *Storia della Massoneria in Italia. I Liberi Muratori Italiani dalle Origini alla Rivoluzione Francese* (Milan: Ghibli, 2013). Texts on the relationship between Freemasonry and Risorgimento abound: see *Storia d'Italia. Annali*, vol. 21, *La Massoneria*, ed. Gian Mario Cazzaniga (Torino: Einaudi, 2006); Aldo A. Mola, *Storia della Massoneria Italiana Dalle Origini ai Giorni Nostri* (Milano: Bompiani, 1992); Maurizio del Maschio, Stefano Momentè, Claudio Nobbio, *Fratelli d'Italia. Memoria del rapporto tra Massoneria e Risorgimento nel 150 anniversario dell'Unità d'Italia* (Foggia: Bastogi, 2011); Fulvio Conti, *Storia della Massoneria italiana. Dal Risorgimento al Fascismo* (Bologna: Il Mulino, 2003).

35. From the minutes of the session, quoted in Augusto Comba, "La Massoneria in Italia dal Risorgimento alla Grande Guerra," in *La Massoneria nella Storia d'Italia*, ed. Aldo A. Mola (Rome: Atanòr, 1981), pp. 71–85 [71].

36. For a more detailed account of the Carboneria, which does not constitute a topic of this chapter, see Pietro Seddio, *La Carboneria* (Rome: Montecovello, 2012); Giovanni Teresi, *Sui Moti Carbonari del 1820–21 in Italia* (Foggia: Bastogi, 2007); Mario Cazzaniga and Marco Marinucci, *Per una Storia della Carboneria dopo l'Unità d'Italia* (Rome: Gaffi, 2014).

37. Carlo Botta, *Storia d'Italia dal 1789 al 1814*, Vol. VI (Capolago: Tipografia Elvetica, 1833), 30–32. Franco Della Peruta, *Mazzini e i Rivoluzionari Italiani: il Partito d'Azione, 1830–1845* (Milan: Feltrinelli, 1974); Denis Mack Smith, *Mazzini* (Milan: Rizzoli, 1993); Antonio Desideri, *Storia e Storiografia*, Vol. II (Messina-Florence: Edizioni D'Anna, 1997); Indro Montanelli and Marco Nozza, *Giuseppe Garibaldi* (Turin: BUR, 2007).

38. Quoted in Sandro Consolato, *Dell'Elmo di Scipio*, Chapter 6, Section 2, Paragraph 7: "Questa rivoluzione è la prima che si sia fatta in Italia da molti secoli senza il soccorso e l'intervento degli stranieri; è la prima che abbia mostrato due popoli italiani che, dalle due estremità della penisola, rispondono l'uno all'altro."

39. *La Carboneria. La Costituzione del Regno delle Due Sicilie*, ed. Francesco Ingravalle (Salerno: Edizioni di Ar, 2011), pp. x–xiii

40. Mario Cervi and Indro Montanelli, *L'Italia del Risorgimento, 1831–1861* (Milan: Rizzoli, 1994), pp. 63–64.

41. For a biography of Filippo Cordova, see his nephew Vincenzo Cordova, *I Discorsi Parlamentari e gli Scritti Editi ed Inediti Preceduti dai Ricordi della Sua Vita*, per Vincenzo Cordova, Vol. 1 (Rome: Edizioni del Senato, 1889).

42. Comba, *Massoneria in Italia*, p. 72: "con il 1865 e lo spostamento della capitale a Firenze, comincia un periodo di 30anni durante il quale ci sarà una forte identificazione tra quel settore politico e la guida della Massoneria Italiana."

43. See Jeffrey Tyssens, "Freemasonry and Nationalism," in *Handbook of Freemasonry*, ed. Henrik Bogdan and Jan A.M. Snoek (Leiden: Brill, 2014), pp. 461-472. For Reghini and the *I Rigeneratori* Lodge, see the next chapter and Di Luca, *Reghini*, pp. 9-11. It must be said, and I will tackle the issue more incisively in Chapter 4, that Freemasons were usually forbidden to bring politics inside masonic lodges, and that this period of Italian history represents an exception to Anderson's *Constitutions*, which had laid the rules and regulation of masonic bodies.
44. Silvio Pellico, *Le Mie Prigioni* (Florence: Adriano Salani Editore, 1832) is a striking first hand account of a member of the *Carboneria* arrested and incarcerated.
45. Ernesto Nathan, "Discorso Inaugurale a Palazzo Giustiniani," *Rivista Massonica* (1912), p. 287, "con la caduta del dominio napoleonico ebbe fine anche questo periodo di sommo splendore della Libera Muratoria e, in parte come conseguenza dell'entrata in scena dei carbonari falsamente parificati ai liberi muratori, furono emesse severe proibizioni [...]. La massoneria non risorse che sulla metà del xix secolo."
46. Conte Camillo di Cavour, "Discorso alla Camera dei Deputati," March 27, 1861, in Cavour, *Discorsi Parlamentari*, pp. 332-353 [334]: "è la necessaria capitale d'Italia, ché senza che Roma sia riunita all'Italia come sua capitale, l'Italia non potrebbe avere un assetto definitivo."
47. Luigi Bulferetti, *Antonio Rosmini nella Restaurazione* (Florence: Le Monnier, 1942), p. 113, "Neoguelfi sono coloro che ritengono elemento basilare del risorgimento politico nazionale il papa, il quale dovrebbe porsi alla testa di una confederazione italiana dei principi della penisola [...] per la lotta contro i Turchi o lo straniero molesto allo stato della Chiesa."
48. Vincenzo Gioberti, *Del Primato Morale e Civile degli Italiani*, 2 vols. (Lausanne: S. Bonamici & Compagnia, 1845).
49. Carlo Alberto di Savoia, "Statuto Albertino," *Gazzetta Piemontese*, March 3, 1848, p. 1.
50. Pius IX, "Non Expedit," *The Catholic Encyclopedia* 11 (New York: Robert Appleton Company, 1911), http://www.newadvent.org/cathen/11098a.htm
51. Lucetta Scaraffia, "Il contributo dei cattolici all'unificazione," in *I Cattolici che hanno fatto l'Italia*, ed. Lucetta Scaraffia (Torino: Lindau, 2011), pp. 223-7; Giancarlo Rocca, *Istituti religiosi in Italia fra Otto e Novecento*, in *Clero e Società nell'Italia contemporanea*, ed. Mario Rosa (Bari, Laterza, 1992), pp. 231 ff.; also see Angela Pellicciari, *L'Altro Risorgimento, Una Guerra di Religione Dimenticata* (Milan: Ares, 2011); Pellicciari, *Risorgimento Anticattolico: la Persecuzione della Chiesa nelle Memorie di Giacomo Margotti* (Casale Monferrato: Piemme, 2004).
52. Anonymous. *Commemorazione del Fratello Filippo Delpino. 25 Settembre 1862. Discorsi dell'Oratore della Loggia Ausonia* (Turin: Marzorati, 1862), p. 8. "Roma, già padrona del mondo, poscia rimasta per secoli contaminata da tanti delitti, dall'opera nefaria dei suoi padroni, in veste di pastor lupi rapaci, tende supplice le mani verso questo lembo di Italia ove regna, adorato dai suoi sudditi, Vittorio Emanuele II." On the *Loggia Ausonia* and its foundation, see Pietro Buscalioni, *La Loggia Ausonia ed il Primo Grande Oriente Italiano* (Cosenza: Brenner Editore, 2001).

53. Allan Kardec, *What Is Spiritism?* (Philadelphia: Allan Kardec Educational Society, [1859] 1999), p. 6; Patrick Deveney, "Spiritualism," in *Dictionary of Gnosis and Western Esotericism* (Leiden: Brill, 2004), pp.1074–1082 [1075].
54. Webb, *Flight*, p.1.
55. For a comprehensive history of the early developments of the Spiritualist movement, see Frank Podmore, *Modern Spiritualism: a History and a Criticism* (Cambridge, MA: Cambridge University Press, [1902] 2011); Amy Lehman, *Victorian Women and the Theatre of Trance: Mediums, Spiritualists and Mesmerists in Performance* (Jefferson, NC: McFarland, 2009); Barbara Weisberg, *Talking to the Dead: Kate and Maggie Fox* (New York: HarperOne, 2004); David Chapin, *Exploring Other Worlds: Margaret Fox, Elisha Kent Kane, and the Antebellum Culture of Curiosity* (Amherst: Massachussetts University Press, 2004); Alex Owen, *The Darkened Room: Women, Power and Spiritualism in Late Victorian England*, 2nd ed. (Chicago: University of Chicago Press, 2004).
56. Deveney, "Spiritualism," p. 1075.
57. Lehman, *Victorian Women*, p. 87.
58. Deveney, "Spiritualism," p. 1076.
59. For this aspect of Mesmerism, see John S. Haller Jr., *Swedenborg, Mesmer, and the Mind/Body Connection: The Roots of Complementary Medicine* (West Chester, PA: Swedenborg Foundation, 2010); Bertrand Mehéust, *Somnambulisme et Médiumnité* (Paris: Les Empêcheurs de penser en rond, 1999); Alan Gauld, *A History of Hypnotism* (Cambridge: Cambridge University Press, 1995).
60. Simona Cigliana, "Spiritismo e Parapsicologia nell'Età Positivistica," in *Storia d'Italia, Annali 25 Esoterismo*, p. 528, "Certo è difficile, oggi, rendersi conto con piena cognizione dell'intensità e dell'estensione del dibattito che si svolse nel corso del xix secolo, e in particolare in età positivistica, quando una sete di meraviglioso soprannaturale sembrò quasi universalmente diffondersi in tutti i ceti sociali, della passione con la quale la scienza positivistica si dedicò a sonnambule e tavole giranti, ad apporti ed ectoplasmi, alternando episodi da *pochade* a spettacolari conversioni, sull'onda dei cosidetti fenomeni di Hydesville."
61. For a sympathetic treatment of Ms. Hayden's case, see Augustus De Morgan's preface in Sophia Elizabeth de Morgan, *From Matter to Spirit: The Result of Ten Years' Experience in Spirit Manifestations. Intended as a Guide to Enquirers* (London: Longman and Green, 1863), pp. v–xlv.
62. Home's séances are discussed by many academic experts on the topic. Some of the most important works are John Casey, *After Lives: A Guide to Heaven, Hell and Purgatory* (Oxford: Oxford University Press, 2009); Ruth Brandon, *The Spiritualists: The Passion for the Occult in the Nineteenth and Twentieth Centuries* (New York: Alfred E. Knopf, 1983); especially the amazingly detailed Rupert Christiansen, "The Psychic Cloud: Yankee Spirit-Rappers," in *The Victorian Visitors: Culture Shock in Nineteenth Century Britain* (New York: Grove/Atlantic, 2001), pp. 130–158.
63. Daniel Dunglas Home, *Incidents in My Life* (New York: A.K.Butts, 1872), p. 96.
64. Ibid., p. 97.

65. Carlos Alvarado, Massimo Biondi, and Wim Kramer, "Historical Notes on Psychic Phenomena in Specialised Journals," *European Journal of Parapsychology* 21, no. 1 (2006), pp. 58–87.
66. Allan Kardec, *Lo Spiritismo alla sua piu' Semplice Espressione. Esposizione Sommaria dell'Insegnamento degli Spiriti e delle Manifestazioni Loro*, prefaced by Vincenzo Scarpa (Turin: Degiorgis and Ferneux, 1863), p. 4, "Tanto in Parigi come in Lione, le due più popolose città della Francia, si é constatato che tutti gli operai, i braccianti e altri lavoranti alla giornata che si sono consacrati alla spiritismo hanno ben presto abbandonato le antiche colpevoli abitudini di imprevidenza e di scialacquo, sono divenuti laboriosi ed economi, e vivono onoratamente confidando in Dio e nella certezza di una vita migliore."
67. Simona Cigliana, "Spiritismo e Psicologia," p. 534, "Gli 'Annali dello Spiritismo' furono [...] il periodico degli anni eroici dello spiritismo in Italia. [...] Lo spiritismo ebbe una parte importante nel sostenere, insieme alla massoneria, i bisogni spirituali del partito progressista, anticlericale e laico, favorendo, anche in conseguenza delle posizioni intransigent assunte dalla Sante Sede, in materia di sovranità popolare, l'indirizzarsi delle aspirazioni religiose verso un orizzonte trascendente non legato alla Chiesa."
68. The best volume on the Turin spiritist scene is still Enrico Imoda, *Fotografie di Fantasmi: Contributo Sperimentale alla Constatazione dei Fenomeni Mediatici con Prefazione del Dott. Prof. Carlo Richet e Numerose Fotografie Stampate dalle Negative Originali* (Turin: Bocca, 1912).
69. For a list of the most prominent groups in Italy, see Massimo Biondi, *Tavoli e Medium: Storia dello Spiritismo in Italia* (Rome: Gremese Editore, 1988), pp. 34–35.
70. Biondi, *Tavoli e Medium*, p. 22.
71. Cigliana, "Spiritismo e Parapsicologia," p. 534, "uno Spiritualista convinto."
72. Giorgio Martellini and Maria Teresa Pichetto, *Massimo d'Azeglio* (Milan: Camunia, 1990), p. 276, "Per casual iniziazione di un non meglio precisato 'Signor Romano,' D'Azeglio si avvicina, nel silenzio notturno della villetta sul Verbano, alle pratiche dello spiritismo. Con l'ospite misterioso, con il pittore Gaetano Ferri, che ha casa lì vicino, con una fanciulla ignota di splendido talento pianistico oltre che medium di rara sensibilità, trascorre serate intere al tavolino a tre gambe, evocando presenze ultraterrene." On this period of d'Azeglio's life, also see Georges Virlogeux, *Massimo d'Azeglio a Canneto* (Novara: Istituto per la Storia del Risorgimento Italiano, 1997).
73. Luigi Capuana, *Spiritismo?* (Catania: Giannotta, 1884); idem, *Mondo Occulto* (Naples: Pierro, 1896).
74. See especially Igino Ugo Tarchetti, *Racconti Fantastici* (Milan: Fratelli Treves, 1869), in which "I Fatali," pp. 5–63 and "Uno Spirito in un Lampone," pp. 116–141 stand out in their relation to Spiritualist themes.
75. For a more nuanced portrait of Positivism in Italy, Piero di Giovanni, *Filosofia e Psicologia nel Positivismo Italiano* (Bari: Laterza, 2006); Augusto Pusceddu, *La Sociologia Positivistica in Italia* (Rome: Bulzoni, 1989); *Cesare Lombroso. Gli scienziati e la nuova Italia*, ed. Silvano Montaldo (Bologna: Il Mulino, 2011).

76. The most comprehensive work on Lombroso's private life, and his extracurricular activities is Delia Frigessi, *Cesare Lombroso* (Turin: Einaudi, 2003); works on Lombroso's theories abound. See Daniele Velo Dalbrenta, *La Scienza Inquieta. Saggio sull'Antropologia Criminale di Cesare Lombroso* (Padova: CEDAM, 2004) and Emilia Musumeci, *Cesare Lombroso e le Neuroscienze: un Parricidio Mancato. Devianza, Libero Arbitrio, Imputabilità tra Antiche Chimere ed Inediti Scenari* (Milano: Franco Angeli, 2012).
77. Giorgio Colombo, *La Scienza Infelice. Il Museo di Antropologia Criminale di Cesare Lombroso* (Torino: Bollati Boringhieri, 2000), p. 4.
78. Cesare Lombroso, Enrico Ferri, Raffaele Garofalo, and Giulio Fioretti, *Polemica in Difesa della Scuola Criminale Positiva* (Bologna: Zanichelli, 1886); Cesare Lombroso, *Studi sull'Ipnotismo con Appendice Critica sullo Spiritismo* (Turin: Bocca, 1886), p. 67: "gli spiriti delle specchiere e delle poltrone" and "ricordatevi che con ciò ritorniamo al Totem, al Feticcio."
79. The literature on Eusapia Palladino is vast: for a basic outlook on her life and séances, see Everard Feilding, W. W. Baggally, and Hereward Carrington, "Report on a Series of Sittings with Eusapia Palladino," *Proceedings of the Society for Psychical Research* 23 (1909), pp. 309–569; Hereward Carrington, *Eusapia Palladino and her Phenomena* (New York: B.W. Dodge & Co., 1909); Enrico Morselli, *Psicologia e Spiritismo Impressioni e Note Critiche sui Fenomeni Medianici di Eusapia Palladino* (Turin: Bocca, 1908); for more recent works, see Simone Natale, *Supernatural Entertainments: Victorian Spiritualism and the Rise of Modern Media Culture* (University Park: Pennsylvania State University Press, 2016); Julian Strube, *Socialismus, Katholizismus un Okkultismus im Frankreich des 19. Jahrhunderts* (Berlin: De Gruyter, 2016); Christopher M. Moreman, *The Spiritualist Movement: Speaking with the Dead in America and around the World* (Westport, CT: Praeger 2013).
80. Cesare Lombroso "Accettazione della Sfida," in *Fanfulla della Domenica* 36 (Sept. 1888), quoted in Cigliana, "Spiritismo e Parapsicologia," p. 543: "vergognato e dolente d'aver combattuto con tanta tenacia la possibilità dei fatti considerati spiritici [...] dico dei fatti [...] perché alla teoria sono contrario. Ma i fatti esistono e io dei fatti mi vanto di essere schiavo."
81. Biondi, *Tavoli e Medium*, p. 140: "Entro pochi anni si sarebbero interessati a lei Charles Richet, il fisiologo Parigino che GIA' da tempo si occupava di fatti spiritici e si sarebbe meritato un Nobel nel 1913 per i suoi studi sui fenomeni immunitari; Myers, Sidgwick, Barrett, cioè il gruppo delle *Societa' per la Ricerca Psichica* inglese; Wagner, il professore di zoologia di Pietroburgo [...]; Ochorowicz, professore di filosofia e psicologia a Varsavia; i coniugi Curie e Flammarion; [...]. Una semi-analfabeta faceva ruotare attorno a sè i più bei nomi della scienza e della cultura europea."
82. Giorgio, *Roma*, pp. 17–27.
83. Riccardo Fubini, "*Gli Storici nei Nascenti Stati Regionali d'Italia*," in Fubini, *Storiografia dell'umanesimo in Italia da Leonardo Bruni ad Annio da Viterbo*, (Rome: Edizioni di Storia e Letteratura 2003), pp. 3–38 (35): "Thus Janus led the humble cities and people and the political alliance, not to excess and lust of domination"; also see Annius

Viterbensis, *Antiquitatum variarum volumina XVII a venerando et sacrae theologiae et praedicatorii ordinis professore Ioanni Annio* (Paris: Josse Bade er Jean Petit, 1512); Roberto Weiss, "Traccia per una Biografia di Annio da Viterbo," in *Italia Medioevale e Umanistica* 5 (1962), pp. 425–441; Giovanni Baffioni and Paola Mattiangeli, *Annio da Viterbo: Documenti e Ricerche*, ed. Giovanni Baffioni (Rome: Multigrafica Editrice per il Consiglio nazionale delle ricerche, 1981).

84. Gianbattista Vico, *De Antiquissima Italorum Sapientia es Linguae Latinae Originibus Eruenda*, trans. L. M. Palmer (Ithaca, NY: Cornell University Press,1988).
85. Quoted in Paolo Galiano, *Roma Prima di Roma: Metastoria della Tradizione Italica* (Rome: Simmetria Edizioni, 2011), p. 45: "[a]rdisco asseveratamente dire che Pitagora non avesse di Ionia portato in Italia la sua dottrina."
86. Ibid., p. 85.
87. See Angelo Mazzoldi, *Delle Origini Italiche e della Diffusione dell'Incivilimento Italiano all'Egitto, alla Fenicia, alla Grecia e a Tutte le Nazioni Asiatiche Poste sul Mediterraneo* (Milan: np, 1840); Giorgio, *Roma*, pp. 26–39, Paolo Galiano, *Roma*, pp. 62–79; Paolo Casini, *L'Antica Sapienza Italica: Cronistoria di un Mito* (Bologna: Il Mulino, 1998), pp. 269–272.
88. Mazzoldi, *Delle Origini*, p. 140, "un'unica divinità, ossia un'arcana causa dell'universo."
89. See Plato, "Timaeus," in Vol. IX of *Plato in Twelve Volumes*, trans. W. R. M. Lamb (Cambridge, MA: Harvard University Press, 1968).
90. Renato Del Ponte, *Il Movimento Tradizionalista Romano nel '900* (Scandiano: SeaR, 1987), p. 23: "era e rimane condizione *imprescindibile* e *necessaria* per ritornare alla realtà geopolitica augustea (e dantesca): quindi per propiziare il rimanifestarsi nella *Saturnia tellus* di quelle forze divine che *ab origine* a quella realtà geografica—consacrata dalla volontà degli dei indigenisono legate."
91. Not all authors back this theory, though. If Sandro Consolato makes a very compelling argument in his three-part essay "Il Risorgimento Come Sviluppo della Storia Sacra di Roma," *Politica Romana* 4 (1997), pp. 125–175; 5 (1998–1989), pp. 48–105; 6 (2004–2005), pp. 109–168; Paolo Casini, in his *L'Antica Sapienza Italica*, is much more dismissive of the sacred aspect of the *Risorgimento*: to him, Mazzoldi's work is a "bizarre rhapsody," p. 269, and he called Mazzoldi's lucubrations and the criteria followed "unrefined and arbitrary," p. 270.
92. Benedetto Croce, "La Storiografia in Italia," *La Critica, Rivista di Letteratura Storia e Filosofia diretta da B. Croce* 13 (1915), pp. 165–192 [178]: "Il testo del Mazzoldi fu generalmente ricevuto con rispetto e studiato seriamente."
93. On the life of Giovanni Mengozzi, philosopher, author, and Italy's foremost expert in homeopathy, see Anonymous, "Cenni Biografici del Comm. Prof. G. E. Mengozzi," *Roma Etrusca* 1, no. 1 (1881), pp. 2–6; on the Scuola Italica founded by Mengozzi, see Giovanni Mengozzi, *La Scuola Italica, Scoieta' Nazionale Filosofica, Medica, Letteraria Residente in Napoli* (Napoli: np, 1865); Giorgio, *Roma Renovata Resurgat*, pp. 17–82.
94. The idea of Pythagoras as a Tyrrenian and non-Greek philosopher was not a new one: Porphyry had claimed a Tyrrenian origin for Pythagoras's father in *Pythagoras*, Diogenes Laertius, and Clement of Alexandria all pointed out to this possibility. Thomas Aquinas, too, and in the twentieth century Reghini and Armentano did too.

95. La Direzione, "Nostro Programma," *Roma Etrusca*, p. 1, "Il Tirreno Pitagora, reduce dall'Oriente, iniziato in quelle arcane dottrine, e raccolta l'avita sapienza dell Roma Etrusca (da Numa altamente propugnata e nobilmente rappresentata) volle ravvivare l'italiana Gloria nella filosofia, recandosi in Crotona, dove sapeva esistere una scuola filosofica incorrotta nei giorni che nella greca Elea il Trovato Italico veniva combattuto e guastato, epperciò pel nostro Pitagora, in Italia miglior campo di Gloria per lui che altrove."
96. See Giorgio, *Roma*, pp. 73-74.
97. Anonymous, "Cenni Biografici," p. 4.
98. Ibid., p. 5, "Io aderisco pienamente al Monoteismo, la cui meta è il culto del vero, la fratellanza delle nazioni e la distruzione in Italia e nel mondo del papato, rappresentante dell'ignoranza e del servaggio."
99. The authors discussed in this paragraph may be the most significant when it comes to the theme I have engaged with, but there were definitely many others who added to a growing corpus of literature on Tyrreno-Pelasgian Italy: see Giuseppe Micali, *L'Italia Avanti il Dominio dei Romani*, 2 vols. (Florence: np, 1810); Camillo Ravioli, *Spedizione Romana in Egitto* (Rome: Tipografia delle Belle Arti, 1870); Ignazio Ciampi, *La Citta' Etrusca* (Rome: Tipografia delle Belle Arti, 1866); Ciro Nispi Landi, *Le Storie d'Italia Narrate in Otto Grandi Eta' dalle piu' Lontane Origini a Noi* (Rome: Salviucci, 1879).
100. Arguably, the most useful overview of the Neapolitan milieu from the seventeenth to the nineteenth century is Gian Mario Cazzaniga, "Ermetismo ed Egizianesimo a Napoli dai Lumi alla Fratellanza di Miriam," in *Annali d'Italia 25: Esoterismo*, pp. 547-566.
101. For a useful introduction to di Sangro's ties to Freemasonry, see Domenico Vittorio Ripa Montesano, *Raimondo di Sangro Principe di San Severo Primo Gran Maestro del Rito Egizio Tradizionale* (Naples: np, 2011); for more general biographies on di Sangro, see Antonio Emanuele Piedimonte, *Raimondo di Sangro Principe di Sansevero, La Vita, le Opere, i Libri, la Cappella, le Leggende, i Misteri* (Naples: Intra Moenia, 2012) or the standard reference biography by Lidia Sansone Vagni, *Raimondo di Sangro Principe di San Severo*, 2nd ed. (Foggia: Bastogi, 1992).
102. Federico d'Andrea, *Raimondo di Sangro, Principe di Sansevero e la Tradizione Egizia Napoletana*, accademiakremmerziana, accademiakremmerziana.it/Home_03_09_08.htm: "Ricerche accurate, svolte in archivi particolari, attestano la fondazione da parte del Principe Raimondo di Sangro di Sansevero di un *Antiquus Ordo Aegypti*, nel quale operò il *Rito di Misraim seu Aegypti*, il 10 dicembre 1747. Ricerche fatte da vari studiosi in seguito a fortunati ritrovamenti, hanno dimostrato la formazione da parte del Principe di Sangro di una loggia segreta, ad indirizzo chiaramente ermetico e rosicruciano, chiamato "Rosa d'Ordine Magno."
103. See Gennaro Ruggiero, *Le Piazze di Napoli* (Rome: Newton Compton, 1998) and Comitato per il Restauro della Statua del Corpo di Napoli, *Lo Sguardo del Nilo: Storia e Recupero del "Corpo di Napoli"* (Napoli: Colonnese, 1993); for the hermetic symbols in the San Severo Chapel, see Edoardo Nappi, *La Famiglia, il Palazzo,*

la Cappella dei Principi di Sansevero (Geneva: Droz, 1975) and Antonella Golia, *Cappella Sansevero, Il Tempio della Virtu' e dell'Arte* (Naples: Akroamatikos, 2009).

104. Only a few articles have been written about Kremmerz and his works in languages other than Italian; among these see Massimo Introvigne, "De l'Hypertrophie de la Filiation: le Milieu Kremmerzien en Italie," in *ARIES—Association pour la Recherche et l'Information sur l'Ésotérisme, Symboles et Mythes dans les Mouvements Initiatiques et Ésotériques (XVII et XXe siècles): Filiations et emprunts* (Paris: Archè – La Table d'Émeraude, 1999), pp. 148–156 and Hans T. Hakl, "The Theory and Practice of Sexual Magic, Exemplified by Four Magical Groups in the Early Twentieth Century," in *Hidden Intercourse: Eros and Sexuality in the History of Western Esotericism*, ed. Wouter J. Hanegraaff and Jeffrey J. Kripal (New York: Fordham University Press, 2011), pp. 445–478. For standard works on Kremmerz's life in Italian, see Jah-Hel, *La Pietra Angolare Miriamica: Storia Documentata della Fratellanza di Miriam di Giuliano Kremmerz* (Viareggio: Rebis, 1989), *Il Maestro Giuliano Kremmerz. L'Uomo - La Missione - L'Opera*, ed. Pier Luca Pierini (Rebis: Viareggio, 1985) and the more philosophical-analytical Piero Di Vona, *Giuliano Kremmerz* (Salerno: Edizioni di Ar, 2005).

105. See Massimo Introvigne, "De l'hypertrophie de la Filiation," pp. 151–156.

106. Giorgio, *Roma*, p. 150: " i contributi che questi ambienti diedero alla causa Unitaria non erano, all fine, solo di natura culturale, visto che tutti coloro che sono descritti come i massimi esponenti dell'Ordine Egizio parteciparono 'con vero Spirito Romano,' alle insurrezioni del Risorgimento."

107. *Il Geronta Sebezio* (Naples: Torchi del Tramaner, 1835–1837).

108. Domenico Bocchini, *Gli Arcani Gentilizi*, Vol. III (Naples: Torchi del Tramaner, 1837), p. 22, "Il Labirinto Romano di cui ci parlano i classici era il sovrano Palladio di Roma di cui Eusebio parlò alla plebe [. . .]. E Plinio ci dice, che per averne solo parlato, Valerio Solano perse la testa. [. . .] Creadiamo che come Labirinto Italiano dobbiamo intendere gli elementi Orfici in tutta Italia."

109. Domenico Bocchini, *La Sapienza degli Arcani Vetusti*, p. 136 of the manuscript, republished in Riccardo Donato, *La Chiave della Sapienza Ermetica*, Vol. II, p. 201, "Cosicché pare che il nome di Pitagora fosse come quello di Zoroastro, di Alcide, di Giove, di Mercurio Trismegisto, e degli altri *Hierophanti* primi; per cui solo il Ministero, e non nella persona era il nome. E con questa idea si conciliano una infinita quantità di anacronismi, che si veggiono nè Poeti Greci e Latini."

110. On Lebano, see Ely-Isis, "Giustiniano Lebano ed i Misteri Classici Antichi," in *Ignis Rivista di Studi Iniziatici* 1 (1990), pp. 25–27; Gaetano Lo Monaco, *L'Ordine Osirideo Egizio e la Trasmissione Pitagorica* (Naples: Carpe Librum, 2000); Michele E. Barraco *Giustiniano Lebano e la Scuola di Napoli* (Nove: Libreria Editrice "Letture S . . . consigliate," 1999).

111. Publisher Victrix has published many of Lebano's writings, collecting them in five volumes. The subjects range from the cure of obscure illnesses to a work dedicated to the topic of hell; for more interesting documents, which had been until now been consulted in manuscript form only, see Riccardo Donato, *La Chiave della Sapienza Ermetica secondo Giuliano Kremmerz, Domenico Bocchini e Giustiniano Lebano*,

Vols. I–II (Rebis: Viareggio, 2012-2014). Never before have so many documents by Lebano been made available to the general public.

112. See Giuseppe Maddalena Capiferro and Cristian Guzzo, *L'Arcano degli Arcani: Storia dell'Ermetismo Egizio-Partenopeo fra i Secoli XVIII–XX* (Viareggio: Rebis, 2005); also see G. Lo Monaco, "Edward Bulwer Lytton e l'Ambiente Iniziatico Partenopeo Nilense," *Atrium* VI, no. 3 (2004), pp. 6–57, for a discussion on Bulwer Lytton's probable involvement with Lebano.

113. Giustianiano Lebano, *Del Morbo Oscuro chiamato Areteo Ociphon Sincope impropriamente creduto dagli europei Cholera Morbus* (Naples: Tocco & C., 1881), p. 10: "aree del Tartaro, creato dalle arti magiche di sacerdoti stranieri."

114. Ibid., pp. 1–2.

115. On the Neapolitan occult milieu, see G. Maddalena Capiferro, Cristian Guzzo, Gaetano Lo Monaco, and Michele Di Iorio, *Sairitis Hus. Gli Antri, le Sirene, la Luce, l'Ombra. Appunti Biografici Ermetici della Napoli Ottocentesca* (Mussolente: Carpe Librum, 2001); G. Maddalena Capiferro and Cristian Guzzo, *L'Arcano degli Arcani, Lungo il Nilo dell'Ordine Osirideo Egizio. Il Mito dell'Eterno Ritorno, ovvero la Lampada della Vita dall'Ombra delle Piramidi alla luce del Sebeto* (Viareggio: Rebis, 2005). On the Lebano-Levi and Lebano-Dumas connections, see Gian Mario Cazzaniga, "Ermetismo ed Egizianesimo."

116. Giusitiano Lebano, *Manuscript*, quoted in Riccardo Donato, *La Chiave della Sapienza Ermetica*, p. 99, "Noi conosciamo dove sono i preziosi metalli, i Sacri Segni e i Sacri Oggetti dei Padri dell'Urbe. A suo tempo indicheremo dove stanno, perché ora i tempi non sono maturi."

117. Giuliano Kremmerz, "Piccola Posta—M.O. Firenze," *Commentarium* 2, no. 2–3 (1911), p. 131, "Delle profezie su Roma ne conosco molte, da molto tempo [. . .]. Ve n'è una, per esempio, che predice nientemeno che una Roma Imperiale e la resurrezione della Gloria Latina e della missione di giustizia della grande civiltà della terza Roma laica."

118. Giuliano Kremmerz, *I Dialoghi sull'Ermetismo*, Vol. 1 (Spoleto: Arti Grafiche Panetto e Petrelli, 1929), p. 14, "Se l'Urbe occulta conobbe in eredità, etrusca e greco-egizia, gli arcani della scienza della psiche umana, la mitologia poetica dei nostri progenitori non può aver celato le verità di una scienza concreta dello spirito dell'uomo? Perché è preferibile fare l'indiano coi simboli di Budda, di Brama, o dei Parsi, quando Giove e le deità maggiori dell'Olimpo Latino possono tenere onorevolmente il paragone?"

Chapter 3

1. Capuana, *Mondo Occulto*, p. 221: "La nuova religione muove il passo con la modernità: non ha apostoli, ma riviste, non martiri, ma vittime che finiscono per riempire manicomi con i loro cervelli colpiti da esaltazioni nervose."

2. The term *Scapigliatura* was originally used in the title of Cletto Arrighi's *La Scapigliatura e il 6 Febbrajo* (Milan: Sonzogno, 1861), in which the author described a new type of Italian, or better, Milanese artist, heavily influenced by the French *bohéme*, in whose works the line between life and art was often blurred and whom Arrighi described as "real pandemonium of the century [. . .], reservoir of the spirit of revolt and opposition to all established order" (p. 6). To be a *Scapigliato*, literally, "with unkept hairstyle" or "dishevelled," meant to oppose the status quo, in every facet of life: figurative arts, music, literature, and in life itself. Its main representatives were without a doubt Cesare Emilio Praga (1839–1875), more famous for his poetry collections *Tavolozze* (Milan: Casa Editrice Autori-Editori, 1862) and *Penombre* (Milano: Casa Editrice Autori-Editori, 1864), and his friend and fellow author Iginio Ugo Tarchetti (1839–1869), most famous for the masterpiece among the literature of the *Scapigliatura*, *Fosca* (Milan: Sonzogno, 1869). Influenced by foreign decadent literature, the *Scapigliati* were influenced by Charles Baudelaire, E. T. A. Hoffmann, and Heinrich Heine, to mention but three: the *Scapigliati* sought to break literary conventions of the time by writing about subjects as taboo and diverse as orgies, drug use, the allure of death, and the exaltation of ugliness. With different aims, as we shall see, but with the same iconoclasm, the group of artists who gathered around Papini and Prezzolini at the turn of the century certainly earned their entry into the roster of the *Scapigliati*, giving birth to a Florentine version of the *Scapigliatura*. On the phenomenon of the Florentine *Scapigliatura*, see Paolo Casini, *Alle Origini del Novecento, "Il Leonardo," 1903–1907* (Bologna: Il Mulino, 2002); Augusto Hermet, *La Ventura delle Riviste* (Florence: Vallecchi, 1941); *La Cultura Italiana del '900 Attraverso le Riviste, Volume Primo, "Leonardo," "Hermes," "Il Regno,"* ed. Delia Frigessi (Turin: Einaudi, 1960); Eugenio Garin, *Cronache di Fliosofia Italiana, 1900/1943* (Rome-Bari: Editori Laterza, 1975); Frigessi, *Intellettuali Italiani del XX Secolo* (Rome: Editori Riuniti, 1974); Nicola Lisi, *Parlata dalla Finestra di Casa* (Florence: Vallecchi, 1973); Antonietta Grippo, *L'Avanguardia Esoterica* (Potenza: Literalia, 1997); and possibly the most relevant study by Lucia Strappini, Claudia Micocci, and Alberto Abruzzese, *La Classe dei Colti: Intellettuali e Societa' nel Primo Novecento Italiano* (Bari: Laterza, 1970).

3. The friendship and relationship between these two authors and thinkers was a productive and long-lasting one, and ended only in 1956, the year of Papini's death. The vast correspondence between the two, which I shall be utilizing in this chapter, has been first collected in the *Fondazione Primo Conti* in Fiesole, Tuscany, and then published in an annotated, three-volume set, of which I will be consulting the first, Giovanni Papini and Giuseppe Prezzolini, *Carteggio I (1900–1907)* (Rome: Edizioni di Storia e Letteratura, 2003). For a basic bibliography on Giovanni Papini, focusing on the period this chapter will deal with, see Papini and Prezzolini, *Il Crepuscolo dei Filosofi* (Milan: Societa' Editrice Lombarda, 1906); *Un Uomo Finito* (Florence: Libreria della Voce, 1913); *Il Non Finito, Diario 1900 e Scritti Inediti Giovanili*, ed. Anna Casini Paszkowski (Florence: Casa Editrice Le Lettere, 2005); *Passato Remoto (1885–1914)* (Florence: L'Arco, 1948). For Prezzolini, especially for the timeframe this chapter treats

and the themes tackled, see *Cos'è il Modernismo?* (Milan: Fratelli Treves Editori, 1908); Benedetto Croce, *Con Bibliografia, Ritratto e Autografo* (Naples: Riccardo Ricciardi Editore, 1909); *Studi e capricci sui mistici tedeschi. Saggio sulla libertà mistica—Meister Eckehart [sic]—La Deutsche Theologie —Paracelso—Novalis—Giovanni Von Hooghens* (Florence: Casa Editrice Italiana, 1912).

4. In her work *Futurismo Esoterico, Contributi per una Storia dell'Irrazionalismo Italiano tra Otto e Novecento* (Naples: Liguori Editore, 2002), p. 78, Simona Cigliana is very clear in linking Reghini to Papini's and Prezzolini's fundamental views on life: "Just as Reghini, Borgese and the group around the journal 'Hermes'—who had declared themselves as 'idealists in philosophy' as they were 'aristocratic' in the arts and individualists in life, the youths writing on the journal 'Leonardo' [edited by Papini and Prezzolini] had too confessed of being idealists." The influence of Reghini on this milieu will be all the more clear as the chapter will quote many authors and philosophers writing about Reghini and his pivotal role in 1900s Florence.

5. Pasi, "The Modernity of Occultism," p. 63.

6. René Guénon, *Orient et Occident* (Paris: Payot, 1924): "[L]'élite intellectuelle n'aurait pas besoin d'être fort nombreuse, au début surtout, pour que son influence puisse s'exercer d'une manière très effective, même sur ceux qui ne se douteraient aucunement de son existence ou qui ne soupçonneraient pas le moins du monde la portée de ses travaux." See also Émile Durkheim, "L'Élite Intellectuelle et la Démocratie," *Revue Bleu* 5, no. 1 (1904), pp. 705–706.

7. For the most important study on the Theosophical Society in Italy in the first years of the twentieth century, see Marco Pasi, "Theosophy and Anthroposophy in Italy During the First Half of the Twentieth Century," trans. Joscelyn Godwin, *Theosophical History* 16, no. 2 (2012), pp. 81–119. Also see Paola Giovetti, "La Societa' Teosofica nel Mondo," in *Helena Petrovna Blavatsky e la Societa' Teosofica* (Rome: Edizioni Mediterranee, 2010), pp. 160–166; vvaa; James Santucci, *La Societa' Teosofica* (Turin: Elledici, 1999). A seminal work on Theosophy in Italy has been recently edited by Antonio Girardi, *La Societa' Teosofica: Storia, Valori, Realta' Attuale* (Vicenza: Edizioni Teosofiche Italiane, 2014): the third section of the book *La Societa' Teosofica in Italia*, pp. 69–88, is especially useful. For a more general account of the Theosophical Society and its history, see Joscelyn Godwin, "The Parting of East and West," in *The Theosophical Enlightenment* (Albany: SUNY Press, 1994), pp. 363–379); Bruce F. Campbell, *The Theosophical Movement* (Los Angeles: University of California Press, 1980), and *The Handbook of the Theosophical Current*, ed. Olav Hammer and Mikael Rothstein (Leiden: Brill, 2013), with a focus on the chapters by Nicholas Goodrick-Clarke, "Western Esoteric Traditions and Theosophy," pp. 261–308 and Gary W. Trompf, "Theosophical Macrohistory," pp. 375–404.

8. See Sestito, *Figlio del Sole*, p. 24: "In this ill-boding hodgepodge, not too promising for the awakening of esotericism in Italy, which was Reghini's wish, arose in him the decision to leave the Theosophical Society, while waiting for better times and better men." See Di Luca, *Arturo Reghini*, p. 24: "It was not still a question of taking his distance from occultism and theosophism, but only a discrimination between a 'serious' and a 'non-serious' occultism. Reghini was vocally in favour of the 'great' occultists

(Martinez de Pasqually, Louis-Claude de Saint-Martin, Eliphas Lévi, Papus), according to a very eclectic and equally improbable filiation, which was nevertheless one supported by the Martinist Order."

9. See Mario Foti, "La Riscoperta di Arturo Reghini negli Anni '80. Da 'Il Ghibellino' alla Associazione Pitagorica," in *La Cittadella* VI/VII: 23-4-5, *la Sapienza Pitagorica*, pp. 230–240.
10. Reghini, *Considerazioni*, pp. v–xv.
11. Most of my research on Reghini's early life is based on Renato del Ponte's excellent archival work, and often, when consulting archives which I thought would allow me to glean more about the topic at hand, I, too, had to stop where del Ponte has, for a total lack of extra documentation, found in my research. See Renato del Ponte, "Un'Antica Famiglia Italiana—Una Nota sulla Stirpe dei Reghini," in *La Sapienza Pitagorica*, pp. 177–183.
12. di Luca, *Arturo Reghini*, p. 8.
13. Sestito, *Figlio del Sole*, p. 16.
14. *Genealogie di Famiglie Pontremolesi*, ed. Nicola Michelotti (Pontremoli: np, 1993) has been the greatest source of information, as has Bernardino Campi, *Memorie Storiche della Citta' di Pontremoli* (Pontremoli: Artigianelli, 1975). Less useful, but still containing references to the Reghini family throughout the ages are Roberto Ricci, *Poteri e Territorio in Lunigiana Storica (VII–XII secolo). Uomini, Terre e Poteri in una Regione di Confine* (Spoleto: CISAM, 2002); Emanuele Gerini, *Illustri Scrittori e Uomini Insigni della Lunigiana* (Bologna: Forni, 1986); Ottaviano Giannetti, *Memorie Francescane della Lunigiana e della Lucchesia* (Florence: Pagnini, 2012).
15. del Ponte, "Antica Famiglia," p. 179.
16. Gerini, *Illustri Scrittori*, p. 223.
17. del Ponte, "Antica Famiglia," p. 180.
18. Nicola Michelotti, *Almanacco Pontremolese 2011* (Pontremoli: Artigianelli, 2011), p. 11; see also Pietro Ferrari, "Un Seminarista in Camicia Rossa: Teodoro Reghini," *Corriere Apuano* 19 (1941), pp. 45–49: "fuggì da Genova, calandosi da una finestra."
19. del Ponte, "Antica Famiglia," p. 178.
20. Roberto Sani, *Maestri e istruzione popolare in Italia tra Otto e Novecento* (Milano: Vita e Pensiero, 2003), pp. 81–84; see also Marco Civra, *I Programmi della Scuola Elementare dall'Unità d'Italia al 2000* (Turin: Marco Valerio, 2002); Angelo Gaudio, "Legislazione e Organizzazione della Scuola, Lotta Contro l'Analfabetismo," in *Storia d'Italia nel Secolo Ventesimo: Strumenti e Fonti—Vol. I: Elementi Strutturali*, ed. Ministero per i Beni e le Attività Culturali, Dipartimento per i Beni Archivistici e Librari (Rome: Ministero per i Beni e le Attività culturali, Dipartimento per i Beni Archivistici e Librari, 2006), pp. 355–373.
21. Rosmini has also been a great influence on twentieth-century Catholics, and books dedicated to his figure and his approach to religion and philosophy abound. Fundamental primary sources include Antonio Rosmini, *Nuovo Saggio sull'Origine delle Idee* (Rome: Tipografia Salviucci, 1830), especially the third book; Rosmini, *Aristotele Esposto ed Esaminato* (Turin: Scoieta' Editrice di Libri di Filosofia, 1857); Rosmini, *Massime di Perfezione Cristiana* (Milan: Tip. Ed. L.F. Cogliati, 1883).

Major secondary sources which facilitate the comprehension of Rosminian theories are Michele Dossi, *Profilo filosofico di Antonio Rosmini* (Brescia: Morcelliana, 1998); Fulvio De Giorgi, *Rosmini e il Suo Tempo. L'educazione dell'Uuomo Moderno tra Riforma della Filosofia e Rinnovamento della Chiesa (1797–1833)* (Brescia: Morcelliana, 2003); Giuseppe Goisis, *Il Pensiero Politico di Antonio Rosmini e Altri Saggi fra Critica ed Evangelo* (S. Pietro in Cariano: Gabrielli Editori, 2009); and of course, the most important text on Rosmini, the seminal Michele Federico Sciacca, *La Filosofia Morale di Antonio Rosmini* (Milano: Bocca, 1955), where Rosmini's role in the Risorgimento is dealt with with clarity and rigour.

On Vincenzo Gioberti, see his *Del Primato Morale e Civile degli Italiani* (Capolago: Tipografia Elvetica, 1844); Gioberti, *Degli Errori Filosofici di Antonio Rosmini* (Capolago: Tipografia Elvetica, 1846); Gioberti, *Il Gesuita Moderno* (Naples: C. Batelli, 1848-9). Out of the vast secondary literature, for an introduction to the works and life of Vincenzo Gioberti, see Giorgio Rumi, *Gioberti* (Bologna: Il Mulino, 1999) and Marcello Mustè, *La Scienza Ideale. Filosofia e Politica in Vincenzo Gioberti* (Soveria Mannelli: Rubbettino, 2000).

22. See Pietro de Nardi, *Rosmini e Kant: Studio Comparativo* (Forlì: Tipografia Sociale, 1902) and Bernardino Visintainer, *Kant e Rosmini e il Problema Gnoseologico* (Rovereto: Notizie Scolastiche del Ginnasio Superiore di Rovereto, 1885), but most importantly, Donato Jaja, *Saggio Storico sulle Categorie e Forme dell'Essere di A. Rosmini* (Bologna: Regia Tipografia, 1878), for its theories on Rosmini's overcoming of Kant's restrictive philosophical categories in his later years.

23. Carlo Cattaneo was a philosopher and political activist. His main works include Carlo Cattaneo, *Opere Edite ed Inedite di Carlo Cattaneo*, ed. Agostino Bertani (Florence: Le Monnier, 1891–1892); Cattaneo, *Una Teoria della Libertà: Scritti Politici e Federalisti*, ed. Walter Berberis (Turin: Einaudi, 2011); Cattaneo, *Lettere 1821*, ed. Carlo G. Lacaita (Milan: Mondadori, 2003); Cattaneo, *Dell'Insurrezione di Milano nel 1848 e della Successiva Guerra*, ed. Luigi Ambrosoli (Milan: Mondadori, 2001); *I Volti di Carlo Cattaneo 1801–1869. Un Grande Italiano del Risorgimento*, ed. F. Della Peruta, C. G. Lacaita, and F. Mazzocca (Milan: Skira, 2001).

24. See *Filosofia Civile e Federalismo nel Pensiero di Carlo Cattaneo*, ed. Gastone Gazzarri (Firenze: Nuova Italia, 1996); Carlo Cattaneo, *Industria e Scienza Nuova*, ed. Delia Castelnuovo Frigessi (Turin: Einaudi 1972); Cattaneo, *Uno Stato è una Gente e una Terra*, ed. Ettore A. Albertoni (Milan, RARA, 1994); Franco della Peruta, *Carlo Cattaneo Politico* (Milan: Franco Angeli, 2001); Giuseppe Armani, *Cattaneo Riformista: la Linea del 'Politecnico'* (Venezia: Marsilio, 2004).

25. See, for example, Carlo Cattaneo, *Interdizioni* (Turin: Einaudi, 1962); Luca Meldolesi, *Carlo Cattaneo e lo Spirito Italiano* (Soveria Mannelli: Rubbettino, 2013); Nadia Urbinati, *Le Civili Libertà: Positivismo e Liberalismo nell'Italia Unita*, pref. by Norberto Bobbio (Venice: Marsilio, 1990).

26. Still fundamental to this day is Guido Oldrini, *Il Primo Hegelismo Italiano* (Florence: Vallecchi, 1969); Eugenio Garin also paints a clear picture of the Hegelian School in his chapter "Problemi e Polemiche dell Hegelismo Italiano dell'Ottocento, 1832–1860"

and Guido Oldrini, "L'Hegelismo Ortodosso in Italia," both in *Incidenza di Hegel*, ed. F. Tessitore (Naples, Morano 1970), pp. 625–662 and 663–682, respectively.

27. For primary sources, consult Bertrando Spaventa, *Principii di Filosofia*, 2 vols. (Naples: Stabilimento Tip. Ghio, 1867); Spaventa, *Studi sull'Etica di Hegel* (Naples: Stamperia della Regia Università, 1869); Spaventa, *La Filosofia Italiana nelle Sue Relazioni con la Filosofia Europea*, ed. Giovanni Gentile, Bari: Laterza, 1909); Francesco de Sanctis, *Saggi Critici* (Naples: Morano, 1869); de Sanctis, *Mazzini e la Scuola Democratica* (Turin: Einaudi, 1951); important secondary sources include Eugenio Garin, *Bertrando Spaventa* (Naples: Bibliopolis, 2007); Luigi Gentile, *Coscienza Nazionale e Pensiero Europeo in Bertrando Spaventa* (Chieti: Ed. NOUBS, 2000); Sergio Landucci, *Cultura e Ideologia in Francesco De Sanctis* (Milan: Feltrinelli, 1964).

28. See Augusto Guerra, *Il Mondo Della Sicurezza: Ardigò, Labriola, Croce* (Florence: Sansoni, 1963); Santo Mandolfo, *I Positivisti Italiani (Angiulli-Gabelli-Ardigò)* (Padua: CEDAM, 1966); *Il Pensiero Pedagogico del Positivismo*, ed. Ugo Spirito (Florence: Giuntine, 1956).

29. See Roberto Ardigò, *La Morale dei Positivisti* (Milan: Marzorati, [1879] 1973; Ardigò, *Scritti Varii* (Florence: Le Monnier, 1922); Giovanni Landucci, "Note sulla Formazione del Pensiero di Roberto Ardigò," *Giornale Critico della Filosofia Italiana* 53 (1974), pp. 16–60; Mario Quaranta, *Il Positivismo Veneto* (Rovigo: Minelliana, 2003).

30. Eugenio Garin, *Cronache di Filosofia Italiana 1900/1943*, 7th ed. (Rome-Bari: Laterza, [1955] 1975), p. 5: "fosse davvero nato in Italia il filosofo dei tempi nuovi, il teorico dello Stato laico, e meglio sarebbe dire, con espressione fortunata, il teologo della nuova Italia democratica e anticlericale."

31. Antonio Banfi, "Verità e Umanità nella Filosofia Contemporanea," *Critica Filosofica* VIII (1947), pp. 83–198 [97]: "gli epigoni del positivismo furon dei contriti in cerca di un'assoluzione, intesi a diluire il progressismo borghese e la socialdemocrazia in un umanitarismo da comizio domenicale."

32. Eugenio Garin, *La Filosofia*, p. 8: "i [...] veri responsabili furono, non già gli idealisti, come certi ottusi ripetitori ricantano, ma proprio quei positivisti sprovveduti che con le loro generiche illazioni determinarono la sfiducia degli scienziati più avvedutie le critiche dei filosofi più accorti, che vennero travolgendo, non gia' la scienza- come taluno credette- ma l'ingenua metafisica che voleva passare da contrabbando sotto panni scientifici."

33. Fundamental works on Corradini and early Italian nationalism include Riccardo Gatteschi, *Un Uomo Contro: Enrico Corradini, Letterato e Politico* (Florence: Ellecidi, 2003) and Pier Ludovico Occhini, *Corradini* (Florence: Rinascimento del Libro, 1933). Useful articles in English on Corradini include Mauro Marsella, "Enrico Corradini's Italian Nationalism: The 'Right Wing' of the Fascist Synthesis," *Journal of Political Ideologies* 9, no. 2 (2004), pp. 203–224, and Tullio Pagano, "From Diaspora to Empire: Enrico Corradini's Nationalist Novels," *Modern Language Notes* 119, no. 1 (2004), pp. 67–83.

34. A complete bibliography on Croce, one of the most important thinkers of Italy's twentieth century, would be impossible. I will here limit myself to texts which could provide the reader with a clearer understanding of his neo-Idealist philosophical theories: Benedetto Croce, *Ciò che è Vivo e ciò che è Morto della Filosofia di Hegel: Studio Critico Seguito da un Saggio di Bibliografia Hegeliana* (Bari: Laterza, 1907); Croce, *La Critica* (Bari: Laterza, 1903–1944); Croce, *Logica come Scienza del Concetto Puro* (Bari: Laterza, 1909); Croce, *Materialismo Storico ed Economia Marxistica* (Naples: Sandron, 1900); Croce, *Saggio su Hegel Seguito da Altri Scritti di Storia della Filosofia* (Bari: G. Laterza & Figli, 1913); for secondary literature, see Giuseppe Galasso, *Croce e lo Spirito del Suo Tempo* (Milan: Il Saggiatore, 1990); Marcello Musté, *La Filosofia dell'Idealismo Italiano* (Rome: Carrocci, 2008); Fausto Nicolini, *Benedetto Croce* (Turin: UTET, 1962); Gennaro Sasso, *Filosofia e Idealismo I—Benedetto Croce* (Naples: Bibliopolis, 1994); Guido Verucci, *Idealisti all'Indice: Croce, Gentile e la Condanna del Santo Uffizio* (Bari: Laterza, 2006).

35. See especially Marco Burgalassi, "Il Giovane Croce e il Positivismo," in Burgalassi, *Itinerari di una Scienza: La Sociologia in Italia tra Otto e Novecento* (Milan: Franco Angeli, 1996), pp. 174–182 [176]: "In this way, he began by distinguishing 'proper sciences' from 'improper sciences' and proposing a differentiation between 'a description which is classification, which is trying to find the general in the particular, which going beyond the object which one focuses on' from 'the description which is reproducing said object in its individuality, since it exists in space and takes place in time.'"

36. See Garin, *Cronache di Filosofia*, p. 30: "Now, in the light of an implicit theorising on freedom, which made every framework of positivist conceptions explode, one pointed towards the idea, not only [to find] the postulation of a reality, but the capacity to create the reality thus postulated."

37. Historian Guido Pescosolido has written many texts on the subject of Italy's backward economical condition in the early twentieth century: see Guido Pescosolido, *Agricoltura e Industria nell'Italia Unita* (Bari: Laterza, 1994); Pescosolido, *Unità Nazionale e Sviluppo Economico 1750–1913* (Bari: Laterza, 1998); see also Emilio Sereni, *Il Capitalismo nelle Campagne (1860–1900)* (Turin: Einaudi, 1968); Francesco Barbagallo, *Stato, Parlamento e le Lotte Politico-Sociali nel Mezzogiorno, 1900–1914* (Naples: Arte Tipografica, 1976); finally see also Edward Banfield, *The Moral Basis of a Backward Society* (Glencoe, IL: Free Press, 1958).

38. See Antonio Labriola, "Come Nacque e Come Morì il Marxismo Teorico in Italia (1895–1900)," in Labriola,, *La Concezione Materialistica della Storia, Nuova ed. con un'Aggiunta di B. Croce sulla Critica del Marxismo in Italia dal 1895 al 1900* (Bari Laterza, 1942), pp. 89–97; see also Antonio Labriola, *Lettere a Benedetto Croce 1885–1904* (Naples: Istituto Italiano per gli Studi Storici, 1975), pp. 34–42.

39. Croce was a strong defender of the lay state and opposed the Lateran Pacts of 1929, which brought the Vatican under papal power once more and declared Catholicism to be state religion. See Antonio Di Mauro, *Il Problema Religioso nel Pensiero di Benedetto Croce* (Milan: Franco Angeli, 2001).

40. See Gianfranco Contini, "L'Influenza Culturale di Benedetto Croce," in Contini, *Altri Esercizi (1942–1971)* (Turin: Einaudi, 1972), pp. 31–70; Karl Vosserl, "Dialettica e

Carattere," in *L'Opera Filosofica, Storica e Letteraria di Benedetto Croce* (Bari: Laterza & Figli, 1942), pp. 22–27.

41. Benedetto Croce, "Introduzione," *La Critica* 1, no. 1 (1903), p. 3: "E, poiché filosofia non può essere se non idealismo, egli è seguace dell'idealismo: dispostissimo a riconoscere che dell'idealismo nuovo, in quanto procede più cauto di una volta e vuol dar conto d'ogni passo che muove, può ben designarsi come idealismo critico, o come idealismo realistico, e perfino (ove per metafisica s'intendano le forme arbitrarie del pensiero) come idealismo anti-metafisico."

42. Croce and Papini corresponded during these years, debating on philosophy, but also on politics and more mundane affairs. In a letter written to Papini, dating March 24, 1903, Croce commented gleefully on Papini's article "Chi Sono I Socialisti?," which had been published in *Leonardo*, writing: "I have read your article 'Who are the Socialists?,' which contains many sagacious remarks. However, I think you ask too much of Socialists: that they even cease to be [considered] men...," in Archivio Papini, Fondazione Primo Conti, Ref. 19030324.

43. "Gli scrittori del *Leonardo* sono legati tra loro da una concezione filosofica ch'è l'idealismo, appreso specialmente nella forma che gli va dando uno dei più fini pensatori contemporanei, il Bergson, quale filosofia della contingenza, della libertà, dell'azione. E sono scrittori vivaci e mordaci, anime scosse ed inebriate per virtù d'idee; non pedestri infilzatori di brani e di periodi altrui con frigidi commenti propri, a scopo scolastico e professionale, quali di solito coloro che riempiono le riviste filosofiche. Ciò non può non attirare fortemente la nostra simpatia." Benedetto Croce, "Leonardo," *La Critica* 1, no. 4 (1903), pp. 287–291 [287].

44. Mario Manlio Rossi, *Lo Spaccio dei Maghi* (Rome: Doxa, 1929), p. 4: "Nel tumulto ogni tanto, qualche tenebrosa illuminazione. Ora, la grassa canizie della Besant alle Giubbe Rosse. Ora, l'astrologia scientifica di un anglo-americano chiamato Dodsworth [...]. Su tutto, l'alta statura, il viso da bonzo, la generosità signorile ed infantile del mago Reghini, che forse fu il mio migliore amico-.

45. *La Cultura Italiana del '900 Attraverso le Riviste "Leonardo," "Hermes," "Il Regno,"* ed. Delia Frigessi, Vol. II (Turin: Einaudi, 1979), pp. 373–374: "Tra l' "Hermes" il "Leonardo" ed "Il Regno" sarà scambievole collaborazione. Il "Leonardo" in un ambito più strettamente filosofico, "Il Regno" in un ambito più strettamente politico proseguono fini non lontani e non dissimili da quelli dell' "Hermes." I tre fratelli areranno da buoni vicini ciascuno il proprio campo."

46. Archivio Papini, Fondazione Primo Conti, Ref. 19021117: "Carissimo, io sto compiendo una funzione scientifica: istituisco un'esperienza. Non si tratta però di ossidi dai barbari nomi o innocui conigli, ma bensì di uomini e superuomini. Si tratta, come comprendi, del Leonardo..."

47. Gabriele d'Annunzio, "Anniversario Orfico," *Leonardo* 1, no. 2 (1903), p. 1.

48. William James, "La Concezione della Coscienza," *Leonardo* 3, no. 3 (1905), p. 77; William James, "Le Energie degli Uomini," *Leonardo* 5, no. 1 (1907), pp. 1–25.

49. Miguel de Unamuno, "Sobre el Quijotismo," *Leonardo* 5, no. 1 (1907), pp. 38–45.

50. Benedetto Croce, "Estratto dalla Critica," *Leonardo* 11–2, no. 1 (1903), p. 21.

51. Gianfalco, "Offese a Giosué Carducci," *Leonardo* 1, no. 3 (1903), 8.

52. See, for example, Adolfo de Karolis, "Cattolicesimo e Paganesimo," *Leonardo* 1, no. 8 (1903), p. 7; Giuliano il Sofista, "La Malattia del Kantismo," *Leonardo* 2, no. 3 (1904), p. 35; Gianfalco, "Come sta di Salute il Positivismo," *Leonardo* 3, no. 1 (1905), p. 38.
53. Gianfalco, "Programma Sintetico," *Leonardo* 1, no. 1, p. 1: "gruppo di giovani."
54. Ibid., p. 1: "Nella Vita son pagani e individualisti- amanti della bellezza e dell'intelligenza [. . .]. Nel Pensiero sono personalisti e idealisti, cioè superiori ad ogni sistema ed a ogni limite, convinti che ogni filosofia non è che un personal modo di vita- negatori di ogni altra esistenza oltre al pensiero. Nell'Arte amano la trasfigurazione ideale della vitae ne combattono le forme inferiori."
55. See Arturo Reghini, "Giordano Bruno Smentisce Rastignac," *Leonardo* 4, no. 5, pp. 51–54; "Istituzioni di Scienze Occulte," 4, no. 2, pp. 155–160; "La Massoneria come Fattore Individuale," 4, no. 4, pp. 297–310; "Il Punto di Vista dell'Occultismo," 5, no. 2, 144–156; the reviews of G. Giordano "La Pensée Ésotérique de Léonard de Vince," 4, no. 4, pp. 382–384 and of W. Williamson, "The Great Law," 5, no. 2, pp. 248–250.
56. Casini, *Origini del Novecento*, p. 51: "La risposta va cercata sul terreno dei miti positivistici subentrati alla crisi della mentalità postrisorgimentale: la vulgata del darwinismo sociale, l'esaltazione del superuomo, l'insorgere di un più' aggressivo sentimento di patria e appartenenza di classe."
57. Giuliano il Sofista, "Imperialismo Intellettuale," *Leonardo* 1, no. 1, pp. 1–2: "Voi affermate di essere avversari della democrazia, della borghesia, della civiltà e del progresso democratico e borghese. Ora anche noi siamo feroci nemici di tali cose, ma non siamo né saremo con voi [. . .]. Aspiriamo ad una preda più vasta e più degna: all'impero intellettuale di tutte le essenze dell'universo."
58. See for example a letter from Bergson to Papini dating October 21, 1903: "J'aurai grand plaisir a lire l'article dont vous voulez bien m'annoncer l'envoi. Je vous en remercie a l'avance, et je vous prie d'agréer, Monsieur, l'assurance de mes sentiments distingués." Archivio Papini, Fondazione Primo Conti, Ref. 19031021b.
59. Giuseppe Antonio Borgese, "Leonardo," *Hermes* 1, no. 1 (1904), p. 59.
60. For comprehensive studies on William James, see the classic Gerald E. Myers, *William James: His Life and Thought* (New Haven, CT: Yale University Press, 1986); more recent works include *The Heart of William James*, ed. Robert D. Richardson (Cambridge, MA: Harvard University Press, 2010) and Wesley Cooper, *The Unity of William James's Thought* (Nashville, TN: Vanderbilt Press, 2002).
61. See William James, "G. Papini and the Pragmatist Movement in Italy," *The Journal of Philosophy, Psychology and Scientific Method* 3, no. 13 (1906), pp. 328–341.
62. Gianfalco, "Gli Psicologi a Roma," *Leonardo* 3, no. 3 (1905), p. 123: "Oggi non si tratta di scegliere un nome piuttosto che un altro, si tratta di aumentare il nostro potere di agire [. . .]. Il vincitore del Congresso, dunque, avrebbe dovuto essere il Pragmatismo, il quale, veramente, ha trionfato a Roma nella persona di uno dei più celebri suoi rappresentanti, William James [. . .]."
63. Casini, *Origini del Novecento*, p. 164: "intesa come un fenomeno psicologico e sociale autonomo alla pretesa egemonia dei filosofi neoidealisti, ma anche come vocazione personale."

64. Ibid., p. 165: "non è certo facile distinguere tra gli intenti 'scientifici' di quell dipo di ricerche e le sue ricadute o aderenze di genere teosofico, iniziatico, esoterico, dilaganti all'inizio del secolo XX [...]."
65. Papini, *Uomo Finito*, p. 23: "Il famoso pragmatismo non m'importava [...]. Io guardavo più in sù. In me sorgeva allora il sogno taumaturgico: il bisogno, il desiderio di purificare e rafforzare lo spirito per farlo capace d'agir sulle cose [...] e giungere così al miracolo, all'onnipotenza."
66. Papini, *Diario 1900*, p. 237.
67. Giovanni Papini and Giuseppe Prezzolini, *Carteggio*, Vol. I, ed. Sandro Gentili and Gloria Manghetti (Rome: Edizioni Storia e Letteratura, 2003), p. 836: "uno dei soliti dilettanti ciarlatani delle scienze magiche ma era uno spirito acuto [...], arricchito da una cultura assai vasta, agguerrito dall'esercizio delle analisi matematiche."
68. Giovanni Papini and Giuseppe Prezzolini, "La Fine," *Leonardo* 5, no. 2 (1907), p. 257: "dai quali ci siamo definitivamente staccati."
69. Giuliano il Sofista, "Alle Sorgenti dello Spirito," *Leonardo* 1, no. 1, p. 4: "Tutto questo puzzo di acido fenico, di grasso e di fumo, di sudor popolare, questo stridor di macchine, questo affaccendarsi commerciale, questo chiasso di *réclame*, son cose legate non solo razionalmente, ma che si tengon tutte per mano sentimentalmente, che ce le farebbe avere in disdegno se fossero lontane, che ce le fa invece odiare perché sono vicine."
70. Research in the old rosters of the Theosophical Society in the early 1900s show that Ida Carlotta Reghini, Arturo's cousin, joined the Society in Bologna, on October 2, 1905, while Arturo Reghini had already joined in Turin on June 4, 1902, eventually receiving the status of "drop-out" on April 17, 1906." Data collected at *The Theosophical Society General Register*, ed. Marty Bax, tsmembers.org, http://tsmembers.org/ts-general-register-1875-1942/book-6-10/.
71. d'Uva, "Il Pitagorismo Iniziatico e Magico di Arturo Reghini," pp. 124–125: "Alle premesse teoretiche universaliste del teosofismo" and "l'universale, un'ingenua e volgare idea della reincarnazione, la tendenza a valorizzare e a specializzarsi in dottrine orientali, un'indulgenza adolescenziale verso i postulati pratico-sentimentali [...] dell'etica Cristiana."
72. Sestito, *Figlio del Sole*, pp. 16–37.
73. See McNeil Christian Taylor, *Disqualified Knowledge: Theosophy and the Revolt of the Fin de Siècle* (Middletown, CT: Unpublished thesis, 2013).
74. Pasi, "Theosophy and Anthroposophy," p. 82.
75. Di Luca, *Arturo Reghini*, p. 9: "crisi di lunga data."
76. See H. P. Blavatsky, *The Secret Doctrine: The Synthesis of Science, Religion, and Philosophy* (Adyar: Theosophical University Press, 1888), pp. 507–8. "History shows in every race and even tribe, especially in the Semitic nations, the natural impulse to exalt its own tribal deity above all others to the hegemony of the gods; and proves that the god of the Israelites was such a *tribal God*, and no more, even though the Christian Church, following the lead of the 'chosen' people, is pleased to enforce the worship of that one particular deity, and to anathematize all the others."
77. Pasi, "Theosophy and Anthroposophy," pp. 87–88.

78. See Pasi, "Theosophy and Anthroposophy," p. 88 and Paola Giovetti, *Helena Petrovna Blavatsky e la Società Teosofica* (Rome: Edizioni Mediterranee, 1991), pp. 163-164.
79. Parise, "Una Nota," p. v.
80. Among the most important titles published by *Ars Regia*, see H. Blavatsky, *Dalle Caverne e dale Giungle dell'Indostan* (Milan: Ars Regia, 1912); Annie Besant, *Teosofia e Vita Umana* (Milan: Ars Regia, 1909); G. R. S. Mead and M. L. Kirby, *Frammenti di una Fede Dimenticata* (Milan: Ars Regia, 1909); C. W. Leadbeater, *Il Piano Astrale* (Milan: Ars Regia, 1913).
81. The international heads of the Theosophical Society were very aware of the difficulties Cooper-Oakley would have encountered on her mission in Italy; see "Italy," *The Theosophist* XXII, no. 4 (1901), p. 246. "The Italians are so inexperienced as a people, in methodical conduct of business, and Theosophy, as a system, is so new to them, that Mrs. Cooper-Oakley, is sure to find in her way many obstacles that will have to be removed before the movement can have free scope to spread."
82. The minutes of the "First Convention of the Italian Section of the Italian Section of the Theosophical Society," republished in 2002, exactly one hundred years since the event in *Rivista Italiana di Teosofia* LVIII, no. 2 (2002), pp. 5-11, are a clear indicator of this.
83. Ida Carlotta Reghini,"Isabel Cooper-Oakley," *Societa' Teosofica: Bollettino della Sezione Italiana* 14, no. 3 (1914), pp. 113-114. "Era tra coloro che facevano sgorgare acqua dalle rocce con la sua bacchetta magica, e la sua bacchetta magica era la sua volontà, la sua smisurata devozione alla causa della Società Teosofica, al suo Maestro," and "in lei si avvertiva il riflesso di quei tempi eroici, che richiedevano un'assoluta e completa dedizione del proprio essere. Dobbiamo a questi gran lavoratori, se oggi possiamo appoggiarci e trovare ristoro alle grandi verità della Teosofia."
84. See Giovanni Papini, *Passato Remoto, 1885-1914*, ed. Anna Casini Paszkowski (Florence: Ponte delle Grazie, 1994), p. 102.
85. Guido Ferrando, in Simona Cigliana, *Futurismo Esoterico*, p. 34: "La Società Teosofica sorse quando il materialismo nella filosofia e nella scienza aveva raggiunto il suo grado più alto; e quando già cominciavano le prime e isolate proteste contro la novissima dottrina che riduceva tutta la vita a un meccanismo e negava ogni attività libera dello spirito."
86. VVAA, *Ritorno*, p. 13.
87. Marino Biondi, "Hermet, Epica e Liturgia delle Riviste," in *Augusto Hermet, La Ventura delle Riviste (1903-1940)*, 2nd ed. (Florence: Vallecchi, 1987), p. 17: "un luogo dove i misteri erano a portata di mano" and "gli spazi chiusi dell'idealismo magico, movimenti iniziatici Evoliani, in cui si poteva parlare di imperialismo pagano, di razze superiori destinate a dominare e vibravano tutte le manie Nietzsciane del tradizionalismo esoterico."
88. Cigliana, *Futurismo Esoterico*, p. 57: "si finisce col chiedersi quale e quanta parte abbia avuto la Biblioteca [...] di Arturo Reghini nella circolazione di alcune idee che sembrarono poi radicarsi nella cultura italiana, sotto forma di parole o idee-chiave, le stesse che andarono a fecondare il substrato di tanto irrazionalismo e di tante confusioni idealistiche, fino a costituire, da una parte, alcune delle linee

ideologiche della involuzione politica italiana, dall'altra alcuni *leitmotifs* della elaborazione letteratio-avanguardistica del futurismo."

89. Nicola Lisi, *Parlata dalla Finestra di Casa*, p. 113; and Paolo Casini, *Alle Origini del Novecento. Leonardo, 1903–1907)*, p. 161.
90. Giovanni Papini, "Biblioteca Filosofica," *Leonardo* IV, no. 4 (1906), pp. 170 ff.: Papini describes Reghini's library as "one of the best signs of an intellectual reawakening of Florence and of the rising interest in Italy for the problems of the spirit."
91. Hermet, *La Ventura*, p. 17: "Reghini apparteneva al tipo di aristocratico di gran cultura, un'immagine ideale per i giovani che volessero elevarsi sopra le masse [. . .], che facevano dell'aristocrazia un punto programmatico del loro percorso intellettuale."
92. Lisi, *Parlata*, p. 112: "Reghini, e ormai i più lo sanno, era un filosofo / matematico che seguiva l'esempio degli antichi. Un Pitagorico, amava definirsi."
93. Cigliana, *Futurismo Esoterico*, p. 66: "elementi aristocratici e antidemocratici."
94. Helena Petrovna Blavatsky, *The Key to Theosophy* (Mumbai: Theosophy Company, 1887), p. 5.
95. Alfred Percy Sinnett, *Esoteric Buddhism* (London: 1883). For a general approach to the subject, see Godwin, *Theosophical Enlightenment*, pp. 363–379.
96. Quoted in Isaac Lubelsky, "Mythological and Real Race Issues in Theosophy," in *Handbook of the Theosophical Current*, ed. Olav Hammer and Mikael Rothstein (Leiden: Brill, 2013), pp. 335–356 [337].
97. Reghini, "Giordano Bruno." The quote is from Marco Pasi, "Theosophy and Anthroposophy," p. 92.
98. Julius Evola, *Il Cammino del Cinabro*, 3rd exp. ed. (Rome: Mediterranee, [1963] 2014), pp. 143–144.
99. Renato del Ponte, "L'Iniziazione Pitagorica di Arturo Reghini in Apuania," *Arthos* 20 (2014), pp. 7–16.
100. Pasi, "Theosophy and Anthroposophy," p. 91.
101. Decio Calvari, "Resumé du Mouvement Théosophique en Italie," in *Transactions of the First Annual Congress of the Federation of European Sections of the Theosophical Society*, ed. Johan Van Manen (Brill: Leiden, 1906), pp. 381–382: "Un autre travail a aussi débuté et aura un plus grand dévelopment dans l'automne prochain. Il consiste dans l'étude particuliere de notre tradition mystique qui a de si nombreaux points de contact avec notre inseignement, comme le démotrarent les recherches dans les oevres des grands écrivains et penseurs de la Renaissance. Par l'institution d'une Bibliotheque Philosophique Religeuse et d'une Société pour Conférence Publiques, on essaiera de revivifier a Florence la grand e idée neo-platonicienne qui a eu dans le 15iesme siècle de si grands représentants tells que Marsilio Ficino et Leonardo da Vinci."
102. Arturo Reghini, "Le Basi Spirituali della Massoneria," in *Rassegna Massonica* 8–9 (1923), reprinted in *Paganesimo, Pitagorismo, Massoneria* (Furnari: Mantinea, 1984), p. 34: "la filosofia della schola italica lasciò il suo marchio forte e indelebile in tutta la successiva filosofia platonica e neo-platonica, e quindi su tutto il pensiero classico."

103. Alaya [Arturo Reghini], "Mors Osculi," *Leonardo* 4 (1906), pp. 142–143; Svasamvedana [Arturo Reghini], "Istituzioni di Scienza Occulta," *Leonardo* 4 (1906), pp. 156–160.
104. Helena Petrovna Blavatsky, *The Voice in the Silence: Being Chosen Fragments from the Book of Golden Precepts* (London: Theosophical Publishing Company, 1889).
105. Blavatsky, *The Secret Doctrine*, p. 29.
106. Blavatsky, *The Voice in the Silence*, p. 24.
107. See d'Uva, "Il Pitagorismo Magico," pp. 132–133; and Sestito, *Figlio del Sole*, pp. 17–19.
108. Reghini, "Imperialismo Pagano," pp. 70–85.
109. See, for example, T. H. Meyer and Elisabeth Vreede, *The Bodhisattva Question: Krishnamurti, Steiner, Tomberg and the Mystery of the Twentieth Century Master* (Forest Row: Temple Lodge Publishing, 2006).
110. See Nitzan Lebovic, *The Philosophy of Life and Death: Ludwig Klages and the Rise of a Nazi Biopolitics* (London: Palgrave Macmillan, 2013) and Ludwig Klages, *Der Geist als Widersacher der Seele*, 4 vols. (Leipzig: J. A. Barth, 1929–1932).
111. Alfred Mombert, *Aeon: Dramatische Trilogie* (Berlin: Schuster & Loeffler, 1907–1911); see also Raymond Furness, *Zarathustra's Children: A Lost Generation of German Writers* (Rochester, NY: Camden House, 2000), pp. 49–75.
112. Helena Petrovna Blavatsky, "The Fall of Ideas," in *The Collected Works Vol. XII* (London: Theosophical Publishing House, 1980), p. 40.
113. Annie Besant, letter of April 24, 1903, in *Ignis* 5 (1992), p. 83.
114. Svasamvedana [Arturo Reghini], "Istituzioni di Scienza Occulta," p. 160: "Dobbiamo tracciare un ponte sopra l'abisso che separa il pensiero moderno con i suoi pregiudizi scientifico-positivisti dal vecchio ma sempre nuovo pensiero esoterico: strappare via il lettore da un'errata e ordinaria concezione della vita e iniziarlo nello spirito dell'occultismo."
115. See Arturo Reghini, "Il Dominio Dell'Anima," in *Paganesimo, Pitagorismo, Massoneria*, pp. 1–12; Arturo Reghini, "La Vita dello Spirito," in *Paganesimo, Pitagorismo, Massoneria*, pp. 13–25; Arturo Reghini, "Per una Concezione Spirituale della Vita," in Arturo Reghini, Giuliano Balbino, and Guido Ferrante, *Per una Concezione Spirituale della Vita* (Firenze: Seeber, 1908).
116. Reghini, "Il Dominio dell'Anima," p. 2: "il problema della morte, della natura e della sopravvivenza dell'anima."
117. See William Q. Judge, *The Ocean of Theosophy* (New York: The Path, 1893), p. 1: "Theosophy is that ocean of knowledge which spreads from shore to shore of the evolution of sentient beings; unfathomable in its deepest parts, it gives the greatest minds their fullest scope, yet, shallow enough at its shores, it will not overwhelm the understanding of a child. [...] Embracing both the scientific and the religious, theosophy is a scientific religion and a religious science."
118. Reghini, "Il Dominio dell'Anima," p. 3: "Ma vi è ancora un'altra categoria di anime, la cui sete di conoscenza non è saziata da nessuna delle due fonti. Queste anime, e sono più numerose di quanto pensiate, non pensano sia necessario scegliere tra scienza

e religione; non giudicano indispensabili nessuna delle due, ma le considerano inadeguate, separate o insieme, a spegnere completamente quella sete di conoscere."
119. Ibid., p. 9: "concentriamo le nostre [energie] sull'evoluzione della nostra coscienza, seguendo sia con la volontà, la fede e gli eroici furori l'impulso naturale, sia le varie tecniche evolutive e dello yoga."
120. Ibid., p. 12: "solo il silenzio ne esprime il nome ineffabile."
121. Reghini, "La Vita dello Spirito," pp. 16–17: "ciascuno di noi possa provare a raggiungere il vasto Oceano della Coscienza e possa sentire la sua immane immanenza."
122. Ibid., 19: "fece risuonare le sponde del Gange, un secolo fa, con la sua *vita*."

Chapter 4

1. Dottor Hermes [Eduardo Frosini], *Massoneria Italiana e Tradizione Iniziatica* (Pescara, Ettore Croce, 1911), p. 153: "Oh, Grande spirito di Pitagora . . . perdona I poveri pofani che profanano l'iniziazione, riducendola a vuota coreografia, perdonali!"
2. The definitive study on the *Rito Filosofico Italiano* is Roberto Sestito, *Storia del Rito Filosofico Italiano e dell'Ordine Orientale Antico e Primitivo di Memphis e Misraim* (Florence: Libreria Chiari, 2003); other studies which briefly touch upon the history of the *Rito Filosofico Italiano* are A. Aldo Mola, *Storia della Massoneria Italiana dale Origini ai Giorni Nostri* (Milan: Bompiani, 1992), pp. 328–329; Gastone Ventura, *I Riti Massonici di Misraim e Memphis* (Todi: Atanor, 1980); Arturo Reghini, *Considerazioni*.
3. According to the scholar of Freemasonry Arturo de Hoyos, Rites may be defined as masonic systems, explained as "the linking of masonic degrees for initiation or instruction, under administrative or governmental authority." See Arturo de Hoyos, "Masonic Rites and Systems," in *Handbook of Freemasonry*, ed. Henrik Bogdan and Jan Snoek (Leiden: Brill, 2014), pp. 355–377.
4. The concept of fringe Masonry has created many debates in academic circles: it was first used in an openly emic and disparaging way in Ellic Howe, "Fringe Masonry in England: 1870–85," *Ars Quatuor Coronatorum* 85 (1972), pp. 242–280, in order to describe those Rites, which had briefly flourished in England without the approval of the United Grand Lodge of England (est. 1717). As Henrik Bogdan and Jan Snoek have pointed out in "Introduction," *Handbook*, pp. [1] 1–10, the scholarly consensus has decided to drop the terms "fringe" and "irregular" for such lodges, preferring a more neutral definition of the two dominant versions of Freemasonry as "regular," for the pre-existing Grand Lodge, and "liberal," for the other Rites that claimed independence from said pre-existing authority. For the sake of clarity, as linking Reghini's preference for the "liberal" Rites would clash with his opposite, conservative, and elitist view of life, I will be referring throughout the chapter to fringe masonic Rites, rather than using the possibly misguiding term "liberal."

5. Reghini, as will be discussed in this chapter, was initiated in a Rite replete with occult overtones. About it, Francesco Brunelli, in his *Rituali dei gradi simbolici di Memphis e Misraim* (Foggia: Bastogi, 1981), p. 45, would write: "the Rite is a visible, tangible nexus between the lower sphere and the higher sphere. It provides the keys to the Arcana, and the means in which they may be revealed and practiced."
6. See especially, Aldo A. Mola, "Promana da Nord-Ovest la Vera Luce d'Oriente," in Mola, *Storia della Massoneria*, pp. 60–80.
7. Ibid., pp. 65–74.
8. See Conti, "Massoneria e Sfera Pubblica," pp. 579–610.
9. Ibid., 580–581; Mola, *La Massoneria*, pp. 69–70.
10. *Costituzioni della Massoneria Italiana Discusse e Votate dalla Prima Assemblea Costituente Massonica Italiana nelle Tenute delli 27, 28, 29, 30, 31 Dicembre 1861, Valle di Torino 5861* (Turin: np., 1861), p. 1: "a) Indipendenza ed unità delle singole nazioni, e fraternità delle medesime; b) Tolleranza di qualunque religione, ed uguaglianza assoluta dei culti; c) Progresso morale e materiale delle masse."
11. Conti, "Massoneria e Sfera Pubblica," pp. 583–584.
12. Ibid., p. 586: "Di conseguenza, l'universalismo cosmopolita sbandierato nelle costituzioni lasciò progressivamente spazio a un patriottismo che, almeno ai vertici dell'obbedienza, non conobbe flessioni o tentennamenti."
13. Quoted in Conti, "Massoneria e Sfera Pubblica," p. 587: "Prima dobbiamo provvedere alle cose nostre, poi a quelle di fuori. Gli altri popoli non pensano e non agiscono diversamente. Saremo forse in tal modo più Italiani che umanitari? Non credo . . . D'altronde io so che l'amore della famiglia è fonte prima dell'amore alla Patria: ciò posto, chi non amasse la patria, potrebbe amare l'umanità?"
14. Conti, "Massoneria e Sfera Pubblica," pp. 606–610.
15. In the same year, another Supreme Council would be created in Naples under the supervision of Domenico Angherà, Italian patriot and founder of the *Loggia Sebezia*. See Gian Mario Cazzaniga, "Ermetismo ed Egizianesimo a Napoli," in *Storia d'Italia*, p. 560. See also Luigi Sessa, *I Sovrani Grandi Commendatori e Breve Storia del Supremo Consiglio d'Italia del Rito Scozzese Antico ed Accettato. Palazzo Giustiniani dal 1805 ad Oggi* (Foggia: Bastogi, 2004).
16. For a definitive biography on Mazzoni, see Guglielmo Adilardi, *Memorie di Giuseppe Mazzoni (1808–1880). L'uomo, il Politico, il Massone*, 2 vols. (Pisa: Pacini, 2008–2016).
17. Fulvio Conti, "Massoneria e Sfera Pubblica," p. 596: "il nucleo più consistente (23%) era rappresentato dagli impiegati, dagli insegnanti e dai pensionati, seguito da quello dei commercianti, dei negozianti e degli esercenti, che arrivavano al 17.5%."
18. Irredentism (from *irredento* or unredeemed) was a political movement which aimed to reclaim and reoccupy a geographic area subtracted by another state. For its Italian manifestation at the turn of the century, see Giulio Vignoli, *I territori Italofoni non Appartenenti alla Repubblica Italiana* (Milan: Giuffrè, 1995); Vignoli, *Gli Italiani dimenticati. Minoranze italiane in Europa* (Milan: Giuffrè, 2000); Gabriele Zaffiri, *L'Impero che Mussolini Sognava per l'Italia* (Pozzuoli: The Boopen, 2008).

19. See Aldo Mola, "Sempre più Scomunicati," in Mola, *Storia della Massoneria*, pp. 81–101; Beatrice Bisogni, *Sette Enigmi*; Conti, "Massoneria e Sfera Pubblica," 594–602; Luigi Pruneti, *La Sinagoga di Satana. Storia dell'antimassoneria, 1725–2002* (Bari: Laterza, 2002); Pruneti, *Oh, Setta Scellerata ed Empia. Appunti su Oltre Due Secoli di Pubblicistica Antimassonica* (Florence: Il Campanile, 1992).
20. Conti, "Massoneria e Sfera Pubblica," p. 597: "Uno degli elementi accomunanti dell'attivismo massonico del secondo Ottocento fu senza dubbio l'anticlericalismo. L'avversione per la Chiesa cattolica e per il ruolo che essa svolgeva nella vita sociale e politica—peraltro ricambiata da sentimenti del tutto analoghi sul versante ecclesiastico – ebbe toni di particolare asprezza […]."
21. See *L'istruzione in Italia tra Sette e Ottocento*, ed. Angelo Bianchi (Brescia: La Scuola, 2007); Angelo Gaudio, "Legislazione e Organizzazione della Scuola, Lotta Contro l'Analfabetismo," in *Storia d'Italia nel Secolo Ventesimo: Strumenti e Fonti—Vol. I: Elementi Strutturali*, ed. Claudio Pavone (Rome: Ministero per i Beni e le Attività Culturali, 2006), pp. 355–373; Benedetto Vertecchi, *La scuola italiana da Casati a Berlinguer* (Milan: Franco Angeli, 2001).
22. See Antonio Gualano, *Il Congresso Antimassonico Internazionale di Trento: L'Ultima Crociata* (Trapani: np, 2010), pp. 105–118.
23. Ibid., 105: "l'ultima crociata."
24. Ibid., 105–106: "potenziare le organizzazioni dei laici cattolici giacché solo con una forza unita […], si sarebbe potuto combattere il nemico non più segreto."
25. Anonymous, "Il Congresso Antimassonico," *Osservatore Romano*, August 8, 1896, p. 2: "Oh! benvenuto sia il Congresso antimassonico, e la nuova Crociata che esso intraprende contro la rea setta, sia l'alba novella di quel giorno fortunato che, dispersi dalla faccia della terra i nemici della nostra santa religione, ritorni su tutti gli uomini il dolce regno di Gesù Cristo."
26. Quoted in Gualano, "Congresso," pp. 107–108: "inconcepibile battaglia contro gli adoratori di Lucifero, contro i sanguinari che non indugiavano a tramare contro il legittimo potere nelle segrete in cui si ordivano le cose piu' indegne ed indecorose per il genere umano."
27. Mola, *La Massoneria*, p. 280: "Non molto più temibili erano le ricorrenti 'rivelazioni' di ecclesiastici che di quando in quando 'scoprivano' la vera trama e le occulte intese ordite in vista dell'imminente rivoluzione destinata a spazzar via ogni ordine, istituzione, fondamento morale. Ben oltre le inquietudini esoteriche di fine secolo, angosciosamente dibattute tra isteria sensuale, eccitamenti mistici, stimoli esalanti naturalismo contraffatto e morbosità religiosa (si rivada al classico *Là-Bas* di Joris Karl Huysmans) assaporando la smodata voluttà di eresia serpeggiante tra i cattolici, 'tentati come mai dal fascino dell'Avversario.'"
28. On the Taxil hoax, see Benvenuti, "Il Congresso"; also see the classic Arthur Edward Waite, *Devil-Worship in France or the Question of Lucifer* (London: George Redway, 1896); Robert Rossi, *Léo Taxil (1854–1907): Du Journalisme Anticlérical à la Mystification Transcendante* (Marseille: Quartiers Nord Éditions, 2015); Marie-France James, *Ésotérisme, Occultisme, Franc-Maçonnerie et Christianisme aux XIXe et XXe Siècles, Explorations Bio-Bibliographiques* (Paris: Lanore, 2008); Fabrice

Hervieu, "Catholiques Contre Francs-Maçons: l'Affaire Léo Taxil," *L'Histoire* 145 (1991), pp. 32-39; on Domenico Margiotta, see Hervieu, *Le Palladisme: Culte de Satan-Lucifer Dans les Triangles Maçonniques* (Grenoble: H. Falque, 1895); Hervieu, *Le Culte de la Nature dans la Franc-Maçonnerie Universelle* (Grenoble: H. Falque 1896).

29. For Ettore Ferrari, sculptor and mason, see Ettore Passalalpi Ferrari, *Ettore Ferrari: Tra le Muse e la Politica* (Città di Castello: Edimond, 2005); *Il Progetto Liberal-Democratico di Ettore Ferrari: Un Percorso tra Politica e Arte*, ed. Anna Maria Isastia (Milan: Franco Angeli, 1997).

30. For the *Piazza del Gesù* reality at the beginning of the twentieth century and Saverio Fera's work, see Michele Moramarco, *Piazza del Gesu', Documenti Rari e Inediti della Tradizione Massonica Italiana* (Reggio Emilia: CE.S.A.S., 1992); Luigi Pruneti, *La Tradizione Masonica Scozzese in Italia: Storia del Supremo Consiglio e della Gran Loggia d'Italia degli A.L.A.M. Obbedienza di Piazza del Gesu' dal 1805 a Oggi* (Rome: EDIMAI, 1994); Arnaldo Francia, *1908-1978: Settant'Anni di Vita Massonica dell'Obbedienza di Piazza del Gesù* (Turin: Orienti Piemontesi, 1978).

31. See on the subject, Jeffrey Thyssen, "Freemasonry and Nationalism," in *Handbook of Freemasonry*, pp. 461-472; Maria Adelaide Frabotta and Guglielmo Salotti, *Propaganda ed Irredentismo nel Primo Novecento* (Florence: Leo S. Olschki, 1990).

32. Conti, "Massoneria e Sfera Pubblica," p. 609: "Il riformismo borghese, un viscerale laicismo, un internazionalismo umanitario che soffocava ogni velleità espansionistica della nazione, una perenne tendenza al compromesso e agli accordi clientelari che imbrigliava le energie vitali e spingeva l'Italia verso una degenerazione morale e spirituale."

33. See, for example, Franco Gaeta, *Il Nazionalismo Italiano* (Rome-Bari: Laterza, 1981).

34. See Rocco D'Alfonso, "Il Nazionalismo Italiano e le Premesse Ideologico-Politiche del Concordato," in Marco Mugnaini, *Stato, Chiesa e Relazioni Internazionali* (Milano: FrancoAngeli, 2007), p. 69.

35. See Tullia Caralan, "Le Società Irredentiste e la Massoneria Italiana," in *Storia d'Italia Annali 21 La Massoneria*, pp. 611-656.

36. Catalan, "Le Società Segrete," p. 619: "lo scoppio di petardi e di bombe rudimentali davanti ad edifici rappresentativi dello Stato Austriaco; la distribuzione di volantini e di opuscoli inneggianti all'Italia durante rappresentazioni teatrali o visite di rappresentanti ufficiali del governo austriaco [...]."

37. *Senso*, directed by Luchino Visconti (1954; Italy: Lux Film, 2011), DVD.

38. Catalan, "Le Società Segrete," pp. 611-618.

39. Reghini, "La Massoneria come Fattore," p. 307: "Una mano di vernice verde non basta a trasformare in liberi pensatori delle marionette che hanno sempre pensato colla testa altrui, e dimenar la testa da destra a sinistra e viceversa non è più intelligente che farla oscillare dall'alto al basso."

40. Ibid., p. 310: "I muratori del nostro tempo preferiscono rimanere pietra greggia al divenire pietra polita: e Platone redivivo rifiuterebbe ancora una volta di spiegare a questi indegni iniziati il mistero della pietra cubica. Spiegandola ne uscirebbe

una croce ermetica, ed i frammassoni la prenderebbero per la croce della Chiesa cattolica."
41. Bisogni, "Sette Enigmi," p. 84: "Come sempre accade le energie possono allora agitarsi convulse e confuse ma anche nella loro apparente e troppo spesso accettata irrazionalità, esse testimoniano un atteggiamento di ribellione ed una volonta' gnoseologica [...]."
42. Ibid., pp. 84–103.
43. See Sestito, "Pitagorismo e Tradizione Romana," in Sestito, *Storia del Rito*, pp. 69–74.
44. See Emmanuel Rebold, *Histoire des Trois Grandes Loges de Francs-Maçons* (Paris: Collignon, 1864), p. 596; Gastone Ventura, *Les Rites Maçonnique de Misraïm et Memphis* (Paris: Maisonneuve et Larose, 1986), pp. 72–89.
45. Parise, "Nota," pp. i–ii; Maurizio Nicosia, "Reghini, Arturo," in *Encyclopédie de la Franc-Maçonnerie*, ed. E. Saunier (Paris: Librairie Générale Française, 2000), quoted in de Luca, *Arturo Reghini*, p. 10.
46. Quoted in Ferdinando Cordova, *Massoneria e Politica in Italia: 1892-1908* (Bari: Laterza, 1985), pp. 219–220: "Democratizzazione della Massoneria, mediante la riduzione dei tributi, acciò possano accedervi le intelligenze sprovviste di mezzi; Riforma del simbolo: 'Alla Gloria del Grande Architetto dell'Universo'; Riduzione delle formalità di Rito; Maggiore sviluppo dell'opera della Massoneria nella vita pubblica pur sempre mantenendone il proprio carattere [...]."
47. Quoted in de Luca, *Reghini*, p. 16: "La Comunione Italiana, non discostandosi nei principi e nel fine da quanto l'Ordine Mondiale professa e si propone, propugna il principio democratico nell'ordine politico e sociale."
48. Reghini, "La Massoneria come Fattore," p. 300: "Subentrati ai cabalisti ed ai mistici i materialisti, i monisti, i positivisti, i socialisti le acque limpide dell'esoterismo sono state intorbidate, ed è difficile riconoscere l'origine di questa pozzanghera che è l'odierna Massoneria."
49. Giuseppe Armentano, "Gli Incontri Fatali," in Armentano, *Massime di Scienza Iniziatica*, pp. 70–102 [70].
50. Ibid., p. 70.
51. Nicola Lisi, *Parlata*, p. 114-115: "Il Reghini solo in un'occasione rinunziava con semplicità di convinzione alla investitura di maestro che gli era, del resto, congeniale. La deroga di ogni volta che appariva un forte e singolare personaggio il cui nome era Armentano. I suoi precedenti erano da tutti, e credo anche da Reghini, sconosciuti. Si sapeva che [...] abitava in un castello su un promontorio della costa calabrese."
52. Augusto Hermet, *La Ventura*, p. 140: "Reghini allora, secondo il suo principio metafisico desunto dalla tradizione ermetico-pitagorica-orfico-eleusina-taoistico-zohariana, disse: 'Non cogito, ergo sum.' E il fraterno jerofante Armentano, tarchiato corpo di rossa testa leonina con atletiche mandibole, l'uomo dalla mazza col grosso pomo d'avorio, musicista negligente e divorator di prosciutti, gli plaudì dicendo: 'Nihil nihil.' Nelle grotte sotto il suo castello sul mare calabro cantavano le superstiti sirene."
53. The *Torre Talao* is mentioned more than once in Aleramo, *Amo Dunque Sono*. The epistolary novel contains letters by Sibilla to her lover Giulio Parise, a disciple of Reghini who was at the time spending a magical retreat in Scalea.

54. Sestito, *Figlio del Sole*, p. 41: "Amedeo mi ha semplicemente resuscitato. Quando Amedeo mi è venuto a trovare io mi ero ormai rassegnato a vivere senza scopo, senza meta, senza speranza."
55. Ibid., "Anche nei miei sogni di occultismo, quando sole cose che io desiderava era il contatto con la Fraternità, mai avrei pensato di avere la quotidiana felicità di una comunione sempre crescente col mio amico, fratello e Maestro."
56. See Arturo Reghini, *I Numeri Sacri nella Tradizione Pitagorica e Massonica* (Rome: Ignis, 1947); Reghini, "Le basi spirituali della Massoneria," in *Paganesimo, Pitagorismo, Massoneria*, pp. 33–43; Reghini, "Sull'Origine del Simbolismo Massonico," in *Paganesimo, Pitagorismo, Massoneria*, pp. 49–63.
57. René Guénon, *L'Ésotérisme de Dante* (Paris: Gallimard, 1925), p. 24: "de Pythagore à Virgile et de Virgile à Dante, la 'chaîne de la tradition' ne fut sans doute pas rompue sur la terre d'Italie."
58. Reghini, "Del Simbolismo e della Filologia in Rapporto alla Scienza Metafisica," in *Paganesimo, Pitagorismo, Massoneria*, pp. 117–150 [149]: "La Scuola Italica non ebbe miti; il suo simbolismo fu il più puro ed astratto possibile, il simbolismo numerico. In essa poche cerimonie, nonostante l'origine italica di questa parola; una dura palestra spirituale, un misticismo sensista, integrale, empirico e trascendente, una visione metafisica eppure sociale; e la serenità luminosa del puro cielo calabrese."
59. Enrico Cornelio Agrippa, *La Filosofia Occulta o la Magia*, intr. by Arturo Reghini, 3 vols. (Milan: Fidi, 1927), p. 40: "Esiste la tradizione 'orale' della sapienza occulta che non è possibile trasmettere con le parole (profanamente percepite ed intese); ed esiste tuttora, in Occidente, una tradizione seria, al di fuori della gazzarra carnevalesca delle parodie e delle pretese del così detto occultismo contemporaneo."
60. Rumon, "Note sulla Schola Italica di Amedeo R. Armentano," *Pietas* 3, no. 6 (2012), pp. 31–43 [35]: "L'uomo romano, come il pitagorico, non concepisce stacco netto tra le varie dimensioni in cui si articola la personalità umana, dall'esoterismo alla politica, il politico ponendosi anzi, secondo taluni, come l'ultimo grado della Scuola pitagorica [. . .]. Non sarebbe azzardato affermare che il fine della Scuola di Pitagora risiedeva nella costituzione di una élite fondata nel Sacro, vale a dire radicata nella conoscenza diretta del Sacro."
61. Arturo Reghini, "Del Simbolismo," pp. 146–147: "Il linguaggio e la razza non sono le cause della superiorità metafisica; essa appare connaturata al luogo, al suolo, all'aria stessa. Roma, Roma caput mundi, la città eterna, si manifesta anche storicamente come una delle regioni magnetiche della terra."
62. For a purely geographical knowledge of the area, I have resorted to the following texts: Marco Lapi and Florenzo Ramacciotti, *Apuane Segrete* (Il Labirinto: np, 1995); Frederick Bailey and Enrico Medda, *Alpi Apuane, Guida al Territorio del Parco* (Pisa: Pacini, 1992); Giorgio Giannelli, *Uomini sulle Apuane* (Forte dei Marmi: Galleria Pegaso Editore, 1999): the latter publication is the narration of the explorations of all the famous authors who have visited or written about the Apuan Alps, from Pliny to Dante, to author Ludovico Ariosto.
63. Quoted in Renato del Ponte, "L'Iniziazione Pitagorica di Reghini in Apuania," *Arthos* 4, no. 20 (2012), pp. 7–16 [8].

64. Ibid., p. 8: "Le Apuane [. . .] si trovano nel luogo esatto in cui la penisola si stacca da continente. Un punto di cambiamento, una soglia ed un luogo di incontro tra condizioni ambientali assai diverse. Questa specificità fece di tali monti un'area di 'cerniera' e di trapasso tra culture e popoli senza che venissero mai del tutto cancellate condizioni pregresse."
65. Ibid., p. 10: "Il passo, una piccola radura in un boschetto, è proprio sul limite dell'abisso."
66. Sestito, *Figlio del Sole*, p. 50: "uno spaventoso precipizio, un abisso, un salto nel vuoto di centinaia di metri."
67. Ibid., p. 50: "nell'oscuro baratro della coscienza esterrefatta e smarrita."
68. Parise omits the whole episode in his short description of Reghini's life; Sestito devotes one page to the description of the place and Armentano's supposed intent, while de Luca, following Parise's example, chooses to ignore this fundamental step in Reghini's life.
69. Quoted in Del Ponte, "L'Iniziazione Pitagorica," p. 12: "a questo abisso interiore può corrispondere all'esterno, quale theatrum dramatis, sia una profonda cavità sotterranea, sia una voragine alpestre, fermo restando che tali eseriori ambienti fisici hanno soltanto lo scopo di propiziare un'esperienza che si consuma unicamente sub specie interioritatis."
70. Henrik Bogdan, *From Darkness to Light, Western Esoteric Rituals of Initiation* (Göteborg: Göteborgs Universitet, 2003), pp. 48–50.
71. Ibid., pp. 49–50.
72. Parise, "Nota," p. Vi–vii: "ricondurre la massoneria alla sua funzione iniziatica, sfrondandola dagli elementi deteriori; orientare la società verso un ordinamento basato su valori spirituali."
73. Sestito, *Figlio del Sole*, p. 51: "Sento che potrei forse lasciarmi prendere e sprofondare in qualcheduna delle mie antiche stupide passioncelle, ma anche sento che per quanto sprofondassi, non potrei mai annegare la percezione incipiente in me di una vita nuova serena ed esente dai meschini piaceri e dolori di quell'io che non vuole arrendersi."
74. Ibid., p. 51: "Io ho bisogno di occultismo come la pianta dell'acqua [. . .]. Che farei io mai della mia vita, se non avessi davanti a me il compito sublime che mi hai additato, che tu mi hai riconfortato a vedere ed a mirare?"
75. Hammer, "The Appeal to Tradition," in *Claiming Knowledge*, pp. 68–157.
76. Ibid., pp. 68–69.
77. Reghini, "Giordano Bruno," pp. 53–54.
78. Ibid., p. 53–54: Reghini, "Giordano Bruno," p. 53: "Né fu precursore del determinismo ma un mistico ed un occultista. Opere essenzialmente mistiche sono gli *Eroici Furori*, il *Sigillus Sigillorum*, e il libro dei *trenta sigilli* per non citare altro; sì che egli credette il regno di Dio essere in noi, e la divinitade abitare in noi per forza del riformato intelletto [. . .]. Il De Monade, e la Cabala non sono altro che trattati di filosofia cabalistica e pitagorica; alla magia consacro' tre opere intiere piu' numerosi brani di altre opere."

79. Reghini, "La Massoneria," p. 299: "ed è un fatto innegabile che i rituali compilati dal Rosacroce Eliah Ashmole nel 1648 [...] sono basati sopra i misteri egiziani come Jamblico ce li ha tramandati [...]."
80. Hammer, "Appeal to Tradition," p. 72.
81. Armentano, *Massime*, p. 153: "Toscano e non di Samo, discepolo di Numa e non viceversa."
82. Reghini, 'L'Impronta Pitagorica nella Massoneria," *Atanòr* 1-2 (1924), pp. 31-46. See also Gennaro d'Uva, "La Tradizione Italica," *Politica Romana* 5 (1998/1989), pp. 106-125.
83. Hobsbawm and Ranger, *The Invention of Tradition*, p. 1.
84. Ibid., p. 1.
85. Ibid., p. 10.
86. Armentano, *Massime*, pp. 148-156: "58—Gli uomini sono uguali innanzi a Dio e non lo sono fra loro. 170—La democrazia è una parola che non ha significato reale; è un'idea ironica di governo. 171—Popolo e governo sono due elementi antitetici 221—Le cose per essere vere non hanno bisogno di essere conosciute dal volgo."
87. See di Luca, *Arturo Reghini*, p. 46n.
88. For a brief yet complete analysis of the French Occult Revival, see Christopher McIntosh, *Eliphas Lévi and the French Occult Revival*, 2nd ed. (Albany: SUNY Press, [1972] 2011).
89. di Luca, *Reghini*: "la *Societas Rosacruciana in Anglia, l'Order of the Golden Dawn in Outer,* il Rito di Memphis e Mizraim, il Rito Nazionale Iberico, il Rito di Swedemborg, l'*Ordo Templi Orientis* etc. Alle sigle in questione, in realtà, facevano capo per solito scarsi seguaci, tra i quali erano generosamente ripartiti 'gradi,' titoli roboanti e correlate dignità, elargiti con pari larghezza a soci *ad honorem* ed a rappresentanti all'estero [...]."
90. Sestito, *Storia del Rito*, p. 43.
91. de Luca, *Reghini*, p. 45: "Così robustamente munito di 'patenti,' ancorché provenienti da massonerie 'irregolari,' nel marzo del 1909 a Firenze con alcuni seguaci alla fondazione di una 'loggia centrale Ausonia' e di un 'Supremo Gran Consiglio Generale dell'Ordine Antico e Primitivo di Memphis e Misraim,' sotto la denominazione di *Rito Filosofico Italiano*."
92. Frosini, *Massoneria Italiana*.
93. See Sestito, *Figlio del Sole*, p. 25-28; di Luca, *Reghini*, pp. 7-27.
94. A slip in the first edition of the book warned the reader that the author had felt no need to provide an *errata corrige*.
95. Frosini, *Tradizione*, p. 15: "teorie esoteriche tramandateci dalle antiche società iniziatiche [...]. La integrazione con la Scuola Italiana con la tradizione Simbolica sarebbe dunque già fatto compiuto se vi fosse stata la preparazione filosofica."
96. Frosini, *Tradizione*, p. 76: "ha nella propria scuola di Giordano Bruno, Telesio, Campanella, i *germi* di un affratellamento tra Filosofia e Religione, dal quale scenderanno le istituzioni che solo possono rifare grande la Patria."

97. Frosini, Tradizione, p. 158: "Papus è cristiano mistico-esoterico ed è sinarchista. Noi della Scuola Italica, pitagorici e mazziniani, siamo teosofi cosmico-umanisti ed alla sinarchia contrapponiamo l'isocrazia."
98. Sestito, Storia del Rito, pp. 53–59.
99. Sestito, Figlio del Sole, p. 61.
100. Ibid., pp. 62–63: "Frosini mi offre un posto nel Supremo Consiglio del Rito Filosofico con piena libertà di lavoro," and "In ogni caso il Rito Filosofico e annessi è in mano nostra, perché chi fa tutto è Bolaffi, E Bolaffi è nostro."
101. Sestito, Storia del Rito, p. 121: "insieme alla 'Hermes' di Firenze, 'I Pitagorici' a Milano e la 'Sebezia' di Napoli [fu] tra le più dinamiche e frequentate."
102. Ibid., p. 138: "Roma sempre risorse tra le ceneri come la Phenice e che l'Italia si riscosse, lottò massonicamente e vinse attraverso l'epopea garibaldina e l'apostolato Mazziniano."
103. Ibid., p. 139: "Ed è per questa tradizione vivente ed immanente che l'Italia guidata dai principi che noi, del Rito Filosofico Italiano, sosteniamo e difendiamo, assurgerà a quella grandezza e a quel dominio morale del Mondo che Roma Eterna e tutto il glorioso pensiero italico additano, preconizzano, vogliono ed avranno!"
104. Ibid., pp. 147–149.
105. Sestito, Figlio del Sole, pp. 71–73.
106. de Luca, Reghini, p. 50; Sestito, Figlio del Sole, pp. 70–71.
107. Reghini, 'La Tradizione Italica," Ultra (Aug. 1914): 67–68 [68]: "Il nostro lavoro, puramente metafisico e quindi naturalmente esoterico, è sempre stato volontatiamente segreto. A noi non occorreva rendere pubblica ragione l'esistenza di questa Scuola; e se il Frosini, non avesse poniamo per inavvertenza, fatto un passo che può ingenerare equivoci, saremmo rimasti bella nostra penombra."
108. Sestito, Storia del Rito, p. 156: "La morte civile (bruciamento massonico) è stata inflitta all'avv. Guido Bolaffi di Firenze e al dott. Arturo Reghini per ALTO TRADIMENTO. Fin dal 14 gennaio 1914 e.v., questi due signori NON HANNO PIU' NULLA DI COMUNE CON LA NOSTRA FAMIGLIA."
109. Ibid., p. 120: "Sì, fu quello il nostro squillo di battaglia—vale a dire del Rito Filosofico Italiano (che piu' che un Rito fu una Scuola vera e propria, massonico ma fino a un certo punto)—per un imperialismo pagano sul serio."

Chapter 5

1. Julius Evola, Imperialismo Pagano (Rome: Mediterranee, [1928] 2004), p. 310: "Ben a ragione Dante diceva che [. . .] il mondo fu distrutto da Costantino."
2. Sestito, "Figlio del Sole," p. 81.
3. For Italo Tavolato, see Contro la morale sessuale (Firenze: Gonnelli, 1913), and mostly his article, famous for being banned for explicit sexual contents, "Elogio della prostituzione," in Bestemmia contro la Democrazia, ed. Anna K. Valerio (Padova: Edizioni di Ar, [1914] 2009), pp. 35–42.

4. See Aldo Palazzeschi, *Il Codice Perelà* (Milan: Edizioni futuriste di Poesia, 1911); Palazzeschi, *Riflessi* (Florence: Cesare Blanc, 1908); *Roma* (Florence: Vallecchi, 1954).
5. A very useful primary source and first hand account of the Battle of Adua is Carlo Diotti, *Prigioniero d'Africa. La Battaglia di Adua e l'Impresa Coloniale del 1895-96 nel Diario di un Caporale Italiano* (Como: Nodolibri, 2006); Emilio Bellavita, *La Battaglia di Adua* (Rome: Gherardo Casini Editore, 2012); Domenico Quirico, *Adua: La Battaglia che Cambiò la Storia d'Italia* (Milano: Mondadori, 2004).
6. For the *Trattato degli Uccialli* see Indro Montanelli, *Storia d'Italia, vol. 6, 1861–1919* (Milan: RCS, 2006), p. 221; a more in-depth narration on the event is written in Angelo Del Boca, *Gli italiani in Africa orientale*, Vol. 1 (Milan: Mondadori, 1992), pp. 343–357.
7. Alfredo Rocco, *Cos'è il Nazionalismo e Cosa Vogliono i Nazionalisti*, 3rd ed. (Rome: Associazione Nazionalista, 1914), p. 10: "I nazionalisti quindi non sono liberali moderati, o per meglio dire non sono essenzialmente liberali moderati, non sono conservatori, non sono clericali, non sono democratici, né radicali, né repubblicani; non sono, infine, socialisti; sebbene non disconoscano il valore dei problemi che taluno di questi partiti pone innanzi (il che spiega che con taluni di essi, in date circostanze, possano andare d'accordo) restano sempre, caratteristicamente nazionalisti, perché danno valore assoluto solo al problema nazionale e considerano tutti gli altri come subordinati."
8. Francesco Perfetti, "La Dottrina Politica del Nazionalismo Italiano: Origini e Sviluppo Fino al Primo Conflitto Mondiale," in *Il nazionalismo in Italia e in Germania fino alla Prima Guerra Mondiale*, ed. Rudolfo Lill (Bologna: Il Mulino, 1983), pp. 226–227: "codardia contemporanea," "ignobile socialismo," and "degrado morale."
9. See Elena Papadia, *Nel Nome della Nazione. L'Associazione Nazionalista Italiana in Età Giolittiana* (Roma: Archivio Guido Izzi, 2006), where the concept is often reiterated.
10. Ettore Bassan, *Lotte Nazionali nella Venezia Giulia* (Rome: Pinci, 1915), pp. 6–7: "L'Italia sa che entro i confini *immutabilmente prescritti dalla sua storia e dalla sua gloria*, vi è un popolo d'eroi che per la difesa del focolare e del sangue disperatamente combatte la guerra più feroce che mai fosse combattuta, solo e meraviglioso. [. . .] L'Italia sa che da Trieste a Pola, da Capo d'Istria a Trento, da Spalato a Fiume, una è la favela, una l'anima, una la speranza, una la voce che reclama il concorso di tutti gli italiani per l'ultima difesa."
11. For the momentum of the Socialist Party in the years preceeding the war, see Gaetano Arfé, *Storia del socialismo italiano 1892–1926* (Turin: Einaudi, 1965); Andrea Spiri, *Socialismo italiano. Cento anni di storia. Il PSI 1892–1992* (Milan: M&B Publishing, 2003); Girogio Spini, *Le origini del socialismo* (Turin: Einaudi, 1982).
12. Ministero dell'Interno, *Compendio dei Risultati delle Elezioni Politiche dal 1848 al 1958* (Rome: Istituto Poligrafico dello Stato, 1963), pp. 56–57.
13. Sestito, *Figlio del Sole*, p. 100: "La situazione politica si fa di nuovo seria. Coll'Austria va a finire in una guerra; pare che l'Austria la desideri subito perché noi non siamo ancora rimessi dalla Libia, e la Russia non è pronta [. . .]. Certo è che non passano dieci giorni senza una questione nuova."

14. In truth, it was a society created ad hoc by FIAT vice-president Dante Ferraris (1868–1931), which allowed the *Idea Nazionale* (*National Idea*) to become a daily paper, after a long existence as a weekly journal.
15. Sestito, *Figlio del Sole*, p. 100: "Il momento sarebbe giunto per agire in senso imperiale."
16. Ibid., p. 102: "Fu un'estate ricca di incontri e di riunioni, nel corso delle quali le discussioni politiche si intrecciavano con discussioni storiche e filosofiche dell'unità spirituale degli italiani, mentre la guerra europea batteva rumorosamente ai confini irredenti della patria."
17. Ibid., p. 102.
18. Ibid., p. 103: "We took one pill each, and then I showed him [friend Giannotto Bastianelli (1883–1927)] and Franchi what I desired. I will only say that at my *fiat lux* a lightbulb three meters away from us switched on; and then at another *fiat lux* it switched on and off, along with all the lights along the road." For more on the mysterious mystic nettle substance, see Piero Fenili, "La Scuola Italica e l'Ortica Mistica," *Politica Romana* 6 (2000–2004), pp. 309–313.
19. Ibid., p. 103: "Tu capisci che può ben servire contro i Gesuiti e gli Austriaci. Io mi metterei a disposizione di Cadorna, dopo avergliene dato la prova. Non credere che esageri; né perda la testa. Ho voluto provare, la cosa è riscuta; per lo meno vi è una trasmissione di pensiero che è già qualcosa."
20. Ibid., p. 105: "e se non fosse la possibilità di dimenticare tutto dentro le mie ricerche filolofiche passerei dei brutti momenti [. . .]. Ma ho fede in tutto quel prodigioso trascendente di cui abbiamo avuto tante volte il contatto!"
21. Sestito, *Figlio del Sole*, p. 103: "Ti basti dire che al mio fiat lux si accese a tre metri da noi una lampada elettrica; e poi ad un altro fiat lux si accese e si rispense insieme a tutte quelle della strada."
22. Ibid., p. 103: "Ieri ho addormentato Vitali. Senza dirgli una sola parola, col semplice contatto sulla fronte della tua lettera, ha potuto vederti. Ti ha visto che ridevi in trincea con uno con una barbetta nera, che ha poi riconosciuto per Rossaro. Vi ha visto in battaglia: gli Austriaci erano presso una chiesetta, dietro il camposanto (?!) [. . .]. Che c'è di vero in questo? Bada che io non gli ho detto una parola; e tutto questo è stato visto in pochi minuti. È successo qualcosa di simile il 13 Luglio?"
23. Ibid., p. 106: "Così sono condannato a fare il soldato semplice. Due soldi al giorno e la promiscuità continuata con i miei simili! Ma pensa tu che cosa sarebbe per me dovere vivere nella continua promiscuità di una massa di bruti, e, senza colpa, senza motivo, dover essere oggetto della loro derisione, e che derisione, e non poter né fuggire, né rivoltarsi!"
24. Ibid., p. 107.
25. Ibid., pp. 108–109.
26. Lisi, "Parlata," p. 115–117: "Ero così, solo, sdraiato a lamentarmi che vidi, scendere dall'alto e venirmi incontro, uno il quale mi parve, più del mago che dell'ufficiale. Fu a un tratto che lo riconobbi per il Reghini [. . .]. Prima di lasciarci [. . .] restai d'accordo col Reghini [. . .] per un incontro del giovedì sera a leggere, per lui rileggere, Platone."
27. Sestito, *Figlio del Sole*, p. 117: "PER OPERA NOSTRA, L'AUSTRIA MUORE."

28. See Harold Lasswell, *The Structure and Function of Communication in Society: The Communication of Ideas* (New York: Institute for Religious and Social Studies, 1948), p. 117.
29. For an improvement on Lasswell's formula, see Richard Braddock, "An Extension of the 'Lasswell Formula,'" *Journal of Communication* 8 (1958), pp. 88–93.
30. Sestito, *Figlio del Sole*, p. 78. "A Firenze si mormorava che il vero capo dei futuristi fosse proprio lui e che il futurismo non fosse un movimento animato solo da ambizioni artistiche e letterarie, ma che in esso si celasse un'anima filosofica e pagana."
31. For a brief analysis of the spokesperson in modern esotericism and New Religious Movements, see Olav Hammer, *Claiming Knowledge*, pp. 28–31, where Bruce Lincoln's theories on power and authority are re-elaborated and adapted to an esoteric framework. See also Bruce Lincoln, *Authority: Construction and Corrosion* (Chicago: University Press of Chicago, 1994)
32. For more information on Däubler in English, see the seminal Raymond Furness: "Theodor Däubler," in *Zarathustra's Children* (Rochester, NY: Camden House, 2000), pp. 152–172; Carola von Edlinger, *Cosmogonic and Mythical World Designs of Inter-Discursive Perspective. Studies on Phantasus (Arno Holz), Northern Lights (Theodor Däubler) and The Ball (Otto zur Linde)* (Frankfurt am Main: Peter Lang, 2002); Thomas Keller, "World Experience and Foreign Experience: The Mythology in Theodor Daubler," in *Mysticism and Modernity in Germany around 1900*, ed. Moritz Bassler and Hildegard Chatellier (Strasbourg: Presses Universitaires, 1998), pp. 255–278.
33. Augusto Agabiti, close friend of Reghini's, would be one of the many intellectuals to find his death during the Great War, succumbing to Spanish fever while on leave in Rome. Staunch Theosophist and editor of the journal *Ultra* in 1914, he was a virulent anti-vivisectionist and an admirer of the figure of philosopher Hypatia of Alexandria. For more on his works, see Augusto Agabiti, *Il Problema della Vivisezione: Testi delle Principali Disposizioni Legislative Vigenti negli Stati Moderni* (Rome: Enrico Voghera, 1911); Agabiti, *Ipazia, la Prima Martire della Libertà di Pensiero* (Rome: Enrico Voghera, 1914); and his posthumous memoir from the front, *Sulla Fronte Giulia: Note di Taccuino 1915–1916–1917* (Naples: Società Editrice Partenope, 1919).
34. Sestito, *Figlio del Sole*, p. 78.
35. Ibid., p. 79.
36. Hermet, *La Ventura*, p. 282.
37. As I have written in the previous chapter, Mori had met Reghini in 1904, when Reghini had been initiated in the *Lucifero* lodge in Florence. Mori then followed Reghini and Armentano after the foundation of the *Rito Filosofico Italiano*.
38. See René Guénon, *Le Théosophisme*.
39. Arturo Reghini, "I Santi Padri della Teosofia: Besant, Leadbeater, Steiner" (Florence: unpublished manuscript, 1914), manuscript to be found in the Reghini-Armentano Archive of Roberto Sestito in Sao Paulo, Brazil.
40. Sestito, *Figlio del Sole*, p. 81. "gli attirò addosso, come era da aspettarsi, le critiche della stragrande maggioranza dei lettori digiuni di cultura classica e padana."
41. Ibid., pp. 82–83.

42. Ibid., p. 82: "universale cretineria. Finirà col prevalere la volontà di far andare le cose avanti a dispetto i tutto e tutti; vale a dire imponendosi a forza di cultura, di arte e di botte."
43. Ibid., p. 82.
44. Ibid., p. 82: "molti giovani che frequentavano i caffè letterari di Firenze rimasero affascinati dal suo patriottismo e vedremo un Däubler, poeta lirico raffinato, travolto dal nuovo misticismo imperialista, comporre gli *Inni All'Italia* di esuberante bellezza." The actual name of Däubler's composition was *Hymne an Italien*, in the singular form; see Theodor Däubler, *Hymne an Italien* (Munich: Georg Muller, 1916).
45. Ibid., p. 82: "'Imperialismo Pagano' fu l'articolo destinato a segnare una svolta nel mondo esoterico italiano, perché ruppe una consuetudine di timori e di sottomissione dell'orgoglio e della dignità italiana verso i potentati politici e religiosi, nella maggior parte stranieri o di origine straniera, rottura modellata sul pensiero dei grandi vati nazionali."
46. Dante's *Monarchia* (and not *De Monarchia*, as many, Reghini himself, tend to write) deals with the then thorny issue of temporal power: where Dante did not dispute the power the Pope had in spiritual matters, or any idea pertaining to life after death, which Dante saw possessing a higher quality than worldly life: he was adamant that temporal power should be assigned to a new Holy Roman Emperor, who would balance theocratic power, which was a strong force in early fourteenth-century Italy. Pope Boniface VIII (ca. 1230–1303) had made claims to temporal power in Florence, and this might have been the reason behind Dante's distrust of the Holy See. The book was banned in 1585 by the Catholic Church.
47. Reghini, "Imperialismo Pagano," p. 70: "Nelle recenti elezioni politiche il suffragio universale, estremo colrollario dei postulati democratici, ci ha portato al trionfo del semplicismo. I due partiti, infatti, che più han visto aumentare il numero dei propri voti sono stati senza dubbio il clericale ed il socialista. Segno evidente che le argomentazioni e le promesse usate da questi partiti erano per loro natura piu' accessibili e più gradite alla mentalità della grande maggioraza, analfabeta, degli elettori, che non potessero esserlo le idee degli altri partiti."
48. In reality, according to the data provided by the Italian *Ministero degli Interni*, the election of 1913 did not really go the way Reghini describes it: Giovanni Giolitti's *Partito Liberale Italiano* (Italian Liberal Party) gained 47.6 percent of the votes, granting 270 of its politicians a seat in Parliament. It is true that through the Gentiloni Pact, named after Count Vincenzo Ottorino Gentiloni, the *Unione Elettorale Cattolici Italiana* (Electoral Italian Catholic Union) were allies with the Liberals, but only a 4.2 percent of the Italian people voted for this party. The other clerical party that ran for these elections, *Cattolici Conservarori* (Conservative Catholics), gained mere 1.8 percent. Where Reghini was right in his political commentary was his analysis of the *Partito Socialista Italiano* (Italian Socialist Party), which, with 17.2 percent of the votes, was the second biggest party in the country.
49. Reghini, "Imperialismo Pagano," p. 71: "Analfabetismo, semplicismo ed internazionalismo, stretti in fascio, han dunque vinto insieme a maggior gloria del regime democratico."

50. Ibid., p. 71: "[. . .] ora in Italia nessun partito col quale la coscienza nazionale possa fiduciosamente identificarsi."
51. See Pier Ludovico Occhini, *Enrico Corradini e la Coscienza Nazionale* (Florence: Vallecchi, 1915), pp. 24–35.
52. Ezio Maria Gray, "Untitled," *La Nazione*, January 8, 1914, p. 12: "Noi affermiamo la necessità di un'associazione che assuma la difesa del grande istituto nazionale minacciato dal socialismo. Tutti gli interessi di classe verranno valutati non nella loro separazione, bensì nella loro unione coordinata nell'interesse nazionale."
53. Ezio Maria Gray was a fundamental figure during the early years of the Fascist regime. Part of six legislatures under the Mussolini government, he was vice-president of the Chamber of Deputies in the XXIX Legislation, from 1935 to 1939. He was staunch anti-socialist and close to the strong powers of high finance and politics: for more on this figure, see Philip Rees, *Biographical Dictionary of the Extreme Right Since 1890* (New York: Schuster & Son, 1991), p. 266; Philip Rees, *Fascism and Pre-fascism in Europe, 1890–1945: A Bibliography of the Extreme Right* (New York: Barnes & Noble, 1984); an Italian biography was published in 2015: Valerio Zinetti, *Ezio Maria Gray. Un Italiano Fedele alla Patria* (Milan: Edizioni Ritter, 2015); Paolo Nello, "La Vocazione Totalitaria del Fascismo e l'Equivoco del Filofascismo Liberale e Democratico: Il caso di Pisa (1919–1925)," *Storia Contemporanea* 20, no. 4 (1989), pp. 656–663.
54. Modernism, or Theological Modernism, was an attempt to link religious preoccupation with the major happenings and themes of the twentieth century: revelation was thus not a message from God, or Jesus, but the realization of one's subconscious at work; the Bible was a collection of myths and in no way a narration of factual events; faith was no longer considered to be an objective fact, but a subjective feeling, different for every person. For a history of the Theological Modernist phenomenon, see Maurilio Guasco, *Modernismo* (Rome: Edizioni Paoline, 1995); Marvin O'Connell, *Critics on Trial: An Introduction to the Catholic Modernist Crisis* (Washington, DC: Catholic University of America Press, 1994); Roberto de Mattei, "Modernismo e antimodernismo nell'epoca di Pio X," in *Don Orione Negli Anni del Modernismo*, ed. Nichele Busi, Roberto De Mattei, Antonio Lanza, and Flavio Peloso (Milan: Jaca Book, 2002), pp. 29–86; a book that connects esotericism to the birth of Theological Modernism is Adele Cerreta, *Le Origini Esoteriche del Modernismo: Padre Gioacchino Ambrosini e la Teologia Modernista* (Chieti: Edizioni Solfanelli, 2012), especially "Le Origini Esoteriche del Modernismo," pp. 59–70, where ties between occultism, the Theosophical Society, and Theological Modernism are attempted and listed.
55. Quoted in John Cornwell, *Hitler's Pope: The Secret History of Pius XII* (London: Penguin, 2008), p. 37. Pius X died in the same year "Imperialismo Pagano" was published, but his battle against Theological Modernism began in 1907, with the publication of *Pascendi Dominici Gregis* (*Feeding the Lord's Flock*), where in point 39, Pius X had written, after a lengthy analysis of the phenomenon: "can anybody who takes a survey of the whole system be surprised that We should define it as the synthesis of all heresies?" An oath against Modernism was introduced in 1910 in *Motu Proprio Sacrorum Antistitum* (*Bishops, Out of Their Own Accord*), a true Antimodernist oath, whereby any member of the clergy had to declare that "I am completely opposed to the error

of the modernists who hold that there is nothing divine in sacred tradition," or "reject that method of judging and interpreting Sacred Scripture which, departing from the tradition of the Church, the analogy of faith, and the norms of the Apostolic See, embraces the misrepresentations of the rationalists." See Pius X, "Motu Proprio Sacrorum Antistitum," in *Acta Apostolicae Sedis* vol. II (1910), n. 17, pp. 655–680.

56. Reghini, "Imperialismo Pagano," p. 73: "*Mala Tempora Currunt!* E magro conforto ait anti guai é il progredire del Cattolicesimo nei paesi protestanti: in Germania dove l'Imperatore ha bisogno dei voti del centro cattolico; in Inghilterra e negli Stati Uniti dove il culto cattolico, più *pittoresco* dei vari gruppi protestanti, guadagna continuamente terreno."

57. Ibid., "In questo modo anche il guaio più grosso che sia capitato alla Chiesa di Roma, la formazione dell'Italia a nazione unita e indipendente, finirà col ridursi a nostro beneficio."

58. Ibid., p. 74–75.

59. Ibid., p. 74: "Ora nel nostro caso vi è contrasto naturale, fatale, profondo, incomponobile. Nella lunga serie dei secoli, dalla fondazione della Chiesa di Roma in poi, il Papato, sempre e poi sempre, è stato il naturale nemico di Roma e d'Italia. La civiltà latina, eclettica, serena, aperta, in una parola *gentile*, e l'impero romano con essa furono soffocati dalla mentalità esotica, intollerante, fanatica, dogmatica del cristianesimo. E questo è un delitto che attende ancora espiazione."

60. For text that exemplify Roman tolerance in conquered regions when it came to religious matters, see the fundamental work of Mary Beard, John North, and Simon Price, *Religions of Rome: A History*, 2 vols. (Cambridge: Cambridge University Press, 1998); John B. Lott, *The Neighborhoods of Augustan Rome* (Cambridge: Cambridge University Press, 2004); Amy Chua, *Day of Empire: How Hyperpowers Rise to Global Dominance and Why They Fall* (New York: Doubleday, 2007), especially "Tolerance in the Roman Empire, Gladiators, Togas and Imperial Glue," pp. 29–59; Jasmine Merced, *Roman Isis and the Pendulum of Tolerance in The Empire* (unpublished thesis, 2008); Jo-Ann Shelton, *As Romans Did: A Sourcebook in Roman Social History* (London: Oxford University Press, 2008); David Frankfurter, *Religion in Roman Egypt: Assimilation and Resistance* (Cambridge, MA: University Press, 1998), especially "Idiom, Ideology, and Iconoclasm: A Prolegomenon to the Conversion of Egypt," pp. 265–285. Of course, intolerance was also shown, usually when the Emperor was not recognised as being of divine origins, and persecutions brought to the Jewish Wars and the persecution of Christians, in the first three centuries CE.

61. Vergil, "The Eclogues," IV:6, in *Loeb Classical Library 63 and 64: The Georgics, The Eclogues, The Aeneid Book I–VI*, trans. and ed. H. R. Fairclough (Cambridge, MA: Harvard University Press, 1916): "The Virgin maiden finally comes to us, and the reign of Saturn is back."

62. The full translation of the segment from which Reghini drew the verse recites thus: "Now the Virgin returns, the reign of Saturn returns; now a new generation descends from heaven on high. Only do you, pure Lucina, smile on the birth of the child, under whom the iron brood shall at last cease and a golden race spring up throughout the world!"

63. Kenneth Reckford, "Some Appearances of the Golden Age," *The Classical Journal* 54, no. 2 (1958), p. 80.
64. Vergil, Aeneid, 1. 291–296: "And the stern age be soften'd into peace: Then banish'd Faith shall once again return, / And Vestal fires in hallow'd temples burn; / And Remus with Quirinus shall sustain / The righteous laws, and fraud and force restrain. / Janus himself before his fane shall wait, / And keep the dreadful issues of his gates / With bolts and iron bar'; 6. 791–794: "And this in truth is he whom/ you so often hear promised you, / Augustus Caesar, son of a god, / who will again establish a golden age in Latium / amid fields once ruled by Saturn."
65. Ella Bourne, "The Messianic Prophecy in Vergil's Fourth Eclogue," *The Classical Journal* 11, no. 7 (1916), p. 390. Other works discussing this fascinating and intricate topic include Edwin Floyd, "Vergil's Eclogue 4," *The Explicator* 56, no. 1 (1997), p. 3; Cindy Vitto, *The Virtuous Pagan in Middle English Literature* (Philadelphia: American Philosophical Society, 1989); Gian Biagio Conte, *Latin Literature: A History* (Baltimore: John Hopkins, 1999); Bruce Arnold, "The Literary Experience of Vergil's Fourth 'Eclogue,'" *The Classical Journal* 90, no. 2 (1997), pp. 143–160; Paul Carus, *Virgil's Prophecy on the Saviour's Birth: the Fourth Eclogue* (Chicago: Open Court Publishing, 1918); for a Roman Traditionalist approach to the subject matter, see Nuccio d'Anna, *Virgilio e le Rivelazioni Divine* (Genoa: ECIG, 1989).
66. Ella Bourne, "Messianic Prophecy," p. 391.
67. See Jan Ziolkowski, "Vergil, Abelard, Eloise and the End of Neumes," *Nottingham Medieval Studies* 56 (2012), pp. 447–466.
68. Reghini, "Imperialismo Pagano," pp. 74–75: "e profetizzato la venuta di un *veltro* che i distruttori dell'ideale virgiliano hanno avuto l'impudenza di identificare con Gesù; ed ecco un megalomane ipocondriaco e sentimentale, cui la visione del mondo creato dal suo Dio moveva a compassione ed al pianto, si credette il primo, l'unico savio spuntato in questa valle di lacrime, e fece la peregrina scoperta che per accomodare le faccende dell'umanità bastava rendere gli uomini migliori."
69. Dante Alighieri, *La Divina Commedia, Inferno* (Foligno: Johann Neumeister), I: 110–111: "Questi non ciberà terra né peltro, / ma sapïenza, amore e virtute."
70. For similar interpretations of the figure of the greyhound, see Robert Hollander, *Allegory in Dante's Commedia* (Princeton, NJ: Princeton University Press, 1969), pp. 89–91; Nicolo' Mineo, *Profetismo e Apocalittica in Dante* (Catania: Facoltà Lettere e Filosofia, 1968); Paul Renucci, "Dantismo Esoterico nel Secolo Presente," *Atti Congresso Internazionale di Studi Danteschi*, I (1965), pp. 305–332; Bruno Nardi, "Il Concetto dell'Impero nello Svolgimento del Pensiero Dantesco," *Giornale Storico* LXXVIII (1921), pp. 1–52; on Luigi Valli, one of Dante's greatest esoteric exegesists, see the comprehensive study by Stefano Sarzani, *Luigi Valli e l'Esoterismo di Dante* (San Marino, Il Cerchio, 2014).
71. Reghini, "Imperialismo Pagano," p. 76.
72. Ibid., p. 76: "Quando gli imperatori si accorsero della novità era troppo tardi. L'infezione si era rapidamente diffusa tramite l'Impero, era giunta sino nell'Urbe; ed il ferro ed il fuoco usati anche più generosamente di quanto pur troppo non lo siano stati non avrebbero potuto salvare l'Occidente."

73. Ibid., p. 76–77: "Un misticismo morboso sentimentale annegava la sana e serena praticità italiana, l'italica *prudentia*; e l'aquila romana, agli ampli voli avvezza, s'impiastricciava gli artigli nel dolciume appiccicoso dell'amore universale."
74. For an exhaustive account on the figure of the pontifex maximus, see Renato Del Ponte, *La religione dei Romani* (Milano: Rusconi, 1982).
75. Ibid., p. 77: "l'unità politica e la coscienza dell'unità nazionale perduta per secoli e secoli, il naufragio della cultura, del pensiero, delle lettere, delle arti [...]."
76. Ibid., p. 78: "Pure i fatti si incaricarono di farne sentire la necessita."
77. Ibid., p. 78: "Un'altra religione, rampollando dall'ebraismo e dal cristianesimo, minacciava dall'Asia. Il fanatismo musulmano non faceva cattiva figura a petto di quello cristiano; dall'estrema Asia le orde asiatiche salivano su su verso l'Europa, e strada facendo convertivano e conquistavano i popoli con l'argomento della scimitarra."
78. A thorough bibliography on the figure of Charles the Great is beyond the scope of this chapter. For a basic introduction to the times and life of this historical figure, see Matthias Becher, *Charlemagne*, trans. David S. Bachrach (New Haven, CT: Yale University Press, 2003); Rosamond McKitterick, *Charlemagne: The Formation of a European Identity* (Cambridge: Cambridge University Press, 2008); Derek Wilson, *Charlemagne: The Great Adventure* (London: Hutchinson, 2005); for a focus on Islam in Europe during the days of Charlemagne, see especially Henri Pirenne, *Mohammed and Charlemagne* (Mineola, NY: Dover, 2001); Jeff Sypeck, *Becoming Charlemagne: Europe, Baghdad, and The Empires of A.D. 800* (New York: Ecco/HarperCollins, 2006).
79. Reghini, "Imperialismo Pagano," p. 78: "l'idea di un impero romano, attuata da Carlo Magno, restava oramai presente nella coscienza dei popoli, e diveniva a poco per volta la segreta speranza di tutti gli eretici, il fine ultimo di tutte le società segrete che dal mille al millequattrocento e dopo pullularono per tutta l'Europa."
80. Reghini, "Imperialismo Pagano," p. 78: "Non è possibile penetrare nel vero spirito dei rivolgimenti di quel tempo senza una conoscenza dello gnosticismo, del manicheismo, del paganesimo di quasi tutte le eresie d'allora, senza aver divinato il segreto mistico e politico della cavalleria, senza aver compreso la gaia scienza d'amore dei trovatori, ed il gergo ed il simbolismo delle società segrete, e senza aver scoperto l'affinita' e gli occulti vincoli che incatenavano tra loro eretici e ghibellini, lombardi e tolosani, fraticelli, trovatori e cavalieri del Tempio."
81. Ibid., p. 79: "e gli altri grandi italiani venuti dopo."
82. Ibid., p. 79: "Perché Dante, per il sommo Giove e per il buon Apollo che egli invocava, non era cattolico ed il suo imperialismo era pagano e romano!"
83. Ibid., p. 80: "L'isagogia è la stessa nei due, é l'esposizione categorica della metamorfosi dell'uomo in Dio; politicamente poi Virgilio e Dante non fanno che l'esaltazione dell'Impero Romano!"
84. Publio Vergilius Maro, *Aeneid*, trans. Robert Fitzgerald (New York: Random House, 1983), VI-788-194: "huc geminas nunc flecte acies, hanc aspice gentem / Romanosque tuos. hic Caesar et omnis Iuli / progenies magnum caeli ventura sub axem / hic vir, hic est, tibi quem promitti saepius audis, / Augustus Caesar, divi genus,

aurea condet / saecula qui rursus Latio regnata per arva / Saturno quondam [...]."
On the political allegories and interpretation of the Aeneid, see Michael C. J. Putnam, *Virgil's Aeneid: Interpretation and Influence* (Chapel Hill: University of South Carolina Press, 1995); Gunther Gottlieb, "Religion in the Politics of Augustus: Aeneid 1.278–291, 8.714–723, 12.791–842," in *Vergil's Aeneid: Augustan Epic and Political Context*, ed. Hans-Peter Stahl (London: Duckworth, 1998), pp. 21–36; Philip Hardie, *Virgil's "Aeneid": Cosmos and Imperium* (Oxford: Clarendon Press, 1989); Francis Cairns, *Virgil's Augustan Epic* (Cambridge: Cambridge University Press, 1989); Eve Adler, *Vergil's Epic: Political Thought in the Aeneid* (Oxford: Rowman & Littlefield, 2003).

85. Reghini, "Imperialismo Pagano," p. 37: "il santo uccello che fé i Romani al mondo reverendi" and "che non é la rosa mistica ma sibbene la rosa settaria del Roman de la rose."
86. See *Debating the Roman de la Rose: A Critical Anthology*, trans. Earl Jeffrey Richards, ed. Christine McWebb (New York: Routledge, 2007).
87. For comprehensive studis on the Cathars and their practices, see Stephen O'Shea, *The Perfect Heresy: The Revolutionary Life and Death of the Medieval Cathars* (New York: Walker & Company, 2000); Andrew Roach, *The Devil's World: Heresy and Society 1100-1320* (Harlow: Pearson Longman, 2005); Malcolm Lambert, *The Cathars* (Oxford: Blackwells, 1998); Jonathan Sumption, *The Albigensian Crusade* (London: Faber and Faber, 1978); Uwe Brunn, *Des Contestataires aux "Cathares": Discours de Réforme et Propagande Antihérétique dans les Pays du Rhin et de la Meuse Avant l'Inquisition* (Paris: Institut d'Études Augustiniennes, 2006).
88. William Anderson, *Dante the Maker* (London: Routledge & Keagan Paul, 1980), p. 80.
89. The classic text is Luigi Valli, *Il Linguaggio Segreto di Dante e dei Fedeli d'Amore* (Rome: Optima, 1928–1930).
90. Reghini, "Imperialismo Pagano," p. 81: "Ma altra volta ci occuperemo più ampiamente del paganesimo e dell'imperialismo di Dante."
91. The *Età dei Comuni*, or Age of Communes, was a medieval period in Italy, where small cities ruled over the immediate land around its extension. The phenomenon, started during the eleventh century, expanded to France, Germany, and, to a certain extent, England. It could be argued that the phenomenon manifested itself as the most obvious opposition to the feudal system. For the Italian manifestation of this trend, see Franco Cardini and Marina Montesano, *Storia Medievale* (Firenze: Le Monnier Università, 2006); Mario Ascheri, *Le Città-Stato* (Bologna: Il Mulino, 2006); Giuliano Milani, *I Comuni Italiani: Secoli XII–XIV* (Bari: Laterza, 2015); Indro Montanelli and Roberto Gervaso, *Storia d'Italia Vol. 2: L'Italia dei Comuni: Il Medioevo dal 1000 al 1250* (Turin: Biblioteca Universale Rizzoli, 2010); for a thorough review of this historical period, see *Italy in the Central Middle Ages: 1000–1300*, ed. David Abulafia (Oxford: Oxford University Press, 2004), especially Edward Coleman, "Cities and Communes," pp. 27–57.
92. Cola di Rienzo (or dé Rienzi) was a medieval politician, hailed by Petrarch as the new Brutus and Romulus, who attempted an ill-fated unification of Italy: his legacy has been impressive, ranging from literary works (Edward Bulwer-Lytton's *Rienzi, the last of the Roman tribunes* (1835) and *Childe Harold's Pilgrimage* (1814–1818) by Lord Byron) to musical compositions such as Richard Wagner's *Rienzi* (1842).

For academic treatments of this historical figure, see Amanda Collins, *Greater Than Emperor: Cola di Rienzo (ca. 1313-54) and the World of Fourteenth Century Rome* (Ann Arbor: University of Michigan Press, 2002); Ronald Musso and Ronald G. Musto, *Apocalypse in Rome. Cola di Rienzo and the Politics of the New Age* (Berkeley: University of California Press, 2003); Elizabeth Beneš, "Mapping a Roman Legend: The House of Cola di Rienzo from Piranesi to Baedeker," *Italian Culture* 26 (2008), pp. 53-83.

93. See, for example, Francesco Petrarch, *The Revolution of Cola di Rienzo*, 3rd ed., ed. Ronald Musto (New York: Italica Press, 1996); G. Baldassari, *Unum in locum. Strategie Macrotestuali nel Petrarca Politico* (Milan: LED Edizioni Universitarie, 2006); Guido Cappelli, "Petrarca e l'Umanesimo Politico del Quattrocento," *Verbum* VII, no. 1 (2005), pp. 53-75; Michele Feo, "Politicità del Petrarca," *Quaderni Petrarcheschi* IX-X (1992-1993), pp. 116-128; for the standard text on Petrarch studies, see Victoria Kirkham and Armando Maggi, *Petrarch: A Critical Guide to the Complete Works* (Chicago: University of Chicago Press, 2009).

94. Two bibliographies, one old and one more recent are Roberto Ridolfi, *The Life of Niccolò Machiavelli* (Chicago: University of Chicago Press, 1963) and Paul Oppenheimer, *Machiavelli: a Life Beyond Ideology* (New York: Continuum, 2011); see also L. J. Andrew Villalon, "Machiavelli's *Prince*, Political Science or Political Satire?: Garrett Mattingly Revisited," *Mediterranean Studies* 12 (2003), pp. 73-101; Harvey Mansfield Jr., "Machiavelli's Political Science," *The American Political Science Review* 75, no. 2 (1981), pp. 293-305; Maurizio Viroli, *Redeeming "The Prince": The Meaning of Machiavelli's Masterpiece* (Princeton, NJ: Princeton University Press, 2014).

95. Reghini, "Imperialismo Pagano," p. 82: "come Dante non aveva veduto morire di doglia la lupa vaticana, anche il Machiavelli morì senza che alcun principe lo ascoltasse; e la politica machiavellica veniva di poi ripresa ed applicata dalla Compagnia di Gesù a danno e non a prò dell'Italia e dell'idea imperialista."

96. Ibid., p. 82: "neo-pitagorici meridionali."

97. Secondary sources on Giordano Bruno include Yates, *Giordano Bruno and the Hermetic Tradition* (Chicago: University of Chicago Press, 1964); Paul Richard Blum, *Giordano Bruno: An Introduction* (New York: Rodopi, 2012); Blum, *Giordano Bruno* (Munich: Beck Verlag, 1999); Ingrid D. Rowland, *Giordano Bruno: Philosopher/Heretic* (New York: Farrar, Staus and Giroux, 2008).

98. See *Bernardino Telesio e la Cultura Napoletana. Atti del Convegno Internazionale, Napoli 15-17 Dicembre 1989*, ed. Raffaelo Sirri and Maurizio Torrini (Napoli: Guida, 1992), especially Mario Agrimi, "Telesio nel Seicento Napoletano," in *Bernadino Telesio e la Cultura Napoletana*, pp. 331-372; Luigi de Franco, *Bernardino Telesio. La Vita e l'Opera* (Cosenza: Edizioni Periferia, 1989); Guido Giglioni, "The First of the Moderns or the Last of the Ancients? B.T. on Nature and Sentience," *Bruniana e Campanelliana* 16, no. 1 (2010), pp. 69-87.

99. See Germana Ernst, *Religione, Ragione e Natura: Ricerche su Tommaso Campanella e il Tardo Rinascimento* (Milan: Franco Angeli, 1991); Ernst, *Tommaso Campanella: il Libro e il Corpo della Natura* (Bari: Laterza, 2002); John M. Headley, *Tommaso Campanella and the Transformation of the World* (Princeton, NJ: Princeton University Press, 1997); D. P. Walker, *Spiritual and Demonic Magic from Ficino to Campanella* (London: Warburg Institute, 1958).

17. Ministero per l'Industria, il Commercio ed il Lavoro, Ufficio Centrale di Statistica, *Statistica delle Elezioni Generali Politiche per la XXVI Legislatura. (15 Maggio 1919)* (Roma: Stabilimento Poligrafico per l'Amministrazione della Guerra, 1920).
18. On a total, the Blocchi received 19.1 percent of the votes, trailing only to the Socialist Party and the Liberal Party.
19. See Angelo D'Orsi, *La rivoluzione antibolscevica* (Milan: Franco Angeli 1985): the rise in Fascist violence was justified by the Squadristi as a form of repression of alleged Bolshevik uprisings.
20. See Renzo de Felice, *Benito Mussolini—La Conquista del Potere (1921-1925)* (Turin: Einaudi, 2002), p. 273.
21. The rally in Naples has been called the dress rehearsal of the March on Rome. Mussolini held two speeches in one day: one at the *San Carlo* theater, for the bourgeoisie, and a more conventional one for his followers, in the bigger *Piazza San Carlo*.
22. See Benito Mussolini, *I Discorsi della Rivoluzione* (Milan: Società Editrice Barbarossa).
23. "O ci daranno il governo o lo prenderemo calando a Roma," see Mussolini, *Discorsi*, p. 89.
24. See Pier Luigi Bellini, *La Questione Elettorale nella Storia d'Italia da Salandra a Mussolini* (Rome: Camera dei Deputati, Archivio Storico, 2011), pp. 34ff.
25. For a clear picture of the relationship between the king and Mussolini, see Antonio Spinosa, *Vittorio Emanuele III:l'Astuzia di un Re* (Milan: Mondadori, 1991).
26. Marco Palla, *Mussolini e il fascismo* (Florence: Giunti Editore, 1994), p. 29.
27. Roger Griffin, *Modernism and Fascism: A Sense of a New Beginning under Mussolini and Hitler* (London: Palgrave Macmillan, 2006), p. 1.
28. Frank Kermode's *The Sense of an Ending: Studies in the Theories of Fiction* (Oxford: Oxford University Press), p. 103
29. Theodor W. Adorno, Else Frenkel Brunswik, Daniel Levinson, and Nevitt Sanford, *The Authoritarian Personality* (New York: Harper, 1950): the discussion on the F-Scale may be found in chapters VII, "The Measurement of Implicit Antidemocratic Trends," pp. 222-278.
30. Frank Kermode, "Apocalyptic Modernity," in *The Sense of an Ending*, pp. 93-124.
31. William Butler Yeats, "Second Coming," in *The Collected Poems of W.B. Yeats* (London: Macmillan, 1982), p. 211.
32. Yeats, "Second Coming," p. 211, vv. 1-6.
33. Griffin, *Modernism and Fascism*, p. 7.
34. Ibid., p. 7.
35. Ibid., p. 9.
36. Ibid., p. 9.
37. Ibid., p. 45.
38. Ibid., p. 45.
39. Ibid., p. 46.
40. Ibid., p. 46.
41. Ibid., p. 55.
42. Benito Mussolini, *Scritti e Discorsi*, vol. 7 (Milan: Hoepli, 1934), p. 256: "Fate che le glorie del passato siano superate dalle glorie dell'avvenire."

43. Ibid., Vol. 2, p. 335: "La democrazia ha tolto lo «stile» alla vita del popolo. Il fascismo riporta lo «stile» nella vita del popolo: cioè una linea di condotta; cioè il colore, la forza, il pittoresco, l'inaspettato, il mistico; insomma, tutto quello che conta nell'animo delle moltitudini."
44. Filippo Tommaso Marinetti, "Manifesto du Futurisme," *Le Figaro* (Feb. 20, 1909), p. 1.
45. See Mimmo Franzinelli and Paolo Cavassini, *Fiume: l'Ultima Impresa di D'Annunzio* (Milan: Mondadori, 2009); Claudia Salaris, *Alla Festa della Rivoluzione. Artisti e Libertari con D'Annunzio a Fiume* (Bologna: Il Mulino, 2002); Renzo de Felice, *D'Annunzio Politico (1918–1928)* (Bari: Laterza, 1978).
46. For primary sources, see Ezra Pound, *L'America, Roosevelt e le Cause della Guerra Presente* (Venice: Casa Editrice delle Edizioni Popolari, 1944); Pound, *Oro et Lavoro: alla Memoria di Aurelio Baisi* (Rapallo: Moderna, 1944); Pound, *Lavoro ed Usura* (Milan: All'Insegna del Pesce d'Oro, 1954); for secondary sources, see *The Ezra Pound Encyclopedia*, ed. Demetres Tryphonopoulos and Stephen Adams (Westport, CT: Greenwood, 2005); *The Cambridge Companion to Ezra Pound*, ed. Ira B. Nadel (Cambridge: Cambridge University Press, 1985); James Wilhelm, *Ezra Pound: The Tragic Years 1925–1972* (University Park: Pennsylvania State University Press, 1994).
47. Quoted in Griffin, *Modernism and Fascism*, p. 200; see Walter Adamson, *Avant-Garde Florence: From Modernism to Fascism* (Cambridge, MA: Harvard University Press, 1993).
48. Ibid., p. 200.
49. Ibid., p. 200.
50. Griffin, "A Primordialist Definition of Modernity," in Griffin, *Modernism and Fascism*, pp. 100–126.
51. Ibid., p. 101.
52. Ibid., p. 102–104.
53. Maurice Bloch, *Prey into Hunter* (Cambridge: Cambridge University Press, 1992), pp. 4–5.
54. Arnold van Gennep, "The Classification of Rites," in van Gennep, *The Rites of Passage* (London: Routledge & Kegan Paul, [1909] 1960), pp. 1–15.
55. Ibid., "Individual Groups," pp. 26–40.
56. Quoted in Griffin, *Modernity and Fascism*, p. 105.
57. Ibid., pp. 132–135.
58. Ibid., p. 131.
59. Ibid., p. 131.
60. Quoted in ibid., p. 133.
61. Martin Clark, *Mussolini: Profiles in Power* (London: Pearson Longman, 2005), p. 139.
62. Griffin, "Modernity, Modernism, and Fascism," p. 17.
63. Jeffrey Alexander, *The Dark Side of Modernity* (Cambridge: Polity Publishing, 2013).
64. Griffin, *Modernity and Fascism*, p. 138.
65. Ibid., p. 138.
66. Nicholas Goodrick-Clarke, *The Occult Roots of Nazism: The Ariosophists of Austria and Germany, 1890–1935* (Wellingborough: Aquarian Press, 1985), p. 217.
67. Louis Pawels and Jacques Bergier, *Le Matin des Magiciens* (Paris: Gallimard, 1960).

68. Quoted in Goodrick-Clarke, *Occult Roots*, p. 219.
69. For more on Eckart, see Ralph Engelman, *Dietrich Eckart and the Genesis of Nazism* (Ann Arbor: UMI Press, 1971).
70. See Christopher Hale, *Himmler's Crusade: The Nazi Expedition to Find the Origins of the Aryan Race* (Hoboken, NJ: John Wiley & Sons, 2003); Isrun Engelhardt, "Tibet in 1938–1939: Photographs from the Ernst Schäfer Expedition to Tibet," *Serindia* (2007), pp. 11–61; Peter Mierau, *Nationalsozialistische Expeditionspolitik. Deutsche Asien-Expeditionen 1933–1945* (Munich: Herbert Utz Verlag, 2006).
71. Rudolf von Sebottendorf [Dietrich Bronder], *Bevor Hitler kam: Urkundlich aus der Frühzeit der Nationalsozialistischen Bewegung* (Munich: Deukula-Grassinger, 1933).
72. At the Nuremberg Rally of 1938, Adolf Hitler had declared: "We will not allow mystically-minded occult folk with a passion for exploring the secrets of the world beyond to steal into our Movement. Such folk are not National Socialists, but something else—in any case, something which has nothing to do with us. At the head of our program there stand no secret surmisings but clear-cut perception and straightforward profession of belief. But since we set as the central point of this perception and of this profession of belief the maintenance and hence the security for the future of a being formed by God, we thus serve the maintenance of a divine work and fulfill a divine will—not in the secret twilight of a new house of worship, but openly before the face of the Lord," quoted in Rainer Bucher, *Hitler's Theology: A Study in Political Religion* (London: Continuum, 2011), p. 39.
73. Trevor Ravenscroft, *The Spear of Destiny: The Occult Power behind the Spear Which Pierced the Side of Christ* (London: Neville Spearman, 1972).
74. Jean-Michel Angebert, *Les Mystiques du Soleil* (Paris: Robert Laffont, 1971).
75. Alan Baker, *Invisible Eagle—The History of Nazi Occultism* (London: Virgin Books, 2000).
76. *Reassessing Nazi Occultism: Histories, Realities, Legacies*, ed. Monica Black and Eric Kurlander (Rochester, NY: Camden House, 2015), p. 1.
77. Goodricke-Clarke, *Occult Roots*, p. vii.
78. See Jörg Lanz von Liebenfels, *Der Weltkrieg als Rassenkampf der Dunklen gegen die Blonden* (Vienna: np, 1927) and especially von Liebenfels, *Bibliomystikon oder die Geheimbibel der Eingeweihten*, 10 vols. (Pforzheim: np, 1929–1934).
79. Quoted in Giorgio Galli, *Hitler e la Cultura Occulta* (Milan: Rizzoli, 2015), p. 302: "Hitler ha un cuore di acciaio [. . .] di indomabile acciaio. Il cervello tuttavia è confuso. Ha del mago e del filosofante da mercato rionale. Si è fatto, a suo uso e consumo, una storia, una politica, una geografia del mondo, e non beve che da quel pozzo."
80. Gianfranco de Turris "Introduzione: Un'Ipotesi di Lavoro," in *Esoterismo e Fascismo*, p. 10: "Se si può parlare, senza troppo sbagliare, di un 'esoterismo nazista', dati i documenti venuti alla luce dopo le clamorose ma generiche rivelazioni de *Il Mattino dei Maghi*, di Louis Pawels e Jacques Bergier, non si può invece parlare—checché ne possa pensare qualcuno- di un 'esoterismo fascista', vale a dire di una dimensione esoterica né ufficiale né ufficiosa del fascismo: le personalità che ne erano a capo, la loro cultura e la loro predisposizione spirituale (nonostante i molteplici contatti con

la massoneria) non risultavano tali da poter dare vita ad una dimensione 'esoterica', 'occulta', né tantomeno 'tradizionale' del fascismo."
81. Emilio Bodrero, *Inchiesta sulla Massoneria* (Milan: Mondadori, 1925), p. xxxi.
82. Ibid., p. 20: "Alle tre domande rispondo con tre 'no.'"
83. Ibid., p. 5: "La futilità dei segreti nella vita politica moderna" and "l'ideologia dei partiti democratici di oggi contrasta grandemente con i bisogni e le mete della società Italiana."
84. Ibid., p. 28: "Come l'Antica Roma-nel 186 av. C., col senatoconsulto *de bacchanalibus*-così l'Italia nostra spalanchi al sole ogni avanzo di società clandestine: *Il sole uccide gli invisibili.*"
85. Ibid., p. 241.
86. Quoted in "Documenti,"*Esoterismo e Fascismo*, p. 39: "In Germania, in Inghilterra, in America i massoni sono una confraternita caritatevole e filantropica. In Italia, invece, i massoni costituiscono un' organizzazione politica segreta. Di più e di peggio, essi dipendono completamente dal Grande Oriente di Parigi. Io auspico che i massoni italiani diventino quello che sono gli inglesi e gli americani: una confraternita apolitica di mutuo soccorso."
87. Bodrero, *Inchiesta*, p. i–xxviii.
88. Quoted in Venzi, *Massoneria e Fascismo*, p. 56: "tutti i fascisti che sono massoni a scegliere tra l'appartenere al Partito Nazionale Fascista o alla Massoneria, poiché non vi è per i fascisti che una sola disciplina del Fascismo; che una sola gerarchia, la gerarchia del Fascismo; che una sola obbedienza assoluto, devote e quotidiana, al Capo e ai capi del Fascismo."
89. Anonymous [Roberto Farinacci], "Untitled column," *Cremona Nuova*, February 14, 1925, p. 2: "fucilarli in massa, come traditori della patria."
90. See Santi Fedele, *La Massoneria Italiana nell'Esilio e nella Clandestinità* (Milan: Franco Angeli, 2005), pp. 45–70.
91. Ibid., p. 84ff.
92. Primary sources by René Guénon have been listed throughout the book; secondary sources of relevance include David Bisson, *René Guénon: Une Politique de l'Esprit* (Paris: Pierre-Guillaume de Roux, 2013); Jean-Pierre Laurant, *René Guénon, Les Enjeux d'une Lecture* (Paris: Dervy, 2006); Robin Waterfield, *René Guénon and the Future of the West* (Hillsdale, NY: Sophia Perennis, [1987] 2002); Graham Rooth, *Prophet for a Dark Age: A Companion to the Works of René Guénon* (Brighton: Sussex Academic Press, 2008); Sedgwick, *Modern World*.
93. Quoted in Sestito, *Figlio del Sole*, p. 189: Letter of Guerrieri to Armentano of May 1, 1910: "I am often in the company of Guénon and I must retract what I wrote to you last time; luckily I will leave, otherwise this mysterious man would drive me crazy for how terrible he is."
94. Laurant, *Enjeux*, pp. 33–57.
95. Bisson, "La Tradition comme Pensée Gnostique," Bisson, *Guénon*, pp. 25–96.
96. Waterfield, *Guénon*, pp. 13–16.
97. Bisson, *Guénon*, p. 28.
98. Ibid., p. 28.

99. On Papus, see Chapter 4.
100. Bisson, *Guénon*, p. 29: "le catalyseur d'une culture en pleine effervescence."
101. Ibid., p. 29.
102. See Albert de Pouvourville and Léon Champrenaud, *Les Enseignments Secrets de la Gnose* (Milan: Arché, [1907] 1999).
103. Sedgwick, *Modern World*, p. 40.
104. Bisson, *Guénon*, p. 29: "restaurer la tradition occidentale et faire de l'occultisme un science à l'égale de celle qu'on enseigne dans les universités."
105. Ibid., pp. 30–31.
106. See Meir Hatina, "Where East Meets West: Sufism as a Lever for Cultural Rapprochement," *International Journal of Middle East Studies* 39 (2007), pp. 389–409; Waterfield, *Guénon*, pp. 28–30.
107. See Waterfield, *Guénon*, p. 29.
108. Bisson, *Guénon*, p. 31: "l'origine divine et immémoriale d'une tradition, un monde sous l'empris du mal, et la nécéssité d'une conversion initiatique."
109. Aristotle, *Metaphysics*, trans. Hugh Tredennick (Cambridge, MA: Harvard University Press, 1996).
110. Waterfield, *Guénon*, pp. 56–66.
111. René Guénon, *Introduction Générale à l'Étude des Doctrines Hindoues* (Paris: Marcel Rivière, 1921).
112. Ibid., p. 296: "la manie des textes, des 'sources' et de la bibliographie."
113. Ibid., pp. 254–255.
114. Ibid., pp. 141 and 156.
115. Bisson, *Guénon*, p. 45: "il inaugure une lecture originale de l'Orient qui ne se fonde pas sure un 'système de fiction ideologique', mais plutôt sure un modèle traditionnel idéalisé."
116. Guénon, *Théosophisme*, and Guénon, *Erreur*.
117. Guénon, *Erreur*, p. 420: "ne costitue qu'un épisode de la foridable déviation mentale que characterise l'Occident moderne."
118. René Guénon, *La Crise du Monde Moderne* (Paris: Bossard, 1927).
119. Bisson, *Guénon*, p. 53: "comment contribuir à la formation de l'élite intellectuelle?"
120. René Guénon, *Orient et Occident* (Paris: Payot, 1924), p. 10: "Nous avon déja fait allusion au role que pourrait jouer une élite intellectuelle, si elle arrivait à se constituer dans le monde occidental, où elle agirait à la façon d'un 'ferment' pour preparer et diriger dans le sens le plus favourable une transformation mentale qui deviendra inevitable un jour ou l'autre, qu'on le veuille ou non."
121. Bisson, *Guénon*, p. 58.
122. Guénon, *Ésotérisme*, p. 28: "une allégorie métaphysico-ésotérique, qui voile et expose en même temps les phases successives par lesquelles passé la conscience de l'initié pour atteindre l'immortalité."
123. See René Guénon, *Le Symbolisme de la Croix* (Paris: Véga, 1931) and Guénon, *Les États Multiples de l'Être* (Paris: Véga, 1932).
124. Bisson, *Guénon*, pp. 210–215.

125. Reghini, *Parole Sacre*, p. 195: "Il lettore ben intenzionato può dunque scegliere. Tutte le tradizioni sono a sua disposizione; quella indiana, quella cinese, l'ebraica, la rosacroce, la druidica, l'araba, perché tutti i popoli sono stati maestri di civiltà e hanno prodotto maestri e iniziati, tranne s'intende l'Italia!"
126. Ibid., p. 195: "Con un certo stupor constatiamo che anche il GUENON condivide questo apprezzamento. Pure egli riconosce che un movimento per riavvicinare l'Occidente all'Oriente, circa la tradizione metafisica, non può partire che dai paesi latini (p. 342). Esclusa l'Italia, il compito spetta evidentemente alla Francia. Cicero pro domo sua?"
127. Sestito, *Figlio del Sole*, p. 190.
128. Quoted in ibid., p. 190: "egli ritiene disgraziatamente assai improbabile che esistano ancora in Occidente delle individualità anche isolate."
129. Quoted in ibid., p. 191: "centro del mondo."
130. Guénon, *Orient et Occident*, pp. 169-170: "Les aptitudes que nous avons en vue quand nous parlons de l'élite, étant de l'ordre de l'intellectualité pure, ne peuvent [170] être déterminées par aucun critérium extérieur, et ce sont là des choses qui n'ont rien à voir avec l'instruction 'profane' [...]".
131. Ibid., p. 171: "Trop rares et trop isolés."
132. Ibid., p. 174: "une société constituée avec des statuts, des règlements, des réunions, et toutes les autres manifestations extérieures que ce mot implique nécessairement."
133. Ibid., p. 176: "C'est en Orient seulement qu'on peut trouver actuellement les exemples dont il conviendrait des'inspirer; nous avons bien des raisons de penser que l'Occident a eu aussi, au moyen âge, quelques organisations du même type, mais il est aumoins douteux qu'il en ait subsisté des traces suffisantes pour qu'on puisse arriver à s'en faire une idée exacte autrement que par analogie avec ce qui existe en Orient, analogie basée d'ailleurs, non sur des suppositions gratuites, mais sur dessignes qui ne trompent pas quand on connaît déjà certaines choses."
134. Sestito, *Figlio del Sole*, p. 191: "che attitudine devo prendere alla sua manifesta proposta di far parte dell'elite intellettuelle per permettere all'Occidente di ricevere la Tradizione Orientale?"
135. Ibid., p. 192: "organizzare qualche cosa insieme."
136. Ibid., p. 194: "Tu avrai visto nel 'Re del Mondo' con quanta indulgenza e buona disposizione tratti il cristianesimo, e io forse non gli avrei proposto di farne la traduzione se avessi potuto prevedere che si sarebbe spinto fino a codesto punto."
137. Ibid., p. 195: "Ho saputo da altri, che nella sua difficile situazione a Parigi, lo si è udito più spesso pronunciare il mio nome quasi ad invocarmi; e penso che il mostrargli in questo momento vera e intelligente simpatia oltre ad essere più che giusto può forse anche essere una buona idea che il suo tentativo era illusorio, e che non è coi preti che si può fare l'elite che egli vagheggia nè l'ottenere *le redressement* dell' Occidente."
138. Ibid., pp. 197-198: "mentre Guénon e altri esoteristi come lui, teorizzavano sulla *tradizione occidentale* stando con le mani in mano in attesa della venuta di miracolosi 'avatar' orientali, Reghini a Roma scendeva coraggiosamente in campo con lo scopo manifesto di coagulare intorno alle sue riviste le forze pure della cultura e dell'intellettualità occidentali."

139. See my translation of "Imperialismo Pagano" in the Appendix.
140. "La Corrispondenza di René Guénon con Arturo Reghini," in René Guénon, *Il Risveglio della Tradizione Occidentale: I testi Pubblicati da Atanòr e Ignis* (ed. Mariano Bizzarri (Roma: Atanòr, 2003), pp. 105–143.
141. I will be referring to this part of the correspondence, kindly provided to me by the heirs of René Guénon, as the Archive Guénon, or AG, followed by the date of the letter.
142. AG: December 17, 1923.
143. AG: January 8, 1924: "Je savais que vous avez prepare un uvrage sure le Vedanta; et j'en suis enchanté, car j'ai beaucoup regrette de ne pas voir la fin de votre etude sure le Vedanta dans la Gnose."
144. AG: March 16, 1924: "deja lu et meme traduit votre article avec un veritable plaisir de l'esprit. Vos écrits me sont désormais tellement familiers que je peux le suivre jusque dans eurs nuances, et m'amuser avec votre ironie discrète."
145. Guénon, *Risveglio*, p. 120: "19 Giugno 1924 . . . Grazie per ciò che dite a proposito del mio saggio; vedo che siamo sempre d'accordo sull'essenziale. In quanto all'osservazione che mi rivolgete a proposito della persistenza della tradizione occidentale, questa è molto giusta, e corrisponde ad una questione che mi preoccupa tanto quanto voi; se, a tutt'oggi, esistono rappresentanti autentici di questa tradizione, come è possibile entrare in contatto con loro? C'è qui una difficoltà che voi probabilmente siete meglio collocato per poterla risolvere, dato che, sotto il profilo intellettuale, io sono molto più vicino all'Oriente che non all'Occidente. Sareste tanto gentile da dirmi cosa pensate su questo argomento?"
146. AG: September 14, 1926: "Il me semble que ce petit écrit est d'une très grande importance."
147. AG: September 14, 1926: "'l'existence, aujourd'hui . . . d'un centre spirituel suprême' and 'les arguments nombreaux avec le quels vous appuyes votre 'revelation.''"
148. AG: November 5, 1924: "Dans le manuel bibliographice de Caillet, en parlant de Saint-Yves d'Alveidre et de l'Agartha on dit que la Blavatsky aussi en parle."
149. Fermi [Benito Mussolini], "Cronache del Pensiero Religioso," *Gerarchia* (1924), pp. 637–642.
150. Arturo Reghini, "Campidoglio e Golgota," *Atanòr* 1, no. 3 (1924), p. 146.
151. Bizzarri, *Risveglio*, p. 132: "Chiunque sia l'autore di quell'articolo, mostra chiaramente, verso la fine, che non ha compreso la distinzione essenziale tra la conoscenza metafisica ed iniziatica e il sapere profano (quando parla di "Nuova Accademia," etc.) ed altresì che non conosce nulla delle dottrine orientali: la sua classificazione delle opere "mistiche" e "morali" è piuttosto divertente!"
152. Ibid.: "Il numero 6 di *Atanòr* mi è pervenuto il giorno dopo avervi scritto. Come avevate previsto ho delle riserve solo al riguardo dell'articolo di Evola; anche se voi lo avete presentato nel modo migliore. Che necessità c'è a complicare le cose con tutta quelle considerazioni ricalcate dalla filosofia tedesca?"
153. AG: December 13, 1924: "A' propos d'Evola, qui est très jeune et très persuadé d'être quelque chose de special, je vous conterai que après avoir lu 'Orient et Occident' il vu

a critique en vous accusant d'être un rationaliste. Pour lui on doit se porter à un tel point que la volonté aoit absolutament puissante."

154. AG: April 13, 1925: "Savez vous que Evola qui prepara un ouvrage sur le Tantra ne connait pas le Sanscrit? Il doit connaitre très mal aussi le latin e le grec car il n'a pas fait les études classiques; e pourtant quel luxe de grec!"

155. Bizzarri, *Risveglio*, p. 138: "Il Signor de Giorgio mi chiede che valore può avere la traduzione del Tao fatta da Evola; non l'ho letta, però, in base a quanto Egli mi ha detto, non mi fido dato che l'autore non conosce la lingua. A proposito di Evola, a che punto sta il suo lavoro sul Tantra? Sarà senza dubbio una riproduzione più o meno arangiata delle opera di Sir John Woodroffe; malauguratamente anche quest'ultimo sa ben poco di sanscrito e ciò che è ancor più singolare è che commette errori inversolimili anche quando scrive in inglese, che, se non vado errato, è la sua lingua madre."

156. Sestito, *Figlio del Sole*, p. 123.

157. Reghini, *Parole Sacre*, p. i: "A volere che una setta o una repubblica viva lungamente è necessario ritrarla spesso verso il suo principio' and 'quelle alterazioni sono a salute che le riconducono verso i principi loro."

158. Ibid., p. vii: "è supremamente importante restituire alle parole, alle cerimonie, il loro valore tradizionale, cosicché, attraverso il loro aiuto l'intelletto possa imparare l'autocontrollo e penetrarne il loro valore segreto."

159. Ibid., *Parole Sacre*, p. 25: "L'idea centrale è dunque l'antica idea mediterranea della sopravvivenza privilegiata, della resurrezione alla immortalità dalla morte, della palingenesi insomma conseguita attraverso la morte mistica."

160. Sestito, *Figlio del Sole*, p. 154: "la conoscenza; l'immortalità; la beatitudine e la perfezione."

161. Found at Biblioteca Nazionale di Firenze, *Manoscritto Magliabechiano*, Classe VIII, codex 6, eighteenth century, 20 x 28 cm, 557 folios.

162. Reghini, *Le Parole Sacre*, p. 79: "È una pagina insuperata nella letteratura tecnica iniziatica, e la tradizione esoterica occidentale per opera di questo neo-pitagorico dell'Italia Meridionale getta vividi bagliori di luce, sfidando eroicamente l'ignoranza e la ferocia cristiana. Non ci sembra che tra i transalpini ce ne siano molti che possano competere per sapienza metafisica con questo erede ed esponente della Scuola Italica."

163. di Luca, *Reghini*, p. 65–66.

164. Reghini, "Due Parole al Dottor Frosini," *Rassegna Massonica* 6–7 (1921), quoted in di Luca, *Reghini*, p. 65: "Io ho un quadernetto in cui [. . .] vado segnalando gli sfarfalloni e le marronate stampate dai vari autori massonici. Capolista nell'elenco è il Fr. Ulisse Bacci, ma il Frosini non rimane indietro di molto, e poiché è ancora giovane e la sua intelligenza si sviluppa floridamente, io ritengo che anche in questo finirà coll'emergere sopra tutti. È solo una questione di tempo [. . .]."

165. See Anonymous, "La Massoneria Fuorilegge," in Sestito, *Figlio del Sole*, pp. 136–145.

166. Ibid., p. 143.

167. Quoted in di Luca, *Reghini*, p. 71: "obbediscono devotamente alla gerarchia fascista, superiore a tutte le contingenze e quindi possono continuare a servire la Patria e

l'organizzione Fascista, fedeli e disciplinati al supremo duce Benito Mussolini ed al suo governo."
168. Arturo Reghini, "L'Intolleranza Cattolica e lo Stato," in *Paganesimo, Pitagorismo, Massoneria*, pp. 159-164 [159]: "I Cattolici, i nazionalisti e tutti i figli di preti' and 'una dedizione della politica italiana alle pretese clericali possa essere nelle intenzioni di Mussolini, non ci sembra dunque che possa sostenersi onestamente."
169. Marco Rossi, "L'Interventismo Politico," p. 499: "il Reghini si trova distante dalla loggia di Piazza Giustiniani a causa delle simpatie fasciste e per personali convinzioni antidemocratiche, ciò spiega la sua attività nel supremo consiglio di Piazza del Gesù; ma nello stesso tempo non concorda affatto con la linea mussoliniana votata alla ricerca di un accordo con la chiesa cattolica, linea [. . .] che il suo superiore Palermi appoggiava incondizionatamente."
170. Sestito, *Figlio del Sole*, p. 146: "mi pare che il momento sia venuto in cui abbamo finalmente un poco di base e i tempi vanno maturando per la istituzione di un movimento, di una Rivista e di un Ordine nostro."
171. Ibid., p. 148: "Nel ricevimento della nostra delegazione ieri, Mussolini mostrò molta cordialità e vi fu uno scambio di idee e di propositi importanti [. . .]."

Chapter 7

1. Il Gruppo dei Dioscuri, *Rivoluzione Tradizionale e Sovversione: Documenti per il Fronte della Tradizione 21* (Rome: Raido, 2004), p. 11: Per l'uomo della Tradizione, rivolgersi verso il passato e non verso l'Alto significherebbe voler bere allo stagno, potendo invece bere alla fonte.
2. Sestito, *Figlio del Sole*, p. 107: "Alvi è un buon scrittore ed è stato uno dei combattenti per l'idealismo in questi quindici anni. Ci siamo trovati d'accordo su tutto. Vuole l'Impero anche lui e il primato degli italiani [. . .] Insomma mi è sembrata una persona più naturalmente vicina a noi di quante ne abbiamo incontrate sinora. Ho invitato anche lui a visitarci a Scalea."
3. Most of the data has been obtained from the Archivio Centrale dello Stato, Casellario Politico Centrale, Fascicolo 82: Alvi, Ciro, Scheda Biografica; Gianfranco de Turris, "Il Gruppo di Ur: Tra Magia e Superfascismo," *Abstracta* II, no. 16 (1987), pp. 12-21; Philip Baillet, "Le Rapports de Julius Evola avec le Fascisme et le National Socialisme," *Politica Hermetica* 1 (1987), p. 66.
4. Both De Turris and Baillet state that Alvi was not a Freemason, although Fabrizio Giorgio argues that the lodges in Umbria in his time were plenty, and one lodge in Todi actually did exist, although this does not really provide us with conclusive evidence: see Giorgio, *Roma Renovata Resurgat*, p. 314.
5. Ciro Alvi, *Verso la Purificazione—Ricordi di un Mellonarca* (Todi: Armuzzi & Orsini Editori, 1899); Ciro Alvi, *La Vita Nuova—Il Culto dell'Avvenire* (Todi: self-published, 1901).
6. Ciro Alvi, *S. Francesco d'Assisi* (Milan: Sandron, 1903).

7. "molto discusso dalla critica, sono state fatte varie edizioni. Fu messo all'indice," in Teodoro Rovito, *Letterati e Giornalisti Italiani Contemporanei: Dizionario Bio-Bibliografico*, 2nd ed. (Naples: Teodoro Rovito Editore, 1907), p. 10.
8. See the exhaustive volume edited by Mariano Bianca, *Atanòr: 1912–2012*, especially "La Fondazione della casa editrice Atanòr," pp. 23–25.
9. Ibid., p. 24: "la sua fondazione, che rappresentò la soddisfazione di un'esigenza della cultura italiana dell'epoca, si collocò all'interno di un vasto movimento culturale, promosso anche dal rafforzamento e consolidamento europeo della Massoneria, delle sue istituzioni e del suo pensiero, che pose all'attenzione culturale quella dimensione esoterica e spirituale che sembrava sperdersi all'interno della diffusione della scienza e del pensiero positivista od ancora entro le diverse dottrine e pratiche religiose."
10. Fabrizio Giorgio, in my opinion, correctly identifies the Alvi's fictional character of Arturo Cemberli with Alvi himself, and Cemberli's desire to found and Imperialist party is coherent with the author's ideas: see Ciro Alvi, "Aurea Atque Felix Italia," in *Arcobaleno* (Todi: Atanòr, 1912), pp. 23–32.
11. Sestito, *Figlio del Sole*, p. 107.
12. Ciro Alvi, *Per lo Spirito la Carne Esaltare* (Todi: Atanòr, 1923): "I primi cittadini si occupavano del benessere, quelli favoriti dagli Dei, e solo essi potevano lavorare per il benessere materiale dei modesti."
13. Ibid., p. 194.
14. Ciro Alvi, *L'Incendio di Roma* (Todi: Atanòr, 1928); for theories on the 64 CE fire in Rome, see Publius Cornelius Tacitus, *Annales*, XV; for secondary sources, see Michael Gray-Fow, "Why the Christians? Nero and the Great Fire," *Latomus* 57, no. 3 (1998), pp. 595–616; Paul Keresztes, "Nero, the Christians and the Jews in Tacitus and Clement of Rome," *Latomus* 43, no. 2 (1984), pp. 404–413; Edward Champlin, "Nero Reconsidered," *New England Review* 19, no. 2 (1998), pp. 97–108; monographs that probably influenced Alvi include Carlo Pascal, *L'incendio di Roma e i Primi Cristiani* (Turin: Loescher, 1900) and Attilio Profumo, *Le Fonti e i Tempi dell'Incendio Neroniano* (Rome: Forzani, 1905).
15. Alvi, *Incendio*, p. 29: "Ascolta Fabio Gemino. Rifletti. Per noi cristiani Roma è la nemica, è l'abominio, è di Satana il regno."
16. Vittore Marchi, *La Missione di Roma nel Mondo* (Todi: Atanòr, 1915) and Enrico Caporali, *La Sapienza Italica*, 3 vols. (Todi: Atanòr, 1914–1946).
17. Giorgio, *Roma Renovata Resurgat*, Vol. I, p. 327: "Fu sicuramente la medesima fede negli ideali imperialistico pagani che sppinse Alvi ad intraprendere, in un momento politico così delicato, una avventura editoriale così rischiosa che esponeva lui e la sua casa editrice."
18. The most complete biographical work on Giulio Parise is without a doubt Simone Caltabellotta, *Un amore degli anni Venti*; he also features prominently in Marco Rossi's articles "L'interventismo politico-culturale delle riviste tradizionali degli anni Venti" and Caltabellotta, "Neopoaganesimo e Arti Magiche nel Periodo Fascista," in *Storia d'Italia, Annali 25, Esoterismo*, pp. 599–628.

19. Parise, *Nota*, p. viii–ix: "conobbi A.R. quando stava preparando il suo volume su 'Le Parole Sacre e di Passo ed il Massimo Mistero Massonico', pubblicato nel 1922. Abitava allora in una modesta stanza dove la cosa più interessante, dopo la sua persona, era uno scaffaletto con i suoi libri."
20. Sestito, *Figlio del Sole*, p. 151: "Caro Maestro, questo libro è frutto del lavoro tuo e mio. Spero non mi manchi il tuo aiuto futuro per poter compiere altra opera maggiormente degna di te. Arturo Reghini."
21. Ibid., pp. 154–155: " Una vera gioia ho avuto dalla lettura del libro del nostro Arturo. Ci sono pagine di profondità veramente geniale; nell'insieme lo giudico politicamente inabile, in quanto urta molte suscettibilità, anzi tutte. Forse valeva meglio attenuare certe asprezze polemiche nella prima edizione e riservarle ad un secondo volume quando fosse stata indiscussa e indiscutibile l'autorità veramente superiore dello scrivente nel campo dell'esoterismo iniziatico."
22. For Eduardo Frosini and the Rito Filosofico debacle, refer to the previous chapters.
23. Nicolò Machiavelli, *Degli Discorsi di Nicolo' Machiavelli, Cittadino & Secretario Fiorentino, sopra la Prima Decade di Tito Livio a Zanobi Buondelmonti & a Cosimo Rucellai* (Florence: Bernardo Giunti, 1531), p. 145: "A volere che una setta o una repubblica viva lungamente, è necessario ritrarla spesso verso il suo principio."
24. Arturo Reghini, *Le Parole Sacre e di Passo*, p. ii: "L'analisi delle cerimonie e delle leggende rituali dei varii gradi mostra all'evidenza l'ispirazione dai Misteri pagani, gli Eleusini e gli Isiaci in specie, ed il libro delle costituzioni dell'Anderson fa fede del sano spirito razionalista che animava l'Ordine nei suoi storici primordii (1717)"; for *The Constitutions of the Freemasons*, which established the rules adopted by the lodges in London and Westminster, see *The Constitutions of the Freemasons*, ed. Rev. James Anderson (London: J. Senex & J. Hooke, 1723).
25. The texts most used for his work throughout his work are certainly Jean-Marie Ragon, *Orthodoxie Maçonnique* (Paris: E. Dentu, 1853); Ragon, *Cours Philosophic et Interpretatif des Initiations Anciennes et Modernes* (Paris: Berlandier, 1841); Gottfried Findel, *Histoire de la Francmaçonnerie*, Vol. II (Paris: Librerie Internationelle, 1866); Eliphas Lévi, *Dogme*; William Hutchinson, *The Spirit of Masonry* (London: J. Wilkie & W. Goldsmith, 1775); Baron de Tschoudy, *L'Etoile Flamboyant—A l'Orient chez le Silence* (Paris: np, 1766); Samuel Prichard, *Masonry Dissected* (London: J. Wilford, 1730).
26. Reghini, *Le Parole Sacre*, p. 8: "è agevole riconoscere nel frasario massonico un insieme di voci e di frasi il cui simbolismo ha un carattere più profondo e determinato."
27. Reghini, *Le Parole Sacre*, p. 21: "Hiram muore e risorge e diviene in tal modo un Maestro. Similmente Osiride, Dioniso, Gesù, venivano uccisi, discendevano agli inferi, resuscitavano e divenivano immortali. L'avere attribuito a Hiram una funzione di questo genere dimostra l'evidente intenzione di riallacciare l'iniziazione massonica a quelle classiche, la isiaca e la eleusina in ispecie."
28. See Publius Vergilius Maro, *Aeneid*, Book VI, vv. 185–204: "'O if now that golden bough would show itself to us on the tree in the deep wood! For all things truly—ah, too truly—did the seer say of you, Misenus.' Scarce had he said these words when

under his very eyes twin doves, as it chanced, came flying from the sky and lit on the green grass. Then the great hero knew them for his mother's birds, and prays with joy: 'Be my guides, if any way there be, and through the air steer a course into the grove, where the rich bough overshades the fruitful ground! And you, goddess-mother, fail not my dark hour!' So speaking, he checked his steps, marking what signs they bring, where they direct their course. As eyes could keep them within sight; then, when they came to the jaws of noisome Avernus, they swiftly rise and, dropping through the unclouded air, perch side by side on their chosen goal—a tree, through whose branches flashed the contrasting glimmer of gold"; on the masonic symbolism of the sprig of acacia, see Irène Mainguy, *La Symbolique Maçonnique du Troisième Millénaire*, 3rd ed. (Paris: Dervy Éditions, [2001] 2006); Alain Pozarnik, *A la Lumière de l'Acacia* (Paris: Dervy Éditions, 2002); for an entheogenic approach to the role of Acacia in antiquity, see Benny Shanon, "Biblical Entheogens: A Speculative Hypothesis in Time and Mind," *The Journal of Archaeology, Consciousness and Culture* I, no. 1 (2008), pp. 51–74.

29. See Chapter 5.
30. Vergil, *Aeneid*, Book III, vv. 19–68: "By chance, hard by there was a mound, on whose top were cornel bushes and myrtles bristling with crowded spear shafts. I drew near, and essaying to tear up the green growth from the soil, that I might deck the altar with leafy boughs, I see an awful portent, wondrous to tell. For from the first tree which is torn from the ground with broken roots trickle drops of black blood and stain the earth with gore. A cold shudder shakes my limbs, and my chilled blood freezes with terror. Once more, from a second also I go on to pluck a tough shoot and probe deep the hidden cause; from the bark of the second also follows black blood. Pondering much in heart, I prayed to woodland Nymphs, and father Gradivus, who rules over the Getic fields, duly to bless the vision and lighten the omen. But when with greater effort I assail the third shafts, and with my knees wrestle against the resisting sands—should I speak of be silent?—a piteous groan is heard from the depth of the mound, and an answering voice comes to my ears. 'Woe is me! why, Aeneas, do you tear me? Spare me in the tomb at last; spare the pollution of your pure hands! I, born of Troy, am no stranger to you; not from a lifeless stock oozes this blood. Ah! flee the cruel land, flee the greedy shore! For I am Polydorus. Here an iron harvest of spears covered my pierced body, and grew up into sharp javelins.' Then, indeed, with mind borne down with perplexing dread, I was appalled, my hair stood up, and the voice choked in my throat."
31. Reghini, *Le Parole Sacre*, p. 25: "è l'idea egizia, orfica, pitagorica, ermetica; è la ragione precipua per i misteri di Eleusi, di Cerere, di Mitra [...]."
32. Aleister Crowley, *Liber 777 Vel Prolegoma Symbolica Ad Systemam Sceptico-Mysticae Viae Explicande, Fundamentum Hieroglyphicum Sanctissimorum Scientiae Summae* (London: Walter Scott Publishing, 1909).
33. Pherecydes and Plutarch are mentioned on p. 54; Pliny and Catullus are on p. 73.
34. Arturo Reghini, *Le Parole Sacre*, p. 105: "Oggi si crede che la verità si possa raggiungere colla discussione, e sembra naturale che l'allievo si metta a tu per tu, a battibecco col suo maestro. Col pregiudizio dell'eguaglianza, e colle sue derivazioni: libertà, diritti

dell'uomo, popolo sovrano, fratellanza obbligatoria, utopie economiche ecc. ecc., ogni principio di autorità è stato minato, ogni superiorità spirituale e intellettuale svalutata, la gerarchia misconosciuta od invertita, e la deferenza e la reverenza verso il maestro sono scomparse."

35. Reghini, *Le Parole Sacre*, p. 141.
36. Ibid., p. 147: "come la notte segue il giorno, il sonno dal ridestarsi, l'inverno dalla primavera."
37. Ibid., p. 167: "le sole cui partecipava la grande massa"; "quegli effetti interior di cui parlano Apuleio e Plutarco." Lucius Apuleius Madaurensis (124–170) is the author of the *Golden Ass*, or *Metamorphosis*, the first Roman novel that has come to us preserved in its entirety, and narrates the account of a young man named Lucius, who is first tempted by magic spells and philtres, which turn him into a donkey, and his travels throughout Numidia. He regains his human shape by eating some rose petals consecrated to Isis, and therefore may evolve to human form again. See chapter 23: "I drew near to the confines of death, treading the very threshold of Proserpine. I was borne through all the elements and returned to earth again. At the dead of night, I saw the sun shining brightly. I approached the gods above and the gods below, and worshipped them face to face. See, I have told you things which, though you have heard them, you still must know nothing about. I will therefore relate only as much as may, without committing a sin, be imparted to the understanding of the uninitiate." Plutarch, in his Περὶ τῶν Ἐκλελοιπότων Χρηστηρίων, or *On the Failure of Oracles*, talks about the ancient mysteries, and admits to having participated to an initiation, and that he may not disclose the secrets learned under penalty of death. See 422c., where Plutarch also writes, "Opportunity to see and to contemplate these things is vouchsafed to human souls once in ten thousand years if they have lived goodly lives; and the best of the initiatory rites here are but a dream of that highest rite and initiation."
38. Ibid., p. 193: "frammassoni, i rosacroce, i templari, gli gnostici, gli ermetisti, i cabalisti, gli astrologhi, gli alchimisti, i teosofi, gli antroposofi' and 'tra qualche decennio saranno tutti iniziati!."
39. Ibid., p. 208: "In cambio vi faremo sperimentare, se ve ne venisse voglia, qualcheduna delle sensazioni di cui parlano Apuleio e Plutarco; e ci contenteremo di ridere quando al primo traballare della *vostra* psiche darete manifesti segni di avere capito che il mare aperto dei naviganti non è pileggio da piccioletta barca."
40. Ibid., pp. 212–213: "sì da assumere quasi l'aspetto di una delle tante sette protestanti che ivi allignano' and 'se non si vuole consegnare l'Ordine e il paese alla mercè del cristianesimo."
41. Ibid., p. 228.
42. Ibid., p. 228.
43. Ibid., p. 228–229: "Ma noi siamo pagani; ed ai massoni italiani ricordiamo ancora una volta che la scienza massonica non ha nulla a che fare colla religione di Gesù, o con qualsiasi altra; ed invece è la stessa sapienza che la civiltà classica custodiva e perpetuava nei sacri misteri."

44. Di Luca, *Reghini*, p. 67: "Reghini è stato il primo in Italia a discutere, con cognizione di prima mano, di questi materiali e di autori come lo Hutchinson, lo Hawkins, il Mickey, il Findel, il Preston, lo Tschoudy, il Thory, il de Bonneville, l'Oliver, il Pike etc."
45. Anonymous, "Recensione de Le Parole Sacre e di Passo e del Massimo Mistero Massonico," in *Cronache d'Attualità*, VI-6-10 (1922), p. 82, quoted in Marco Rossi, "Neopaganesimo e Arti Magiche nel Periodo Fascista," in *Storia d'Italia*, pp. 599-627: "Quest'opera dei nostri tremendi amici Arturo Reghini, autore, e Ciro Alvi, editore, ci raccapriccia come molte di quelle pubblicate dal mago dell'Umbria. La quale era verde, ma con tanti suffumigi sarà, oramai, diventata nerofumo."
46. For biographical news on Armentano between the years 1919–1924, see Giuseppe Armentano, "Gli Anni piu' Difficili: 1919-1924," in Armentano, *Massime*, pp. 91-101; due to a law against marriage between blood relations in Brasil, the wedding had to be organized hastily in Montevideo, Uruguay.
47. See Rossi, "Neopaganesimo," p. 600; Rossi, "L'interventismo politico-culturale," pp. 457-504; also see chapter 3 of this volume, on avant-garde and tradition: "dopotutto esisteva una connessione tra la ricerca spirituale e culturale delle avanguardie artistiche, l'ambiente della Massoneria esoterica e le origini del movimento fascista."
48. La Direzione, "Ai Lettori," *Atanòr* 1, no. 1-2 (1924), pp. 1-3.
49. Ibid., p. 1: "con speciale riguardo alla tradizione italiana, da Pitagora ai nostri tempi"; "Alla smania pel nuovo, l'originale, il maraviglioso, preferirà l'esame dei fatti e l'appuramento della verità, vecchia o nuova."
50. Ibid., p. 3: "Non possiamo ammettere la pretesa di quelle religioni e credenze che presumono sottrarre alla scienza ed avocare alla fede il dominio dell'indagine spirituale. Né possiamo ammettere le abdicazioni di una scienza che vuole arbitrariamente escludere dal campo dell'esperienza scientifica le esperienze spirituali, né l'irragionevole ostinazione che vuole per forza imporre in questo campo criteri e metodi inadatti, subordinando l'argomento da studiare al sistema di indagine e non viceversa."
51. Wouter J. Hanegraff, "Knowledge," in *Western Esotericism: A Guide for the Perplexed* (London: Bloomsbury, 2013), pp. 86-101.
52. Ibid., p. 89 [86-101].
53. René Guénon, "L'Insegnamento Iniziatico," *Atanòr* 1, no. 1-2, pp. 12-18.
54. René Guénon, "L'Insegnamento Iniziatico," *Atanòr* 1, no. 1-2 (1924), pp. 12-18 [17]: "L'unità e l'immutabilità del principio non esigono affatto l'unità e l'immobilità, dall'altra parte irrealizzabile, delle forme esteriori."
55. Frithjof Schuon, *The Transcendent Unity of Religions* (Varanasi: Indica Books, [1952] 2005).
56. "L'Esoterismo di Dante," *Atanòr* spans through issues 1, no. 4, pp. 103-116; 1, no. 5, pp. 140-145; 1, no. 7, pp. 193-201; 1, no. 8-9, pp. 252-267; "Il Re del Mondo," *Atanòr* can be found on issue 1, no. 12, pp. 353-370.
57. Arturo Reghini, "L'Impronta Pitagorica nella Massoneria," *Atanòr* 1, no. 1-2, pp. 31-46; 1, no. 7, pp. 210-219; and 1, no. 8-9, pp. 268-275.

58. Aniceto del Massa, "Palingenesi e Reincarnazione," *Atanòr* 1, no. 8-9, p. 231 [221-236]: "Per i Pitagorici scopo dell'uomo è di divenire simile a Dio. La chiave del sistema pitagorico è il seguire Dio [. . .].L'autorità di Aristotile ci permette di asserire che i Pitagorici dividevano le cose razionali viventi in Dei, uomini e simili a Pitagora."
59. Pythagoras, *Golden Verses*, ed. Florence M. Firth (San Francisco: Theosophical Publishing House, 1904), p. 22..
60. Reghini, "Imperialismo Pagano," pp. 69-85.
61. Ibid., p. 70: "Né simile questione è priva di importanza anche dal punto di vista politico, soprattutto quando si parli o si pensi ad una politica imperiale e si voglia avviare un paese ad una grandezza spirituale e non soltanto mercantile. Ed in particolar modo sarebbe savio pensarvi quando la religione ufficiale, priva o dimentica della sapienza iniziatica, usurpa in terra il loco mio che vaca, come diceva Dante parlando del Sommo Pontificato, lasciando L'Italia e l'Occidente, almeno in apparenza, in una posizione di inferiorità spirituale."
62. Arturo Reghini, "Campidoglio e Golgota," *Atanòr* 1, no. 5, p. 146.
63. Ibid., p. 148: "*Il colle del Campidoglio*' egli ha detto 'dopo il Golgota *è certamente da secoli il più sacro alle genti civili*."
64. Ibid., p. 148: "Noi ci rifiutiamo di subordinare ad una collinetta asiatica il sacro colle del Campidoglio."
65. Arturo Reghini, "Morale e Peccato," *Atanòr* 1, no. 6, pp. 161-170.
66. Ibid., p. 162: "La religion Cristiana che deriva da quella Ebraica essenzialmente *politica*, cambiando territorio si è fatta *apolitica* e magari *impolitica*. Mentre a Roma attaccare la religion significava attaccare lo stato, nei paesi Cristiani si pensa che lo Stato possa anche essere una cosa separata dalla Chiesa e questa ha una sua gelosa teoria di supremazia sullo Stato."
67. In a letter to Armentano, published in the reprint of *Ignis* (Associazione Culturale Ignis, "Presentazione," in *Ignis*, ed. by Arturo Reghini, p. 7), Reghini had confessed that Alvi's lack of reliability had engraged the Florentine philosopher, his Florentine dialect words being, "Alvi mi ha fatto ingrullire," roughly translatable to "Alvi drove me nuts."
68. Arturo Reghini, "Ai Lettori," *Ignis* 1, no. 1-2 (1925), pp. 1-3 [1]: "il titolo e l'indirizzo postale."
69. See Arturo Reghini, "Cagliostro in Documenti Inediti del Santo Uffizio," *Ignis* 1, no. 1-2 (1925), pp. 14-27; the article carried on in *Ignis* 1, no. 3, pp. 79-83; Reghini, "Una Pagina Ermetica e Cabalistica di Osvaldo Crollio," *Ignis* 1, no. 1-2 (1925), pp. 47-63; Reghini, "Bevi Note sul Cosmopolita e i suoi Scritti," *Ignis* 1, no. 3 (1925), pp. 82-88; carried on in *Ignis* 1, no. 4-5, pp. 127-143.
70. In Sestito, *Figlio del Sole*, p. 155, Mario Gallinaro, close friend of Armentano's, thus commented on Reghini's research in a letter dated October 20, 1922: "Reghini must write for his and our gain; few have his clarity of ideas, his vastness of culture, and his sure grip on the Italian language, vigorous and certain."
71. Julius Evola, "La Donna come Cosa," *Ignis* 1, no. 1-2, pp. 18-29; Evola, "Che cosa vuole l'Antroposofia di Steiner," *Ignis* 1, no. 6-7, p. 185.

72. Evola, "La Donna," p. 18: "La sua sostanza è affatto negativa—non vivendo per sé stessa [. . .] bensì per la morte della vita perfetta—per la decomposizione e l'impurità, essa è a sé medesima contigente."
73. Ibid., p. 19: "L'esperienza mostra che soltanto la passione ha reso possibile ciò in cui la donna si è elevata da una vita amorfa ed ottusa. Lo stesso misticismo femminile è in massima parte giustiziabile con della sensualità deviata o refoulée. Il che spiega il fatto—notato da tanti autori—dell'assoluta mediocrità (per non dire nullità) dell'opera femminile in quelle categorie in quelle categorie quali la scienza, la filosofia, la creazione di religioni ecc. che implicano un principio di mediazione e positiva iniziativa."
74. Evola, "Che cosa vuole," p. 185: "si tratta di una deformazione e di una comprensione imperfetta di elementi della sapienza orientale, aggravata, di contro alla teosofia propriamente detta (Blavatsky)—da una parte dal pregiudizio cristiano, dall'altra da ciò che vi è di più deteriore in Occidente, v.d. da una mentalità positivo-empiristica e progressistico-umanitaria."
75. Maximus [Arturo Reghini], "Associazioni Vecchie e Nuove," *Ignis* 1, no. 6–7 (1925), pp. 211–224.
76. Ibid., p. 213: "gli istituti massonici [propugnano] una dottrina inspirata ad una specie di razionalismo mistico, che, assurdo per sé stesso, è poi quanto di più antitetico si possa immaginare con il carattere fondamentale del sentimento e del pensiero italiano."
77. Ibid., p. 215: "Noi, imperialisti dal 1910 (quando tanta gente di cui è inutile fare il nome seguiva ideologie straniere ed internazionaliste e derideva sino il nome imperialismo), noi che primi in Italia nel 1912 abbiamo festeggiato il Natale di Roma (quando tanti illustri ipernazionali di oggi non sapevano neanche cosa volesse dire), noi interventisti della prima ora, noi che per nostra volontà siamo stati al fronte, noi aristocratici che non accettiamo il principio di nazionalità appunto perché imperialisti, abbiamo sempre pensato che nessuna considerazione poteva assolvere i rinunciatarii a terre italiane in nome della democrazia, come non possiamo applaudire i cosiddetti nazionalisti che han consegnato l'Italia ai preti."
78. Ibid., p. 224: "E non riteniamo il Campidoglio meno glorioso del Golgota. Anzi!"
79. Maximus, "Eccessi di Parte Guelfa," *Ignis* 1, no. 10 (1925), pp. 318–320.
80. Ibid., pp. 319–320: "Il Governo, che si allarma in modo così esagerato ed ingiustificato per le possibili inframettenze della gerarchia massonica a danno di quella dello Stato e di quella fascista (che non sono e non devono essere la stessa cosa), non farebbe male se considerasse un pò attentamente le conseguenze cui lo espone (e con lui il paese) la inframettenza di un'altra gerarchia, più subdola e più vicina, che antepone esplicitamente gli interessi confessionali a quelli italiani, anche perché i veri capi ne sono stranieri, ed il vero ispiratore ha un carattere internazionale e nettamente antiitaliano."
81. See Paolo Cacace, *Quando Mussolini Rischiò di Morire* (Rome: Fazi Editore, 2007).
82. Sestito, *Figlio del Sole*, p. 203; for a exhaustive literature on *Ur* and the *Ur* Group, see Renato del Ponte, *Evola e il Magico "Gruppo di Ur": Studi e Documenti per Scrivere la Storia di 'Ur-Krur'* (Borzano: SeaR, 1994); Evola, *Il Cammino del Cinabro*,

pp. 157–176; Gianfranco de Turris, "La Concezione Magica dell'Uomo e del Mondo," *Vie della Tradizione* 1, no. 2 (1971), pp. 59–70; Renato del Ponte, "Evola e l'Esperienza del 'Gruppo di Ur,'" *Arthos* 2–3, no. 4–5 (1973), pp. 177–191; Marco Mori, "Il Gruppo di 'Ur,'" *Yghieia* 3, no. 1–4 (1986), pp. 6–7; Gianfranco de Turris, "Il Gruppo di Ur tra Magia e Superfascismo," *Abstracta* 2–6, pp. 12–21; del Ponte, *Il Movimento Tradizionalista*. Most recently, the first English article on the subject has been published: Hans Thomas Hakl, "Julius Evola and the UR Group," *Aries* 12, no. 1 (2012), pp. 53–89.

83. For the identity behind the pseudonyms, see the list by del Ponte, *Magico Gruppo di Ur*, pp. 179–182.
84. Hakl, "Ur Group," p. 69.
85. Anonymous [Julius Evola], "Ai Lettori," *Ur* 2, no. 1 (1928), pp. i–vii [v]: "iniziatico, gerarchico, tradizionale, Occidentale, ed elitario."
86. del Ponte, *Magico Gruppo di Ur*, p. 67: "dottrina e cultura esoterica," "pratica," "edizione o traduzione di testi esoterici," "inquadramenti dottrinari sintetici."
87. Pietro Negri [Arturo Reghini], "Della Tradizione Occidentale: Prima Parte," *Ur* 2, no. 1 (1928), pp. 47–74.
88. Ibid., p. 52: "1) l'occidentalità del Cristianesimo 2) il carattere Cristiano della tradizione iniziatica occidentale."
89. Pietro Negri [Arturo Reghini], "Avventure e Disavventure in Magia," *Ur* 1, no. 10 (1927), pp. 388–395: "Impugno ritualmente la spada, inforco gli occhiali, prendo con la sinistra un rotolo di carta appositamente preparato in modo da poterlo svolgere usanto una sola mano per leggere la lunga invocazione scrittavi su, mi volgo ad oriente, metto la spada in direzione del segno e dell'operazione e ben conscio di quanto faccio comincio lentamente e fortemente a dire: 'Potenza somma di ogni potenza.' Constato con piacere che la luce della lampada mi permette di seguire a mio agio le parole dell'invocazione e che tutto sta procedendo. Ma che cosa succede? Che cosa è questo vento? Proprio ora si desta per agitar le fiammelle e disturbar la lettura!? Ed ora che accade? Non ci vedo più! Per tutti gli Dei dell'Olimpo, mi si sono appannati gli occhiali!"
90. de Luca, *Reghini*, p. 73.
91. Anonymous, "Ai Lettori," quoted in Hakl, "Ur Group," p. 76: "Conoscenza di sé, e, in sé, dell'Essere. Questo, o nulla."
92. Ibid., p. 77.
93. Ibid., p. 78.
94. See Renato del Ponte, "E come Esoterismo," in *Il Maestro della Tradizione: Dialoghi su Julius Evola*, ed. Marco Iacona (Naples: Controcorrente, 2008), pp. 81–92 [83–84].
95. Hakl, p. 84; de Luca, pp. 108–109.
96. Evola, *Cammino del Cinabro*, p. 163.
97. Julius Evola, *Imperialismo Pagano: Il Fascismo Dinnanzi al Pericolo Euro-Cristiano* (Rome: Atanòr, 1928).
98. See de Luca, *Reghini*, p. 109: "the robust hands of my co-editor of 'Ignis,'" wrote Reghini, "are without a doubt quite experienced in slapping who deserves it and will not respond."

99. Ibid., p. n112: "in Italy a book by Evola has been published titled 'Imperialismo Pagano,' which, starting from the title is a complete unconfessed plagiarism of my writings; he took all: ideas, arguments, maxims, entire sentences, even my jokes. What he didn't copy from me he took from Guénon, you [Armentano] (without quoting you), Celsus and Rougier."
100. See del Massa, *Pagine Esoteriche*, pp. 53–54: "Evola offered the tribunal a complete recantation and after the addenda and the clarifications wanted by Reghini, he signed the recantation which will have to be published at his expenses on *Roma Fascista*."

Chapter 8

1. Quoted in Caliel [Luigi Petriccioli], *Frammenti dal Sacramentario delle Fratellanze Ermetiche* (Viareggio: Rebis, 2011), p. 4: "Così credo nell'uno che tutto in sé contiene, moto, forza, intelligenza, bene, amore e morte. Credo nell'ascenzo dell'uomo all'uno infinito, nella legge universa di ciò che fu, che è, e che in eterno sarà."
2. Di Luca, *Arturo Reghini*, p. 125.
3. Sestito, *Figlio del Sole*, p. 290.
4. Ibid., p. 290.
5. Parise, "Nota," p. x: "il suo alto valore, la sua padronanza della materia ed il metodo didattico l'avevan posto tra i primissimi, nella stima degli allievi, dei colleghi, degli scienziati."
6. Sestito, *Figlio del Sole*, p. 290.
7. For Tacchi Venturi's unofficial but highly influential role as Mussolini's connection with the higher echelons of the Vatican hierarchy, see Giuseppe Castellani, *Notizie Biografiche del P. Pietro Tacchi Venturi S.I.* (Rome: Pontificiae Universitatis Gregorianae, 1958); Amedeo Giannini, "Padre Tacchi in funzione diplomatica," *Doctor Communis 9* (1956), pp. 227–236; for a reliable source in English, see David I. Kertzer, *The Pope and Mussolini: The Secret History of Pius XI and the Rise of Fascism in Europe* (Oxford: Oxford University Press, 2014).
8. Quoted in Sestito, *Figlio del Sole*, p. 293: "a quanto mi è stato detto Mussolini avrebbe subito esclamato: No, questo imperialista lo conosco io. [. . .] Come vedi, non si può dire che i pionieri dell'imperialismo non abbiano ritratto i loro frutti. Tu mi dirai che sono un pò magri, ed io ti rispondo che son già contento."
9. Ibid., p. 294: "la semplice ed esclusiva erudizione non gli era sufficiente."
10. Ibid., p. 295: "Quanto alla mia venuta in Brasile sono convinto che ne avrei tutta la convenienza perché qui ci si ammazza dalla fatica per non guadagnare che lo stretto necessario. Ma vi sono due ragioni che mi terranno probabilmente qui; una è mia madre cui darei un dispiacere che sicuramente non potrebbe sopportare e non vorrei in nessun modo dovermi rimproverare di averla fatta morire; e l'altra è che malgrado tutte le guerre e le difficoltà e malgrado gli incredibili trionfi dei nemici della romanità spero e credo che vi sia da fare ancora qualche cosa; e siccome fino

ad oggi non ho fatto transazioni né ho abbandonato il campo, desidero di seguitare nello stesso modo sino a che non mi sia impossibile di vivere a Roma."
11. See Archivio Centrale dello Stato, Ministero dell'Interno, Divisione Polizia Politica. *Fascicolo per Persone: Busta 1105. Fascicolo 35 Reghini, Dottor Arturo*; Archivio Centrale dello Stato, Ministero dell'Interno. Divisione Polizia Politica, *Fascicolo per Materie. Busta 100. Fascicolo 8 Ordine Teosofico (1927-1930)*; Archivio Centrale dello Stato, Ministero dell'Interno. Divisione Polizia Politica, *Fascicolo per Materie. Busta 95. Fascicolo 5. Massoneria.*
12. *Fascicolo 8 Ordine Teosofico (1927-1930)*, p. 2: "il Capo del Governo può benissimo credere di servirsi di questi uomini per scopi immediati, ma non è inutile farvi osservare che si tratta di uomini che non hanno scrupoli, che ostentano disprezzo per le leggi morali, che obbediscono a motivi settari secolari [...]."
13. Ibid., p. 2: "cose non realizzabili nell'Evo storico (ad esempio la valutazione come fatto dei miti pagani)."
14. See Fabio Fucci, *Le Polizie di Mussolini. La Repressione dell'Antifascismo nel "Ventennio"* (Milan: Mursia, 2019), pp. 98 and 235–236; Mimmo Franzinelli, *I Tentacoli dell'OVRA: Agenti, Collaboratori e Vittime della Polizia Politica Fascista* (Turin: Bollati Boringhieri, 1999), p. 256.
15. Archivio Centrale dello Stato. Ministero dell'Interno. PS-G1. Busta 129. *Fascicolo 416. Logge Teosofiche. Nota informativa della Regia Questura di Roma del 18 Dicembre 1934*, p. 1.
16. See Sestito, *Figlio del Sole*, pp. 242–245.
17. Parise, *Nota*, p. xii: "si giocava a scacchi; si ragionava sui guai politici del momento, ma sopratutto si parlava di quanto più ci stava a cuore: della possibilità, ancora troppo lontana, di migliori forme avvenire di vita civile, d'un ritorno della massoneria [...]."
18. Di Luca, *Arturo Reghini*, p. 128: "there is reason to believe [...] that a 'pythagorean' group gravitated around him."
19. Del Massa, *Pagine Esoteriche*, pp. 53–54: "Stasera Reghini è stato qui, nel mio studio [...]. Quando andrò a Roma spero di essere ammesso alle esperienze che si svolgono in un circolo da lui diretto e intorno al quale mi ha brevemente accennato."
20. Sestito, *Figlio del Sole*, p. 299.
21. Arturo Reghini, "Il Fascio Littorio," *Docens* 10–11 (1934), republished in Reghini, *Il Simbolismo Duodecimale e il Fascio Etrusco*, ed. Renato del Ponte (Genoa: Edizioni del Basilisco, 1980).
22. Arturo Reghini, *Per la Restituzione della Geometria Pitagorica* (Rome: IGNIS, 1935).
23. *Dei Numeri Pitagorici*, finished only two years before Reghini's death, was never printed during his lifetime: the prologue and the first three books have been published in recent years: see Arturo Reghini, *Dei Numeri Pitagorici: Prologo* (Ancona: Associazione Culturale Ignis, 2003); Reghini, *Dei Numeri Pitagorici, Parte Prima—Volume Primo—Dell'equazione Indeterminata di Secondo Grado con Due Incognite* (Milan: Archè/Pizeta, 2006); Reghini, *Dei Numeri Pitagorici, Parte Prima—Volume Secondo—Delle Soluzioni Primitive dell'Equazione di Tipo Pell $x^2-Dy^2=B$ e del loro Numero* (Milan: Archè/Pizeta, 2012); Reghini, *Dei Numeri*

Pitagorici (Libri sette) —Parte Seconda—Volume Terzo—Dei Numeri Triangolari, dei Quadrati e dei Numeri piramidali a Base Triangolare o Quadrata (Milan: Archè/Pizeta, 2018).

24. Arturo Reghini, "Il Fascio Littorio," *Docens* 10–11 (1934), republished as Reghini, *Il Simbolismo Duodecimale e il Fascio Etrusco*, ed. Renato del Ponte (Genoa: Edizioni del Basilisco, 1980).
25. Ibid., p. 22: "il valore occulto e tradizionale del glorioso simbolo del fascio littorio."
26. In Ancient Rome, magistrates were accompanied by twelve carriers of the Fasces, a symbol of law and order, or *insignia imperii* in Latin. The twelve reeds were bundled together by red leather strips, and an iron or brone axe head was attached to the upper part of the rod, thus creating the famous Anciet Roman and Fascist symbol for legislative power.
27. Ibid., pp. 22–23.
28. Ibid., p. 35: "Ben lieti di vedere tornati in onore i fasci littori, che veneriamo profondamente, con spirito pagano, immune da esotiche infezioni, auspichiamo ad essi favorevoli i fati; auspichiamo un ritorno sempre più consapevole e profondo all romanità, in tutto e per tutto, senza submittere fasces ad influenze avverse o diverse."
29. A fascinatng take on this topic can be found in Alfredina Storchi Marino, *Numa e Pitagora: Sapientia Constituendae Civitatis* (Naples: Liguori, 1999); see also Anonimo Romano, "Il Genio di Roma," *Politica Romana* 3 (1996), p. 150n204.
30. Massimiliano Vittori, "Storia e Simbologia del Fascio Littorio," in *Esoterismo e Fascismo*, ed. Gianfranco de Turris (Rome: Mediterranee, 2006) , pp. 15–19 [15]: "Il fascis era composto da un insieme di 12 verghe di olmo o di betulla, lunghe circa 150 cm, tenute insieme da corregge di cuoio rosse (simbolo del coraggio e dell'amore), nelle quali era inserita, lateralmente o sopra, una scure. Veniva portato sulla spalla sinistra dai littori (lat. *lictor*, forse da licére, 'citare in giudizio'), che erano degli ufficiali subalterni al servizio dei magistrati romani e di alcuni sacerdoti."
31. Ibid., pp. 15–16: "popoli e civiltà affini, contrassegnati da stessi simboli e culti. È il caso della civiltà cretese-micenea o pre-ellenica, che ebbe come centro Creta anteriormente al 1000 a.C."
32. Reghini, "Il Fascio," p. 2: "Vetulonia fu un tempo decoro della gente Meonia (cioè della Lidia): fu la prima città a far precedere dodici fasci ed a cui congiunse ad essi, con silenzioso terrore, altrettante scuri."
33. Ibid., p. 3: "si impone la determinazione di una ragione più profonda e di una natura meno contingente anche per spiegare la sua presenza nei fasci littorii."
34. Quoted by Reghini in ibid., p. 3: "con tali litui, presi gli auspicii, che lo comandassero, dettavano le pene ai loro figli."
35. Ibid., p. 3: "non è invero strano che il bastone del re sia stato ad un tempo lo scettro regale, il bastone della giustizia, ed il lituo o verga magica." The lituus was an Etruscan, and then Roman, curved augural staff or a curved war trumpet: see Renato Meucci, "Roman Military Instruments and the Lituus," *The Galpin Society Journal* 42 (1989), pp. 85–97.
36. Quoted in ibid., p. 4: "chiama l'Etruria una nazione religiosa per eccellenza."

37. See Herodotus, *Histories*, ed. A. D. Godley (Oxford: Oxford University Press, 1921), 2.4.2: "Furthermore, the Egyptians (they said) first used the names of twelve gods (which the Greeks afterwards borrowed from them); and it was they who first assigned to the several gods their altars and images and temples, and first carved figures on stone."
38. Reghini, "Il Fascio," p. 5.
39. Ibid., p. 6: "La Cina, il Giappone, il Siam usano un anno lunare di dodici mesi e un anno luni-solare con una tredicesima lunazione. Una tribù selvaggia dell'Africa Orientale, i *kikuyos*, divide anche essa l'anno in dodici parti. In India infine, troviamo dodici *adityas*, forme ed emblemi del sole per ogni mese dell'anno [...]. La corrispondenza tra i dodici *adityas* hindù e i 12 *dei consentes* dell'olimpo etrusco-greco-romano è evidente."
40. For more on the extant fragments of the *Carmen Saliare*, see H. S. Versnel, *Inconsistencies in Greek and Roman Religion: Transition and Reversal in Myth and Ritual* (Leiden: Brill, 1994).
41. Reghini, "Il Fascio," p. 7: "tutti fatti ed elementi della massima importanza, ed il fatto che dodici era il numero dei littori che precedevano re e consoli non si può considerare isolatamente, ma va evidentemente inquadrato in questa considerazione e venerazione del numero dodici che si ritrova alla base stessa della fondazione di Roma."
42. Reghini's intimate knowledge of all the alchemical texts quoted earlier can be seen in his introduction to Agrippa's *De Occulta Philosophia*, published by Fidi in 1926, and in another introduction which was supposed to shed more light on the works of Michael Sendovigius, but that was never published because of Reghini's tarnished reputation in the late 1920s.
43. Vittori, "Storia e Simbologia," p. 17.
44. René Guénon, "Il Fascio Littorio," *Le Voile d'Isis* (Mai 1935), p. 15: "Une question qui est soulevée ici et qui mériterait d'être examinée de plus près, c'est celle de la place qu'il convient d'assigner à la correspondance zodiacale parmi les autres applications du duodénaire; tout ceci se rapportant aux nombres cycliques, peut d'ailleurs être rattaché aussi au 'symbole de l'Univers' pythagoricien, le dodécaèdre, dont il est traité dans l'autre ouvrage dont nous avons parlé ci-dessus."
45. Sestito, *Figlio del Sole*, p. 298.
46. Ibid., p. 298.
47. Ibid., p. 299.
48. Di Luca, *Arturo Reghini*, p. 127.
49. The two books that deal with the Reale Accademia d'Italia in the most thorough way are Marinella Ferrarotto, *L'Accademia d'Italia. Intellettuali e Potere Durante il Fascismo* (Naples: Liguori, 1977) and Cesco Giulio Baghino and Enzo Marino, *L'Accademia d'Italia. Motore della Cultura* (Reggio Calabria: Iriti Editore, 2001).
50. See Arturo Reghini, "Il Teoremia di Pitagora," "I Poliedri Regolari," "Dimostrazione del Postulato di Euclide," in Reghini, *Per la Restituzione*, respectively pp. 32–50, 69–97, 114–135.

51. Reghini, *Per la Restituzione*, p. 60: "Le ragioni per le quali il pentalfa fu prescelto come simbolo della nostra Scuola non sono tutte di natura geometrica," "data la connessione tra la geometria, le altre scienze e la cosmologia pitagorica."
52. Ibid., p. 67: "quella salvezza o sopravvivenza privilegiata indicata alla fine dei 'Versi d'Oro.'" The last of the *Golden Verses*, number 71, reads: "Thou shalt be a God, immortal, incorruptible, and Death shall have no more dominion over thee."
53. Ibid., p. 67: "Questo antico simbolo pitagorico appare qua e là nella tradizione esoterica occidentale, designato di solito come 'la figura di Pitagora.' Talora al centro si trova scritta la lettera G, iniziale di Geometria, come ad esempio nella 'flaming Star' di un noto Ordine Occidentale avente per scopo il perfezionamento dell'uomo, ossia alla lettera, la *teleté* dei misteri."
54. Ibid., p. 68: "Diremo soltanto [. . .] che il pentalfa ed il fascio littorio (tra quale passa più di un legame) sono i soli importanti simboli spirituali veramente occidentali. Il resto, buono o cattivo che sia, vien dall'Oriente."
55. Sestito, *Figlio del Sole*, p. 297: "Il Reghini doctor mathematicus che noi vogliamo ricordare è ovviamente l'autore 'Dei Numeri Pitagorici' e non l'instancabile professore che si guadagnava faticosamente da vivere insegnando l'algebra e le equazioni nelle scuole romane. È il misterioso Archimede che lasciava perplessi gli amici convenuti come lui nei ritiri spirituali alla Torre Talao quando lo vedevano da solo, con l'abaco in mano, seduto in riva al Tirreno immerso nei calcoli e nei disegni geometrici."
56. Parise, "Nota," p, vi: "gli ultimi quindici anni furono dedicati ad un'attività prevalentemente scientifica, tendente a restaurare i valori ed il metodo di ricerca della Scuola Italica."
57. Sestito, *Figlio del Sole*, pp. 297–298: "Dobbiamo ritenere, sulla base di quanto riferito dai suoi amici, che si dedicasse all' 'opera numerica' evitando l'interferenza di persone estranee; sarebbe facile attribuire alla personalità 'esoterica' e alla sua naturale riservatezza l'osservanza di così gelosa cautela, ma è attraverso la scienza dei numeri che egli intuiva alcuni segreti mai rivelati dell'antica Scuola Italica e che per la loro ineffabilità rimasero sepolti nel fondo della sua anima."
58. For a "scientific" biography of Lagrange's contributions, see Maria Teresa Borgato and Luigi Pepe, *Lagrange, Appunti per una Biografia Scientifica* (Turin: La Rosa, 1990).
59. Reghini, *Dei Numeri*, p. 109.
60. Homer, *Odyssey, Volume 2: Books 13–24*, trans. A. T. Murray, ed. George E. Dimock (Cambridge, MA: Harvard University Press, 1919), XIX-177.
61. Reghini, *Dei Numeri*, p. 18: "ci sembra verosimile e naturale l'intervento di qualche altra più importante influenza, conforme al genio della scuola, e cioè il riconoscimento immediato, spirituale, della grande legge ternaria universale, di cui appariva nel linguaggio e nella magia il riflesso e la manifestazione."
62. Ibid., p. 18: "l'esistenza di un esoterismo pitagorico."
63. Ibid., p. 18: "la scienza moderna ignora o disprezza."
64. Ibid., p. 18: "l'intuzione, il senso estetico, l'anamnesi, la esperienza interior e le pratiche dei misteri."

65. See Paul Antoine Meillet, *Aperçu d'une Histoire de la Langue Greque* (Paris: Hachette, 1913), pp. 98–99; Abel Rey, *La Jeunesse de la Science Greque* (Paris: La Renaissance du Livre, 1933), pp. 34ff.
66. Reghini, *Dei Numeri*, p. 20: "residui sentimentali, credenze cotennose e di tabù sessuali."
67. Ibid., p. 21: "Il moralismo dei Pitagorici non è altro che una tecnica spirituale esoterica."
68. Ibid., p. 22.
69. Ibid., p. 22: "L'orfismo ne faceva oggetto di pratiche religiose e muniva di un 'viatico' i propri morti, il pitagoreismo ne faceva oggetto di esperienza e di esercizio spirituale per condurre i propri vivi alla palingenesi."
70. Ibid., p. 23: "Facendo il viso dell'arme a tutto quanto odora di iniziatico e di esoterico e confinandosi nelle posizioni in cui si trincera e limita, il pensiero occidentale moderno, ci si condanna alla incomprensione delle altre mentalità ed in particolare dello spirito pitagorico; prendendo invece la stessa attitudine e compiendo le medesime pratiche deve, o meglio dovrebbe, essere per lo meno possibile pervenire a risultati identici o consimili a trame conlusioni corrispondenti."
71. Ibid., p. 24: "Anche a noi occidentali, che, addestrandosi seriamente, quotidianamente, in certi riti ed esercizi spirituali [...], è possibile, dopo mesi, anni o decenni arrivare alla percezione del silenzio interiore."
72. Ibid., p. 26: "non vi è altro. Riassumendo, l'esperienza dell'ascesi conduce al riconoscimento successivo della monade, della diade e della triade."
73. Matila Costiescu Ghyka, *Esthétique des Proportions dans la Nature et dans les Arts* (Paris: Gallimard, 1927); for a brief summary of Ghyka's ideas on aesthetics, see Cornel-Florin Moraru: "Art and Mathematics in Matila Ghyka's Philosophical Aesthetics: A Pythagorean Approach on Contemporary Aesthetics," *Hermeneia* 20 (2018), pp. 42–58.
74. Reghini, *Dei Numeri—Prologo*, p. 86: "La concezione pitagorica va d'accordo con quanto dice la Bibbia quando afferma che Dio fece tutte le cose *in numero, pondere et mensura*; ed è espressa da Platone secondo cui Dio sempre geometrizza (sempre e non soltanto illo tempore)."
75. Ibid., p. 90: "Il pitagoreismo si prefiggeva tra le altre cose di accordare gli individui tra loro, di armonizzare la società e di accordare l'individuo singolo col tutto, senza per altro sacrificare gli individui alla massa."
76. See Salvatore Cognetti de Martiis, "L'Istituto Pitagorico," *Atti della Reale Accademia delle scienze di Torino* XXIV (1889), pp. 208–225.
77. Ibid., p. 91: "fondato e diretto da Pitagora, ossia da un essere spiritualmente elevatissimo, costituito a somiglianza ed esempio delle fratellanze celesti, ordinate e rette secondo l'ordine sacro e cementate dalle affinità spirituali, sembra appartenere alla leggenda anziché alla storia."
78. Ibid., p. 92: "Secondo molti sostenitori dell'eguaglianza, tutti gli uomini sono eguali perché sono figli dello stesso Padre; ma anche se questa frase, tipicamente anglosassone e cristiana, avesse un senso intelligibile ed effettivo, questa non sarebbe una buona ragione perché nelle famiglie non sono uguali neppure i gemelli [...]."

Gesù, come quasi tutti gli ebrei, considerava gli ebrei come il popolo eletto; e chiamava figliuoli i figli degli ebrei e cagnuoli ossia figli di cani i figli di non ebrei."

79. Ibid., p. 94: "La salute spirituale veniva raggiunta mediante palingenesi, ossia la rinascita, o la nuova nascita o la nascita alla vita nuova."
80. Ibid., p. 94: "metempsicosi o metemsomatosi, o migrazione [...]."
81. Ibid., p. 95: "un lavoro, anzi è la 'grande opera,' attuata deliberatamente e tecnicamente, secondo un apposito rito o τέχνη che Platone e Massimo di Tiro chiamano 'arte regia.'"
82. Ibid., p. 101: "in modo affatto misterioso ed in certi casi irrazionale."
83. Ibid., pp. 101–102: "Le storie convenzionali prendono per garantito che ogni fatto è stato scoperto mediante una serie naturale di deduzioni da fatti precedenti e dedicano spazio considerevole a tentare di ricostruire tale sequela. Ma gli esperti in ricerche sanno che almeno i germi di molti importanti risultati sono stati scoperti mediante una improvvisa e misteriosa intuizione, risultato forse di uno sforzo mentale subcosciente, anche se tali intuizioni devono essere in seguito sottoposte ai processi delle facoltà critiche." See also L. E. Dickson, *The History of the Theory of Numbers* (Washington, DC: Carnegie Institution of Washington, 1919–1923).
84. Ibid., p. 102: "Pertanto la sapienza divina non è riducibile a sistema filosofico; essa è per così dire necessariamente 'incerta,' e non può essere umanamente *compresa*. Capir quest è già molto perché bisogna riconoscere I propri limiti per poterli oltrepassare. La scienza divina o 'sapienza' di cui i pitagorici si professavano amici è quindi raggiungibile solo transumanando, transumanazione che va attuata non *per verba* ma esssenzialmente mediante la palingenesi che dal verme umano forma l'angelica farfalle che vola alla giustizia senza schermi."
85. *La Prattica* has already been mentioned in Chapter 6.
86. Quoted in Reghini, *Dei Numeri—Prologo*, p. 104: "et quando l'anima si trova depurata proporselo davanti, e allora gli parrà di avere un chiarissimo e risplendente lume, mediante il quale non se gli nasconde verità nessuna."
87. Ibid., p. 105.
88. Sestito, *Figlio del Sole*, p. 243: "Ho visto Arturo poche sere fa, e con rammarico mi da la notizia che tra giorni si trasferirà a Bologna per insegnare alla Scuola Italica che è ancora viva ed è tenuta dalla signora Partengo rimasta devota a Salvi."
89. Camilla Partengo volunteered as a nurse in World War I and then obtained a degree in physics at the University of Bologna. Though being offered a position at the university, Camilla created a network of private schools that could offer postelementary education to youths living in small centers. It is through these networks that she met Enrico Salvi and helped found the *Schola Italica Lux et Ars* in the small town of Budrio. During World War II, she would host her lessons in her private house, Villa Giacomelli.
90. Sestito, *Figlio del Sole*, p. 245: "Permetterà di fare una Geometria che si basi sul Teorema di Pitagora e che riaffermi nella scala di valori il primato italiano, quando la attuale pazzia dilagante a base di atomismo, in cui il progresso tecnico e la perfezione alla quale tende l'umanità sono sinonimo di massacro, avrà dovuto lasciare il passo ad un ordinamento spirituale predominante."

91. Ibid., p. 250: "Nei primi anni le cose sono andate bene, anche grazie all'aiuto del Comune. Poi il segretario del fascio repubblicano ci ha cacciato con la forza in mezzo alla strada; e sono cominciate le difficoltà e le ostilità di ogni specie: i fascisti, gli sfollati, i tedeschi che si sono installati anche in casa per dieci mesi e ci hanno costretto a chiudere la scuola (ho guadagnato 80 lire in un anno!) poi i bombardamenti aerei di giorno e di notte ed infine il bombardamento dell'artiglieria inglese e tedesca per quattro giorni ininterrotti."
92. Ibid., p. 253: "Degli amici che avrebbero voluto darmi un aiuto, nessuno ci è riuscito; Cavalli si è suicidato, Moretto è fallito, tu sei dove sei, altri mi hanno abbandonato."
93. Ibid., p. 253.
94. Ibid., p. 253: "l'intelligenza, la memoria e la resistenza al lavoro [sono] quelle di prima."
95. Quoted in Sestito, *Figlio del Sole*, p. 270: "Egli era l'esempio di quella calma spirituale propria di chi vive in un mondo superiore e non teme nulla."
96. Ibid., p. 270: "Eroe nel linguaggio della tradizione classica era non solo il nume tutelare di città o famiglie, ma anche il Maestro di Magia che aveva conseguito in vita e nel post-mortem l'immortalità."
97. Parise, *Nota*, p. xiv: "Il primo giorno del mese di Luglio del 1946, lo spirito di Arturo Reghini scioglieva i legami corporei e passava nell'Eterna Luce. Era la quinta ora pomeridiana. Il segno era apparso. Arturo Reghini si volse verso il sole declinante per l'ultimo saluto, per l'ultimo rito; poi si appoggiò con la destra al vicino scaffale, piegò la gigantesca statura verso la Grande Madre, eretto il busto: e fu libero."
98. Mario Coen Belifanti, "Le Ultime Ore del Filosofo," in Julius Evola, *Il Cammino del Cinabro*, pp. 415–416: "Essere portato 'in piedi' davanti alla finestra di fronte al Gianicolo e lì la sua forte fibra aveva ceduto."
99. Ibid., p. 416.

Chapter 9

1. Sestito, *Figlio del Sole*, p. 254: "egli era l'esempio di quella calma spirituale propria di chi vive in un mondo superiore e non teme nulla."

Appendix: English Translation of Imperialismo Pagano

1. I have stuck to Reghini's inconsistency in capitalization and punctuation, in order to preserve Reghini's original and highly idiosyncratic style.
2. Dante, *Monarchia*, II-6, "The Roman People have been ordained to rule by nature."
3. "Already doth the Virgin return, the Reign of Saturn returns," Vergil, Eclogue 4, v. 6.
4. "To improve and convert Mankind," Johann Wolfgang von Goethe, Faust, ed. A. Wilbrandt (Padeborn: Salzwasser Verlag, [1895] 2014), p. 19.

5. "Harm no one, give one his due, live honestly," attributed to Gnaeus Domitius Annius Ulpianus's lost *Regulae*.
6. *Prudentia* may be translated as wisdom or knowledge.
7. Dante Alighieri, *La Divina Commedia: Paradiso* (Venice: Gabriel Giolito de Ferrari, 1555), v. 114: "made shields and lances out of the gospel."
8. Dante Alighieri, *La Divina Commedia: Purgatorio*, v. 18: "already seen human corpses alight."
9. Dante Alighieri, *La Divina Commedia: Paradiso*, v127-9: "As he who is silent but really wants to speak/Beatrice drew me to her and said: Look at/The size of the crowd in white stoles!"
10. Reghini describes this as a verse from Valentinus's gnostic prayer: "Oh come, sweet visions to the white stoles." See Gastone Ventura, *Cosmogonie Gnostiche: Saggio Storico-Critico sulle Principali Teogonie Gnostiche* Cristiane (Rome: Atanòr, 1975).
11. Lucius Annaeus Seneca, *Epistles to Lucilius*, 107, no. 11, 5: "Fate leads the willing, drags the unwilling."

Bibliography

Primary Sources

Agabiti, Augusto. *Il Problema della Vivisezione: Testi delle Principali Disposizioni Legislative Vigenti negli Stati Moderni*. Rome: Enrico Voghera, 1911.
Agabiti, Augusto. *Ipazia, la Prima Martire della Libertà di Pensiero*. Rome: Enrico Voghera, 1914.
Agabiti, Augusto. *Sulla Fronte Giulia: Note di Taccuino 1915–1916–1917*. Naples: Società Editrice Partenope, 1919.
Agrippa, Enrico Cornelio. *La Filosofia Occulta o la Magia*. Introduction and translation by Arturo Reghini. 3 vols. Milan: Fidi, 1927.
Aleramo, Sibilla. *Amo Dunque Sono*. Milano: Mondadori, 1927.
Alvi, Ciro. *Verso la Purificazione—Ricordi di un Mellonarca*. Todi: Armuzzi & Orsini Editori, 1899.
Alvi, Ciro. *La Vita Nuova—Il Culto dell'Avvenire*. Todi: np, 1901.
Alvi, Ciro. *S. Francesco d'Assisi*. Milan: Sandron, 1903.
Alvi, Ciro. *L'Arcobaleno*. Todi: Atanòr, 1912.
Alvi, Ciro. *Per lo Spirito la Carne Esaltare*. Todi: Atanòr, 1923.
Alvi, Ciro. *L'Incendio di Roma*. Todi: Atanòr, 1928.
Amendola, Giovanni. *Carteggio 1897–1909*. Bari: Laterza, 1986.
Angebert, Jean-Michel. *Les Mystiques du Soleil*. Paris: Robert Laffont, 1971.
Anonimo, Romano. "Il Genio di Roma." *Politica Romana* 3 (1996), p. 150, n. 204.
Anonymous [Benito Mussolini]. "Programma di San Sepolcro." *Il Popolo d'Italia*, June 6, 1919, pp. 2–4.
Anonymous [Julius Evola]. "Ai Lettori." *Ur* 2, no. 1 (1928), pp. i–vii.
Anonymous. *Commemorazione del Fratello Filippo Delpino. 25 Settembre 1862. Discorsi dell'Oratore della Loggia Ausonia*. Turin: Marzorati, 1862.
Anonymous. "Cenni Biografici del Comm. Prof. G. E. Mengozzi." *Roma Etrusca* 1, no. 1 (1881), pp. 2–6.
Anonymous. "Italy." *The Theosophist* 22, no. 4 (1901), p. 246.
Anonymous. "Il Congresso Antimassonico." *Osservatore Romano*, August 8, 1896, p. 2.
Ardigò, Roberto. *La Morale dei Positivisti*. Milan: Marzorati, (1879) 1973.
Ardigò, Roberto. *Scritti Varii*. Florence: Le Monnier, 1922.
Armentano, Amedeo Rocco. *Massime di Scienze Iniziatica*. Ancona: Ignis, 1992.
Arrighi, Cletto. *La Scapigliatura e il 6 Febbrajo*. Milan: Sonzogno, 1861.
Atti del Primo Congresso Massonico Internazionale: Trento XXVI–XXX settembre MDCCCCXCVI. Monauni: Unione Antimassonica Universale, 1898.
Baker, Alan. *Invisible Eagle–The History of Nazi Occultism*. London: Virgin Books, 2000.
Bassan, Ettore. *Lotte Nazionali nella Venezia Giulia*. Rome: Pinci, 1915.
Bedeschi, Lorenzo, ed. *Diario di Don Minzoni*. Brescia: Morcelliana, 1965.
Belifanti, Mario Coen. "Le Ultime Ore del Filosofo." In *Il Cammino delCinabro*, edited by Julius Evola, pp. 415–416. Roma: Mediterranee, 2014.

Benso, Camillo Conte di Cavour. *Discorsi Parlamentari Del Conte Camillo di Cavour Raccolti e Pubblicati per Ordine della Camera dei Deputati*. Rome: Eredi Botta, 1872.
Berchet, Giovanni. "All'Armi! All'Armi." In *Canti e Poesie*, vv. 1-6.
Besant, Annie. *Teosofia e Vita Umana*. Milan: Ars Regia, 1909.
Berchet, Giovanni. Letter of April 24, 1903. *Ignis* 5 (1992), p. 83.
Bianca, Mariano. *Atanòr 1912-2012*. Rome: Atanòr, 2012.
Blavatsky, H. P. *The Key to Theosophy*. Mumbai: Theosophy Company, 1887.
Blavatsky, H. P. *The Secret Doctrine: The Synthesis of Science, Religion, and Philosophy*. Adyar: Theosophical University Press, 1888.
Blavatsky, H. P. *The Voice in the Silence: Being Chosen Fragments from the Book of Golden Precepts*. London: Theosophical Publishing Company, 1889.
Blavatsky, H. P. *Dalle Caverne e dale Giungle dell'Indostan*. Milan: Ars Regia, 1912.
Blavatsky, H. P. "The Fall of Ideas." In *The Collected Works Vol. XII*, edited by Boris De Zirkoff, pp. 40-45. London: Theosophical Publishing House, 1980.
Bocchini, Domenico. *Gli Arcani Gentilizi*. Vol. 3. Naples: Torchi del Tramaner, 1837.
Bodrero, Emilio. *Inchiesta sulla Massoneria*. Milan: Mondadori, 1925.
Borella, Jean. *Ésotérisme Guénonien et Mystère Chrétien*. Lausanne: L'Age d'Homme, 1997.
Borgese, Giuseppe Antonio. "Leonardo." *Hermes* 1, no. 1 (1904), p. 59.
Botta, Carlo. *Storia d'Italia dal 1789 al 1814*. 6 vols. Capolago: Tipografia Elvetica, 1833.
Caliel [Luigi Petriccioli]. *Frammenti dal Sacramentario delle Fratellanze Ermetiche*. Viareggio: Rebis, 2011.
Calvari, Decio. "Resumé du Mouvement Théosophique en Italie." In *Transactions of the First Annual Congress of the Federation of European Sections of the Theosophical Society*, edited by Johan Van Manen, 381-382. Brill: Leiden, 1906.
Capparelli, Vincenzo. *Il Messaggio di Pitagora: Il Pitagorismo nel Tempo*. Rome: Edizioni Mediterranee, (1944) 2003.
Capuana, Luigi. *Spiritismo?* Catania: Giannotta, 1884.
Capuana, Luigi. *Mondo Occulto*. Naples: Pierro, 1896.
Carrington, Hereward. *Eusapia Palladino and her Phenomena*. New York: B. W. Dodge & Co., 1909.
Cattaneo, Carlo. *Opere Edite ed Inedite di Carlo Cattaneo*. Edited by Agostino Bertani. Florence: Le Monnier, 1891-1892.
Cattaneo, Carlo. *Industria e Scienza Nuova*. Edited by Delia Frigessi. Turin: Einaudi, 1972.
Cattaneo, Carlo. *Uno Stato è una Gente e una Terra*. Edited by Ettore A. Albertoni. Milan, RARA, 1994.
Cattaneo, Carlo. *Filosofia Civile e Federalismo nel Pensiero di Carlo Cattaneo*. Edited by Gastone Gazzarri. Florence: Nuova Italia, 1996.
Cattaneo, Carlo. *Dell'Insurrezione di Milano nel 1848 e della Successiva Guerra*. Edited by Luigi Ambrosoli. Milan: Mondadori, 2001.
Cattaneo, Carlo. *I Volti di Carlo Cattaneo 1801-1869. Un Grande Italiano del Risorgimento*. Edited by F. della Peruta, C. G. Lacaita, and F. Mazzocca. Milan: Skira, 2001.
Cattaneo, Carlo. *Lettere 1821*. Edited by Carlo G. Lacaita. Milan: Mondadori, 2003.
Cattaneo, Carlo. *Una Teoria della Libertà: Scritti Politici e Federalisti*. Edited by Walter Berberis. Turin: Einaudi, 2011.
Ciampi, Ignazio. *La Citta' Etrusca*. Rome: Tipografia delle Belle Arti, 1866.
Cicero, Marcus T. *De Officiis*. Translated by Walter Miller. Cambridge, MA: Harvard University Press, 1913.

Cognetti de Martiis, Salvatore. "L'Istituto Pitagorico." *Atti della Reale Accademia delle scienze di Torino* XXIV (1889), pp. 208–225.
Comitato per il Restauro della Statua del Corpo di Napoli. *Lo Sguardo del Nilo: Storia e Recupero del "Corpo di Napoli."* Napoli: Colonnese, 1993.
Consolato, Sandro. "Il Risorgimento Come Sviluppo della Storia Sacra di Roma." *Politica Romana* 4 (1997), pp. 125–175; 5 (1998–1999), pp. 48–105; 6 (2004–2005), pp. 109–168.
Consolato, Sandro. *Dell'Elmo di Scipio: Risorgemento, Storia d'Italia e Memoria di Roma.* e-book. Rome: flower-ed, 2012.
Copenhaver, Brian P. trans. *Hermetica: The Greek Corpus Hermeticum and the Latin Asclepius in a New English Translation, with Notes and Introduction.* Cambridge: Cambridge University Press, 1995.
Cordova, Vincenzo. *I Discorsi Parlamentari e gli Scritti Editi ed Inediti Preceduti dai Ricordi della Sua Vita, per Vincenzo Cordova.* Vol. 1. Rome: Edizioni del Senato, 1889.
Costituzioni della Massoneria Italiana Discusse e Votate dalla Prima Assemblea Costituente Massonica Italiana nelle Tenute delli 27, 28, 29, 30, 31 Dicembre 1861, Valle di Torino 5861. Turin: np, 1861.
Croce, Benedetto. *Materialismo Storico ed Economia Marxistica.* Naples: Sandron, 1900.
Croce, Benedetto. "Introduzione." *La Critica* 1, no. 1 (1903), p. 3.
Croce, Benedetto. "Leonardo." *La Critica* 1, no. 4 (1903), pp. 287–291.
Croce, Benedetto. "Estratto dalla Critica." *Leonardo* 1–2, no. 1 (1903), p. 21.
Croce, Benedetto. *Ciò che è Vivo e ciò che è Morto della Filosofia di Hegel: Studio Critico Seguito da un Saggio di Bibliografia Hegeliana.* Bari: Laterza, 1907.
Croce, Benedetto. *Logica come Scienza del Concetto Puro.* Bari: Laterza, 1909.
Croce, Benedetto. *Saggio su Hegel Seguito da Altri Scritti di Storia della Filosofia.* Bari: G. Laterza & Figli, 1913.
Croce, Benedetto. "La Storiografia in Italia." *La Critica: Rivista di Letteratura Storia e Filosofia diretta da B. Croce* 13 (1915), pp. 165–192.
Croce, Benedetto. *Storia d'Italia. Dal 1871 al 1915.* Edited by Giuseppe Galasso. Milan: Adelphi, (1928) 1991.
Crowley, Aleister. *Magick in Theory and Practice—Book 4 Part III.* Paris: Lecram Press, 1929.
Crowley, Aleister. *The Book of Thoth.* London: OTO, 1944.
Crowley, Aleister. *The Confessions of Aleister Crowley: An Autohagiography.* London: Routledge and Kegan Paul, 1979.
d'Anna, Nuccio. *Virgilio e le Rivelazioni Divine.* Genoa: ECIG, 1989.
d'Annunzio, Gabriele. "Anniversario Orfico." *Leonardo* 1, no. 2 (1903), p. 1.
Däubler, Theodor. *Hymne an Italien.* Munich: Georg Muller, 1916.
de Amicis, Edmondo. *Cuore.* Milano: Fratelli Treves, 1886.
de Karolis, Adolfo. "Cattolicesimo e Paganesimo." *Leonardo* 1, no. 8 (1903), p. 7.
de Morgan, Sophia Elizabeth. *From Matter to Spirit: The Result of Ten Years' Experience in Spirit Manifestations. Intended as a Guide to Enquirers.* Preface by Augustus de Morgan. London: Longman and Green, 1863.
de Pouvourville, Albert, and Léon Champrenaud. *Les Enseignments Secrets de la Gnose.* Milan: Arché, (1907) 1999.
de Saint-Martin, Louis-Claude. *Des Erreurs et de la Vérité ou les Hommes Rappeliés au Principe Universel de la Science.* Endinburgh: np, 1775.
de Saint-Martin, Louis-Claude. *Tableau Naturel des Rapports qui Unissent Dieu, l'Homme et l'Universe.* Edinburgh: np, 1782.

de Tschoudy, Baron. *L'Etoile Flamboyant—A l'Orient chez le Silence*. Paris: np, 1766.
de Unamuno, Miguel. "Sobre el Quijotismo." *Leonardo* 5, no. 1 (1907), pp. 38–45.
del Massa, Aniceto. *Pagine Esoteriche*. Lavis: La Finestra, (1928) 2001.
del Massa, Aniceto. "Palingenesi e Reincarnazione." *Atanòr* 1, no. 8–9 (1924), pp. 221–236.
di Savoia, Carlo Alberto. "Statuto Albertino." *Gazzetta Piemontese* 3 March (1848), p. 1.
d'Uva, Gennaro. "La Tradizione Italica." *Politica Romana* 5 (1998/9), pp. 106–125.
Dickson, L. E. *The History of the Theory of Numbers*. Washington, DC: Carnegie Institution of Washington, 1919–1923.
Diotti, Carlo. *Prigioniero d'Africa. La Battaglia di Adua e l'Impresa Coloniale del 1895–96 nel Diario di un Caporale Italiano*. Como: Nodolibri, 2006.
Direzione. "Nostro Programma." *Roma Etrusca* 1, no. 1 (1921), p. 1.
Donato, Riccardo. *La Chiave della Sapienza Ermetica secondo Giuliano Kremmerz, Domenico Bocchini e Giustiniano Lebano*. 2 vols. Rebis: Viareggio, 2012–2014.
Duprey, Jacques, *Un Fils de Napoleón dans les Pays de la Plata au Temps de Rosas*. Paris-Montevideo: Casa Barrero y Ramos, 1937.
Durkheim, Émile. "L'Élite Intellectuelle et la Démocratie." *Revue Bleu* 5, no. 1 (1904), pp. 705–706.
Ely-Isis. "Giustiniano Lebano ed i Misteri Classici Antichi." *Ignis Rivista di Studi Iniziatici* 1 (1990), pp. 25–27.
Éncausse, Gerard [Papus]. *Traité Méthodique de Science Occulte*. 3 vols. Paris: Georges Carré, 1888–1891.
Éncausse, Gerard [Papus]. *La Science des Mages et ses Applications Théoriques et Pratiques*. Paris: Chamuel Editeur, 1892.
Éncausse, Gerard [Papus]. *Kabbalah: Tradition Secret de l'Occident*. Paris: Georges Carré, 1892.
Evola, Julius. "La Donna Come Cosa." *Ignis* 1, no. 1–2 (1925), pp. 13–14.
Evola, Julius. "Che cosa vuole l'Antroposofia di Steiner." *Ignis* 1, no. 6–7 (1925), p. 185.
Evola, Julius. *Imperialismo Pagano: Il Fascismo Dinnanzi al Pericolo Euro-Cristiano*. Rome: Mediterranee, (1928) 2004.
Evola, Julius. *Orientamenti, Undici Punti*. Rome: Imperium, 1950.
Evola, Julius. *La Metafisica del Sesso*. Rome: Mediterranee, (1958) 1996.
Evola, Julius. *Il Cammino del Cinabro*. 3rd exp. ed. Rome: Mediterranee, (1963) 2014.
Evola, Julius. *Heathen Imperialism*. Kemper: Thompkins and Cariou, 2007.
Feilding, Everard, W. W. Baggally, and Hereward Carrington. "Report on a Series of Sittings with Eusapia Palladino." *Proceedings of the Society for Psychical Research* 23 (1909), pp. 309–569.
Fermi [Benito Mussolini]. "Cronache del Pensiero Religioso." *Gerarchia* 3, no. 1 (1924), pp. 637–642.
Ferrari, Pietro. "Un Seminarista in Camicia Rossa: Teodoro Reghini." *Corriere Apuano* 19 (1941), pp. 45–49.
Findel, Gottfried. *Histoire de la Francmaçonnerie*. 2 vols. Paris: Librerie Internationelle, 1866.
"First Convention of the Italian Section of the Italian Section of the Theosophical Society." *Rivista Italiana di Teosofia* 68, no. 2 (2002), pp. 5–11.
Flaccus, Quintus Horatius. *Satyrarum Libri*. 23 BCE.
Frosini, Eduardo. *Massoneria Italiana e Tradizione Iniziatica*. Pescara: Ettore Croce, 1911.
Gabrieli, Francesco, ed. *Giornata di Studio nel Cinquantenario della Morte di Leone Caetani* Rome: Fondazione Leone Caetani dell'Accademia Nazionale dei Lincei, 1985.

Galliano, Paolo. *Roma prima di Roma, Metastoria della Tradizione Italica*. Rome: Simmetria Edizioni, 2011.

Gatto Chanu, Tersilla. *Canti Popolar del Vecchio Piemonte*. Rome: Newton Compton, 2007.

Gatto Chanu, Tersilla. *Il Geronta Sebezio*. Naples: Torchi del Tramaner, 1835–1837.

Ghyka, Matila Costiescu. *Esthétique des Proportions dans la Nature et dans les Arts*. Paris: Gallimard, 1927.

Gioberti, Vincenzo. *Del Primato Morale e Civile degli Italiani*. 2 vols. Lausanne: S. Bonamici & Compagnia, 1845.

Gioberti, Vincenzo. *Degli Errori Filosofici di Antonio Rosmini*. Capolago: Tipografia Elvetica, 1846.

Gioberti, Vincenzo. *Il Gesuita Moderno*. Naples: C. Batelli, 1848–1849.

Gray, Ezio Maria. "Untitled." *La Nazione*, January 8, 1914, p. 12.

Gruppo dei Dioscuri. *Rivoluzione Tradizionale e Sovversione: Documenti per il Fronte della Tradizione 21*. Rome: Raido, 2004.

Guénon, René. *Introduction Générale à l'Étude des Doctrines Hindoues*. Paris: Marcel Rivière, 1921.

Guénon, René. *Le Théosophisme, Histoire d'une pseudo-Religion*. Paris: Editiones Traditionelles, 1921.

Guénon, René. *L'Erreur Spirite*. Paris: Editiones Traditionelles, 1923.

Guénon, René. *Orient et Occident*. Paris: Payot, 1924.

Guénon, René. "L'Esoterismo di Dante." Translated by Arturo Reghini. *Atanòr* 1, no. 4 (1924), pp. 103–116.

Guénon, René, "L'Esoterismo di Dante." Translated by Arturo Reghini. *Atanòr* 1, no. 5 (1924), pp. 140–145.

Guénon, René, "L'Esoterismo di Dante." Translated by Arturo Reghini. *Atanòr* 1, no. 7 (1924), pp. 193–201.

Guénon, René, "L'Esoterismo di Dante." Translated by Arturo Reghini. *Atanòr* 1, no. 8–9 (1924), pp. 252–267.

Guénon, René. "L'Insegnamento Iniziatico." *Atanòr* 1, no. 1–2 (1924), pp. 12–18.

Guénon, René. *L'Ésotérisme de Dante*. Paris: Ch. Bosse Libraire, 1925.

Guénon, René. *La Crise du Monde Moderne*. Paris: Bossard, 1927.

Guénon, René. *Le Symbolisme de la Croix*. Paris: Véga, 1931.

Guénon, René. *Les États Multiples de l'Être*. Paris: Véga, 1932.

Guénon, René. "Il Fascio Littorio." *Le Voile d'Isis* 185 (Mai 1935), p. 15.

Guénon, René. *Le Règne de la Quantité et les Signes des Temps*. Paris: Gallimard, 1945.

Guénon, René. *Aperçus sur l'Initiation*. Paris: Éditions Traditionelles, 1946.

Guénon, René. *Comptes Rendus*. Paris: Éditions Traditionelles, 2000.

Guénon, René. *Il Risveglio della Tradizione Occidentale: I testi Pubblicati da Atanòr e Ignis*. Edited by Mariano Bizzarri. Rome: Atanòr, 2003.

Hermet, Augusto. *La Ventura delle Riviste*. Florence: Vallecchi, 1941.

Herodotus. *Histories*. Edited by A. D. Godley. Oxford: Oxford University Press, 1921.

Home, Daniel Dunglas. *Incidents in My Life*. New York: A. K. Butts, 1872.

Homer. *Odyssey, Volume 2: Books 13–24*. Translated by A. T. Murray. Edited by George E. Dimock. Cambridge, MA: Harvard University Press, 1919.

Hossein, Sayed Nasr. *The Need for a Sacred Science*. Albany: SUNY Press, 1993.

Hutchinson, William. *The Spirit of Masonry*. London: J. Wilkie & W. Goldsmith, 1775.

Huxley, Aldous. *The Perennial Philosophy*. New York: Harper & Brothers, 1945.

Imoda, Enrico. *Fotografie di Fantasmi: Contributo Sperimentale alla Constatazione dei Fenomeni Mediatici con Prefazione del Dott. Prof. Carlo Richet e Numerose Fotografie Stampate dalle Negative Originali.* Turin: Bocca, 1912.

Jah-Hel. *La Pietra Angolare Miriamica: Storia Documentata della Fratellanza di Miriam di Giuliano Kremmerz.* Viareggio: Rebis, 1989.

James, William. "La Concezione della Coscienza." *Leonardo* 3, no. 3 (1905), p. 77.

James, William. "G. Papini and the Pragmatist Movement in Italy." *Journal of Philosophy, Psychology and Scientific Method* 3, no. 13 (1906), pp. 328–341.

James, William. "Le Energie degli Uomini." *Leonardo* 5, no. 1 (1907), pp. 1–25.

Judge, William Q. *The Ocean of Theosophy.* New York: The Path, 1893.

Kardec, Allan. *What Is Spiritism?* Philadelphia: Allan Kardec Educational Society, (1859) 1999.

Kardec, Allan. *Lo Spiritismo alla sua piu' Semplice Espressione. Esposizione Sommaria dell'Insegnamento degli Spiriti e delle Manifestazioni Loro.* Preface and translation by Vincenzo Scarpa. Turin: Degiorgis and Ferneux, 1863.

Kirkham, Victoria, and Armando Maggi. *Petrarch: A Critical Guide to the Complete Works.* Chicago: University of Chicago Press, 2009.

Klages, Ludwig. *Der Geist als Widersacher der Seele.* 4 vols. Leipzig: J.A. Barth, 1929–1932.

Kleuker, Johann Friedrich. *Magikon oder das Geheime System einer Gesellschaft Unbekannter Philosophen.* Hannover: np, 1784.

Kremmerz, Giuliano. "Piccola Posta—M.O. Firenze." *Commentarium* 2, no. 2–3 (1911), p. 131.

Kremmerz, Giuliano. *I Dialoghi sull'Ermetismo.* Vol. 1. Spoleto: Arti Grafiche Panetto e Petrelli, 1929.

Labriola, Antonio. "Come Nacque e Come Morì il Marxismo Teorico in Italia (1895–1900)." In Labriola, *La Concezione Materialistica della Storia, Nuova ed. con un'Aggiunta di B. Croce sulla Critica del Marxismo in Italia dal 1895 al 1900*, pp. 89–97. Bari: Laterza, 1942.

Labriola, Antonio. *Lettere a Benedetto Croce 1885–1904.* Naples: Istituto Italiano per gli Studi Storici, 1975.

Leadbeater, C. W. *Il Piano Astrale.* Milan: Ars Regia, 1913.

Lebano, Giustianiano. *Del Morbo Oscuro chiamato Areteo Ociphon Sincope impropriamente creduto dagli europei Cholera Morbus.* Naples: Tocco & C., 1881, p. 10.

Lévi, Eliphas. *Dogme et Rituel de Haute Magie.* Paris: Librairie Medical de Germer Ballière, 1856.

Lisi, Nicola. *Parlata dalla Finestra di Casa.* Florence: Vallecchi, 1973.

Lo Monaco, Giuseppe. *L'Ordine Osirideo Egizio e la Trasmissione Pitagorica.* Bassano del Grappa: np, 1999.

Lo Monaco, Giuseppe. "Edward Bulwer Lytton e l'Ambiente Iniziatico Partenopeo Nilense." *Atrium* 6, no. 3 (2004), pp. 6–57.

Lombroso, Cesare, Enrico Ferri, Raffaele Garofalo, and Giulio Fioretti. *Polemica in Difesa della Scuola Criminale Positiva.* Bologna: Zanichelli, 1886.

Lombroso, Cesare, Enrico Ferri, Raffaele Garofalo, and Giulio Fioretti. *Studi sull'Ipnotismo con Appendice Critica sullo Spiritismo.* Turin: Bocca, 1886.

Machiavelli, Nicolò. *Degli Discorsi di Nicolò Machiavelli, Cittadino & Secretario Fiorentino, sopra la Prima Decade di Tito Livio a Zanobi Buondelmonti & a Cosimo Rucellai.* Florence: Bernardo Giunti, 1531.

Maddalena Capiferro, Cristian Guzzo, Gaetano Lo Monaco, and Michele Di Iorio. *Sairitis Hus. Gli Antri, le Sirene, la Luce, l'Ombra. Appunti Biografici Ermetici della Napoli Ottocentesca*. Mussolente: Carpe Librum, 2001.

Maddalena Capiferro, Cristian Guzzo, Gaetano Lo Monaco, Michele Di Iorio, and Cristian Guzzo. *L'Arcano degli Arcani: Storia dell'Ermetismo Egizio-Partenopeo fra i Secoli XVIII-XX*. Viareggio: Rebis, 2005.

Maddalena Capiferro, Cristian Guzzo, Gaetano Lo Monaco, Michele Di Iorio, and Cristian Guzzo. *L'Arcano degli Arcani, Lungo il Nilo dell'Ordine Osirideo Egizio. Il Mito dell'Eterno Ritorno, ovvero la Lampada della Vita dall'Ombra delle Piramidi alla luce del Sebeto*. Viareggio: Rebis, 2005.

Manzoni, Alessandro. "1821." In Associazione Amici dell'Accademia dei Lincei, *Canti e Poesie*, Rome: Accademia dei Lincei, 2011, vv. 5-8.

Marchi, Vittore. *La Missione di Roma nel Mondo*. Todi: Atanòr, 1915.

Marinetti, Filippo Tommaso. "Il Manifesto Futurista." In *I Manifesti del Futurismo Lanciati da Marinetti – Boccioni – Carrà – Russolo – Balla – Severini – Pratella*. Edited by Filippo Tommaso Marinetti. Florence: Lacerba, 1914, pp. 3-11.

Maro, Publius Virgilius. "The Eclogues." In *Loeb Classical Library 63 and 64: The Georgics, The Eclogues, The Aeneid Book I-VI*, translated and edited by H. R. Fairclough, pp. 23-97. Cambridge, MA: Harvard University Press, 1916.

Mazzini, Giuseppe. *Dei Doveri dell'Uomo*. Milan: RCS Libri, (1860) 2010.

Mazzoldi, Angelo. *Delle Origini Italiche e della Diffusione dell'Incivilimento Italiano all'Egitto, alla Fenicia, alla Grecia e a Tutte le Nazioni Asiatiche Poste sul Mediterraneo*. Milan: np, 1840.

Mead, G. R. S., and M. L. Kirby. *Frammenti di una Fede Dimenticata*. Milan: Ars Regia, 1909.

Meillet, Paul Antoine. *Aperçu d'une Histoire de la Langue Greque*. Paris: Hachette,1913.

Mengozzi, Giovanni. *La Scuola Italica, Scoieta' Nazionale Filosofica, Medica, Letteraria Residente in Napoli*. Napoli: np, 1865.

Micali, Giuseppe. *L'Italia Avanti il Dominio dei Romani*. 2 vols. Florence: np, 1810.

Ministero per l'Industria, il Commercio ed il Lavoro, Ufficio Centrale di Statistica. *Statistica delle Elezioni Generali Politiche per la XXV Legislatura. (16 Novembre 1919)*. Roma: Stabilimento Poligrafico per l'Amministrazione della Guerra, 1920.

Ministero per l'Industria, il Commercio ed il Lavoro, Ufficio Centrale di Statistica. *Statistica delle Elezioni Generali Politiche per la XXVI Legislatura. (15 Maggio 1919)*. Roma: Stabilimento Poligrafico per l'Amministrazione della Guerra, 1920.

Ministero dell'Interno. *Compendio dei Risultati delle Elezioni Politiche dal 1848 al 1958*. Rome: Istituto Poligrafico dello Stato, 1963.

Mombert, Alfred. *Aeon: Dramatische Trilogie*. Berlin: Schuster & Loeffler, 1907-1911.

Montini, Giovanni Battista. "Una Nuova Rivista." *Studium* 26, no. 6 (1928), pp. 323-324.

Morselli, Enrico. *Psicologia e Spiritismo Impressioni e Note Critiche sui Fenomeni Medianici di Eusapia Palladino*. Turin: Bocca, 1908.

Mussolini, Benito. "Dalla Assoluta Neutralità alla Neutralità Attiva." *Avanti!* October 18, 1914, p. 3.

Mussolini, Benito. *Scritti e Discorsi*. Vol. 7. Milan: Hoepli, 1934.

N. R., Caesar Augustus. "NON CONFUNDITUR—Ovvero se debba avere fine la polemica sull'identità di N.R. Ottaviano con Leone Caetani." *Elixir* 2, pp. 27-90. Viareggio: Rebis, 2006.

Nathan, Ernesto. "Discorso Inaugurale a Palazzo Giustiniani." *Rivista Massonica* 5, no. 33 (1912), p. 287.
Nievo, Ippolito. *Le Confessioni di un Italiano*. Turin: Einaudi, (1867) 1964.
Nispi Landi, Ciro. *Le Storie d'Italia Narrate in Otto Grandi Eta' dalle piu' Lontane Origini a Noi*. Rome: Salviucci, 1879.
Nitti, Francesco. *La Disgregazione dell'Europa, Saggio su Alcune Verita' Impopolari*. 2nd ed. Rome: Faro, 1946.
La Nuova Crociata: Numero Unico 1 (1896), pp. 1–18
Pal, Bipin Chandra. *Memoirs of My Life and Times*. Vol. 1. Calcutta: np, 1932.
Palazzeschi, Aldo. *riflessi*. Florence: Cesare Blanc, 1908.
Palazzeschi, Aldo. *Il Codice Perelà*. Milan: Edizioni futuriste di Poesia, 1911.
Palazzeschi, Aldo. *Roma*. Florence: Vallecchi, 1954.
Palermo, Giangiacomo. *Inni e canti del Risorgimento*. Milan: Mondadori, 2012.
Pallis, Marco. *A Treasury of Traditional Wisdom: An Encyclopedia of Humankind's Spiritual Truth*. Louisville, KY: Fons Vitae, 2000.
Palumbi, Nicola. *Don Giovanni Minzoni. Educatore e Martire*. Milan: Nicola Palumbi, 2003.
Papini, Giovanni, and Giuseppe Prezzolini. "Programma Sintetico." *Leonardo* 1, no. 1(1903), p. 1.
Papini, Giovanni, and Giuseppe Prezzolini. "Offese a Giosué Carducci." *Leonardo* 1, no. 3 (1903), p. 8.
Papini, Giovanni, and Giuseppe Prezzolini. "Come sta di Salute il Positivismo." *Leonardo* 3, no. 1 (1905), p. 38.
Papini, Giovanni, and Giuseppe Prezzolini. "Gli Psicologi a Roma." *Leonardo* 3, no. 3 (1905), p. 123.
Papini, Giovanni, and Giuseppe Prezzolini. "Biblioteca Filosofica." *Leonardo* 4, no. 4 (1906), p. 170.
Papini, Giovanni, and Giuseppe Prezzolini. *Il Crepuscolo dei Filosofi*. Milan: Società Editrice Lombarda, 1906.
Papini, Giovanni, and Giuseppe Prezzolini. "La Fine." *Leonardo* 5, no. 2 (1907), p. 257.
Papini, Giovanni, and Giuseppe Prezzolini. *Un Uomo Finito*. Florence: Libreria della Voce, 1913.
Papini, Giovanni, and Giuseppe Prezzolini. *Passato Remoto (1885–1914)*. Florence: L'Arco, 1948.
Papini, Giovanni, and Giuseppe Prezzolini. *Carteggio I (1900–1907)*. Rome: Edizioni di Storia e Letteratura, 2003.
Papini, Giovanni, and Giuseppe Prezzolini. *Il Non Finito, Diario 1900 e Scritti Inediti Giovanili*. Edited by Anna Casini Paszkowski. Florence: Casa Editrice Le Lettere, 2005.
Parise, Giulio. "Nota sulla Vita dell'Autore." In Arturo Reghini, *Considerazioni sul Rituale dell'Apprendista Muratore, con una nota sulla vita e sull'Attività Massonica dell'Autore*, pp. i–xviii. Naples: Edizioni di Studi Iniziatici, 1946.
Pascal, Carlo. *L'incendio di Roma e i Primi Cristiani*. Turin: Loescher, 1900.
Pauwels, Louis, and Jacques Bergier. *Le Matin des Magiciens*. Paris: Gallimard, 1960.
Pellico, Silvio. *Le Mie Prigioni*. Florence: Adriano Salani Editore, 1832.
Petrarca, Francesco. "Italia Mia Perché 'l Parlar sia Indarno." In *Sonetti, Canzoni e Trionfi*. Edited by Giovannantonio de Nicolini da Sabio. Florence: Giovanniantonio de Nicolini da Sabio, 1541, p. 14.

Pierini, Pier Luca, ed. *Il Maestro Giuliano Kremmerz. L'Uomo - La Missione - L'Opera*. Rebis: Viareggio, 1985.

Pius X. "Motu Proprio Sacrorum Antistitum." *Acta Apostolicae Sedis*, vol. II (1910), n. 17, pp. 655–680.

Plato. "Timaeus." In Vol. IX of *Plato in Twelve Volumes*, translated by W. R. M. Lamb, pp. 1–255. Cambridge, MA: Harvard University Press, 1968.

Pound, Ezra. *L'America, Roosevelt e le Cause della Guerra Presente*. Venice: Casa Editrice delle Edizioni Popolari, 1944.

Pound, Ezra. *Oro et Lavoro: alla Memoria di Aurelio Baisi*. Rapallo: Moderna, 1944.

Pound, Ezra. *Lavoro ed Usura*. Milan: All'Insegna del Pesce d'Oro, 1954.

Praga, Cesare Emilio. *Tavolozze*. Milan: Casa Editrice Autori-Editori, 1862.

Praga, Cesare Emilio. *Penombre*. Milan: Casa Editrice Autori-Editori, 1864.

Prezzolini, Giuseppe. "Alle Sorgenti dello Spirito." *Leonardo* 1, no. 1 (1903), p. 4.

Prezzolini, Giuseppe. *Cos'è il Modernismo?* Milan: Fratelli Treves Editori, 1908.

Prezzolini, Giuseppe. "La Malattia del Kantismo." *Leonardo* 2, no. 3 (1904), p. 35.

Prezzolini, Giuseppe. *Benedetto Croce. Con Bibliografia, Ritratto e Autografo*. Naples: Riccardo Ricciardi Editore, 1909.

Prezzolini, Giuseppe. *Studi e Capricci sui Mistici Tedeschi. Saggio sulla Libertà Mistica – Meister Eckehart* [sic] *- La Deutsche Theologie - Paracelso - Novalis – Giovanni Von Hooghens*. Florence: Casa Editrice Italiana, 1912.

Pritchard, Samuel. *Masonry Dissected*. London: J. Wilford, 1730.

Profumo, Attilio. *Le Fonti e i Tempi dell'Incendio Neroniano*. Rome: Forzani, 1905.

Pythagoras. *Golden Verses*. Edited by Florence M. Firth. San Francisco: Theosophical Publishing House, 1904.

Ragon, Jean-Marie. *Cours Philosophic et Interpretatif des Initiations Anciennes et Modernes*. Paris: Berlandier, 1841.

Ragon, Jean-Marie. *Orthodoxie Maçonnique*. Paris: E. Dentu, 1853.

Ravenscroft, Trevor. *The Spear of Destiny*. New York: Bantam, 1974.

Ravioli, Camillo. *Spedizione Romana in Egitto*. Rome: Tipografia delle Belle Arti, 1870.

Rebold, Emmanuel. *Histoire des Trois Grandes Loges de Francs-Maçons*. Paris: Collignon, 1864.

Reghini, Arturo. "Giordano Bruno Smentisce Rastignac." *Leonardo* 4, no. 5 (1906), pp. 51–54.

Reghini, Arturo. Review of G. Giordano "La Pensée Ésotérique de Léonard de Vince." *Leonardo* 4, no. 4 (1906), pp. 382–384.

Reghini, Arturo. "Mors Osculi." *Leonardo* 4, no. 2 (1906), pp. 142–143.

Reghini, Arturo. "Istituzioni di Scienze Occulte." *Leonardo* 4, no. 2 (1906), pp. 155–160.

Reghini, Arturo. "La Massoneria come Fattore Individuale." *Leonardo* 4, no. 4 (1906), pp. 297–310.

Reghini, Arturo. "Il Punto di Vista dell'Occultismo." *Leonardo* 5, no. 2 (1907), pp. 144–156.

Reghini, Arturo. Review of W. Williamson, "The Great Law." *Leonardo* 5, no. 2 (1907), pp. 248–250.

Reghini, Arturo. "Il Dominio dell'Anima." In *Paganesimo, Pitagorismo e Massoneria*, edited by Gennaro d'Uva, pp. 1–12. Furnari: Societa' Editrice Mantinea, 1988.

Reghini, Arturo. "Il Dominio Dell'Anima." In *Paganesimo, Pitagorismo, Massoneria*, pp. 1–12. Furnari: Mantinea, 1986.

Reghini, Arturo. "La Vita dello Spirito." In *Paganesimo, Pitagorismo, Massoneria*, pp. 13–25. Furnari: Mantinea, 1986.

Reghini, Arturo. "Le basi spirituali della Massoneria." In *Paganesimo, Pitagorismo, Massoneria*, pp. 33–43. Furnari: Mantinea, 1986.
Reghini, Arturo. "Sull'Origine del Simbolismo Massonico." In *Paganesimo, Pitagorismo, Massoneria*, pp. 49–63. Furnari: Mantinea, 1986.
Reghini, Arturo. "Del Simbolismo e della Filologia in Rapporto alla Scienza Metafisica." In *Paganesimo, Pitagorismo, Massoneria*, pp. 117–150. Furnari: Mantinea, 1986.
Reghini, Arturo. "L'Intolleranza Cattolica e lo Stato." In *Paganesimo, Pitagorismo, Massoneria*, pp. 159–164. Furnari: Mantinea, 1986.
Reghini, Arturo. "La Tradizione Italica." *Ultra* 7, no. 2 (1914), pp. 68–70.
Reghini, Arturo. *Le Parole Sacre e di Passo e il Massimo Mistero Massonico*. Todi: Atanòr, 1922.
Reghini, Arturo. "Ai Lettori." *Atanor* 1, no. 1–2 (1924), pp. 1–2.
Reghini, Arturo. "Imperialismo Pagano." *Atanòr* 1, no. 3 (1924), pp. 69–85.
Reghini, Arturo. "Campidoglio e Golgota." *Atanor* 1, no. 5 (1924), p. 146.
Reghini, Arturo. "L'Impronta Pitagorica nella Massoneria." *Atanòr* 1 (1924), pp. 31–46.
Reghini, Arturo. "Morale e Peccato." *Atanòr* 1, no. 6 (1924), pp. 161–170.
Reghini, Arturo. "Ai Lettori." *Ignis* 1, no. 1–2 (1925), pp. 1–3.
Reghini, Arturo. "Brevi Note sul Cosmopolita e i suoi Scritti' *Ignis* 1, no. 3 (1925), pp. 82–88.
Reghini, Arturo. "Cagliostro in Documenti Inediti del Santo Uffizio." *Ignis* 1, no. 1–2 (1925), pp. 14–27.
Reghini, Arturo. "Una Pagina Ermetica e Cabalistica di Osvaldo Crollio." *Ignis* 1, no. 1–2 (1925), pp. 47–63.
Reghini, Arturo. "Associazioni Vecchie e Nuove." *Ignis* 1, no. 6–7 (1925), pp. 211–224.
Reghini, Arturo. "Eccessi di Parte Guelfa." *Ignis* 1, no. 10 (1925), pp. 318–320.
Reghini, Arturo. "Trascendenza di Spazio e di Tempo." *Mondo Occulto* 6, no. 6 (1926), pp. 69–107.
Reghini, Arturo. "Avventure e Disavventure in Magia." *Ur* 1, no. 10 (1927), pp. 388–395.
Reghini, Arturo. "Della Tradizione Occidentale: Prima Parte." *Ur* 2, no. 1 (1928), pp. 47–74.
Reghini, Arturo. *Per la Restituzione della Geometria Pitagorica*. Rome: IGNIS, 1935.
Reghini, Arturo. *Considerazioni sul Rituale dell'Apprendista Muratore, con una nota sulla vita e sull'Attività Massonica dell'Autore*. Naples: Edizioni di Studi Iniziatici, 1946.
Reghini, Arturo. *I Numeri Sacri nella Tradizione Pitagorica e Massonica*. Rome: Ignis, 1947.
Reghini, Arturo. *Il Simbolismo Duodecimale e il Fascio Etrusco*. Edited by Renato del Ponte. Genoa: Edizioni del Basilisco, 1980.
Reghini, Arturo. *Dei Numeri Pitagorici: Prologo*. Ancona: Associazione Culturale Ignis, 2003.
Reghini, Arturo. *Dei Numeri Pitagorici, Parte Prima - Volume Primo - Dell'equazione Indeterminata di Secondo Grado con Due Incognite*. Milan: Archè/Pizeta, 2006.
Reghini, Arturo. *Dei Numeri Pitagorici, Parte Prima - Volume Secondo - Delle Soluzioni Primitive dell'Equazione di Tipo Pell $x^2-Dy^2=B$ e del loro Numero*. Milan: Archè/Pizeta, 2012.
Reghini, Arturo. *Dei Numeri Pitagorici, Parte Seconda - Volume Terzo - Dei Numeri Triangolari, deiQuadrati e dei Numeri piramidali a Base Triangolare o Quadrata*. Milan: Archè/Pizeta, 2018.
Reghini, Arturo, Giuliano Balbino, and Guido Ferrante. *Per una Concezione Spirituale della Vita*. Firenze: Seeber, 1908.

Reghini, Ida Carlotta. "Isabel Cooper-Oakley." *Società Teosofica: Bollettino della Sezione Italiana* 14, no. 3 (1914), pp. 113–114.
Rey, Abel. *La Jeunesse de la Science Greque*. Paris: La Renaissance du Livre, 1933.
Ridolfi, Pierluigi, ed. *Poesie per un Italia Unita—1821-1861*. Preface by Carlo Azeglio Ciampi. Rome: Accademia dei Lincei, 2011.
Rocco, Alfredo. *Cos'è il Nazionalismo e Cosa Vogliono i Nazionalisti*. 3rd ed. Rome: Associazione Nazionalista, 1914.
Rosmini, Antonio. *Nuovo Saggio sull'Origine delle Idee*. Rome: Tipografia Salviucci, 1830.
Rosmini, Antonio. *Aristotele Esposto ed Esaminato*. Turin: Scoieta' Editrice di Libri di Filosofia, 1857.
Rosmini, Antonio. *Massime di Perfezione Cristiana*. Milan: Tip. Ed. L.F. Cogliati, 1883.
Rossi, Mario Manlio. *Lo Spaccio dei Maghi*. Rome: Doxa, 1929.
Rumon. "Note sulla Schola Italica di Amedeo R. Armentano." *Pietas* 3, no. 6 (2012), pp. 31–43.
Salvemini, Gaetano. *La politica estera dell'Italia (1871-1914)*. Turin: Barbera Editore, 1944.
Sani, Roberto. *Maestri e Istruzione Popolare in Italia tra Otto e Novecento*. Milan: Vita e Pensiero, 2003.
Seneca, Lucius Annaeus. *Epistles to Lucilius*. Translated by Richard Gummere. Cambridge, MA: Harvard University Press, 1917.
Sinnett, Alfred Percy. *Esoteric Buddhism*. London: np, 1883.
Smith, Huston. *The World's Religions: Our Great Wisdom Traditions*. New York: Harper & Brothers, 1958.
Spaventa, Bertrando. *Principii di Filosofia*. 2 vols. Naples: Stabilimento Tip. Ghio, 1867.
Spinetti, Gastone Silvano, and Elisabetta. *Sintesi della Dottrina Fascista*. Edited by Marco Piraino and Stefano Fiorito. Bologna: np, 2015.
Stefecius, Edoardo Carlo, and Giuseppe Poli. *Inno Antimassonico: Composto in Occasione del I Congresso Antimassonico Internazionale di Trento*. Rome: Unione Antimassonica Universale, 1897.
Steuco, Agostino. *De Perenni Philosophia*. New York: Johnson Reprint Corp., 1972.
Stevenson, Robert L. *Lo Strano Caso del Dottor Jekyll e del Signor Hyde*. Translated by Arturo Reghini. Rome: Voghera, 1923.
Tarchetti, Igino Ugo. *Racconti Fantastici*. Milan: Fratelli Treves, 1869.
Tarchetti, Igino Ugo. *Fosca*. Milan: Sonzogno, 1869.
Tavolato, Italo. *Contro la Morale Sessuale*. Firenze: Gonnelli, 1913.
Tavolato, Italo. "Elogio della prostituzione." In *Bestemmia contro la Democrazia*, edited by Anna K. Valerio, pp. 35–42. Padova: Edizioni di Ar, (1914) 2009.
Valli, Luigi. *L'Allegoria di Dante Secondo Pascoli*. Bologna: Zanichelli, 1922.
Valli, Luigi. *Il Linguggio Segreto di Dante e i Fedeli d'Amore*. Rome: Optima, 1928–30.
Valli, Luigi. *La Chiave della Divina Commedia*. Bologna: Zanichelli, 1929.
Vico, Gianbattista. *De Antiquissima Italorum Sapientia es Linguae Latinae Originibus Eruenda*. Translated by L. M. Palmer. Ithaca, NY: Cornell University Press, (1710) 1988.
Viterbensis, Annius. *Antiquitatum variarum volumina XVII a venerando et sacrae theologiae et praedicatorii ordinis professore Ioanni Annio*. Paris: Josse Bade er Jean Petit, 1512.
von Sebottendorf, Rudolf [Adam Glauer]. *Bevor Hitler kam: Urkundlich aus der Frühzeit der Nationalsozialistischen Bewegung*. Munich: Deukula-Grassinger, 1933.
Waterfield, Robin. *René Guénon and the Future of the West*. Hillsdale, NY: Sophia Perennis, (1987) 2002.

Yarker, John. *The Various Rites and Degrees of Free and Accepted Masonry*. London: J. Hogg, 1872.
Yarker, John. *Two Lectures on High Grade Masonry*. Liverpool: np, 1886.
Yarker, John. *The Arcane Schools*. Belfast: Carswell and Son, 1909.
Yarker, John. *The Ancient Constitutional Charges of the Guild Free Masons: To Which Is Added a Comparison with York Freemasonry*. Belfast: William Tait, 1909.
Yeats, William Butler. "Second Coming." In *The Collected Poems of W.B. Yeats*. Edited by Robert Mighall, p. 211. London: Macmillan, 1982.

Secondary Sources

Adamson, Walter. "Modernism and Fascism: The Politics of Culture in Italy, 1903–1922." *The American Historical Review* 95, no. 2 (1990), pp. 359–390.
Adamson, Walter. *Avant-Garde Florence: From Modernism to Fascism*. Cambridge, MA: Harvard University Press, 1993.
Adler, Eve. *Vergil's Epic: Political Thought in the Aeneid*. Oxford: Rowman & Littlefield, 2003.
Adilardi, Guglielmo. *Memorie di Giuseppe Mazzoni (1808–1880): L'uomo, il Politico, il Massone*. 2 vols. Pisa: Pacini, 2008–2016.
Adorno, Theodor, Else Frenkel Brunswik, Daniel Levinson, and Nevitt Sanford. *The Authoritarian Personality*. New York: Harper, 1950.
Adorno, Theodor, Else Frenkel Brunswik, Daniel Levinson, and Nevitt Sanford. "Theses Against Occultism." In *The Stars Down to Earth and Other Essays on the Irrational in Culture*, edited and introduction by Stephen Crook, pp. 172–180. London: Routledge, (1974) 1994.
Albanese, Giulia. *La Marcia su Roma*. Bari: Laterza, 2006.
Alexander, Jeffrey C. *The Dark Side of Modernity*. Malden, MA: Polity, 2013.
Almond, Gabriel A., R. Scott Appleby, and Emmanuel Sivan. *Strong Religion: The Rise of Fundamentalisms around the World*. Chicago: University of Chicago, 2003.
Alvarado, Carlos, Massimo Biondi, and Wim Kramer. "Historical Notes on Psychic Phenomena in Specialised Journals." *European Journal of Parapsychology* 21, no. 1 (2006), pp. 58–87.
Anand, Vidya Sagar. "L'India di Mazzini nel Risorgimento Italiano." In *Il Pensiero Mazziniano* 6 (1969), pp. 47–51.
Anderson, William. *Dante the Maker*. London: Routledge & Keagan Paul, 1980.
André, Marie-Sophie, and Christophe Beaufils. *Papus, Biographie: La Belle Époque de l'Occultisme*. Paris: Berg International, 1995.
Arfé, Gaetano. *Storia del Socialismo Italiano 1892–1926*. Turin: Einaudi, 1965.
Arnason, Johann P. "The Theory of Modernity and the Problematic of Democracy." *Thesis Eleven* 26 (1990), pp. 20–46.
Arnold, Bruce. "The Literary Experience of Vergil's Fourth "Eclogue." *The Classical Journal* 90, no. 2 (1997), pp. 143–160.
Ascheri, Mario. *Le Città-Stato*. Bologna: Il Mulino, 2006.
Asprem, Egil. *The Problem of Disenchantment: Scientific Naturalism and Esoteric Discourse, 1900–1939*. Leiden: Brill, 2015.
Asprem, Egil. "The Disenchantment of Problems: Musings on a Cognitive Turn in Intellectual History." *Journal of Religion in Europe* 8 (2015), pp. 304–319.

Bacci, Roberto. *La Trasmutazione della Coscienza nell'Esoterismo Italiano del Periodo Fascista: Spaccio dei Maghi (1929) di Mario Manlio Rossi e Maschera e Volto dello Spiritualismo Contemporaneo (1932) di Julius Evola*. Unpublished thesis. Providence, RI: Brown University, 2014.

Baffioni, Giovanni, and Paola Mattiangeli. *Annio da Viterbo: Documenti e Ricerche*. Rome: Multigrafica Editrice per il Consiglio nazionale delle ricerche, 1981.

Baghino, Cesco Giulio, and Enzo Marino. *L'Accademia d'Italia. Motore della Cultura*. Reggio Calabria: Iriti Editore, 2001.

Bailey, Frederick, and Enrico Medda. *Alpi Apuane, Guida al Territorio del Parco*. Pisa: Pacini, 1992.

Baldassari, G. *Unum in Locum. Strategie Macrotestuali nel Petrarca Politico*. Milan: LED Edizioni Universitarie, 2006.

Banfi, Antonio. "Verità e Umanità nella Filosofia Contemporanea." *Critica Filosofica* 8 (1947), pp. 83–198.

Banfield, Edward. *The Moral Basis of a Backward Society*. Glencoe, IL: Free Press, 1958.

Banti, Alberto Mario. *La Nazione del Risorgimento. Parentela, Santità ed Onore alle Origini dell'Italia Unita*. Turin: Einaudi, 2000.

Banti, Alberto Mario. *Immagini della Nazione nell'Italia del Risorgimento*. Edited by Roberto Bizzocchi. Roma: Carocci, 2002.

Banti, Alberto Mario, and Paul Ginsborg. "Per una Nuova Storia del Risorgimento." In *Storia d'Italia Gli Annali 22, Il Risorgimento*, edited by Alberto Mario Banti and Paul Ginsborg, pp. i–lxvi. Turin: Giulio Einaudi Editore, 2007.

Banti, Alberto Mario, and Paul Ginsborg. *Nel nome dell'Italia. Il Risorgimento nelle Testimonianze, nei Documenti e nelle Immagini*. Bari: Laterza, 2010.

Banti, Alberto Mario, and Paul Ginsborg. *Sublime Patria Nostra: la Nazione Italiana dal Risorgimento al Fascismo*. Bari: Giuseppe Laterza e Figli, 2011.

Barbagallo, Francesco. *Stato, Parlamento e le Lotte Politico-Sociali nel Mezzogiorno, 1900–1914*. Naples: Arte Tipografica, 1976.

Baroni, Francesco. *Benedetto Croce e l'Esoterismo*. Bologna: Il Mulino, 2011.

Barraco, Michele E. *Giustiniano Lebano e la Scuola di Napoli*. Nove: Libreria Editrice "Letture S. consigliate," 1999.

Beard, Mary, John North, and Simon Price. *Religions of Rome: A History*. 2 vols. Cambridge: Cambridge University Press, 1998.

Beckford, James. "The Disenchantment of Postmodernity." *New Blackfriars* 73, no. 913 (2007), pp. 121–128.

Bellavita, Emilio. *La Battaglia di Adua*. Rome: Gherardo Casini Editore, 2012.

Beneš, Elizabeth. "Mapping a Roman Legend: The House of Cola di Rienzo from Piranesi to Baedeker." *Italian Culture* 26 (2008), pp. 53–83.

Benvenuti, Sergio. "Il Congresso Antimassonico di Trento del 1896 e le Mistificazioni di Leo Taxil." *Bollettino del Museo del Risorgimento e della Lotta per la Libertà* 37 (1988), pp. 45–61.

Beraldo, Michele. "Le Riviste Spiritualistiche, Occultiste ed Esoteriche durante il Regime." In *Esoterismo e Fascismo*, edited by Gianfranco de Turris, pp. 383–387. Rome: Mediterranee, 2006.

Berman, Marshall. *All That Is Solid Melts into Air: The Experience of Modernity*. London: Verso, (1982) 2010.

Bertelli, Italo. *L'itinerario umano e poetico di Giovanni Berchet*. Ghezzano: Giardini, 2005.

Borgato, Maria Teresa, and Luigi Pepe. *Lagrange, Appunti per una Biografia Scientifica*. Turin: LaRosa, 1990.
Borsa, Giorgio, and P. Beonio Brocchieri, eds. *Garibaldi, Mazzini e il Risorgimento nel Risveglio dell'Asia e dell'Africa*. Milan: Franco Angeli, 1982.
Bucher, Rainer. *Hitler's Theology: A Study in Political Religion*. London: Continuum, 2011.
Biagi, Enzo, ed. *Storia del Fascismo*. 3 vols. Florence: Sadea-Della Volpe, 1964.
Bianchi, Angelo, ed. *L'istruzione in Italia tra Sette e Ottocento*. Brescia: La Scuola, 2007.
Biguzzi, Stefano. *Cesare Battisti*. Turin: UTET, 2008.
Biondi, Marino. "Hermet, Epica e Liturgia delle Riviste." In Augusto Hermet, *La Ventura delle Riviste (1903-1940)*, 2nd ed., pp. 8-27. Florence: Vallecchi, 1987.
Biondi, Massimo. *Tavoli e Medium: Storia dello Spiritismo in Italia*. Rome: Gremese Editore, 1988.
Bisogni, Beatrice. *Sette Enigmi di Storia Massonica*. Foggia: Bastogi, 1983.
Bisson, David. *René Guénon: Une Politique de l'Esprit*. Paris: Pierre-Guillaume de Roux, 2013.
Black, Monica, and Eric Kurlander, eds. *Reassessing Nazi Occultism: Histories, Realities, Legacies*. Rochester, NY: Camden House, 2015.
Bloch, Maurice. *Prey into Hunter*. Cambridge: Cambridge University Press, 1992.
Blum, Paul Richard. *Giordano Bruno*. Munich: Beck Verlag, 1999.
Blum, Paul Richard. *Giordano Bruno: An Introduction*. New York: Rodopi, 2012.
Bogdan, Henrik. *From Darkness to Light, Western Esoteric Rituals of Initiation*. Göteborg: Göteborgs Universitet, 2003.
Bonfiglioli, Giorgio. *Manzoni, la Vita e le Opere*. Milan: Genio, 1949.
Bonivecchio, Claudio. "La Polemica su Imperialismo Pagano." In Julius Evola, *Imperialismo Pagano*, pp. 297-332. Rome: Mediterranee, 2004.
Borofsky, Robert. *Making History: Pukapukan and Anthropological Construction of Knowledge*. Cambridge: Cambridge University Press, 1981.
Braddock, Richard. "An Extension of the 'Lasswell Formula.'" *Journal of Communication* 8 (1958), pp. 88-93.
Brandon, Ruth. *The Spiritualists: The Passion for the Occult in the Nineteenth and Twentieth Centuries*. New York: Alfred E. Knopf, 1983.
Brunelli, Francesco. *Rituali dei gradi simbolici di Memphis e Misraim*. Foggia: Bastogi, 1981.
Bryman, Alan. *Social Research Methods*. 2nd ed. New York: Oxford University Press, 2004.
Bulferetti, Luigi. *Antonio Rosmini nella Restaurazione*. Florence: Le Monnier, 1942.
Burgalassi, Marco. "Il Giovane Croce e il Positivismo." In Burgalassi, *Itinerari di una Scienza: La Sociologia in Italia tra Otto e Novecento*, pp. 174-182. Milan: Franco Angeli, 1996.
Buscalioni, Pietro. *La Loggia Ausonia ed il Primo Grande Oriente Italiano*. Cosenza: Brenner Editore, 2001.
Butler, Alison. "Making Magic Modern: Nineteenth-Century Adaptations." *The Pomegranate* 6, no. 2 (2004), pp. 212-230.
Butler, Alison. *Victorian Occultism and the Making of Modern Magic: Invoking Tradition*. New York: Palgrave Macmillan, 2011.
Cacace, Paolo. *Quando Mussolini Rischiò di Morire*. Rome: Fazi Editore: 2007.
Cairns, Francis. *Virgil's Augustan Epic*. Cambridge: Cambridge University Press, 1989.
Caltabellotta, Simone. *Un'Amore degli Anni Venti: Storia Erotica e Magica di Sibilla Aleramo e Giulio Parise*. Milan: Adriano Salani, 2015.

Campbell, Bruce F. *The Theosophical Movement*. Los Angeles: University of California Press, 1980.
Campi, Alessandro, ed. *Giornale di Guerra*. Soveria Mannelli: Rubbettino, 2015.
Campi, Bernardino. *Memorie Storiche della Città di Pontremoli*. Pontremoli: Artigianelli, 1975.
Cappelli, Guido. "Petrarca e l'Umanesimo Politico del Quattrocento." *Verbum* 7, no. 1 (2005), pp. 53–75.
Cardini, Franco, and Marina Montesano. *Storia Medievale*. Firenze: Le Monnier Università, 2006.
Carus, Paul. *Virgil's Prophecy on the Saviour's Birth: The Fourth Eclogue*. Chicago: Open Court, 1918.
Casey, John. *After Lives: A Guide to Heaven, Hell and Purgatory*. Oxford: Oxford University Press, 2009.
Casini, Paolo. *L'Antica Sapienza Italica*. Bologna: Il Mulino, 1998.
Casini, Paolo. *Alle Origini del Novecento, "Il Leonardo," 1903–1907*. Bologna: Il Mulino, 2002.
Castellani, Giuseppe. *Notizie Biografiche del P. Pietro Tacchi Venturi S.I.* Rome: Pontificiae Universitatis Gregorianae, 1958.
Catalan, Tullia. "Le Società Irredentiste e la Massoneria Italiana." In *Storia d'Italia Anni 21 La Massoneria*, edited by Gian Mario Cazzaniga, pp. 611–656. Turin: Einaudi, 2006.
Cazzaniga, Gian Mario. "Dante Profeta dell' Unità d'Italia." In *Storia d'Italia Annali 25 L'Esoterismo*, edited by Gian Mario Cazzaniga, pp. 455–476. Turin: Einaudi, 2010.
Cazzaniga, Gian Mario. "Ermetismo ed Egizianesimo a Napoli dai Lumi alla Fratellanza di Miriam." In *Annali d'Italia 25: Esoterismo*, pp. 547–566. Turin: Einaudi, 2010.
Cazzaniga, Gian Mario, and Marco Marinucci. *Per una Storia della Carboneria dopo l'Unita' d'Italia*. Rome: Gaffi, 2014.
Ceci, Luca. *L'Interesse Superiore: Il Vaticano e l'Italia di Mussolini*. Bari: Laterza & Figli, 2013.
Celenza, Christopher S. "Paul Oskar Kristeller and the Hermetic Tradition." In *Kristeller Reconsidered: Essays on His Life and Scholarship*, edited by John Monfasani, pp. 71–80. Ithaca, NY: Cornell University Press, 2006.
Cerreta, Adele, *Le Origini Esoteriche del Modernismo: Padre Gioacchino Ambrosini e la Teologia Modernista*. Chieti: Edizioni Solfanelli, 2012.
Champlin, Edward. "Nero Reconsidered." *New England Review* 19, no. 2 (1998), pp. 97–108.
Chapin, David. *Exploring Other Worlds: Margaret Fox, Elisha Kent Kane, and the Antebellum Culture of Curiosity*. Amherst: Massachusetts University Press, 2004.
Chiron, Yves. *Pio XI: Il Papa dei Patti Lateranensi e dell'Opposizione ai Totalitarismi*. Rome: San Paolo, 2006.
Christiansen, Rupert. "The Psychic Cloud: Yankee Spirit-Rappers." In *The Victorian Visitors: Culture Shock in Nineteenth Century Britain*, edited by R. Christiansen, pp. 130–158. New York: Grove/Atlantic, 2001.
Chua, Amy. *Day of Empire: How Hyperpowers Rise to Global Dominance and Why They Fall*. New York: Doubleday, 2007.
Cigliana, Simona. *Futurismo Esoterico, Contributi per una Storia dell'Irrazionalismo Italiano tra Otto e Novecento*. Naples: Liguori Editore, 2002.
Civra, Marco. *I Programmi della Scuola Elementare dall'Unità d'Italia al 2000*. Turin: Marco Valerio, 2002.

Clark, Martin. *Mussolini: Profiles in Power*. London: Pearson Longman, 2005.
Clark, Martin. *The Italian Risorgimento*. 2nd ed. New York: Routledge, 2013.
Collins, Amanda. *Greater Than Emperor: Cola di Rienzo (ca. 1313-54) and the World of Fourteenth Century Rome*. Ann Arbor: University of Michigan Press, 2002.
Colombo, Giorgio. *La Scienza Infelice. Il Museo di Antropologia Criminale di Cesare Lombroso*. Torino: Bollati Boringhieri, 2000.
Comba, Augusto. "La Massoneria in Italia dal Risorgimento alla Grande Guerra." In *La Massoneria nella Storia d'Italia*, edited by Aldo A. Mola, pp. 71-85. Rome: Atanòr, 1981.
Compagnon, Antoine. *Les Antimodernes. De Joseph de Maistre à Roland Barthes*. Paris: Gallimard, 2005.
Conte, Gian Biagio. *Latin Literature: A History*. Baltimore: John Hopkins, 1999.
Conti, Fulvio. *Storia della Massoneria italiana. Dal Risorgimento al Fascismo*. Bologna: Il Mulino, 2003.
Conti, Fulvio. "Massoneria e Sfera Pubblica." In *Storia d'Italia Annali 21 La Massoneria*, edited by Gian Mario Cazzaniga, pp. 579-610. Turin: Einaudi, 2006.
Contini, Gianfranco. "L'Influenza Culturale di Benedetto Croce." In Gianfranco Contini, *Altri Esercizi (1942-1971)*, pp. 31-70. Turin: Einaudi, 1972.
Cooper, Wesley. *The Unity of William James's Thought*. Nashville, TN: Vanderbilt Press, 2002.
Cordova, Ferdinando. *Massoneria e Politica in Italia: 1892-1908*. Bari: Laterza, 1985.
Cornwell, John. *Hitler's Pope: The Secret History of Pius XII*. London: Penguin, 2008.
Crowley, David. "Nationalist Modernisms." In *Modernism 1914-1939, Designing a New World*, edited by Christopher Wilk, pp. 371-373. London: V&A Publications, 2006.
Cummings, William L. "John Yaker: A Study." *Nocalore: Being the Transactions of the North Carolina Lodge of Research No 666*, A.F. & A.M 9 (1939), pp. 76-85.
d'Orsi, Angelo. *La rivoluzione antibolscevica*. Milan: Franco Angeli, 1985.
dal Pozzo, Ugo. *Giuseppe Gaudenzi e il Suo Secolo*. Forlì: P.R.I., 1972.
de Felice, Renzo. *d'Annunzio Politico (1918-1928)*. Bari: Laterza, 1978.
de Felice, Renzo.*Benito Mussolini: Il Fascista: la Conquista del Potere (1921-1925)*. Turin: Einaudi, 2002.
de Felice, Renzo. *Mussolini Il Rivoluzionario 1883-1920*. Turin: Einaudi, 2005.
de Franco, Luigi. *Bernardino Telesio. La Vita e l'Opera*. Cosenza: Edizioni Periferia, 1989.
de Giorgi, Fulvio. *Rosmini e il Suo Tempo. L'educazione dell'Uuomo Moderno tra Riforma della Filosofia e Rinnovamento della Chiesa (1797-1833)*. Brescia: Morcelliana, 2003.
de Hoyos, Arturo. "Masonic Rites and Systems." In *Handbook of Freemasonry*, edited by Henrik Bogdan and Jan Snoek, pp. 355-377. Leiden: Brill, 2014.
de Mattei, Roberto. "Modernismo e antimodernismo nell'epoca di Pio X." In *Don Orione Negli Anni del Modernismo*, edited by Nichele Busi, Roberto De Mattei, Antonio Lanza, and Flavio Peloso, pp. 29-86. Milan: Jaca Book, 2002.
de Turris, Gianfranco. "La Concezione Magica dell'Uomo e del Mondo." *Vie della Tradizione* 1, no. 2 (1971), pp. 59-70.
de Turris, Gianfranco. "Il Gruppo di Ur: Tra Magia e Superfascismo." *Abstracta* 2, no. 16 (1987), pp. 12-21.
de Turris, Gianfranco, ed. *Esoterismo e Fascismo: Storia, Interpretazioni, Documenti*. Rome: Mediterranee, 2006.
del Boca, Angelo. *Gli italiani in Africa orientale*. Vol. 1. Milan: Mondadori, 1992.
del Ponte, Renato. "Evola e l'Esperienza del 'Gruppo di Ur.'" *Arthos* 2-3, no. 4-5 (1973), pp. 177-191.

del Ponte, Renato. *La religione dei Romani*. Milan: Rusconi, 1982.
del Ponte, Renato. *Il Movimento Tradizionalista Romano nel 900*. Scandiano: SeaR, 1987.
del Ponte, Renato. "Un'Antica Famiglia Italiana- Una Nota sulla Stirpe dei Reghini." In Sandro Consolato, *La Cittadella La Sapienza Pitagorica*, pp. 177–183 24–26 (2006).
del Ponte, Renato. "E come Esoterismo." In *Il Maestro della Tradizione: Dialoghi su Julius Evola*, edited by Marco Iacona, pp. 81–92. Naples: Controcorrente, 2008.
del Ponte, Renato. "L'Iniziazione Pitagorica di Arturo Reghini in Apuania." *Arthos* 20 (2014), pp. 7–16.
della Peruta Franco. *Mazzini e i Rivoluzionari Italiani: il Partito d'Azione, 1830–1845*. Milan: Feltrinelli, 1974.
di Giovanni, Piero. *Filosofia e Psicologia nel Positivismo Italiano*. Bari: Laterza, 2006.
di Luca, Natale Mario. *Arturo Reghini: Un Intellettuale Neo-Pitagorico tra Massoneria e Fascismo*. Rome: Atanòr, 2003.
di Mauro, Antonio. *Il Problema Religioso nel Pensiero di Benedetto Croce*. Milan: Franco Angeli, 2001.
di Vona, Piero. *Evola, Guénon, De Giorgio*. Borzano: SeaR, 1993.
di Vona, Piero. *Giuliano Kremmerz*. Salerno: Edizioni di Ar, 2005.
Dalbrenta, Daniele Velo. *La Scienza Inquieta. Saggio sull'Antropologia Criminale di Cesare Lombroso*. Padova: CEDAM, 2004.
Delph, Ronald K. "Renovatio, Reformatio, and Humanist Ambition in Rome." In *Heresy, Culture and Religion in Early Modern Religion*, edited by Ronald K. Delph, Michelle M. Fontaine, and John Jeffries Martin, pp. 73–92. Kirksville, MO: Truman State University Press, 2006.
Desideri, Antonio. *Storia e Storiografia*, Vol .II. Messina-Florence: Edizioni D'Anna, 1997.
Deveney, Patrick. "Spiritualism." In *Dictionary of Gnosis and Western Esotericism*, edited by Wouter J. Hanegraaff, in collaboration with Antoine Faivre, Roelof van den Broek and Jean-Pierre Brach, pp. 1074–1082. Leiden: Brill, 2004.
Dossi, Michele. *Profilo filosofico di Antonio Rosmini*. Brescia: Morcelliana, 1998.
Dy-Lacco, G. S., and R. L. Piedmont. "A Content Analysis of Research in the Social Scientific Study of Religion from 1997 to 2001: Where We Have Been and Where We Hope to Go." *Research in the Social Study of Religion* 14 (2003), pp. 277–288.
Eco, Umberto. *Cinque Scritti Morali*. Milan: Bompiani, 1997.
Eco, Umberto. *Il Fascismo Eterno*. Milan: Bompiani, 1997.
Eisenstadt, S. N., ed. *The Origins and Diversity of the Axial-Age Civilizations*. Albany: State University of New York Press, 1986.
Eisenstadt, S. N., ed. "Multiple Modernities." *Daedalus* 129, no. 1 (2000), pp. 1–29.
Engelman, Ralph. *Dietrich Eckart and the Genesis of Nazism*. Ann Arbor: UMI Press, 1971.
Ernst, Germana. *Religione, Ragione e Natura: Ricerche su Tommaso Campanella e il Tardo Rinascimento*. Milan: Franco Angeli, 1991.
Ernst, Germana. *Tommaso Campanella: il Libro e il Corpo della Natura*. Bari: Laterza, 2002.
Faivre, Antoine. *L'Ésotérisme*. Paris: Presses Universitaires de France, 1992.
Faivre, Antoine. *Access to Western Esotericism*. Albany: SUNY Press, 1994.
Faivre, Antoine. "Questions of Terminology Proper to Study of Esoteric Currents in Modern and Contemporary Europe." In *Western Esotericism and the Science of Religion*, edited by Antoine Faivre and Wouter J. Hanegraaff, pp. 1–10. Louvain: Peeters, 1998.
Faivre, Antoine. "Histoire de la Notion Moderne de Tradition dans ses Rapports avec les Courants Ésotériques (XVe-XXe siècles)." In *Filiation et Emprunts, Aries Special Issue*, pp. 4–47. Milan: Archè/La Table d'Émeraude, 1999.

Faivre, Antoine. *Theosophy, Imagination, Tradition.* Albany: State University of New York Press, 2000.
Farmer, S. A., ed. and trans. *Syncretism in the West: Pico's 900 Theses (1486): The Evolution of Traditional Religious and Philosophical Systems.* Tempe, AZ: Medieval and Renaissance Texts and Studies, 1998.
Fedele, Santi. *La Massoneria Italiana nell'Esilio e nella Clandestinità.* Milan: Franco Angeli, 2005.
Feo, Michele. "Politicità del Petrarca." *Quaderni Petrarcheschi* IX–X (1992–1993), pp. 116–128.
Ferguson, Kitty. *Pythagoras, His Life and the Legacy of a Rational Universe.* London: Walker, 2008.
Ferrari, Ettore Passalalpi. *Ettore Ferrari: Tra le Muse e la Politica.* Città di Castello: Edimond, 2005.
Ferrarotto, Marinella. *L'Accademia d'Italia. Intellettuali e Potere Durante il Fascismo.* Naples: Liguori, 1977.
Festa, Francesco Saverio. "Teosofia ed Esoterismo nelle Riviste Italiane della Prima Metà del 900." In *Pioniere, Poeten, Professoren: Eranos und der Monte Verità in der Zivilisationgeschichte des 20 Jahrhunderts*, edited by Elisabetta Barone, Matthias Riedl, and Alexandra Tischel, pp. 143–154. Wurzburg: Konigshausen & Neumann, 2004.
Foti Mario. "La Riscoperta di Arturo Reghini negli Anni '80. Da "Il Ghibellino" alla Associazione Pitagorica." *La Cittadella* 6–7: 23-4-5 (2006), *la Sapienza Pitagorica*, pp. 230–240.
Frabotta, Maria Adelaide, and Guglielmo Salotti. *Propaganda ed Irredentismo nel Primo Novecento.* Florence: Leo S. Olschki, 1990.
Francovich, Carlo. *Storia della Massoneria in Italia. I Liberi Muratori Italiani dalle Origini alla Rivoluzione Francese.* Milan: Ghibli, 2013.
Franzinelli, Mimmo. *I Tentacoli dell'OVRA: Agenti, Collaboratori e Vittime della Polizia Politica Fascista.* Turin: Bollati Boringhieri, 1999.
Franzinelli, Mimmo. *Squadristi: Protagonisti e Tecniche della Violenza Fascista 1919–1922.* Milan: Mondadori, 2003.
Franzinelli, Mimmo, and Paolo Cavassini, *Fiume: l'Ultima Impresa di D'Annunzio.* Milan: Mondadori, 2009.
Frigessi, Delia, ed. *La Cultura Italiana del '900 Attraverso le Riviste, Volume Primo, "Leonardo," "Hermes," "Il Regno."* Turin: Einaudi, 1960.
Frigessi, Delia, ed. *Cesare Lombroso.* Turin: Einaudi, 2003.
Fubini, Riccardo. "Gli Storici nei Nascenti Stati Regionali d'Italia." In Fubini, *Storiografia dell'Umanesimo in Italia da Leonardo Bruni ad Annio da Viterbo*, pp. 3–38. Rome: Edizioni di Storia e Letteratura 2003.
Fucci, Fabio. *Le Polizie di Mussolini. La Repressione dell'Antifascismo nel "Ventennio."* Milan: Mursia, 2001.
Furness, Raymond. *Zarathustra's Children: a Lost Generation of German Writers.* Rochester, NY: Camden House, 2000.
Gaeta, Franco. *Il Nazionalismo Italiano.* Rome-Bari: Laterza, 1981.
Galasso, Giuseppe. *Croce e lo Spirito del Suo Tempo.* Milan: Il Saggiatore, 1990.
Galbreath, Robert. "Explaining Modern Occultism." In *The Occult in America: New Historical Perspectives*, edited by Howard Kerr and Charles L. Crow, pp. 11–37. Chicago: University of Illinois Press, 1983.

Galiano, Paolo. *Roma Prima di Roma: Metastoria della Tradizione Italica*. Rome: Simmetria Edizioni, 2011.
Galli, Giorgio. *La Politica e i Maghi*. Milan: Rizzoli, 1995.
Galli, Giorgio. *La magia e il potere. L'esoterismo nella politica occidentale*. Turin: Lindau, 2004.
Garin, Eugenio. *Intellettuali Italiani del XX Secolo*. Rome: Editori Riuniti, 1974.
Garin, Eugenio. *Cronache di Fliosofia Italiana, 1900/1943*. Rome-Bari: Editori Laterza, 1975.
Garin, Eugenio. "Divagazioni Ermetiche." *Rivista Critica di Storia della Filosofia* 31 (1979), pp. 462–466.
Garin, Eugenio. *Bertrando Spaventa*. Naples: Bibliopolis, 2007.
Gatteschi, Riccardo. *Un Uomo Contro: Enrico Corradini, Letterato e Politico*. Florence: Ellecidi, 2003.
Gatto Trocchi, Cecilia. *Il Risorgimento Esoterico, Storia Esoterica d'Italia da Mazzini ai Giorni Nostri*. Milano: Mondadori, 1996.
Gatto Trocchi, Cecilia. *Viaggio nella Magia: La Cultura Esoterica nell'Italia di Oggi*. Rome: Laterza, 1996.
Gatto Trocchi, Cecilia. *Storia Esoterica d'Italia*. Milano: Piemme, 2001.
Gaudio, Angelo. "Legislazione e Organizzazione della Scuola, Lotta Contro l'Analfabetismo." In *Storia d'Italia nel Secolo Ventesimo: Strumenti e Fonti— Vol. I: Elementi Strutturali*, edited by Ministero per i Beni e le Attività Culturali, Dipartimento per i Beni Archivistici e Librari, pp. 355–373. Rome: Ministero per i Beni e le Attività culturali, Dipartimento per i Beni Archivistici e Librari, 2006.
Gauld, Alan. *A History of Hypnotism*. Cambridge: Cambridge University Press, 1995.
Gentile, Emilio. "The Myth of National Regeneration in Italy: From Modernist Avant-garde to Fascism." In *Fascist Visions*, edited by Matthew Affron and Mark Antliff, pp. 25–45. Princeton, NJ: Princeton University Press, 1997.
Gentile, Emilio, and Spencer di Scala. *Mussolini Socialista*. Bari: Laterza, 2015.
Gentile, Luigi. *Coscienza Nazionale e Pensiero Europeo in Bertrando Spaventa*. Chieti: Ed. NOUBS, 2000.
Gerini, Emanuele. *Illustri Scrittori e Uomini Insigni della Lunigiana*. Bologna: Forni, 1986.
Germain, Gilbert G. *A Discourse on Disenchantment: Reflections on Politics and Technology*. Albany: SUNY Press, 1993.
Giannelli, Giorgio. *Uomini sulle Apuane*. Forte dei Marmi: Galleria Pegaso Editore, 1999.
Giannetti, Ottaviano. *Memorie Francescane della Lunigiana e della Lucchesia*. Florence: Pagnini, 2012.
Giannini, Amedeo. "Padre Tacchi in funzione diplomatica." *Doctor Communis* 9 (1956), pp. 227–236.
Giddens, Anthony. *Modernity and Self-Identity: Self and Society in the Late Modern Age*. Cambridge: Polity Press, 1991.
Giglioni, Guido. "The First of the Moderns or the Last of the Ancients? B.T. on Nature and Sentience." *Bruniana e Campanelliana* 16, no. 1 (2010), pp. 69–87.
Giorgio, Fabrizio. *Roma Renovata Resurgat*. 2 vols. Rome: Settimo Sigillo, 2011.
Giovetti, Paola. "La Società Teosofica nel Mondo." In Giovetti, *Helena Petrovna Blavatsky e la Società Teosofica*, pp. 160–166. Rome: Edizioni Mediterranee, 2010.
Girardi, Antonio. *La Società Teosofica: Storia, Valori, Realtà Attuale*. Vicenza: Edizioni Teosofiche Italiane, 2014.

Giudice, Christian. "Rome Was Rebuilt in a Play: Roggero Musmeci Ferrari Bravo and the Representation of *Rumon*." *Pomegranate: Journal for Pagan Studies* 14, no. 2 (2012), pp. 212–232.

Godwin, Joscelyn. "The Parting of East and West." In Godwin, *The Theosophical Enlightenment*, pp. 363–379. Albany: SUNY Press, 1994.

Godwin, Joscelyn. *The Golden Thread: The Ageless Wisdom of the Western Mystery Traditions*. Wheaton, IL: Quest Books, 2007.

Goisis, Giuseppe. *Il Pensiero Politico di Antonio Rosmini e Altri Saggi fra Critica ed Evangelo*. S. Pietro in Cariano: Gabrielli Editori, 2009.

Golia, Antonella. *Cappella Sansevero, Il Tempio della Virtù e dell'Arte*. Naples: Akroamatikos, 2009.

Goodrick-Clarke, Nicholas. "The Modern Mythology of Nazi Occultism." In Goodrick-Clarke, *The Occult Roots of Nazism: Aryan Cults and their Influence on Nazi Ideology*, pp. 217–226. Albany: SUNY Press, 2004.

Gottlieb, Gunther. "Religion in the Politics of Augustus: Aeneid 1.278-291, 8.714-23, 12.791.842." In *Vergil's Aeneid: Augustan Epic and Political Context*, edited by Hans-Peter Stahl, pp. 21–36. London: Duckworth, 1998.

Gray-Fow, Michael. "Why the Christians? Nero and the Great Fire." *Latomus* 57, no. 3 (1998), pp. 595–616.

Greeley, Andrew M. "Implications for the Sociology of Reason of Occult Behaviour in the Youth Culture." In *On the Margin of the Visible: Sociology, the Esoteric and the Occult*, edited by Edward A. Tiryakian, pp. 295–302. New York: Wiley, 1974.

Griffin, Roger. *Modernism and Fascism: The Sense of a New Beginning under Hitler and Mussolini*. Basingstoke: Palgrave Macmillan, 2007.

Griffin, Roger. "Modernity, Modernism, and Fascism. A Mazeway Resynthesis." *Modernism/Modernity* 15, no. 1 (2008), pp. 9–24.

Grippo, Antonietta. *L'Avanguardia Esoterica*. Potenza: Literalia, 1997.

Gualano, Antonio. *Il Congresso Antimassonico Internazionale di Trento: L'Ultima Crociata*. Trapani: np, 2010.

Guasco, Maurilio. *Modernismo*. Rome: Edizioni Paoline, 1995.

Guerra, Augusto. *Il Mondo Della Sicurezza: Ardigò, Labriola, Croce*. Florence: Sansoni, 1963.

Guerri, Giordano Bruno. *Fascisti*. Milan: Mondadori, 1995.

Hakl, Hans Thomas. "Nazionalsocialismo ed Occultismo." *Arthos* 1, no. 1 (1997), pp. 16–27.

Hakl, Hans Thomas. "Nazionalsocialismo ed Occultismo." *Arthos* 1, no. 2 (1997), pp. 57–75.

Hakl, Hans Thomas. "Julius Evola and the UR Group." *Aries* 12, no. 1 (2012), pp. 53–90.

Hakl, Hans Thomas. "The Theory and Practice of Sexual Magic, Exemplified by Four Magical Groups in the Early Twentieth Century." In *Hidden Intercourse: Eros and Sexuality in the History of Western Esotericism*, edited by Wouter J. Hanegraaff and Jeffrey J. Kripal, pp. 445–478. Leiden: Brill, 2008.

Hakl, Hans Thomas. *Eranos, an Alternative Intellectual History of the Twentieth Century*. Durham, NC: Acumen Press, 2013.

Hale, Christopher. *Himmler's Crusade: The Nazi Expedition to Find the Origins of the Aryan Race*. Hoboken, NJ: John Wiley & Sons, 2003.

Haller Jr., John S. *Swedenborg, Mesmer, and the Mind/Body Connection: The Roots of Complementary Medicine*. West Chester, PA: Swedenborg Foundation, 2010.

Hammer, Olav. *Claiming Knowledge: Strategies of Epistemology from Theosophy to the New Age*. Leiden: Brill, 2001.

Hammer, Olav, and Mikael Rothstein, eds. *The Handbook of the Theosophical Current*. Leiden: Brill, 2013.

Hamill, John. "John Yarker, Masonic Charlatan?" *Ars Quatuor Coronatum* 109 (1996), pp. 191–214.

Hanegraaff, Wouter J. "Empirical Method in the Study of Esotericism." *Method & Theory in the Study of Religion* 7, no. 2 (1995), pp. 99–129.

Hanegraaff, Wouter J. *New Age Religion and Western Culture: Esotericism in the Mirror of Secular Thought*. Albany: SUNY Press, 1998.

Hanegraaff, Wouter J. "Beyond the Yates Paradigm: The Study of Western Esotericism between Counterculture and new Complexity." *Aries* 1, no. 1 (2001), pp. 5–37.

Hanegraaff, Wouter J. "How Magic Survived the Disenchantment of the World." *Religion* 33 (2003), pp. 357–380.

Hanegraaff, Wouter J. "The Study of Western Esotericism: New Approaches to Christian and Secular Culture." In *New Approaches to the Study of Religion (Regional, Critical, Historical)*, Vol. 1, edited by Peter Antes, Armin W. Geertz, and Randi R. Warne, pp. 489–519. Berlin: De Gruyter, 2004.

Hanegraaff, Wouter J. "The Birth of Esotericism from the Spirit of Protestantism." *Aries* 10, no. 2 (2010), pp. 197–216.

Hanegraaff, Wouter J. *Esotericism and the Academy: Rejected Knowledge in Western Culture*. Cambridge: Cambridge University Press, 2012.

Hanegraaff, Wouter J. "Textbooks and Introductions to Western Esotericism." *Religion* 43, no. 2 (2012), pp. 1–23.

Hanegraaff, Wouter J. *Western Esotericism: A Guide for the Perplexed*. London: Bloomsbury, 2013.

Hardie, Philip. *Virgil's 'Aeneid': Cosmos and Imperium*. Oxford: Clarendon Press, 1989.

Hartley, John. *The Politics of Pictures: The Creation of the Public in the Age of Popular Media*. London: Routledge, 1992.

Harvey, David Allen. *The Condition of Postmodernity*. Oxford: Blackwell, 1989.

Harvey, David Allen. *Beyond Enlightenment: Occultism and Politics in Modern France*. DeKalb: Northern Illinois University Press, 2005.

Hatina, Meir. "Where East Meets West: Sufism as a Lever for Cultural Rapprochement." *International Journal of Middle East Studies* 39 (2007), pp. 389–409.

Hauschild, Thomas. "Making History in Southern Italy." In *Other Histories*, edited by K. Hastrup, pp. 29–44. London: Routledge, 1992.

Headley, John M. *Tommaso Campanella and the Transformation of the World*. Princeton, NJ: Princeton University Press, 1997.

Herf, Jeffrey. *Reactionary Modernism: Technology, Culture and Politics in Weimar and the Third Reich*. Cambridge: Cambridge University Press, (1984) 1998.

Hervieu, Fabrice. *Le Palladisme: Culte de Satan-Lucifer Dans les Triangles Maçonniques*. Grenoble: H. Falque, 1895.

Hervieu, Fabrice. *Le Culte de la Nature dans la Franc-Maçonnerie Universelle*. Grenoble: H. Falque, 1896.

Hobsbawm, Eric, and Terence Ranger, eds. *The Invention of Tradition*. Cambridge: Cambridge University Press, 1992.

Hölkeskamp, Karl-J. *Reconstructing the Roman Republic: An Ancient Political Culture and Modern Research*. Princeton, NJ: Princeton University Press, 2010.

Hollander, Robert. *Allegory in Dante's Commedia*. Princeton, NJ: Princeton University Press, 1969.
Holt, Edgar. *The Making of Italy 1815–1870*. New York: Atheneum, 1971.
Howe, Ellic. "Fringe Masonry in England: 1870–85." *Ars Quatuor Coronatorum* 85 (1972), pp. 242–280.
Huntington, Samuel P. *The Clash of Civilization and the Remaking of World Order*. New York: Simon and Schuster, 1996.
Iacovella, Angelo. "Julius Evola e Arturo Reghini: un Sodalizio "Occulto"." In *Esoterismo e Fascismo*, pp. 155–161. Rome: Edizioni Mediterranee, 2006.
Idinopulos, Thomas A., and Edward A. Yonan. *Religion and Reductionism: Essays on Eliade, Segal, and the Challenge of the Social Sciences in the Study of Religion*. Leiden: Brill, 1994.
Ingravalle, Francesco, ed. *La Carboneria. La Costituzione del Regno delle Due Sicilie*. Salerno: Edizioni di Ar, 2011.
Inkeles, Alex, and David H. Smith. *Becoming Modern: Individual Change in Six Developing Countries*. Cambridge, MA: Harvard University Press, 1974.
Introvigne, Massimo. "De l'Hypertrophie de la Filiation: le Milieu Kremmerzien en Italie." In *ARIES—Association pour la Recherche et l'Information sur l'Ésotérisme, Symboles et Mythes dans les Mouvements Initiatiques et Ésotériques (XVII et XXe siècles): Filiations et emprunts*. Edited by Antoine Faivre, Pierre Deghaye and Roland Edighoffer, pp. 148–156. Paris: Archè–La Table d'Émeraude, 1999.
Isastia, Anna Maria, ed. *Il Progetto Liberal-Democratico di Ettore Ferrari: un Percorso tra Politica e Arte*. Milan: Franco Angeli, 1997.
James, Marie-France. *Ésotérisme, Occultisme, Franc-Maçonnerie et Christianisme aux XIXe et XXe Siècles, Explorations Bio-Bibliographiques*. Paris: Lanore, 2008.
Jesi, Furio. *Cultura di Destra. Con Tre Inediti e un'Intervista*. Edited by Andrea Cavalletti. Rome: Nottetempo, (1993) 2011.
Joost-Gaugier, Christiane L. *Measuring Heaven, Pythagoras and his Influence on Thought and Art in Antiquity and the Middle Ages*. Ithaca, NY: Cornell University Press, 2006.
Kaczynski, Richard. *Perdurabo: The Life of Aleister Crowley*. 2nd ed. Berkeley, CA: North Atlantic Books, 2010.
Kaczynski, Richard. "John Yarker: Masonic Archaeologist." In Kaczynski, *Forgotten Templars: The Untold Origins of Ordo Templi Orientis*, pp. 163–184. Baltimore: np, 2012.
Kaya, Ibrahim. "Modernity, Openness, Interpretation: A Perspective of Multiple Modernities." *Social Science Information* 43, no. 1 (2004), pp. 35–57.
Keller, Thomas. "World Experience and Foreign Experience: The Mythology in Theodor Daubler." In *Mysticism and Modernity in Germany around 1900*, edited by Moritz Bassler and Hildegard Chatellier, pp. 255–278. Strasbourg: Presses Universitaires, 1998.
Kenney, E. J. *The Age of Augustus*. Cambridge: Cambridge University Press, 1982.
Keresztes, Paul. "Nero, the Christians and the Jews in Tacitus and Clement of Rome." *Latomus* 43, no. 2 (1984), pp. 404–413.
Kermode, Frank. *The Sense of an Ending: Studies in the Theory of Fiction*. Oxford: Oxford University Press, 1967.
Kertzer, David I. *The Pope and Mussolini: The Secret History of Pius XI and the Rise of Fascism in Europe*. Oxford: Oxford University Press, 2014.
King, Peter. *The Antimodern Condition: An Argument Against Progess*. London: Ashgate, 2014.
Kolakowski, Leszek. "Modernity on Endless Trial." *Encounter* 66 (1986), pp. 8–12.

Krippendorf, Klaus H. *Content Analysis: An Introduction to Its Methodology.* London: Sage Books, 2004.
Krippendorf, Klaus H. "Reliability in Content Analysis: Some Common Misconceptions and Reccomendations." *Human Communication Reasearch* 30, no. 3 (2004), pp. 411–433.
Kristeller, Paul Oskar. *Supplementum Ficinianum: Marsilii Ficini Florentini Philosophi Platonici Opuscula Inedita et Dispersa Primum Collegit et ex Fontibus Plerumque Manuscriptis Edidit.* 2 vols. Florence: Olschki, 1937.
Kristeller, Paul Oskar. "Marsilio Ficino e Lodovico Lazzarelli: Contributo alla Diffusione delle Idee Ermetiche nel Rinascimento." *Annali della R. Scuola Normale Superiore di Pas, Lettere, Storia e Filosofia* 2 (1938), pp. 237–262.
Landucci, Giovanni. "Note sulla Formazione del Pensiero di Roberto Ardigò." *Giornale Critico della Filosofia Italiana* 53 (1974), pp. 16–60.
Landucci, Sergio. *Cultura e Ideologia in Francesco De Sanctis.* Milan: Feltrinelli, 1964.
Langella, Giuseppe. *Manzoni e Altra Letteratura del Risorgimento.* Novara: Interlinea, 2005.
Lapi, Marco, and Florenzo Ramacciotti. *Apuane Segrete.* Il Labirinto: np, 1995.
Laqueur, Thomas. "Why Margins Matter: Occultism and the Making of Modernity." *Modern Intellectual History* 3, no. 1 (2006), pp. 111–135.
Lasswell, Harold D. *The Structure and Function of Communication in Society. The Communication of Ideas.* New York: Institute for Religious and Social Studies, 1948.
Lasswell, Harold D. *Power and Personality.* New York: W. W. Norton & Company, 1949.
Latour, Bruno. *Nous n'Avons Jamais Été Modernes: Essai d'Anthropologie Symétrique.* Cambridge, MA: Harvard University Press, (1991) 1993.
Laurant, Jean-Pierre. *Guénon.* Paris: Éditions de l'Herne, 1985.
Laurant, Jean-Pierre. *René Guénon, Les Enjeux d'une Lecture.* Paris: Dervy, 2006.
Lawrence, Bruce B. *Defenders of God.* New York: Harper & Row, 1989.
Lebovic, Nitzan. *The Philosophy of Life and Death: Ludwig Klages and the Rise of a Nazi Biopolitics.* London: Palgrave Macmillan, 2013.
Lee, Raymond L. M. "Reinventing Modernity: Reflexive Modernity vs Liquid Modernity vs Multiple Modernities." *European Journal of Social Theory* 9, no. 3 (2006), pp. 355–368.
Lehman, Amy. *Victorian Women and the Theatre of Trance: Mediums, Spiritualists and Mesmerists in Performance.* Jefferson, NC: McFarland, 2009.
Lewis, James R., and Olav Hammer, eds. *The Invention of Sacred Tradition.* Cambridge: Cambridge University Press, 2007.
Lincoln, Bruce. *Authority: Construction and Corrosion.* Chicago: University Press of Chicago, 1994.
Lombardi, Giovanna. *Filoteo Alberini, L'Inventore del Cinema.* Rome: Arduino Sacco, 2008.
Lott, John B. *The Neighborhoods of Augustan Rome.* Cambridge: Cambridge University Press, 2004.
Mandolfo, Santo. *I Positivisti Italiani (Angiulli-Gabelli-Ardigò).* Padua: CEDAM 1966.
Mansfield Jr., Harvey. "Machiavelli's Political Science." *The American Political Science Review* 75, no. 2 (1981), pp. 293–305.
Mariani, Mauro, ed. *I fratelli Giuseppe e Quinto Gaudenzi e Pievequinta.* Forlì: Associazione Amici della Pieve, 2000.
Marsella, Mauro. "Enrico Corradini's Italian Nationalism: The 'Right Wing' of the Fascist Synthesis." *Journal of Political Ideologies* 9, no. 2 (2004), pp. 203–224.
Martellini Giorgio, and Maria Teresa Pichetto. *Massimo d'Azeglio.* Milan: Camunia, 1990.

Marty, Martin E., and R. Scott Appleby. *The Glory and the Power: The Fundamentalist Challenge to the Modern World*. Boston: Beacon Press, 1992.

Marty, Martin E., and R. Scott Appleby, eds. *Fundamentalism Observed*. Chicago: University of Chicago Press, 1994.

McIntosh, Christopher. *Eliphas Lévi and the French Occult Revival*. 2nd ed. Albany: SUNY Press, (1972) 2011.

McKee, Alex. *Textual Analysis*. London: Sage, 2009.

Mehéust, Bertrand. *Somnambulisme et Médiumnité*. Paris: Les Empêcheurs de Penser en Rond, 1999.

Meldolesi, Luca. *Carlo Cattaneo e lo Spirito Italiano*. Soveria Mannelli: Rubbettino, 2013.

Meucci, Renato. "Roman Military Instruments and the Lituus." *The Galpin Society Journal* 42 (1989), pp. 85–97.

Meyer, T. H., and Elisabeth Vreede. *The Bodhisattva Question: Krishnamurti, Steiner, Tomberg and the Mystery of the Twentieth Century Master*. Forest Row: Temple Lodge, 2006.

Michelotti, Nicola, ed. *Genealogie di Famiglie Pontremolesi*. Pontremoli: np, 1993.

Michelotti, Nicola, ed. *Almanacco Pontremolese 2011*. Pontremoli: Artigianelli, 2011.

Milani, Giuliano. *I Comuni Italiani: Secoli XII–XIV*. Bari: Laterza, 2015.

Mineo, Nicolò. *Profetismo e Apocalittica in Dante*. Catania: Facoltà Lettere e Filosofia, 1968.

Mola, Aldo A. *Storia della Massoneria Italiana Dalle Origini ai Giorni Nostri*. Milano: Bompiani, 1992.

Mola, Aldo A. *Fratelli d'Italia. Memoria del Rapporto tra Massoneria e Risorgimento nel 150 Anniversario dell'Unità d'Italia*. Foggia: Bastogi, 2011.

Monroe, John Wayne. "The Way We Believe Now: Modernity and the Occult." *Magic, Ritual and Witchcraft* 2, no. 1 (2007), pp. 68–78.

Montaldo, Silvano, ed. *Cesare Lombroso. Gli scienziati e la nuova Italia*. Bologna: Il Mulino, 2011.

Montanelli, Indro, and Mario Cervi. *L'Italia del Risorgimento, 1831–1861*. Milan: Rizzoli, 1994.

Montanelli, Indro, and Mario Cervi. *Storia d'Italia 1861–1919*, vol. 6. Milan: RCS, 2006.

Montanelli, Indro, Mario Cervi, and Marco Nozza. *Giuseppe Garibaldi*. Turin: BUR, 2007.

Montesano, Domenico Vittorio Ripa. *Raimondo di Sangro Principe di San Severo Primo Gran Maestro del Rito Egizio Tradizionale*. Naples: np, 2011.

Moramarco, Michele. *Piazza del Gesu." Documenti Rari e Inediti della Tradizione Massonica Italiana*. Reggio Emilia: CE.S.A.S., 1992.

Moraru, Cornel-Florin. "Art and Mathematics in Matila Ghyka's Philosophical Aesthetics: A Pythagorean Approach on Contemporary Aesthetics." *Hermeneia* 20 (2018), pp. 42–58.

Moreman, Christopher M. *The Spiritualist Movement: Speaking with the Dead in America and Around the World*. Westport, CT: Praeger 2013.

Mori, Marco. "Il Gruppo di 'Ur.'" *Yghieia* 3, no. 1–4 (1986), pp. 6–7.

Mosse, George. "The Mystical Roots of National Socialism." *Journal of the History of Ideas* 22, no. 1 (1961), pp. 81–96.

Mustè, Marcello. *La Scienza Ideale. Filosofia e Politica in Vincenzo Gioberti*. Soveria Mannelli: Rubbettino, 2000.

Mustè, Marcello. *La Filosofia dell'Idealismo Italiano*. Rome: Carrocci, 2008.

Musso, Ronald. *Apocalypse in Rome*. Berkeley: University of California Press, 2003.

Musumeci, Emilia. *Cesare Lombroso e le Neuroscienze: un Parricidio Mancato. Devianza, Libero Arbitrio, Imputabilità tra Antiche Chimere ed Inediti Scenari.* Milano: Franco Angeli, 2012.

Myers, Gerald E. *William James: His Life and Thought.* New Haven, CT: Yale University Press, 1986.

Nadel, Ira B., ed. *The Cambridge Companion to Ezra Pound.* Cambridge: Cambridge University Press, 1985.

Nardi, Bruno. "Il Concetto dell'Impero nello Svolgimento del Pensiero Dantesco." *Giornale Storico* LXXVIII (1921), pp. 1–52

Nappi, Edoardo. *La Famiglia, il Palazzo, la Cappella dei Principi di Sansevero.* Geneva: Droz, 1975.

Natale, Simone. *Supernatural Entertainments: Victorian Spiritualism and the Rise of Modern Media Culture.* University Park: Pennsylvania State University Press, 2016.

Nello, Paolo. "La Vocazione Totalitaria del Fascismo e l'Equivoco del Filofascismo Liberale e Democratico. Il caso di Pisa (1919–1925)." *Storia Contemporanea* 20, no. 4 (1989), pp. 656–663.

Nicolini, Fausto. *Benedetto Croce.* Turin: UTET, 1962.

O'Connell, Marvin. *Critics on Trial: An Introduction to the Catholic Modernist Crisis.* Washington, DC: Catholic University of America Press, 1994.

O'Meara, Dominic J. *Pythagoras Revived.* Oxford: Oxford University Press, 1989.

Occhini, Pier Ludovico. *Corradini.* Florence: Rinascimento del Libro, 1933.

Oldmeadow, Kenneth. *Traditionalism: Religion in the Light of Perennial Philosophy.* 2nd ed. San Rafael, CA: Sophia Perennis, (2000) 2011.

Oldrini, Guido. *Il Primo Hegelismo Italiano.* Florence: Vallecchi, 1969.

Oppenheimer, Paul. *Machiavelli: A Life beyond Ideology.* New York: Continuum, 2011.

Owen, Alex. *The Disenchantment of the West: British Occultism and the Culture of the Modern.* Chicago: University Press of Chicago, 2004.

Owen, Alex. *The Darkened Room: Women, Power and Spiritualism in Late Victorian England.* 2nd ed. Chicago: University of Chicago Press, 2004.

Pagano, Tullio. "From Diaspora to Empire: Enrico Corradini's Nationalist Novels." *Modern Language Notes* 119, no. 1. (2004), pp. 67–83.

Papadia, Elena. *Nel Nome della Nazione. L'Associazione Nazionalista Italiana in Età Giolittiana.* Roma: Archivio Guido Izzi, 2006.

Parsons, Talcott. "Democracy and Social Structure in Pre-Nazi Germany." In Talcott Parsons editor, *Essays in Sociological Theory*, pp. 104–123. New York: Free Press, 1964.

Pasi, Marco. "The Modernity of Occultism: Reflections on Some Crucial Aspects." In *Hermes in the Academy: Ten Years' Study of Western Esotericism at the University of Amsterdam*, edited by Wouter J. Hanegraaff and Joyce Pijnenburg, pp. 59–74. Leiden: Brill, 1999.

Pasi, Marco. "Occultism." In *The Brill Dictionary of Religion*, edited by Kocku Von Stuckrad and translated by Robert R. Barr, Vol. III, p. 1366. Leiden: Brill, 2006.

Pasi, Marco. "Il Problema della Definizione dell'Esoterismo: Analisi Critica e Proposte per la Ricerca Futura." In *Forme e Correnti dell'Esoterismo Occidentale*, edited by Alessandro Grossato, pp. 205–228. Milan: Medusa, 2008.

Pasi, Marco. "Theosophy and Anthroposophy in Italy during the First Half of the Twentieth Century." *Theosophical History, a Quarterly Journal of Research* 16, no. 2 (2012), pp. 81–119.

Pavloet, Jan. "The Definers Defined: Traditions in the Definition of Religion." *Method and Theory in the Study of Religion* 2 (1990), pp. 180–212.
Pellicciari, Angela. *Risorgimento Anticattolico: la Persecuzione della Chiesa nelle Memorie di Giacomo Margotti*. Casale Monferrato: Piemme, 2004.
Pellicciari, Angela. *L'Altro Risorgimento, Una Guerra di Religione Dimenticata*. Milan: Ares, 2011.
Perfetti, Francesco. *Il Nazionalismo Italiano dalle Origini alla Fusione col Fascismo*. Bologna: Cappelli, 1977.
Perfetti, Francesco. "La Dottrina Politica del Nazionalismo Italiano: Origini e Sviluppo Fino al Primo Conflitto Mondiale." In *Il nazionalismo in Italia e in Germania fino alla Prima Guerra Mondiale*, edited by Rudolfo Lill, pp. 23–45. Bologna: Il Mulino, 1983.
Pertici, Roberto. *Chiesa e Stato in Italia dalla Grande Guerra al Nuovo Concordato (1914–1984)*. Bologna: Il Mulino, 2009.
Pescosolido, Guido. *Agricoltura e Industria nell'Italia Unita*. Bari: Laterza, 1994.
Pescosolido, Guido. *Unità Nazionale e Sviluppo Economico, 1750–1913*. Bari: Laterza, 1998.
Piedimonte, Antonio Emanuele. *Raimondo di Sangro Principe di Sansevero, La Vita, le Opere, i Libri, la Cappella, le Leggende, i Misteri*. Naples: Intra Moenia, 2012.
Podmore, Frank. *Modern Spiritualism: a History and a Criticism*. Cambridge, MA: Cambridge University Press, (1902) 2011.
Politica Hermetica: Doctrine de la Race et Tradition 2 (1988).
Pozzato, Maria Pia. "Due casi di interpretazione aberrante di Dante. Luigi Valli e i 'Fedeli d'amore." In *L'Ansia dell'Interpretazione*, edited by V. Franci, pp. 181–203. Modena: Mucchi, 1989.
Pozzato, Maria Pia. *L'idea Deforme. Interpretazioni Esoteriche di Dante*. Milan: Bompiani, 1989.
Pruneti, Luigi. *Oh, Setta Scellerata ed Empia. Appunti su Oltre Due Secoli di Pubblicistica Antimassonica*. Florence: Il Campanile, 1992.
Pruneti, Luigi. *La Tradizione Masonica Scozzese in Italia: Storia del Supremo Consiglio e della Gran Loggia d'Italia degli A.L.A.M. Obbedienza di Piazza del Gesu' dal 1805 a Oggi*. Rome: EDIMAI, 1994.
Pruneti, Luigi. *La Sinagoga di Satana. Storia dell'antimassoneria, 1725–2002*. Bari: Laterza, 2002.
Pusceddu, Augusto. *La Sociologia Positivistica in Italia*. Rome: Bulzoni, 1989.
Putnam, Michael C. J. *Virgil's Aeneid: Interpretation and Influence*. Chapel Hill: University of South Carolina Press, 1995.
Quaranta, Mario. *Il Positivismo Veneto*. Rovigo: Minelliana, 2003.
Quinn, William W. *The Only Tradition*. Albany: State University of New York Press, 1997.
Quirico, Domenico. *Adua: La Battaglia che Cambiò la Storia d'Italia*. Milano: Mondadori, 2004.
Rees, Philip. *Fascism and Pre-fascism in Europe, 1890–1945: A Bibliography of the Extreme Right*. New York: Barnes & Noble, 1984.
Rees, Philip. *Biographical Dictionary of the Extreme Right Since 1890*. New York: Schuster & Son, 1991.
Renucci, Paul. "Dantismo Esoterico nel Secolo Presente." *Atti Congresso Internazionale di Studi Danteschi* I (1965), pp. 305–332.
Riall, Lucy. *Il Risorgimento: Storia e Interpretazioni*. Roma: Donzelli, 1997.
Ricci, Roberto. *Poteri e Territorio in Lunigiana Storica (VII–XII secolo). Uomini, Terre e Poteri in una Regione di Confine*. Spoleto: CISAM, 2002.

Richards, Earl Jeffrey, trans. *Debating the Roman de la Rose: A Critical Anthology*. Edited by Christine McWebb. New York: Routledge, 2007.
Richardson, Robert D., ed. *The Heart of William James*. Cambridge, MA: Harvard University Press, 2010.
Ridolfi, Roberto. *The Life of Niccolò Machiavelli*. Chicago: University of Chicago Press, 1963.
Riedweg, Christoph. *Pythagoras: His Life, Teaching and Influence*. Ithaca, NY: Cornell University Press, 2005.
Roccucci, Adriano. *Roma Capitale del Nazionalismo, 1908–1923*. Rome: Archivio Guido Izzi, 2001.
Rooth, Graham. *Prophet for a Dark Age: A Companion to the Works of René Guénon*. Brighton: Sussex Academic Press, 2008.
Rosenau, Pauline Marie. *Post-Modernism and the Social Sciences: Insights, Inroads, Intrusions*. Princeton, NJ: Princeton University Press, 1992.
Rosenthal, Bernice, ed. *The Occult in Russian and Soviet Culture*. Ithaca, NY: Cornell University Press, 2005.
Rossi, Marco. "L'Interventismo Politico-Culturale delle Riviste Tradizionaliste negli Anni Venti." *Storia Contemporanea* 18, no. 3 (1987), pp. 457–504.
Rossi, Marco. "Neopaganesimo e Arti Magiche nel Periodo Fascista." In *Storia d'Italia, Annali 25, Esoterismo*, edited by Gian Mario Cazzaniga, pp. 599–628. Turin: Einaudi, 2010.
Rossi, Robert, and Léo Taxil (1854–1907). *Du Journalisme Anticlérical à la Mystification Transcendante*. Marseille: Quartiers Nord Éditions, 2015.
Rovito, Teodoro. *Letterati e Giornalisti Italiani Contemporanei: Dizionario Bio-Bibliografico*. 2nd ed. Naples: Teodoro Rovito Editore, 1907.
Rowland, Ingrid D. *Giordano Bruno: Philosopher/Heretic*. New York: Farrar, Staus and Giroux, 2008.
Ruggiero, Gennaro. *Le Piazze di Napoli*. Rome: Newton Compton, 1998.
Rumi, Giorgio. "Mussolini e il "programma" di San Sepolcro." *Il movimento di Liberazione in Italia* 4-5-6 (1963), pp. 3–26.
Rumi, Giorgio. *Gioberti*. Bologna: Il Mulino, 1999.
Salaris, Claudia. *Alla Festa della Rivoluzione. Artisti e Libertari con D'Annunzio a Fiume*. Bologna: Il Mulino, 2002.
Sale, Giovanni. *La Chiesa di Mussolini*. Milan: Rizzoli, 2015.
Salzani, Stefano. *Luigi Valli e l'Esoterismo di Dante*. Verona: Il Cerchio, 2014.
Santomassimo Gianpasquale. *La Marcia su Roma*. Florence: Giunti, 2000.
Sasso, Gennaro. *Filosofia e Idealismo I—Benedetto Croce*. Naples: Bibliopolis, 1994.
Scaraffia, Lucetta. "Il contributo dei cattolici all'unificazione." In *I Cattolici che hanno fatto l'Italia*, edited by Lucetta Scaraffia, pp. 223–227. Torino: Lindau, 2011.
Schmidt, Volker H. "Multiple Modernities or Varieties of Modernity?" *Current Sociology* 54, no. 1 (2006), pp. 77–97.
Schmitt, Charles. "Perennial Philosophy: Steuco to Leibniz." *Journal of the History of Ideas* 27 (1966), pp. 505–532.
Schroeder, Ralph. "Disenchantment and Its Discontents." *Sociological Review* 43, no. 2 (1995), pp. 227–250.
Sciacca, Michele Federico. *La Filosofia Morale di Antonio Rosmini*. Milano: Bocca, 1955.
Seddio, Pietro. *La Carboneria*. Rome: Montecovello, 2012.

Sedgwick, Mark. *Against the Modern World: Traditionalism and the Secret Intellectual History of the Twentieth Century.* New York: Oxford University Press, 2004.

Segal, Robert. "In Defence of Reductionism." *Journal of the American Academy of Religion* 51 (1983), pp. 97–122

Sereni, Emilio. *Il Capitalismo nelle Campagne (1860–1900).* Turin: Einaudi, 1968.

Sestito, Roberto. *Storia del Rito Filosofico Italiano e dell'Ordine Orientale Antico e Primitivo.* Firenze: Libreria Chiari, 2003.

Sestito, Roberto. *Il Figlio del Sole: Vita e Opere di Arturo Reghini Filosofo e Matematico.* Ancona: Associazione Culturale Ignis, 2006.

Sestito, Roberto, ed. *Ritorno alle Giubbe Rosse.* Ancona: Associazione Culturale Ignis, 2006.

Seton-Watson, Christopher. *Italy from Liberalism to Fascism, 1870–1925.* London: Barnes & Noble, 1967.

Shils, Edward. "Tradition." *Comparative Studies in Society and History: Special Issue on Tradition and Modernity* 13, no. 2 (1971), pp. 122–159.

Shils, Edward. "How Traditional Are the Traditionalists? The Case of the Guenonian Sufis." *Aries* 22 (1999), pp. 3–24.

Shull, Kristina Karin. "Has the Magic Gone? Weber's Disenchantment of the World and Its Implications for Art in Today's World." *Anamesa: An Interdisciplinary Journal* 3, no. 2 (2005), pp. 61–73.

Smith, Denis Mack. *Mazzini.* Milan: Rizzoli, 1993.

Sirri, Raffaelo, and Maurizio Torrini, eds. *Bernardino Telesio e la Cultura Napoletana. Atti del Convegno Internazionale, Napoli 15–17 Dicembre 1989.* Napoli: Guida, 1992.

Snoek, Jan. "Drei Entwicklungsstufen des Meistergrads." *Quatuor Coronati Jahrbuch fur Freimaurerforschung* 41 (2004), pp. 21–46.

Snoek, Jan. "Trois Phases de développement du grade de Maitre." *Acta Macionica* 14 (2004), pp. 9–24.

Spini, Giorgio. *Le origini del socialismo.* Turin: Einaudi, 1982.

Spiri, Andrea. *Socialismo italiano. Cento anni di storia. Il PSI 1892–1992.* Milan: M&B, 2003.

Srivastava, Gita. "Svarkar and Mazzini." *Rassegna Storica del Risorgimento* 71 (1984), pp. 259–264.

Srivastava, Gita. "Historical Biographies of Italian Nationalist Leaders in Indian Literature During the Freedom Movement of India." *Estratti della Rassegna storica del Risorgimento* 83 (1996), pp. 323–338.

Stambaugh, John E. *The Ancient Roman City.* Baltimore: Johns Hopkins University Press, 1988.

Staudenmaier, Peter. *Between Occultism and Fascism: Antroposophy and the Politics of Race in the Fascist Era.* Brill: Leiden, 2014.

Storchi Marino, Alfredina. *Numa e Pitagora: Sapientia Constituendae Civitatis.* Naples: Liguori, 1999.

Strappini, Lucia, Claudia Micocci, and Alberto Abruzzese. *La Classe dei Colti: Intellettuali e Società nel Primo Novecento Italiano.* Bari: Laterza, 1970.

Straude, John. "Alienated Youth and the Cult of the Occult." In *Sociology for the Seventies,* edited by Morris Medley and James E. Conyers. New York: Wiley, 1970, pp. 222–249.

Styers, Randall. *Making Magic: Religion, Magic and Science in the Modern World.* Oxford: Oxford University Press, 2004.

Sunker, Heinz, and Hans-Uwe Otto, eds. *Education and Fascism: Political Identity and Social Education in Nazi Germany.* London: Falmer Press, 1997.

Taylor, Charles. *The Malaise of Modernity*. Toronto: Anansi Press, 1991.
Taylor, McNeil Christian. *Disqualified Knowledge: Theosophy and the Revolt of the Fin de Siècle*. Unpublished thesis. Middletown, CT, 2013.
Tatti, Silvia M. *Il Risorgimento dei Letterati*. Rome: Storia e Letteratura, 2011.
Tessitore, F. ed. *Incidenza di Hegel*. Naples, Morano 1970.
Teresi Giovanni. *Sui Moti Carbonari del 1820-21 in Italia*. Foggia: Bastogi, 2007.
Thomas, Dana Lloyd. "Arturo Reghini: A Modern Pythagorean." *Gnosis* 44 (1997), pp. 52-59.
Thomas, Dana Lloyd. "Arturo Reghini." In *Dictionary of Gnosis and Western Esotericism*, edited by Wouter J. Hanegraaff, Antoine Faivre, Roelof van der Broek, and Jean-Pierre Brach, pp. 979-980. Brill: Leiden, 2006.
Tiezzi, Massimo. *L'Eroe Conteso. La Costruzione del Mito di Cesare Battisti negli anni 1916-1935*. Trento, Museo Storico in Trento, 2007.
Tiryakian, Edward A. "Toward the Sociology of Esoteric Culture." In *On the Margin of the Visible: Sociology, the Esoteric, and the Occult*, edited by Edward A. Tiryakian, pp. 257-281. New York: Wiley, 1974.
Toffetti, Sergio e Mario Musumeci. *Da La presa di Roma a Il Piccolo Garibaldino*. Rome: Gangemi Editore, 2007.
Toth, Lazlo. "Arturo Reghini." *Politica Hermetica* 1 (1987), pp. 143-155.
Trevor-Roper, Hugh. *The Last Days of Hitler*. London: Macmillan, 1974.
Trevor-Roper, Hugh. *Consciousness and Society: The Reorientation of European Social Thought, 1890-1930*. London: Transaction, 2002.
Treitel, Corinna. *A Science for the Soul: Occultism and the Genesis of the German Modern*. Baltimore: Johns Hopkins University, 2004.
Truzzi, Marcello. "The Occult Revival as Popular Culture: Some Random Observations on the Old and Nouveau Witch." *The Sociological Quarterly* 13 (1972), pp. 16-36.
Tryphonopoulos, Demetres, and Stephen Adams, eds. *The Ezra Pound Encyclopedia*. Westport, CT: Greenwood, 2005.
Tyssens, Jeffrey. "Freemasonry and Nationalism." In *Handbook of Freemasonry*, edited by Henrik Bogdan and Jan A. M. Snoek, pp. 461-472. Leiden: Brill, 2014.
Urbinati, Nadia. *Le Civili Libertà: Positivismo e Liberalismo nell'Italia Unita*. Preface by Norberto Bobbio. Venice: Marsilio, 1990.
Vagni, Lidia Sansone. *Raimondo di Sangro Principe di San Severo*. 2nd ed. Foggia: Bastogi, 1992.
van Gennep, Arnold. *The Rites of Passage*. London: Routledge & Kegan Paul, (1909) 1960.
Vené, Gian Franco. *Il Golpe Fascista del 1922. Cronaca e Storia della Marcia su Roma*. Rome: Garzanti, 1975.
Ventura, Gastone. *Cosmogonie Gnostiche, Saggio Storico-Critico sulle Principali Teogonie Gnostiche Cristiane*. Rome: Atanòr, 1975.
Ventura, Gastone. *I Riti Massonici di Misraim e Memphis*. Todi: Atanor, 1980.
Ventura, Gastone. *Les Rites Maçonnique de Misraïm et Memphis*. Paris: Maisonneuve et Larose, 1986.
Versnel, H. S. *Inconsistencies in Greek and Roman Religion: Transition and Reversal in Myth and Ritual*. Leiden: Brill, 1994.
Vertecchi, Benedetto. *La scuola italiana da Casati a Berlinguer*. Milan: Franco Angeli, 2001.
Verter, Bradford. *Dark Star Rising: The Emergence of Modern Occultism*. Unpublished PhD dissertation. Princeton, NJ, 1998.
Versluis, Arthur. "What Is Esoteric." *Esoterica* 4 (2002), pp. 1-15.

Versluis, Arthur. "Antimodernism." *Telos* 132 (2006), pp. 96–130.
Versluis, Arthur. "The New Inquisitions: Heretic Hunting and the Intellectual Origins of Modern Totalitarianism." In *Theodor Adorno and the "Occult,"* pp. 1–14. Oxford: Oxford University Press, 2011.
Verucci, Guido. *Idealisti all'Indice: Croce, Gentile e la Condanna del Santo Uffizio*. Bari: Laterza, 2006.
Vigni, Francesca. *Donna e Massoneria in Italia: dalle Origini ad Oggi*. Foggia: Bastogi Editrice Italiana, 1997.
Vignoli, Giulio. *I territori Italofoni non Appartenenti alla Repubblica Italiana*. Milan: Giuffrè, 1995.
Villalon, L. J. Andrew. *Gli Italiani dimenticati. Minoranze italiane in* Europa. Milan: Giuffrè, 2000.
Villalon, L. J. Andrew. "Machiavelli's *Prince*, Political Science or Political Satire?: Garrett Mattingly Revisited." *Mediterranean Studies* 12 (2003), pp. 73–101.
Virlogeux, Georges. *Massimo d'Azeglio a Canneto*. Novara: Istituto per la Storia del Risorgimento Italiano, 1997.
Vitto Cindy. *The Virtuous Pagan in Middle English Literature*. Philadelphia: American Philosophical Society, 1989.
Vittori, Massimiliano. "Storia e Simbologia del Fascio Littorio." In *Esoterismo eFascismo*, edited by Gianfranco de Turris, pp. 15–19. Rome: Mediterranee, 2006.
Vivarelli, Roberto. *Storia delle Origini del Fascismo—Dalla Grande Guerra alla Marcia su Roma*. Bologna: Il Mulino, 1991.
von Edlinger, Carola. *Cosmogonic and Mythical World Designs of Inter-Discursive Perspective. Studies on Phantasus (Arno Holz), Northern Lights (Theodor Däubler) and The Ball (Otto zur Linde)*. Frankfurt am Main: Peter Lang, 2002.
von Stuckrad, Kocku. "Discursive Study of Religion: From States of the Mind to Communication and Action." *Method & Theory in the Study of Religion* 15 (2003), pp. 255–271.
von Stuckrad, Kocku. *Western Esotericism: A Brief History of Secret Knowledge*. Translated by Nicholas Goodrick-Clarke. London: Equinox, (2005) 2009.
von Stuckrad, Kocku. *Locations of Knowledge in Medieval and Early Modern Europe*. Leiden: Brill, 2010.
von Stuckrad, Kocku. "Reflections on the Limits of Reflection: an Invitation to the Discursive Study of Religion." *Method & Theory in the Study of Religion* 22 (2010), pp. 156–169.
Vosserl, Karl. "Dialettica e Carattere." In *L'Opera Filosofica, Storica e Letteraria di Benedetto Croce*, edited by Edmondo Cione.pp. 22–27. Bari: Laterza & Figli, 1942.
Walker, D. P. *Spiritual and Demonic Magic from Ficino to Campanella*. London: Warburg Institute, 1958.
Webb, James. *Flight from Reason*. London: MacDonald & Co., 1971.
Weber, Max. *The Sociology of Religion*. Boston: Beacon Press, (1922) 1964.
Weisberg, Barbara. *Talking to the Dead: Kate and Maggie Fox*. New York, HarperOne, 2004.
Weiss, Roberto. "Traccia per una Biografia di Annio da Viterbo." *Italia Medioevale e Umanistica* 5 (1962), pp. 425–441.
Wilhelm, James. *Ezra Pound: The Tragic Years 1925–1972*. University Park: Pennsylvania State University Press, 1994.
Wittrock Björn. "Modernity: One, None, or Many?' European Origins and Modernity as Global Condition." *Daedalus* 129, no. 1 (2000), pp. 31–60.

Yates, Frances A. *Giordano Bruno and the Hermetic Tradition*. Chicago: University of Chicago Press, 1964.
Yates, Frances A. *The Art of Memory*. Chicago: University of Chicago Press, 1966.
Yates, Frances A. *The Rosicrucian Enlightenment*. London: Routledge & Kegan Paul, 1972.
Yates, Frances A. *The Occult Philosophy in the Elizabethan Age*. London: Routledge & Kegan Paul, 1979.
Zaffiri, Gabriele. *L'Impero che Mussolini Sognava per l'Italia*. Pozzuoli: The Boopen, 2008.
Zinetti, Valerio. *Ezio Maria Gray. Un Italiano Fedele alla Patria*. Milan: Edizioni Ritter, 2015.
Ziolkowski, Jan. "Vergil, Abelard, Eloise and the End of Neumes." *Nottingham Medieval Studies* 56 (2012), pp. 447–466.
Zolla, Élemire. *Uscite dal Mondo*. Milano: Adelphi, 1992.

Internet Sources

Bax, Marty, ed. *The Theosophical Society General Register*. tsmembers.org, http://tsmembers.org/ts-general-register-1875-1942/book-6-10/. (2010).
d'Andrea, Federico. *Raimondo di Sangro, Principe di Sansevero e la Tradizione Egizia Napoletana*. accademiakremmerziana.it,accademiakremmerziana.it/ Home_03_09_08.htm. (2008).
ISTAT. "Italia in Cifre." istat.it. http://www.istat.it/files/2011/03/italia-in-cifre.pdf. (2011).
Ministry of Defence. "L'Unità d'Italia (1861–1918)." http://www.difesa.it/ Content/150anniversario/Pagine/Unit%C3%A0dItalia.aspx. (2010).
Pius IX. "Non Expedit." *The Catholic Encyclopedia* 11. New York: Robert Appleton Company, 1911. newadvent.org. http://www.newadvent.org/cathen/11098a.htm.
Pius XI. "Vogliamo Anzitutto." w2.vatican.va, http://w2.vatican.va/content/ pius- xi/it/speeches/documents/hf_p-xi_spe_19290213_vogliamo-anzitutto.html. (2002).

Index

For the benefit of digital users, indexed terms that span two pages (e.g., 52–53) may, on occasion, appear on only one of those pages.

Accademia Nazionale, la Scuola Italica (National Academy, Italic School) association, 43–44
Accademia Reale (Royal Academy), 44
Adorno, Theodor, 2, 114–15, 117
   Theses, 6–7
Advaita (nondualism), 127–28
Aeon: Dramatische Trilogie (Mombert), 66–67
Agabiti, Augusto, 97
Agrippa, Cornelius, 6
Agrippa, Heinrich Cornelius, 81–82
Aleramo, Sibilla, 9
Alexander, Jeffrey C., 3–4
Alighieri, Dante. *See* Dante Alighieri
Alvi, Ciro. See also *Atanòr, Rivista di Studi Iniziatici (Atanòr, Journal of Initiatic Studies)*
   background, 142–44
   founding of *Atanòr* publishing house, 142–43
   meeting with Reghini, 142
   repulsion toward Christianity, 143–44
Amendola, Giovanni, 111
Amici, Edmondo de, 30
Anima (Reghini), 66–67
Annals of Islam (Italian Philosophical Rite) (Caetani), 22–23
anthroposophy, 5–6, 156, 166
anti-Catholic Masonic body, 70
anti-clericalism, 35–36, 73–75, 97
The Antimodern Condition: An Argument against Progress (King), 10–11
anti-modernism, 2–3, 10–11. *See also* Fascism; Roman Traditionalism
   Adamson on, 117–18
   Armentano's anti-modern aphorisms, 16
   comparison to positivism, 10–11
   Eisenstadt on, 18–19
   the elite and, 49–50
   Fascism/Roman Traditionalism links with, 114–15
   influence of modernism, 10, 19–20
   modern time existence of, 116
   modern times idea of, 116
   Reghini/Armentano, support for, 70
   sentiments in modern Italy, 1–6
   social occult modernism and, 24
anti-Positivism, 49–50, 53
anti-Semitism, 5
"Apocalyptic Modernity" poem (Kermode), 114–15
Ardigò, Roberto, 52–53
Armentano, Amedeo Rocco, 4–5
   anti-modern aphorisms of, 16
   background, 80–82
   correspondence with Bianchini, 179–80
   correspondence with Gallinaro, 144–45
   correspondence with Guénon, 82
   correspondence with Reghini, 93–98, 132–33, 142, 163, 164
   differences with Corradini on religion, 75–76
   Ermete Cosentino (Hermes of Cosenza) pseudonym of, 88
   expulsion from *Rito Filosofico Italiano*, 89
   Hermet's writings on, 80
   influence/impact on Reghini, 80–81
   initiation of Reghini into *Schola Italica*, 81, 82–84
   Massime di Scienza Iniziatica (Maxims of Initiatic Science), 85–86
   Mazzoldi/Mengozzi, influence on, 47
   meeting with Guénon, 130
   as member of the *élite intellectuelle*, 24, 109–10
   mentorship of Reghini, 14–15, 70
   neo-Pythanorean beliefs, 5–6
   129th Maxim, 85
   possible entrance to *Rito Filosofico Italiano*, 88
   quote on "progress," 1
   Reghini's visits with, 138–39, 140
   RomanTraditionalist outlook of, 45
   Schola Italica and, 69, 75–76, 118–19
Ars Regia publishing house, 61–62
Assagioli, Roberto, 59–60

Associazione Nazionalisti Italiani (Italian Nationalist Association), 23, 75–76, 91, 92–93, 99–100
Associazione Pitagorica (Pythagorean Association), 141
Atanòr, Rivista di Studi Iniziatici (Atanòr, Journal of Initiatic Studies), 6, 23, 134, 141
  important articles on Roman Traditionalism's point of view, 152–53
  publication of Guénon's articles, 153–54
  publication of Reghini's attacks on the Church, 154–55
  publication of Reghini's esoteric articles, 153–54
  publication of Reghini's "Imperialismo Pagano," 154
  publication of Reghini's *Le Parole Sacre e di Passo*, 144–45
  Reghini's founding of, 24–25, 150–52
  variety of authors/books published by, 144
The Authoritarian Personality (Adorno, Brunswick, Levinson, Sanford), 114–15
avant-garde
  Florentine avant-garde, 56–60
  Reghihi's contradictory involvement with, 21–22
  rise of, 4–5

Banfi, Antonio, 53
Banti, Alberto Mario, 28
Baratieri, Oreste, 91
Bauman, Zygmunt, 2
Beals, Derek, 28
Benso, Camillo, 21
Berchet, Giovanni, 31
Bergier, Jacques, 7, 120–21
Bergson, Henri, 57–58
Berman, Marshall, 2–3
Bertolorenzi, Disioniso D., 82–83
Besant, Annie, 62, 64
The Betrothed (I Promessi Sposi) (Manzoni), 31
Bevor Hitler Kam (Before Hitler Came) (Bronder), 122
Beyond Enlightenment: Occultims and Politics in Modern France (Harvey), 9
Bianchini, Amerigo, 165, 170, 179–80
Biblioteca Filosofica, Reghini's lectures, 6, 68
Biblioteca Teosofica (Florence, Italy), 21–22, 49–50, 68
Biondi, Massimo, 41
Blavatsky, Helena Petrovna, 9, 61–62. *See also* Theosophical Society
  Fall of Ideas, 67–68
  The Secret Doctrine, 66–67
  The Voice of the Silence, 66–67
Blocchi Nazionali (National Blocks) political group, 113–14
Bocchini, Domenico, 21, 45–46
Bodrero bill, banning of Freemasonry, 24
Bogdan, Henrik, 83–84
Boggio, Pier Carlo, 71
Borgese, Giuseppe Antonio, 58–59
Bradbury, Malcolm, 116–17
Bronder, Dietrich, 122
Bruno, Giordano, 32–33, 45, 64–65
Brunswick, Else Frenkel, 114–15
Butler, Alison, 7–8
By Scipio's Helm: Risorgimento, Italian History and the Remembrance of Rome (Risorgimento, Dell'Elmo di Scipio: Risorgimento, Storia d'Italia e Memoria di Roma) (Consolato), 32–33

Cadorna, Luigi, 27–28
Caetani, Leone, 22–23
Caffé Giubbe Rosse, 21–22
Calvari, Decio, 22–23
Campanella, Tommaso, 32–33, 45
Caporali, Enrico, 144
Capuana, Luigi, 40, 49
Carboneria (Charcoal BUrners), 33–35
Carducci, Giosué, 21, 75–76
Casini, Paolo, 59–60
Catholicism
  Corradini's upholding of, 75–76
  declaration as the "State Religion," 35–36
  as obsession for Reghini, 99–100
  Papini/Prezzolini, attacks against, 56–57
Catholic-liberal movement, 52
Cattaneo, Carlo, 52
Cavour (Camillo Benso, Count of Cavour), 28, 29–30, 35–36
Che cos'è il Nazionalismo e Cosa Vogliono i Nazionalisti (What Nationalism Is and What Nationalists Want) (Rocco), 92
Chicago School Mircea Eliade, 11, 13
Christianity
  Alvi's repulsion toward, 143–44
  vs. Paganism, in traditionalism, 16–17
  Reghini's blaming of, for the fall of the Roman Empire, 186–87
  Reghini's definition of, 5
  Yates's Hermetic Tradition and, 11–12
Ciconi, Teobaldo, 31–32
Circolo Dante Alighieri (Dante Alighieri Circle) association, 76

Claiming Knowledge: Strategies of Epistemology from Theosophy to the New Age (Hammer), 12–13
Claiming Knowledge: Strategies of Epistemology from Theosophy to the New Age (Hammer), 84–85
Colazza, Giovanni, 5–6
Collodi, Carlo, 21
Colonna di Cesarò, Giovanni Antonio, 5–6
The Confessions of an Italian (Le Confessioni di un Italiano) (Nievo), 33
Congress of Vienna (November 1814-June 1815), 27–28
Considerations (Reghini), 50–51
Consolato, Sandro, 32–33
Conti, Fulvio, 71
Coomaraswamy, Ananda, 120
Cooper-Oakley, Isabel, 62
Coppino, Michele, 71
Corbin, Henri, 11
Corpus Hermeticum (trans. Ficino), 11
Corpus Reghinianum, 6
Corradini, Enrico, 7, 53–54, 56–57, 75–76. See also Associazione Nazionalisti Italiani; *Il Regno (The Kingdom)*, nationalist journal
Corridoni, Filippo, 112, 118–19
counterpositivism, 53–56
Crispi, Francesco, 72–73, 91
La Critica (The Critique) journal (Croce), 53–54, 55–57
Croce, Benedetto (Neopolitan Idealist)
  denunciation of Hegel's Idea, Nature, Spirit triad, 54–55
  flirtation with/attach of Marxist philosophy, 54–55
  Florentine *Scapigliatura* philosophy of, 49–50, 53–54
  founding of *La Critica* journal, 53–54
  and Idealism as counterpositivism, 53–56
  La Critica journal of, 53–54, 55–57
  neo-Idealism philosophical system of, 55
  proponent of Neapolitan Hegelian School, 53–54
Cuore (Heart) (Amici), 30

D'Alveydre, Joseph Saint Yves, 120–21
D'Andrea, Federico, 44–45
D'Annunzio, Gabriele, 56–57, 117
Dante Alighieri, 1, 20, 32–33
  Divina Commedia (Divine Comedy), 103–4, 105, 106–7, 129, 198–99
  influence of Pythagoras, 81
  as "so-called" father of Italian language, 32–33

Dante Alighieri Circle (Circolo Dante Alighieri) association, 76
Darwin, Charles, 44
Daubler, Teodor, 91
d'Azeglio, Massimo, 40
Dei Numeri Pitagorici: Libri Sette (On Pythagorean Numbers: Seven Volumes, 1936-1944)(Reghini), 166, 172–79
Delpino, Filippo, 35–36
"Del Simbolismo e della Filologia in Rapporto alla Scienza Metatisica (On Symbolism and Philology in Relation to Metaphysic Science)" (Reghini), 81, 82
Dialektik der Aufklärung (Dialectic of Enlightenment) (Adorno and Horkheimer), 117
di Fiore, Gigi, 28
Di Luca, Natale Mario, 5, 60–61
Discorsi sulla Prima Deca di Tito Livio (Discourses on the First Deca of Titus Livius) (Machiavelli), 145
Divina Commedia (Divine Comedy) (Dante), 103–4, 105, 106–7, 129, 198–99
Dumas, Thomas-Alexander, 78–79

Eckart, Dietrich, 120–21
Egyptian Great Orient, 45, 46–47
Egyptian hermetic tradition, 44–45
Eisenstadt, S. N., 18–19
Eliade, Mircea, 83–84
elitism/*élite intellectuelle*, 24, 49–50
  as core belief, 60
  cultural elitism, 57–58
  Guénon's condemning of, 120
  relation to occultism, 24–25
  in the *Schola*, 110
English Scandinavian modernity, 19
Eranos meetings, 11, 12
Esoteric Buddhism (Sinnett), 64–65
Ésotérisme de Dante (Dante's Esotericism) (Dante), 81
Eternal City, 1
Ethiopia
  defeat of Italian forces, 91
  Treaty of Uccialli with Italy, 91
Evola, Julius
  Man as Power (L'Uomo come Potenza), 22–23
  Reghini's collaboration with, 158–59, 164
  Reghini's lawsuit against, 161–62, 163, 164, 165
  Ur Group's break with, 160–62
  "Woman as a Thing," 9

Facta, Luigi, 113–14
Faivre, Antoine, 11, 12
Fall of Ideas (Blavatsky), 67–68
Falorsi, Vittorio, 165, 170
Farina, Giuseppe la, 71
Fasci di Azione Rivoluzionaria (Fasces of Revolutionary Action), extra-parliamentary political group, 112
Fasci Italiani di Combattimento (Italian Fighting Fasces), 113–14
Fascism. *See also* Mussolini, Benito
    fascist esotericism, 7
    F-Scale (Fascist Scale), 114–15
    link with occultism, 122–25
    march on Rome, 111–14
    Mussolini and, 109–10
    Occult Fascism, 24
    Reghini's adherence to, 165
    relation with the Vatican, 4–5, 25, 118–19, 158–59, 161–62, 165
    rise to power in Italy, 3–5, 7, 99–100, 112–14
    Roman Traditionalism and, 4–5, 24, 114–18
    shortcomings of, 117
    similarity to Roman Traditionalism, 118
Federzoni, Luigi, 75–76
feminist activism, 9
Ferrari, Giuseppe, 52, 79
the Fetish, 41
Ficino, Marsilio, 11
"*La Filosofia che Muore*" ("*The Dying Philosophy*") (Prezzolini), 4–5
Flight from Reason (Webb), 7
Florentine avant-garde, 56–60. *See also Leonardo* journal
    origins, characteristics of, 56–32
Florentine Renaissance, 11
Fogazzaro, Antonio, 40
For a New History of the Risorgimento (Per una Nuova Storia del Risorgimento) Banti, 29
Formisano, Ciro, 45
Freemasons/Freemasonry (in Italy)
    anti-Catholic Masonic body, 70
    anti-clericalism within, 73–75
    Bodrero bill banning of, 24
    Carboneria and, 33–35
    Les Disciples de Memphis (The Disciples of Memphis) mother lodge, 78–79
    fringe Masonry, 77–78
    Grand Orient (GI) enabled lodges, 71
    history of, 33–35, 71–73
    I Rigeneratori (The Restorers) lodge, Palermo, 78–79
    Loggia Ausonia, Turin Masonic lodge, 35–36, 71
    Lucifero lodge, 79, 82–83
    Michele di Lando lodge, Florence, 79
    Mussolini's stance against, 24
    nationalism/irredentism within, 75–76
    Reghini's interest in/involvement with, 17, 22–23, 78–79, 145
    Reghini's involvement with, 17, 22–23
    Rito Simbolico Italiano (Italian Symbolic Rite), 79
    role in modern Italy, 71–78
    therapeutic masonic circle, 5–6
    Vatican's mocking of, 73–74
French modernity, 19
From Darkness to Light (Bogdan), 83–84
Frosini, Eduardo, 22–23, 145
    charters (titles) held by, 87
    prominence in Italian Masonic milieu, 86
    theories of, 87–88
F-Scale (Fascist Scale), 114–15
Futurists/Futurism, 10–11, 97, 117, 186–87

Gallinaro, Mario, 144–45
Gardner, Frederick Leigh, 7–8
Garibaldi, Giuseppe, 21, 27–28
    advocacy for Italy's unification, 33
    assignation as Freemason Honorary Grand Master, 21, 34–35, 183–84
    conquest of the Two Sicilies, 27–28, 71
    enthusiasm for anti-Papal movement, 44
    as incarnation of Italian imperialist ideas, 109
    influence on Reghini, 183
    as *Risorgimento* hero, 72–73
    Risorgimento ideals of Mazzini/Garibaldi, 72–73
Garin, Eugenio, 53
Gentile, Giovanni, 53–54
Gentiloni, Vincenzo Ottorino, 93, 194–95
Gerini, Emanuele, 50–51
German modernity, 19
Germany
    Munich Cosmic Circle, 66–67
    nineteenth-century occultism, 7–8
    study of patriotic nationalism of, 29
Giddens, Anthony, 1
Ginsborg, Paul, 28
Gioberti, Vincenzo, 35–36, 52
Giolitti, Giovanni, 91
    alliance with Mussolini, 113–14
    strategy for avoiding power of the Socialists, 93

Giordano Bruno and the Hermetic Tradition (Yates), 11
"Giordano Bruno Smentisce Rastignac" ("Giordano Bruno Refutes Rastignac") Reghini, 64–65, 84–85
Giorgio, Fabrizio, 45
Giorgio, Guido de, 5–6
Giovane Italia (Mazzini), 31
Godwin, Joscelyn, 24–25
GOI. *See* Italian Grand Orient (GOI)
Goodricke-Clarke, Nicholas, 120–21
Gori, Gino, 141
Grand Duchy of Tuscany (post-Napoleonic state), 27–28, 50–51
Great Britain
  nineteenth-century occultism, 7–8
  occult order in, 2
Great War. *See* World War I
Griffin, Roger
  description of modernity, 2–3, 116
  Modernism and Fascism: A Sense of a New Beginning under Mussolini and Hitler, 115
  "A Primordialist Definition of Modernity," 118–20
  on rightist social modernism, 120
  theory of occultist social modernism, 119–20
Guénon, René, 6
  articles in *Atanòr*, 153–54
  condemning of elitism, 120
  correspondence with Reghini, 133–38
  focus on *Advaita-Vedanta*, 129–30
  founding of Traditionalism, 81, 125–30
  L'Erreur Spirite (The Spiritist Error: History of a Pseudo-Religion), 128–29
  Le Théosophisme, Histoire d'une Pseudo-Religion (Theosophism: History of a Pseudo-Religion), 128–29
  l'Exposé Orientale phase, 125–26
  l'Intuition Gnostique phase, 125–26
  Orient et Occident, 128–29
  on *philosophia perennis* (perennial philosophy), 120
  Reghini's break with, 16–17, 130–31
  and 1920s Italian Traditionalism, 130–33
  theories for the rise of an *élite intellectuelle*, 24, 49–50
Guerrieri, Giulio, 97

Hakl, Thomas, 22–23
Hammer, Olav, 12–13, 84–85
Hanegraaff, Wouter J., 7, 12–13
Harvey, David, 2
Harvey, David Allan, 9

Hegel, Georg, 52–53, 54–55
  Idea, Nature, Science triad of, 54–55
Hegelian Idealism (philosophy), 53–55
Herf, Jeffrey, 2
Herf, Weiman, 3–4
Hermet, Augusto, 97–98
hermetic currents, 11
  Egyptian hermetic tradition, 44–45
Hermetic Order of the Golden Dawn (Great Britain), 2, 7–8
Hermetic-Pythagorean-Orphic-Eleusnian-Daoist-Zoharian tradition, 80
Hess, Rudolf, 120–21
Himmler, Heinrich, 120–21
Hinduism, 127–28
Hobsbawm, Eric
  The Invention of Tradition, 85–86
  theory on the invention of traditions, ad hoc myths, 20
Honis, Samuel, 78–79
Horkheimer, Max, 2, 117
Humanum Genus, papal encyclical (Leo XII), 74–75
Huntington, Samuel P., 18–19
Huxley, Aldous, 120

"L'Ideale Imperialista" ("The Imperial Ideal") article (Prezzolini), 32
Idealism
  as counterpositivism, 53–56
  Hegelian Idealism, 53–54
  neo-Hegelian Idealism, 52–53
  as a real, trustworthy science, 54–55
  rise of neo-Idealism, 51–56
Ignis (Fire) journal, 155–58
Il Dominio dell'Anima (Control of the Soul) lecture (Reghini), 68
"Il Fascio Littorio" (The *Lictoriae* Fasces) journal article (Reghini), 166–70
Il Popolo d'Italia (The Italian People) newspaper (Mussolini), 112
Il Regno (The Kingdom), nationalist journal, 53–54, 56–57
Il Regno (The Kingdom), nationalist journal, 75–76
"Imperialismo Pagano" ("Pagan Imperialism") (Reghini), 32–33, 95, 96–110. *See also* "Imperialismo Pagano" ("Pagan Imperialism"), textual analysis
  advocacy for the use of force, 117
  context of, 23, 96–101
  contrast with positivist, progressive worldview, 1

"Imperialismo Pagano" ("Pagan Imperialism")
(Reghini) (*cont.*)
  Garibaldi's influence, 183
  importance of, to the political aims of the
    Schola Italica, 109–10
  importance to political aims of the
    Schola, 109–10
  influence of Mazzini, 33
  Machiavelli/Vergii/Dante/Mazzini's
    championing of, 145
  Mazzini's influence, 33, 183
  Papini's criticism of, 98
  publication in *Salamandra*, 1, 93, 97–98
  public reaction in Roman/Florentine circles, 98
  Reghini's advocacy for use of force in, 117
  Reghini's republishing of, 154
  role in pinpointing *Schola Italica* in the
    Italian occult milieu, 110
  Schola's elitist approach and, 85–86
  Sesito's conclusion regarding, 98
  shattering of Regini's dream for, 25
  supposed purpose of, 98
  World War I (the Great War) and, 23, 186–87
"Imperialismo Pagano" ("Pagan Imperialism")
(Reghini), textual analysis, 193–202
  Adeste visiones stolis albis candidae, 199–200
  context of, 23, 96–101
  Die Menschen zu bessern und zu
    bekehren, 196–97
  Empire and Christendom, 195–97
  "Introduction," 99–101
  Jam redit et Virgo, redeunt Saturnia
    regna, 195–96
  "L'Idea Imperiale Dopo Dante" ("The
    Imperial Idea after Dante") section, 107–
    9, 200–2
  "La Tradizione Imperiale Romana" ("The
    Roman Imperial Tradition") section, 104–
    7, 197–200
L'Incendio di Roma (The Fire of Rome)
  (Alvi), 143–44
Innocent X, Pope, 50–51
"Intellectual Imperialism" (Prezzolini), 57–58
The Invention of Tradition (Hobsbawm), 85–86
irredentism
  defined, 239n.18
  ties to Freemasonry, 75–76
Islamicism, 11
"Istituzioni di Scienza Occulta" ("Institutions of
  Occult Sciences") (Reghini), 66–68
Italian Catholic Electoral Union, 93
Italian Grand Orient (GOI), 74–75, 76, 87, 98,
  124–25, 140

Alvi's membership, 142–43
characteristic traits of, 71
Cordova's election as Grand Master, 34–35
de Luca's role as Grand Master, 34–35
Ferrari's role as Grand Master, 79
founding of Supreme Council, 34–35
Frosini's disenchantment with, 87
growth of anti-clericalism within, 73
growth of, in Italy, 71
Lemmi's role as Grand Master, 72
Nathan's role as Grand Master, 35
plenary of Northern lodges in
  Florence, 72–73
ties to irredentist circles, 76, 92
Todi's membership, 142–43
Turin branch of GOI, 72–73
Italian School of Positivist Criminology, 21
Italy
  anti-modern sentiments, 1–6
  attempted conquest of Ethiopia, 91
  fascination with Oriental philosophies, 22–23
  Fascist regime of, 3–5, 7
  Freemasonry in, 33–35
  Garibaldi's advocacy for unification, 33
  late nineteenth-century philosophy, 51–53
  Liquidation of the Ecclesiastic Fund
    (*Liquidazione dell'Asse Ecclesiastico*)
    laws, 35–36
  Mazzini's advocacy for unification, 32–33
  Mussolini's march on Rome, 111–14
  nationalism and, 91–93
  nineteenth-century occultism and, 36–41
  OVRA, Fascist secret police, 25–26
  post-Napoleonic states of, 27–28
  right-wing culture rejection of Reghini, 5
  rise of fascist power, 24
  rise of the Neo-Guelph group, 35–36
  Risorgimento, historical phase, 3–4, 21
  Socialist milieu, 57–58
  Theosophical Society origins in, 5–6, 61–62
  Treaty of Uccialli with Ethiopia, 91

James, William, 56–57, 59–60
Jinarajadasa, Curupullumage, 62

Kabbalah scholarship, 11
Kant, Emmanuel, 52
Kaya, Ibrahim, 19–20
Kermode, Frank, 114–15, 117
King, Peter, 10–11
Kingdom of Two Sicilies (post-Napoleonic
  state), 27–28
Klages, Ludwig, 66–67

INDEX 323

Kremmerz, Giuliano, 5–6, 21, 45
Kristeller, Paul Oskar, 11

Labriola, Antonio, 54–55
Lacerba Futurist journal, 6, 21–22, 91
Laqueur, Thomas, 9–10
Lasswell, Harold, 96–97
La Voce journal, 6
Lazzarelli, Lodovico, 11
Leadbeater, Charles, 62
Lebano, Giustiniano, 21, 45, 46–47
Lee, Raymond R. M., 19–20
Lega Nazionale (National League) association, 76
Leonardo journal, 6, 21–22, 53–54, 56–60
   articles by Prezzolini, 58–59
   founders of, 53–54
   "L'Ideale Imperialista" article, 32
   philosophical environment of, 56–57
   Reghini and, 60
   "Schermaglie" ("Skirmishes") column, 56–57
   three lives/occultist phase of, 32–60
Leo XII, Pope, 74–75
L'Erreur Spirite (The Spiritist Error: History of a Pseudo-Religion) (Guénon), 128–29
L'Ésotérisme (Faivre), 12
Levi, Eliphas, 59–60
Levinson, Daniel, 114–15
l'Intuition Gnostique (the Gnostic Intuition), 125–26
Liquidazione dell'Asse Ecclesiastico (Liquidation of the Ecclesiastic Fund) laws, 35–36
Locations of Knowledge and Early Modern Europe (Stukrad), 12–13
Loggia Ausonia, Turin Masonic lodge, 35–36, 71
Lombardy-Venetia (post-Napoleonic state), 27–28
Lombroso, Cesare, 21, 41

Machiavelli, Niccolò, 145
Malombra (Fogazzaro), 40
Man as Power (L'Uomo come Potenza) (Evola), 22–23
Manifesto of the Futurist Movement (Marinetti), 117
Manzoni, Alessandro, 31
Marchi, Vittore, 144
Marconis de Négre, Gabriel Mathieu, 78–79
Marinetti, Filippo Tommaso, 117
"Marta e Maria (dalla Contemplazione all'Azione)" ("Martha and Mary [from Contemplation to Action])" (Prezzolini), 58–59

Marxism, 54–55
Massa, Aniceto del, 166
Massoneria Italiana e Tradizione Iniziatica (Italian Freemasonry and Initiatiic Tradition) (Frosini), 87–88
Le Matin Des Magiciens (The Morning of the Magicians (Pauwel and Bergier), 120–21
Le Matin Des Magiciens (The Morning of the Magicians) (Pauwel and Bergier), 120–21
Mazzini, Giuseppe, 1, 27, 28
   advocacy for Italy's unification, 32–33
   Giovane Italia, 31
   Risorgimento ideals of *Giovane Italia,* 72–73
Mazzoldi, Angelo, 43
McFarlane, James, 116–17
Mengozzi, Giovanni Ettore, 43
Military Academy of Turin, 96
La Missione di Roma nel Mondo (Rome's Mission in the World) (Marchi), 144
Modernism and Fascism: A Sense of a New Beginning under Mussolini and Hitler (Griffin), 115
modernism (modernity). *See also* anti-modernism
   Berman's description of, 2–3
   Bradbury/McFarlane on, 116–17
   Capuana on, 49
   Fascism/Roman Traditionalism links with, 114–15
   global variances in, 19
   Griffin on, 2–3, 116, 118–20
   Herf on reactionary modernism, 3–4
   Horace's writings on, 3–4
   interaction with occultism, 2
   occultism and, 6–11
   occultism and multiple modernities, 18–20
   rightist social modernism, 120
   social occult modernism, 118–20
   Volker on different accounts of, 2
   Zygmunt's idea of, 2
"The Modernity of Occultism" (Pasi), 7–8
Mombert, Albert, 66–67
Mori, Giovavnni, 97–98
Mors Osculi (Death by a Kiss) (Reghini), 66–67
"Morte e Resurrezione della Filosofia" ("Death and Resurrection of Philosophy") (Prezzolini), 58–59
Mosse, George, 29
mundus imaginalis theory, 11
Munich Cosmic Circle, 66–67
Mussolini, Benito Amilcare Andrea, 24. *See also* Fascism
   background, 111–12

Mussolini, Benito Amilcare Andrea (*cont.*)
  endorsement of Reghini, 164
  expulsion from Socialist Party, 112
  founding of *Gerarchia (Hierarchy)* Fascist newspaper, 113–14
  founding of *Il Popolo d'Italia* newspaper, 112
  march on Rome, 111–14
  membership in *Blocchi Nazionali* political group, 113–14
  rise to power, 18–19, 24, 25, 109–10, 111
  speeches given by, 113
  speech supporting Fascism, 117
  stance against Freemasonry, 24
Mutti, Romolo, 93

Naples, 42–48
  links to Egypt/initiatory knowledge, 44–45
  nineteenth-century occultism in, 44–48
  Rosicrucians, 44–45
Napoleon Bonaparte, 27–28
Natalale de Luca, Mario, 50–51
nationalism
  bourgeois followers of, 23
  comparison, by Lemmi, to internal affairs, 72
  Corradini's version of, 92–93
  evolution of nationalist thought by embodied thinkers, 92
  Gilitti government's nationalists, 92
  Italy and, 91–93
  Mosse's study of, 29
  of Reghini, 32–33
  ties to Freemasonry, 75–76
Naturphilosophie, 66–67
Nazis/Nazi Germany, 7, 10, 24, 120–22
Neapolitan Hegelian School, 52–54
Neo-Guelph group, 35–36
neo-Hegelian Idealism, 52–53
Neo-Idealism, 51–56
  of Croce, 55, 56–57, 58–59
  Hegelian neo-Idealism, 53–55
  rise of, 51–56
neo-Paganism, 5–6, 46–47
Neapolitan Masonic tradition, 44
Neapolitan School, 21
neo-Pythagoreans, 5–6, 21
Nievo, Ippolito, 33
Nigra, Costantino, 71
Nota sulla Vita e l'Attività Massonica dell'Autore (Note on the Life and Masonic Activity of the Author) (Parise), 50–51
Numa Pompilius, King, 1

De Occulta Philosophia Libri Tres (Three Books on The Occult Philosophy) (Agrippa), 6, 81–82
Occult Fascism, 24
occultism
  Adorno's ideas on, 6
  Butler on, 7–8
  Hanegraaff's definition, 7
  Hanegraaff's theory, 7–8
  influence on the Nazis, 24, 120–22
  interaction with modernity, 2
  links with Fascism, 120–25
  modernity and, 6–11
  multiple modernities and, 18–20
  in nineteenth-century Italy, 36–41
  in nineteenth-century Naples, 44–48
  occultist phase of *Leonardo* journal, 57–60
  Pasi's characterization of, 7
  Reghini's experimentation with, 95
  relation to elitism, 24–25
  Truzzi's limited knowledge of, 7
Occult World (Mondo Occulto) (Capuana), 40
Of the Moral and Civil Primacy of the Italians (Del Primato Civile degli Italiani) (Gioberti), 35–36
Oh my Italy, Though Speaking [of unity] is Fruitless (Italia mia, perché 'l parlar sia indarno) (Petrarca), 32–33
Olcott, Henry Steel, 62
On Italic Origins (Delle Origini Italiche) (Mazzoldi), 43
Ordine Egizio (Egyptian Order), 45
Orient et Occident (Guénon), 128–29
Orlando, Vittorio Emanuele, 114
Osirian Egyptian Order (Ordine Egizio Osirideo), 46–47
Ossendowski, Ferdynand, 120–21
OVRA, Fascist secret police, 25–26
Owen, Alex, 2, 7–8, 9

Pagan Imperialism. *See* "Imperialismo Pagano"
Pagine Esoteriche (Massa), 166
Palazzeschi, Aldo, 91
Palladino, Eusapia, 21, 41
Papal States (post-Napoleonic state), 27–28
Papini, Giovanni, 4–5, 21–22, 53–54. *See also Leonardo* journal
  co-founding of *Leonardo* journal, 53–54
  comment on Pragmatism, 59–60
  criticism of "Imperialismo Pagano," 98
  Florentine Scapigliatura philosophy and, 49–50
  letter to Prezzolini, 56–57

straddling of avant-garde and Tradition, 49–50
Parise, Giulio, 5–6, 17
  meeting with Reghini, 144–45
  Note on the Life and Masonic Activity of the Author, 50–51
  Reghini's collaboration with, 158–59
  vouching for Reghini's success, 163
Le Parole Sacre e di Passo dei Primi Tre Gradi ed il Massimo Mistero Massonico- Studio Critico e Iniziatico (The Sacred Words and Pass- Words of the First Three Degrees and the Greatest Masonic Mystery: Critical and Initiatic Study) (Reghini), 6, 130–31
La Parole Sacre e di Passo monograph (Reghini), 144–50
Partito Nazionale Fascista (National Fascist Party), 111, 113–14, 165. *See also* Fascism
Partito Socialista Italiano (Italian Socialist Party), 93, 111–12
Pasi, Marco, 2, 7, 24–25
Patria journal, 6
The Patrol Comes Around (Passa la Ronda) (Ciconi), 31–32
Pauwel, Louis, 120–21
Pauwels, Louis, 7
Per la Restituzione della Geometria Pitagorica (For the Restitution of Pythagorean Geometry) (Reghini), 166, 170–72
Per lo Spirito la Carne Esaltare (To Exalt the Flesh for the Spirit) (Alvi), 143–44
Per una Concezione Spirituale della Vita (For a Spiritual Understanding of Life) lecure (Reghini), 68–69
Petrarca, Francesco, 32–33
Phenomenalism, 52–53
philosophia perennis (perennial philosophy), 120
phrenology, 41
physiognomics, 41
Piedmont (post-Napoleonic state), 27–28
Platonic-Augustinian view of the world, 52
Ponte, Renato del, 50–51
Pontremoli, Reghini di, 50–51
Positivism (Positivist method), 4–5
  anti-Positivist barrage against, 49–50, 53
  arrival in Italy, 41
  attacks against, 56–57
  Cattaneo/Ferrari's promotion of, 52
  conversion of scientists to the Spiritualist cause, 41
  Corradini's critiquing of, 92
  counterpositivism, 53–56

  crisis of (1890s/1900s), 53
  Lombroso's view on, 41
  Neapolitan Hegelian School challenge of, 52–53
  origins in Italy, 41
Pragmatism
  Papini's comment on, 59–60
  Prezzolini's pursuit of, 58–59
Prezzolini, Giuseppe, 4–5, 56–57. *See also Leonardo* journal
  articles by, 32–59
  co-founding of *Leonardo* journal, 53–54
  Florentine Scapigliatura philosophy and, 49–50
  initial belief in Mussolini, 111
  "Intellectual Imperialism" (Prezzolini), 57–59
  Papini's letter to, 56–57
  pursuit of Pragmatism, 58–59
  straddling of avant-garde and Tradition, 49–50
"A Primordialist Definition of Modernity" (Griffin), 118–20
Principi di Scienza Nuova (Principles of New Science) (Vico), 167–68
Pro Patria (For the Fatherland) association, 76

Ranger, Terence, 20
Rassegna Massonica masonic journal, 6
Ravenscroft, Trevor, 7
Reghini, Arturo. *See also Atanòr, Rivista di Studi Iniziatici (Atanòr, Journal of Initiatic Studies)*; "Imperialismo Pagano" ("Pagan Imperialism")
  adherence to Fascism, 165
  advocacy for the use of force, 117
  advocacy for the use of force in "Imperialismo Pagano," 118–19
  anti-Christian stance, 61–62
  appreciation of Guénon's work, 134
  Armentano's mentorship of, 14–15, 70
  articles for *Salamandra*, 93
  attack on the Vatican/Catholic nationalists, 1
  Biblioteca Filosofica lectures, 6, 17
  blaming of Christianity for the fall of the Roman Empire, 186–87
  break with Guénon, 16–17
  brief involvement with Theosophy, 21–22, 50–51, 60–61, 64, 65
  co-editing of *Ur* journal, 17
  collaborations with Parise and Evola, 158–59
  Considerations, 50–51
  contradictory involvement with cultural avant-garde, 21–22

Reghini, Arturo (*cont.*)
    contributions to *Leonardo* journal, 60
    correspondence with Armentano, 93–98, 132–33, 142, 163, 164
    correspondence with Guénon, 133–38
    creation of Pythagorean association in Rome, 141
    criticism of Guénon, 130–31
    decision to cut ties with Masonic past, 165
    differences with Corradini on religion, 75–76
    early life/background, 50–51
    endorsement from Mussolini, 164
    enrollment in Military Academy of Turin, 96
    establishment of *Ars Regia* publishing house, 61–62
    experimentation with occultism, 95
    foray into hermeticism, 169–70
    founding of *Atanòr* journal, 24–25, 150–52
    founding of *Ignis (Fire)* journal, 155–58
    frequentation of cafes by, 93
    Hermet's writings on, 80
    ill health issues, 166
    "Imperialismo Pagano," 23
    initial belief in Mussolini, 111
    initiation into the *Schola Italica*, 80–81, 82–84
    interest in/Freemasonry involvement, 17, 22–23, 78–79, 145
    lawsuit against Evola, 161–62, 163, 164, 165
    leadership role at *Associazione Pitagorica (Pythagorean Association)*, 141
    lectures given by, 68–69
    and *Leonardo* journal, 60
    mathematical works, 166
    Mazzoldi/Mengozzi, influence on, 47
    meeting with Ciro Alvi, 142
    as member of the *élite intellectuelle*, 24, 109–10
    membership in *Partito Nazionale Fascista*, 165
    obsession for Catholicism, 99–100
    La Parole Sacre e di Passo monograph, 144–50
    period of ill health, 166
    possible entrance to *Rito Filosofico Italiano*, 88
    reasons for abandonment of Rome, 25–26
    right-wing culture rejection of, 5
    Roman Traditionalism and, 45, 46–47, 93–96
    shattered dream of Pagan Imperialism, 25
    straddling of avant-garde and Tradition, 49–50
    summering in Scalea with Armentano, 94
    Theosophical writings, 64, 66–69
    visits with Armentano in Scalea, 138–39, 140

Reghini, Cesare, 50–51
Reghini, Ida Carlotta, 62
Reghini, Marcello, 50–51
Reghini, Petricciolo, 50–51
Reghini, Teodoro, 50–51
Risorgimento, 3–4, 21, 27–48
    Amici's children's book on values of, 30
    Banti's description of, 29
    Cavour's characterization of, 29–30
    Consolato's book on, 32–33
    historical overview, 27–32
    influence of spiritualism on the élite, 21–22, 40–41
    key dates, 27–28
    literary expressions/sentiments on, 31–33
    post-Risorgimento forms of thought, 57–58
    pre-World War I ideals of, 23
    primacy metanarrative, 42–44
    primary leaders of, 28
    role of Garibaldi, 33–34
    works of Mazzoldi and, 43
    works of Mengozzi and, 43
Rito Filosofico Italiano (Italian Philosophical Rite), 22–23, 141
    changes/expansion within, 88
    Reghini/Armentano, possible entrance, 88
La Rivoluzione Fascista (The Fascist Revolution), 113–14
Rocco, Alfredo, 92
Roman pagan movements, 22–23
Roman Traditionalism, 4–5
    the beginning of the end, 141
    Consolato's book on, 32–33
    the end of the beginning, 138–41
    Fascism and, 4–5, 24, 91–141
    Guénon's role in founding, 81
    Neopolitan School and, 21
    onset/entrance of, 13–16
    Paganism *vs.* Christianity in, 16–17
    Pythagoras's founding of, 85
    Reghini and, 16–17, 93–96
    roots of, in Consolato's book on, 32–33
    shortcomings of, 117
    similarity to Fascism, 118
    ties with occultists, 17
Rosicrucians, 44–45
Rosmini-Serbati, Antonio, 52
Rossi, Mario Manlio, 56–57

S. Francesco d'Assisi (St. Francis of Assisi) (Alvi), 142–43
Salamandra, Italian cultural publication, 1, 6, 23, 89, 93, 97–98

INDEX   327

Salandra, Antonio, 114
Sanctis, Francesco de, 52–53
Sanford, Nevitt, 114–15
Sangro, Raimondo di, 44
La Sapienza Italica (The Italic Wisdom)
    (Caporali), 144
Satires (Horace), 3–4
Scandinavian modernity, 19
Scapigliatura, Milan literary movement thru
    4–5, 40, 49–50, 49–69, 64
Schiller, F. C. S., 58–59
Schmidt, Volker H., 18–19
Schola Italica (Italic School)
    anti-modernism and, 10–11
    Armentano's links to, 75–76, 84–85
    creation of a Pythagorean association, 141
    elitist approach of, 85–86
    expendability of the members, 165
    importance of "Imperialismo Pagano"
        to, 109–10
    influence of Neopolitan schools on, 21
    invention of sacred traditions, the occult,
        and, 20
    Reghini's links to, 2, 80–81, 82–84
    *Rito Filosofico Italiano (Italian Philosophical
        Rite)* and, 22–23
    search for the Perennial Pythagorean
        Tradition, 119–20
Schola Italica (Traditionalist movement),
    2, 10–11
Schuon, Fritjof, 120, 153–54
Second Coming poem (Yeats), 114–15
The Secret Doctrine (Blavatsky), 66–67
*The Sense of an Ending: Studies in the Theories of
    Fiction* (Kermode), 114–15
Senso film (Visconti), 76
Sestito, Roberto, 5, 25–26, 50–51, 60–61
Sholem, Gershom, 11
Sinnet, A. P., 64–65
social Darwinism, 41, 57–58
Socialist Italian milieu, 57–58
social occult modernism, 118–20
*Lo Spaccio dei Maghi (The Dispatch of the
    Magicians)* (Rossi), 56–57
Spaventa, Bertrando, 52–53
Spaventa, Silvio, 52–53
Spiritism? (Spiritismo?) (Capuana), 40
spiritualism
    Adorno on, 6
    influence on the *Risorgimento* élite, 21–22
    origins and spread of, 37–40
Staudenmaier, Peter, 10
Steiner, Rudolf, 156

*Studiengruppe für Germanisches Altertum
    (Study Group for Germanic Antiquity)*, 122
Sturzo, Luigi, 93
Sulli-Rao, Giuseppe, 61–62

Tavolato, Italo, 91
Theosophical Library, 62–64
Theosophical Society (Theosophy), 5–6, 7–8,
    51. *See also* Blavatsky, Helena Petrovna
    Besant's leadership, 62, 64
    establishment in Italy, 5–6, 61–62
    Guénon's book on, 14–15, 97–98, 128–29
    Reghini's brief involvement with, 21–22,
        60–61, 65
    Reghini's Theosophical writings, 64,
        66–69
    role in providing alternate beliefs, 61–62
    role of Blavatsky in establishing, 61–62
    role of Cooper-Oakley in establishing, 62
    roots of Roman Traditionalism in, 64–66
*Le Théosophisme: Histoire d'une pseudo-religion
    (Theosophism: History of a Pseudo-religion)*
    (Guénon), 14–15, 97–98, 128–29
Theses (Adorno), 6–7
Thomas, Dana Lloyd, 5–6
Thule Gesellschaft (Thule Society), 120–21
Thus Spake Zarathustra (Nietzsche), 96
To Arms! to Arms! (All Armi! All Armi!)
    (Berchet), 31
Tommaseo, Nicolò, 44
Totem, 41
Traditionalist movement *(Schola Italica)*, 2
The Transcendent Unity of Religions
    (Schuon), 153–54
Treaty of Uccialli (Ethiopia and Italy)
    (1889), 91
Treitel, Corinna, 2, 9, 24–25
Truzzi, Marcello, 7
Tucci, Giuseppe, 22–23
Turner, Victor, 119
Turris, Gianfranco de, 7

Ultra theosophical journal, 6
Umberto I, 40
Unamuno, Miguel de, 56–57
*Ur: Rivista di Indirizzi di una Scienza per l'Lo
    (Ur: Journal of Orientations Towards a
    Scicence for the I)*, 158–62
Ur Group *(Gruppo di Ur)*, 142–62
    break with Evola, 160–62
    culture of elitism and, 24
    Reghini's role with, 17, 24–25
d'Uva, Gennaro, 60–61

Van Gennep, Arnold, 118–19
The Varieties of Religious Experience: A Study in Human Nature (James), 59–60
Vatican
　anti-Masonic "crusade" by, 73–74
　Freemasonry and, 35–36
　Reghini's attack on, 1
　Reghini's family ties with, 50–51
　relation with Fascism, 4–5, 25, 118–19, 158–59, 161–62, 165
　relation with occult orders, 4–5
Vedanta, 127–28
Ventura, Gastone, 133–34
La Ventura delle Riviste (The Destiny of Journals) (Hermet), 141
Venturi, Pietro Tacchi, 164
Vergil, 1
Verso la Purificazione (Towards Purification) (Alvi), 142–43
La Via Nuova (The New Way) (Alvi), 142–43
Vico, Giambattista, 167–68
Victor Emmanuel III, King, 111
Visconti, Luchino, 76
La Vita dello Spirito (The Life of the Spirit) lecture (Reghini), 68–69
Vitalists, 66–67
Vittorio Emanuele II, King, 28, 35–36, 40, 44
Vittorio Emanuele III, King, 114
The Voice of the Silence (Blavatsky), 66–67
Von List, Ariosophists Guido, 120–21

von Metternich, Klement, 28
von Stuckrad, Kocku, 12–13
Vril Gesellschaft (Vril Society), 120–21

Wachtmeister, Ulla, 61–62
Wagner, Nietzsche, Pragmatism, 56–57
Webb, James
　definition of occultism, 2
　Flight from Reason, 7
Weber, Max, 1, 2
Westcott, William Wynn, 7–8
Western esotericism, 4–5
　discourse of Hammer, 12–13
　Faivre's definition of, 12–13
　Hermetic Tradition concept (Yates), 11–12
　scholarly debates about, 14–15
　studies of, 11–15
The Wise Man of the Sebetus (Il Geronta Sebezio) journal (Bocchini), 45–46
Wittrock, Björn, 19
"Woman as a Thing" (Evola), 9
Woodroffe, John, 22–23
World War I (Great War)
　"Imperialismo Pagano" and, 23, 91–110

Yates, Dame Frances, 11–12
　Giordano Bruno and the Hermetic Tradition, 11
　Hermetic Tradition concept, 11–12